CROSSED ™

GARTH ENNIS

story

JACEN BURROWS

artwork

JUANMAR
color chapters 2-10, covers, gallery

GREG WALLER
color chapter 1, gallery

WILLIAM CHRISTENSEN editor-in-chief
MARK SEIFERT creative director
JIM KUHORIC managing editor
KEITH DAVIDSEN director of sales and marketing
DAVID MARKS director of events
ARIANA OSBORNE production assistant

 **AVATAR** ™

www.crossedcomic.com   www.avatarpress.com   www.twitter.com/avatarpress

CROSSED VOLUME 1. April 2010. Published by Avatar Press, Inc., 515 N. Century Blvd. Rantoul, IL 61866. ©2011 Avatar Press, Inc. Crossed and all related properties TM & ©2011 Garth Ennis. All characters as depicted in this story are over the age of 18. The stories, characters, and institutions mentioned in this magazine are entirely fictional. Second Printing June 2011. Printed in Canada.

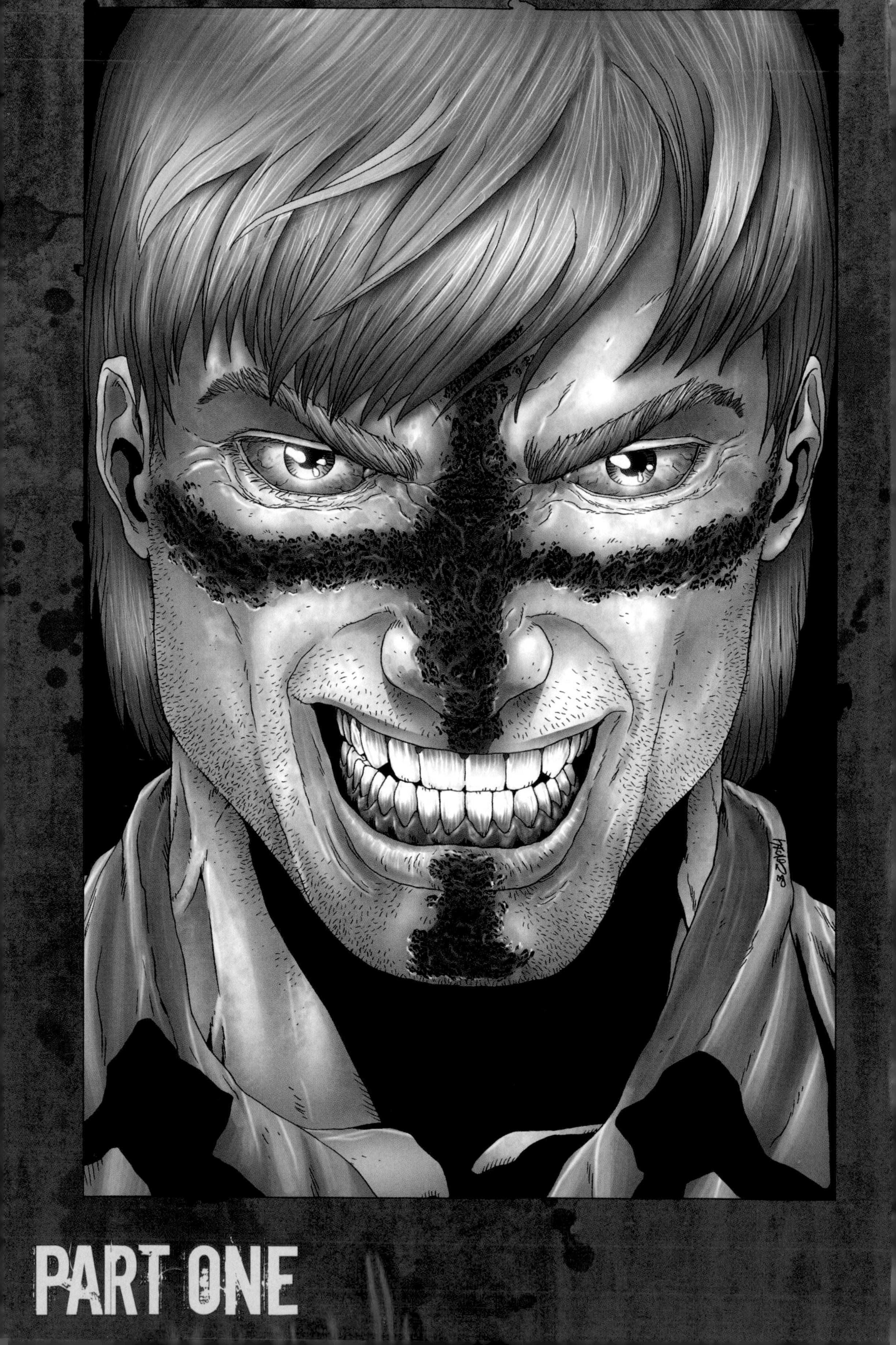

PART ONE

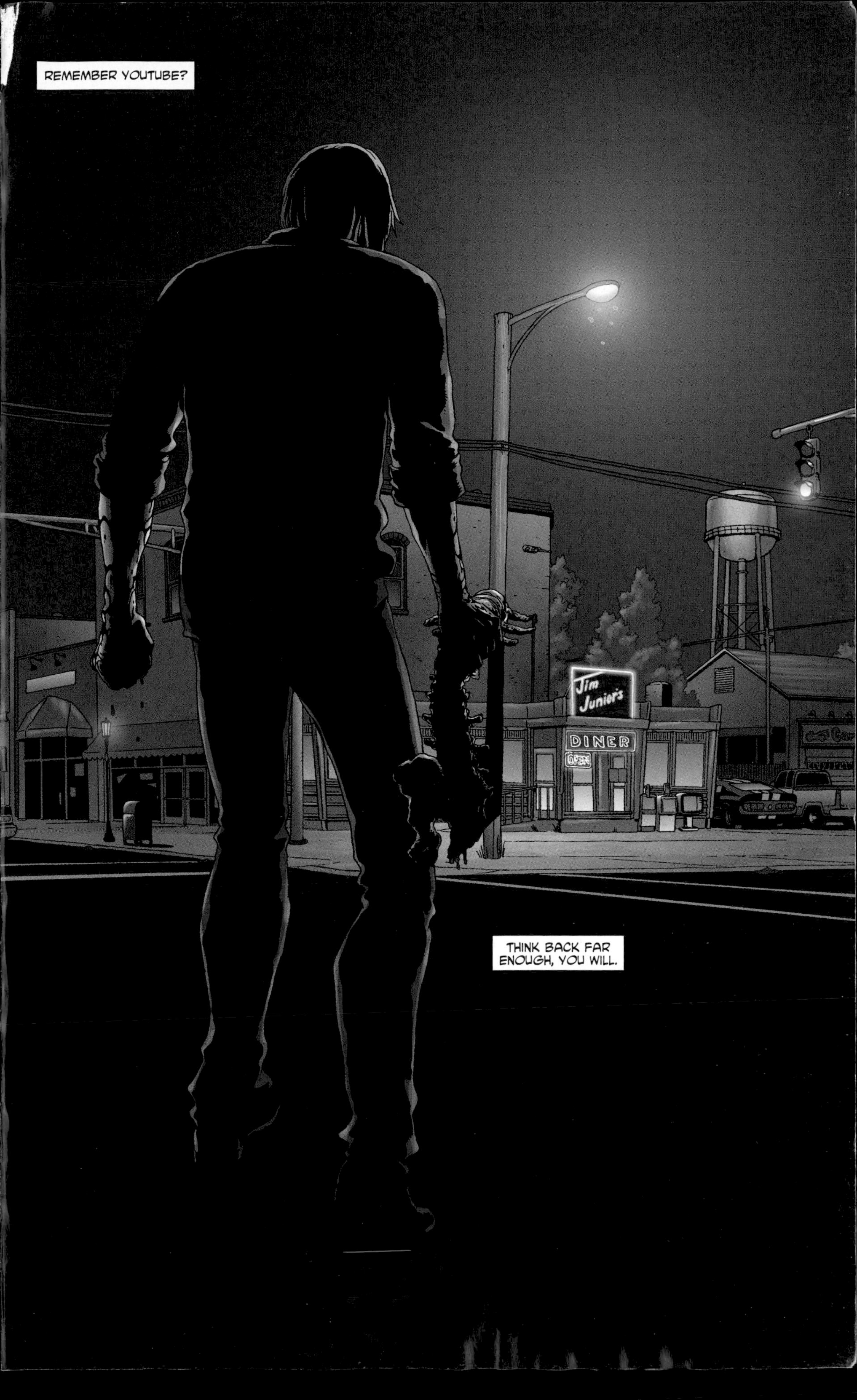
REMEMBER YOUTUBE?
Jim Junior's
DINER
OPEN
THINK BACK FAR ENOUGH, YOU WILL.

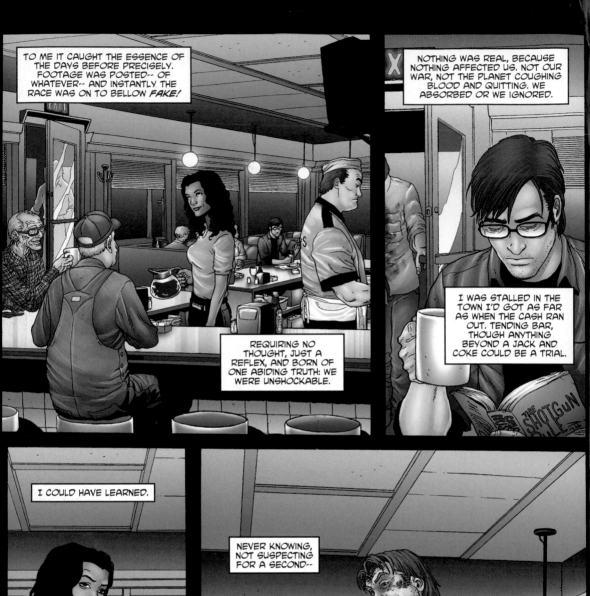

TO ME IT CAUGHT THE ESSENCE OF THE DAYS BEFORE PRECISELY. FOOTAGE WAS POSTED-- OF WHATEVER-- AND INSTANTLY THE RACE WAS ON TO BELLOW *FAKE!*

REQUIRING NO THOUGHT, JUST A REFLEX, AND BORN OF ONE ABIDING TRUTH: WE WERE UNSHOCKABLE.

NOTHING WAS REAL, BECAUSE NOTHING AFFECTED US. NOT OUR WAR, NOT THE PLANET COUGHING BLOOD AND QUITTING. WE ABSORBED OR WE IGNORED.

I WAS STALLED IN THE TOWN I'D GOT AS FAR AS WHEN THE CASH RAN OUT. TENDING BAR, THOUGH ANYTHING BEYOND A JACK AND COKE COULD BE A TRIAL.

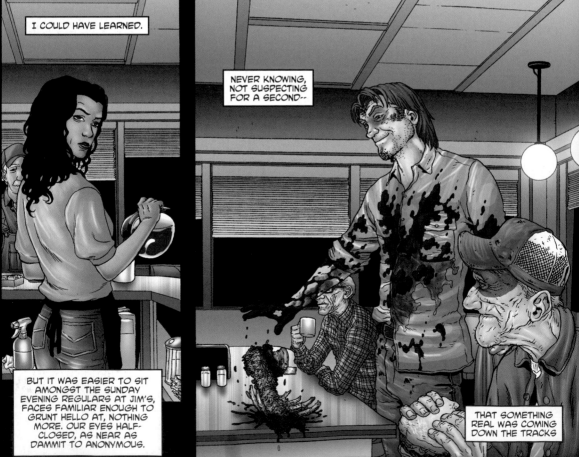

I COULD HAVE LEARNED.

BUT IT WAS EASIER TO SIT AMONGST THE SUNDAY EVENING REGULARS AT JIM'S, FACES FAMILIAR ENOUGH TO GRUNT HELLO AT, NOTHING MORE. OUR EYES HALF-CLOSED, AS NEAR AS DAMMIT TO ANONYMOUS.

NEVER KNOWING, NOT SUSPECTING FOR A SECOND--

THAT SOMETHING REAL WAS COMING DOWN THE TRACKS.

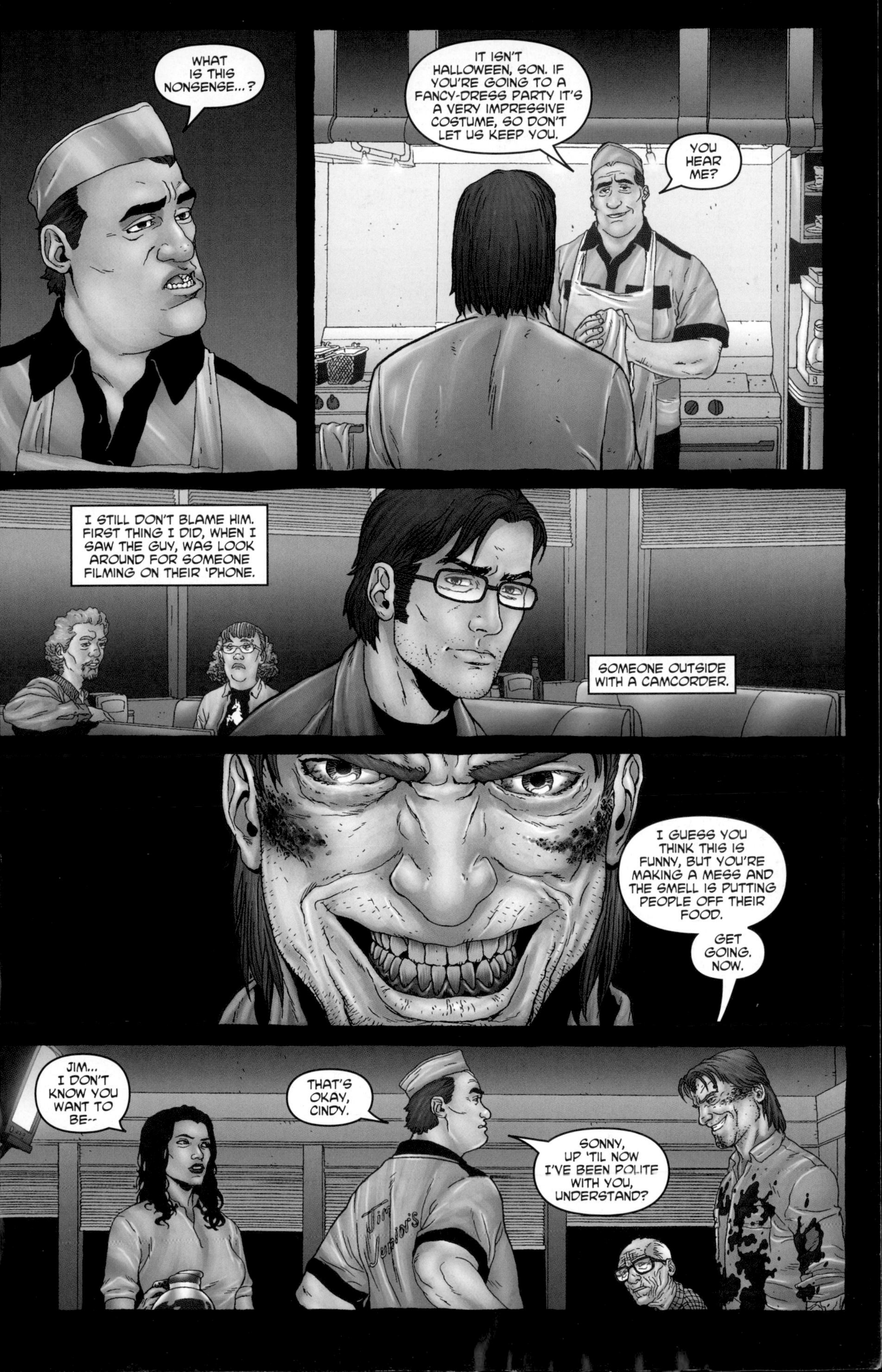
WHAT IS THIS NONSENSE...?
IT ISN'T HALLOWEEN, SON. IF YOU'RE GOING TO A FANCY-DRESS PARTY IT'S A VERY IMPRESSIVE COSTUME, SO DON'T LET US KEEP YOU.
YOU HEAR ME?
I STILL DON'T BLAME HIM. FIRST THING I DID, WHEN I SAW THE GUY, WAS LOOK AROUND FOR SOMEONE FILMING ON THEIR 'PHONE.
SOMEONE OUTSIDE WITH A CAMCORDER.
I GUESS YOU THINK THIS IS FUNNY, BUT YOU'RE MAKING A MESS AND THE SMELL IS PUTTING PEOPLE OFF THEIR FOOD.
GET GOING. NOW.
JIM... I DON'T KNOW YOU WANT TO BE--
THAT'S OKAY, CINDY.
SONNY, UP 'TIL NOW I'VE BEEN POLITE WITH YOU, UNDERSTAND?

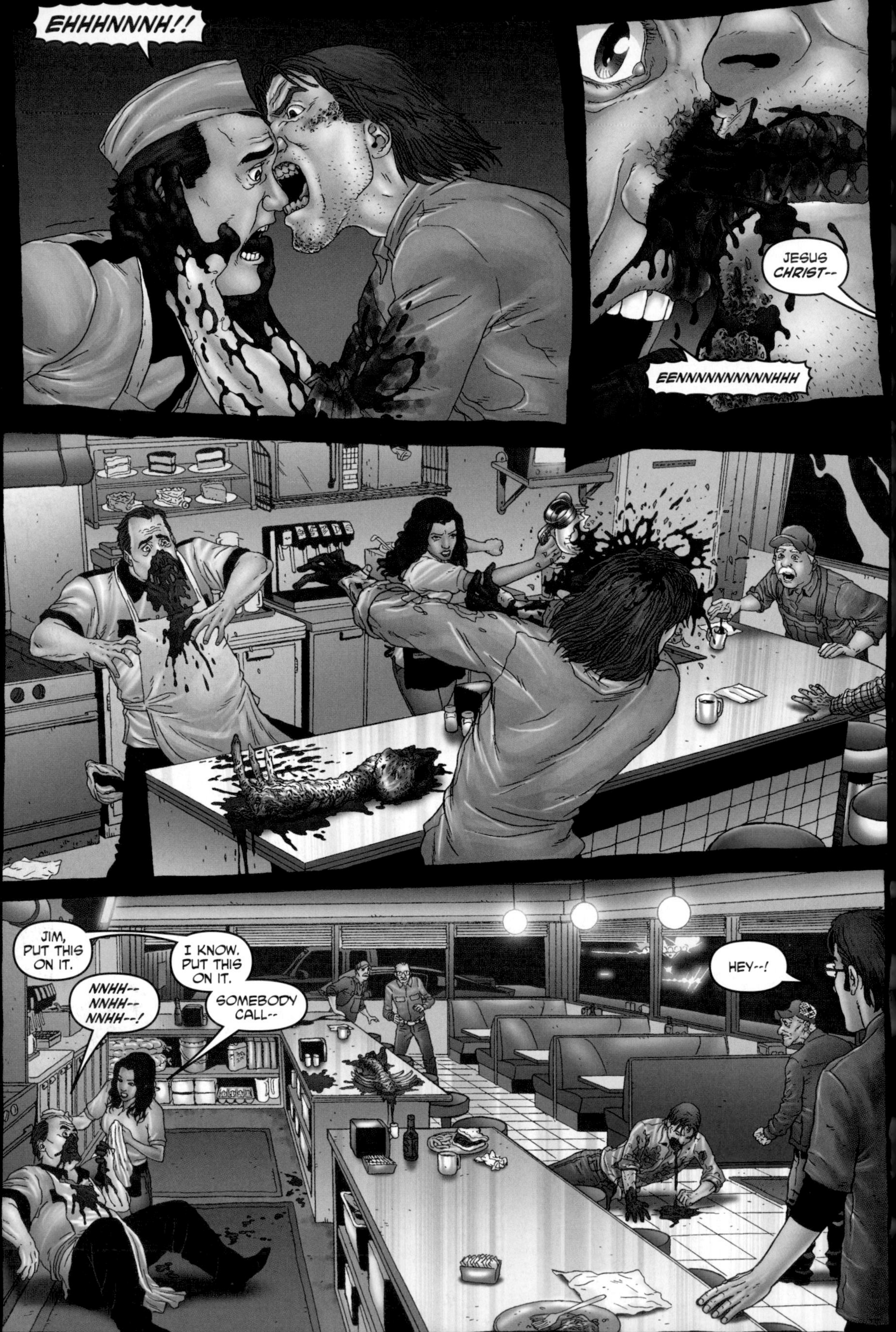
EHHHNNNH!!
JESUS CHRIST--
EENNNNNNNNNNHHH
JIM, PUT THIS ON IT.
I KNOW. PUT THIS ON IT.
NNHH-- NNHH-- NNHH--!
SOMEBODY CALL--
HEY--!

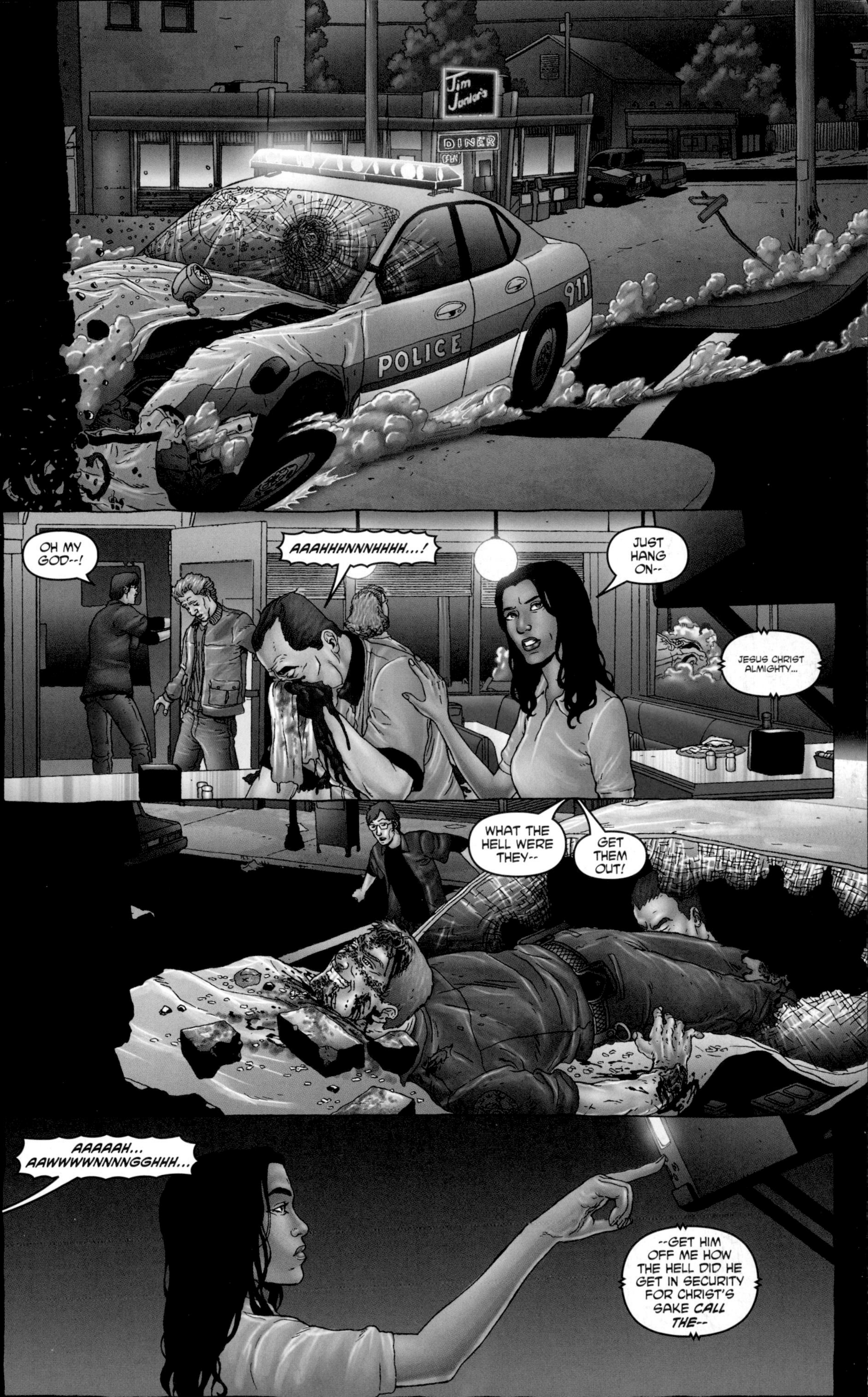
Jim Janlar's
DINER
911
POLICE
OH MY GOD--!
AAAHHHNNNHHHH...!
JUST HANG ON--
JESUS CHRIST ALMIGHTY...
WHAT THE HELL WERE THEY--
GET THEM OUT!
AAAAAH... AAWWWWNNNNGGHHH...
--GET HIM OFF ME HOW THE HELL DID HE GET IN SECURITY FOR CHRIST'S SAKE CALL THE--

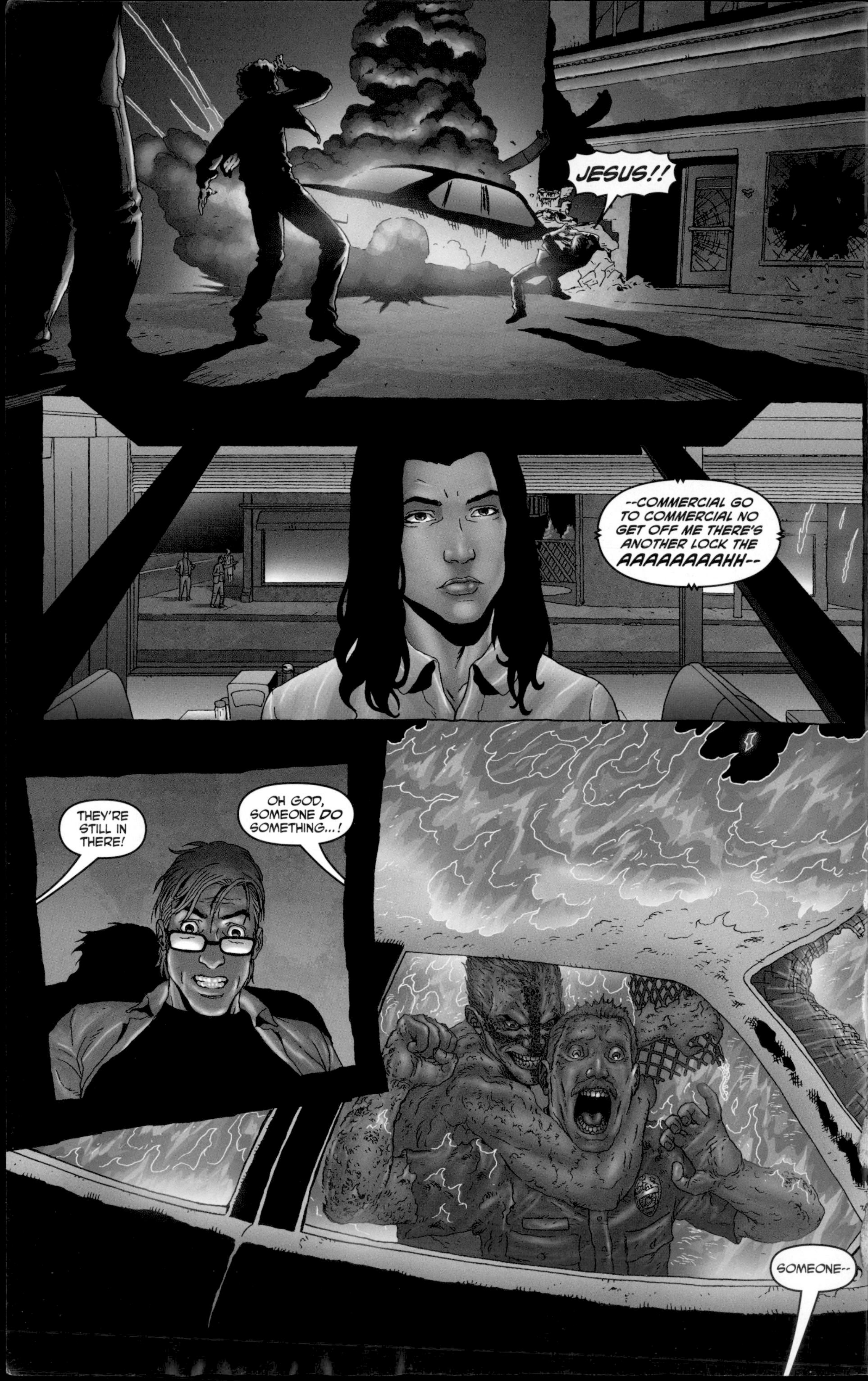
JESUS!!
--COMMERCIAL GO TO COMMERCIAL NO GET OFF ME THERE'S ANOTHER LOCK THE AAAAAAAAHH--
THEY'RE STILL IN THERE!
OH GOD, SOMEONE DO SOMETHING...!
SOMEONE--

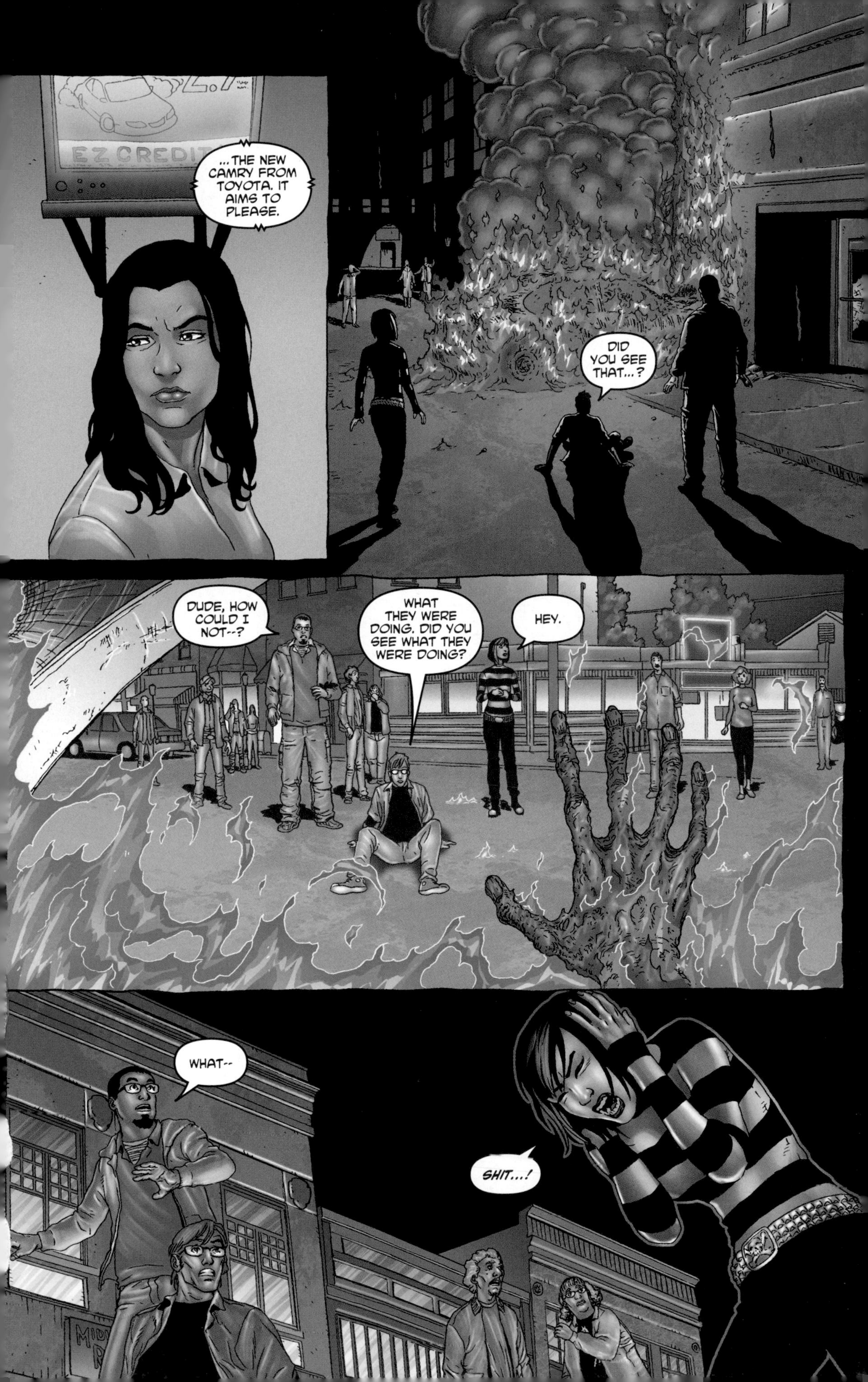

EZ CREDIT
...THE NEW CAMRY FROM TOYOTA. IT AIMS TO PLEASE.
DID YOU SEE THAT...?
DUDE, HOW COULD I NOT--?
WHAT THEY WERE DOING. DID YOU SEE WHAT THEY WERE DOING?
HEY.
WHAT--
SHIT...!

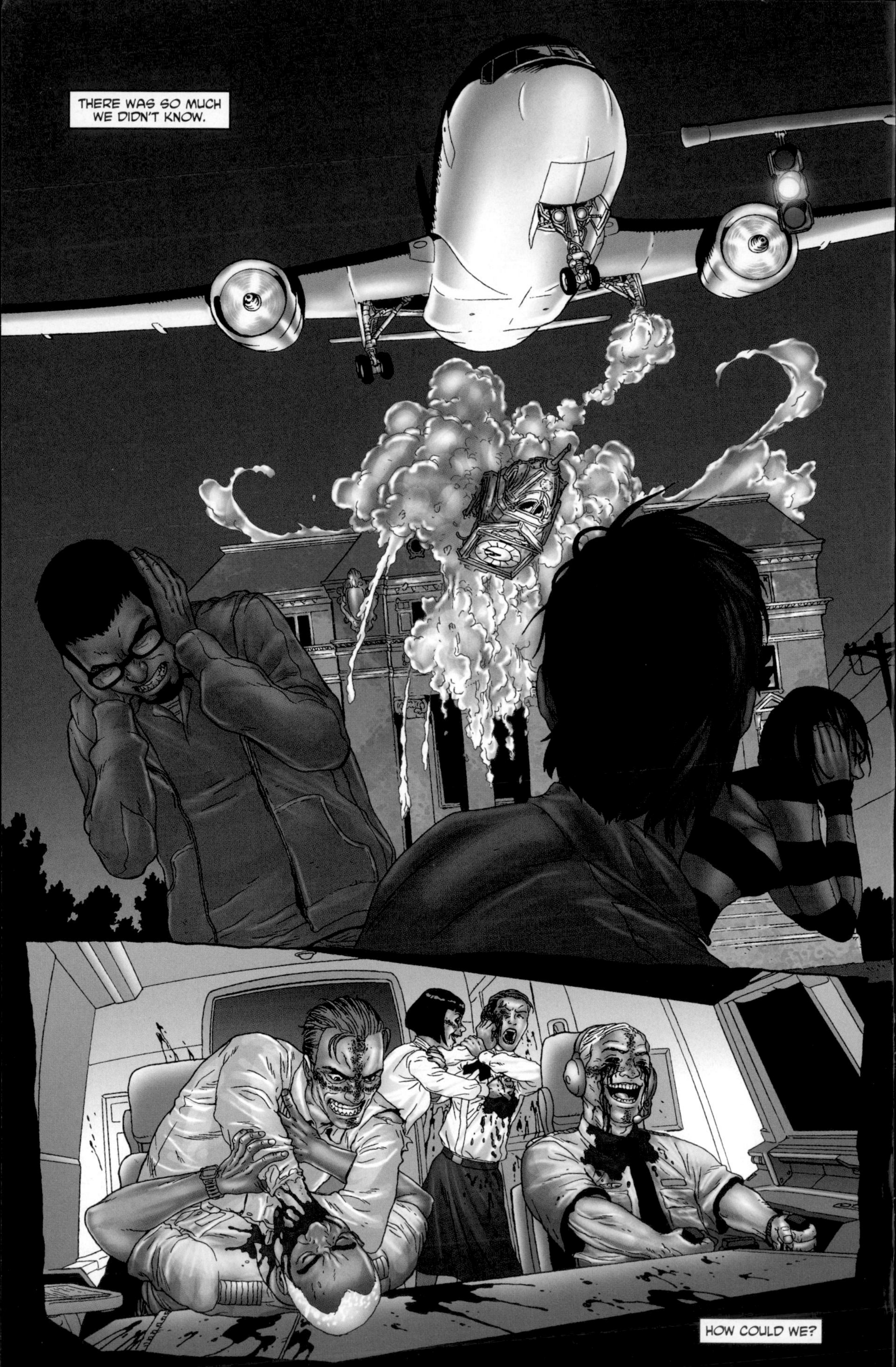
THERE WAS SO MUCH WE DIDN'T KNOW.
HOW COULD WE?

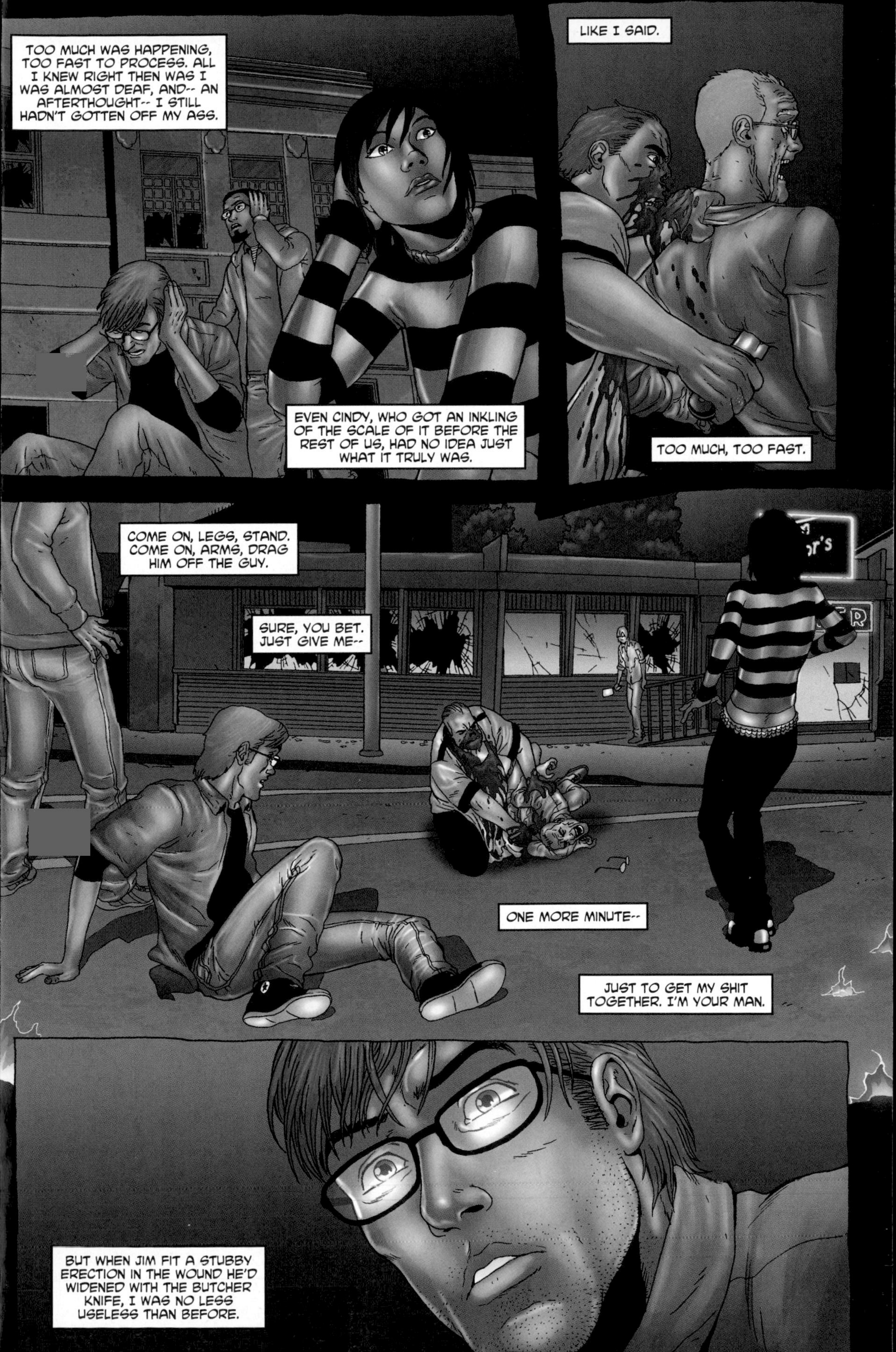
TOO MUCH WAS HAPPENING, TOO FAST TO PROCESS. ALL I KNEW RIGHT THEN WAS I WAS ALMOST DEAF, AND-- AN AFTERTHOUGHT-- I STILL HADN'T GOTTEN OFF MY ASS.
EVEN CINDY, WHO GOT AN INKLING OF THE SCALE OF IT BEFORE THE REST OF US, HAD NO IDEA JUST WHAT IT TRULY WAS.
LIKE I SAID.
TOO MUCH, TOO FAST.
COME ON, LEGS, STAND. COME ON, ARMS, DRAG HIM OFF THE GUY.
SURE, YOU BET. JUST GIVE ME--
ONE MORE MINUTE--
JUST TO GET MY SHIT TOGETHER. I'M YOUR MAN.
BUT WHEN JIM FIT A STUBBY ERECTION IN THE WOUND HE'D WIDENED WITH THE BUTCHER KNIFE, I WAS NO LESS USELESS THAN BEFORE.

AT LEAST I WAS FACING IN THE WRONG DIRECTION.

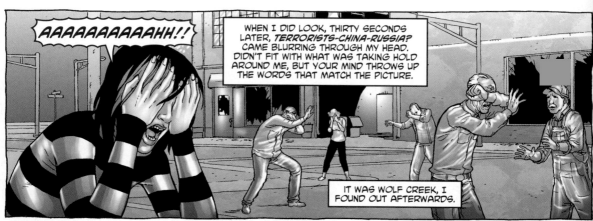

AAAAAAAAAAHH!!

WHEN I DID LOOK, THIRTY SECONDS LATER, *TERRORISTS-CHINA-RUSSIA?* CAME BLURRING THROUGH MY HEAD. DIDN'T FIT WITH WHAT WAS TAKING HOLD AROUND ME, BUT YOUR MIND THROWS UP THE WORDS THAT MATCH THE PICTURE.

IT WAS WOLF CREEK, I FOUND OUT AFTERWARDS.

ONE OF THEM MUST HAVE PULLED THE CONTROL RODS.

ARE YOU--

NAAAAHH!

KELLY! KELLY, RIGHT? IT'S STAN, IT'S STAN FROM THE DINER!

NNNOOO...!

MOTHER

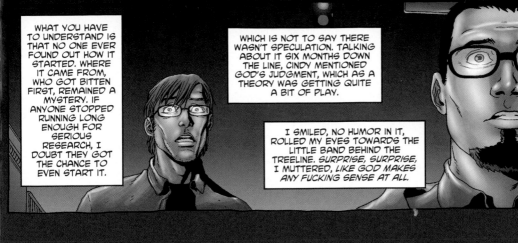

WHAT YOU HAVE TO UNDERSTAND IS THAT NO ONE EVER FOUND OUT HOW IT STARTED. WHERE IT CAME FROM, WHO GOT BITTEN FIRST, REMAINED A MYSTERY. IF ANYONE STOPPED RUNNING LONG ENOUGH FOR SERIOUS RESEARCH, I DOUBT THEY GOT THE CHANCE TO EVEN START IT.

WHICH IS NOT TO SAY THERE WASN'T SPECULATION. TALKING ABOUT IT SIX MONTHS DOWN THE LINE, CINDY MENTIONED GOD'S JUDGMENT, WHICH AS A THEORY WAS GETTING QUITE A BIT OF PLAY.

I SMILED, NO HUMOR IN IT, ROLLED MY EYES TOWARDS THE LITTLE BAND BEHIND THE TREELINE. *SURPRISE, SURPRISE,* I MUTTERED, *LIKE GOD MAKES ANY FUCKING SENSE AT ALL.*

SHE SET THE BUTT OF THE CARBINE TO HER HIP, SHRUGGED AS SHE TURNED TO FACE THE NIGHT. *IT DOES IF HE'S A COCKSUCKER,* SHE SAID, AND I HAD TO ADMIT SHE MIGHT JUST HAVE A POINT.

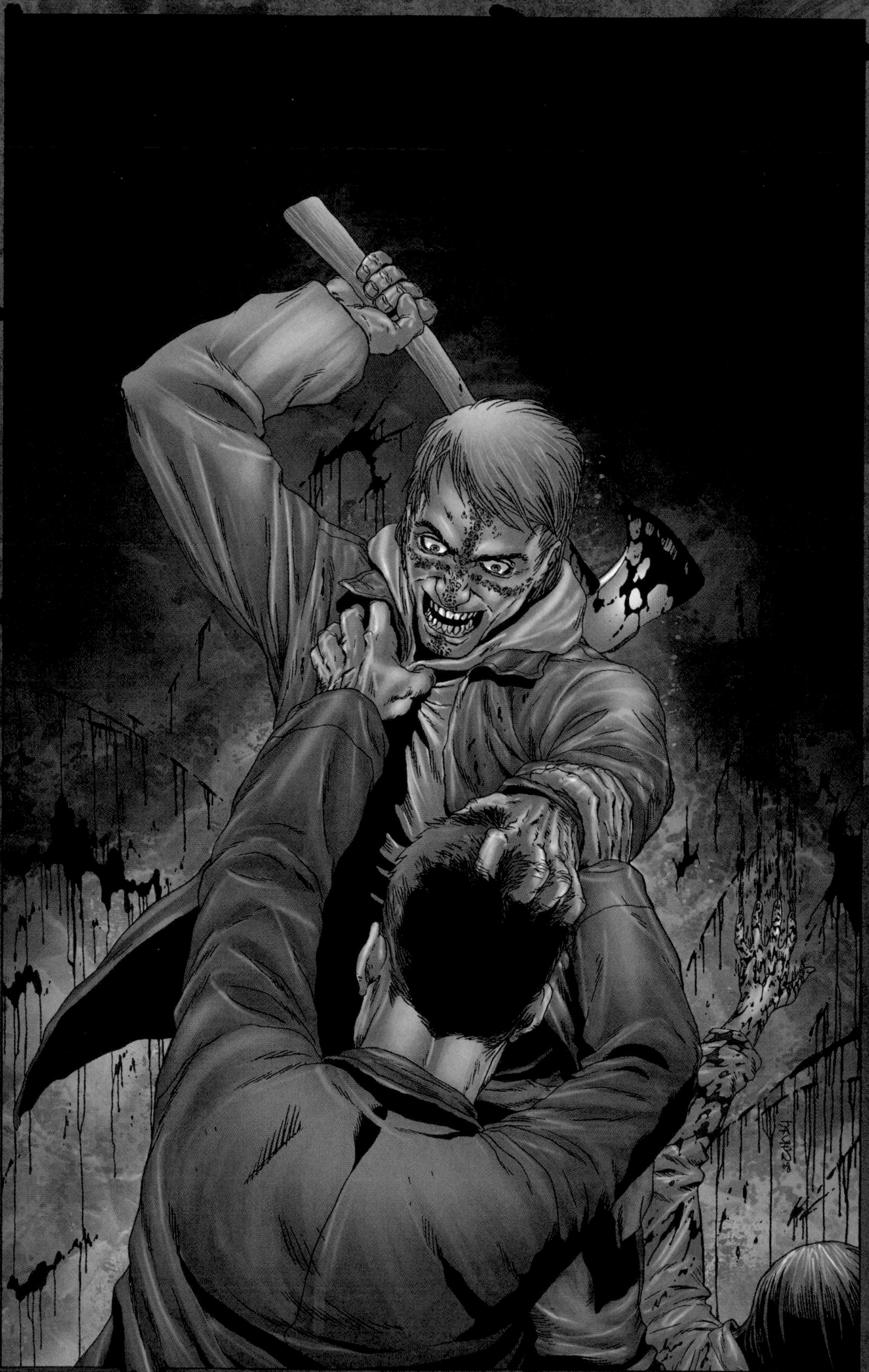

PART TWO

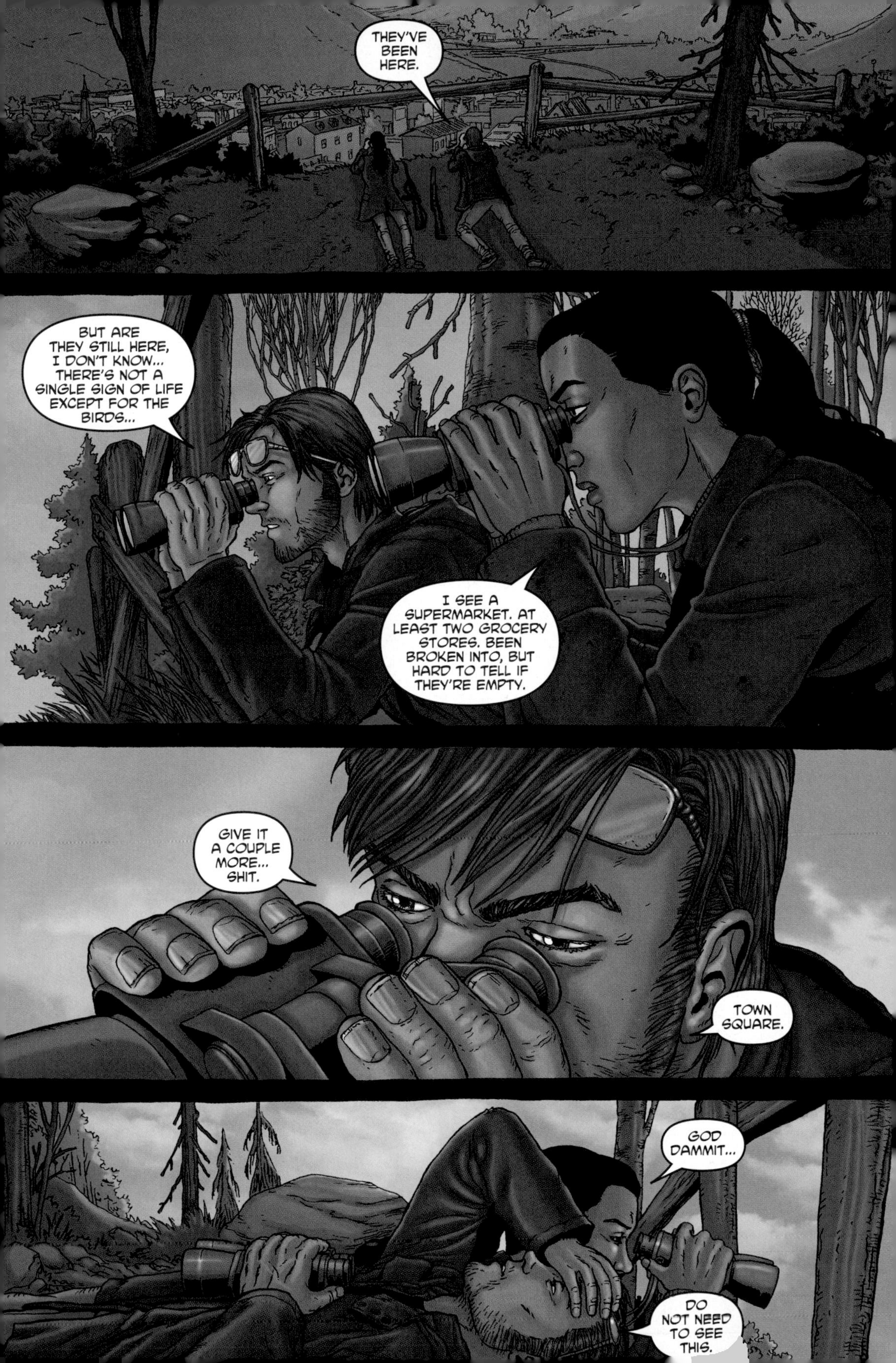
THEY'VE BEEN HERE.
BUT ARE THEY STILL HERE, I DON'T KNOW... THERE'S NOT A SINGLE SIGN OF LIFE EXCEPT FOR THE BIRDS...
I SEE A SUPERMARKET. AT LEAST TWO GROCERY STORES. BEEN BROKEN INTO, BUT HARD TO TELL IF THEY'RE EMPTY.
GIVE IT A COUPLE MORE... SHIT.
TOWN SQUARE.
GOD DAMMIT...
DO NOT NEED TO SEE THIS.

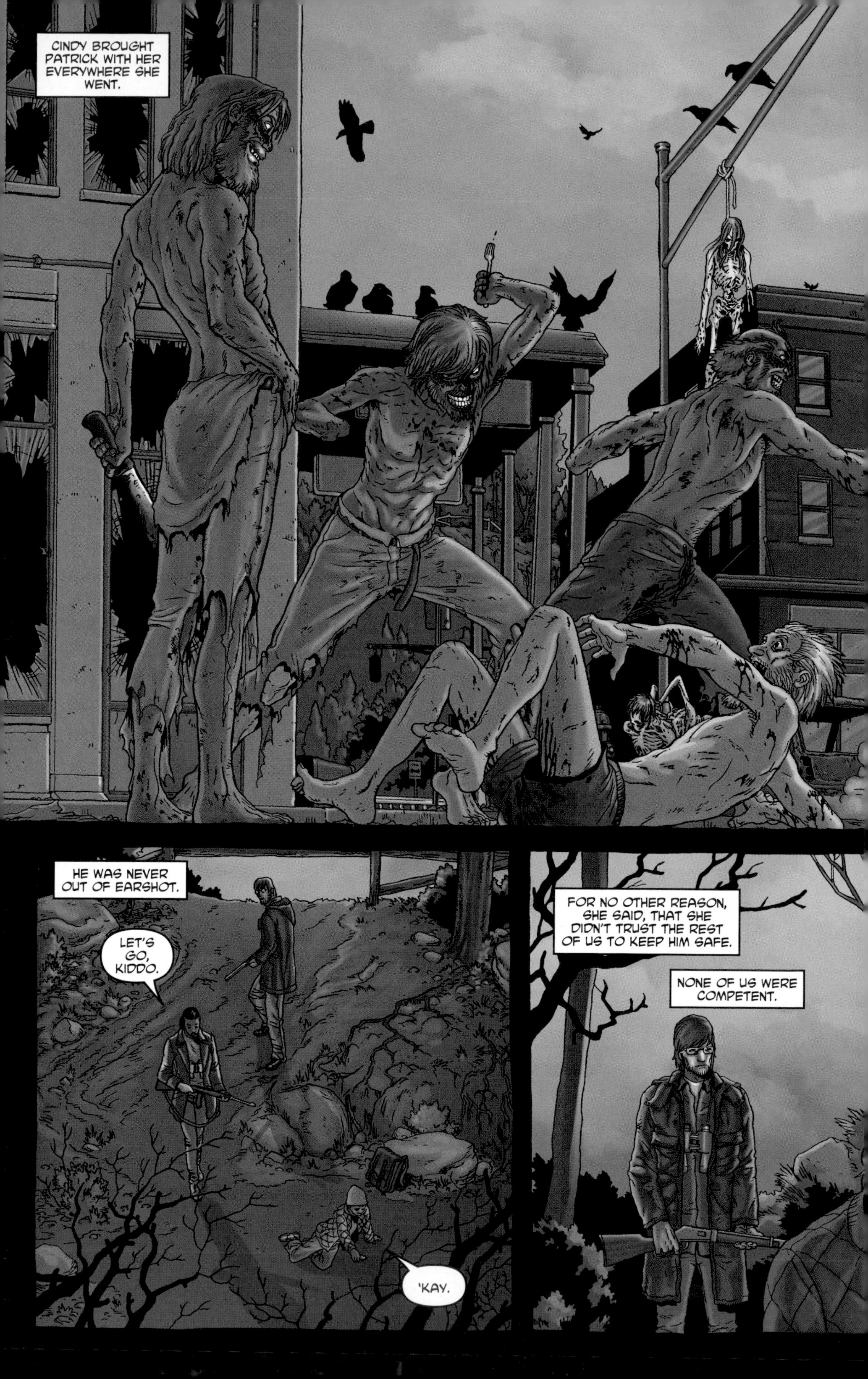
CINDY BROUGHT PATRICK WITH HER EVERYWHERE SHE WENT.
HE WAS NEVER OUT OF EARSHOT.
LET'S GO, KIDDO.
'KAY.
FOR NO OTHER REASON, SHE SAID, THAT SHE DIDN'T TRUST THE REST OF US TO KEEP HIM SAFE.
NONE OF US WERE COMPETENT.

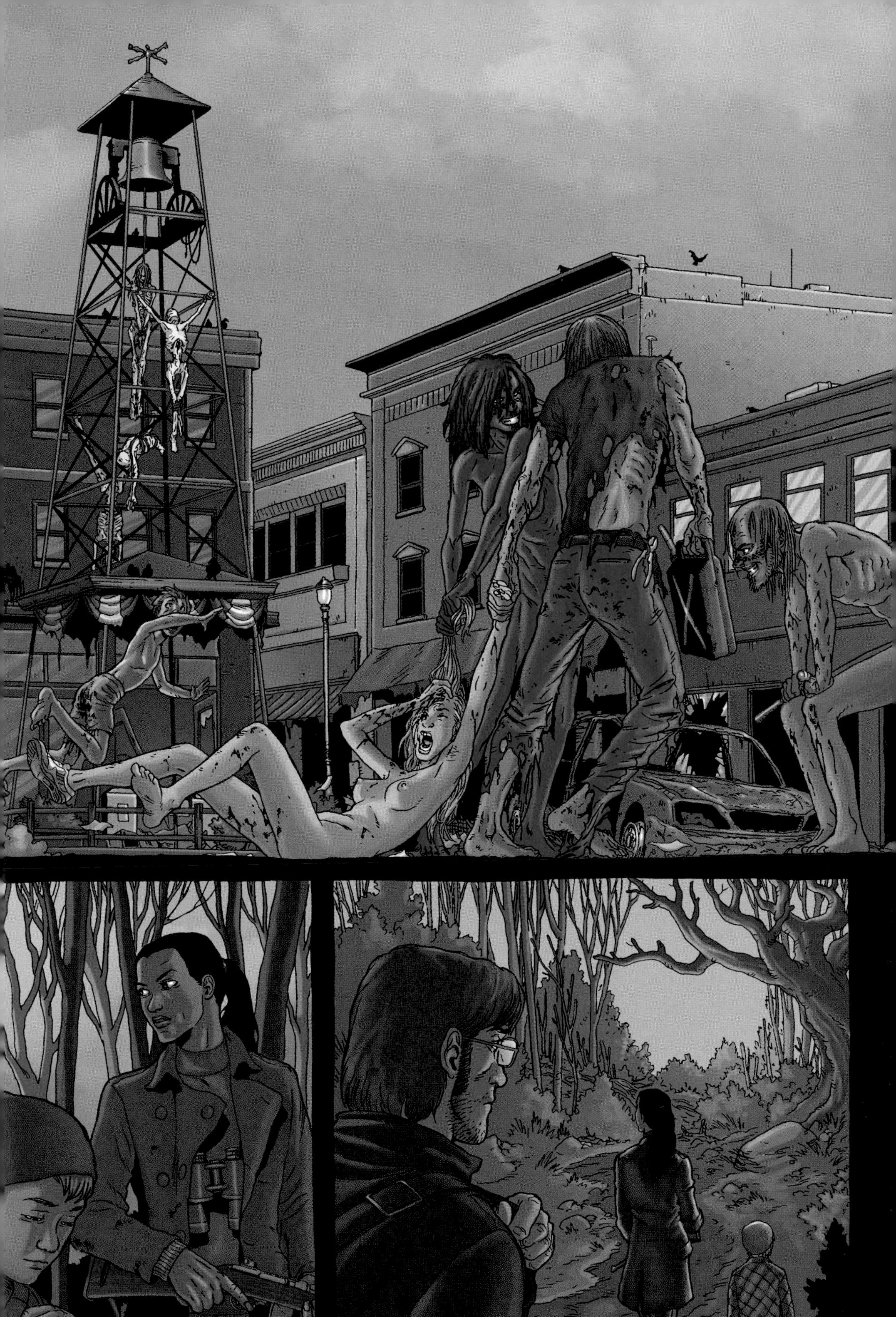
I AGREED.

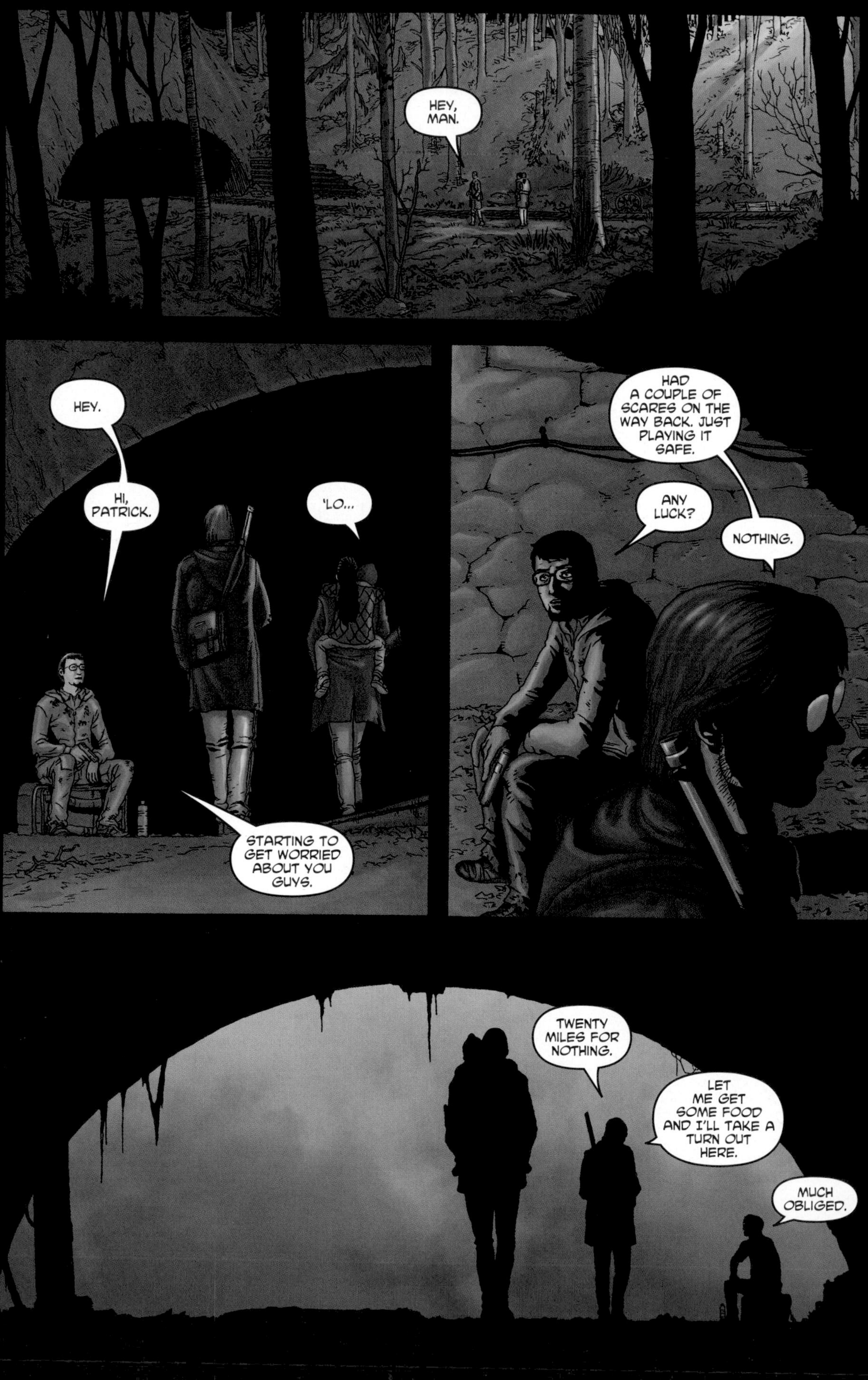
HEY, MAN.
HEY.
HI, PATRICK.
'LO...
STARTING TO GET WORRIED ABOUT YOU GUYS.
HAD A COUPLE OF SCARES ON THE WAY BACK. JUST PLAYING IT SAFE.
ANY LUCK?
NOTHING.
TWENTY MILES FOR NOTHING.
LET ME GET SOME FOOD AND I'LL TAKE A TURN OUT HERE.
MUCH OBLIGED.

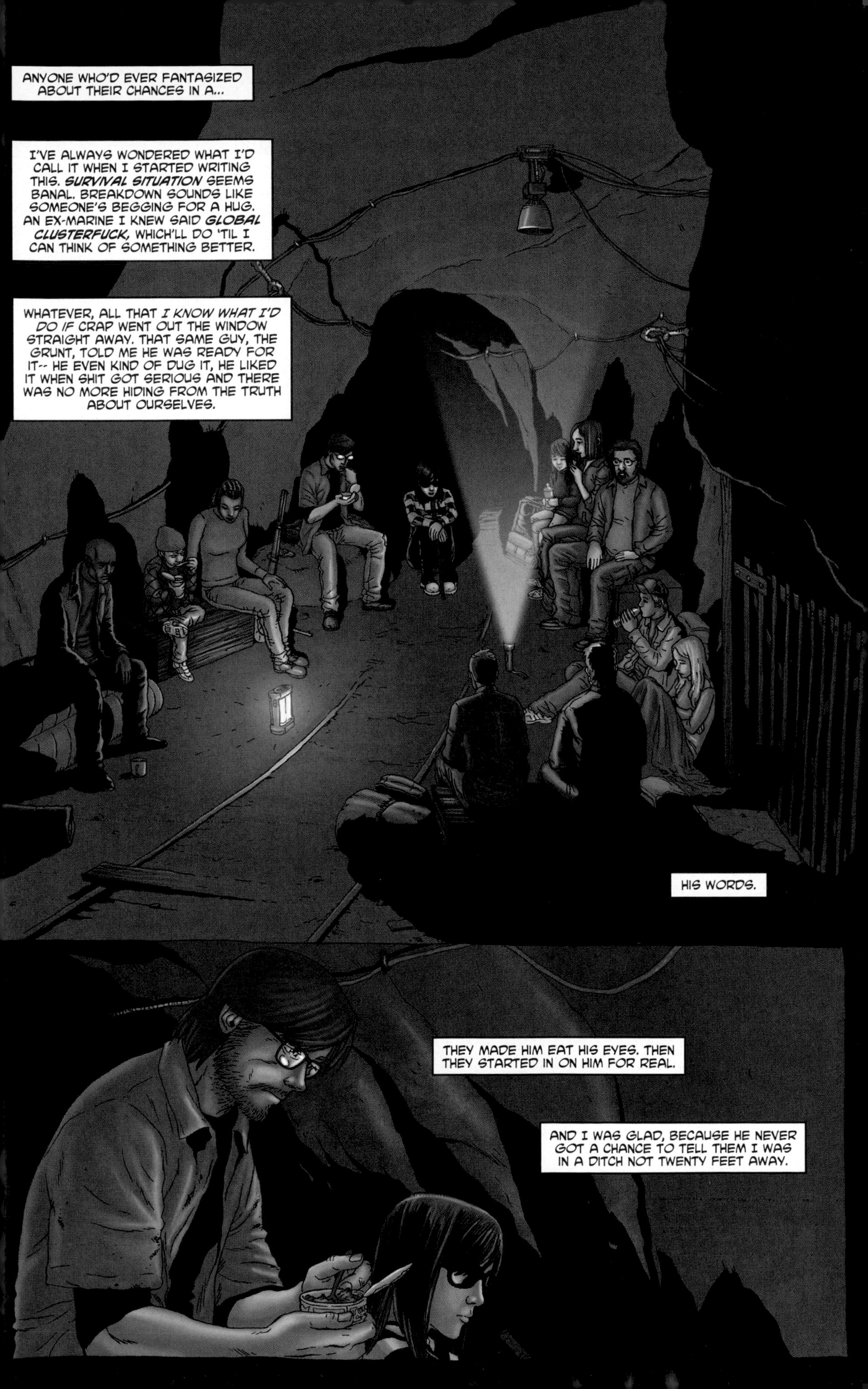
ANYONE WHO'D EVER FANTASIZED ABOUT THEIR CHANCES IN A...
I'VE ALWAYS WONDERED WHAT I'D CALL IT WHEN I STARTED WRITING THIS. *SURVIVAL SITUATION* SEEMS BANAL. BREAKDOWN SOUNDS LIKE SOMEONE'S BEGGING FOR A HUG. AN EX-MARINE I KNEW SAID *GLOBAL CLUSTERFUCK,* WHICH'LL DO 'TIL I CAN THINK OF SOMETHING BETTER.
WHATEVER, ALL THAT *I KNOW WHAT I'D DO IF* CRAP WENT OUT THE WINDOW STRAIGHT AWAY. THAT SAME GUY, THE GRUNT, TOLD ME HE WAS READY FOR IT-- HE EVEN KIND OF DUG IT, HE LIKED IT WHEN SHIT GOT SERIOUS AND THERE WAS NO MORE HIDING FROM THE TRUTH ABOUT OURSELVES.
HIS WORDS.
THEY MADE HIM EAT HIS EYES. THEN THEY STARTED IN ON HIM FOR REAL.
AND I WAS GLAD, BECAUSE HE NEVER GOT A CHANCE TO TELL THEM I WAS IN A DITCH NOT TWENTY FEET AWAY.

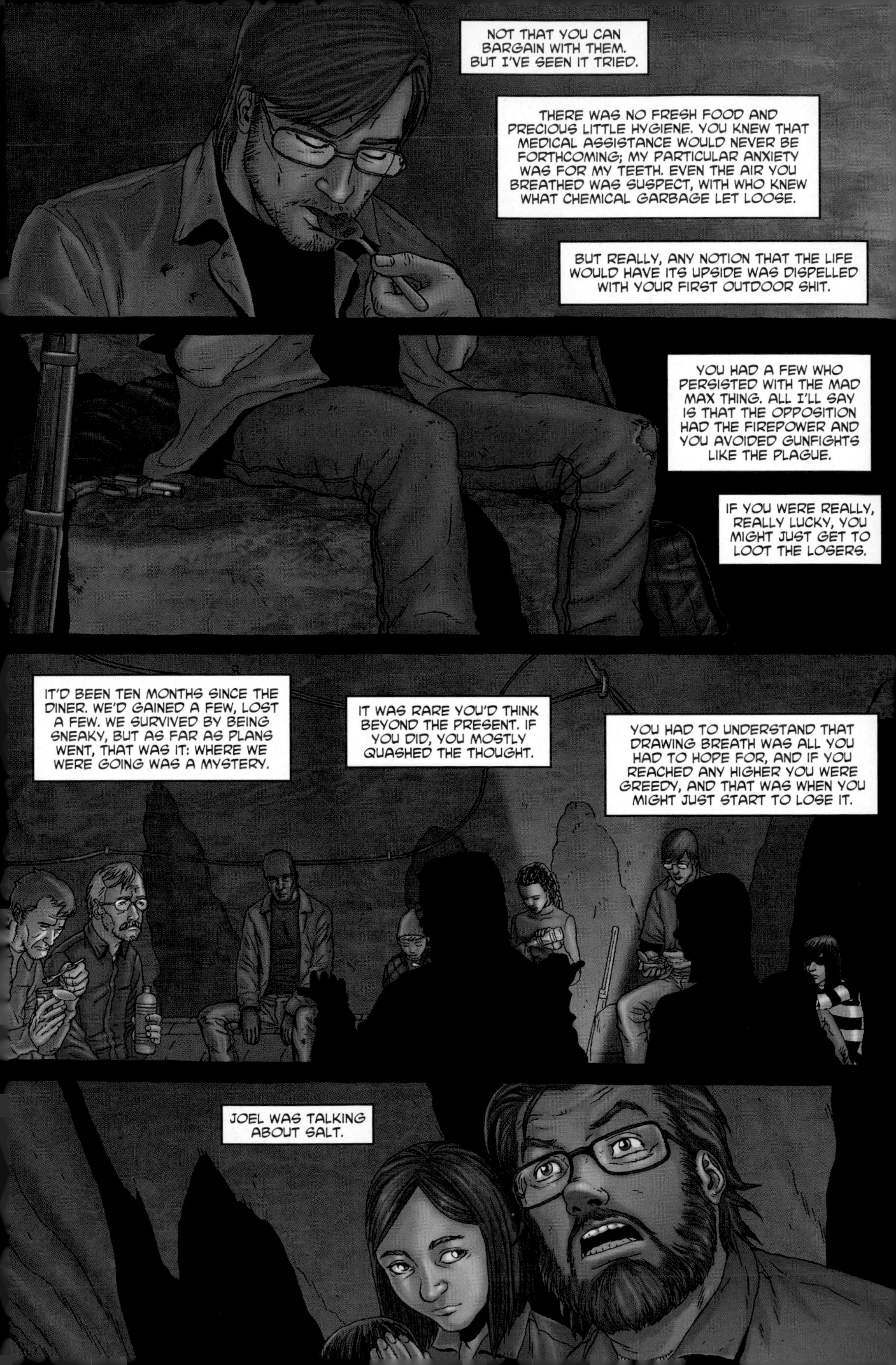
NOT THAT YOU CAN BARGAIN WITH THEM. BUT I'VE SEEN IT TRIED.
THERE WAS NO FRESH FOOD AND PRECIOUS LITTLE HYGIENE. YOU KNEW THAT MEDICAL ASSISTANCE WOULD NEVER BE FORTHCOMING; MY PARTICULAR ANXIETY WAS FOR MY TEETH. EVEN THE AIR YOU BREATHED WAS SUSPECT, WITH WHO KNEW WHAT CHEMICAL GARBAGE LET LOOSE.
BUT REALLY, ANY NOTION THAT THE LIFE WOULD HAVE ITS UPSIDE WAS DISPELLED WITH YOUR FIRST OUTDOOR SHIT.
YOU HAD A FEW WHO PERSISTED WITH THE MAD MAX THING. ALL I'LL SAY IS THAT THE OPPOSITION HAD THE FIREPOWER AND YOU AVOIDED GUNFIGHTS LIKE THE PLAGUE.
IF YOU WERE REALLY, REALLY LUCKY, YOU MIGHT JUST GET TO LOOT THE LOSERS.
IT'D BEEN TEN MONTHS SINCE THE DINER. WE'D GAINED A FEW, LOST A FEW. WE SURVIVED BY BEING SNEAKY, BUT AS FAR AS PLANS WENT, THAT WAS IT: WHERE WE WERE GOING WAS A MYSTERY.
IT WAS RARE YOU'D THINK BEYOND THE PRESENT. IF YOU DID, YOU MOSTLY QUASHED THE THOUGHT.
YOU HAD TO UNDERSTAND THAT DRAWING BREATH WAS ALL YOU HAD TO HOPE FOR, AND IF YOU REACHED ANY HIGHER YOU WERE GREEDY, AND THAT WAS WHEN YOU MIGHT JUST START TO LOSE IT.
JOEL WAS TALKING ABOUT SALT.

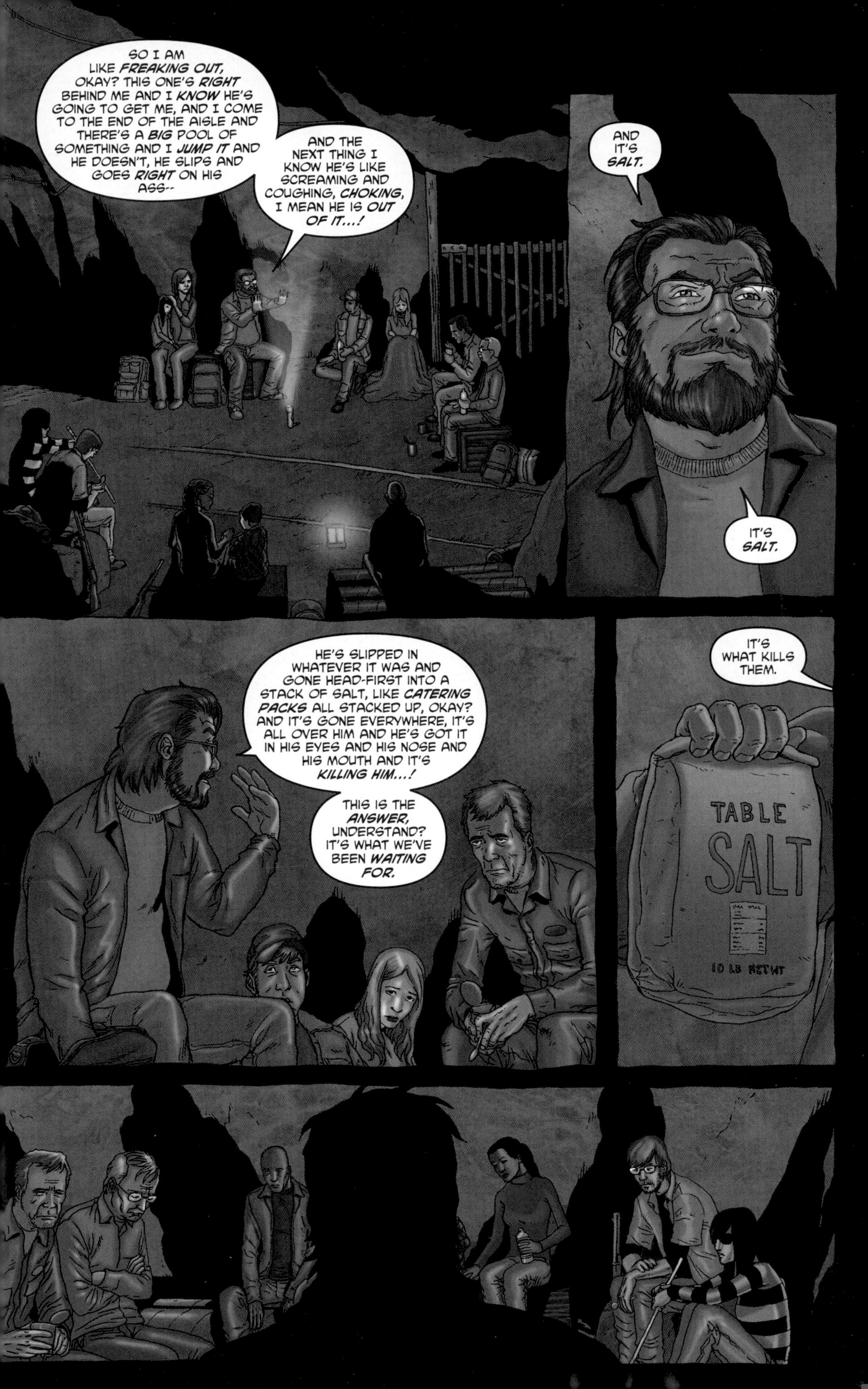
SO I AM LIKE *FREAKING OUT*, OKAY? THIS ONE'S *RIGHT* BEHIND ME AND I *KNOW* HE'S GOING TO GET ME, AND I COME TO THE END OF THE AISLE AND THERE'S A *BIG* POOL OF SOMETHING AND I *JUMP IT* AND HE DOESN'T, HE SLIPS AND GOES *RIGHT* ON HIS ASS--
AND THE NEXT THING I KNOW HE'S LIKE SCREAMING AND COUGHING, *CHOKING*, I MEAN HE IS *OUT OF IT...!*
AND IT'S *SALT.*
IT'S *SALT.*
HE'S SLIPPED IN WHATEVER IT WAS AND GONE HEAD-FIRST INTO A STACK OF SALT, LIKE *CATERING PACKS* ALL STACKED UP, OKAY? AND IT'S GONE EVERYWHERE, IT'S ALL OVER HIM AND HE'S GOT IT IN HIS EYES AND HIS NOSE AND HIS MOUTH AND IT'S *KILLING HIM...!*
THIS IS THE *ANSWER*, UNDERSTAND? IT'S WHAT WE'VE BEEN *WAITING FOR.*
IT'S WHAT KILLS THEM.
TABLE SALT
10 LB NET WT

JOEL, ARE YOU SURE THAT'S NOT JUST WISHFUL THINKING?

WELL-- KELLY-- YOU WEREN'T THERE, OKAY? AND NO OFFENCE OR ANYTHING, BUT EVEN IF YOU *WERE*...

CLASSY.

I GET THE IDEA. BUT I THINK IF ANYONE GOT A FACEFUL OF SALT IT WOULD BE UNCOMFORTABLE; IF ONE OF US GOT IT IN THEIR EYES OR THEIR MOUTH AND CHOKED ON IT, IT WOULD HURT A LOT.

SO DID YOU REALLY SEE THIS ONE DIE...?

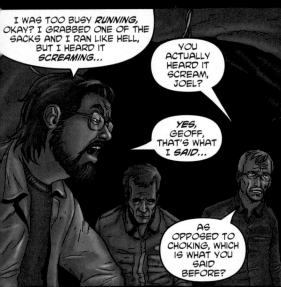

I WAS TOO BUSY *RUNNING*, OKAY? I GRABBED ONE OF THE SACKS AND I RAN LIKE HELL, BUT I HEARD IT *SCREAMING*...

YOU ACTUALLY HEARD IT SCREAM, JOEL?

YES, GEOFF, THAT'S WHAT I *SAID*...

AS OPPOSED TO CHOKING, WHICH IS WHAT YOU SAID BEFORE?

I *KNOW* WHAT I SAID, OKAY?

LOOK, THIS IS *REAL*, THIS IS NOT SOME *DELUSION*. WE'VE BEEN LOOKING FOR A WAY TO STOP RUNNING, TO START THE *FIGHTBACK* AGAINST THESE THINGS...

WE HAVE?

"FIGHTBACK"...

YOU KNOW WHAT THIS IS? THIS IS YOUR SCI-FI SHOWS AND YOUR MOVIES, YOUR DUNGEONS AND DRAGONS GAMES YOU USED TO PLAY...

DUNGEONS AND DRAGONS, DO YOU EVEN *KNOW* WHAT YOU'RE TALKING ABOUT? IT WAS *MAGIC THE*--

WELL, WHATEVER THE FUCK.

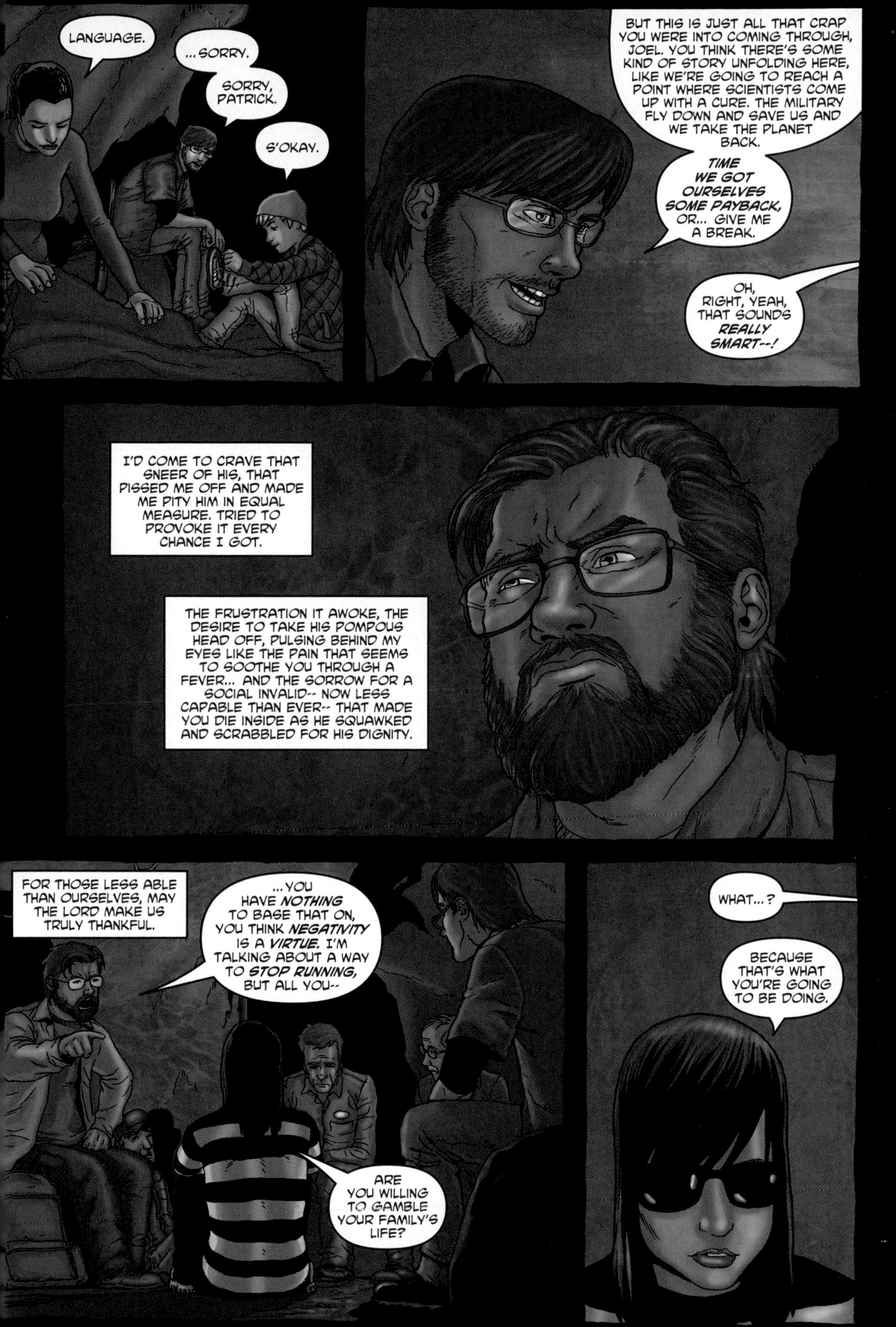
LANGUAGE.
...SORRY.
SORRY, PATRICK.
S'OKAY.
BUT THIS IS JUST ALL THAT CRAP YOU WERE INTO COMING THROUGH, JOEL. YOU THINK THERE'S SOME KIND OF STORY UNFOLDING HERE, LIKE WE'RE GOING TO REACH A POINT WHERE SCIENTISTS COME UP WITH A CURE. THE MILITARY FLY DOWN AND SAVE US AND WE TAKE THE PLANET BACK.
TIME WE GOT OURSELVES SOME PAYBACK, OR... GIVE ME A BREAK.
OH, RIGHT, YEAH, THAT SOUNDS *REALLY SMART--!*
I'D COME TO CRAVE THAT SNEER OF HIS, THAT PISSED ME OFF AND MADE ME PITY HIM IN EQUAL MEASURE. TRIED TO PROVOKE IT EVERY CHANCE I GOT.
THE FRUSTRATION IT AWOKE, THE DESIRE TO TAKE HIS POMPOUS HEAD OFF, PULSING BEHIND MY EYES LIKE THE PAIN THAT SEEMS TO SOOTHE YOU THROUGH A FEVER... AND THE SORROW FOR A SOCIAL INVALID-- NOW LESS CAPABLE THAN EVER-- THAT MADE YOU DIE INSIDE AS HE SQUAWKED AND SCRABBLED FOR HIS DIGNITY.
FOR THOSE LESS ABLE THAN OURSELVES, MAY THE LORD MAKE US TRULY THANKFUL.
...YOU HAVE *NOTHING* TO BASE THAT ON, YOU THINK *NEGATIVITY* IS A *VIRTUE.* I'M TALKING ABOUT A WAY TO *STOP RUNNING,* BUT ALL YOU--
ARE YOU WILLING TO GAMBLE YOUR FAMILY'S LIFE?
WHAT...?
BECAUSE THAT'S WHAT YOU'RE GOING TO BE DOING.

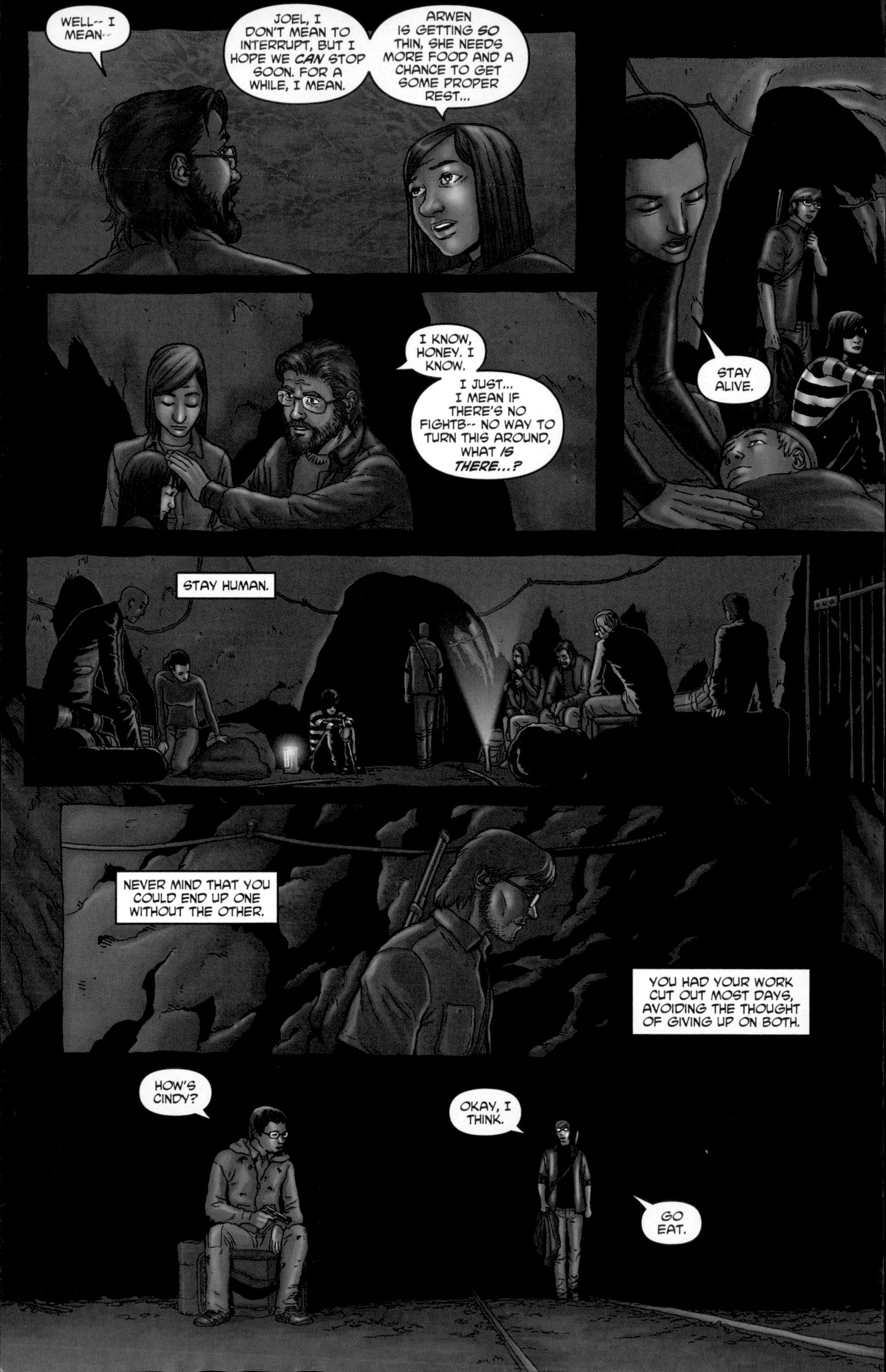
WELL-- I MEAN--
JOEL, I DON'T MEAN TO INTERRUPT, BUT I HOPE WE CAN STOP SOON. FOR A WHILE, I MEAN.
ARWEN IS GETTING SO THIN, SHE NEEDS MORE FOOD AND A CHANCE TO GET SOME PROPER REST...
I KNOW, HONEY. I KNOW.
I JUST... I MEAN IF THERE'S NO FIGHTB-- NO WAY TO TURN THIS AROUND, WHAT IS THERE...?
STAY ALIVE.
STAY HUMAN.
NEVER MIND THAT YOU COULD END UP ONE WITHOUT THE OTHER.
YOU HAD YOUR WORK CUT OUT MOST DAYS, AVOIDING THE THOUGHT OF GIVING UP ON BOTH.
HOW'S CINDY?
OKAY, I THINK.
GO EAT.

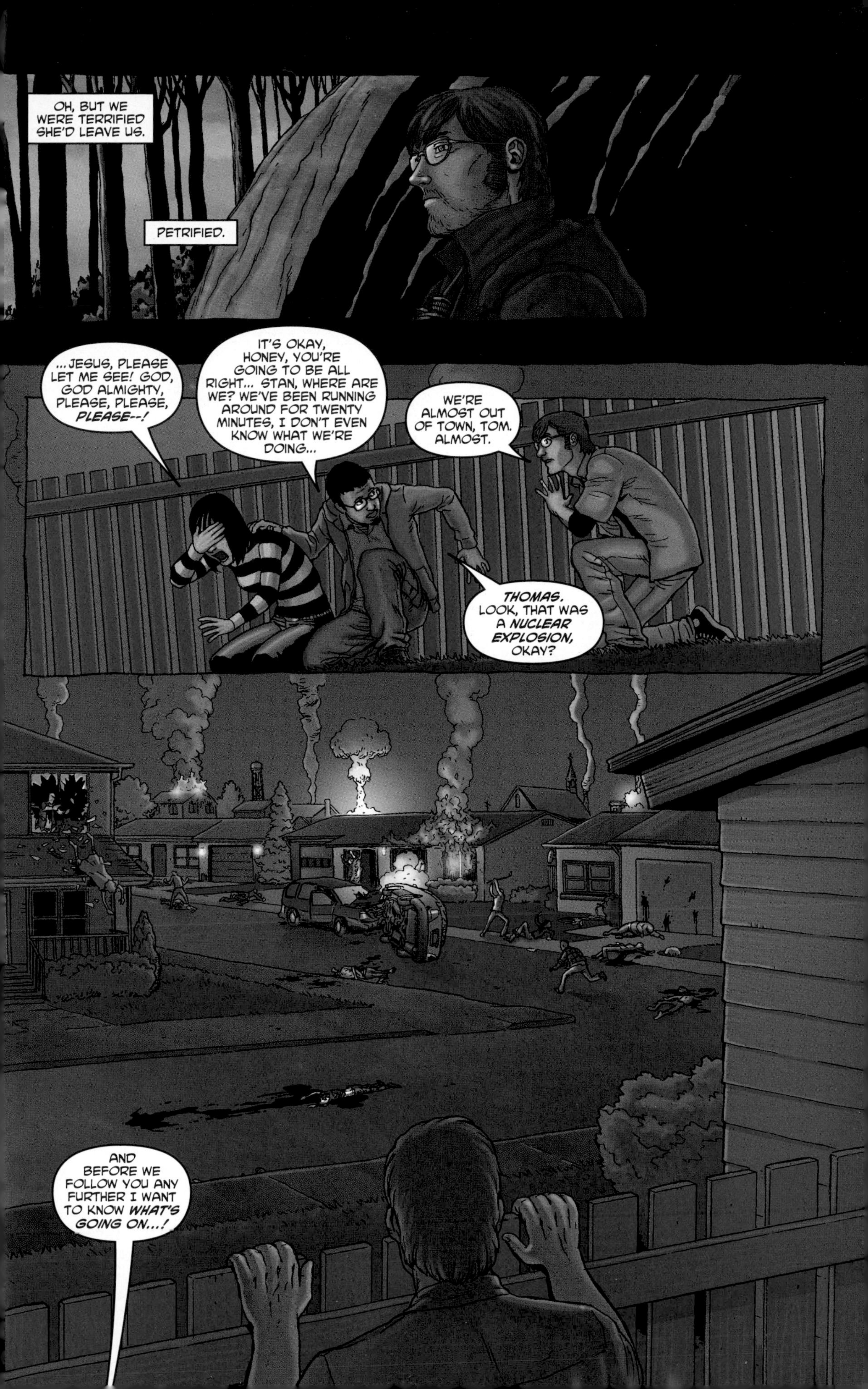
OH, BUT WE WERE TERRIFIED SHE'D LEAVE US.
PETRIFIED.
...JESUS, PLEASE LET ME SEE! GOD, GOD ALMIGHTY, PLEASE, PLEASE, *PLEASE--!*
IT'S OKAY, HONEY, YOU'RE GOING TO BE ALL RIGHT... STAN, WHERE ARE WE? WE'VE BEEN RUNNING AROUND FOR TWENTY MINUTES, I DON'T EVEN KNOW WHAT WE'RE DOING...
WE'RE ALMOST OUT OF TOWN, TOM. ALMOST.
THOMAS. LOOK, THAT WAS A *NUCLEAR EXPLOSION,* OKAY?
AND BEFORE WE FOLLOW YOU ANY FURTHER I WANT TO KNOW *WHAT'S GOING ON...!*

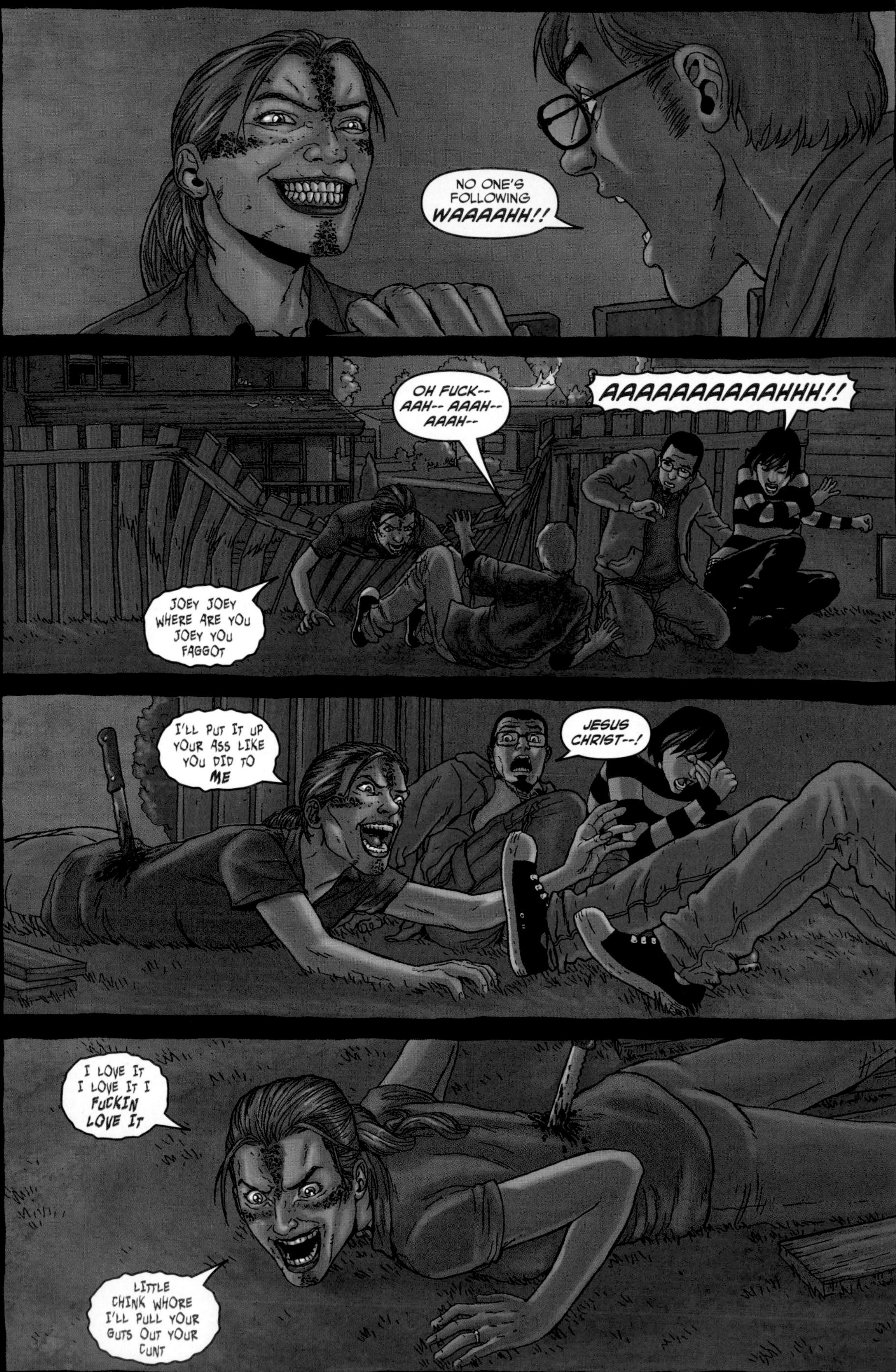
NO ONE'S FOLLOWING WAAAAHH!!
OH FUCK-- AAH-- AAAH-- AAAH--
AAAAAAAAAAAHHH!!
JOEY JOEY WHERE ARE YOU JOEY YOU FAGGOT
I'LL PUT IT UP YOUR ASS LIKE YOU DID TO ME
JESUS CHRIST--!
I LOVE IT I LOVE IT I FUCKIN LOVE IT
LITTLE CHINK WHORE I'LL PULL YOUR GUTS OUT YOUR CUNT

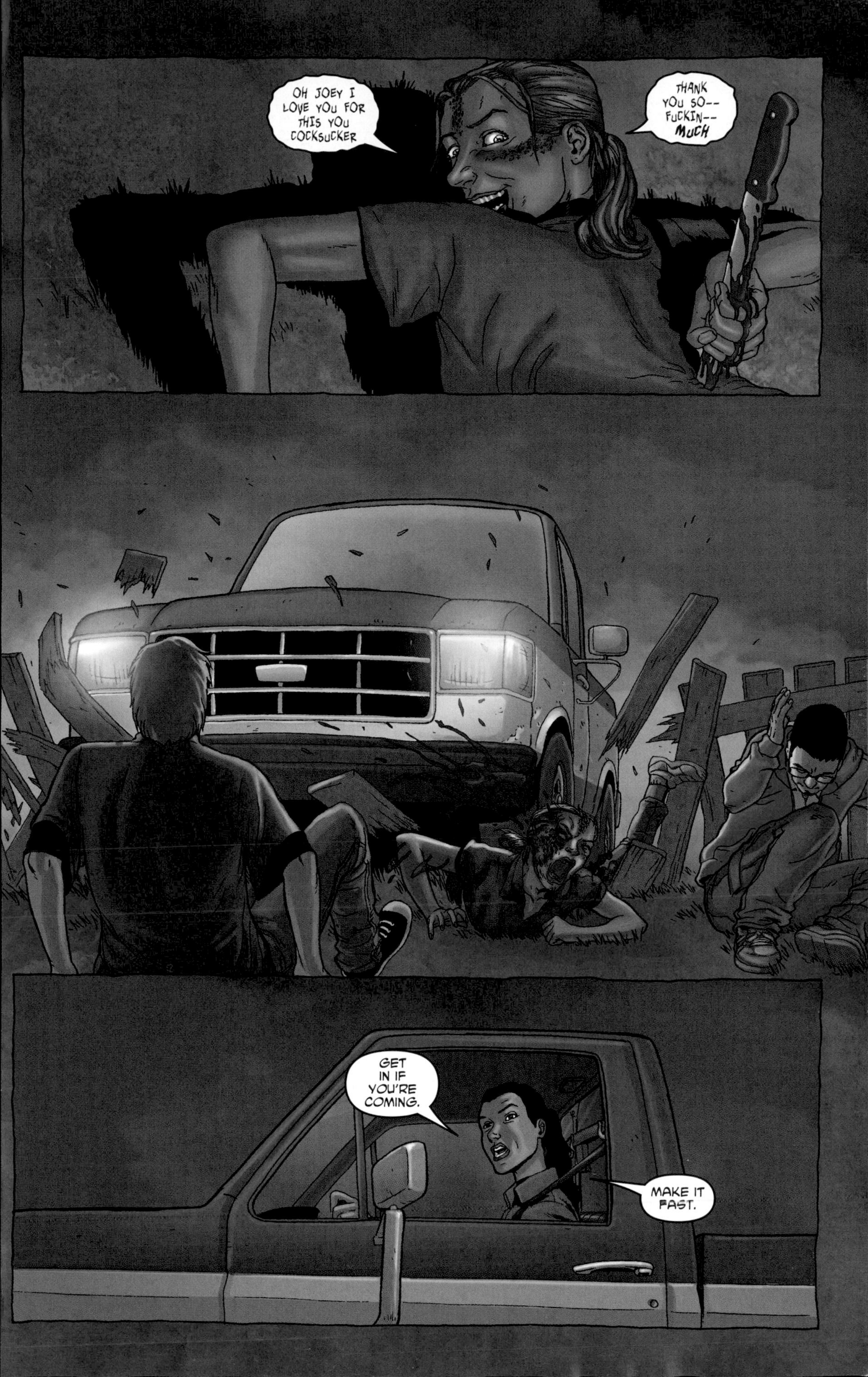
OH JOEY I LOVE YOU FOR THIS YOU COCKSUCKER
THANK YOU SO-- FUCKIN-- MUCH
GET IN IF YOU'RE COMING.
MAKE IT FAST.

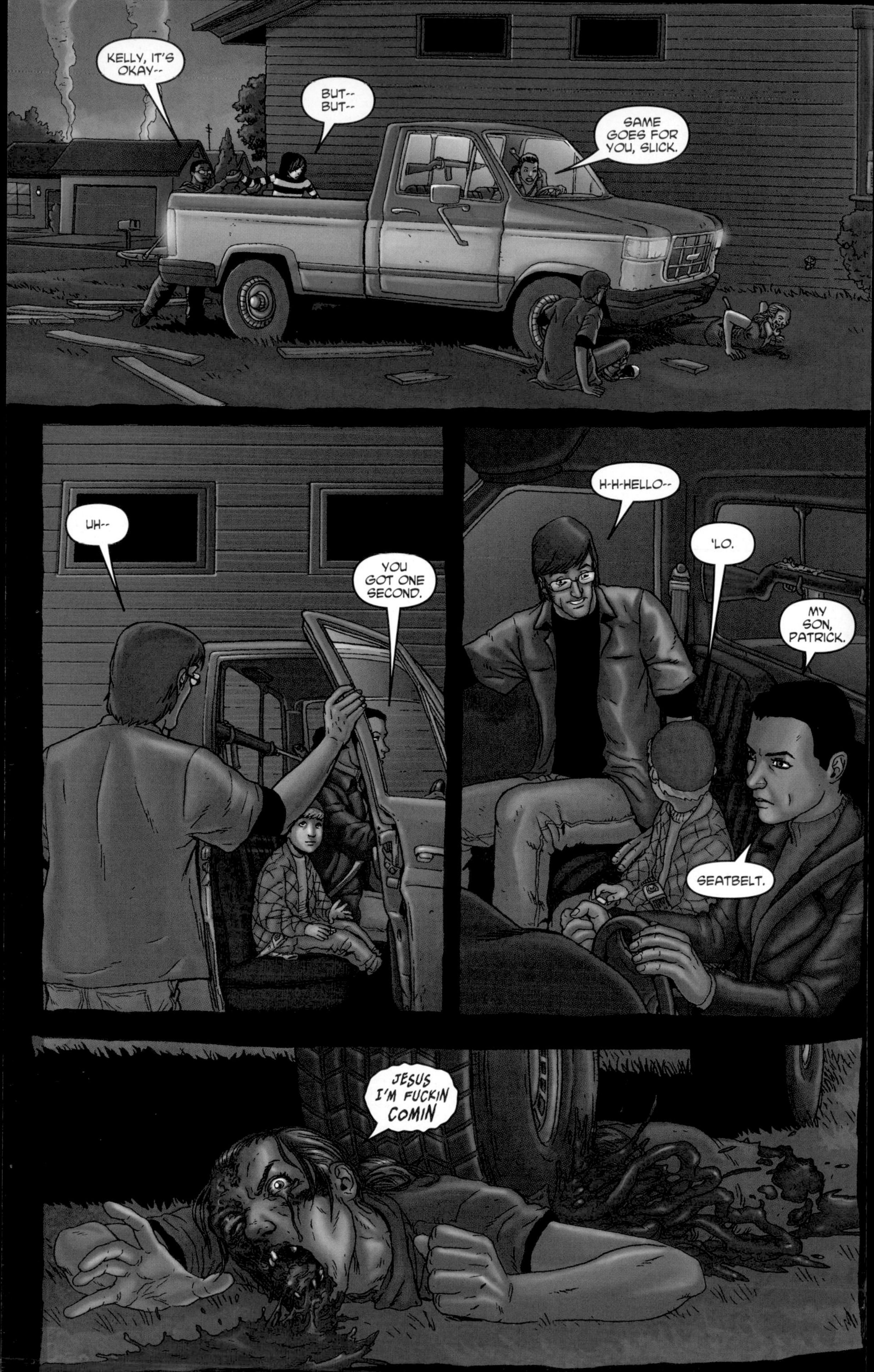
KELLY, IT'S OKAY--
BUT-- BUT--
SAME GOES FOR YOU, SLICK.
UH--
YOU GOT ONE SECOND.
H-H-HELLO--
'LO.
MY SON, PATRICK.
SEATBELT.
JESUS I'M FUCKIN COMIN

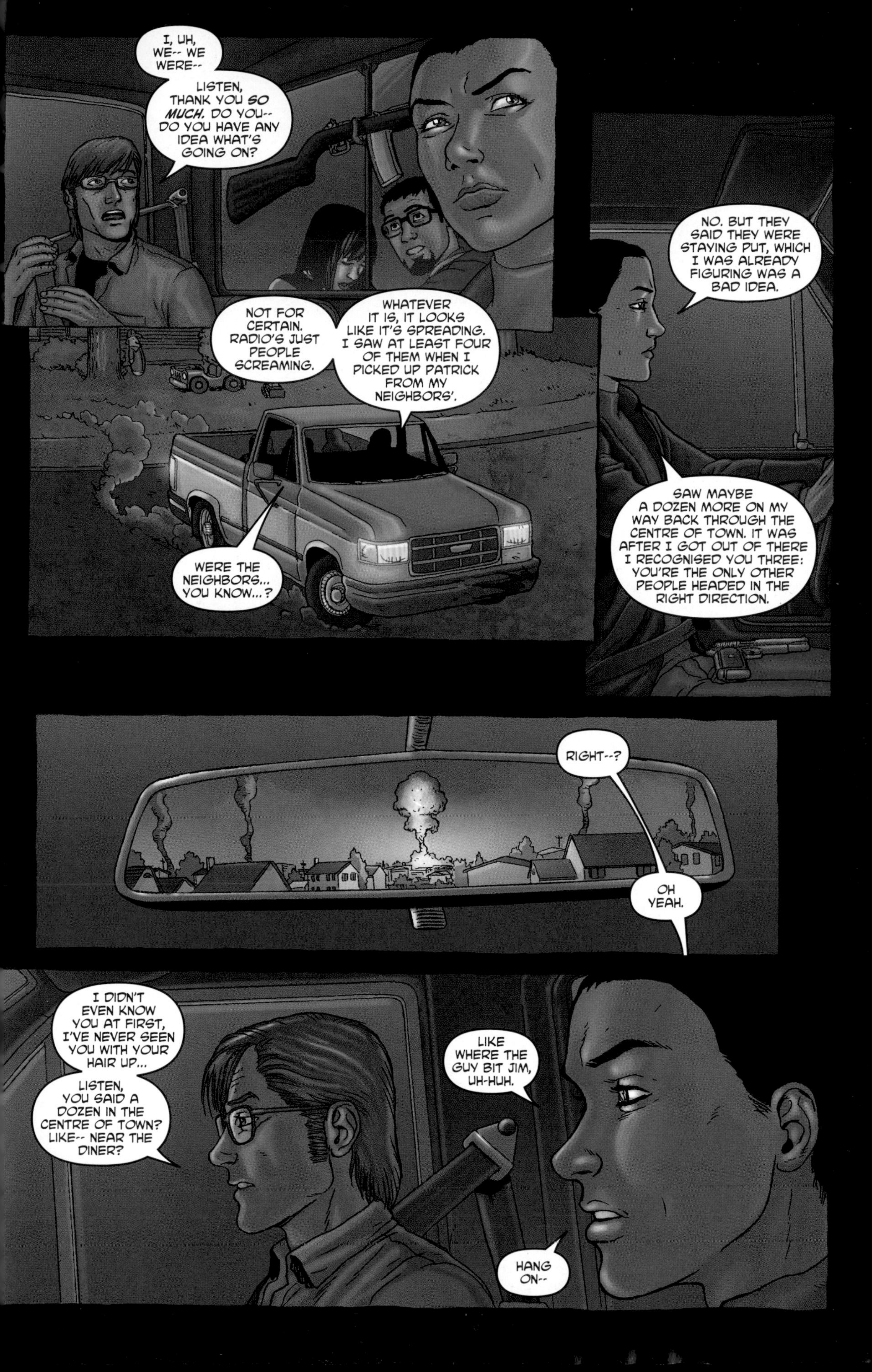
I, UH, WE-- WE WERE--
LISTEN, THANK YOU *SO MUCH.* DO YOU-- DO YOU HAVE ANY IDEA WHAT'S GOING ON?
NO. BUT THEY SAID THEY WERE STAYING PUT, WHICH I WAS ALREADY FIGURING WAS A BAD IDEA.
NOT FOR CERTAIN. RADIO'S JUST PEOPLE SCREAMING.
WHATEVER IT IS, IT LOOKS LIKE IT'S SPREADING. I SAW AT LEAST FOUR OF THEM WHEN I PICKED UP PATRICK FROM MY NEIGHBORS'.
WERE THE NEIGHBORS... YOU KNOW...?
SAW MAYBE A DOZEN MORE ON MY WAY BACK THROUGH THE CENTRE OF TOWN. IT WAS AFTER I GOT OUT OF THERE I RECOGNISED YOU THREE: YOU'RE THE ONLY OTHER PEOPLE HEADED IN THE RIGHT DIRECTION.
RIGHT--?
OH YEAH.
I DIDN'T EVEN KNOW YOU AT FIRST, I'VE NEVER SEEN YOU WITH YOUR HAIR UP...
LISTEN, YOU SAID A DOZEN IN THE CENTRE OF TOWN? LIKE-- NEAR THE DINER?
LIKE WHERE THE GUY BIT JIM, UH-HUH.
HANG ON--

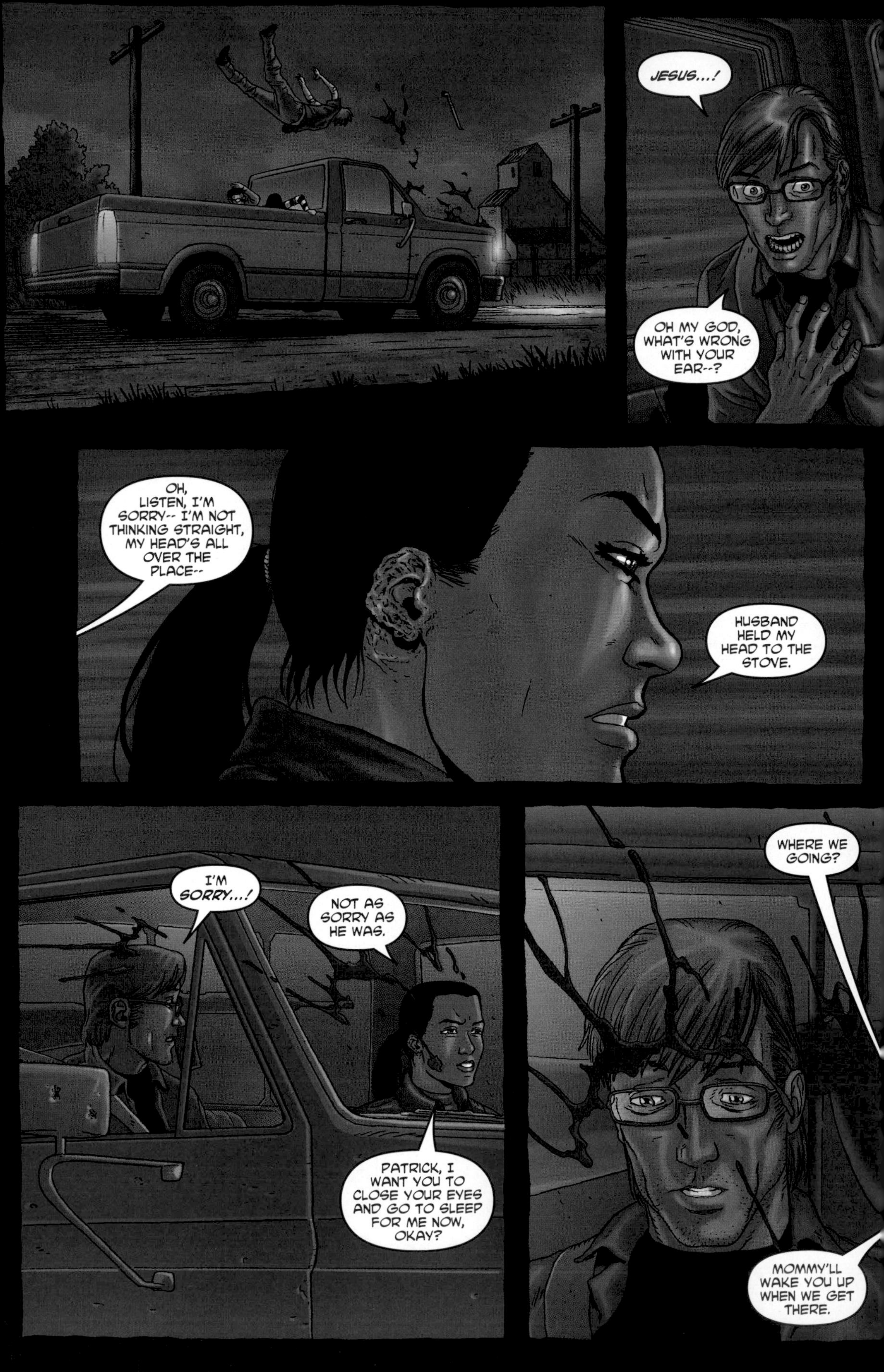
JESUS...!
OH MY GOD, WHAT'S WRONG WITH YOUR EAR--?
OH, LISTEN, I'M SORRY-- I'M NOT THINKING STRAIGHT, MY HEAD'S ALL OVER THE PLACE--
HUSBAND HELD MY HEAD TO THE STOVE.
I'M SORRY...!
NOT AS SORRY AS HE WAS.
PATRICK, I WANT YOU TO CLOSE YOUR EYES AND GO TO SLEEP FOR ME NOW, OKAY?
WHERE WE GOING?
MOMMY'LL WAKE YOU UP WHEN WE GET THERE.

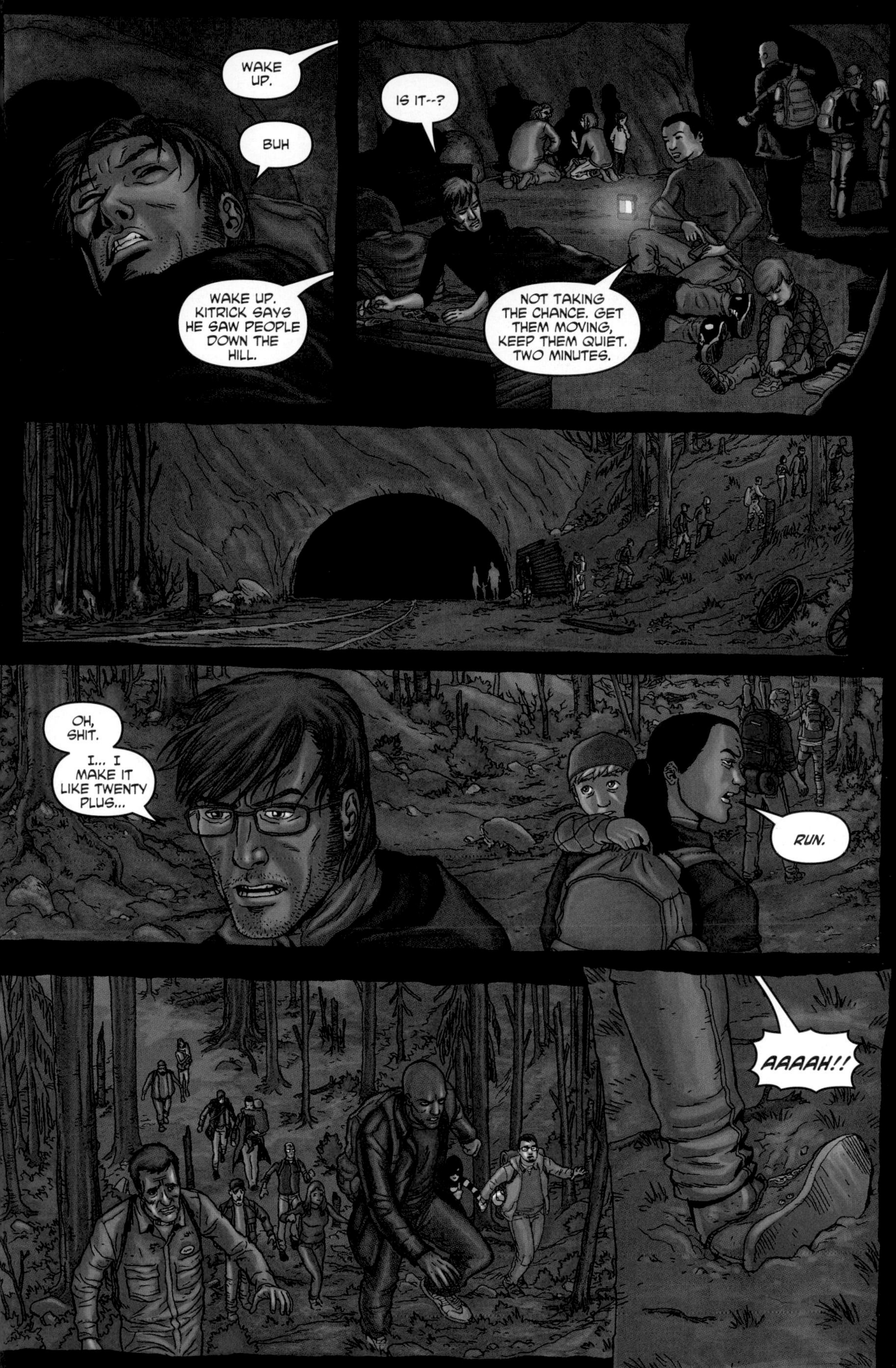
WAKE UP.
BUH
WAKE UP. KITRICK SAYS HE SAW PEOPLE DOWN THE HILL.
IS IT--?
NOT TAKING THE CHANCE. GET THEM MOVING, KEEP THEM QUIET. TWO MINUTES.
OH, SHIT.
I... I MAKE IT LIKE TWENTY PLUS...
RUN.
AAAAH!!

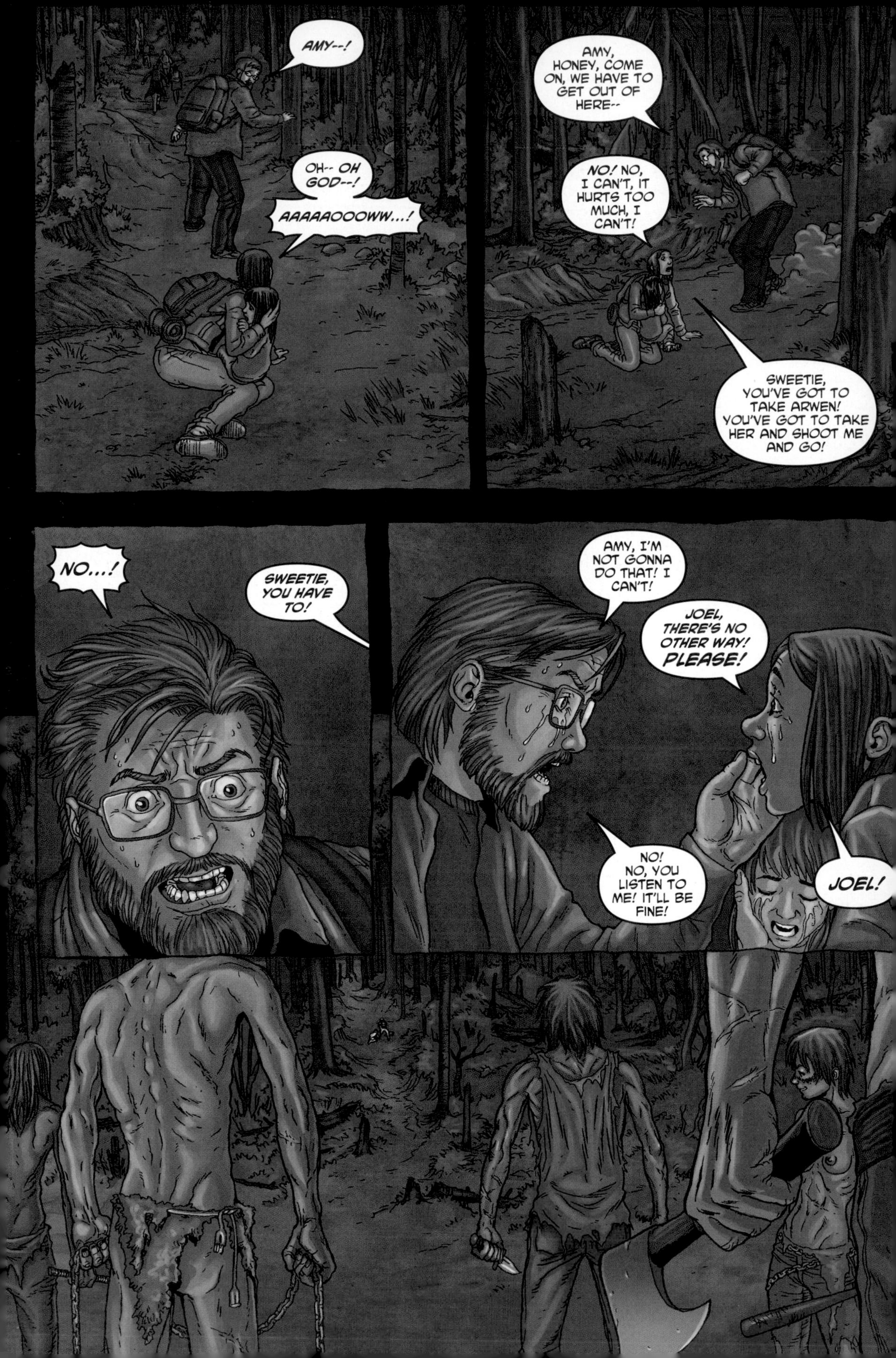
AMY--!
OH-- OH GOD--!
AAAAAOOOWW...!
AMY, HONEY, COME ON, WE HAVE TO GET OUT OF HERE--
NO! NO, I CAN'T, IT HURTS TOO MUCH, I CAN'T!
SWEETIE, YOU'VE GOT TO TAKE ARWEN! YOU'VE GOT TO TAKE HER AND SHOOT ME AND GO!
NO...!
SWEETIE, YOU HAVE TO!
AMY, I'M NOT GONNA DO THAT! I CAN'T!
JOEL, THERE'S NO OTHER WAY! PLEASE!
NO! NO, YOU LISTEN TO ME! IT'LL BE FINE!
JOEL!

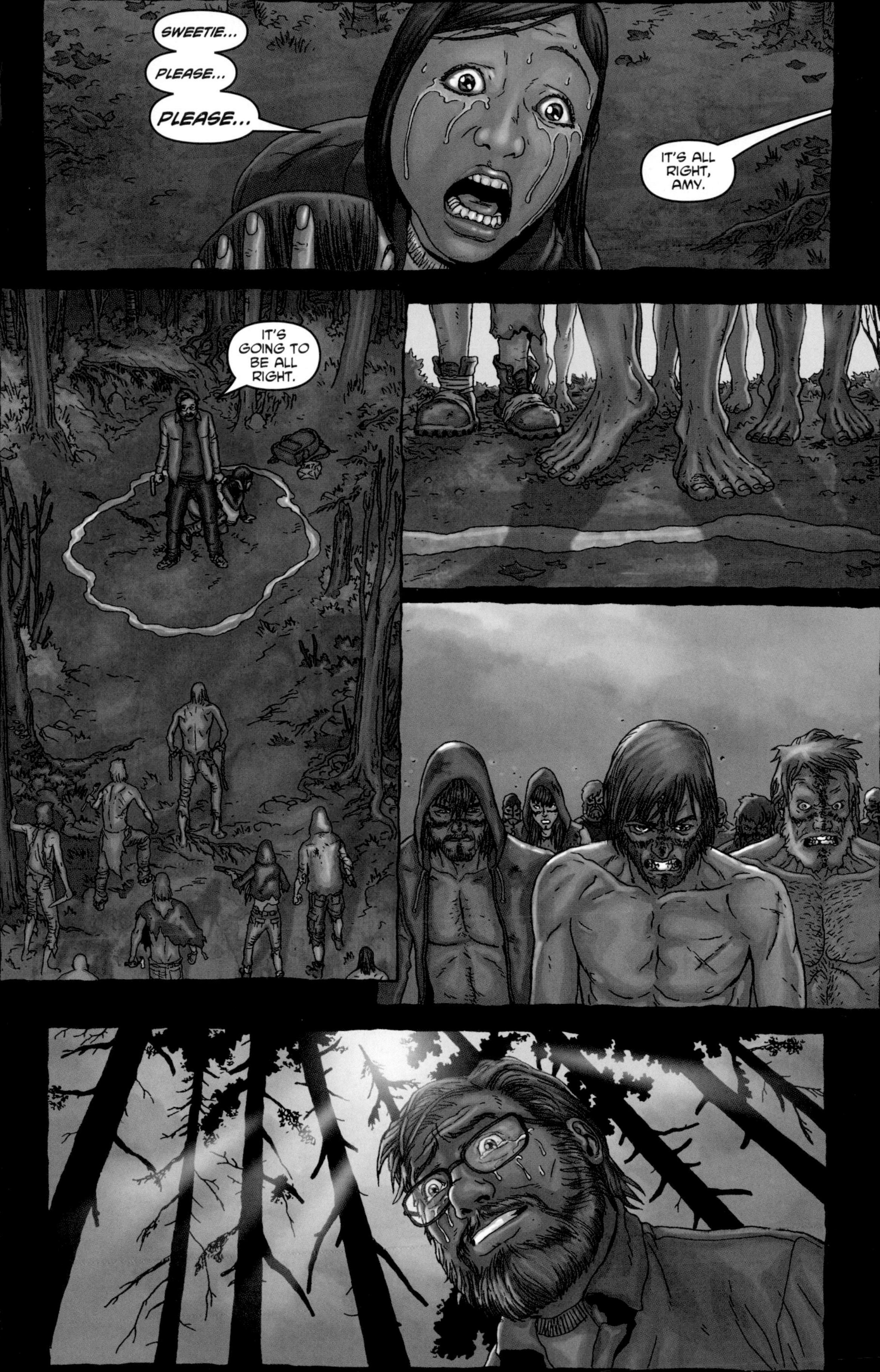
SWEETIE...
PLEASE...
PLEASE...
IT'S ALL RIGHT, AMY.
IT'S GOING TO BE ALL RIGHT.

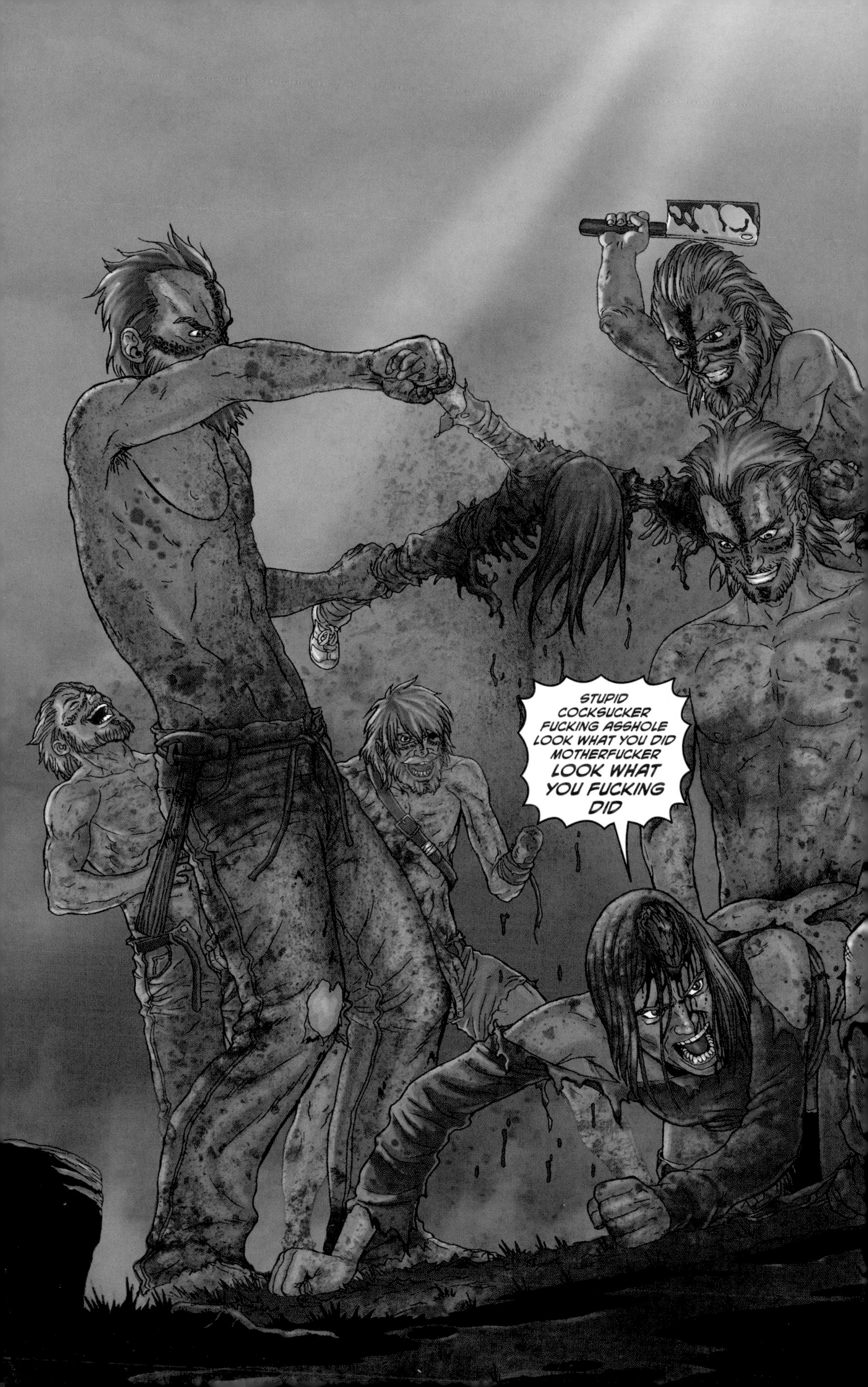
STUPID COCKSUCKER FUCKING ASSHOLE LOOK WHAT YOU DID MOTHERFUCKER LOOK WHAT YOU FUCKING DID

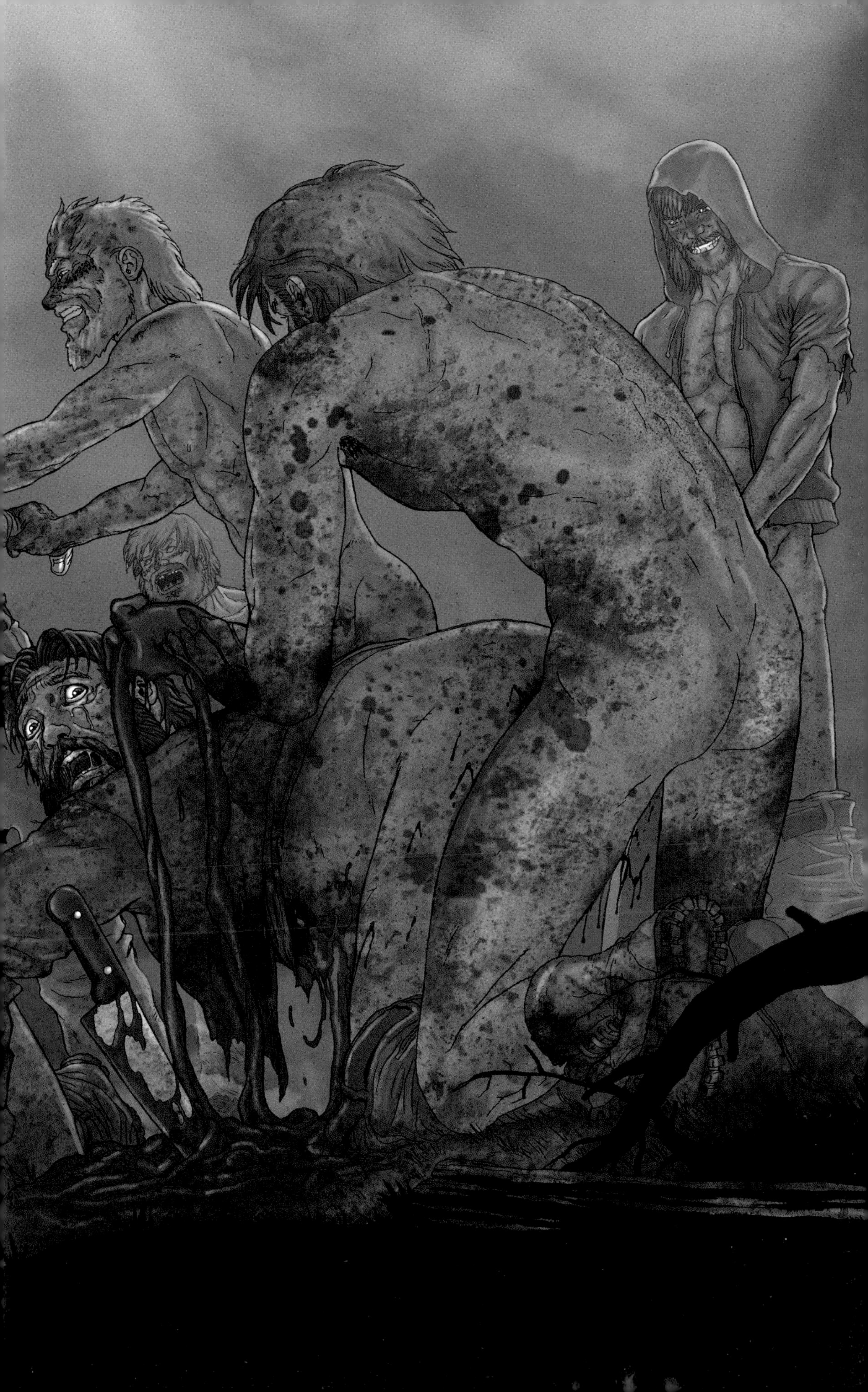

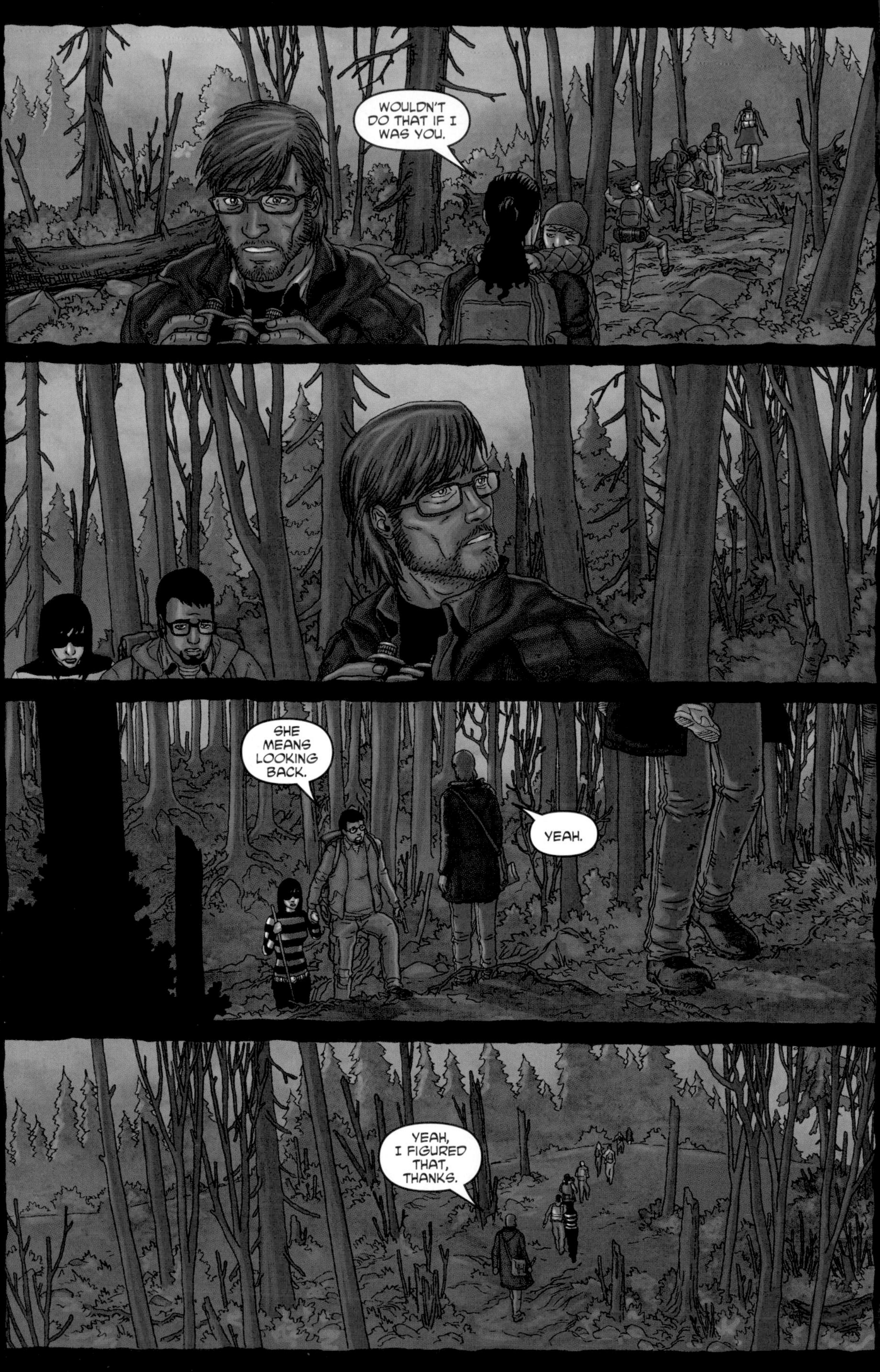
WOULDN'T DO THAT IF I WAS YOU.
SHE MEANS LOOKING BACK.
YEAH.
YEAH, I FIGURED THAT, THANKS.

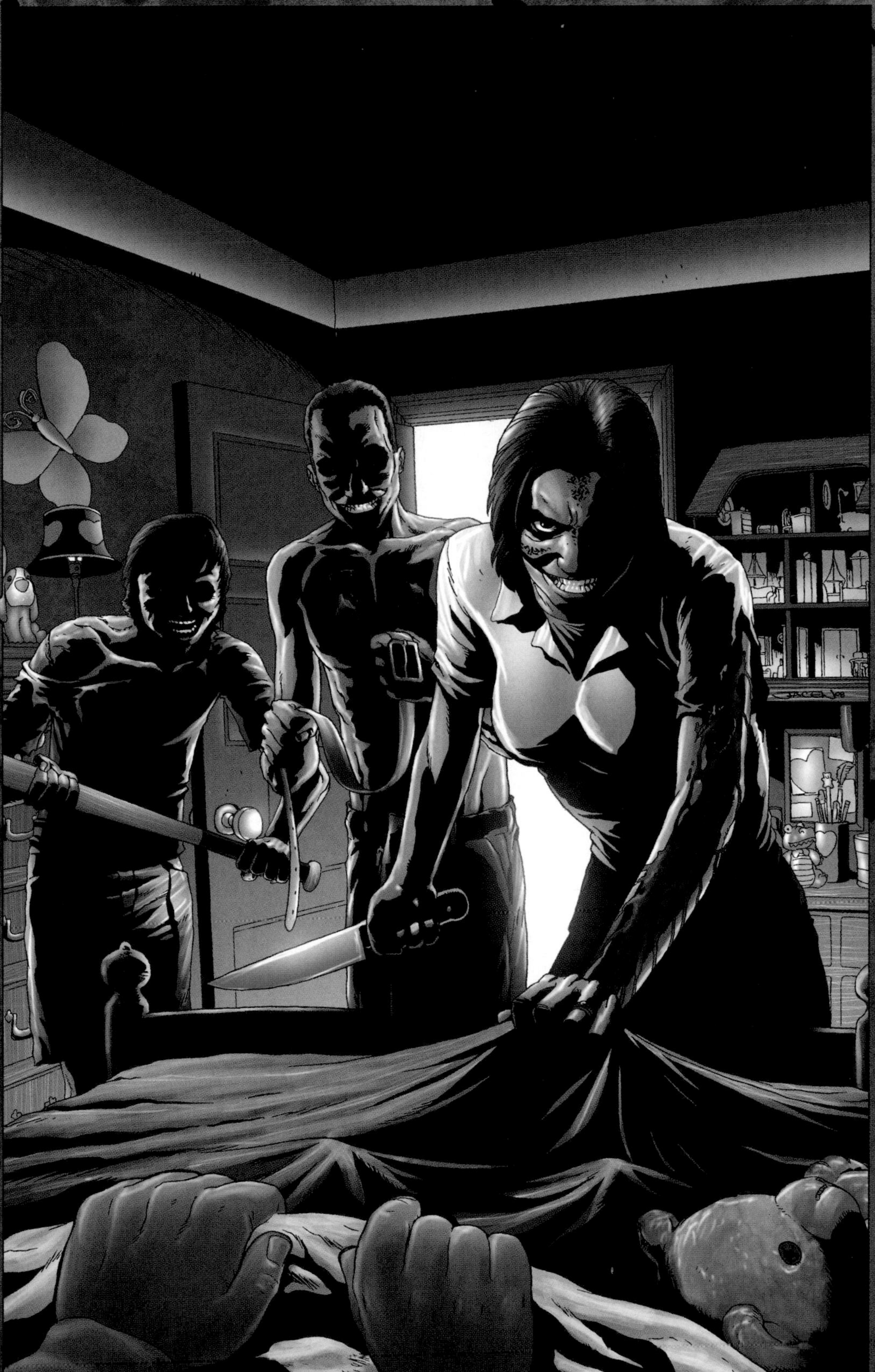

PART THREE

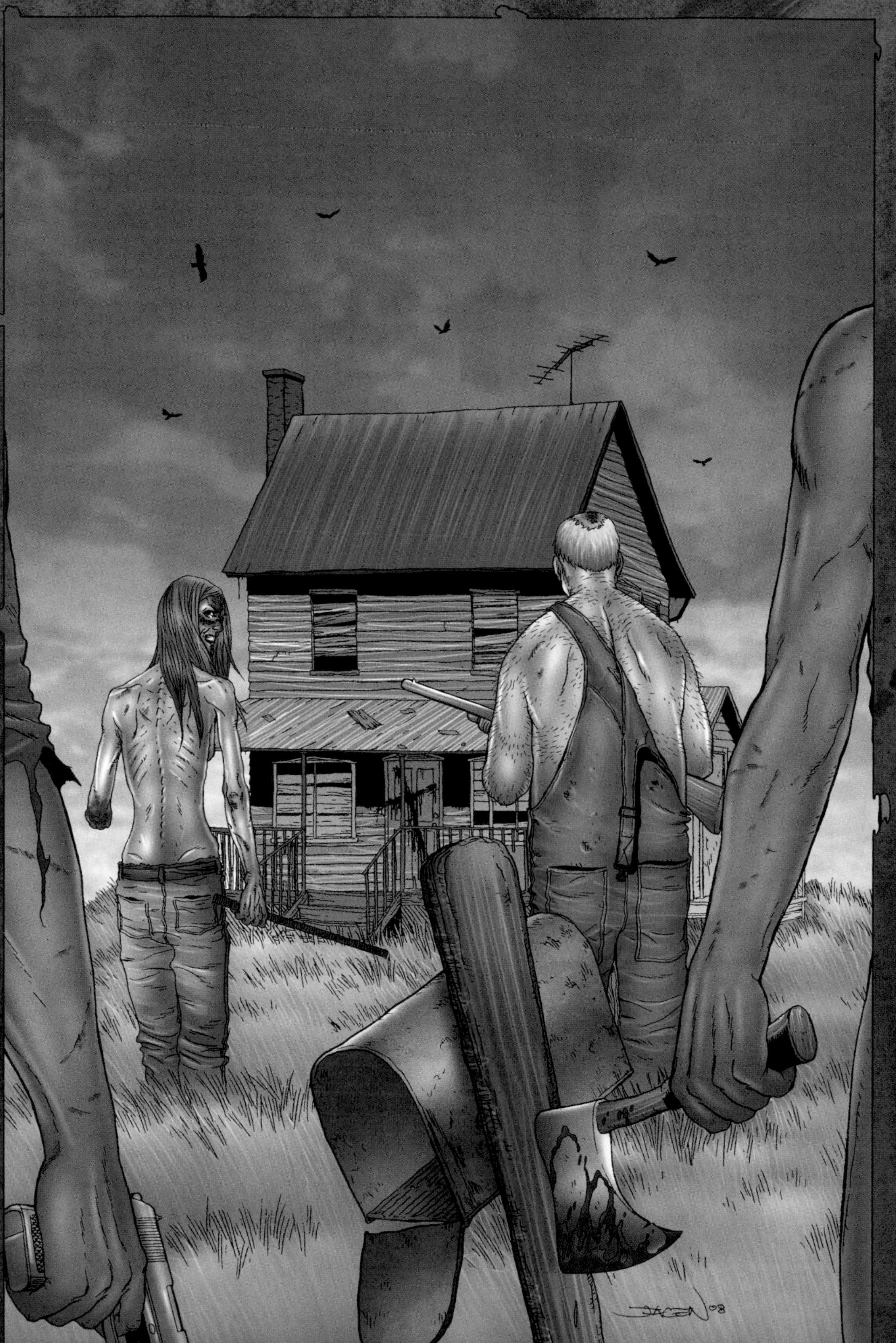

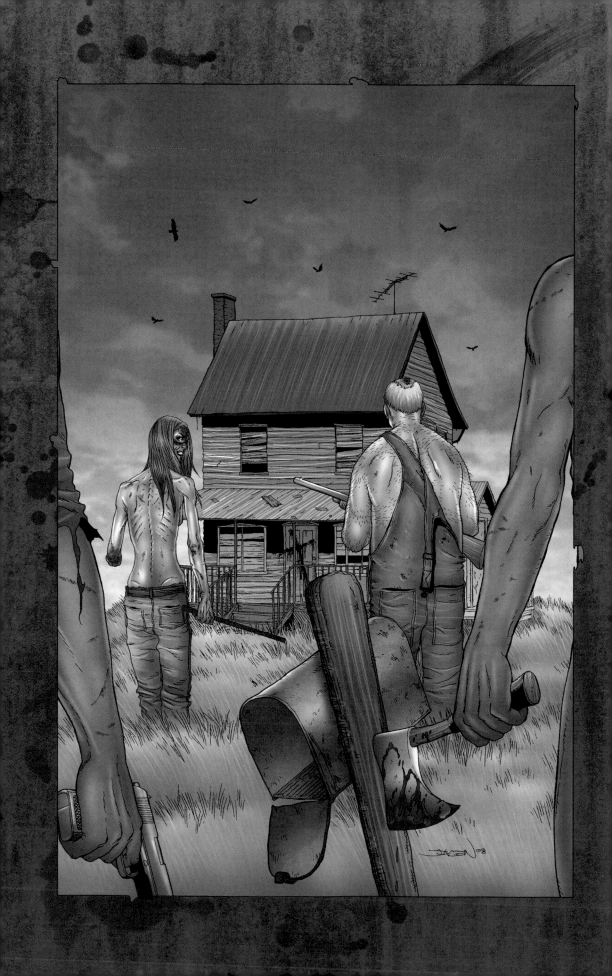

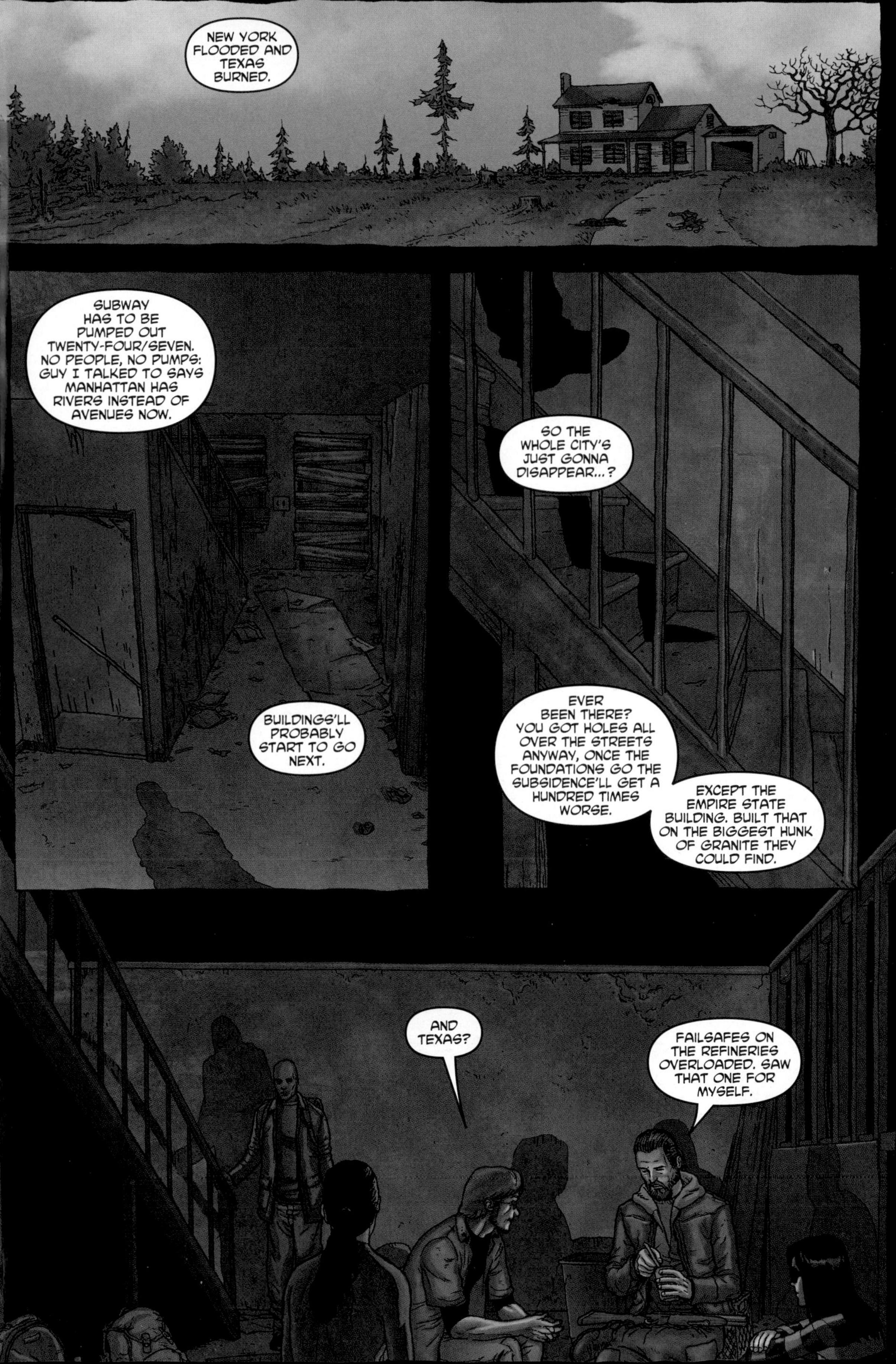
NEW YORK FLOODED AND TEXAS BURNED.
SUBWAY HAS TO BE PUMPED OUT TWENTY-FOUR/SEVEN. NO PEOPLE, NO PUMPS: GUY I TALKED TO SAYS MANHATTAN HAS RIVERS INSTEAD OF AVENUES NOW.
SO THE WHOLE CITY'S JUST GONNA DISAPPEAR...?
BUILDINGS'LL PROBABLY START TO GO NEXT.
EVER BEEN THERE? YOU GOT HOLES ALL OVER THE STREETS ANYWAY, ONCE THE FOUNDATIONS GO THE SUBSIDENCE'LL GET A HUNDRED TIMES WORSE.
EXCEPT THE EMPIRE STATE BUILDING. BUILT THAT ON THE BIGGEST HUNK OF GRANITE THEY COULD FIND.
AND TEXAS?
FAILSAFES ON THE REFINERIES OVERLOADED. SAW THAT ONE FOR MYSELF.

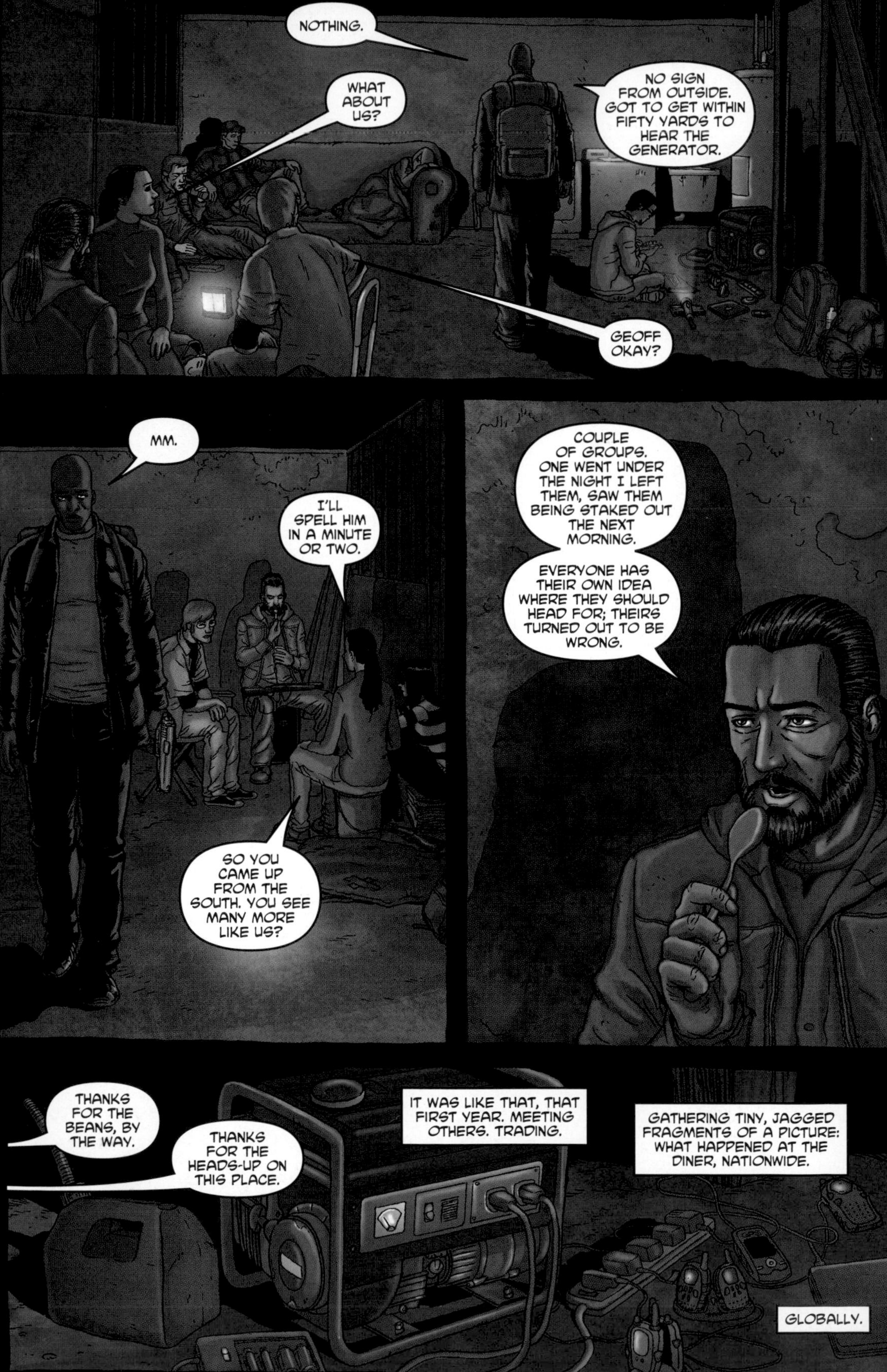
NOTHING.
WHAT ABOUT US?
NO SIGN FROM OUTSIDE. GOT TO GET WITHIN FIFTY YARDS TO HEAR THE GENERATOR.
GEOFF OKAY?
MM.
I'LL SPELL HIM IN A MINUTE OR TWO.
SO YOU CAME UP FROM THE SOUTH. YOU SEE MANY MORE LIKE US?
COUPLE OF GROUPS. ONE WENT UNDER THE NIGHT I LEFT THEM, SAW THEM BEING STAKED OUT THE NEXT MORNING.
EVERYONE HAS THEIR OWN IDEA WHERE THEY SHOULD HEAD FOR; THEIRS TURNED OUT TO BE WRONG.
THANKS FOR THE BEANS, BY THE WAY.
THANKS FOR THE HEADS-UP ON THIS PLACE.
IT WAS LIKE THAT, THAT FIRST YEAR. MEETING OTHERS. TRADING.
GATHERING TINY, JAGGED FRAGMENTS OF A PICTURE: WHAT HAPPENED AT THE DINER, NATIONWIDE.
GLOBALLY.

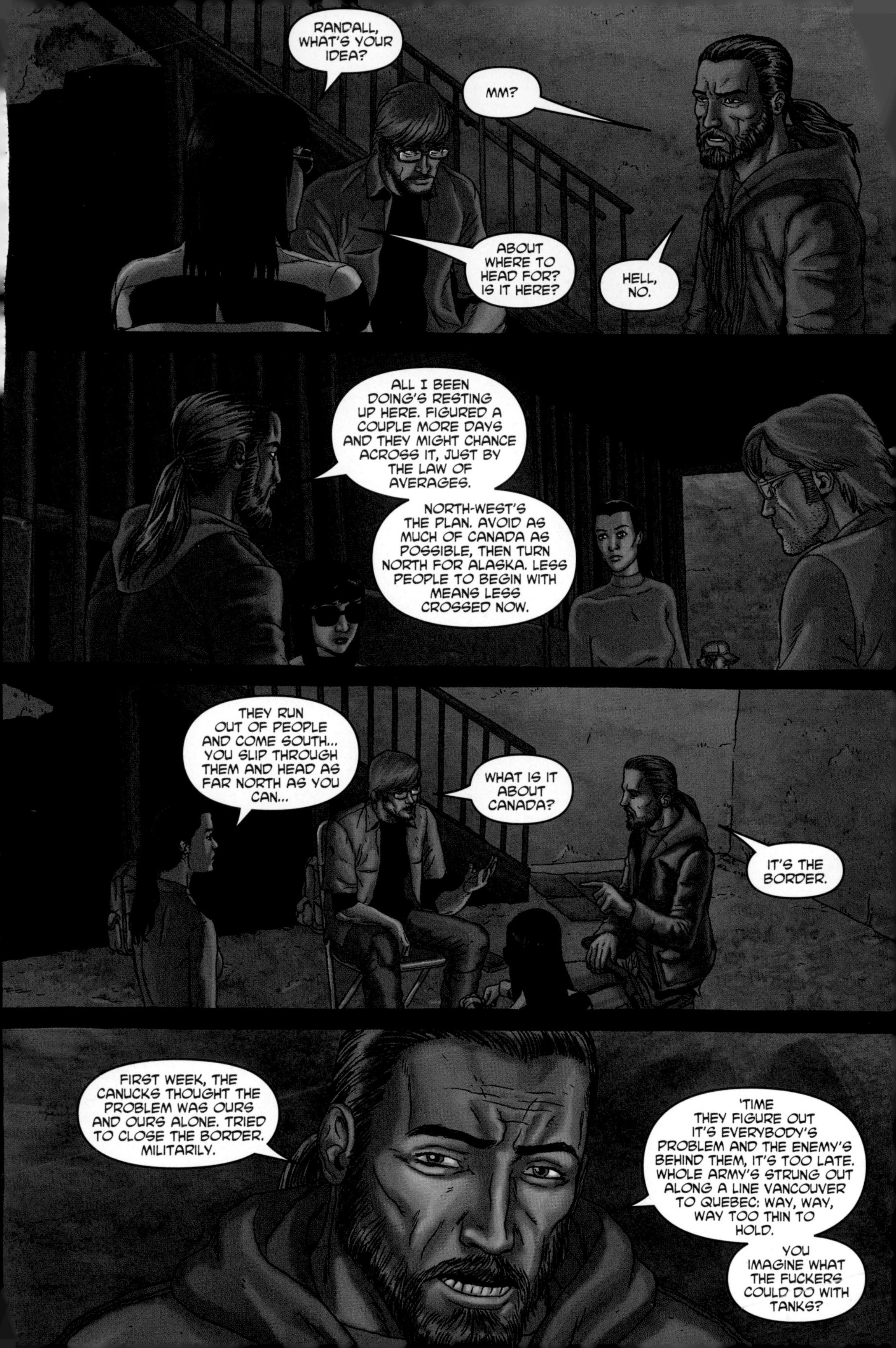
RANDALL, WHAT'S YOUR IDEA?
MM?
ABOUT WHERE TO HEAD FOR? IS IT HERE?
HELL, NO.
ALL I BEEN DOING'S RESTING UP HERE. FIGURED A COUPLE MORE DAYS AND THEY MIGHT CHANCE ACROSS IT, JUST BY THE LAW OF AVERAGES.
NORTH-WEST'S THE PLAN. AVOID AS MUCH OF CANADA AS POSSIBLE, THEN TURN NORTH FOR ALASKA. LESS PEOPLE TO BEGIN WITH MEANS LESS CROSSED NOW.
THEY RUN OUT OF PEOPLE AND COME SOUTH... YOU SLIP THROUGH THEM AND HEAD AS FAR NORTH AS YOU CAN...
WHAT IS IT ABOUT CANADA?
IT'S THE BORDER.
FIRST WEEK, THE CANUCKS THOUGHT THE PROBLEM WAS OURS AND OURS ALONE. TRIED TO CLOSE THE BORDER. MILITARILY.
'TIME THEY FIGURE OUT IT'S EVERYBODY'S PROBLEM AND THE ENEMY'S BEHIND THEM, IT'S TOO LATE. WHOLE ARMY'S STRUNG OUT ALONG A LINE VANCOUVER TO QUEBEC: WAY, WAY, WAY TOO THIN TO HOLD.
YOU IMAGINE WHAT THE FUCKERS COULD DO WITH TANKS?

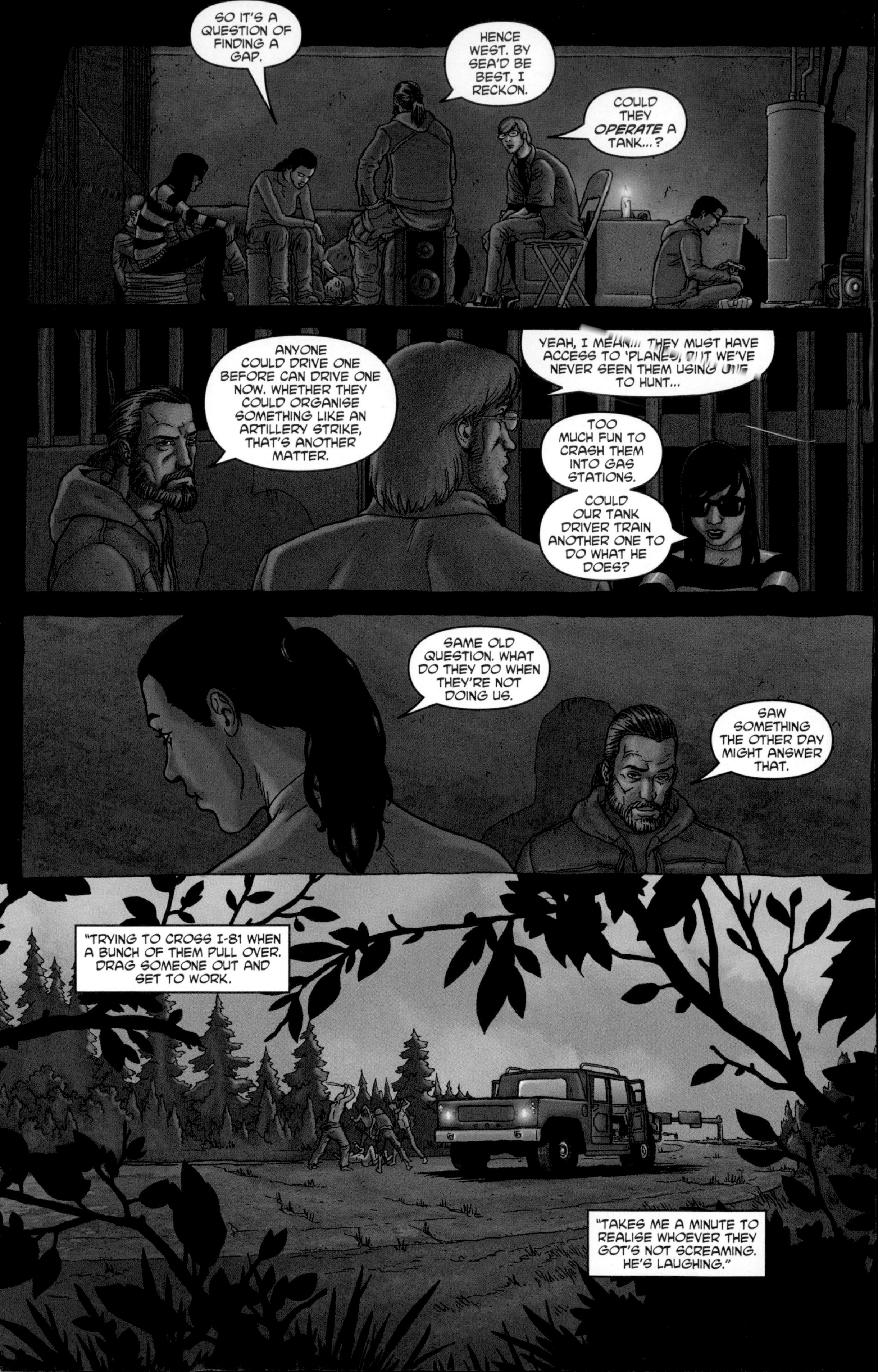

SO IT'S A QUESTION OF FINDING A GAP.
HENCE WEST. BY SEA'D BE BEST, I RECKON.
COULD THEY *OPERATE* A TANK...?
ANYONE COULD DRIVE ONE BEFORE CAN DRIVE ONE NOW. WHETHER THEY COULD ORGANISE SOMETHING LIKE AN ARTILLERY STRIKE, THAT'S ANOTHER MATTER.
YEAH, I ME... THEY MUST HAVE ACCESS TO 'PLANES, ...UT WE'VE NEVER SEEN THEM USING U... TO HUNT...
TOO MUCH FUN TO CRASH THEM INTO GAS STATIONS.
COULD OUR TANK DRIVER TRAIN ANOTHER ONE TO DO WHAT HE DOES?
SAME OLD QUESTION. WHAT DO THEY DO WHEN THEY'RE NOT DOING US.
SAW SOMETHING THE OTHER DAY MIGHT ANSWER THAT.
"TRYING TO CROSS I-81 WHEN A BUNCH OF THEM PULL OVER. DRAG SOMEONE OUT AND SET TO WORK.
"TAKES ME A MINUTE TO REALISE WHOEVER THEY GOT'S NOT SCREAMING. HE'S LAUGHING."

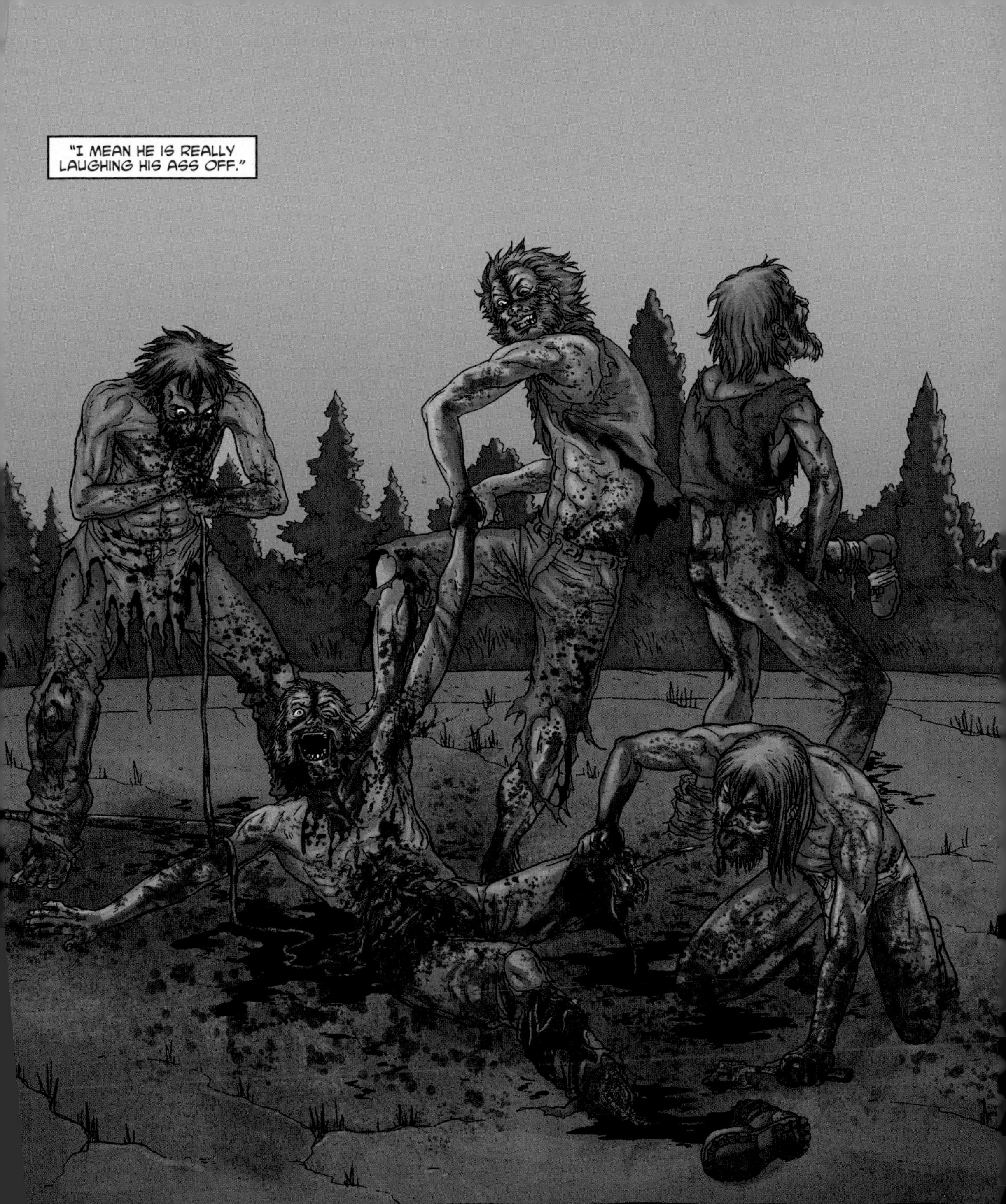
"I MEAN HE IS REALLY LAUGHING HIS ASS OFF."

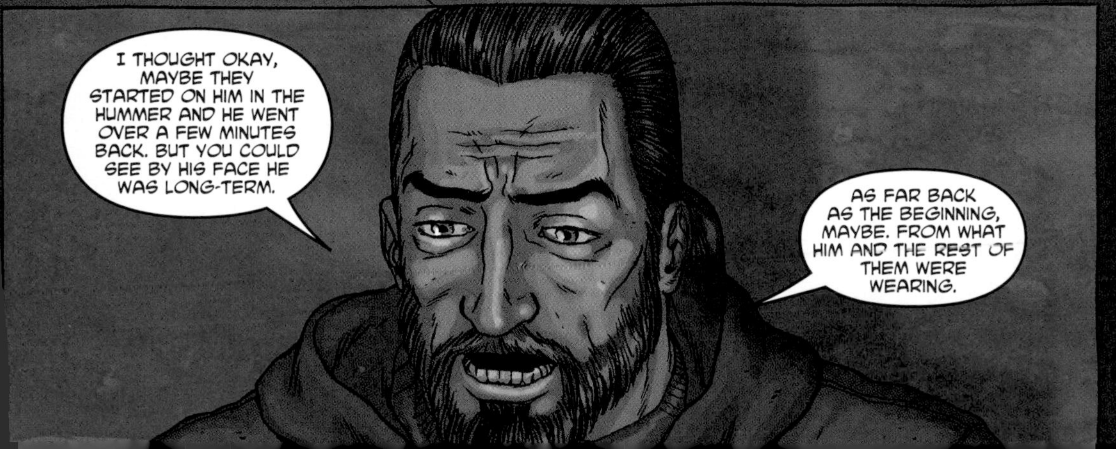
I THOUGHT OKAY, MAYBE THEY STARTED ON HIM IN THE HUMMER AND HE WENT OVER A FEW MINUTES BACK. BUT YOU COULD SEE BY HIS FACE HE WAS LONG-TERM.
AS FAR BACK AS THE BEGINNING, MAYBE. FROM WHAT HIM AND THE REST OF THEM WERE WEARING.

I'VE NEVER HEARD OF THEM KILLING THEIR OWN BEFORE...

I THOUGHT ABOUT IT. HAD PLENTY OF TIME, TOOK THEM ALL AFTERNOON TO FINISH HIM OFF.

BUT WHAT IF... THEY HAVE SO *MUCH* EVIL IN THEM... THAT IT JUST *HAS* TO GET USED UP, NO MATTER WHAT?

EVIL?

I STILL SAY MADNESS.

ANOTHER OLD QUESTION.

SO IF THEY CAN'T FIND A CONVENIENT PERSON, THEY GO FOR ONE OF THEIR OWN? DO THEY DRAW LOTS?

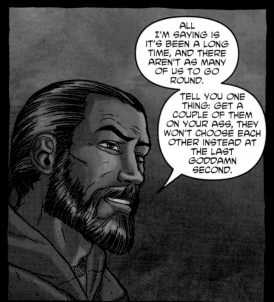

ALL I'M SAYING IS IT'S BEEN A LONG TIME, AND THERE AREN'T AS MANY OF US TO GO ROUND.

TELL YOU ONE THING: GET A COUPLE OF THEM ON YOUR ASS, THEY WON'T CHOOSE EACH OTHER INSTEAD AT THE LAST GODDAMN SECOND.

NO.

NO MAGIC BULLETS.

OH, WE KNOW THAT, ALL RIGHT...

GOING TO TAKE OVER FROM GEOFF.

I'LL JOIN YOU.

MM.

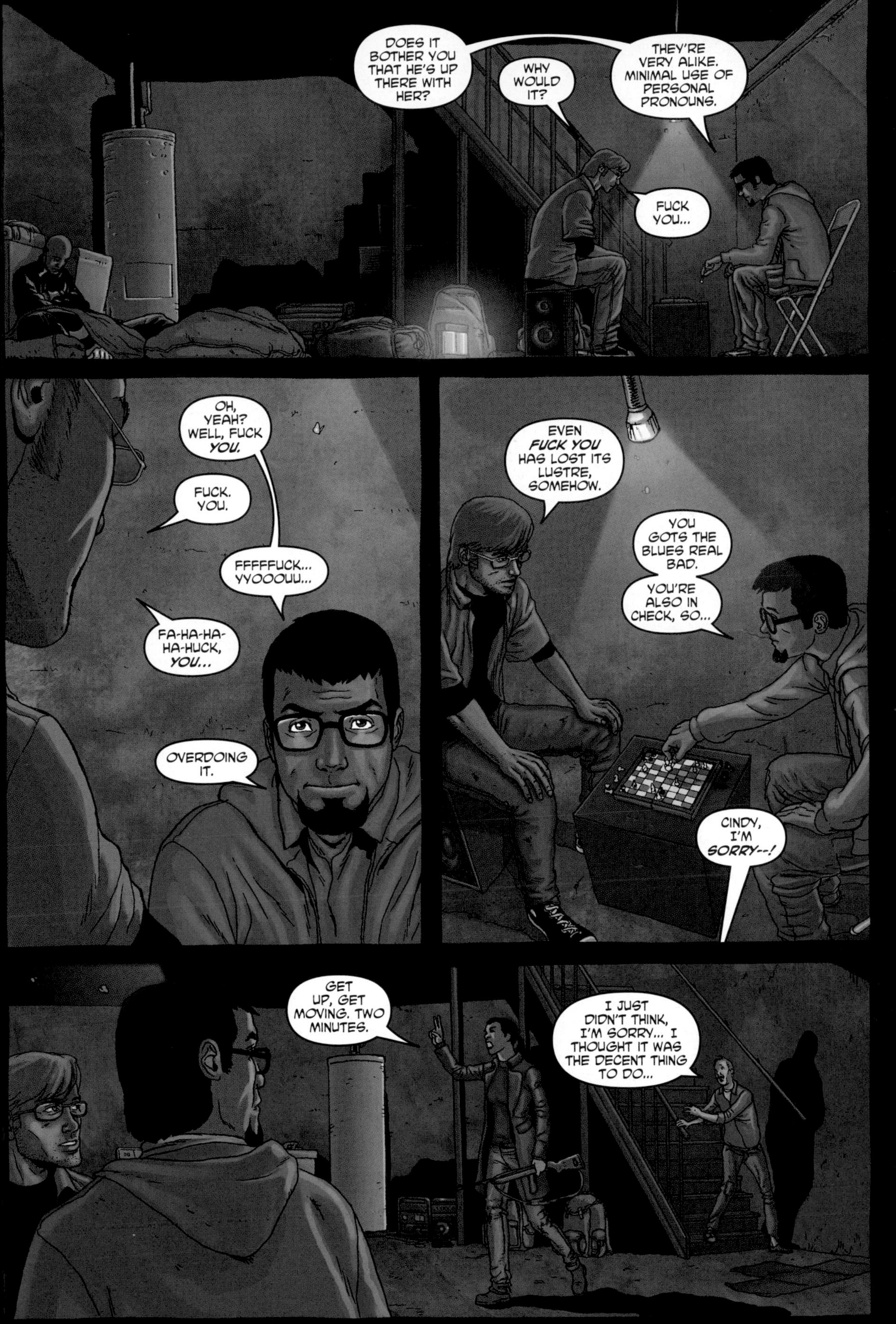
DOES IT BOTHER YOU THAT HE'S UP THERE WITH HER?
WHY WOULD IT?
THEY'RE VERY ALIKE. MINIMAL USE OF PERSONAL PRONOUNS.
FUCK YOU...
OH, YEAH? WELL, FUCK *YOU.*
FUCK. YOU.
FFFFFUCK... YYOOOUU...
FA-HA-HA-HA-HUCK, *YOU...*
OVERDOING IT.
EVEN *FUCK YOU* HAS LOST ITS LUSTRE, SOMEHOW.
YOU GOTS THE BLUES REAL BAD.
YOU'RE ALSO IN CHECK, SO...
CINDY, I'M *SORRY--!*
GET UP, GET MOVING. TWO MINUTES.
I JUST DIDN'T THINK, I'M SORRY... I THOUGHT IT WAS THE DECENT THING TO DO...

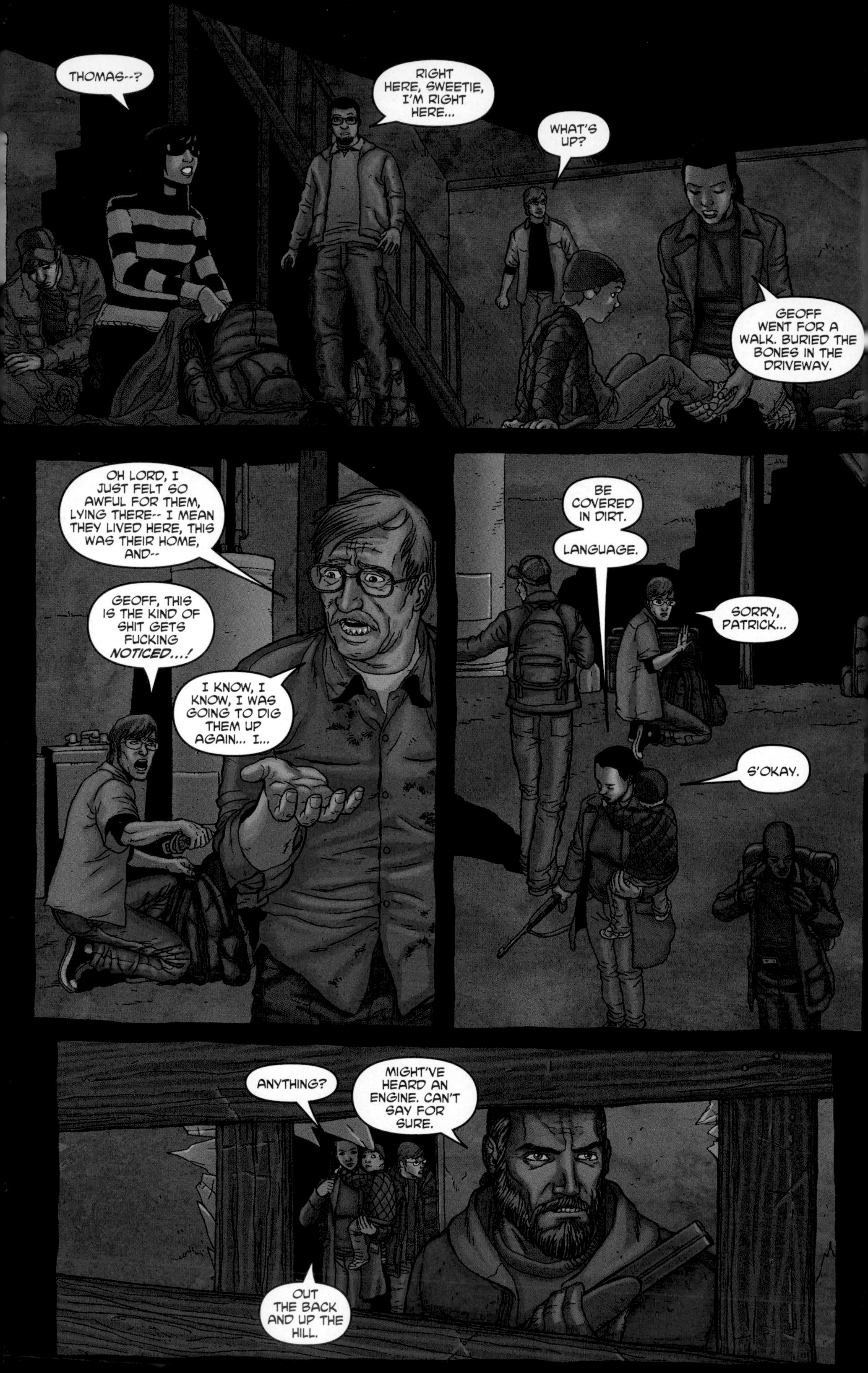
THOMAS--?
RIGHT HERE, SWEETIE, I'M RIGHT HERE...
WHAT'S UP?
GEOFF WENT FOR A WALK. BURIED THE BONES IN THE DRIVEWAY.
OH LORD, I JUST FELT SO AWFUL FOR THEM, LYING THERE-- I MEAN THEY LIVED HERE, THIS WAS THEIR HOME, AND--
GEOFF, THIS IS THE KIND OF SHIT GETS FUCKING *NOTICED...!*
I KNOW, I KNOW, I WAS GOING TO DIG THEM UP AGAIN... I...
BE COVERED IN DIRT.
LANGUAGE.
SORRY, PATRICK...
S'OKAY.
ANYTHING?
MIGHT'VE HEARD AN ENGINE. CAN'T SAY FOR SURE.
OUT THE BACK AND UP THE HILL.

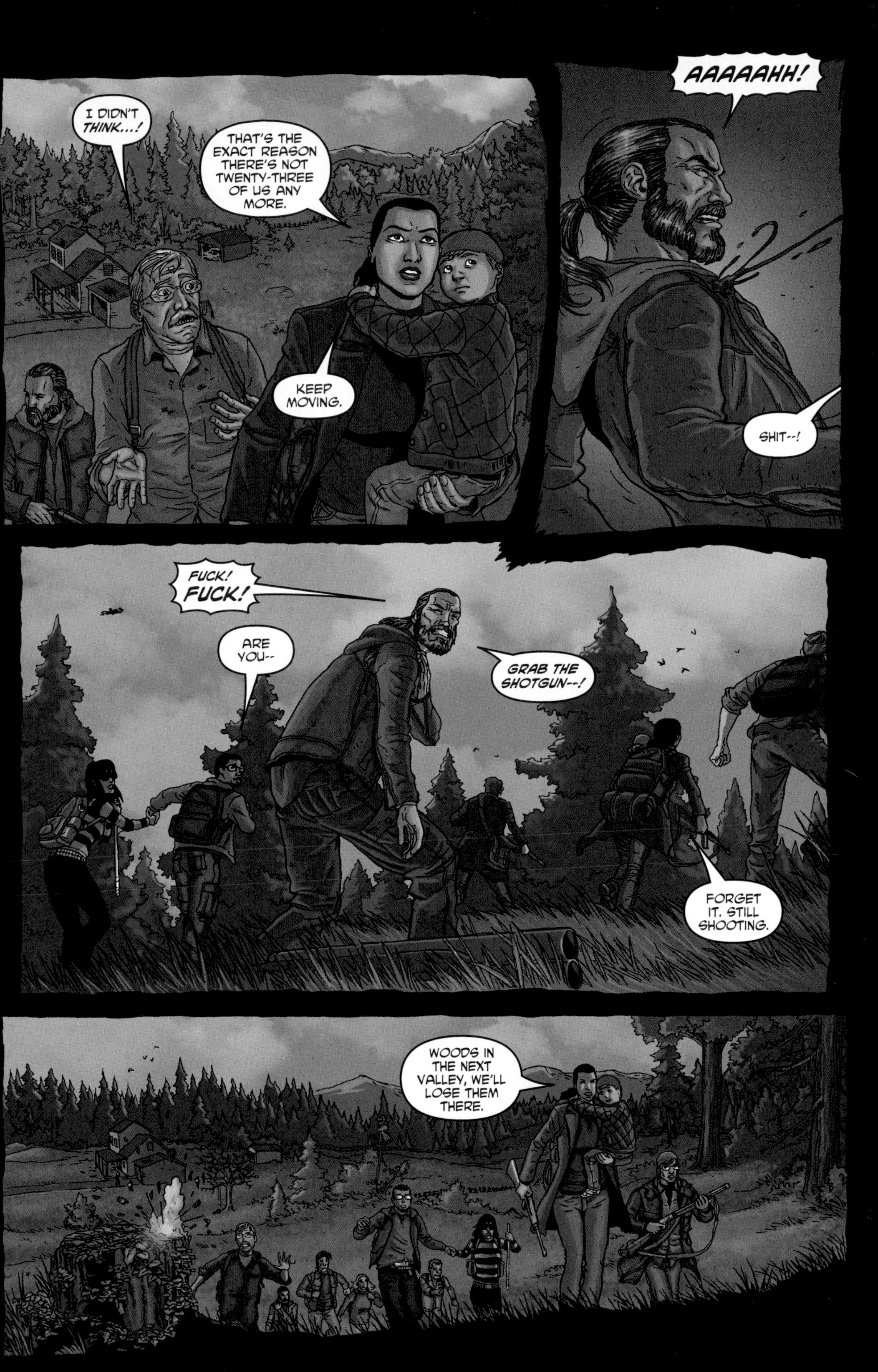
I DIDN'T *THINK...!*
THAT'S THE EXACT REASON THERE'S NOT TWENTY-THREE OF US ANY MORE.
KEEP MOVING.
AAAAAHH!
SHIT--!
FUCK! ***FUCK!***
ARE YOU--
GRAB THE SHOTGUN--!
FORGET IT. STILL SHOOTING.
WOODS IN THE NEXT VALLEY, WE'LL LOSE THEM THERE.

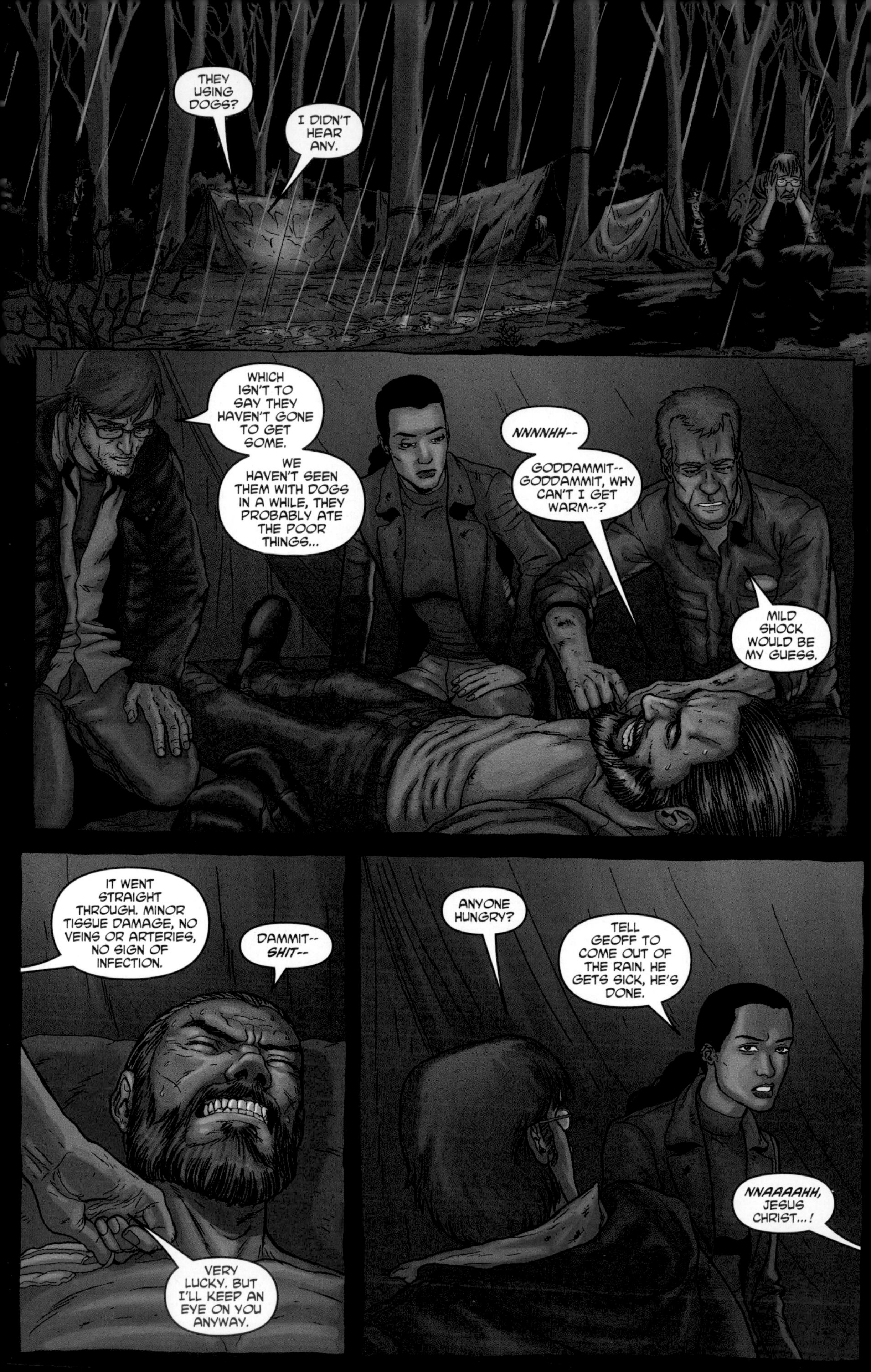
THEY USING DOGS?
I DIDN'T HEAR ANY.
WHICH ISN'T TO SAY THEY HAVEN'T GONE TO GET SOME.
WE HAVEN'T SEEN THEM WITH DOGS IN A WHILE, THEY PROBABLY ATE THE POOR THINGS...
NNNNHH--
GODDAMMIT--GODDAMMIT, WHY CAN'T I GET WARM--?
MILD SHOCK WOULD BE MY GUESS.
IT WENT STRAIGHT THROUGH. MINOR TISSUE DAMAGE, NO VEINS OR ARTERIES, NO SIGN OF INFECTION.
DAMMIT--SHIT--
VERY LUCKY. BUT I'LL KEEP AN EYE ON YOU ANYWAY.
ANYONE HUNGRY?
TELL GEOFF TO COME OUT OF THE RAIN. HE GETS SICK, HE'S DONE.
NNAAAAHH, JESUS CHRIST...!

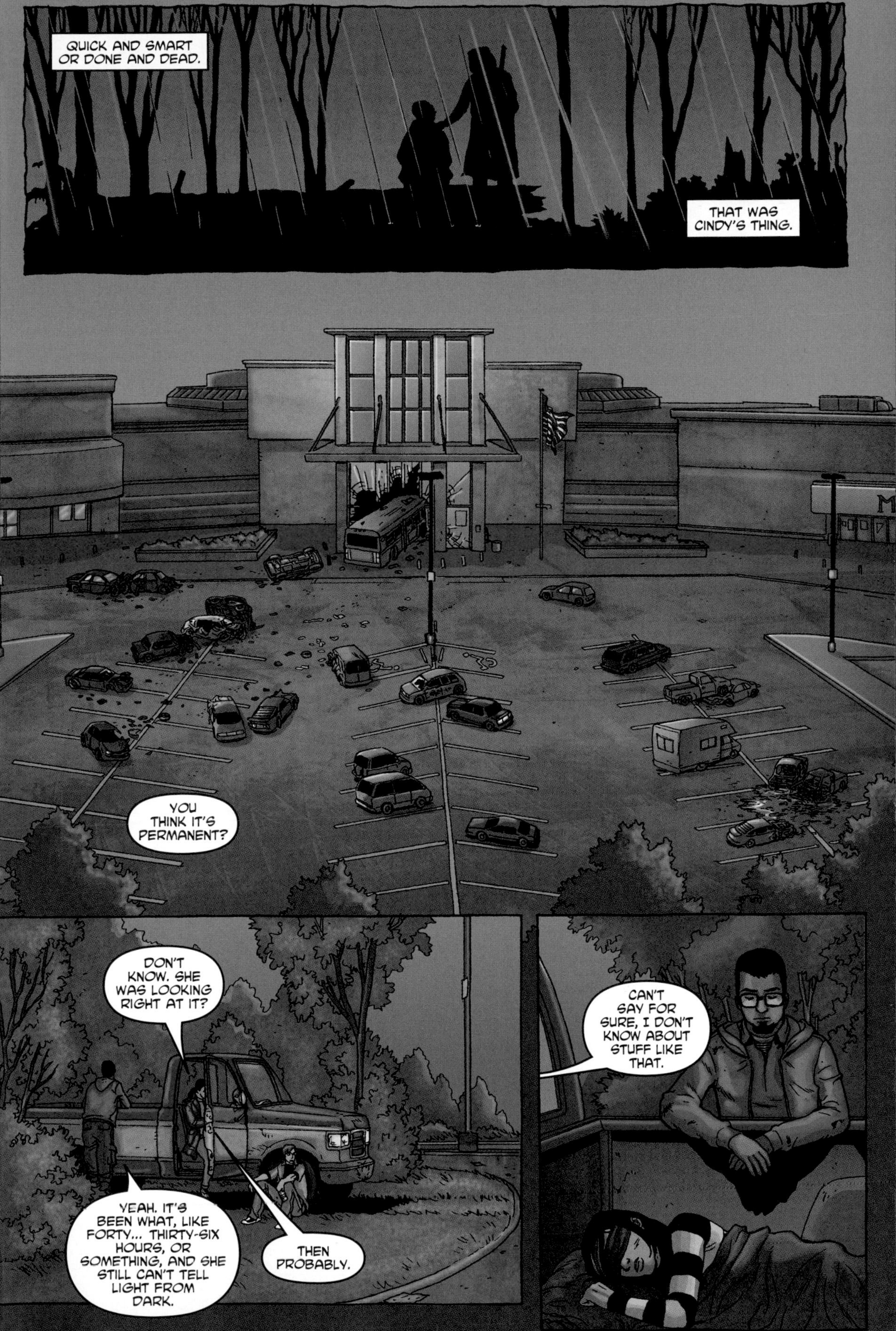
QUICK AND SMART OR DONE AND DEAD.
THAT WAS CINDY'S THING.
YOU THINK IT'S PERMANENT?
DON'T KNOW. SHE WAS LOOKING RIGHT AT IT?
YEAH. IT'S BEEN WHAT, LIKE FORTY... THIRTY-SIX HOURS, OR SOMETHING, AND SHE STILL CAN'T TELL LIGHT FROM DARK.
THEN PROBABLY.
CAN'T SAY FOR SURE, I DON'T KNOW ABOUT STUFF LIKE THAT.

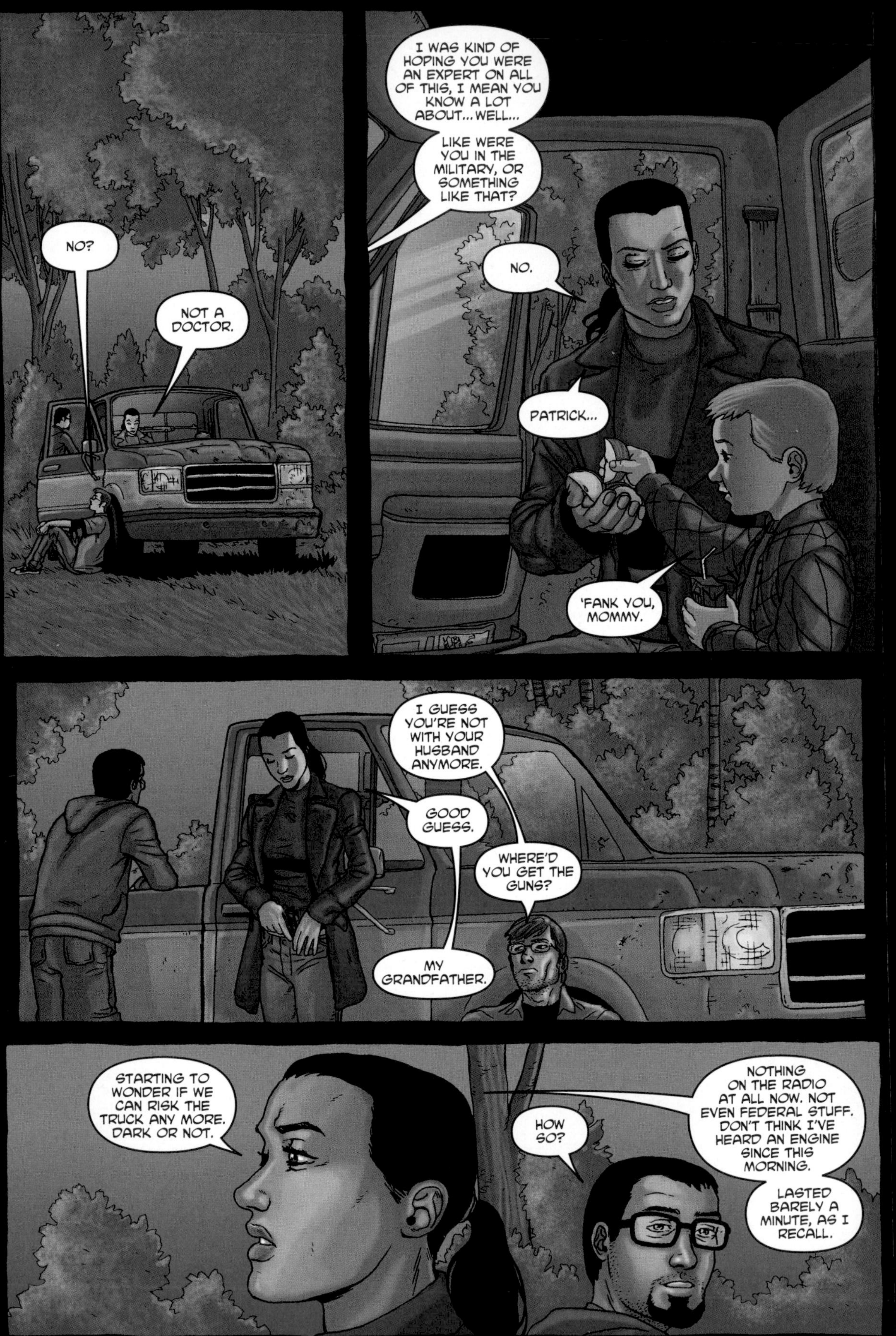
NO?
NOT A DOCTOR.
I WAS KIND OF HOPING YOU WERE AN EXPERT ON ALL OF THIS, I MEAN YOU KNOW A LOT ABOUT... WELL...
LIKE WERE YOU IN THE MILITARY, OR SOMETHING LIKE THAT?
NO.
PATRICK...
'FANK YOU, MOMMY.
I GUESS YOU'RE NOT WITH YOUR HUSBAND ANYMORE.
GOOD GUESS.
WHERE'D YOU GET THE GUNS?
MY GRANDFATHER.
STARTING TO WONDER IF WE CAN RISK THE TRUCK ANY MORE. DARK OR NOT.
HOW SO?
NOTHING ON THE RADIO AT ALL NOW. NOT EVEN FEDERAL STUFF. DON'T THINK I'VE HEARD AN ENGINE SINCE THIS MORNING.
LASTED BARELY A MINUTE, AS I RECALL.

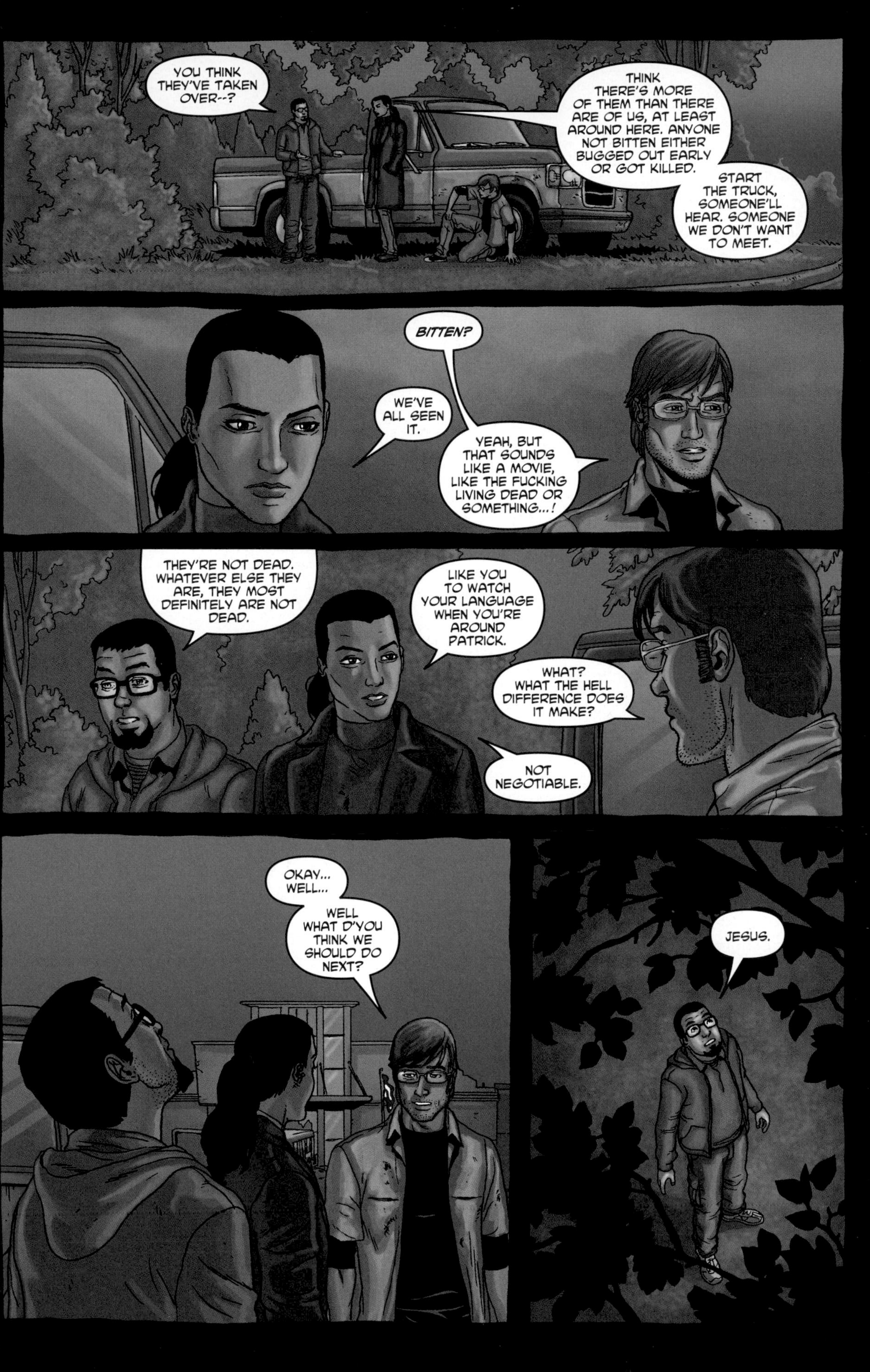

YOU THINK THEY'VE TAKEN OVER--?
THINK THERE'S MORE OF THEM THAN THERE ARE OF US, AT LEAST AROUND HERE. ANYONE NOT BITTEN EITHER BUGGED OUT EARLY OR GOT KILLED.
START THE TRUCK, SOMEONE'LL HEAR. SOMEONE WE DON'T WANT TO MEET.
BITTEN?
WE'VE ALL SEEN IT.
YEAH, BUT THAT SOUNDS LIKE A MOVIE, LIKE THE FUCKING LIVING DEAD OR SOMETHING...!
THEY'RE NOT DEAD. WHATEVER ELSE THEY ARE, THEY MOST DEFINITELY ARE NOT DEAD.
LIKE YOU TO WATCH YOUR LANGUAGE WHEN YOU'RE AROUND PATRICK.
WHAT? WHAT THE HELL DIFFERENCE DOES IT MAKE?
NOT NEGOTIABLE.
OKAY... WELL...
WELL WHAT D'YOU THINK WE SHOULD DO NEXT?
JESUS.

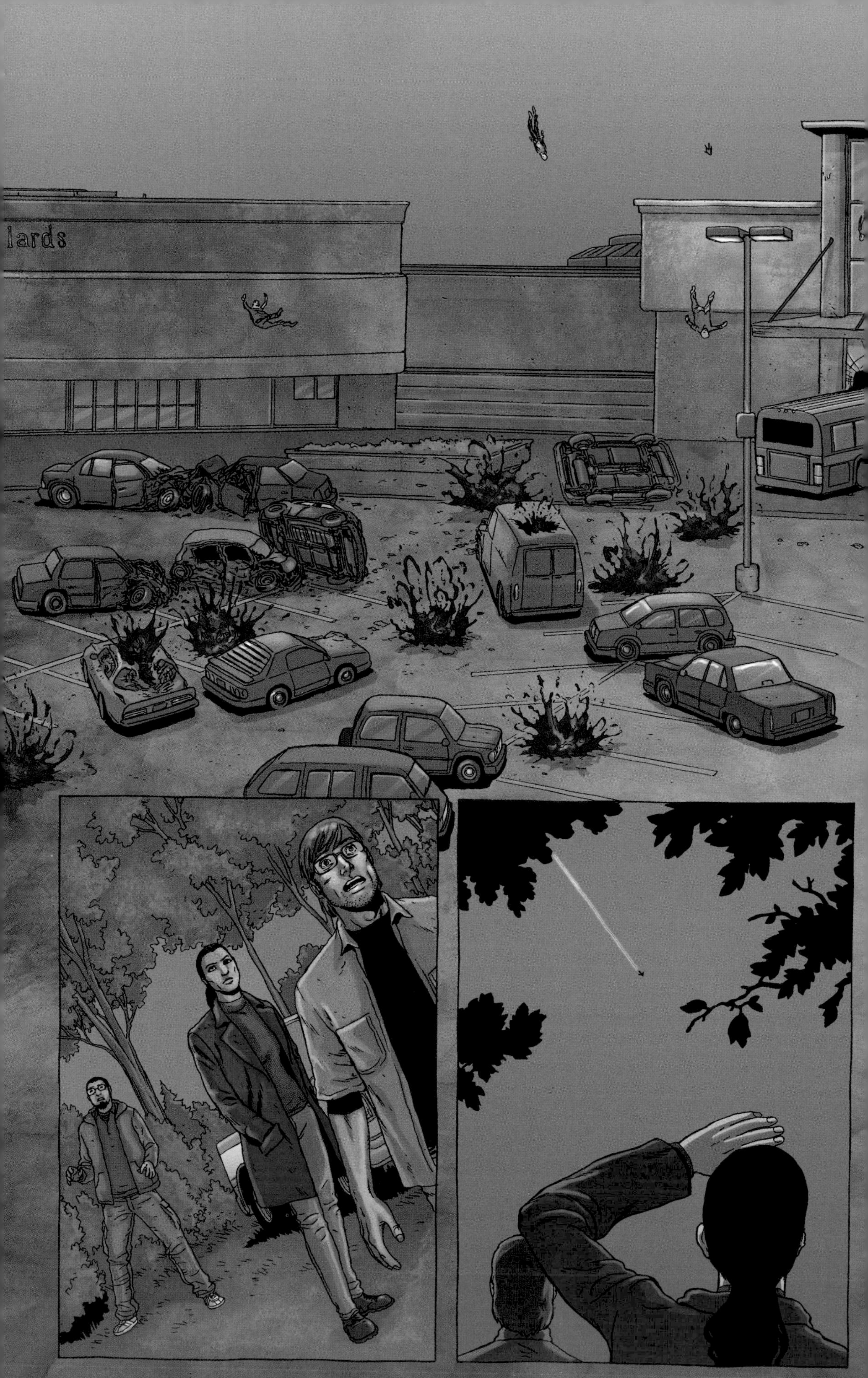
lards

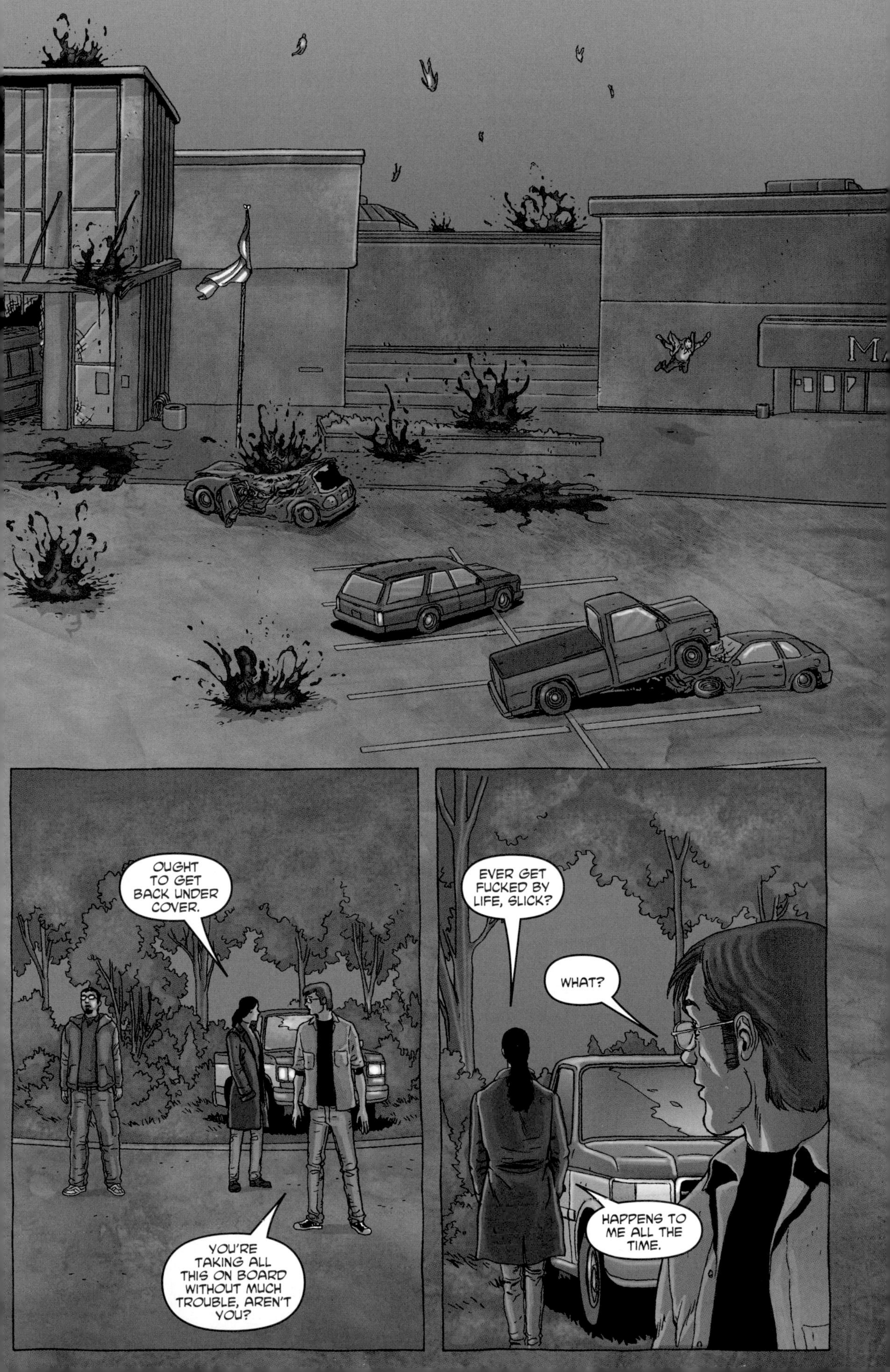
MA
OUGHT TO GET BACK UNDER COVER.
YOU'RE TAKING ALL THIS ON BOARD WITHOUT MUCH TROUBLE, AREN'T YOU?
EVER GET FUCKED BY LIFE, SLICK?
WHAT?
HAPPENS TO ME ALL THE TIME.

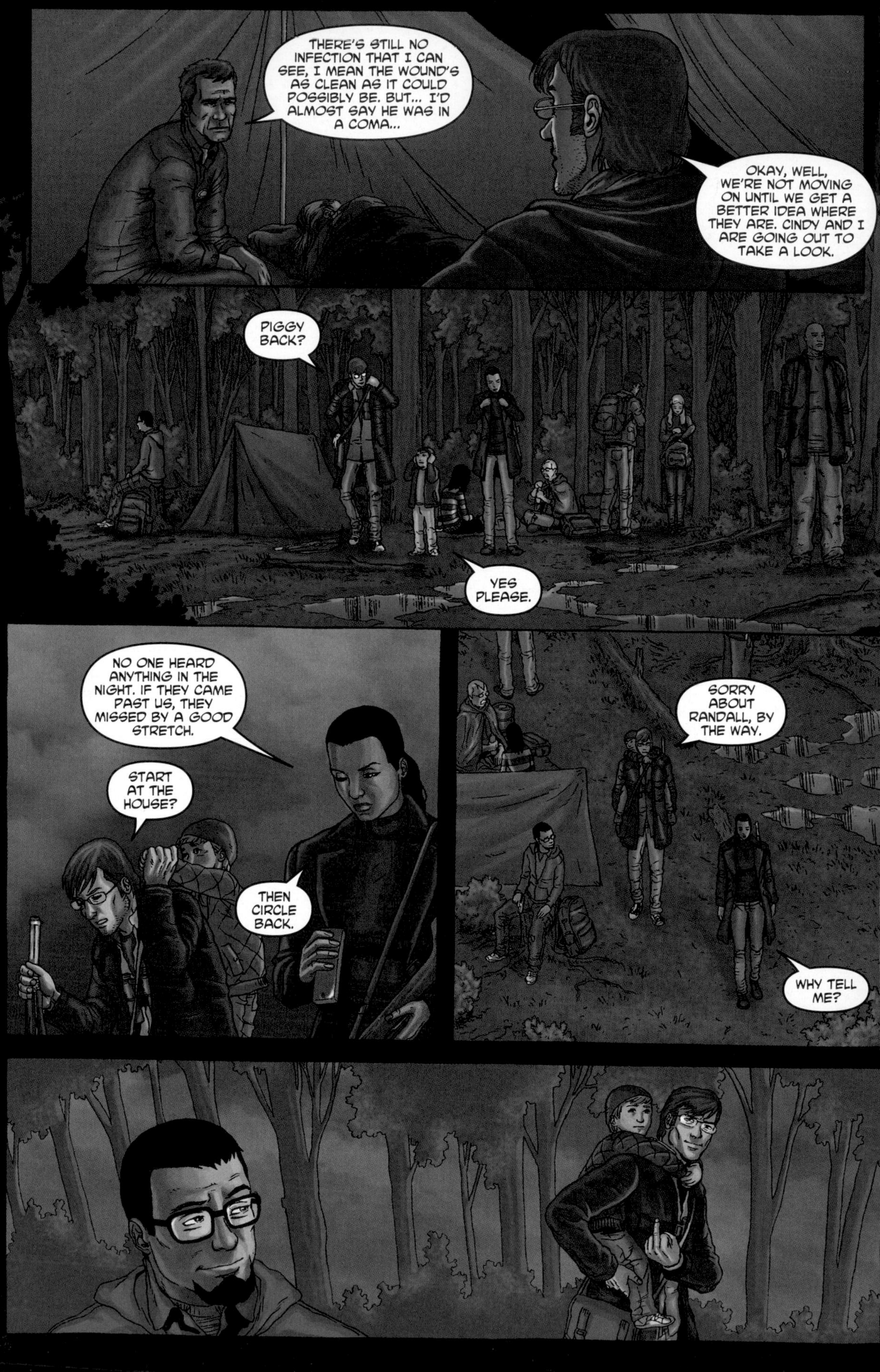

THERE'S STILL NO INFECTION THAT I CAN SEE, I MEAN THE WOUND'S AS CLEAN AS IT COULD POSSIBLY BE. BUT... I'D ALMOST SAY HE WAS IN A COMA...
OKAY, WELL, WE'RE NOT MOVING ON UNTIL WE GET A BETTER IDEA WHERE THEY ARE. CINDY AND I ARE GOING OUT TO TAKE A LOOK.
PIGGY BACK?
YES PLEASE.
NO ONE HEARD ANYTHING IN THE NIGHT. IF THEY CAME PAST US, THEY MISSED BY A GOOD STRETCH.
START AT THE HOUSE?
THEN CIRCLE BACK.
SORRY ABOUT RANDALL, BY THE WAY.
WHY TELL ME?

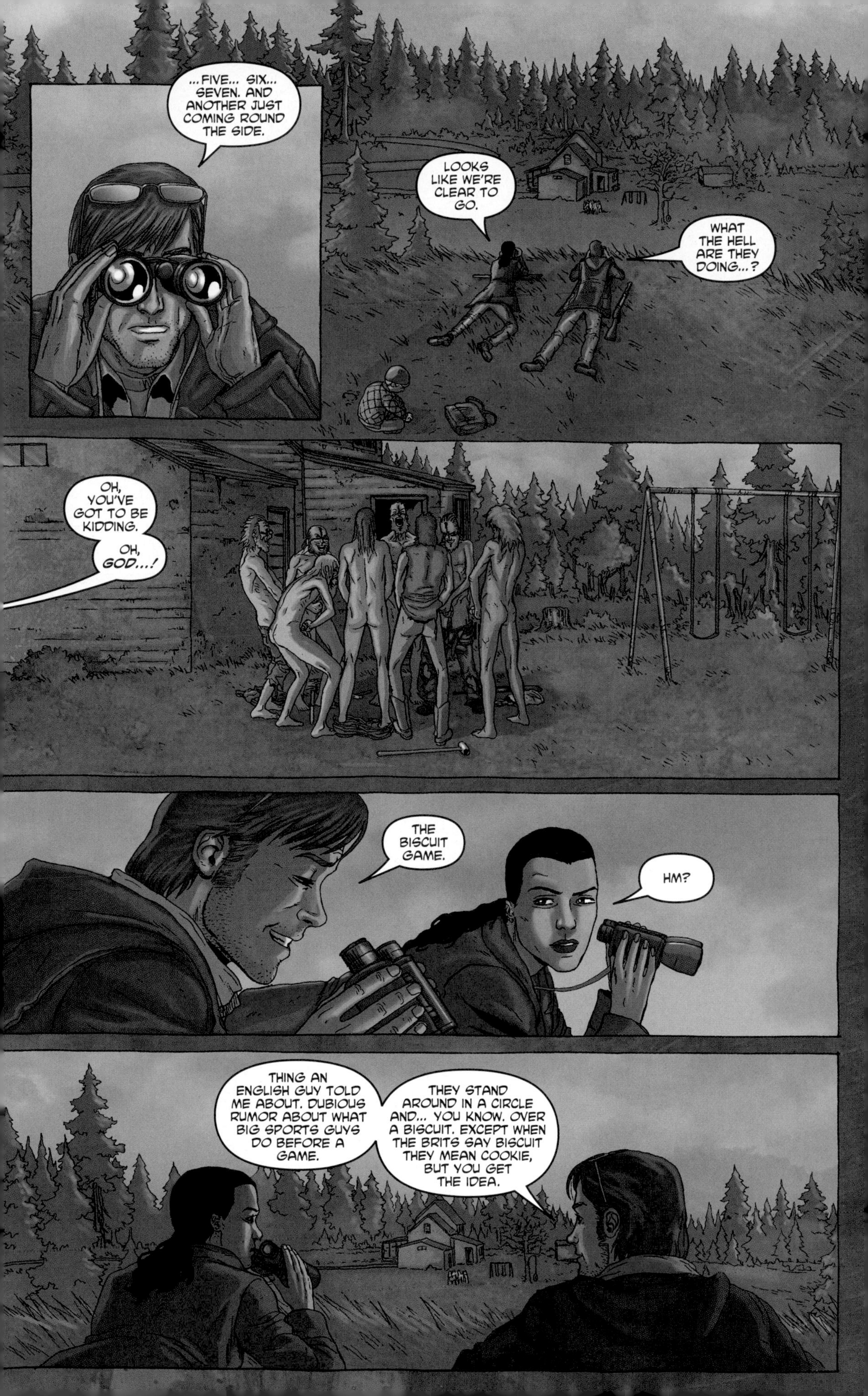
...FIVE... SIX... SEVEN. AND ANOTHER JUST COMING ROUND THE SIDE.
LOOKS LIKE WE'RE CLEAR TO GO.
WHAT THE HELL ARE THEY DOING...?
OH, YOU'VE GOT TO BE KIDDING.
OH, GOD...!
THE BISCUIT GAME.
HM?
THING AN ENGLISH GUY TOLD ME ABOUT. DUBIOUS RUMOR ABOUT WHAT BIG SPORTS GUYS DO BEFORE A GAME.
THEY STAND AROUND IN A CIRCLE AND... YOU KNOW. OVER A BISCUIT. EXCEPT WHEN THE BRITS SAY BISCUIT THEY MEAN COOKIE, BUT YOU GET THE IDEA.

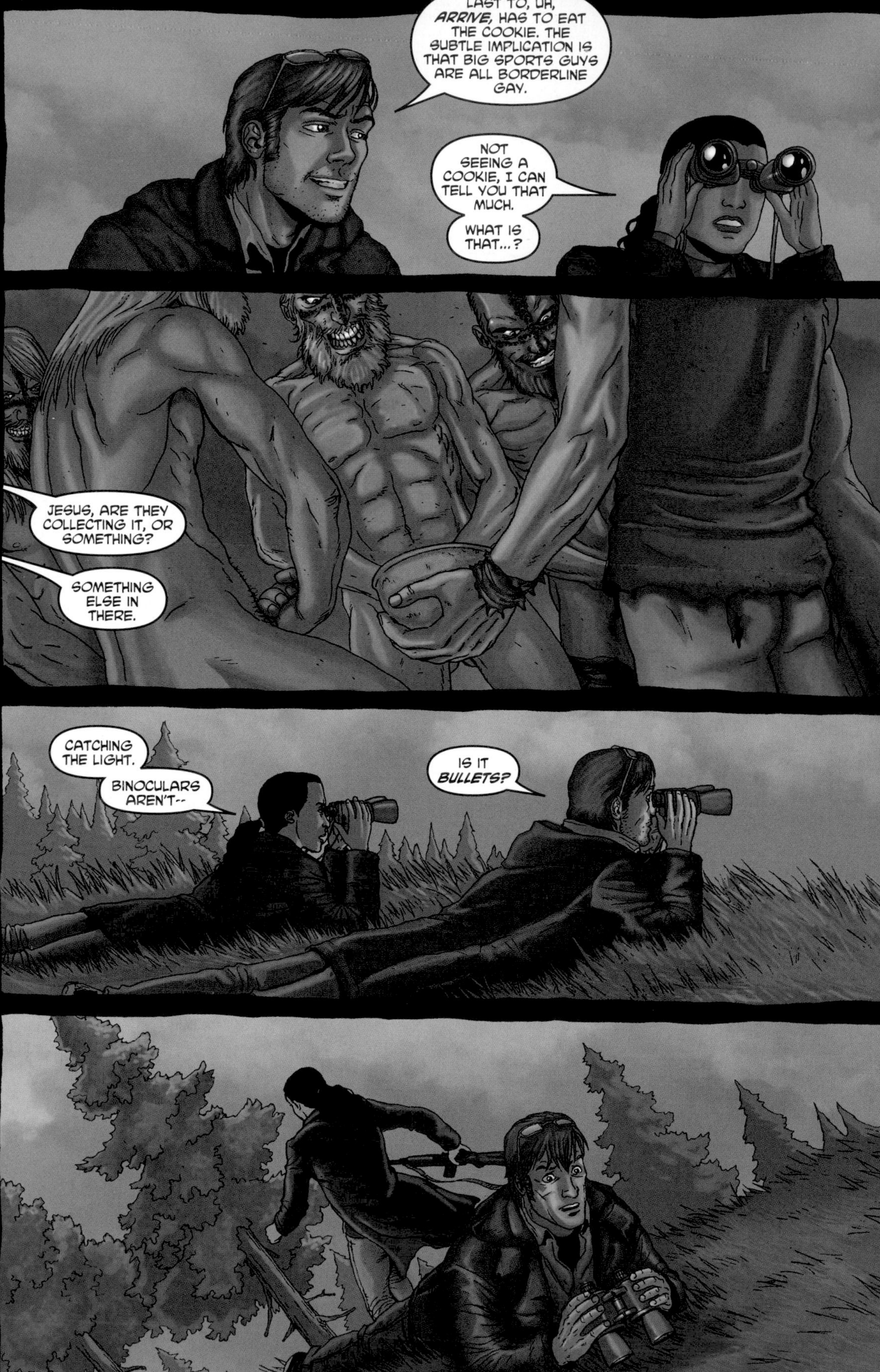
LAST TO, UH, *ARRIVE,* HAS TO EAT THE COOKIE. THE SUBTLE IMPLICATION IS THAT BIG SPORTS GUYS ARE ALL BORDERLINE GAY.
NOT SEEING A COOKIE, I CAN TELL YOU THAT MUCH.
WHAT IS THAT...?
JESUS, ARE THEY COLLECTING IT, OR SOMETHING?
SOMETHING ELSE IN THERE.
CATCHING THE LIGHT.
BINOCULARS AREN'T--
IS IT *BULLETS?*

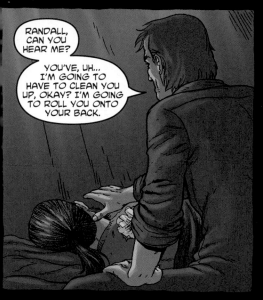

RANDALL, CAN YOU HEAR ME?

YOU'VE, UH... I'M GOING TO HAVE TO CLEAN YOU UP, OKAY? I'M GOING TO ROLL YOU ONTO YOUR BACK.

I'M--

AAAK

SCOTT?

RANDALL?

KELLY--!

I SMELL CUNT

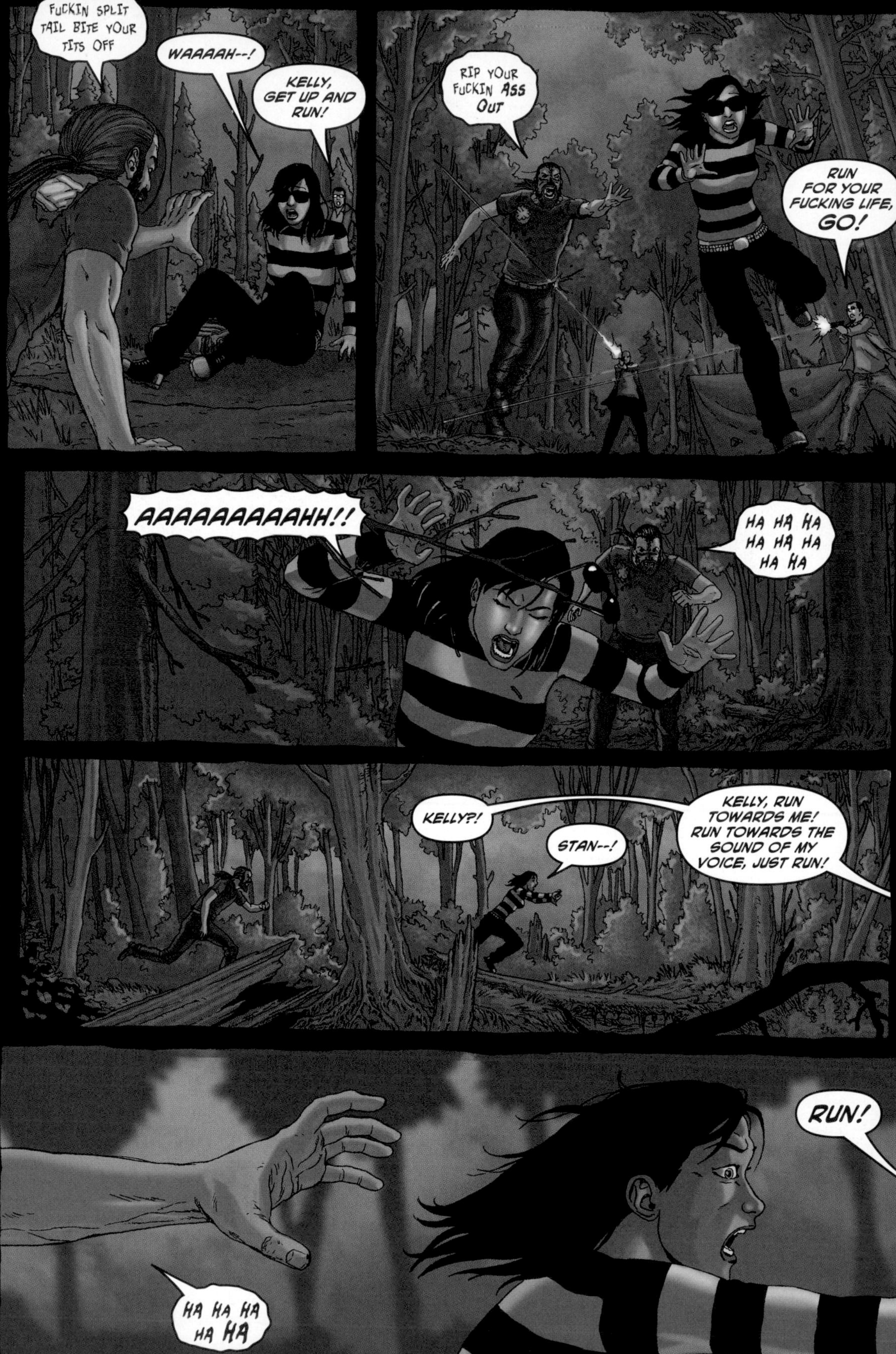
FUCKIN SPLIT TAIL BITE YOUR TITS OFF
WAAAAH--!
KELLY, GET UP AND RUN!
RIP YOUR FUCKIN ASS OUT
RUN FOR YOUR FUCKING LIFE, GO!
AAAAAAAAAHH!!
HA HA HA HA HA HA HA HA
KELLY?!
KELLY, RUN TOWARDS ME! RUN TOWARDS THE SOUND OF MY VOICE, JUST RUN!
STAN--!
RUN!
HA HA HA HA HA

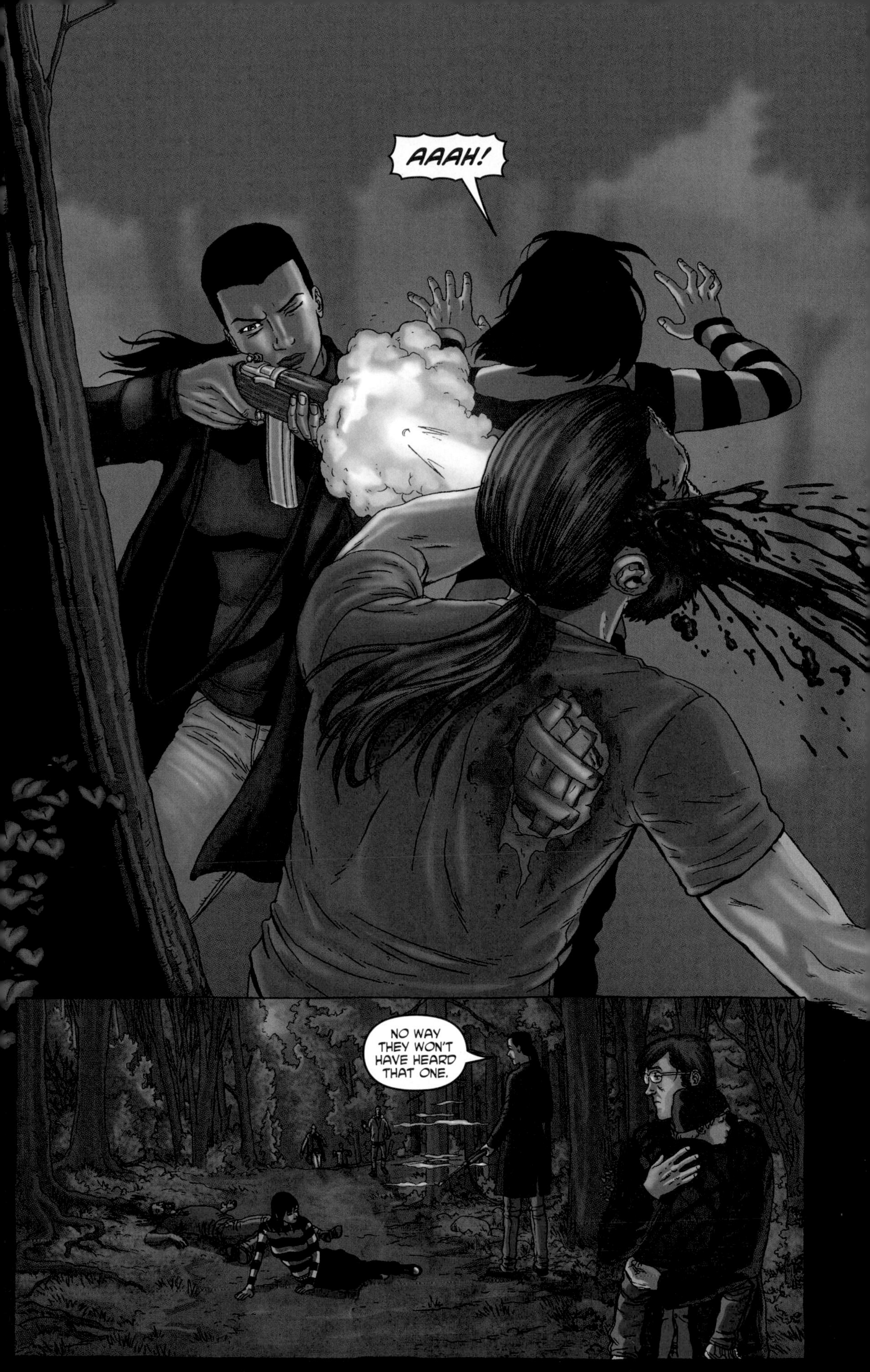
AAAH!
NO WAY THEY WON'T HAVE HEARD THAT ONE.

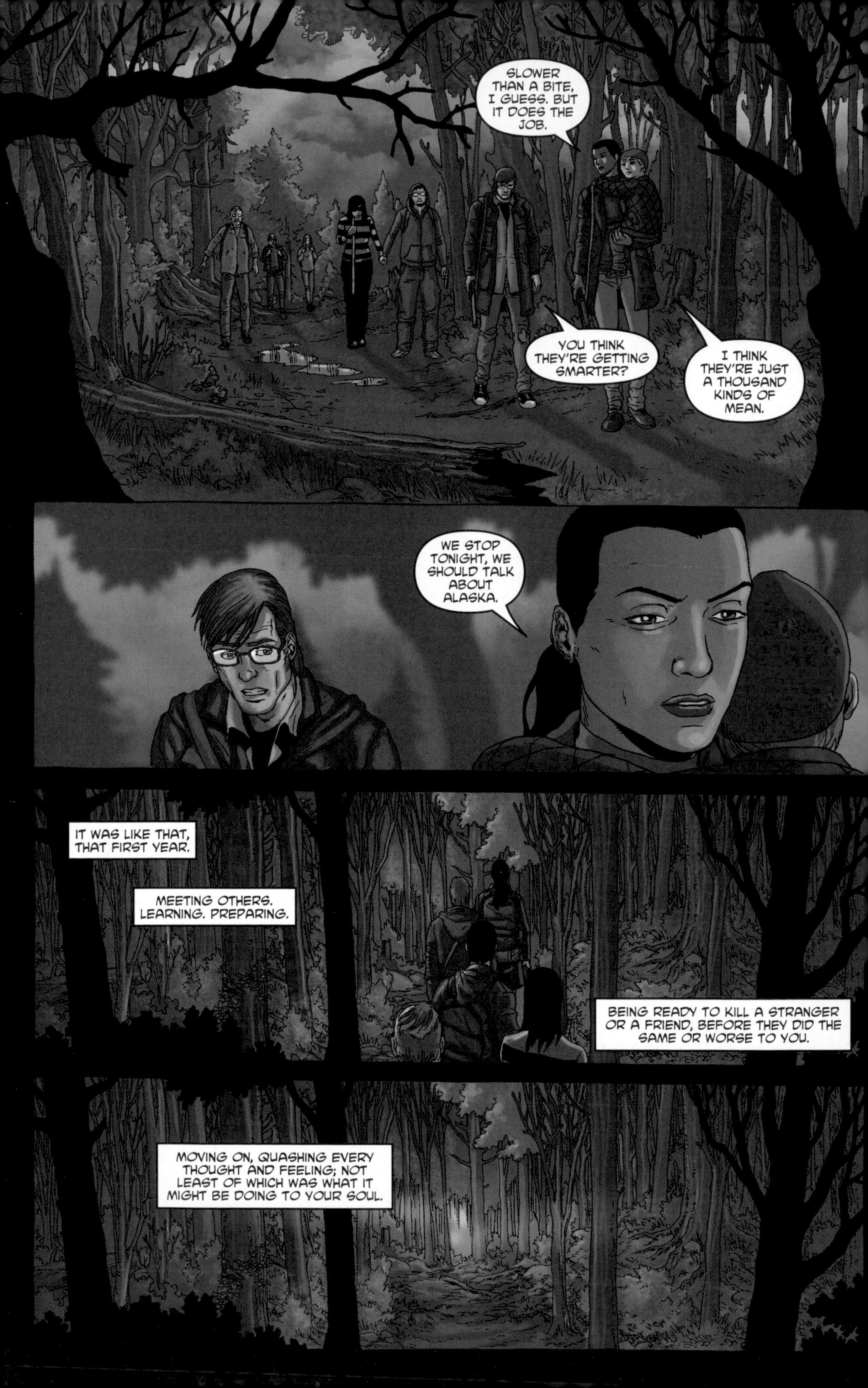
SLOWER THAN A BITE, I GUESS. BUT IT DOES THE JOB.
YOU THINK THEY'RE GETTING SMARTER?
I THINK THEY'RE JUST A THOUSAND KINDS OF MEAN.
WE STOP TONIGHT, WE SHOULD TALK ABOUT ALASKA.
IT WAS LIKE THAT, THAT FIRST YEAR.
MEETING OTHERS. LEARNING. PREPARING.
BEING READY TO KILL A STRANGER OR A FRIEND, BEFORE THEY DID THE SAME OR WORSE TO YOU.
MOVING ON, QUASHING EVERY THOUGHT AND FEELING; NOT LEAST OF WHICH WAS WHAT IT MIGHT BE DOING TO YOUR SOUL.

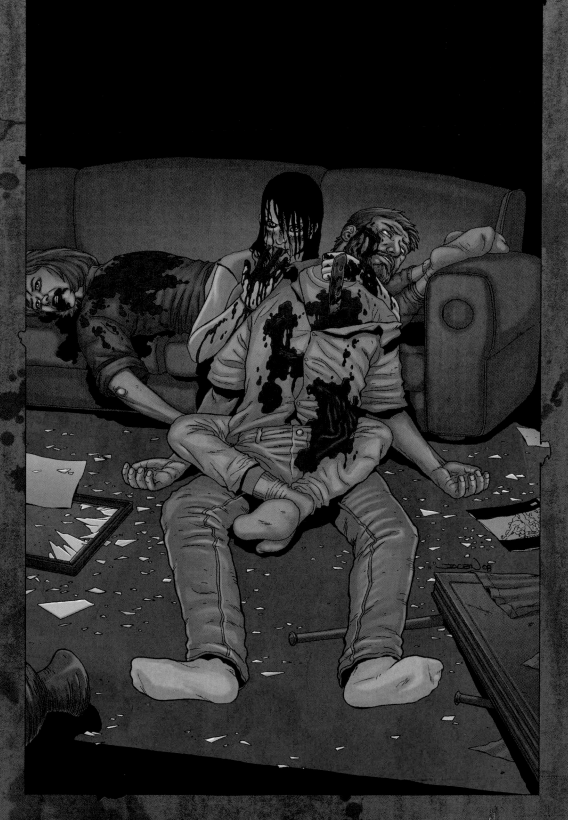

PART FOUR

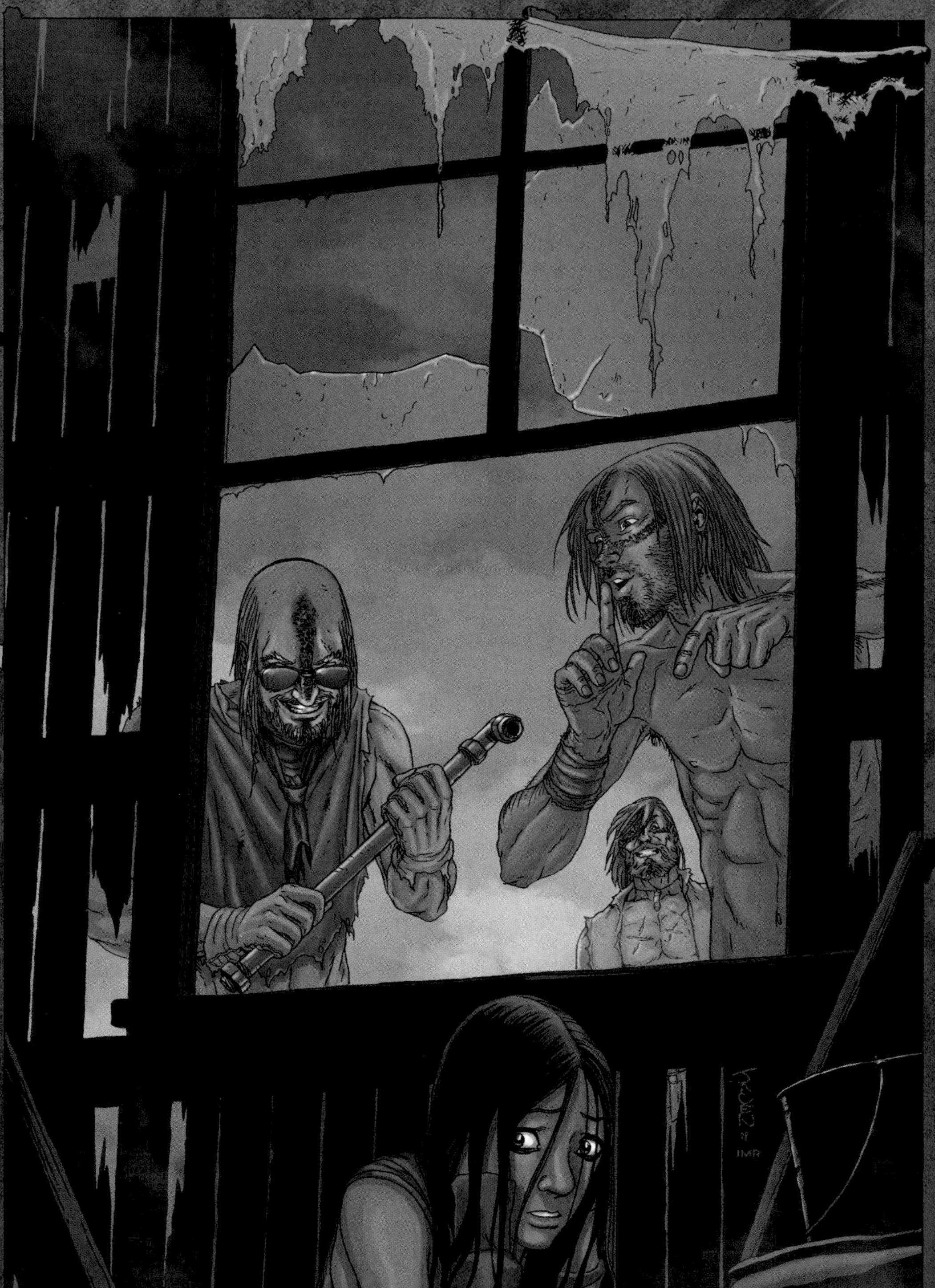

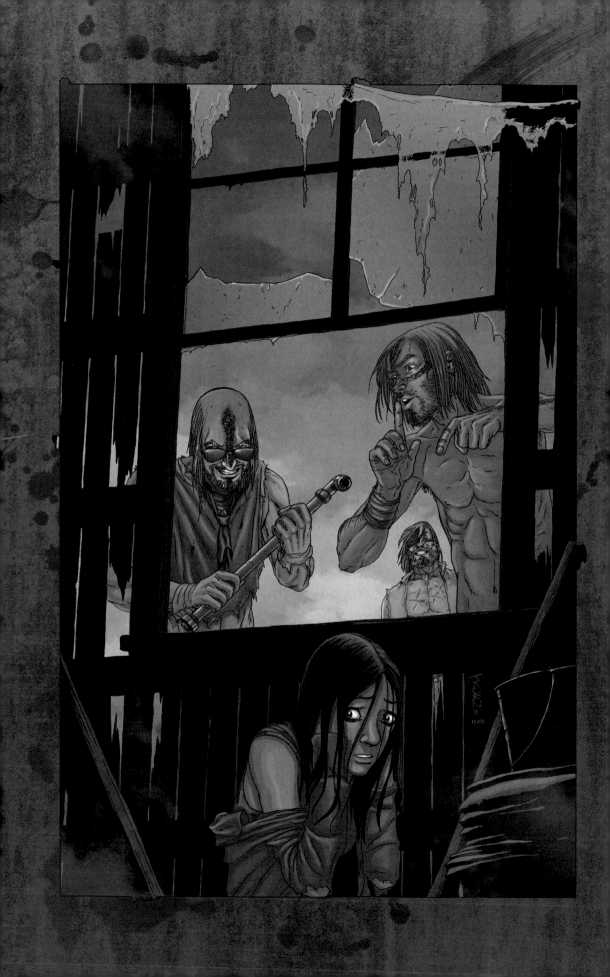

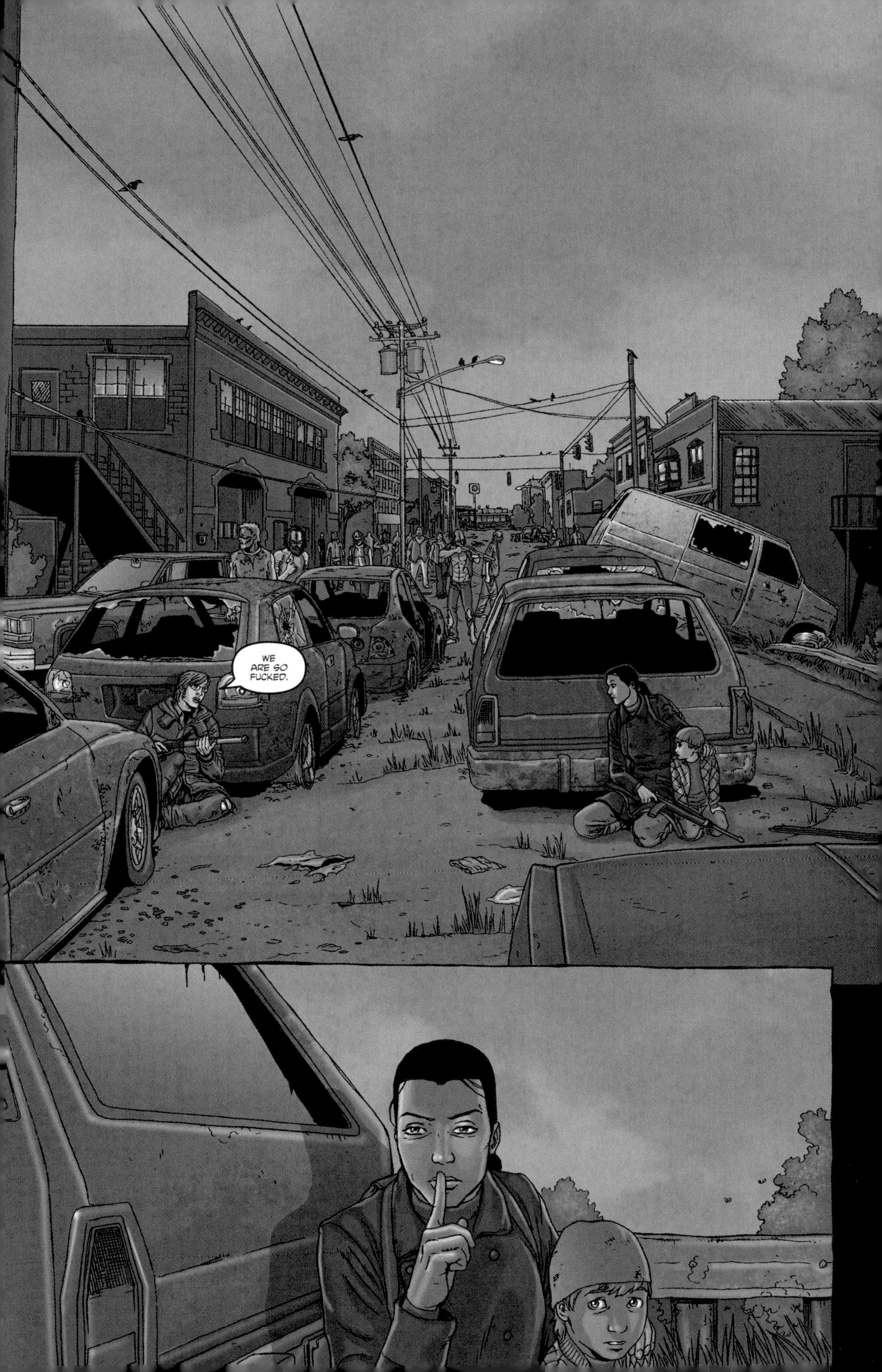
WE ARE SO FUCKED.

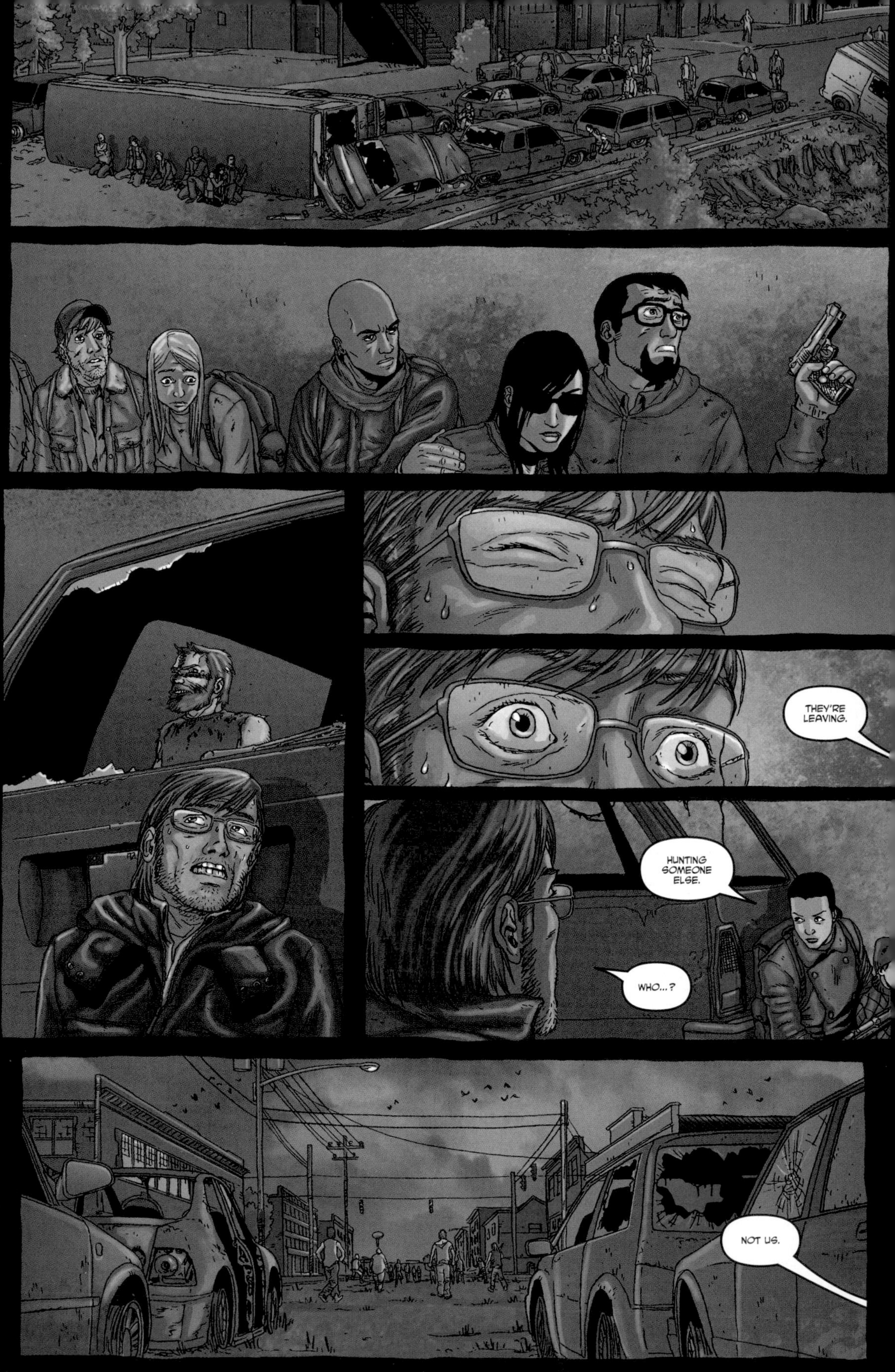
THEY'RE LEAVING.
HUNTING SOMEONE ELSE.
WHO...?
NOT US.

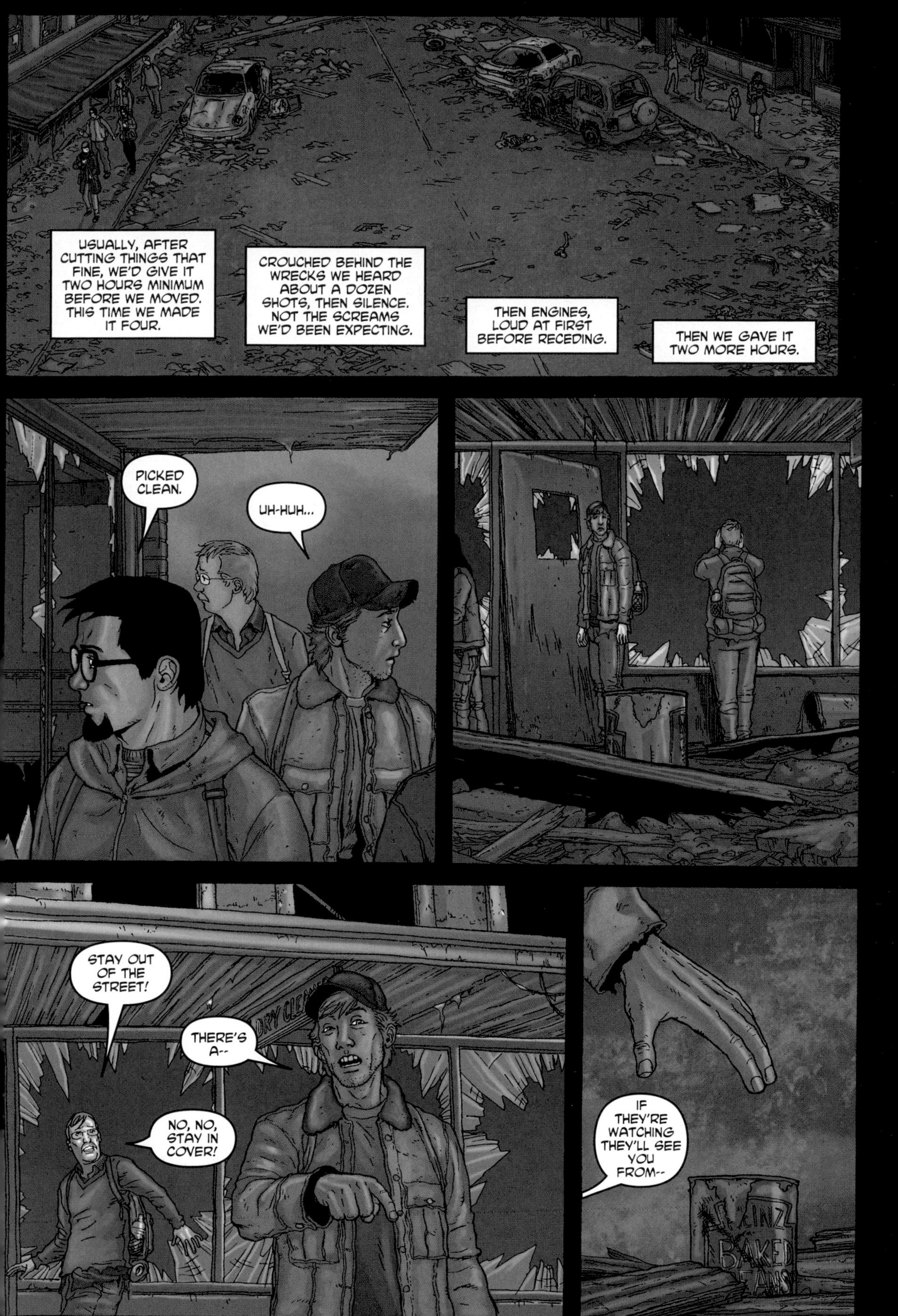
USUALLY, AFTER CUTTING THINGS THAT FINE, WE'D GIVE IT TWO HOURS MINIMUM BEFORE WE MOVED. THIS TIME WE MADE IT FOUR.
CROUCHED BEHIND THE WRECKS WE HEARD ABOUT A DOZEN SHOTS, THEN SILENCE. NOT THE SCREAMS WE'D BEEN EXPECTING.
THEN ENGINES, LOUD AT FIRST BEFORE RECEDING.
THEN WE GAVE IT TWO MORE HOURS.
PICKED CLEAN.
UH-HUH...
STAY OUT OF THE STREET!
THERE'S A--
NO, NO, STAY IN COVER!
DRY CLEANE
IF THEY'RE WATCHING THEY'LL SEE YOU FROM--
BAKED

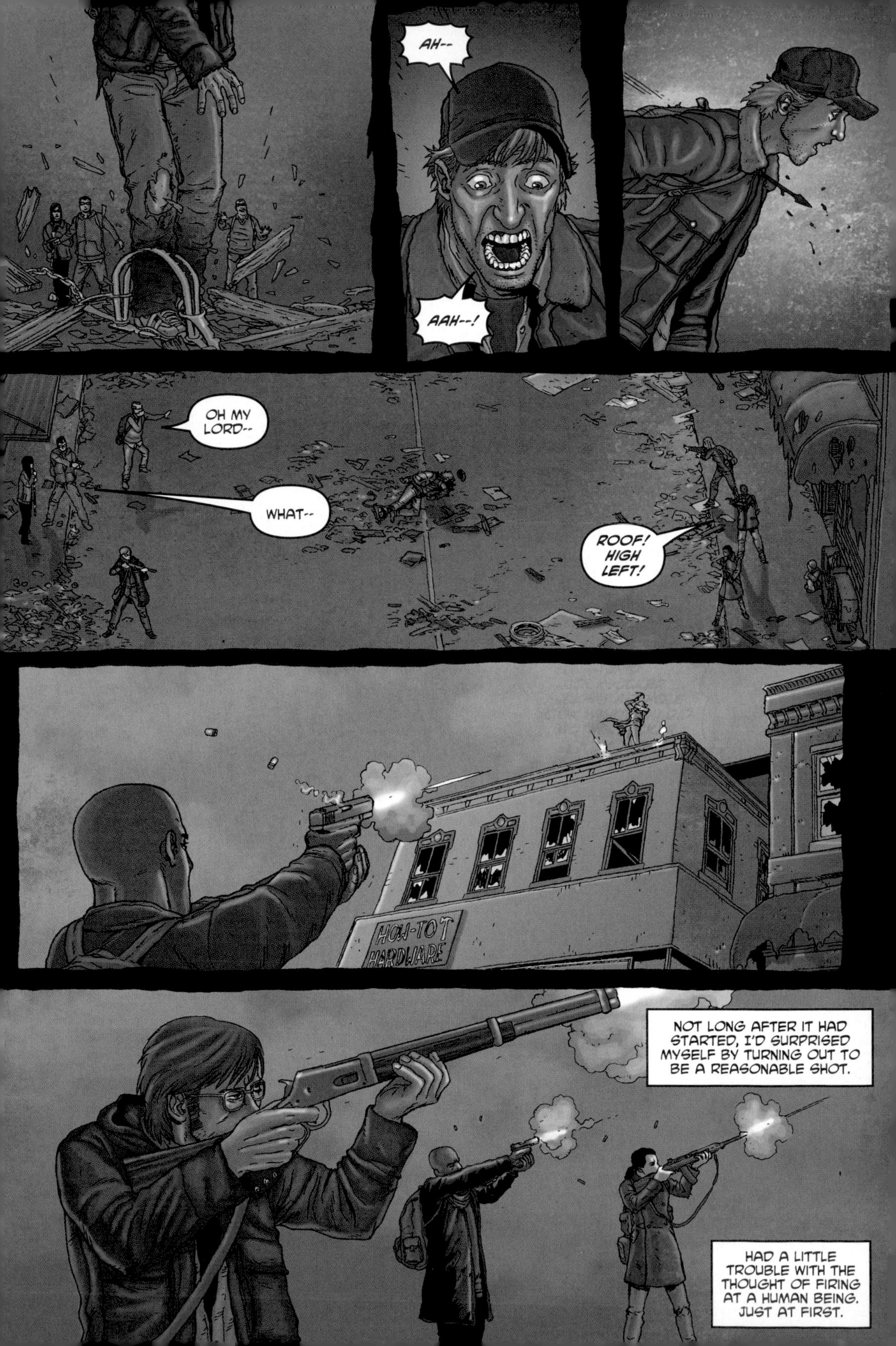
AH--
AAH--!
OH MY LORD--
WHAT--
ROOF! HIGH LEFT!
HOW-TO-T HARDWARE
NOT LONG AFTER IT HAD STARTED, I'D SURPRISED MYSELF BY TURNING OUT TO BE A REASONABLE SHOT.
HAD A LITTLE TROUBLE WITH THE THOUGHT OF FIRING AT A HUMAN BEING. JUST AT FIRST.

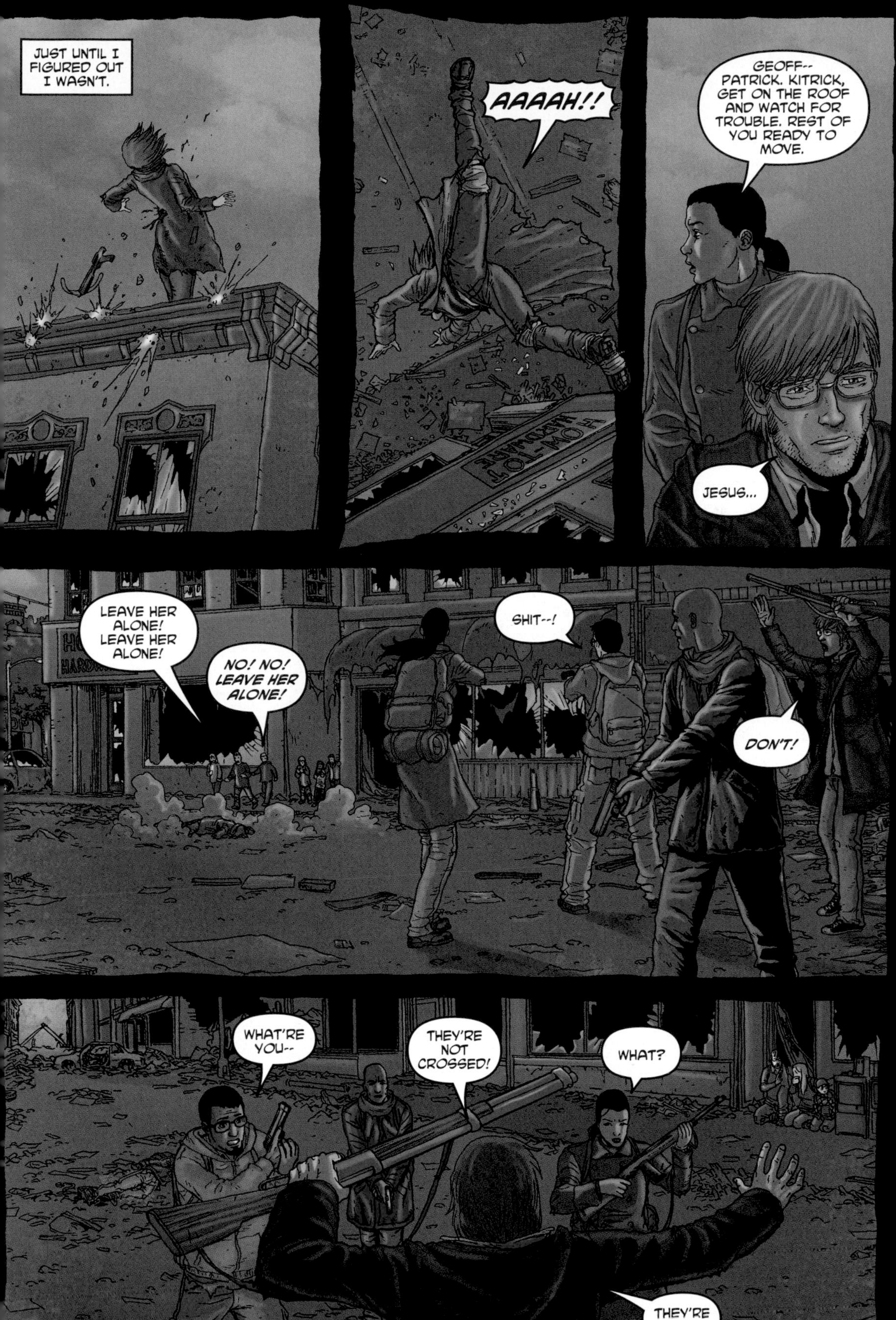
JUST UNTIL I FIGURED OUT I WASN'T.
AAAAH!!
HOW-TOT HARDWARE
GEOFF-- PATRICK. KITRICK, GET ON THE ROOF AND WATCH FOR TROUBLE. REST OF YOU READY TO MOVE.
JESUS...
LEAVE HER ALONE! LEAVE HER ALONE!
NO! NO! LEAVE HER ALONE!
SHIT--!
DON'T!
WHAT'RE YOU--
THEY'RE NOT CROSSED!
WHAT?
THEY'RE NOT!

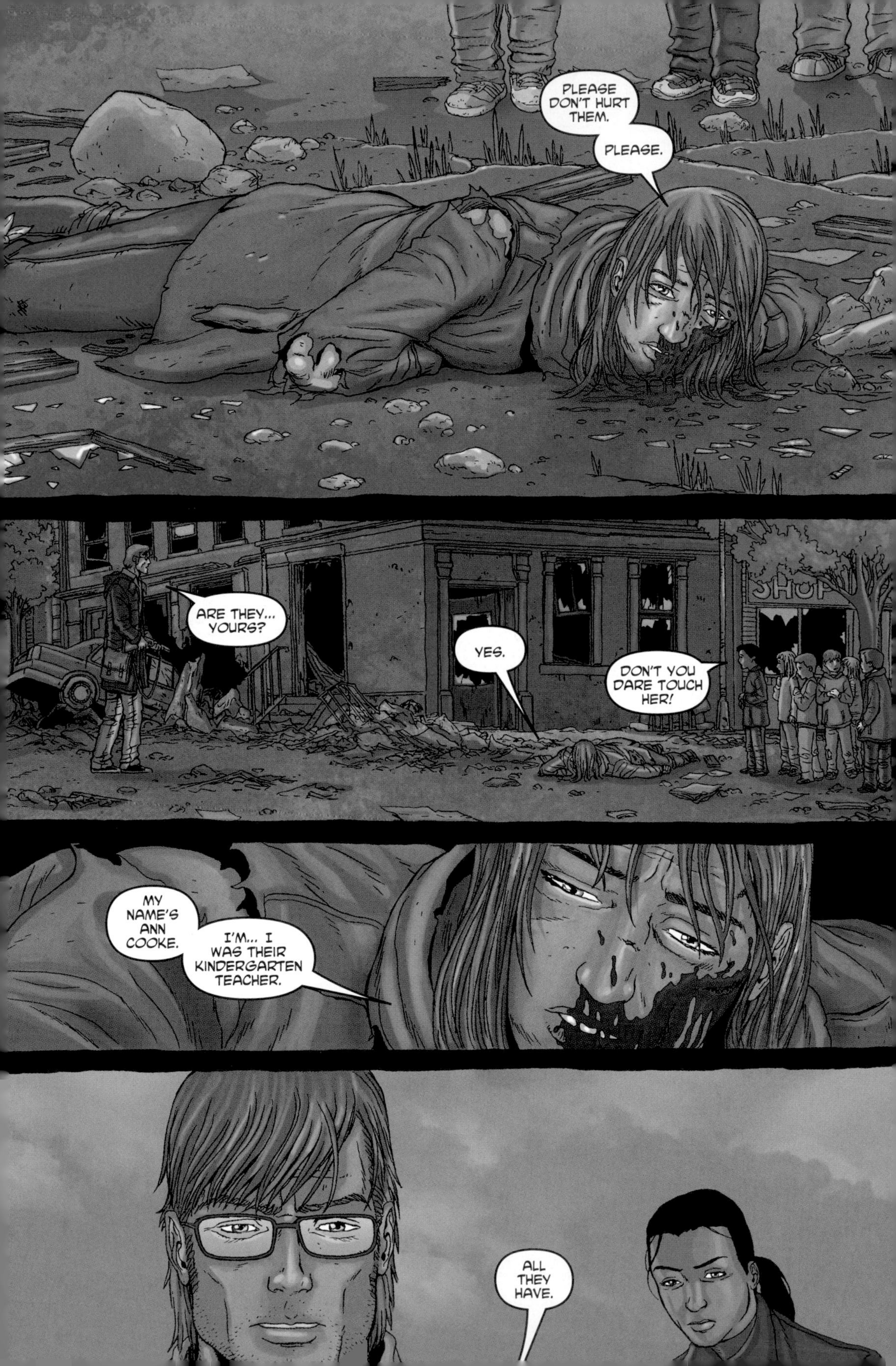

PLEASE DON'T HURT THEM.
PLEASE.
ARE THEY... YOURS?
YES.
DON'T YOU DARE TOUCH HER!
MY NAME'S ANN COOKE.
I'M... I WAS THEIR KINDERGARTEN TEACHER.
ALL THEY HAVE.

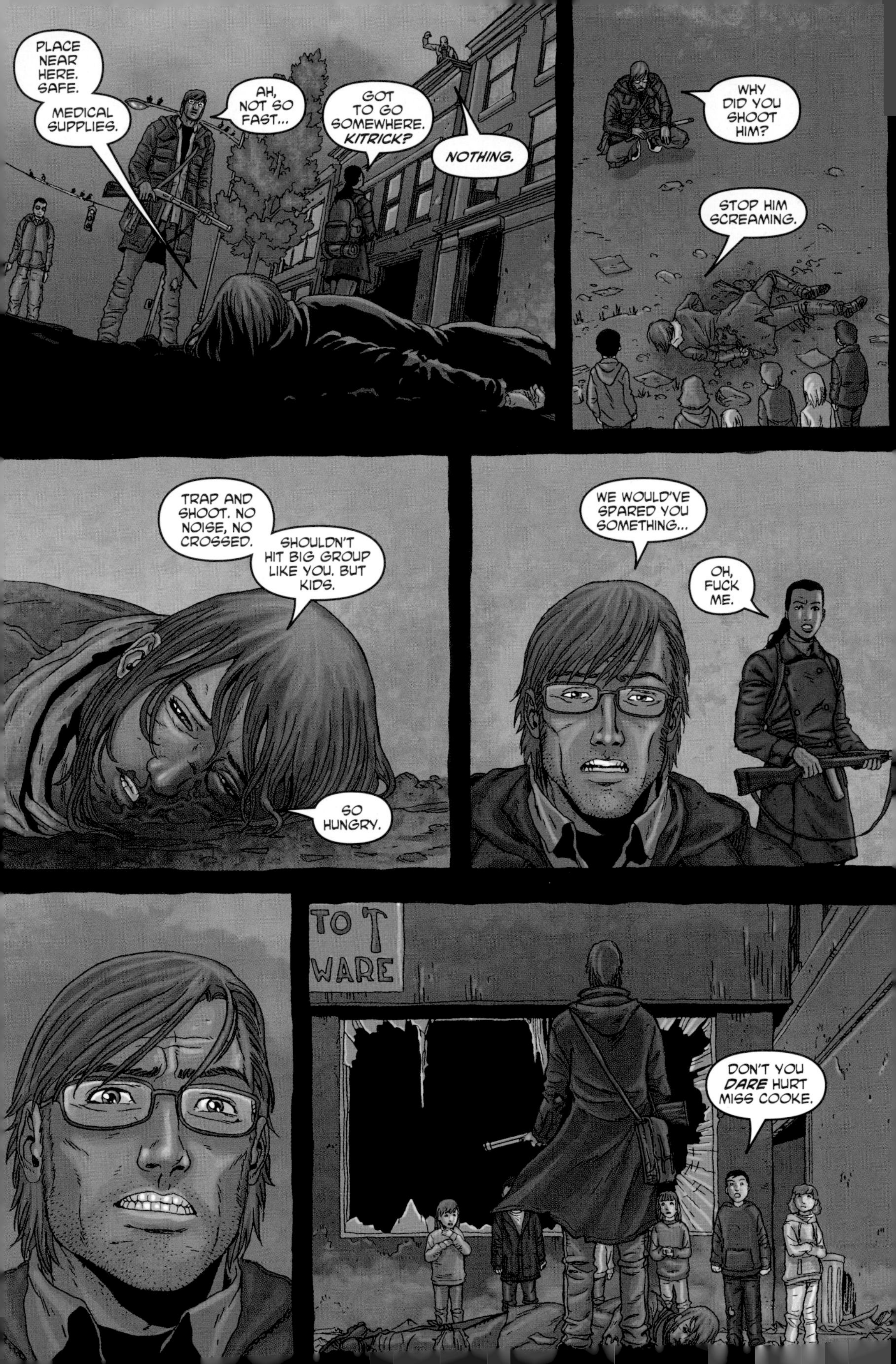
PLACE NEAR HERE. SAFE.
MEDICAL SUPPLIES.
AH, NOT SO FAST...
GOT TO GO SOMEWHERE. *KITRICK?*
NOTHING.
WHY DID YOU SHOOT HIM?
STOP HIM SCREAMING.
TRAP AND SHOOT. NO NOISE, NO CROSSED.
SHOULDN'T HIT BIG GROUP LIKE YOU. BUT KIDS.
SO HUNGRY.
WE WOULD'VE SPARED YOU SOMETHING...
OH, FUCK ME.
TO T
WARE
DON'T YOU *DARE* HURT MISS COOKE.

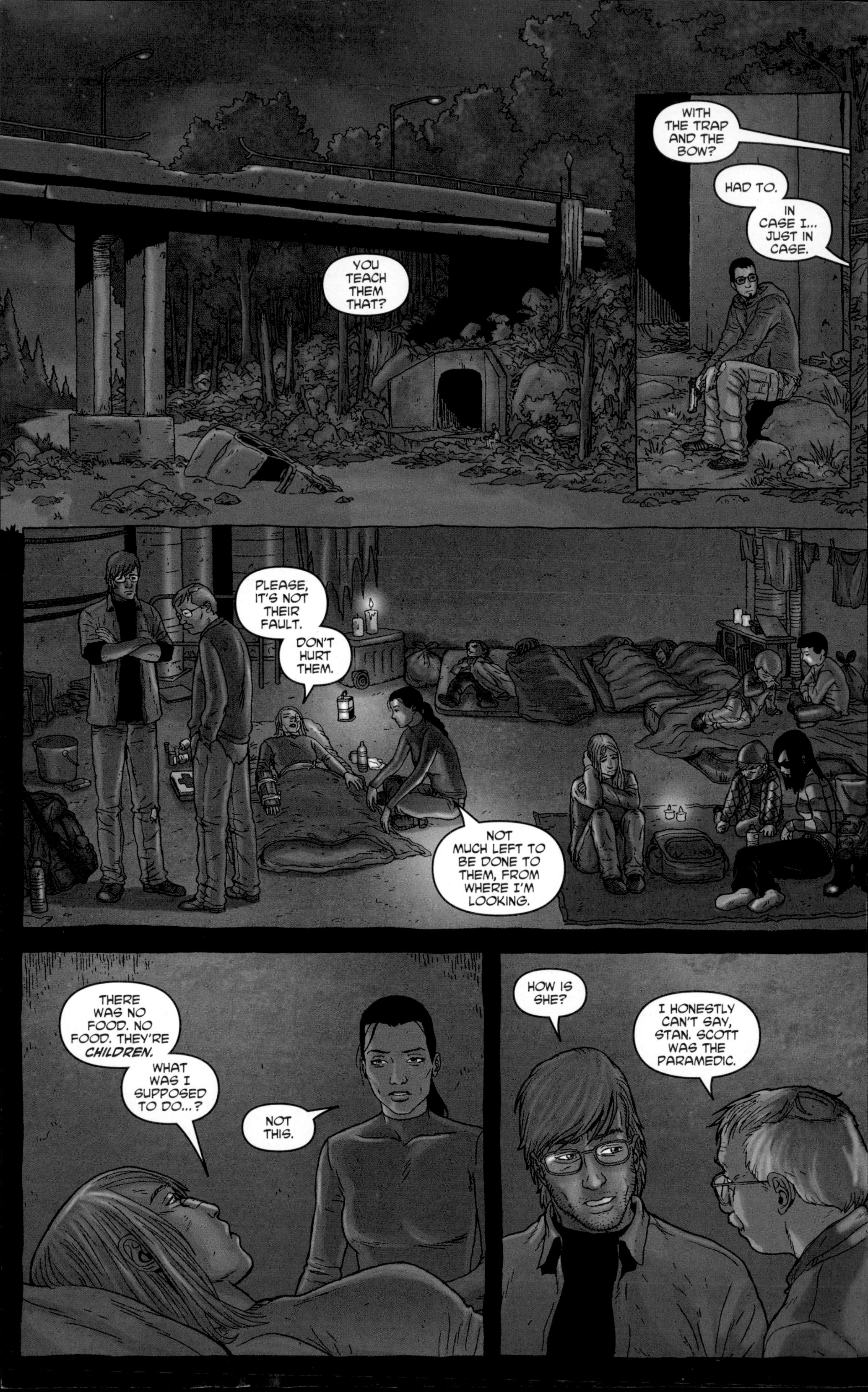
YOU TEACH THEM THAT?
WITH THE TRAP AND THE BOW?
HAD TO.
IN CASE I... JUST IN CASE.
PLEASE, IT'S NOT THEIR FAULT.
DON'T HURT THEM.
NOT MUCH LEFT TO BE DONE TO THEM, FROM WHERE I'M LOOKING.
THERE WAS NO FOOD. NO FOOD. THEY'RE *CHILDREN.*
WHAT WAS I SUPPOSED TO DO...?
NOT THIS.
HOW IS SHE?
I HONESTLY CAN'T SAY, STAN. SCOTT WAS THE PARAMEDIC.

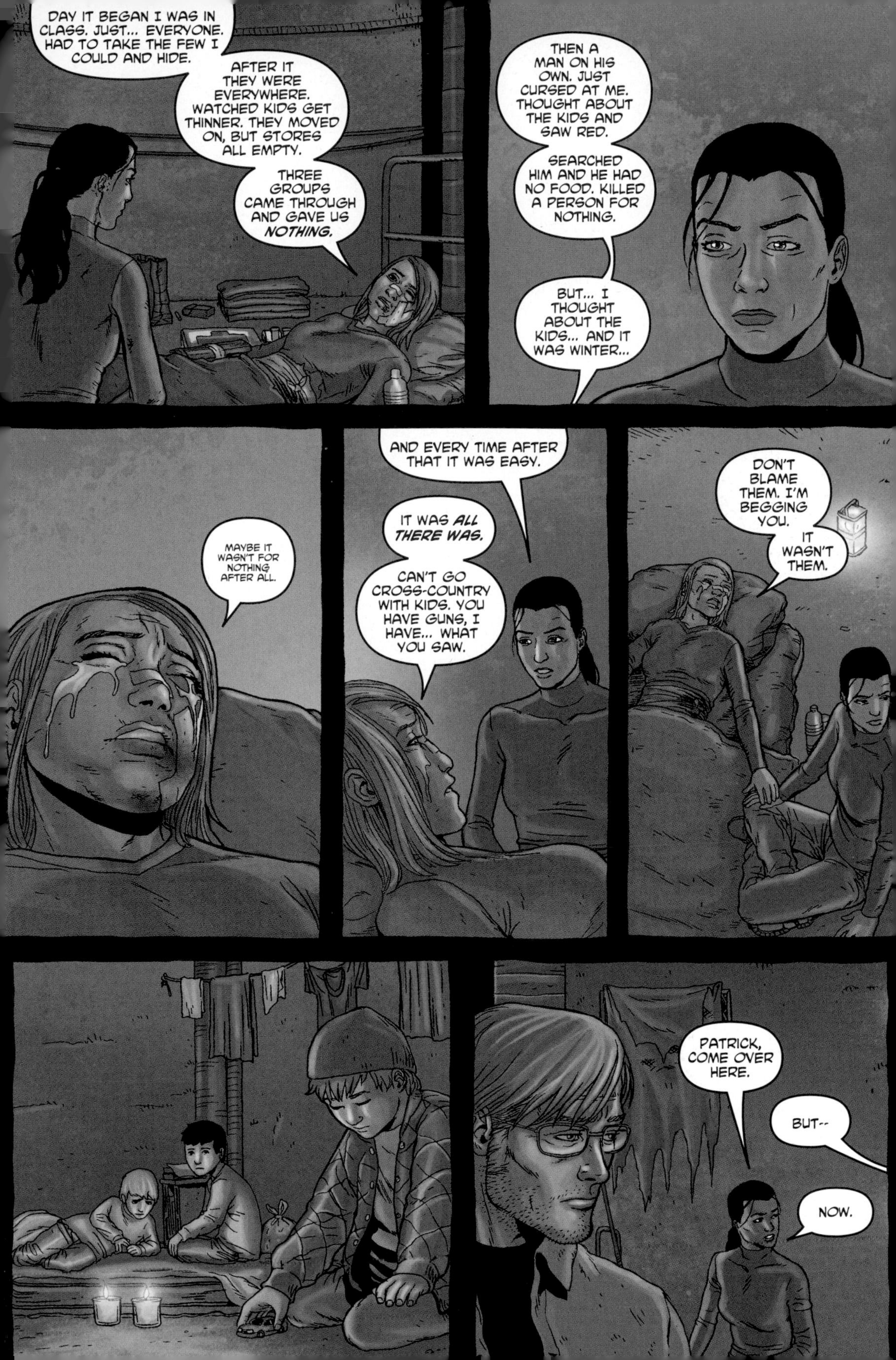
DAY IT BEGAN I WAS IN CLASS. JUST... EVERYONE. HAD TO TAKE THE FEW I COULD AND HIDE.
AFTER IT THEY WERE EVERYWHERE. WATCHED KIDS GET THINNER. THEY MOVED ON, BUT STORES ALL EMPTY.
THREE GROUPS CAME THROUGH AND GAVE US *NOTHING.*
THEN A MAN ON HIS OWN. JUST CURSED AT ME. THOUGHT ABOUT THE KIDS AND SAW RED.
SEARCHED HIM AND HE HAD NO FOOD. KILLED A PERSON FOR NOTHING.
BUT... I THOUGHT ABOUT THE KIDS... AND IT WAS WINTER...
MAYBE IT WASN'T FOR NOTHING AFTER ALL.
AND EVERY TIME AFTER THAT IT WAS EASY.
IT WAS *ALL THERE WAS.*
CAN'T GO CROSS-COUNTRY WITH KIDS. YOU HAVE GUNS, I HAVE... WHAT YOU SAW.
DON'T BLAME THEM. I'M BEGGING YOU.
IT WASN'T THEM.
PATRICK, COME OVER HERE.
BUT--
NOW.

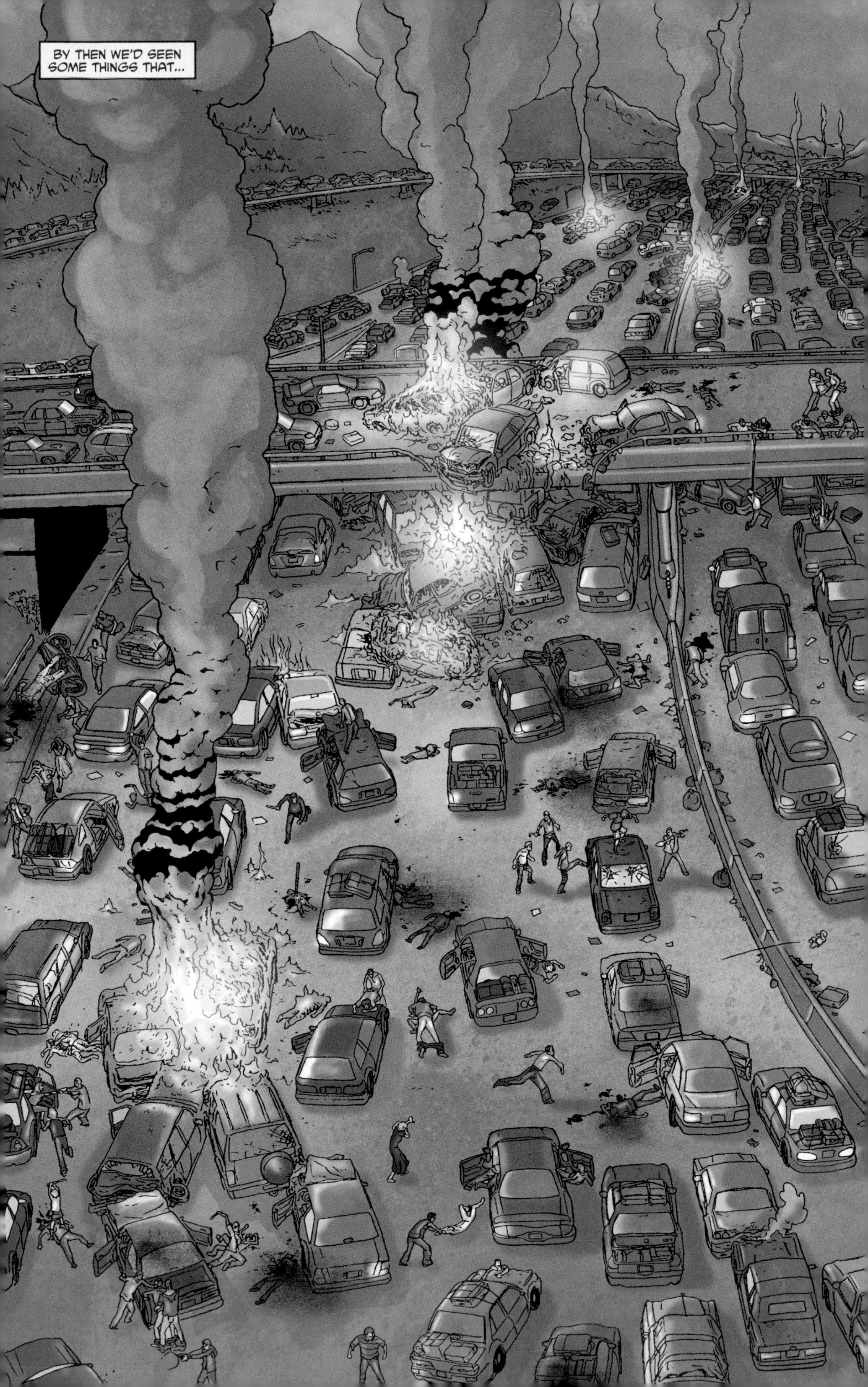
BY THEN WE'D SEEN SOME THINGS THAT...

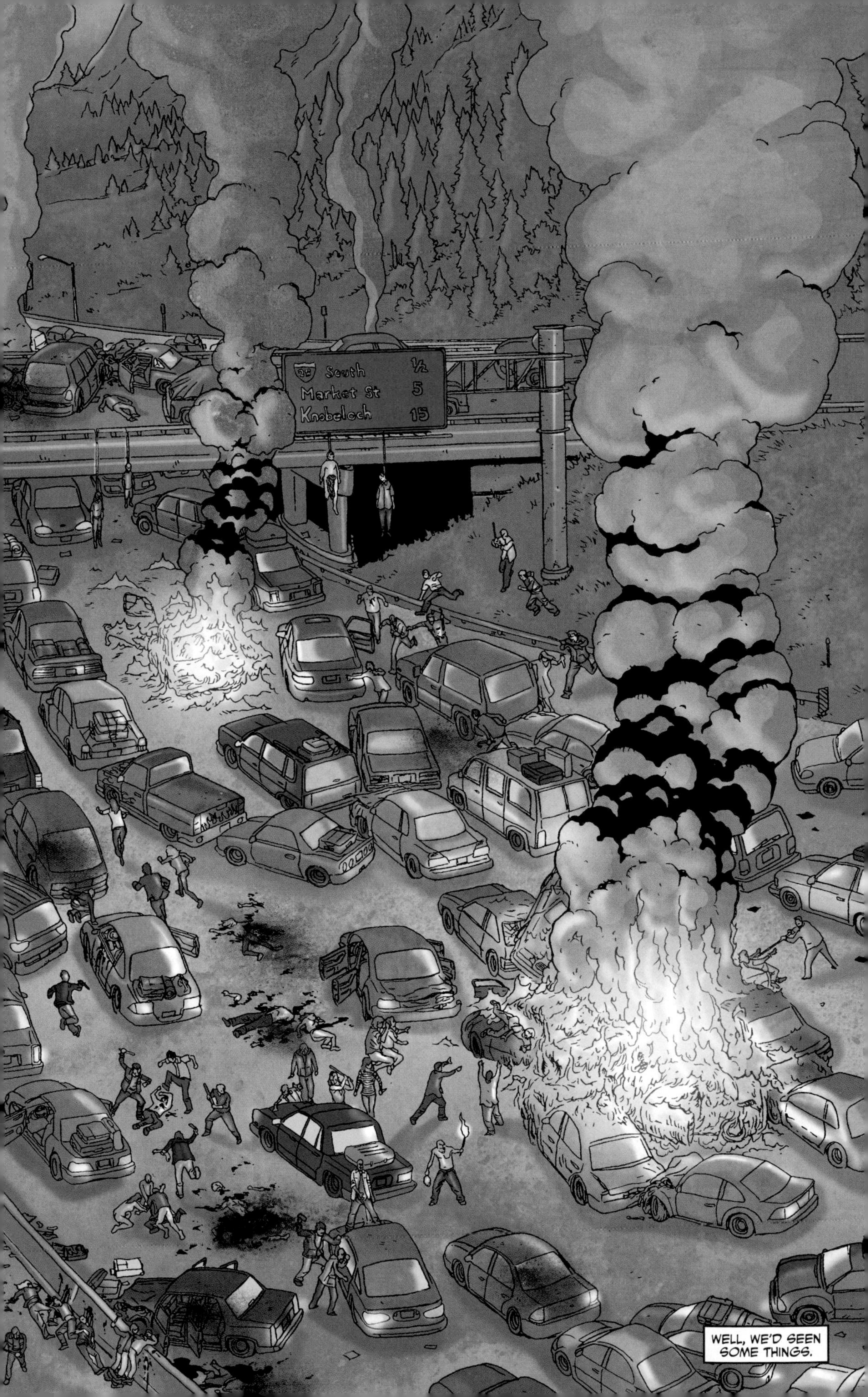
South 1/2
Market St 5
Knobeloch 15
WELL, WE'D SEEN SOME THINGS.

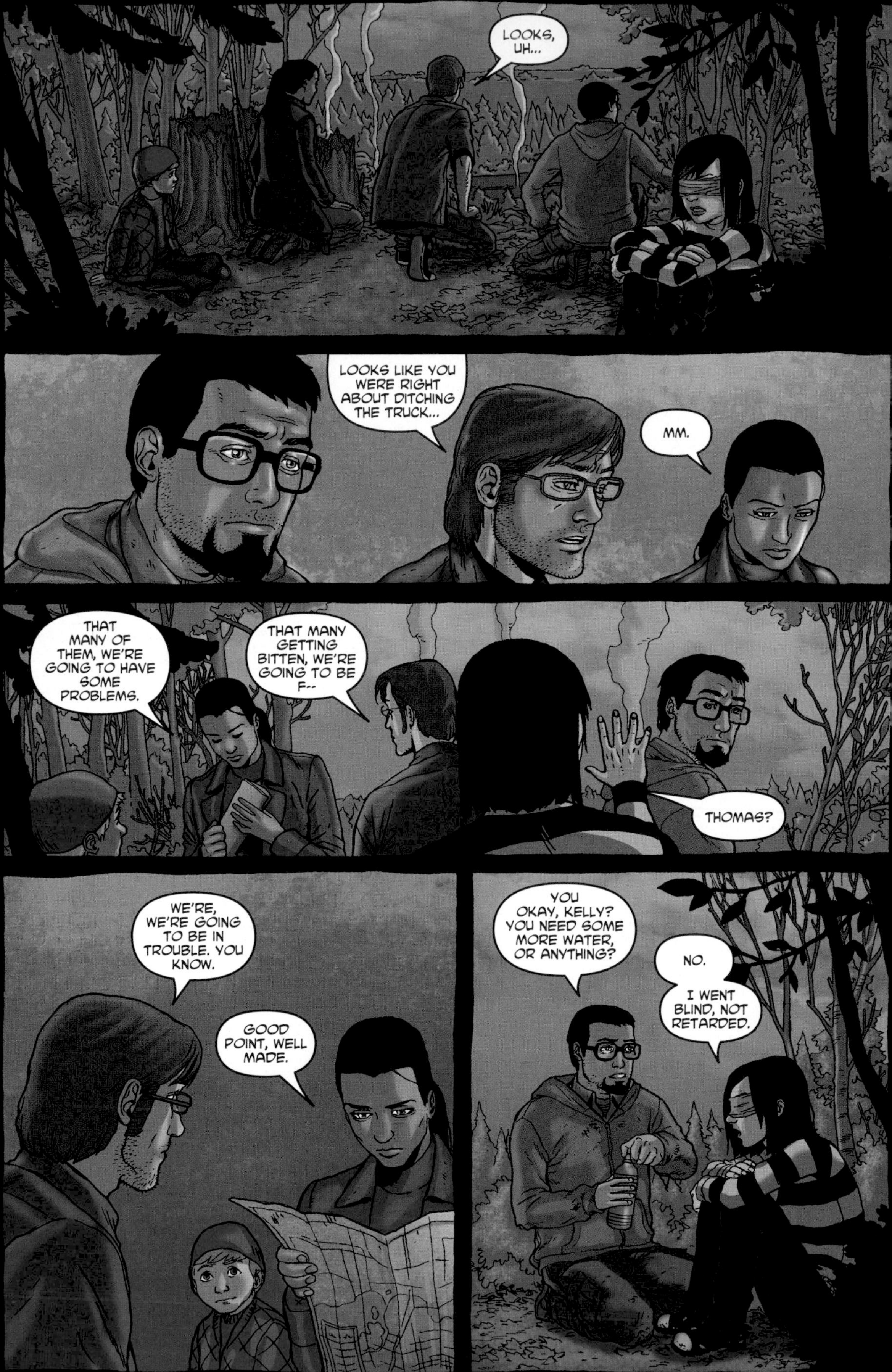
LOOKS, UH...
LOOKS LIKE YOU WERE RIGHT ABOUT DITCHING THE TRUCK...
MM.
THAT MANY OF THEM, WE'RE GOING TO HAVE SOME PROBLEMS.
THAT MANY GETTING BITTEN, WE'RE GOING TO BE F--
THOMAS?
WE'RE, WE'RE GOING TO BE IN TROUBLE. YOU KNOW.
GOOD POINT, WELL MADE.
YOU OKAY, KELLY? YOU NEED SOME MORE WATER, OR ANYTHING?
NO.
I WENT BLIND, NOT RETARDED.

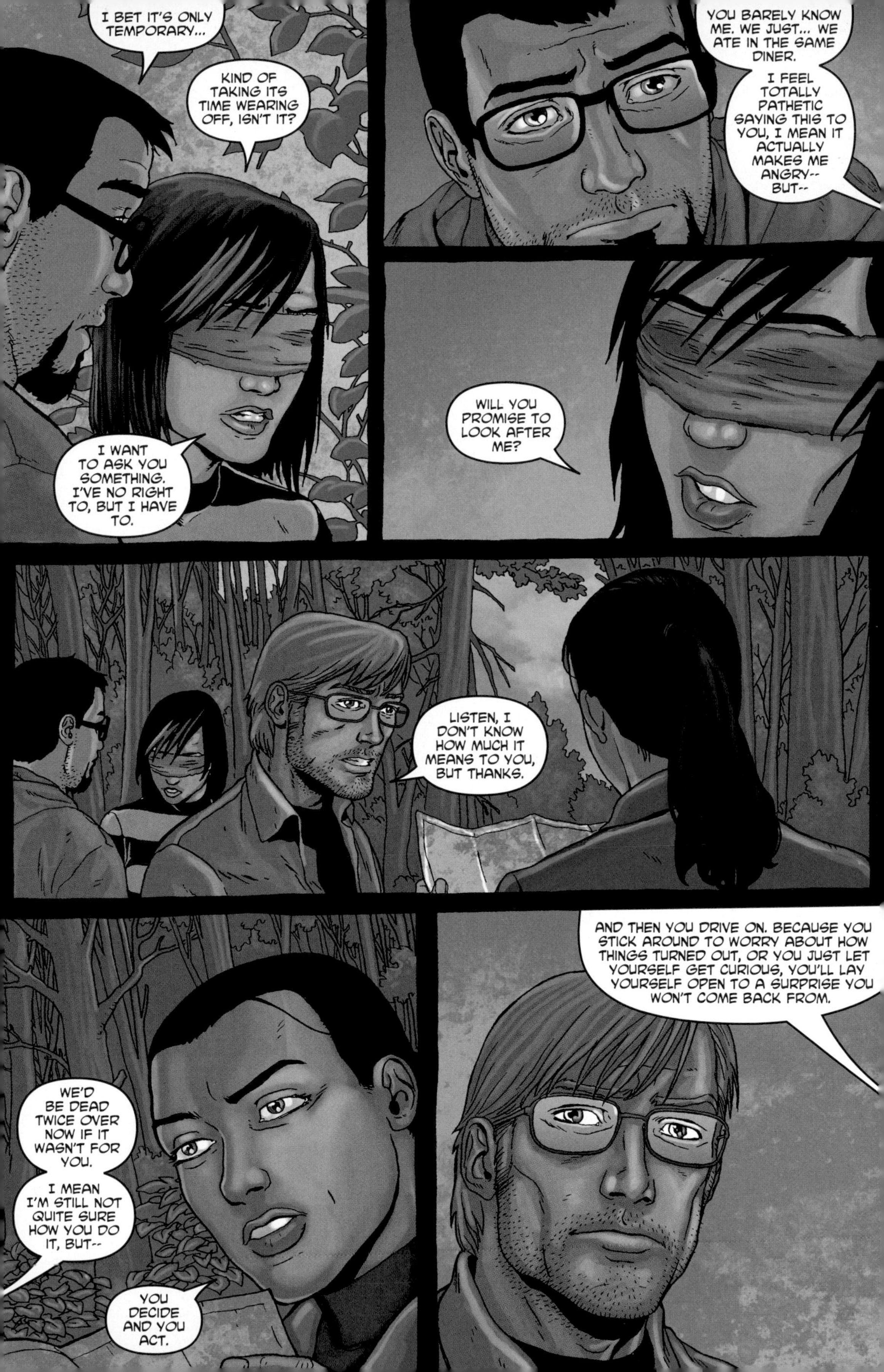
I BET IT'S ONLY TEMPORARY...
KIND OF TAKING ITS TIME WEARING OFF, ISN'T IT?
I WANT TO ASK YOU SOMETHING. I'VE NO RIGHT TO, BUT I HAVE TO.
YOU BARELY KNOW ME. WE JUST... WE ATE IN THE SAME DINER.
I FEEL TOTALLY PATHETIC SAYING THIS TO YOU, I MEAN IT ACTUALLY MAKES ME ANGRY-- BUT--
WILL YOU PROMISE TO LOOK AFTER ME?
LISTEN, I DON'T KNOW HOW MUCH IT MEANS TO YOU, BUT THANKS.
WE'D BE DEAD TWICE OVER NOW IF IT WASN'T FOR YOU.
I MEAN I'M STILL NOT QUITE SURE HOW YOU DO IT, BUT--
YOU DECIDE AND YOU ACT.
AND THEN YOU DRIVE ON. BECAUSE YOU STICK AROUND TO WORRY ABOUT HOW THINGS TURNED OUT, OR YOU JUST LET YOURSELF GET CURIOUS, YOU'LL LAY YOURSELF OPEN TO A SURPRISE YOU WON'T COME BACK FROM.

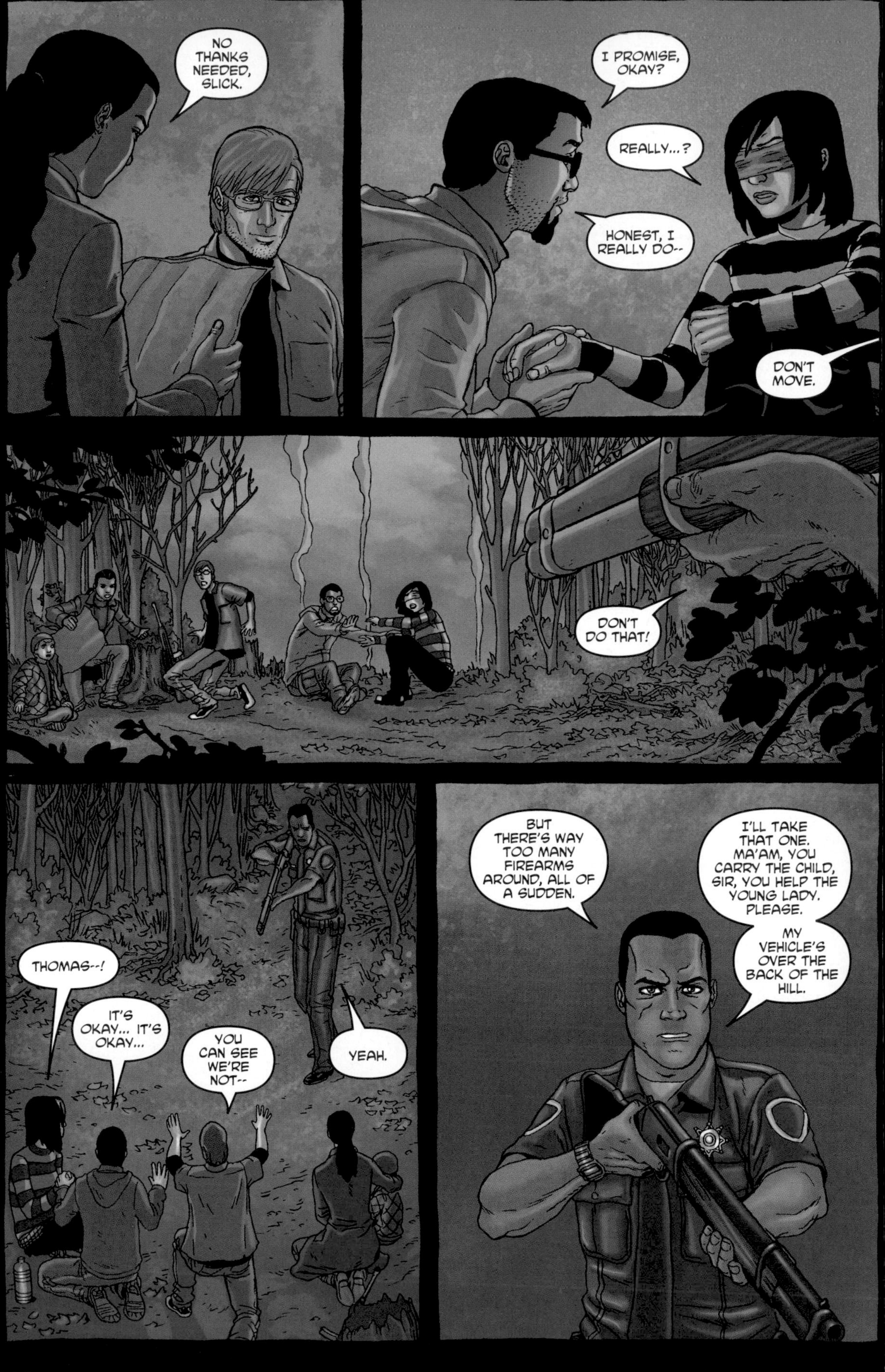
NO THANKS NEEDED, SLICK.
I PROMISE, OKAY?
REALLY...?
HONEST, I REALLY DO--
DON'T MOVE.
DON'T DO THAT!
THOMAS--!
IT'S OKAY... IT'S OKAY...
YOU CAN SEE WE'RE NOT--
YEAH.
BUT THERE'S WAY TOO MANY FIREARMS AROUND, ALL OF A SUDDEN.
I'LL TAKE THAT ONE. MA'AM, YOU CARRY THE CHILD, SIR, YOU HELP THE YOUNG LADY. PLEASE.
MY VEHICLE'S OVER THE BACK OF THE HILL.

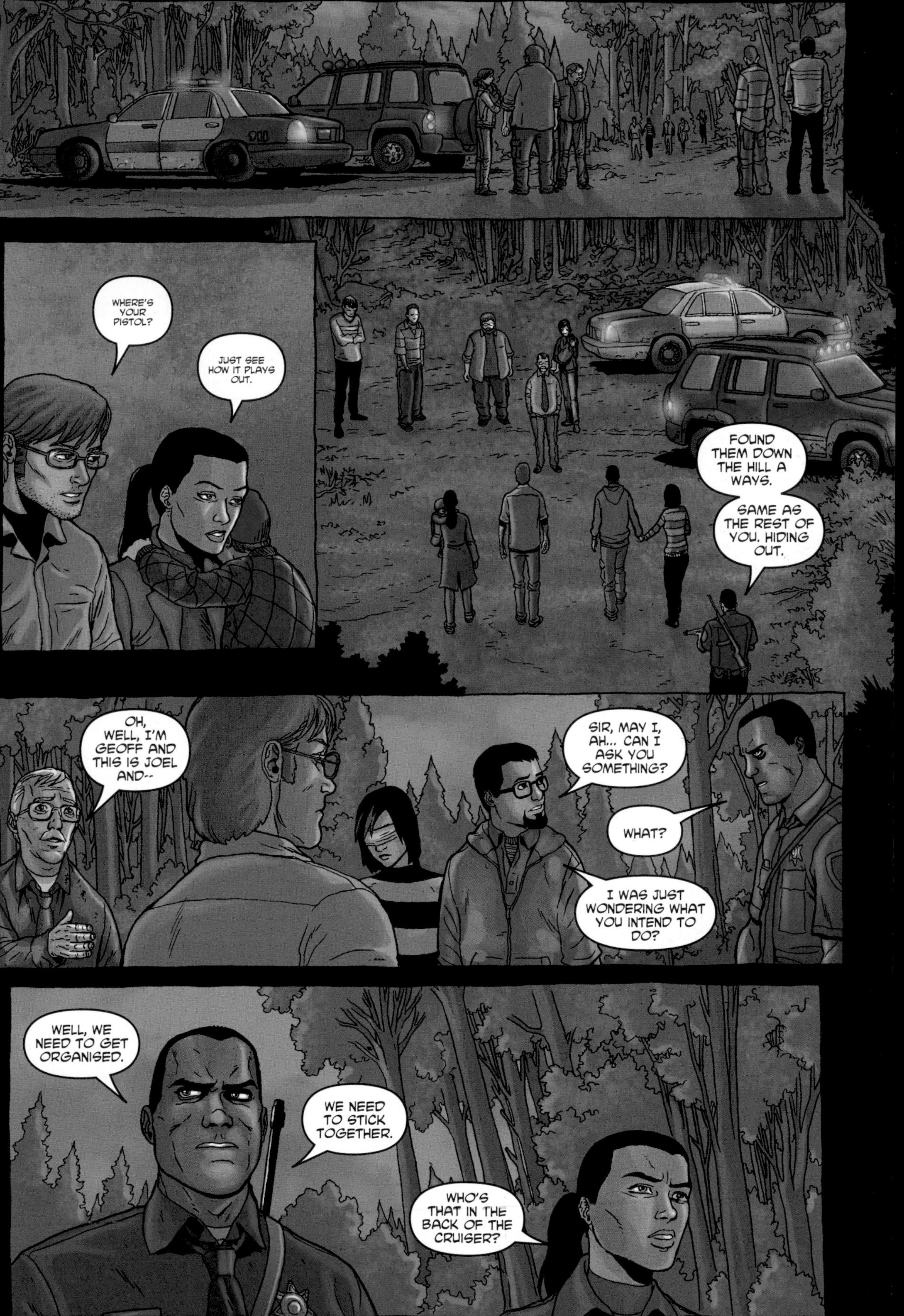
WHERE'S YOUR PISTOL?
JUST SEE HOW IT PLAYS OUT.
FOUND THEM DOWN THE HILL A WAYS.
SAME AS THE REST OF YOU. HIDING OUT.
OH, WELL, I'M GEOFF AND THIS IS JOEL AND--
SIR, MAY I, AH... CAN I ASK YOU SOMETHING?
WHAT?
I WAS JUST WONDERING WHAT YOU INTEND TO DO?
WELL, WE NEED TO GET ORGANISED.
WE NEED TO STICK TOGETHER.
WHO'S THAT IN THE BACK OF THE CRUISER?

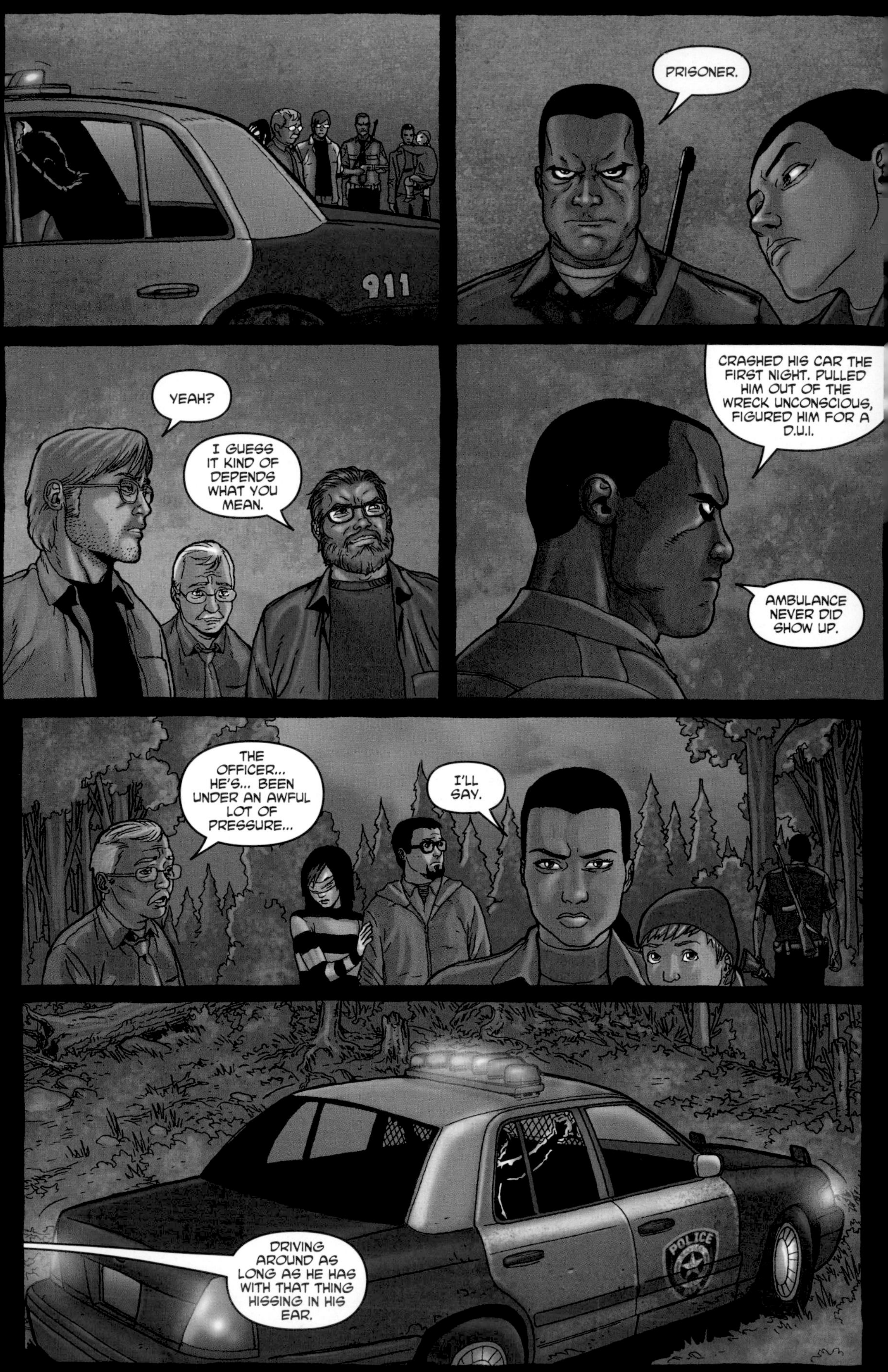
PRISONER.
YEAH?
I GUESS IT KIND OF DEPENDS WHAT YOU MEAN.
CRASHED HIS CAR THE FIRST NIGHT. PULLED HIM OUT OF THE WRECK UNCONSCIOUS, FIGURED HIM FOR A D.U.I.
AMBULANCE NEVER DID SHOW UP.
THE OFFICER... HE'S... BEEN UNDER AN AWFUL LOT OF PRESSURE...
I'LL SAY.
DRIVING AROUND AS LONG AS HE HAS WITH THAT THING HISSING IN HIS EAR.
911
POLICE

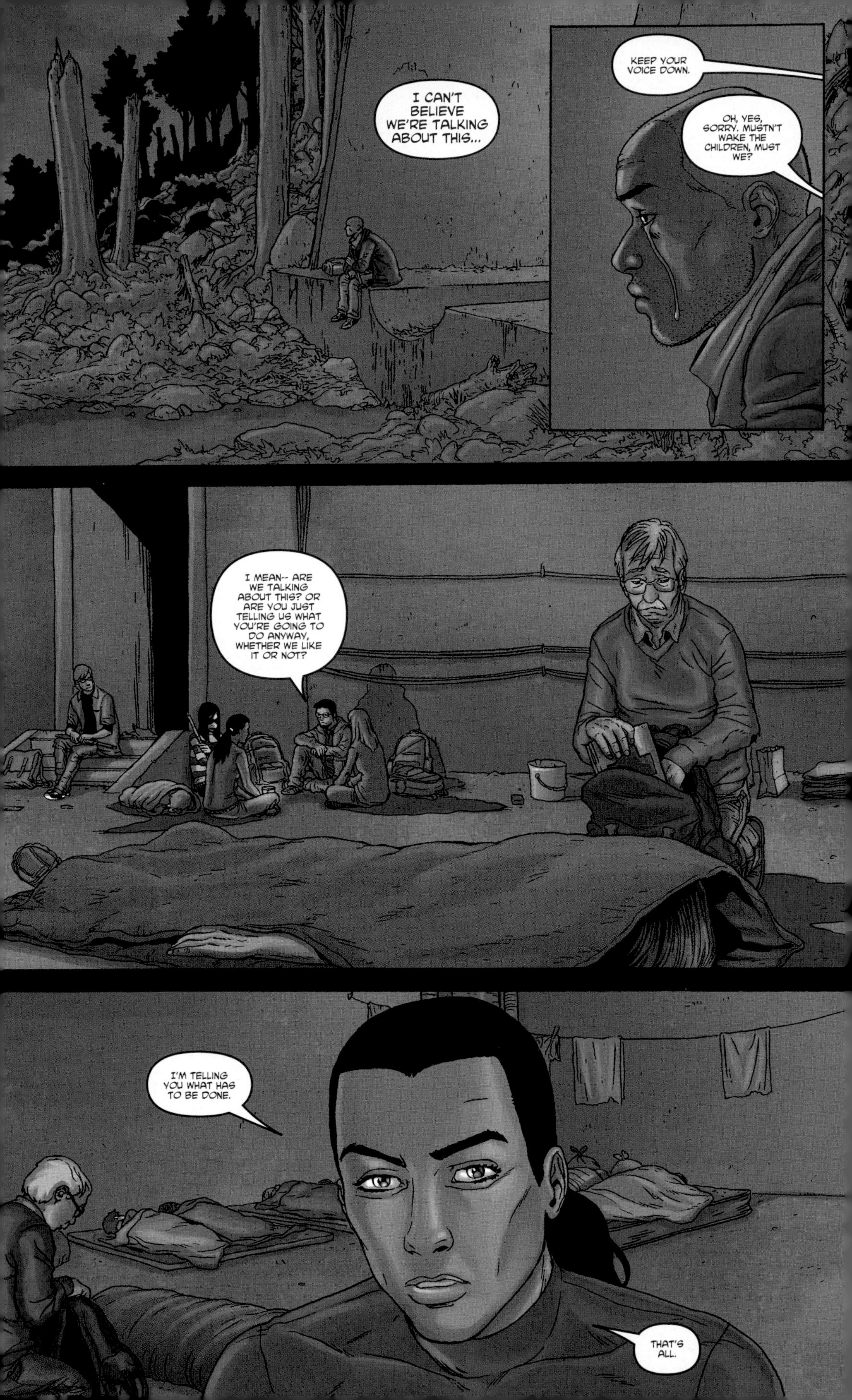
I CAN'T BELIEVE WE'RE TALKING ABOUT THIS...
KEEP YOUR VOICE DOWN.
OH, YES, SORRY. MUSTN'T WAKE THE CHILDREN, MUST WE?
I MEAN-- ARE WE TALKING ABOUT THIS? OR ARE YOU JUST TELLING US WHAT YOU'RE GOING TO DO ANYWAY, WHETHER WE LIKE IT OR NOT?
I'M TELLING YOU WHAT HAS TO BE DONE.
THAT'S ALL.

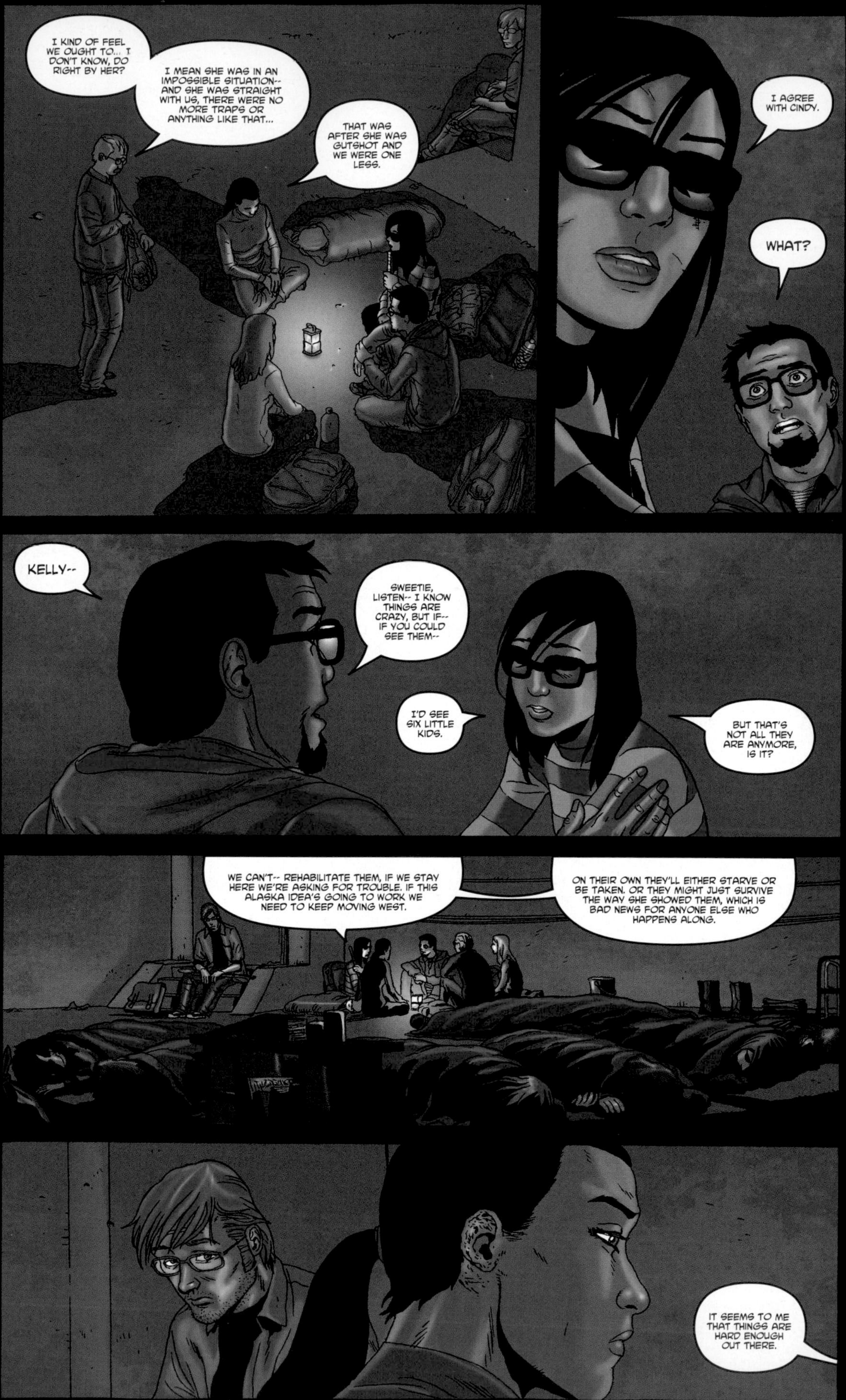
I KIND OF FEEL WE OUGHT TO... I DON'T KNOW, DO RIGHT BY HER?
I MEAN SHE WAS IN AN IMPOSSIBLE SITUATION-- AND SHE WAS STRAIGHT WITH US, THERE WERE NO MORE TRAPS OR ANYTHING LIKE THAT...
THAT WAS AFTER SHE WAS GUTSHOT AND WE WERE ONE LESS.
I AGREE WITH CINDY.
WHAT?
KELLY--
SWEETIE, LISTEN-- I KNOW THINGS ARE CRAZY, BUT IF-- IF YOU COULD SEE THEM--
I'D SEE SIX LITTLE KIDS.
BUT THAT'S NOT ALL THEY ARE ANYMORE, IS IT?
WE CAN'T-- REHABILITATE THEM, IF WE STAY HERE WE'RE ASKING FOR TROUBLE. IF THIS ALASKA IDEA'S GOING TO WORK WE NEED TO KEEP MOVING WEST.
ON THEIR OWN THEY'LL EITHER STARVE OR BE TAKEN. OR THEY MIGHT JUST SURVIVE THE WAY SHE SHOWED THEM, WHICH IS BAD NEWS FOR ANYONE ELSE WHO HAPPENS ALONG.
IT SEEMS TO ME THAT THINGS ARE HARD ENOUGH OUT THERE.

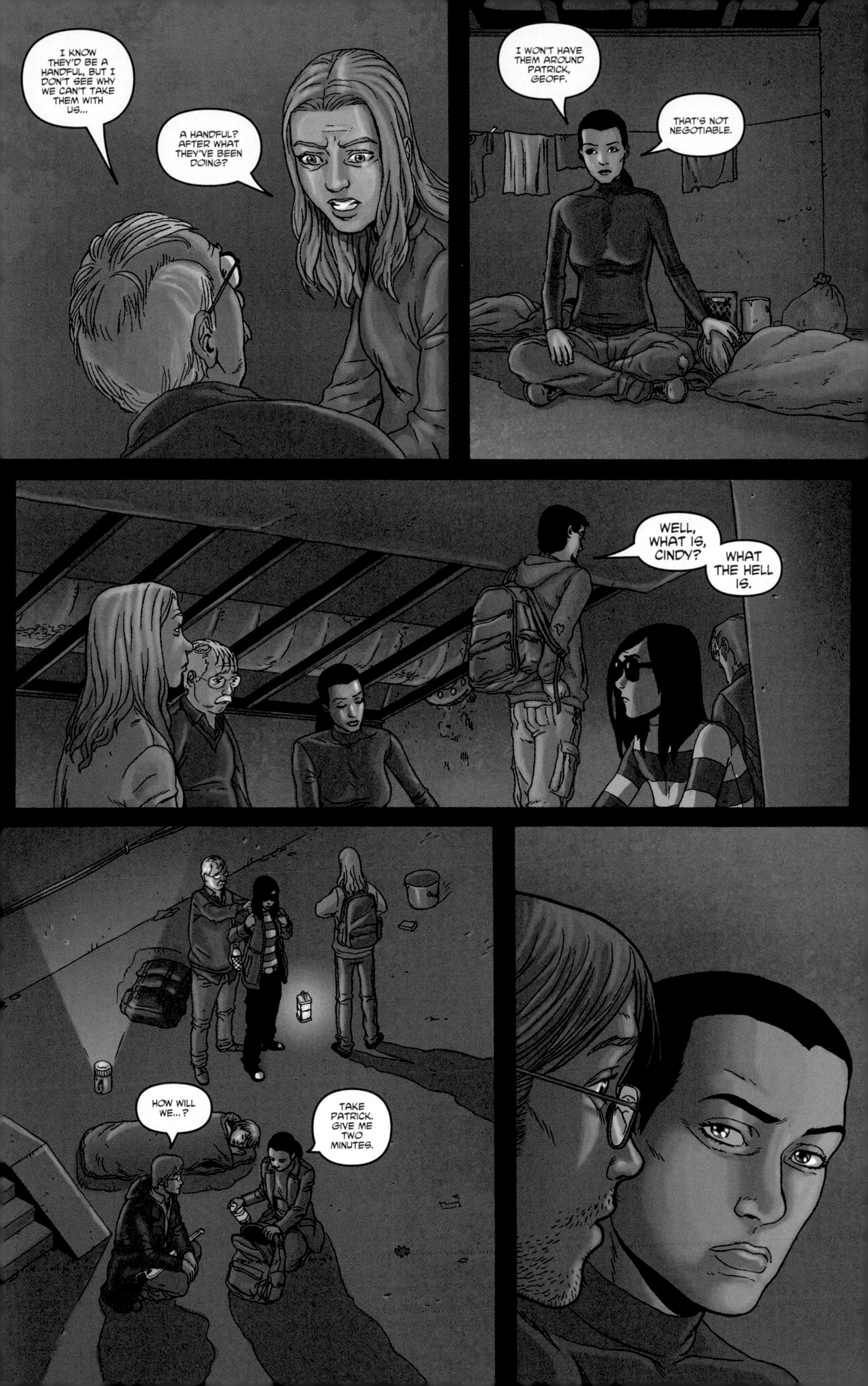
I KNOW THEY'D BE A HANDFUL, BUT I DON'T SEE WHY WE CAN'T TAKE THEM WITH US...
A HANDFUL? AFTER WHAT THEY'VE BEEN DOING?
I WON'T HAVE THEM AROUND PATRICK, GEOFF.
THAT'S NOT NEGOTIABLE.
WELL, WHAT IS, CINDY?
WHAT THE HELL IS.
HOW WILL WE...?
TAKE PATRICK. GIVE ME TWO MINUTES.

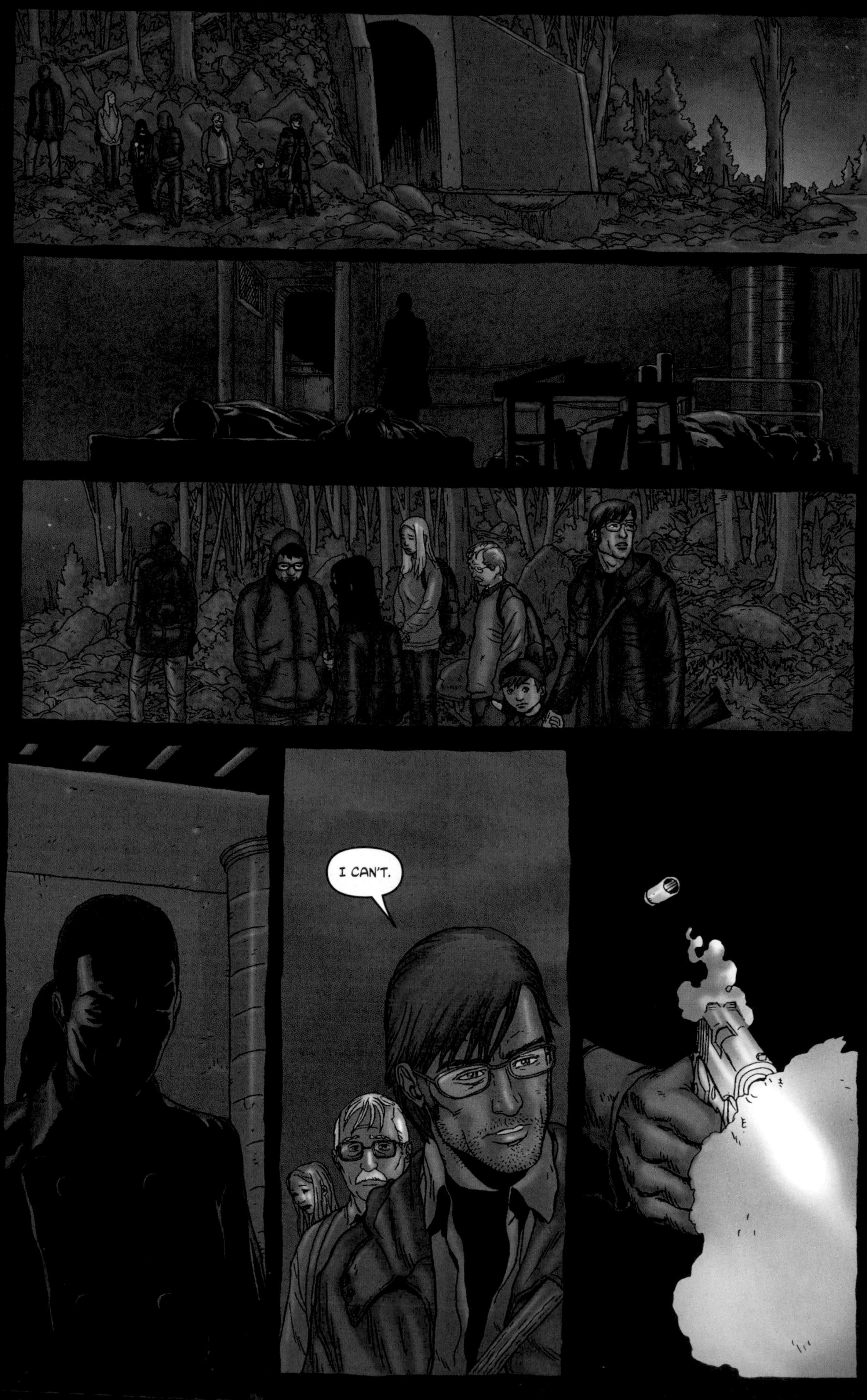
I CAN'T.

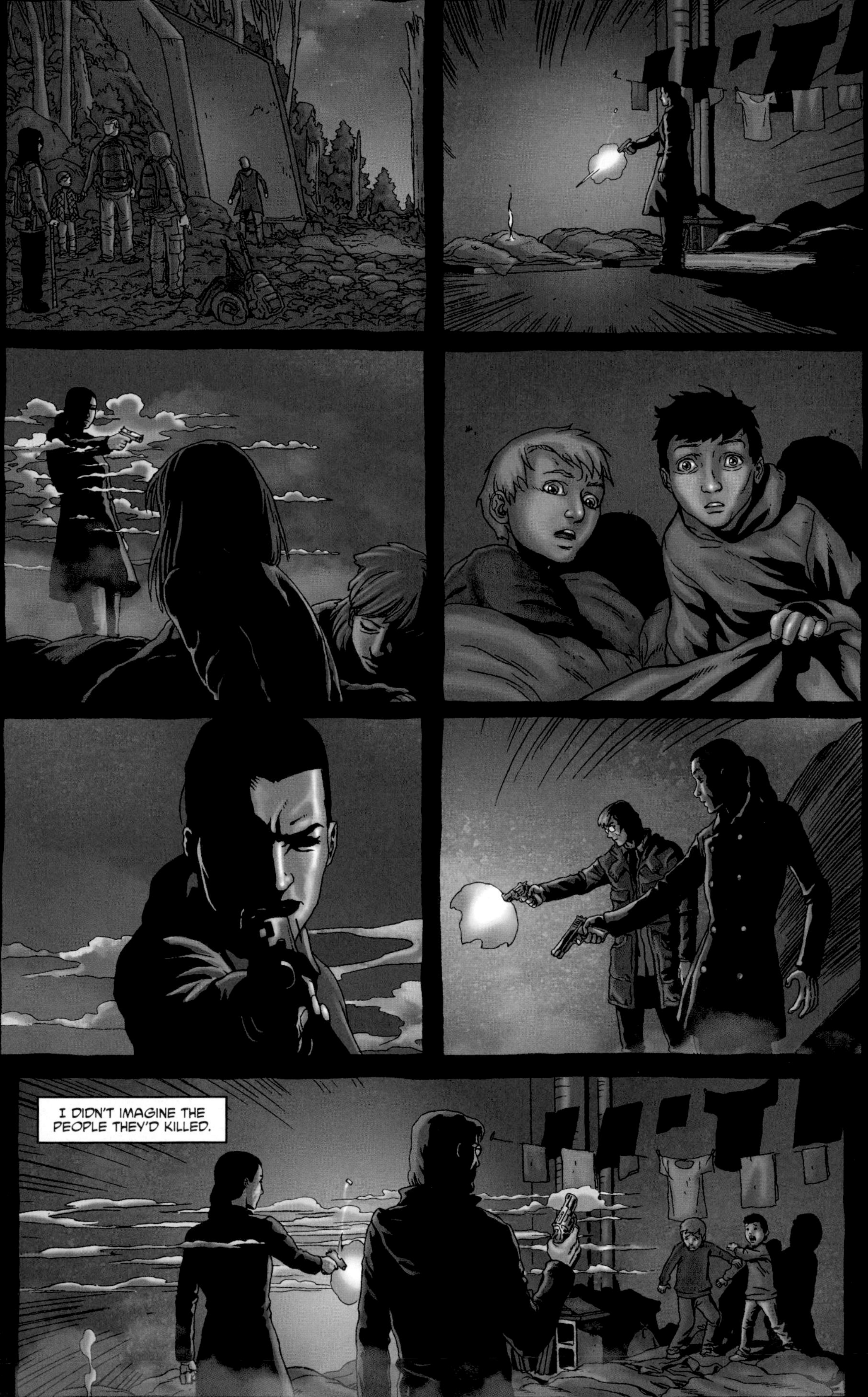
I DIDN'T IMAGINE THE PEOPLE THEY'D KILLED.

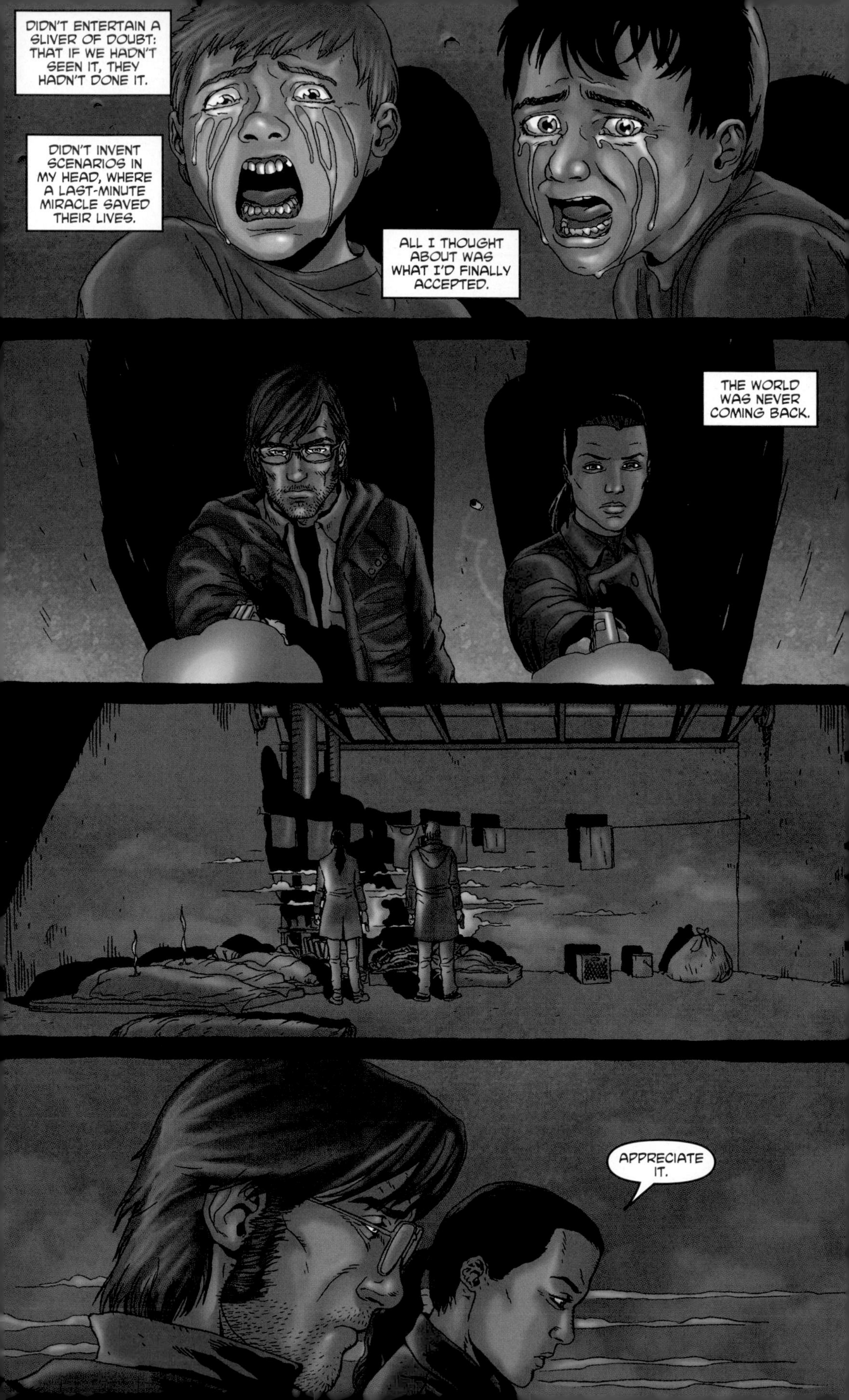
DIDN'T ENTERTAIN A SLIVER OF DOUBT: THAT IF WE HADN'T SEEN IT, THEY HADN'T DONE IT.
DIDN'T INVENT SCENARIOS IN MY HEAD, WHERE A LAST-MINUTE MIRACLE SAVED THEIR LIVES.
ALL I THOUGHT ABOUT WAS WHAT I'D FINALLY ACCEPTED.
THE WORLD WAS NEVER COMING BACK.
APPRECIATE IT.

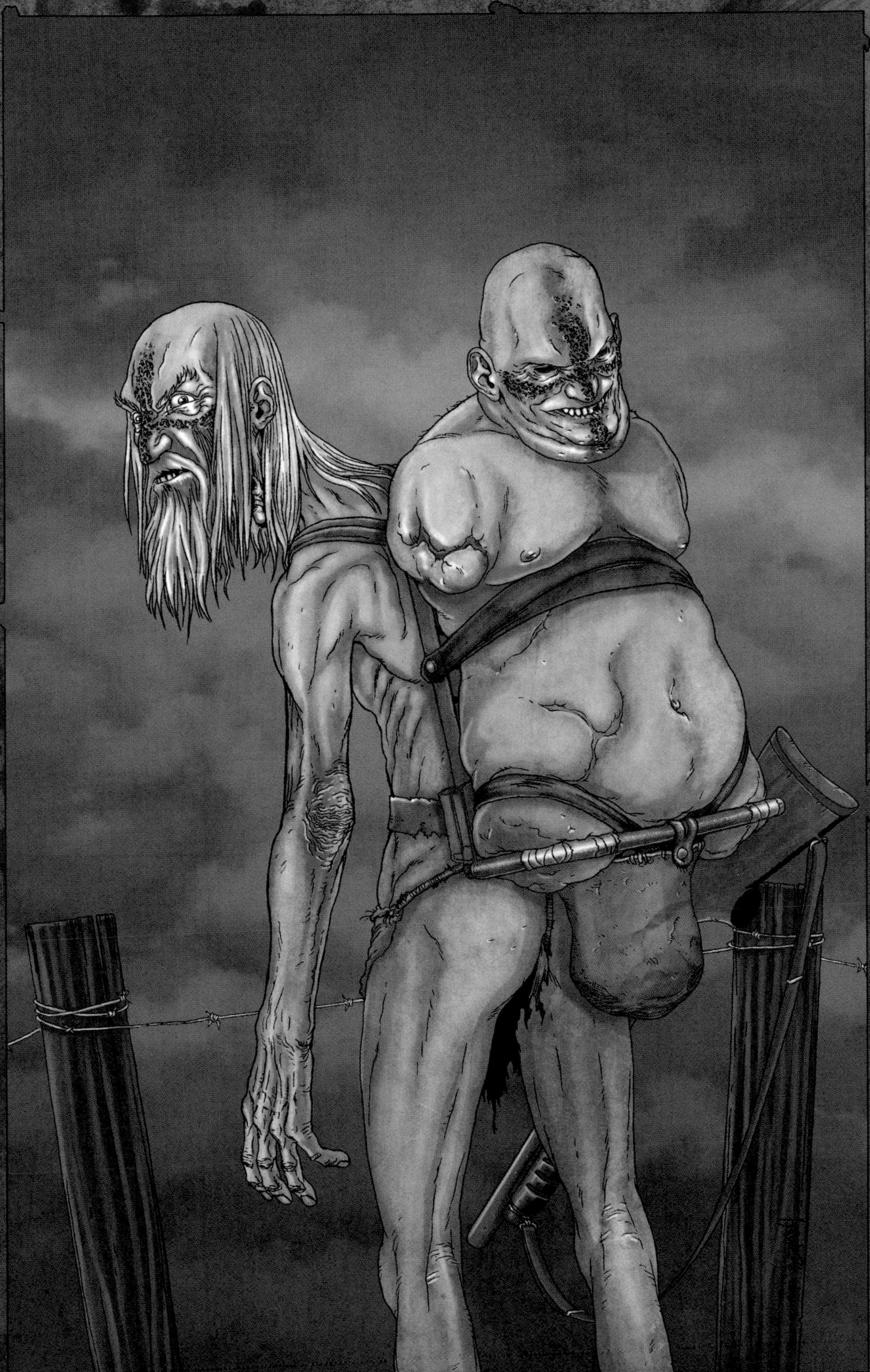

PART FIVE

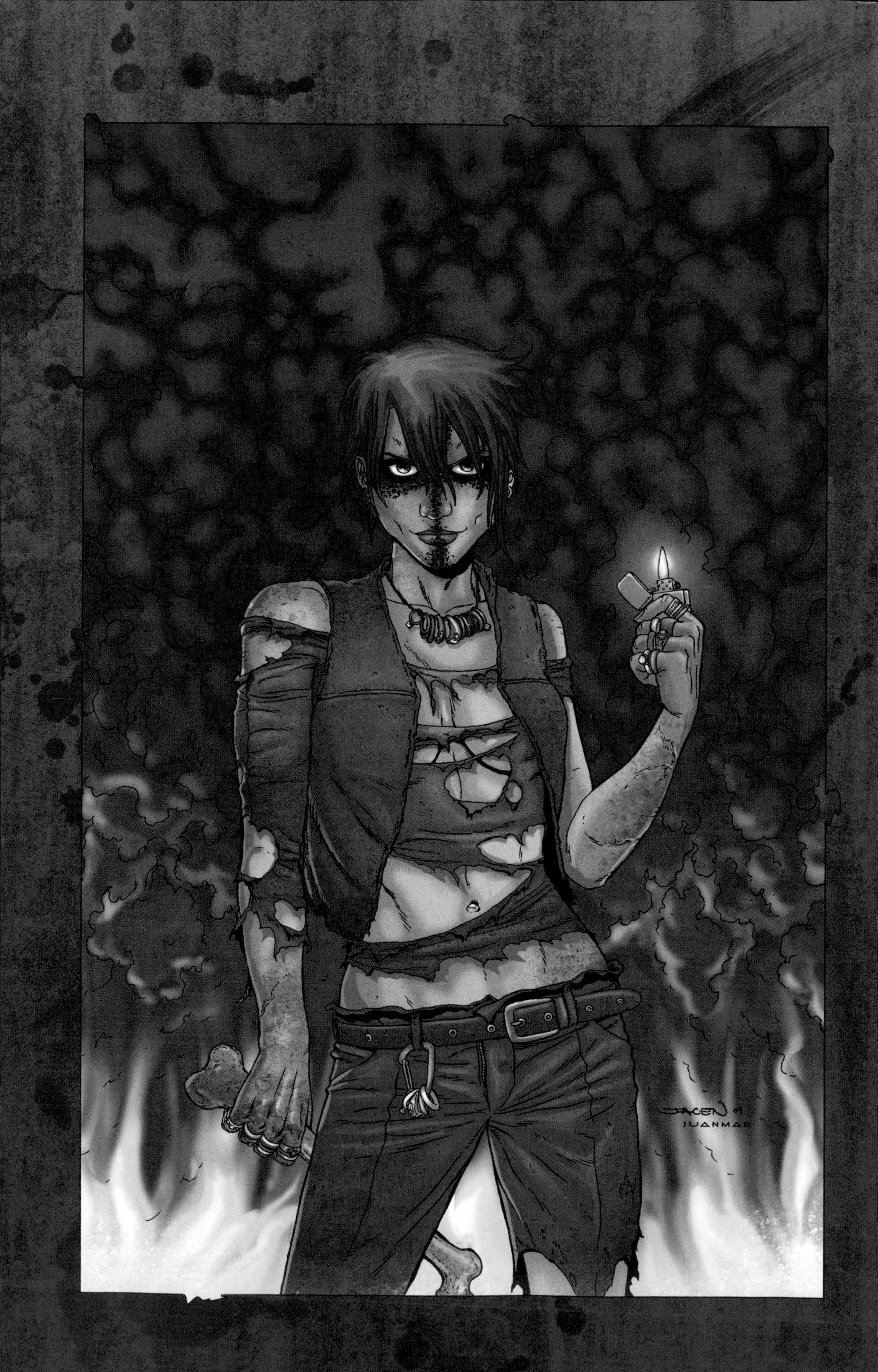

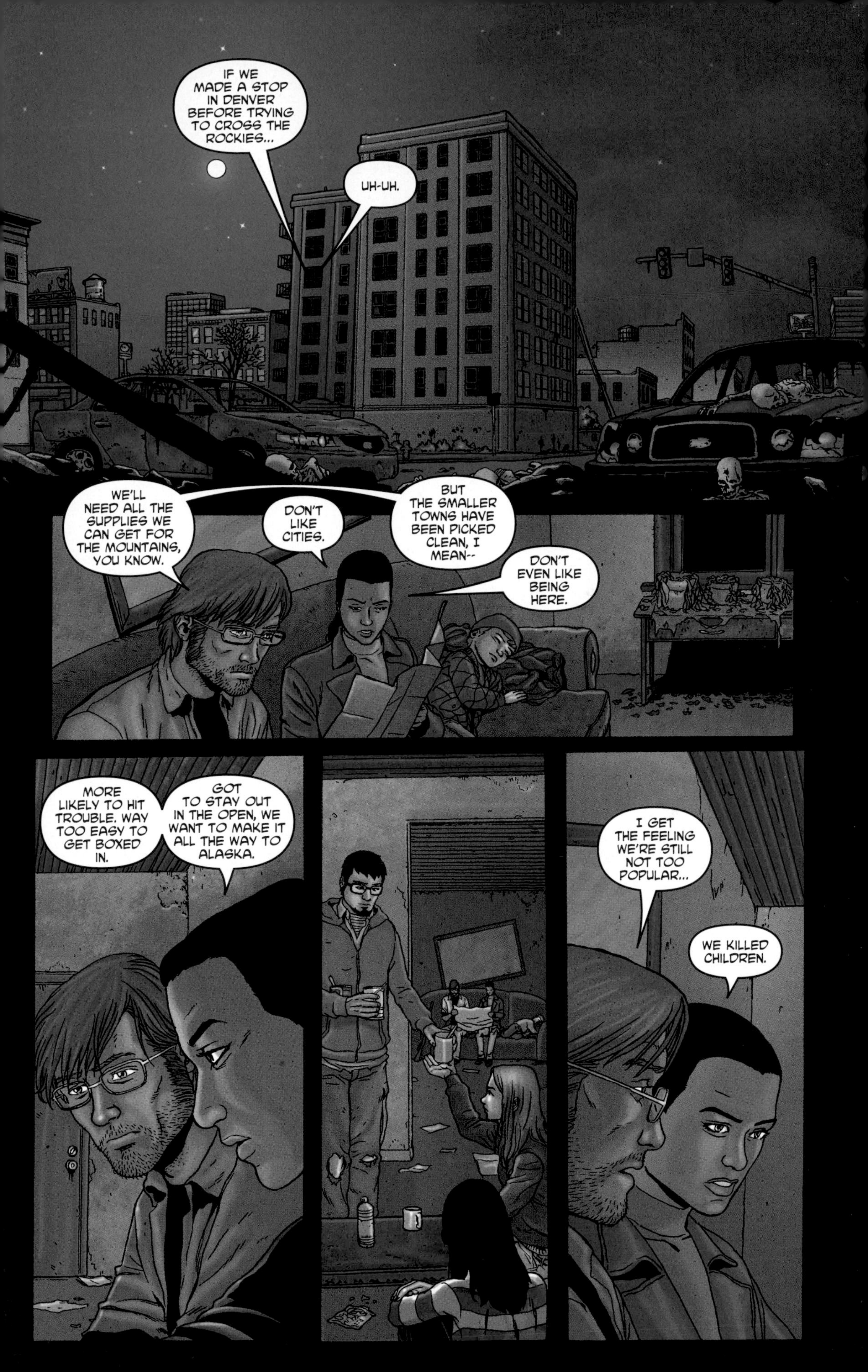
IF WE MADE A STOP IN DENVER BEFORE TRYING TO CROSS THE ROCKIES...
UH-UH.
WE'LL NEED ALL THE SUPPLIES WE CAN GET FOR THE MOUNTAINS, YOU KNOW.
DON'T LIKE CITIES.
BUT THE SMALLER TOWNS HAVE BEEN PICKED CLEAN, I MEAN--
DON'T EVEN LIKE BEING HERE.
MORE LIKELY TO HIT TROUBLE. WAY TOO EASY TO GET BOXED IN.
GOT TO STAY OUT IN THE OPEN, WE WANT TO MAKE IT ALL THE WAY TO ALASKA.
I GET THE FEELING WE'RE STILL NOT TOO POPULAR...
WE KILLED CHILDREN.

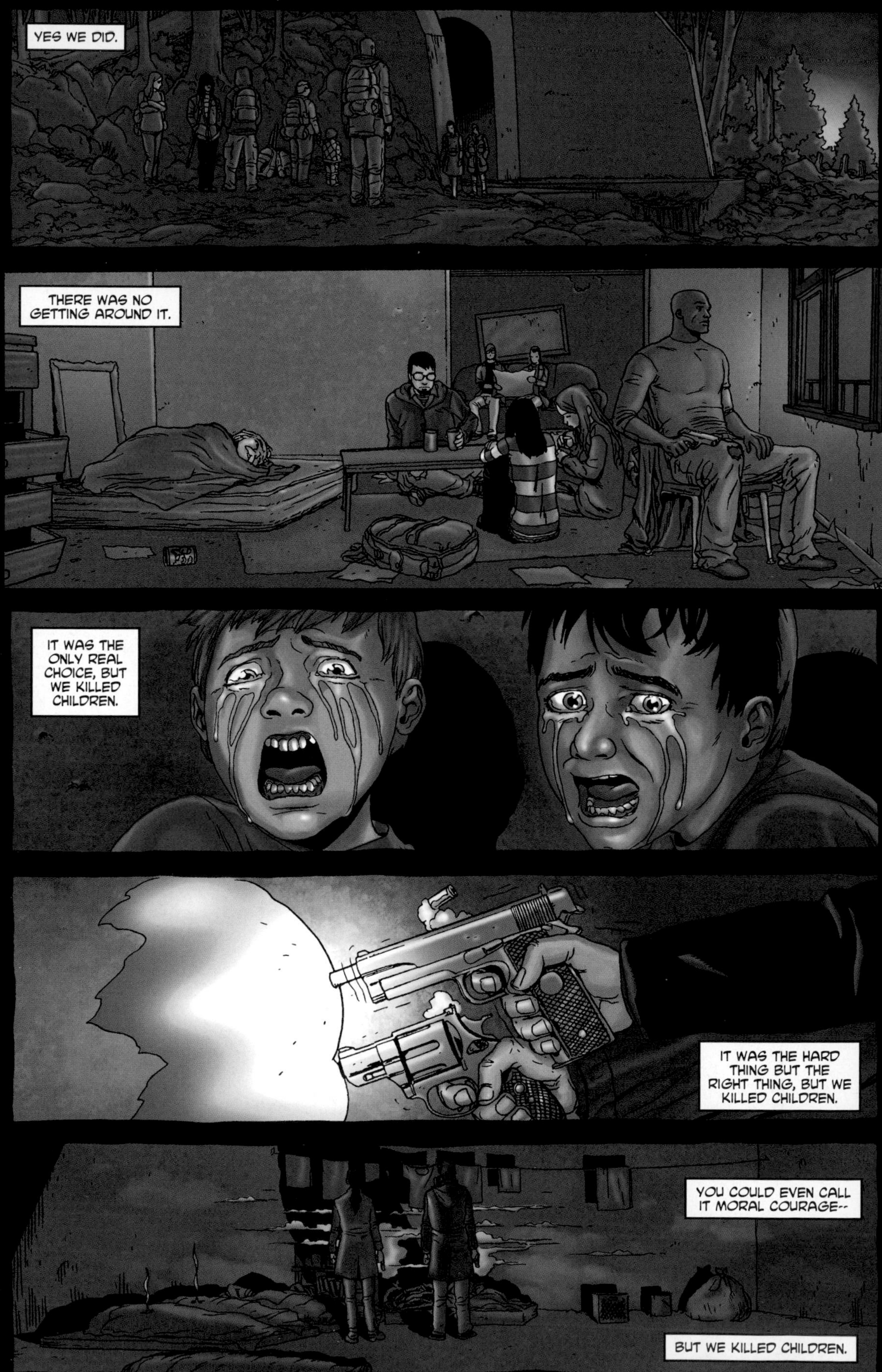
YES WE DID.
THERE WAS NO GETTING AROUND IT.
IT WAS THE ONLY REAL CHOICE, BUT WE KILLED CHILDREN.
IT WAS THE HARD THING BUT THE RIGHT THING, BUT WE KILLED CHILDREN.
YOU COULD EVEN CALL IT MORAL COURAGE--
BUT WE KILLED CHILDREN.

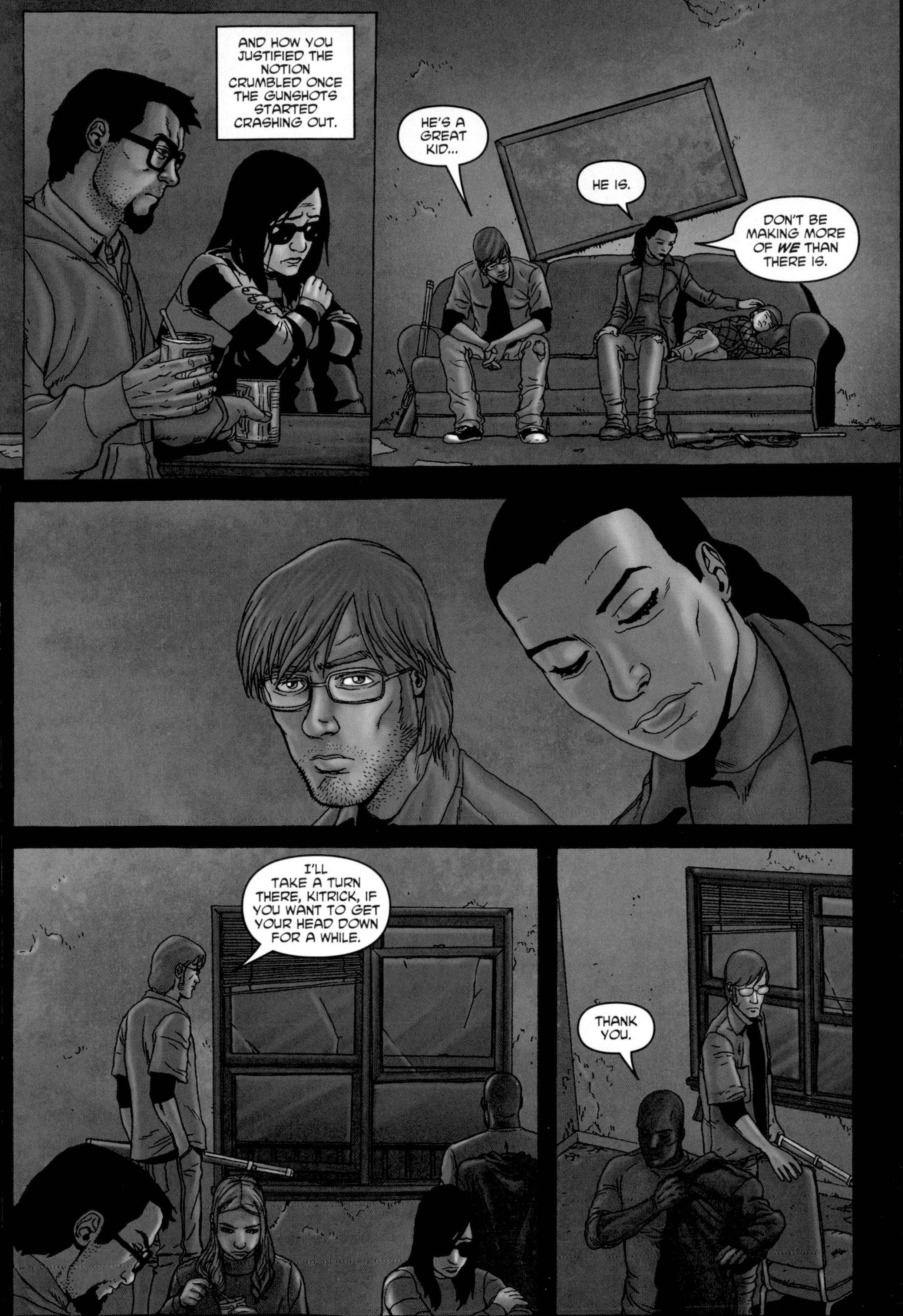
AND HOW YOU JUSTIFIED THE NOTION CRUMBLED ONCE THE GUNSHOTS STARTED CRASHING OUT.
HE'S A GREAT KID...
HE IS.
DON'T BE MAKING MORE OF *WE* THAN THERE IS.
I'LL TAKE A TURN THERE, KITRICK, IF YOU WANT TO GET YOUR HEAD DOWN FOR A WHILE.
THANK YOU.

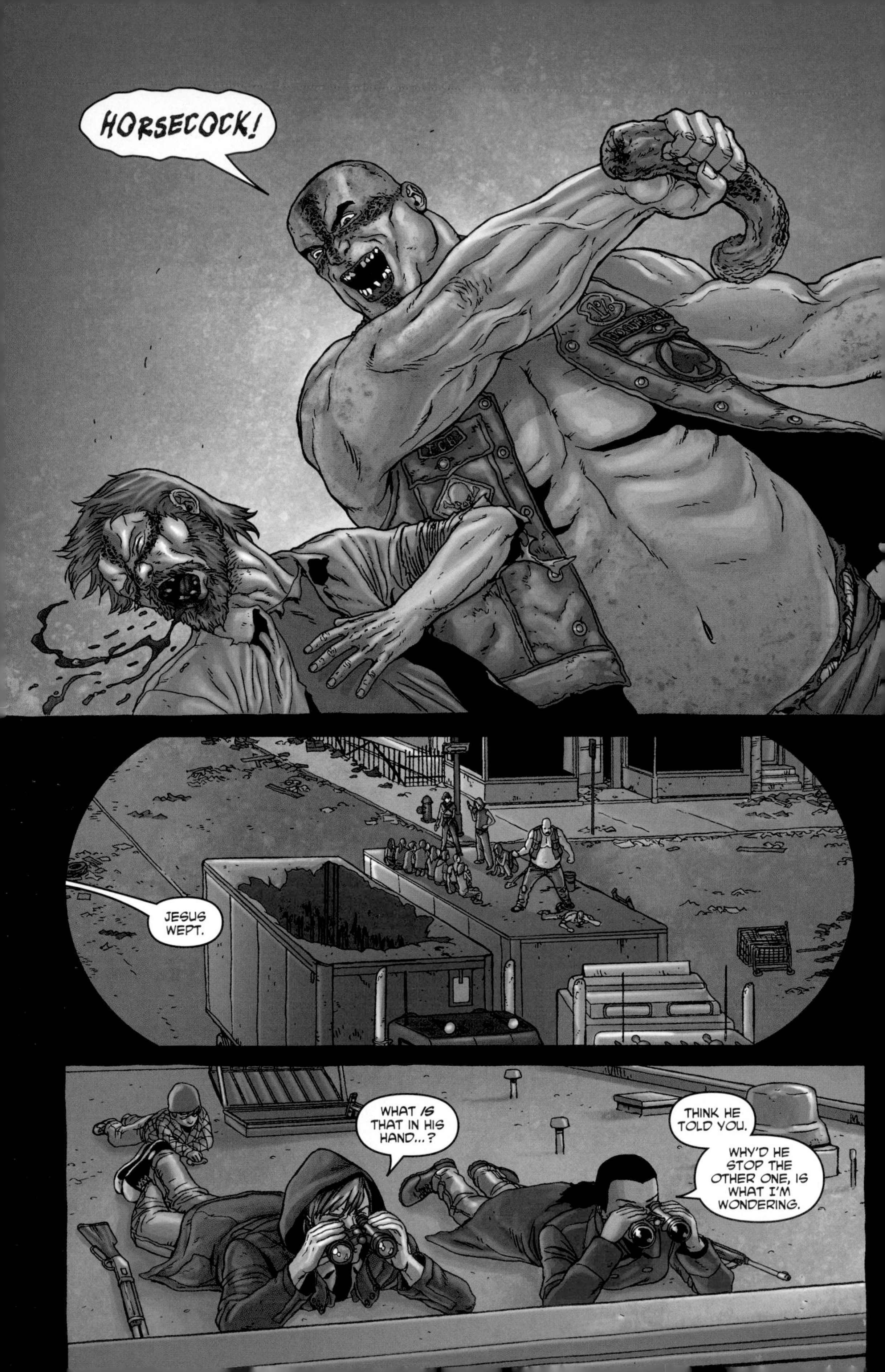
HORSECOCK!
JESUS WEPT.
WHAT IS THAT IN HIS HAND...?
THINK HE TOLD YOU.
WHY'D HE STOP THE OTHER ONE, IS WHAT I'M WONDERING.

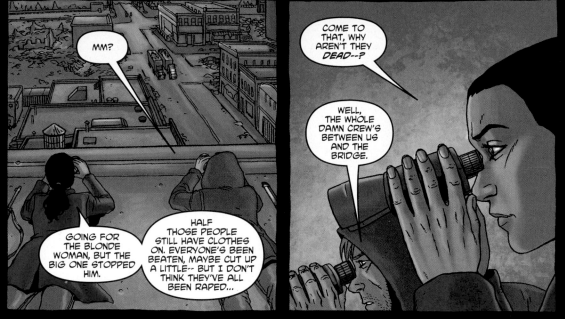

MM?

COME TO THAT, WHY AREN'T THEY *DEAD*--?

WELL, THE WHOLE DAMN CREW'S BETWEEN US AND THE BRIDGE.

GOING FOR THE BLONDE WOMAN, BUT THE BIG ONE STOPPED HIM.

HALF THOSE PEOPLE STILL HAVE CLOTHES ON. EVERYONE'S BEEN BEATEN, MAYBE CUT UP A LITTLE-- BUT I DON'T THINK THEY'VE ALL BEEN RAPED...

AND THAT'S OUR ONLY WAY WEST.

WITHOUT A MASSIVE DETOUR, ANYHOW...

HATE TO DO THAT.

COULD WE... *FIGHT* OUR WAY THROUGH THIS BUNCH?

YOU KNOW IT ISN'T WORTH THE RISK.

THERE'S ONLY FIVE OF THEM. NOT SEEING ANYTHING BUT HANDGUNS.

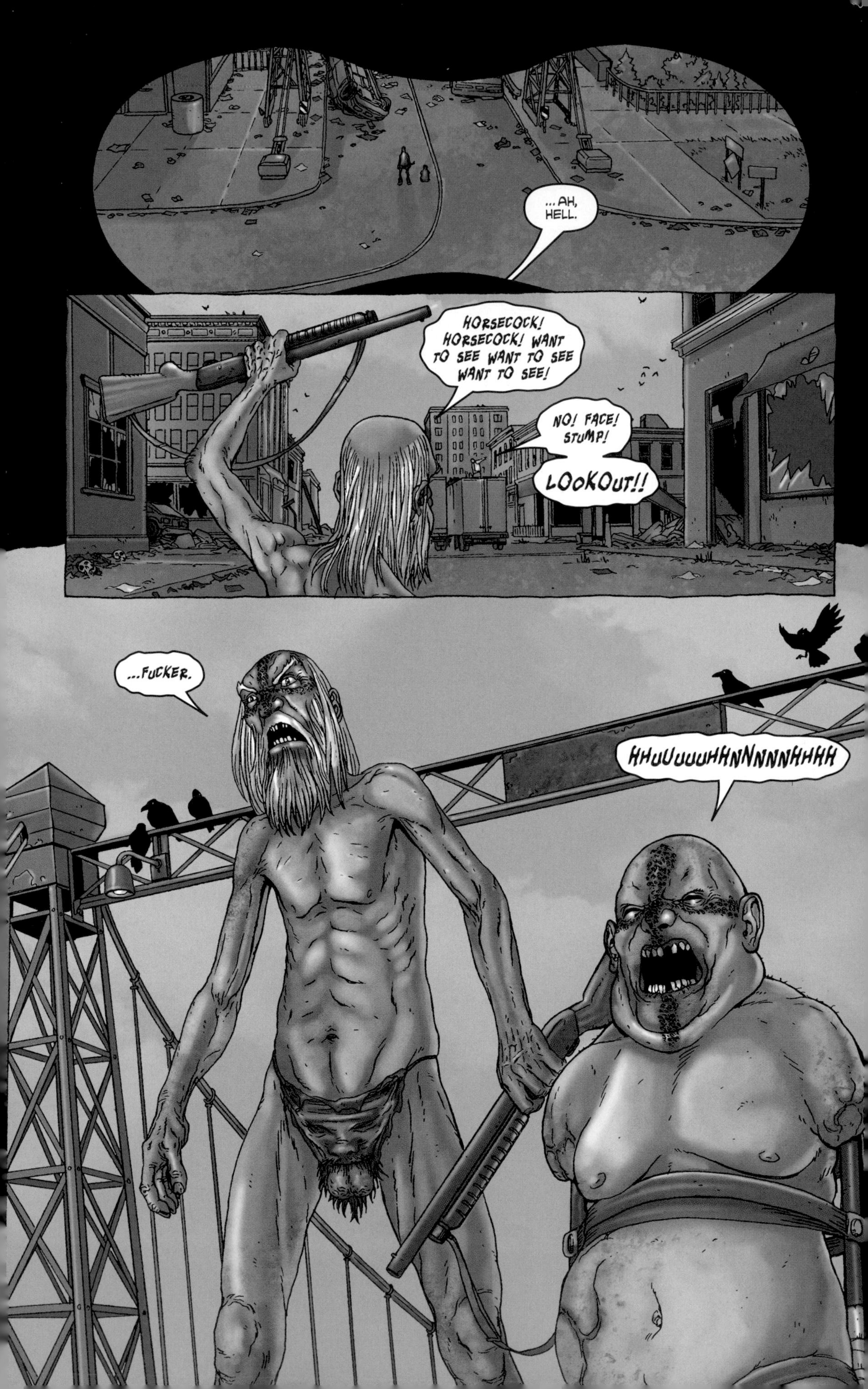
...AH, HELL.
HORSECOCK! HORSECOCK! WANT TO SEE WANT TO SEE WANT TO SEE!
NO! FACE! STUMP!
LOOKOUT!!
...FUCKER.
HHUUUUUHHNNNNNHHHH

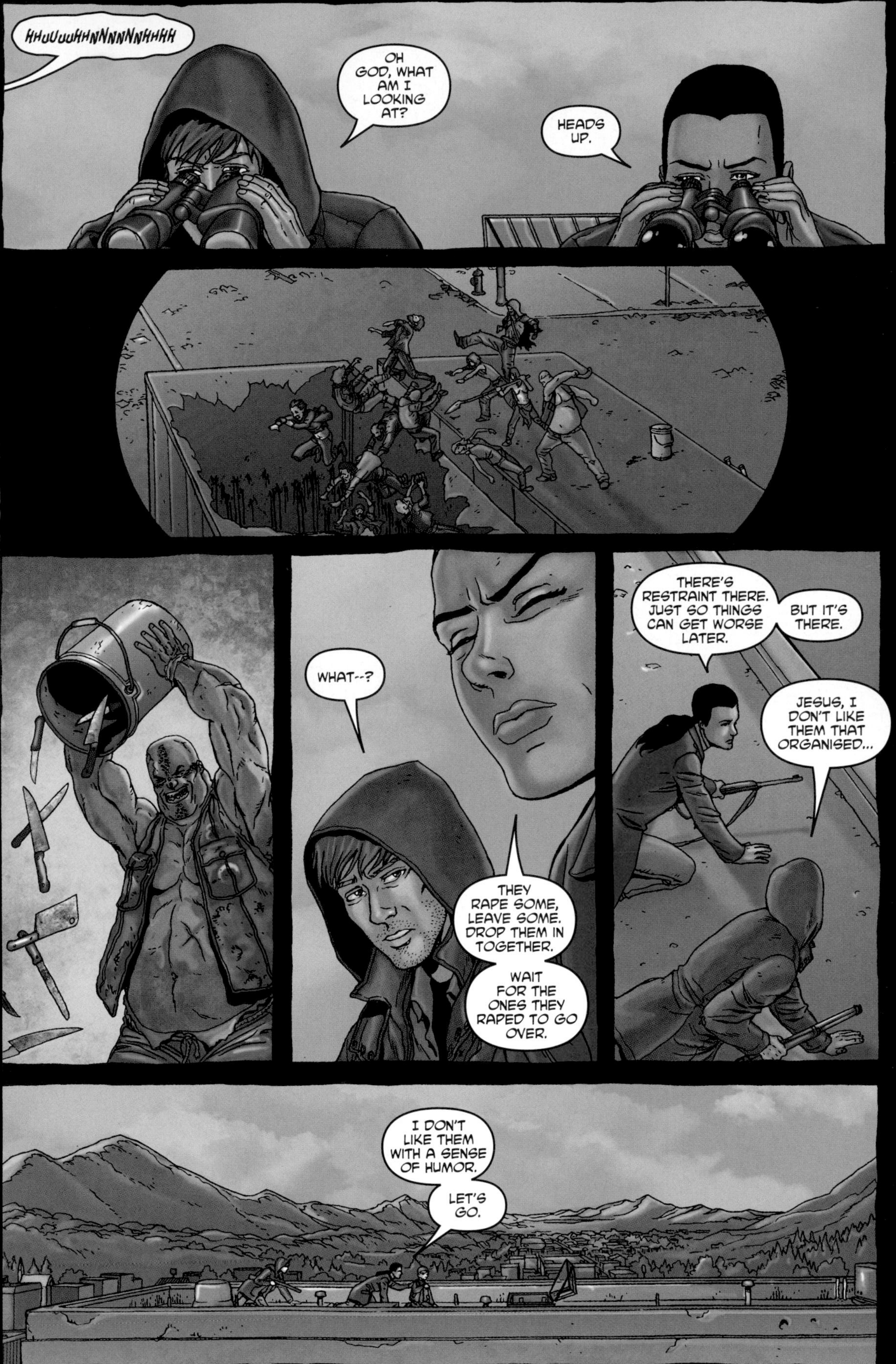
HHUUUUHHNNNNNHHHH
OH GOD, WHAT AM I LOOKING AT?
HEADS UP.
WHAT--?
THEY RAPE SOME, LEAVE SOME. DROP THEM IN TOGETHER.
WAIT FOR THE ONES THEY RAPED TO GO OVER.
THERE'S RESTRAINT THERE. JUST SO THINGS CAN GET WORSE LATER.
BUT IT'S THERE.
JESUS, I DON'T LIKE THEM THAT ORGANISED...
I DON'T LIKE THEM WITH A SENSE OF HUMOR.
LET'S GO.

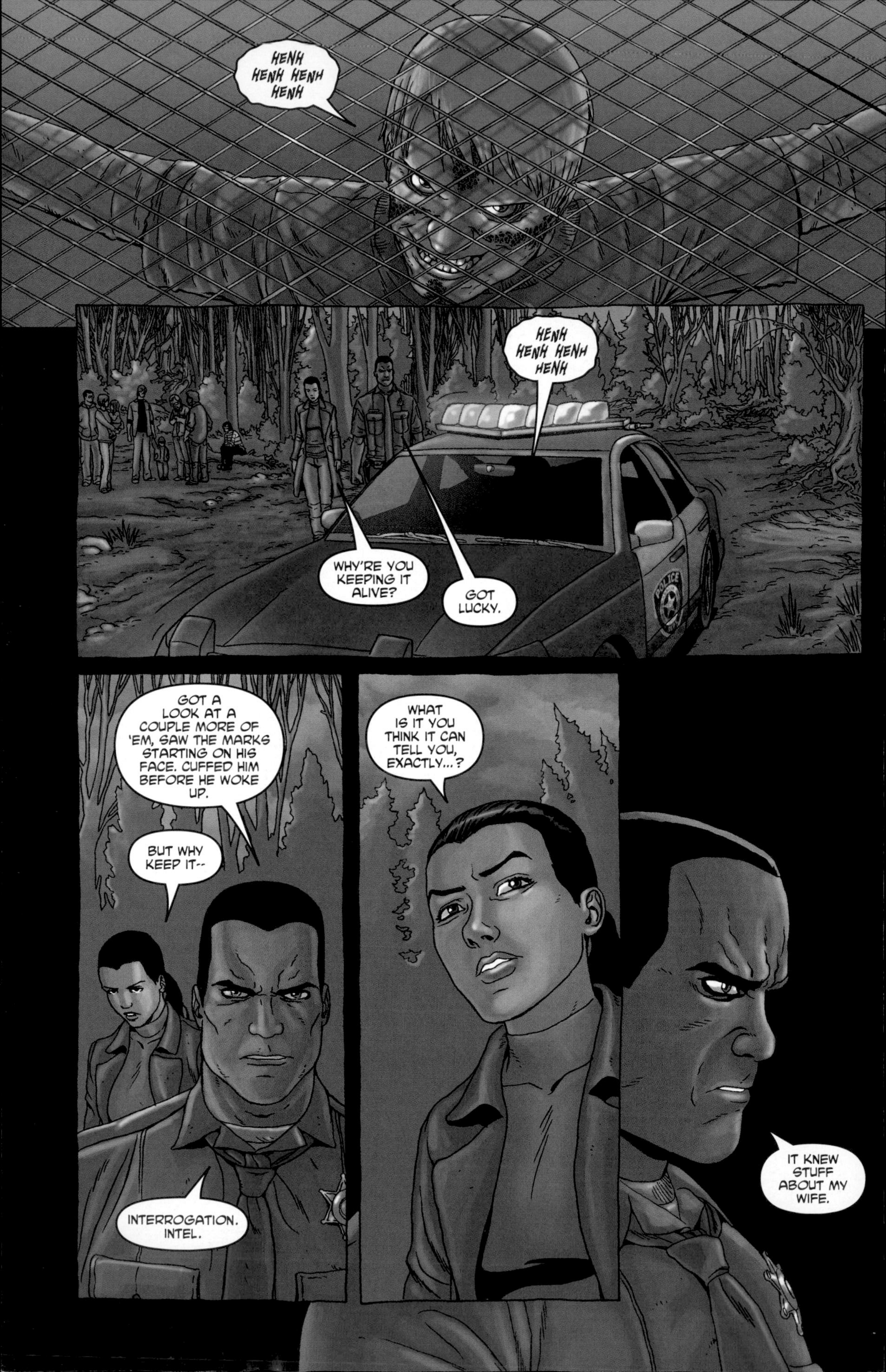
HENH HENH HENH HENH
HENH HENH HENH HENH
WHY'RE YOU KEEPING IT ALIVE?
GOT LUCKY.
GOT A LOOK AT A COUPLE MORE OF 'EM, SAW THE MARKS STARTING ON HIS FACE. CUFFED HIM BEFORE HE WOKE UP.
BUT WHY KEEP IT--
INTERROGATION. INTEL.
WHAT IS IT YOU THINK IT CAN TELL YOU, EXACTLY...?
IT KNEW STUFF ABOUT MY WIFE.

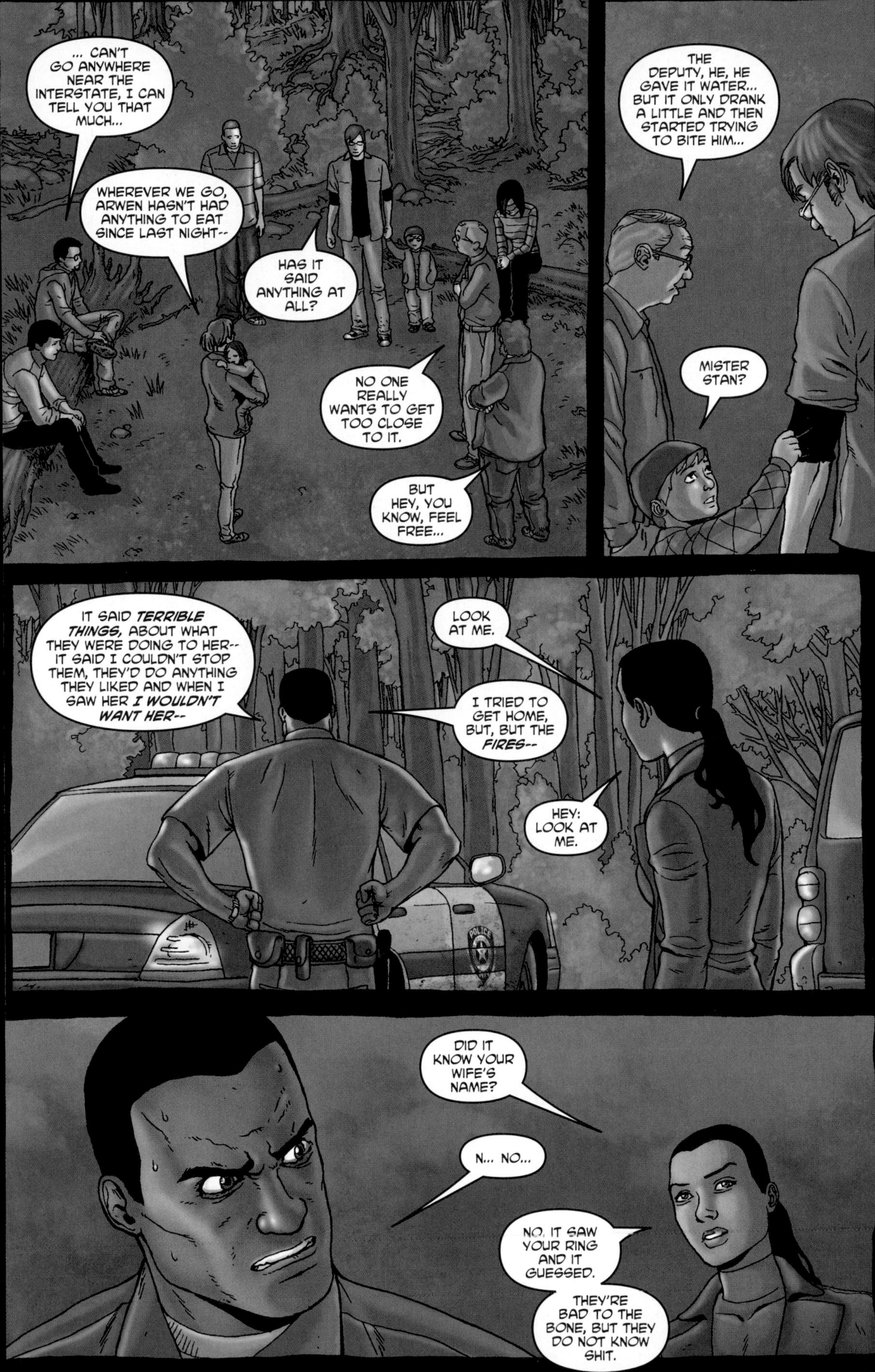
... CAN'T GO ANYWHERE NEAR THE INTERSTATE, I CAN TELL YOU THAT MUCH...
WHEREVER WE GO, ARWEN HASN'T HAD ANYTHING TO EAT SINCE LAST NIGHT--
HAS IT SAID ANYTHING AT ALL?
NO ONE REALLY WANTS TO GET TOO CLOSE TO IT.
BUT HEY, YOU KNOW, FEEL FREE...
THE DEPUTY, HE, HE GAVE IT WATER... BUT IT ONLY DRANK A LITTLE AND THEN STARTED TRYING TO BITE HIM...
MISTER STAN?
IT SAID TERRIBLE THINGS, ABOUT WHAT THEY WERE DOING TO HER-- IT SAID I COULDN'T STOP THEM, THEY'D DO ANYTHING THEY LIKED AND WHEN I SAW HER I WOULDN'T WANT HER--
LOOK AT ME.
I TRIED TO GET HOME, BUT, BUT THE FIRES--
HEY: LOOK AT ME.
POLICE
DID IT KNOW YOUR WIFE'S NAME?
N... NO...
NO. IT SAW YOUR RING AND IT GUESSED.
THEY'RE BAD TO THE BONE, BUT THEY DO NOT KNOW SHIT.

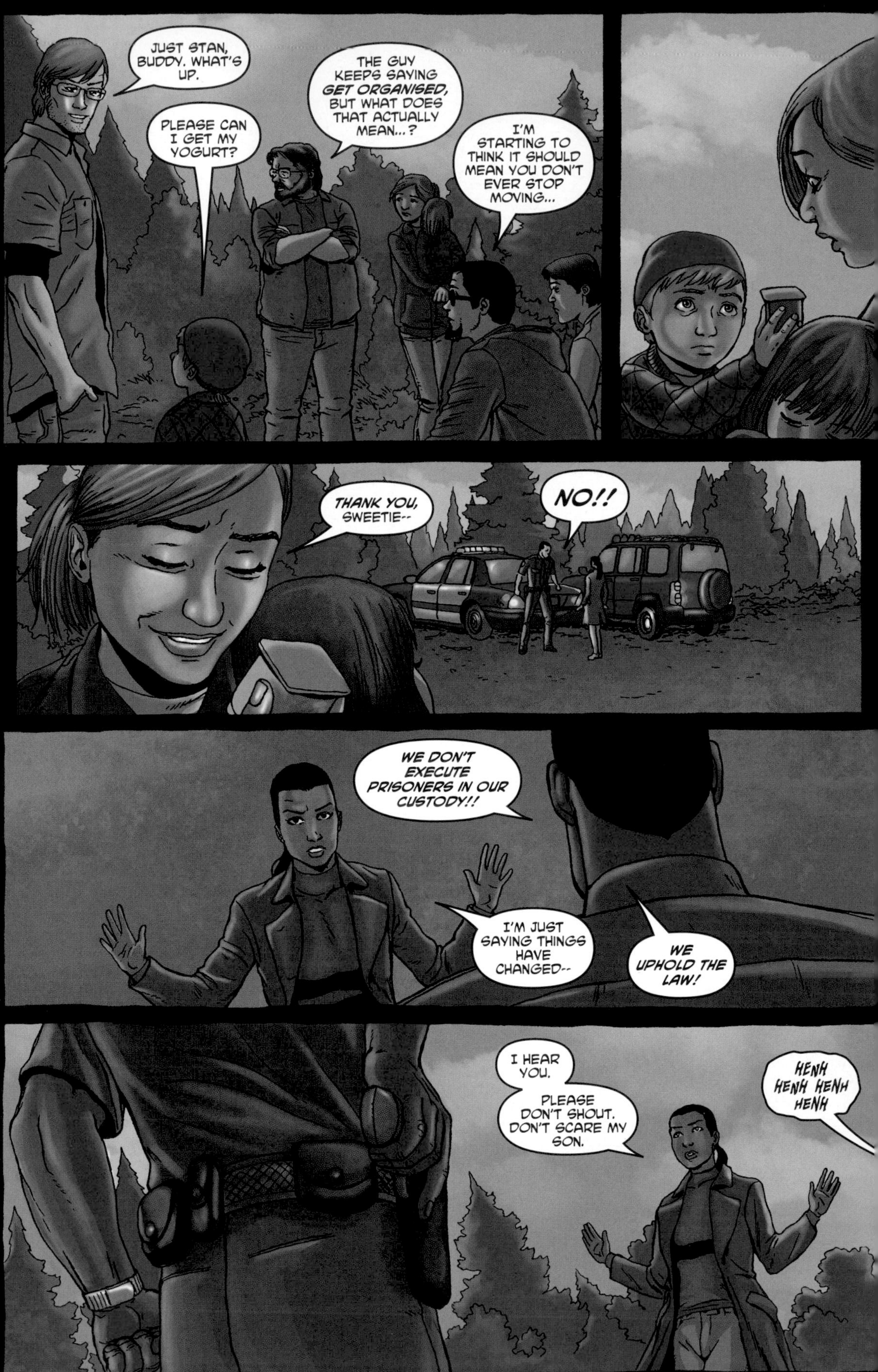
JUST STAN, BUDDY. WHAT'S UP.
PLEASE CAN I GET MY YOGURT?
THE GUY KEEPS SAYING *GET ORGANISED*, BUT WHAT DOES THAT ACTUALLY MEAN...?
I'M STARTING TO THINK IT SHOULD MEAN YOU DON'T EVER STOP MOVING...
THANK YOU, SWEETIE--
NO!!
WE DON'T EXECUTE PRISONERS IN OUR CUSTODY!!
I'M JUST SAYING THINGS HAVE CHANGED--
WE UPHOLD THE LAW!
I HEAR YOU.
PLEASE DON'T SHOUT. DON'T SCARE MY SON.
HENH HENH HENH HENH

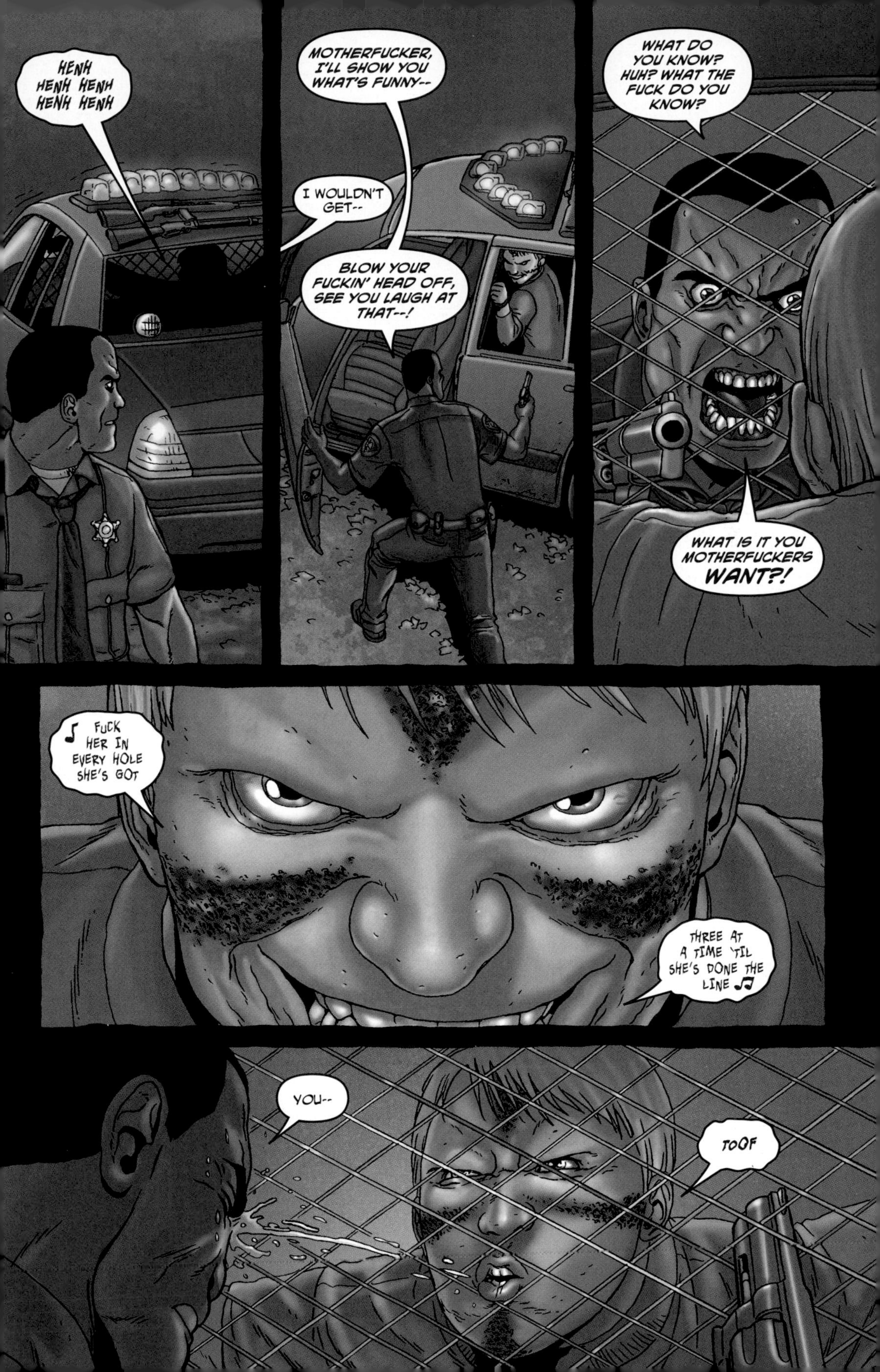
HENH HENH HENH HENH HENH
MOTHERFUCKER, I'LL SHOW YOU WHAT'S FUNNY--
I WOULDN'T GET--
BLOW YOUR FUCKIN' HEAD OFF, SEE YOU LAUGH AT THAT--!
WHAT DO YOU KNOW? HUH? WHAT THE FUCK DO YOU KNOW?
WHAT IS IT YOU MOTHERFUCKERS WANT?!
♪ FUCK HER IN EVERY HOLE SHE'S GOT
THREE AT A TIME 'TIL SHE'S DONE THE LINE ♫
YOU--
TOOF

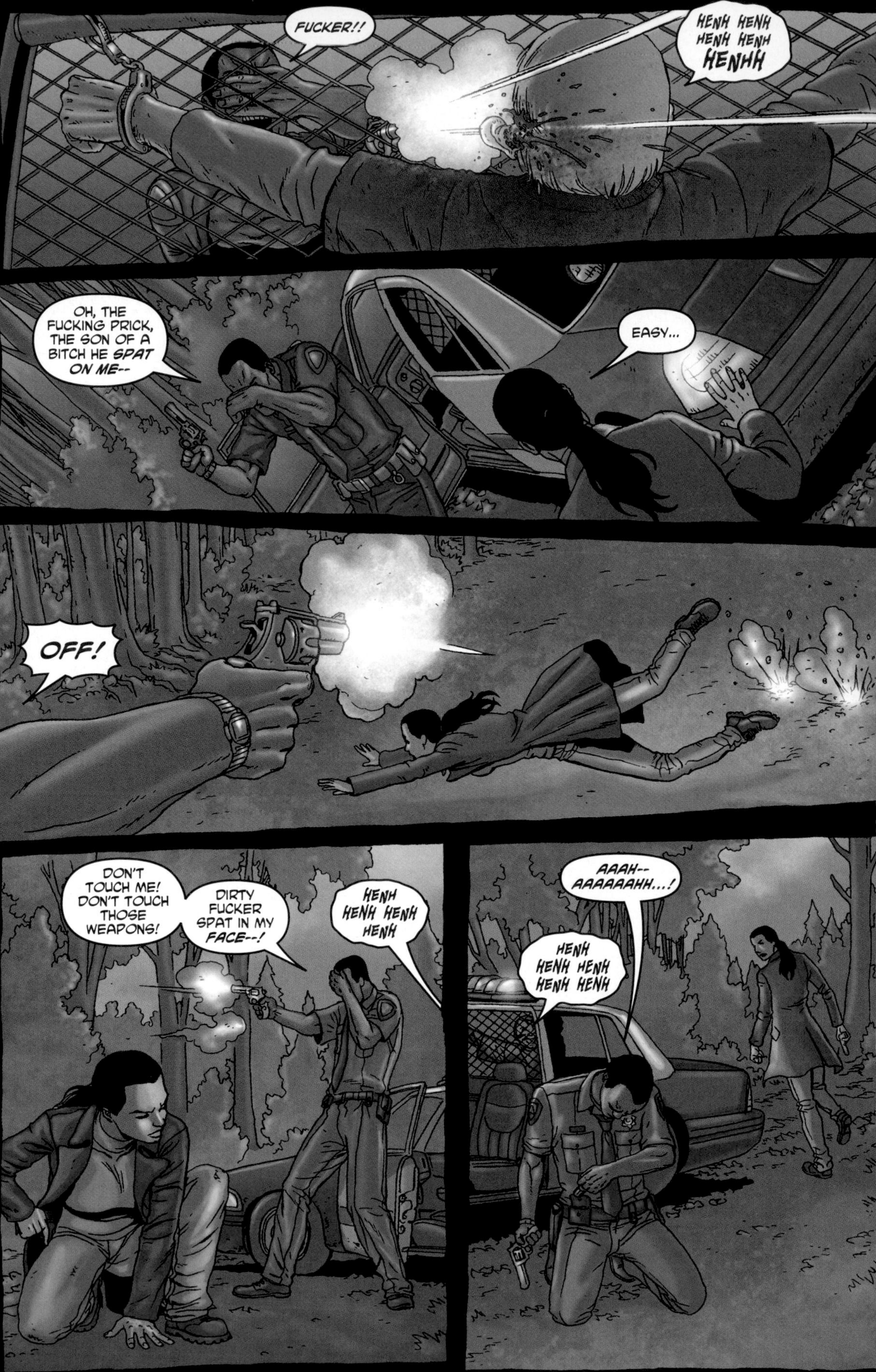
FUCKER!!
HENH HENH HENH HENH HENHH
OH, THE FUCKING PRICK, THE SON OF A BITCH HE SPAT ON ME--
EASY...
OFF!
DON'T TOUCH ME! DON'T TOUCH THOSE WEAPONS!
DIRTY FUCKER SPAT IN MY FACE--!
HENH HENH HENH HENH
AAAH-- AAAAAAHH...!
HENH HENH HENH HENH HENH

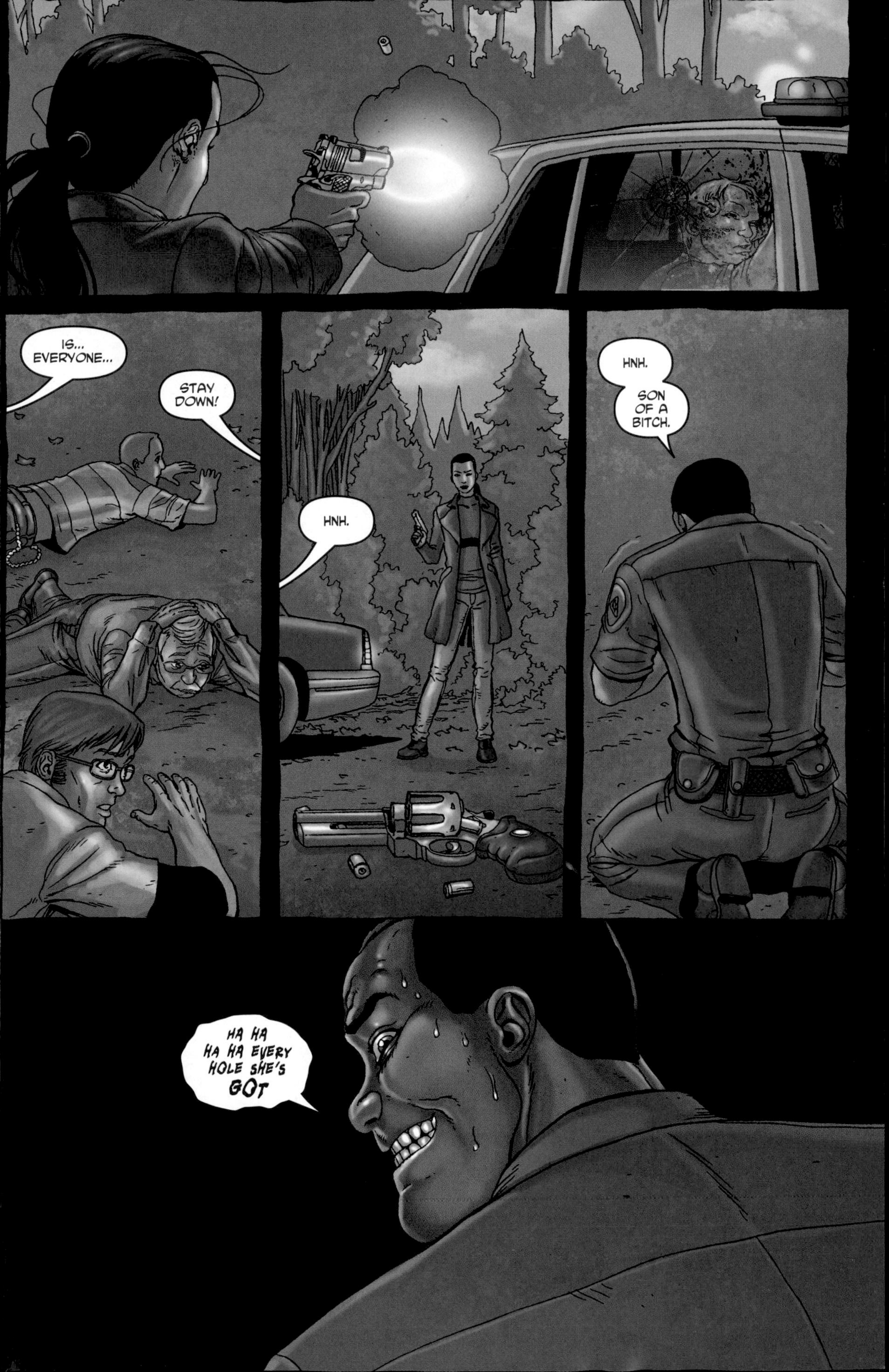
IS... EVERYONE...
STAY DOWN!
HNH.
HNH.
SON OF A BITCH.
HA HA HA HA EVERY HOLE SHE'S GOT

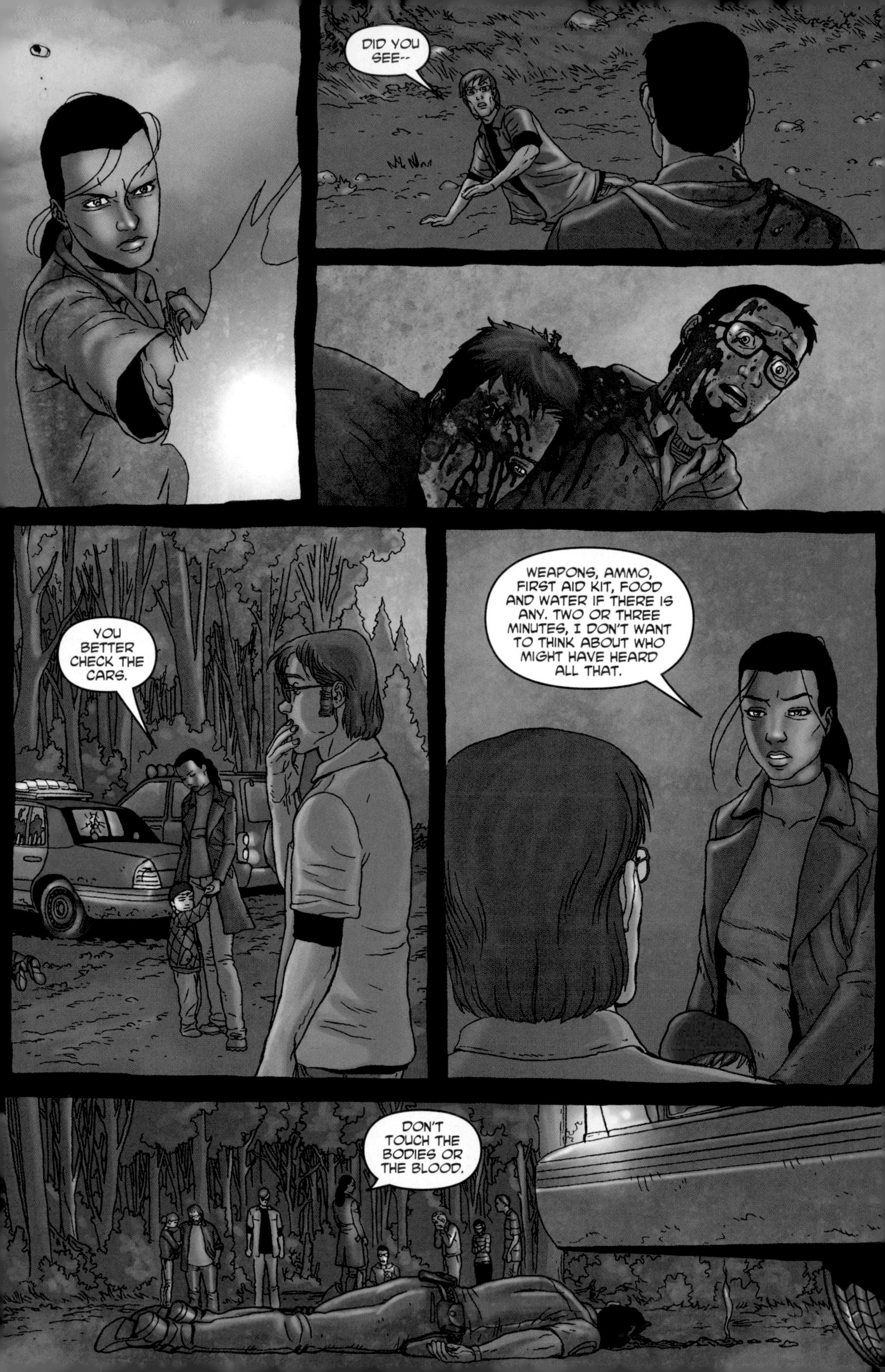
DID YOU SEE--
YOU BETTER CHECK THE CARS.
WEAPONS, AMMO, FIRST AID KIT, FOOD AND WATER IF THERE IS ANY. TWO OR THREE MINUTES, I DON'T WANT TO THINK ABOUT WHO MIGHT HAVE HEARD ALL THAT.
DON'T TOUCH THE BODIES OR THE BLOOD.

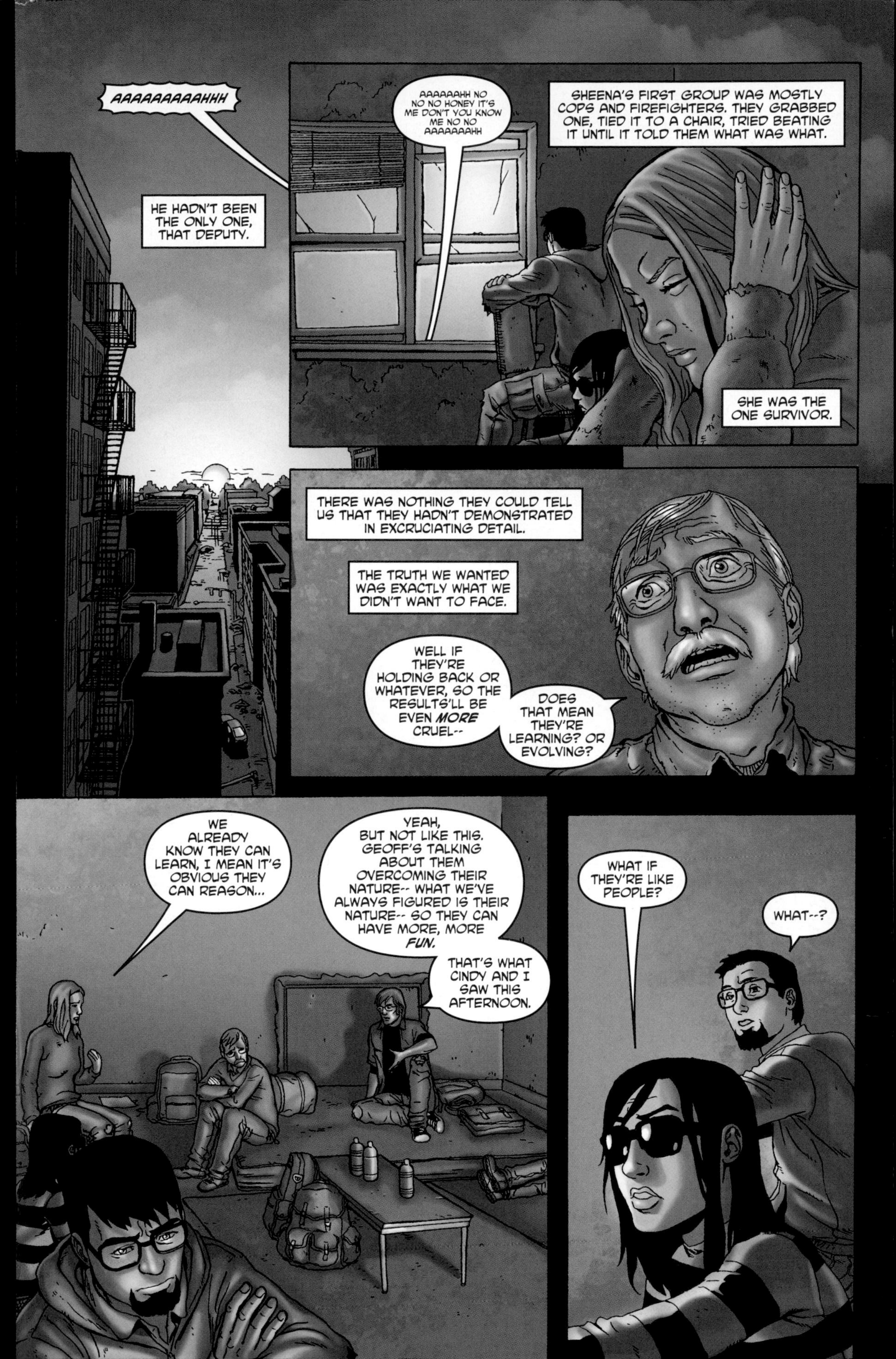
AAAAAAAAAAHHH
HE HADN'T BEEN THE ONLY ONE, THAT DEPUTY.
AAAAAAAHH NO NO NO HONEY IT'S ME DON'T YOU KNOW ME NO NO AAAAAAAHH
SHEENA'S FIRST GROUP WAS MOSTLY COPS AND FIREFIGHTERS. THEY GRABBED ONE, TIED IT TO A CHAIR, TRIED BEATING IT UNTIL IT TOLD THEM WHAT WAS WHAT.
SHE WAS THE ONE SURVIVOR.
THERE WAS NOTHING THEY COULD TELL US THAT THEY HADN'T DEMONSTRATED IN EXCRUCIATING DETAIL.
THE TRUTH WE WANTED WAS EXACTLY WHAT WE DIDN'T WANT TO FACE.
WELL IF THEY'RE HOLDING BACK OR WHATEVER, SO THE RESULTS'LL BE EVEN MORE CRUEL--
DOES THAT MEAN THEY'RE LEARNING? OR EVOLVING?
WE ALREADY KNOW THEY CAN LEARN, I MEAN IT'S OBVIOUS THEY CAN REASON...
YEAH, BUT NOT LIKE THIS. GEOFF'S TALKING ABOUT THEM OVERCOMING THEIR NATURE-- WHAT WE'VE ALWAYS FIGURED IS THEIR NATURE-- SO THEY CAN HAVE MORE, MORE FUN.
THAT'S WHAT CINDY AND I SAW THIS AFTERNOON.
WHAT IF THEY'RE LIKE PEOPLE?
WHAT--?

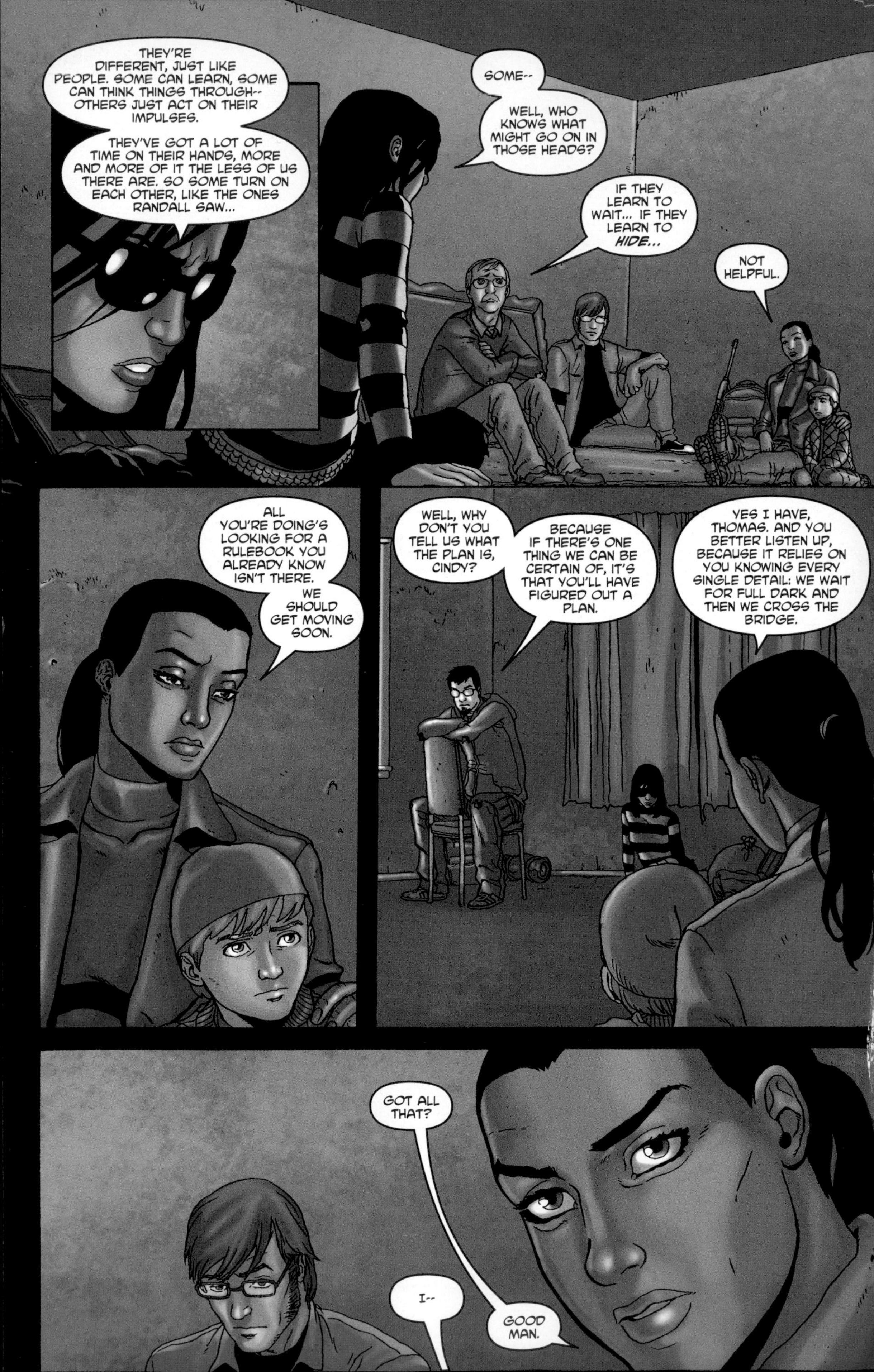

THEY'RE DIFFERENT, JUST LIKE PEOPLE. SOME CAN LEARN, SOME CAN THINK THINGS THROUGH-- OTHERS JUST ACT ON THEIR IMPULSES.
THEY'VE GOT A LOT OF TIME ON THEIR HANDS, MORE AND MORE OF IT THE LESS OF US THERE ARE. SO SOME TURN ON EACH OTHER, LIKE THE ONES RANDALL SAW...
SOME--
WELL, WHO KNOWS WHAT MIGHT GO ON IN THOSE HEADS?
IF THEY LEARN TO WAIT... IF THEY LEARN TO *HIDE*...
NOT HELPFUL.
ALL YOU'RE DOING'S LOOKING FOR A RULEBOOK YOU ALREADY KNOW ISN'T THERE.
WE SHOULD GET MOVING SOON.
WELL, WHY DON'T YOU TELL US WHAT THE PLAN IS, CINDY?
BECAUSE IF THERE'S ONE THING WE CAN BE CERTAIN OF, IT'S THAT YOU'LL HAVE FIGURED OUT A PLAN.
YES I HAVE, THOMAS. AND YOU BETTER LISTEN UP, BECAUSE IT RELIES ON YOU KNOWING EVERY SINGLE DETAIL: WE WAIT FOR FULL DARK AND THEN WE CROSS THE BRIDGE.
GOT ALL THAT?
I--
GOOD MAN.

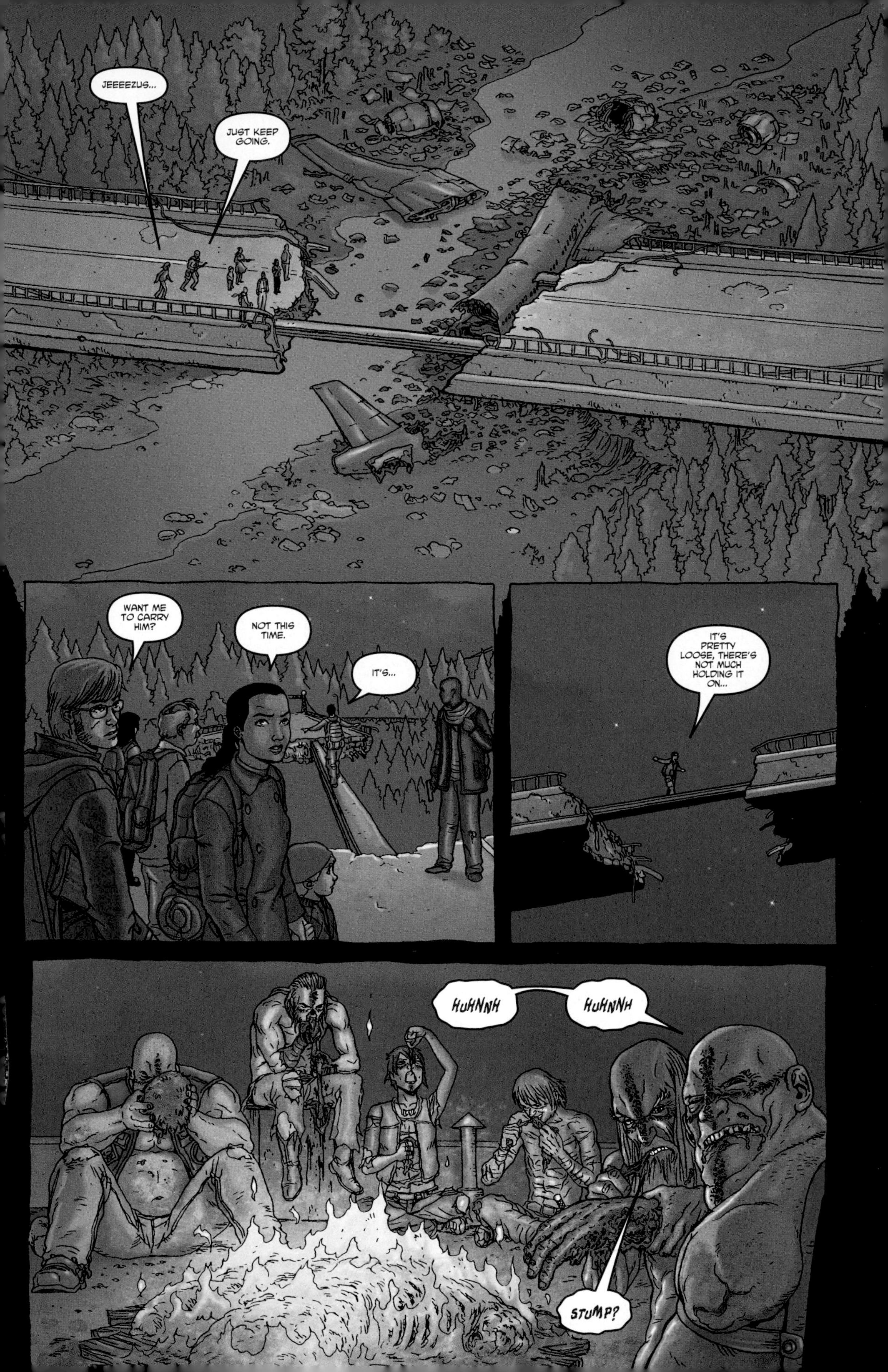
JEEEEZUS...
JUST KEEP GOING.
WANT ME TO CARRY HIM?
NOT THIS TIME.
IT'S...
IT'S PRETTY LOOSE, THERE'S NOT MUCH HOLDING IT ON...
HUHNNH
HUHNNH
STUMP?

HHUuuHHNNKHHHH

HHUuuHHNNKHHHH

WAS THAT--

THAT'S THE NOISE THE ONE WITH THE, YOU KNOW, THE AMPUTEE--

PATRICK, GET BEHIND MOMMY. STAY THERE.

GEOFF, HURRY IT UP.

OH GOD, AM I CLOSE TO THE EDGE?

KELLY, WE'VE GOT TO--

NO! NO-NO-NO, I'LL FALL!

OH, CHRIST...!

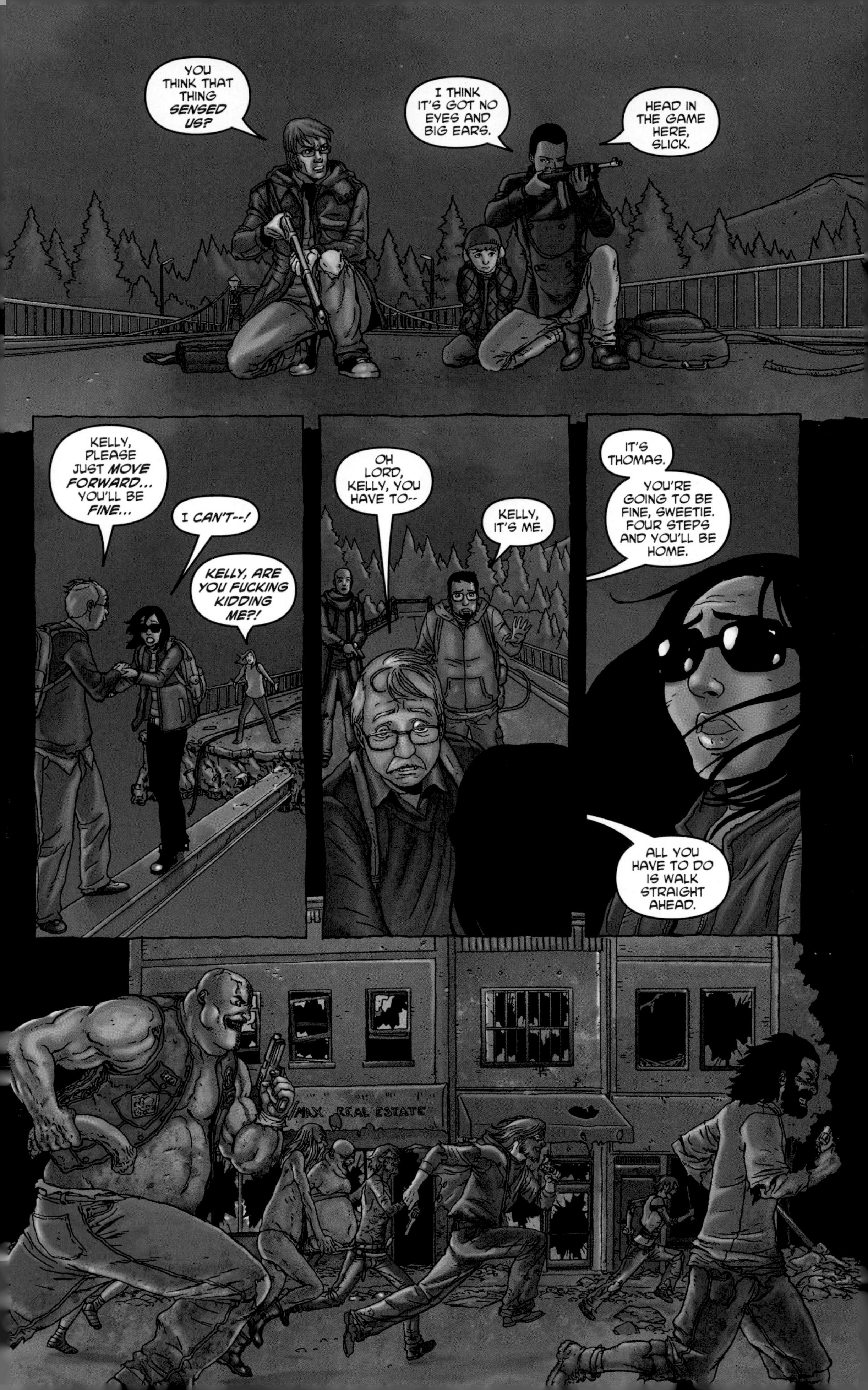
YOU THINK THAT THING SENSED US?
I THINK IT'S GOT NO EYES AND BIG EARS.
HEAD IN THE GAME HERE, SLICK.
KELLY, PLEASE JUST MOVE FORWARD... YOU'LL BE FINE...
I CAN'T--!
KELLY, ARE YOU FUCKING KIDDING ME?!
OH LORD, KELLY, YOU HAVE TO--
KELLY, IT'S ME.
IT'S THOMAS.
YOU'RE GOING TO BE FINE, SWEETIE. FOUR STEPS AND YOU'LL BE HOME.
ALL YOU HAVE TO DO IS WALK STRAIGHT AHEAD.
MAX REAL ESTATE

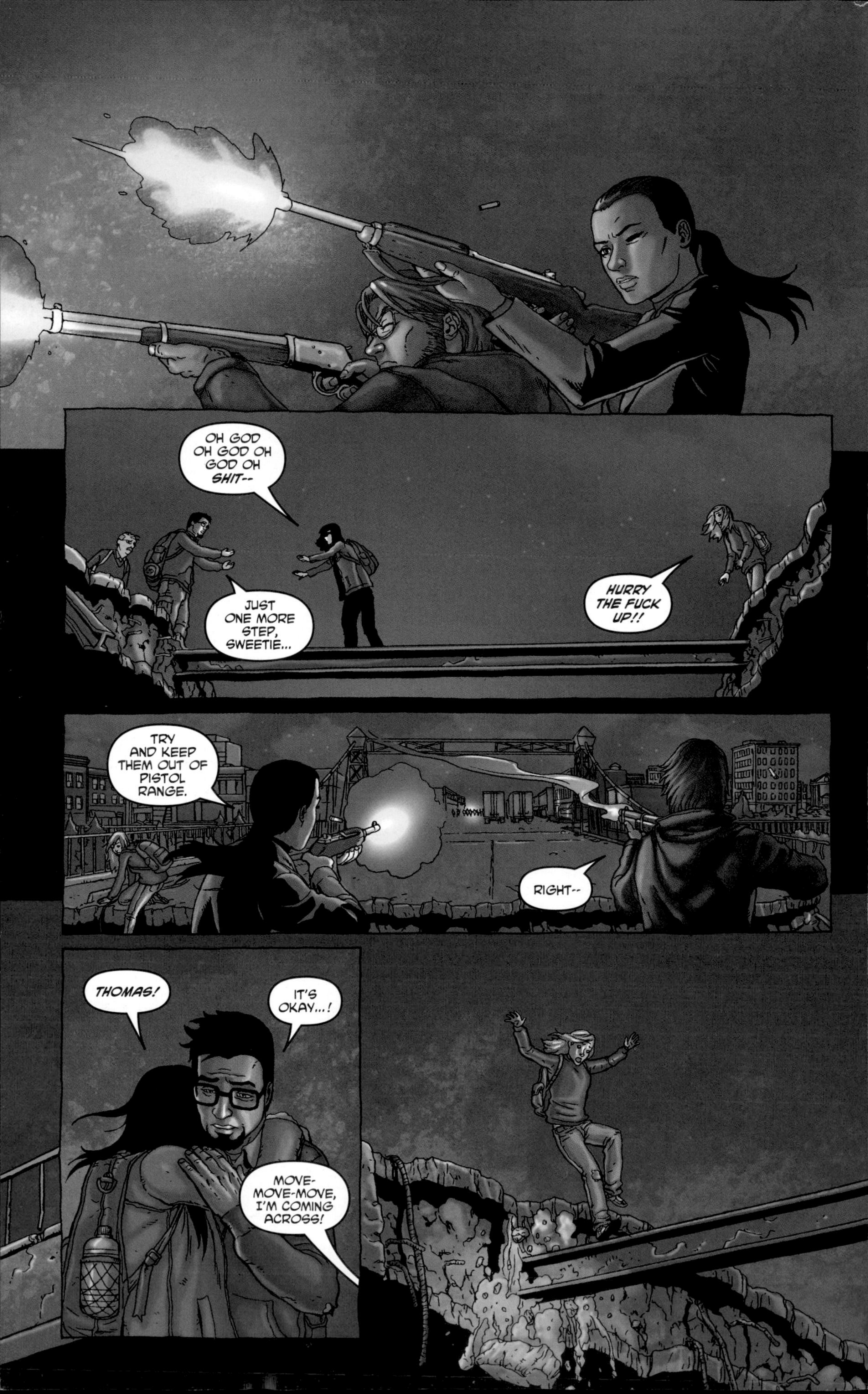
OH GOD OH GOD OH GOD OH SHIT--
JUST ONE MORE STEP, SWEETIE...
HURRY THE FUCK UP!!
TRY AND KEEP THEM OUT OF PISTOL RANGE.
RIGHT--
THOMAS!
IT'S OKAY...!
MOVE-MOVE-MOVE, I'M COMING ACROSS!

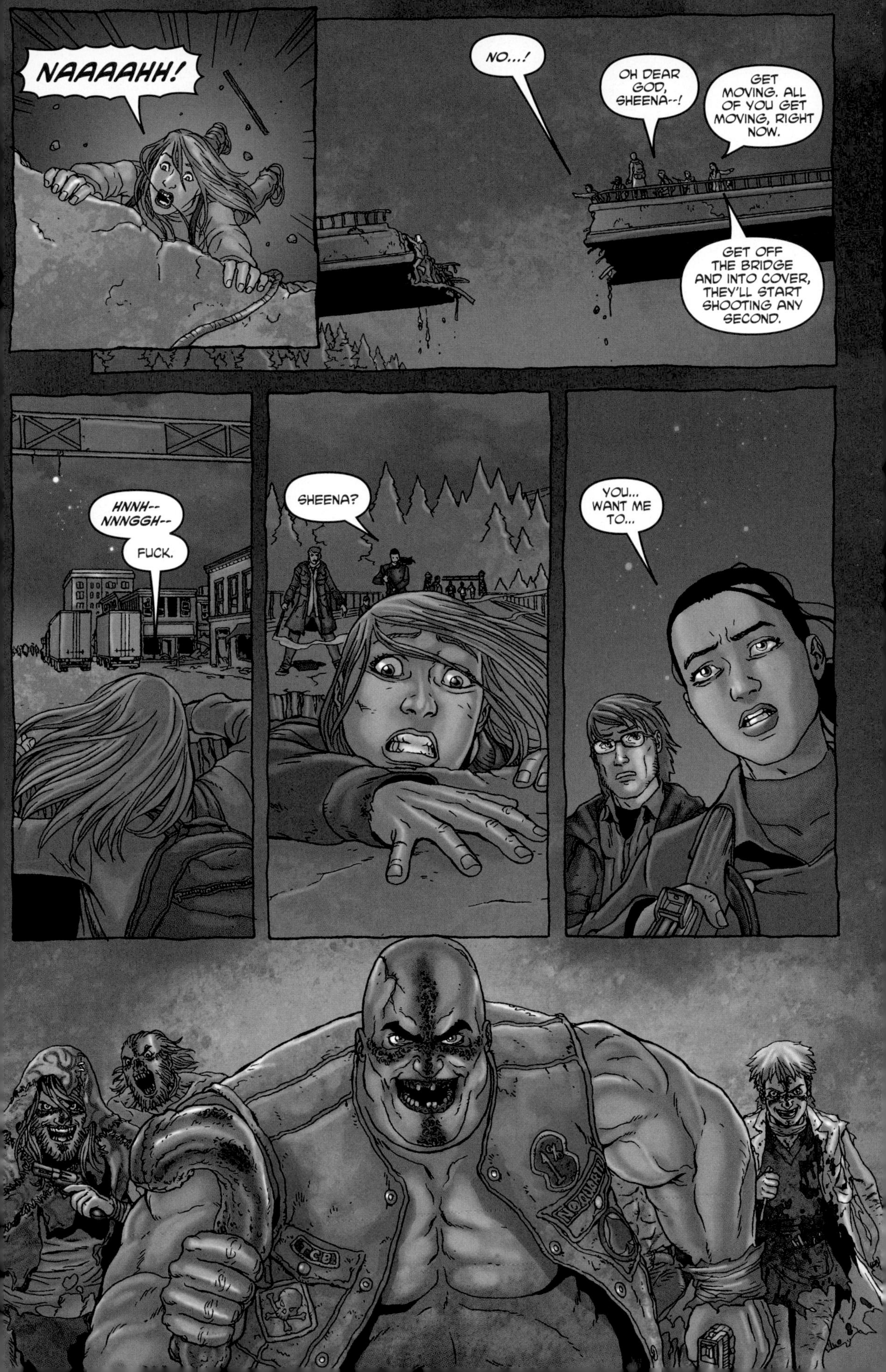
NAAAAHH!
NO...!
OH DEAR GOD, SHEENA--!
GET MOVING. ALL OF YOU GET MOVING, RIGHT NOW.
GET OFF THE BRIDGE AND INTO COVER, THEY'LL START SHOOTING ANY SECOND.
HNNH-- NNNGGH--
FUCK.
SHEENA?
YOU... WANT ME TO...

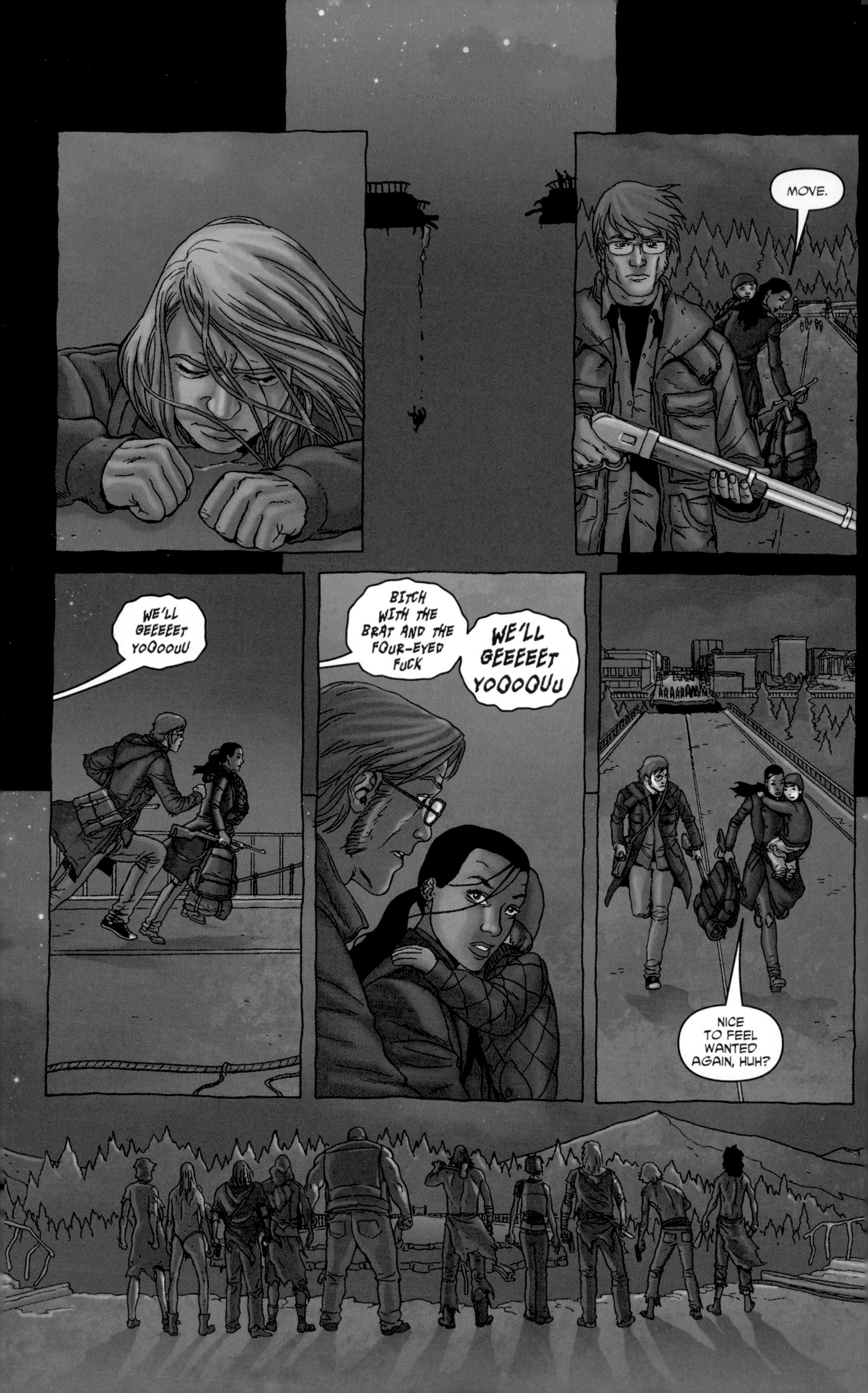
MOVE.
WE'LL GEEEEET YOOoouu
BITCH WITH THE BRAT AND THE FOUR-EYED FUCK
WE'LL GEEEEET YOOOOUU
NICE TO FEEL WANTED AGAIN, HUH?

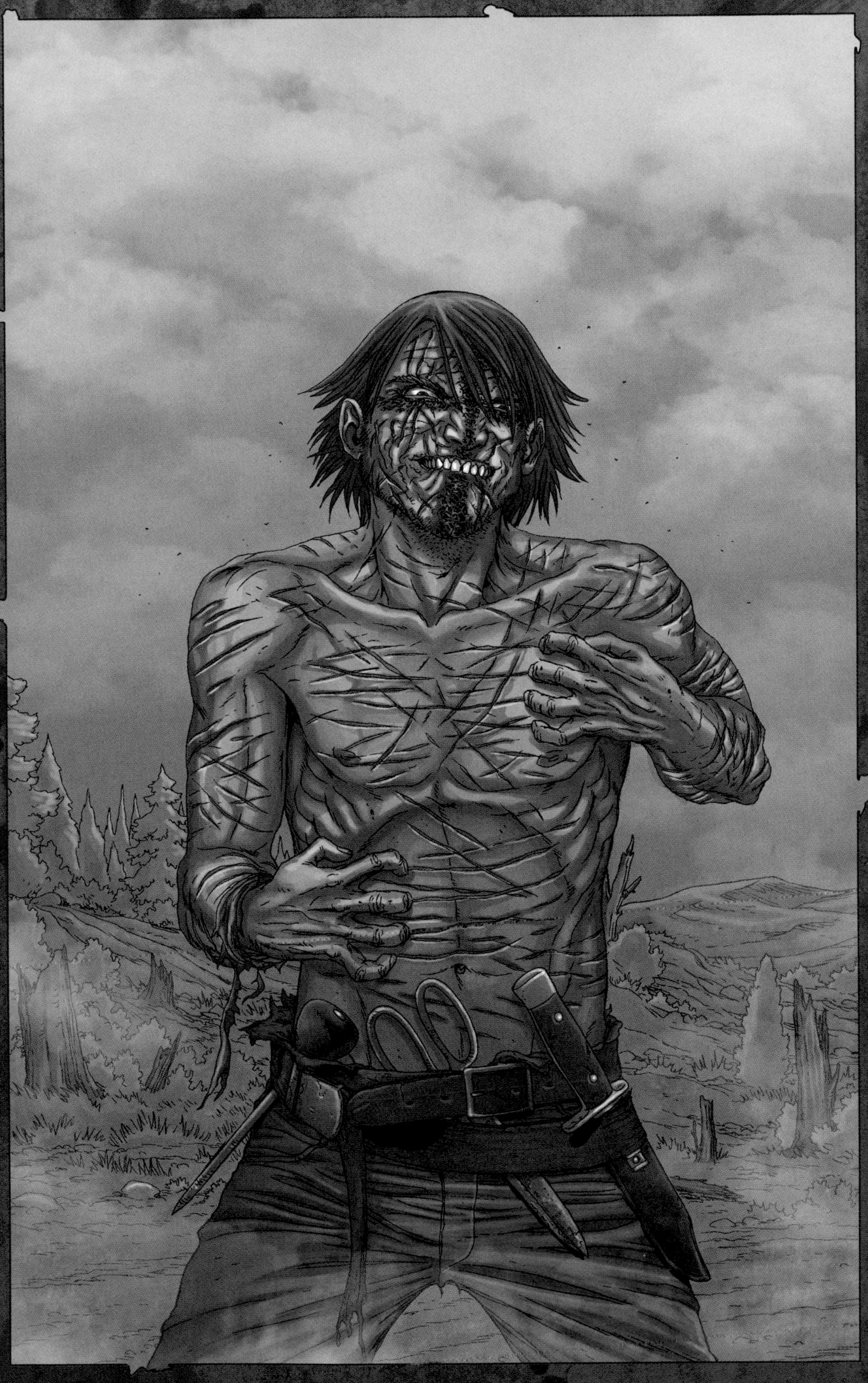

PART SIX

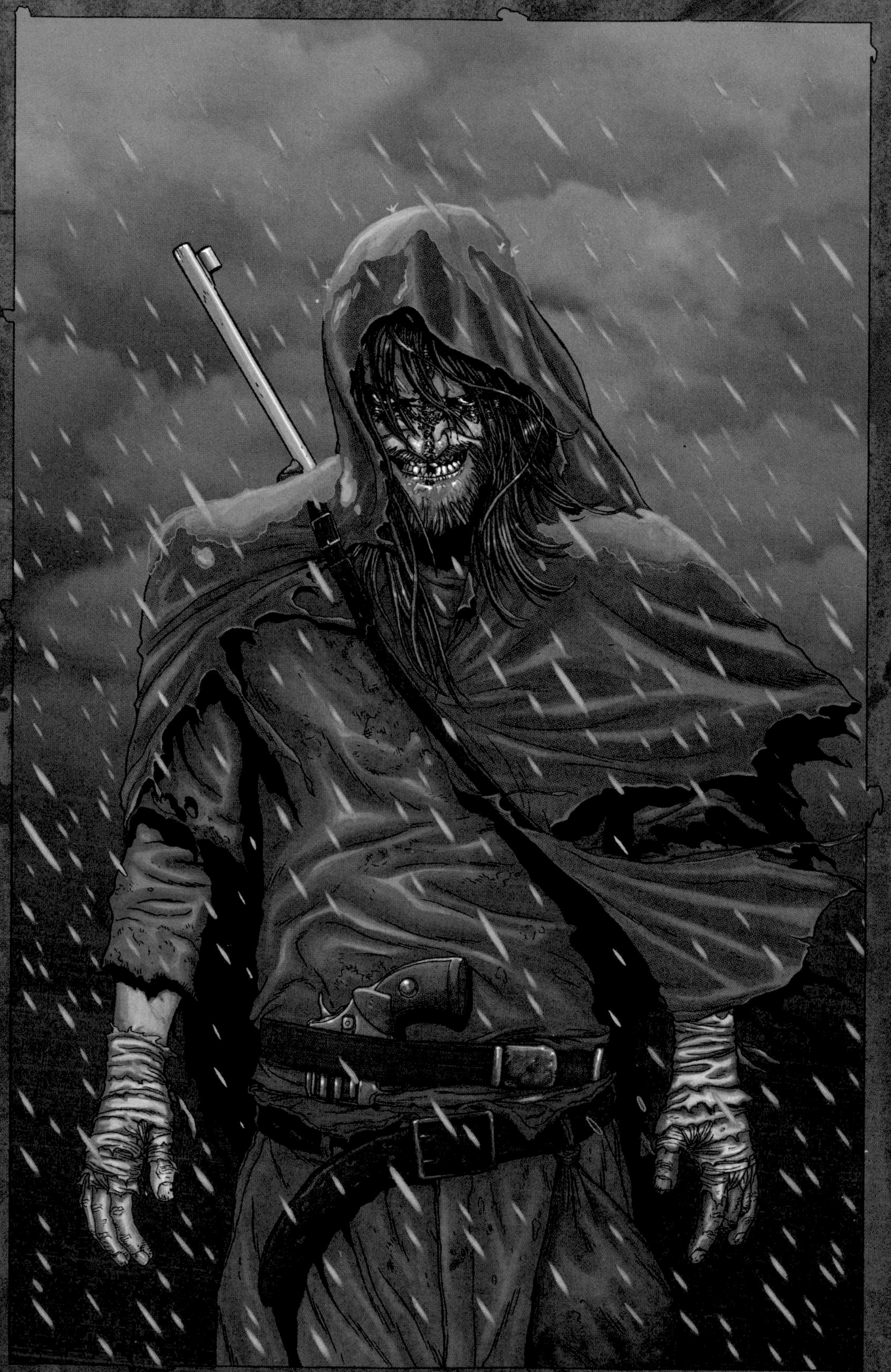

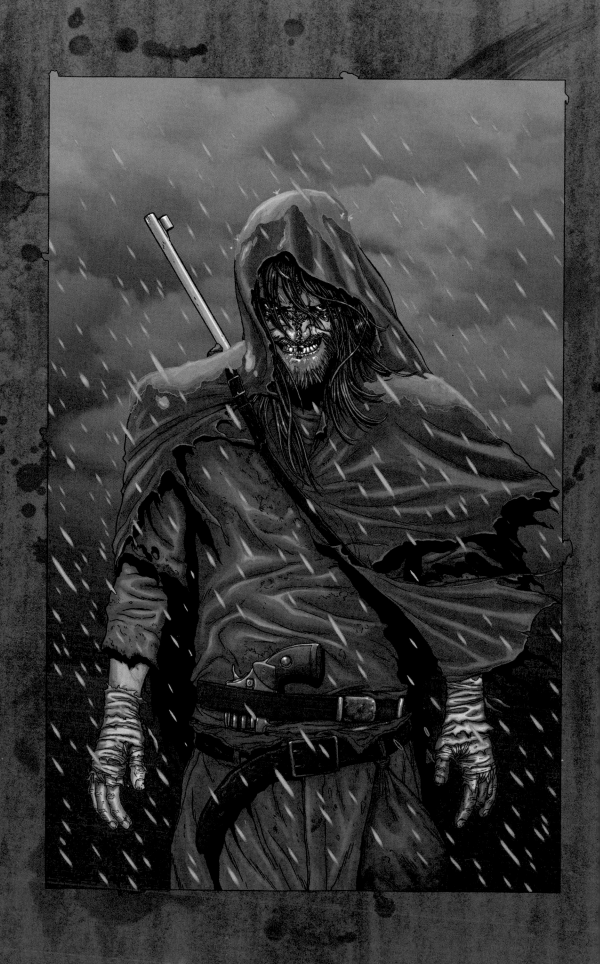

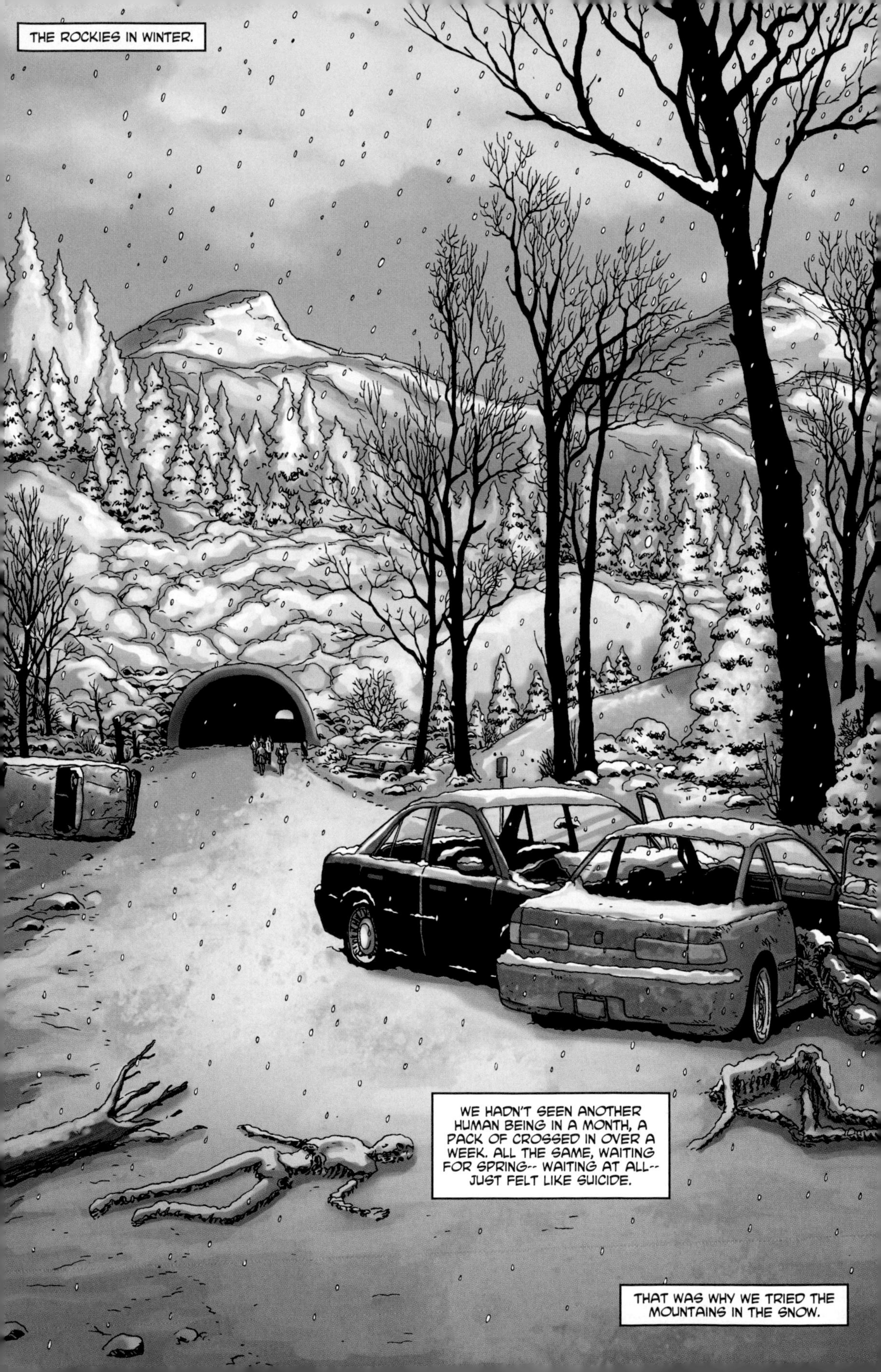
THE ROCKIES IN WINTER.
WE HADN'T SEEN ANOTHER HUMAN BEING IN A MONTH, A PACK OF CROSSED IN OVER A WEEK. ALL THE SAME, WAITING FOR SPRING-- WAITING AT ALL-- JUST FELT LIKE SUICIDE.
THAT WAS WHY WE TRIED THE MOUNTAINS IN THE SNOW.

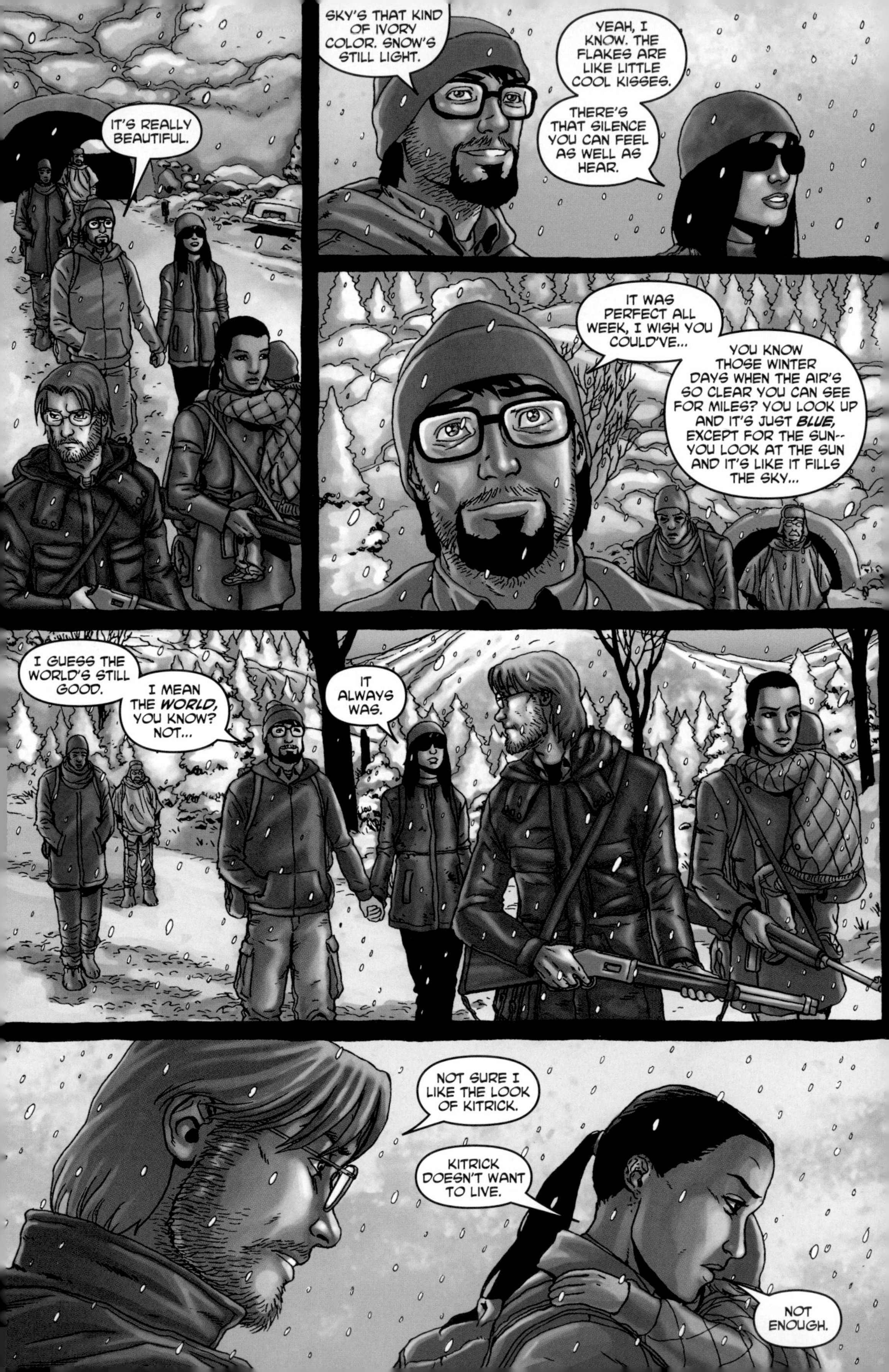
IT'S REALLY BEAUTIFUL.
SKY'S THAT KIND OF IVORY COLOR. SNOW'S STILL LIGHT.
YEAH, I KNOW. THE FLAKES ARE LIKE LITTLE COOL KISSES.
THERE'S THAT SILENCE YOU CAN FEEL AS WELL AS HEAR.
IT WAS PERFECT ALL WEEK, I WISH YOU COULD'VE...
YOU KNOW THOSE WINTER DAYS WHEN THE AIR'S SO CLEAR YOU CAN SEE FOR MILES? YOU LOOK UP AND IT'S JUST *BLUE,* EXCEPT FOR THE SUN-- YOU LOOK AT THE SUN AND IT'S LIKE IT FILLS THE SKY...
I GUESS THE WORLD'S STILL GOOD.
I MEAN THE *WORLD,* YOU KNOW? NOT...
IT ALWAYS WAS.
NOT SURE I LIKE THE LOOK OF KITRICK.
KITRICK DOESN'T WANT TO LIVE.
NOT ENOUGH.

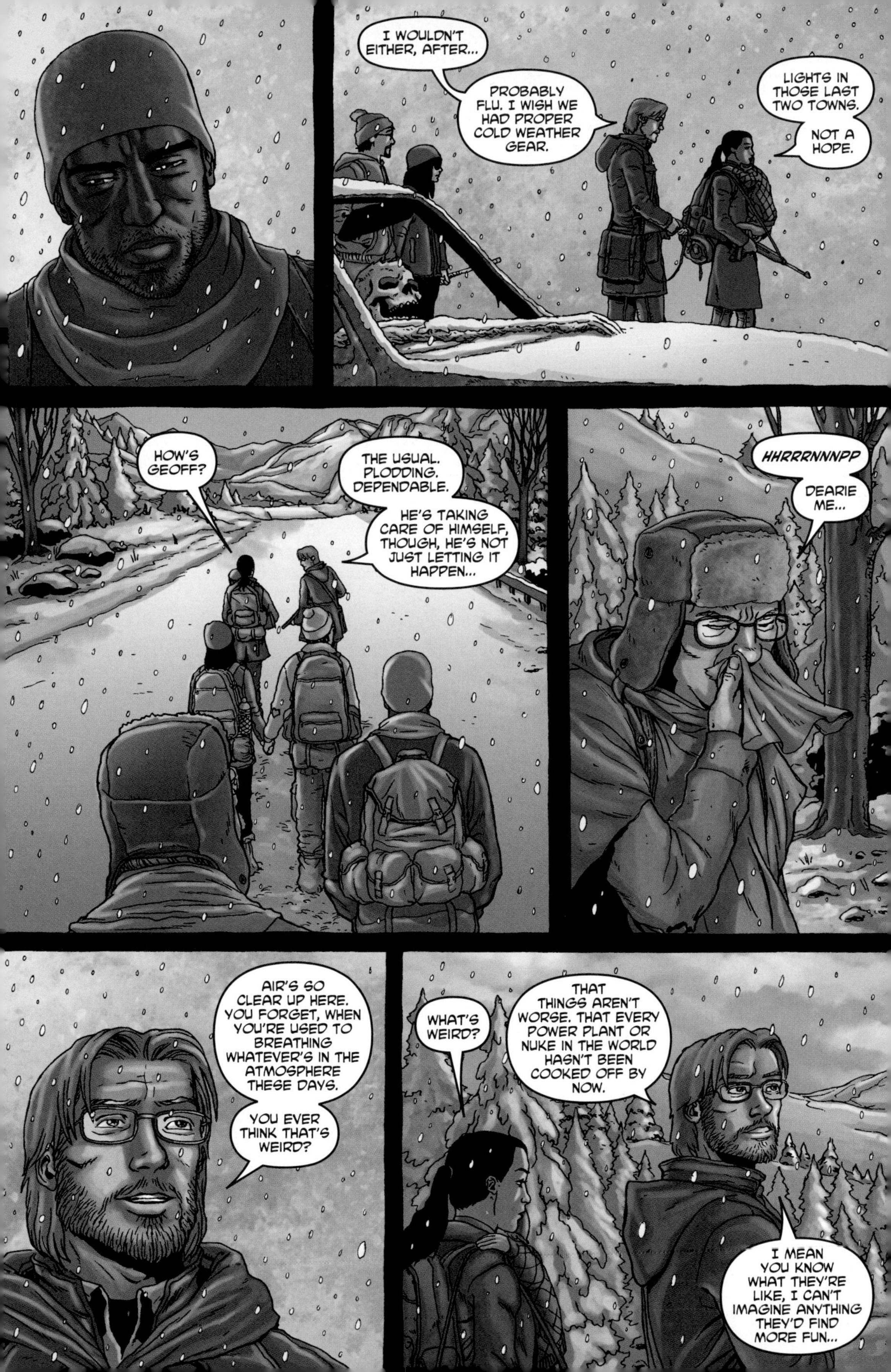
I WOULDN'T EITHER, AFTER...
PROBABLY FLU. I WISH WE HAD PROPER COLD WEATHER GEAR.
LIGHTS IN THOSE LAST TWO TOWNS.
NOT A HOPE.
HOW'S GEOFF?
THE USUAL. PLODDING. DEPENDABLE.
HE'S TAKING CARE OF HIMSELF, THOUGH, HE'S NOT JUST LETTING IT HAPPEN...
HHRRRNNNPP
DEARIE ME...
AIR'S SO CLEAR UP HERE. YOU FORGET, WHEN YOU'RE USED TO BREATHING WHATEVER'S IN THE ATMOSPHERE THESE DAYS.
YOU EVER THINK THAT'S WEIRD?
WHAT'S WEIRD?
THAT THINGS AREN'T WORSE. THAT EVERY POWER PLANT OR NUKE IN THE WORLD HASN'T BEEN COOKED OFF BY NOW.
I MEAN YOU KNOW WHAT THEY'RE LIKE, I CAN'T IMAGINE ANYTHING THEY'D FIND MORE FUN...

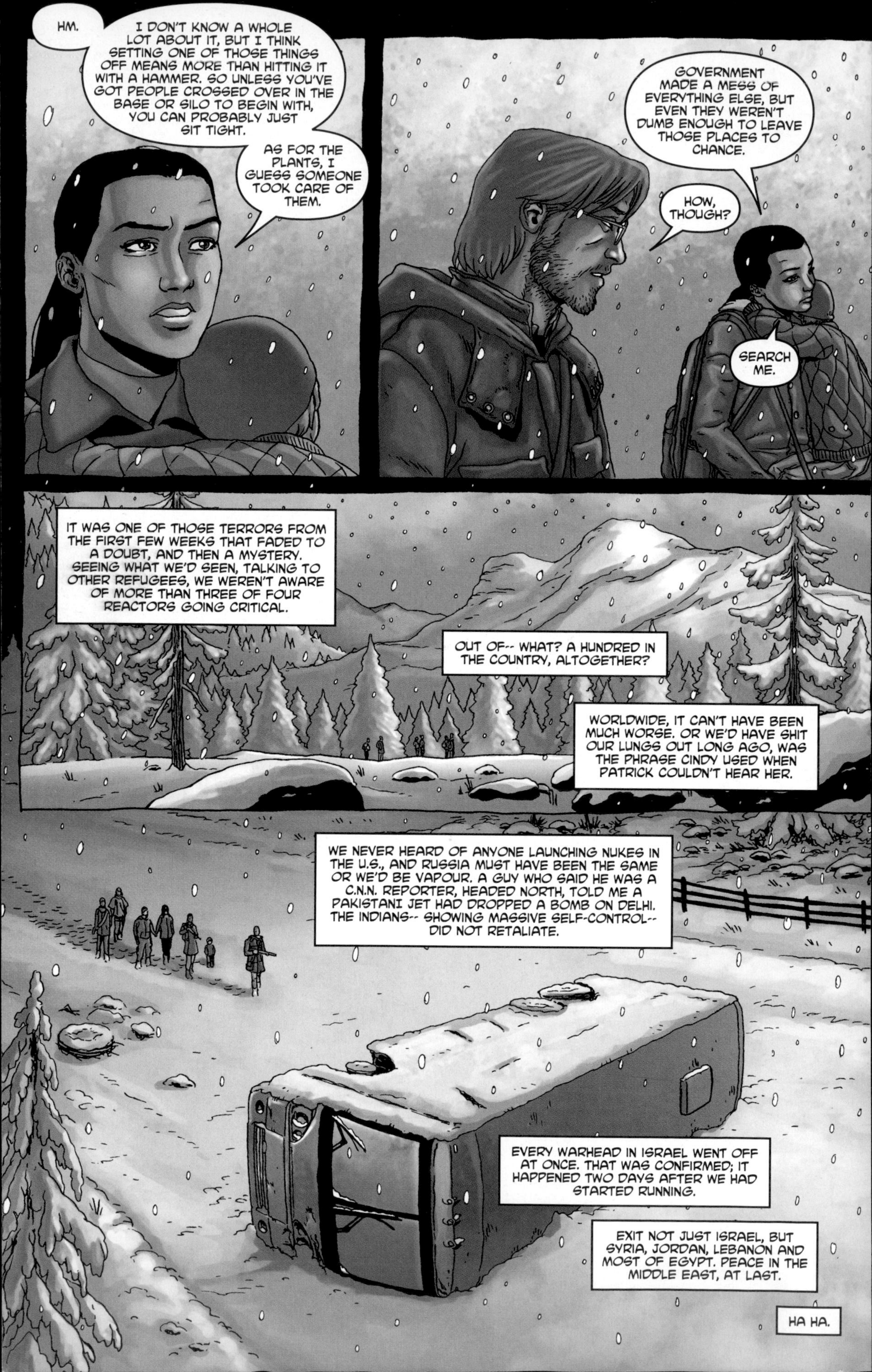
HM.
I DON'T KNOW A WHOLE LOT ABOUT IT, BUT I THINK SETTING ONE OF THOSE THINGS OFF MEANS MORE THAN HITTING IT WITH A HAMMER. SO UNLESS YOU'VE GOT PEOPLE CROSSED OVER IN THE BASE OR SILO TO BEGIN WITH, YOU CAN PROBABLY JUST SIT TIGHT.
AS FOR THE PLANTS, I GUESS SOMEONE TOOK CARE OF THEM.
GOVERNMENT MADE A MESS OF EVERYTHING ELSE, BUT EVEN THEY WEREN'T DUMB ENOUGH TO LEAVE THOSE PLACES TO CHANCE.
HOW, THOUGH?
SEARCH ME.
IT WAS ONE OF THOSE TERRORS FROM THE FIRST FEW WEEKS THAT FADED TO A DOUBT, AND THEN A MYSTERY. SEEING WHAT WE'D SEEN, TALKING TO OTHER REFUGEES, WE WEREN'T AWARE OF MORE THAN THREE OF FOUR REACTORS GOING CRITICAL.
OUT OF-- WHAT? A HUNDRED IN THE COUNTRY, ALTOGETHER?
WORLDWIDE, IT CAN'T HAVE BEEN MUCH WORSE. OR WE'D HAVE SHIT OUR LUNGS OUT LONG AGO, WAS THE PHRASE CINDY USED WHEN PATRICK COULDN'T HEAR HER.
WE NEVER HEARD OF ANYONE LAUNCHING NUKES IN THE U.S., AND RUSSIA MUST HAVE BEEN THE SAME OR WE'D BE VAPOUR. A GUY WHO SAID HE WAS A C.N.N. REPORTER, HEADED NORTH, TOLD ME A PAKISTANI JET HAD DROPPED A BOMB ON DELHI. THE INDIANS-- SHOWING MASSIVE SELF-CONTROL-- DID NOT RETALIATE.
EVERY WARHEAD IN ISRAEL WENT OFF AT ONCE. THAT WAS CONFIRMED; IT HAPPENED TWO DAYS AFTER WE HAD STARTED RUNNING.
EXIT NOT JUST ISRAEL, BUT SYRIA, JORDAN, LEBANON AND MOST OF EGYPT. PEACE IN THE MIDDLE EAST, AT LAST.
HA HA.

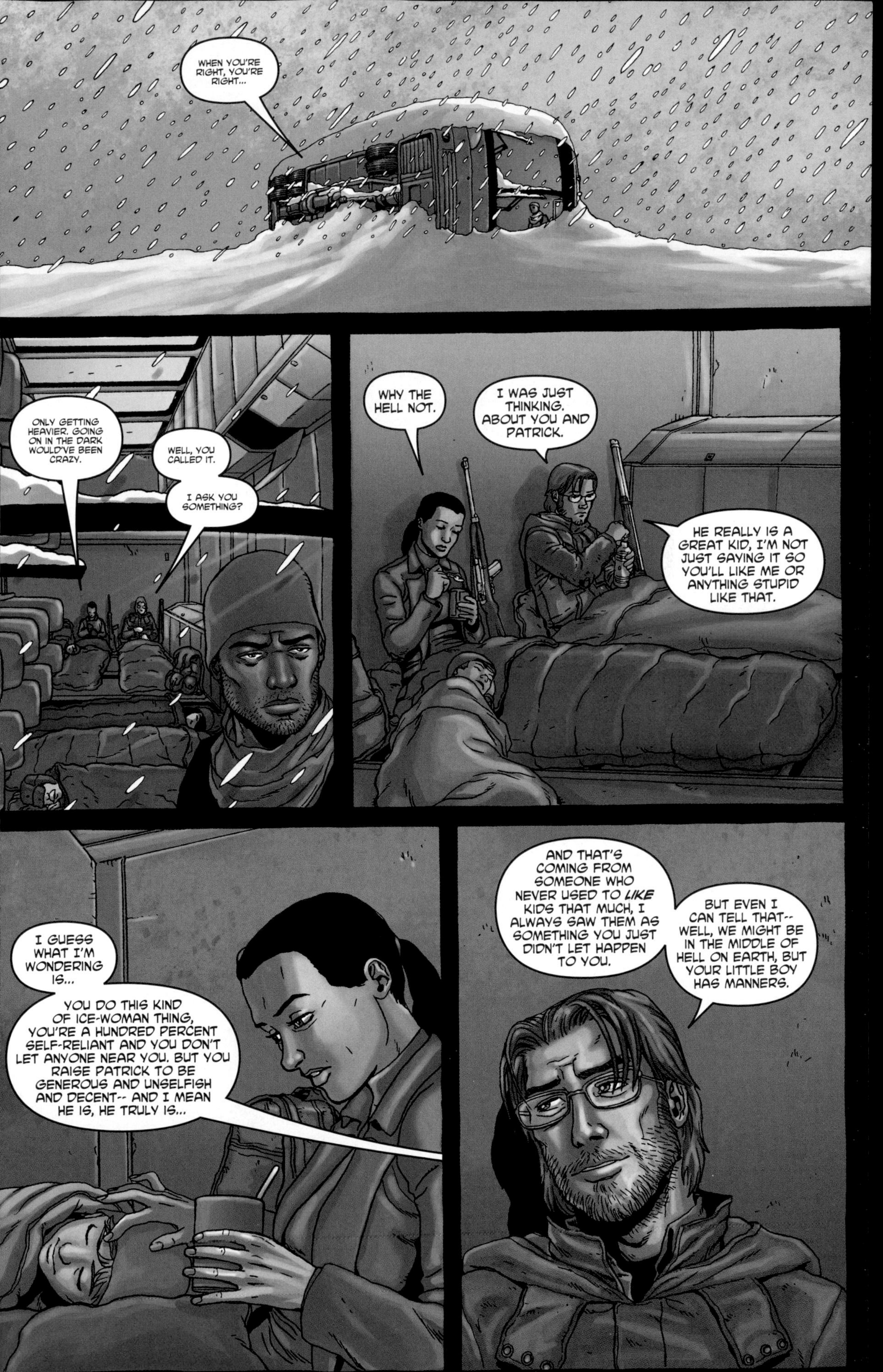
WHEN YOU'RE RIGHT, YOU'RE RIGHT...
ONLY GETTING HEAVIER. GOING ON IN THE DARK WOULD'VE BEEN CRAZY.
WELL, YOU CALLED IT.
I ASK YOU SOMETHING?
WHY THE HELL NOT.
I WAS JUST THINKING. ABOUT YOU AND PATRICK.
HE REALLY IS A GREAT KID, I'M NOT JUST SAYING IT SO YOU'LL LIKE ME OR ANYTHING STUPID LIKE THAT.
AND THAT'S COMING FROM SOMEONE WHO NEVER USED TO LIKE KIDS THAT MUCH, I ALWAYS SAW THEM AS SOMETHING YOU JUST DIDN'T LET HAPPEN TO YOU.
BUT EVEN I CAN TELL THAT-- WELL, WE MIGHT BE IN THE MIDDLE OF HELL ON EARTH, BUT YOUR LITTLE BOY HAS MANNERS.
I GUESS WHAT I'M WONDERING IS...
YOU DO THIS KIND OF ICE-WOMAN THING, YOU'RE A HUNDRED PERCENT SELF-RELIANT AND YOU DON'T LET ANYONE NEAR YOU. BUT YOU RAISE PATRICK TO BE GENEROUS AND UNSELFISH AND DECENT-- AND I MEAN HE IS, HE TRULY IS...

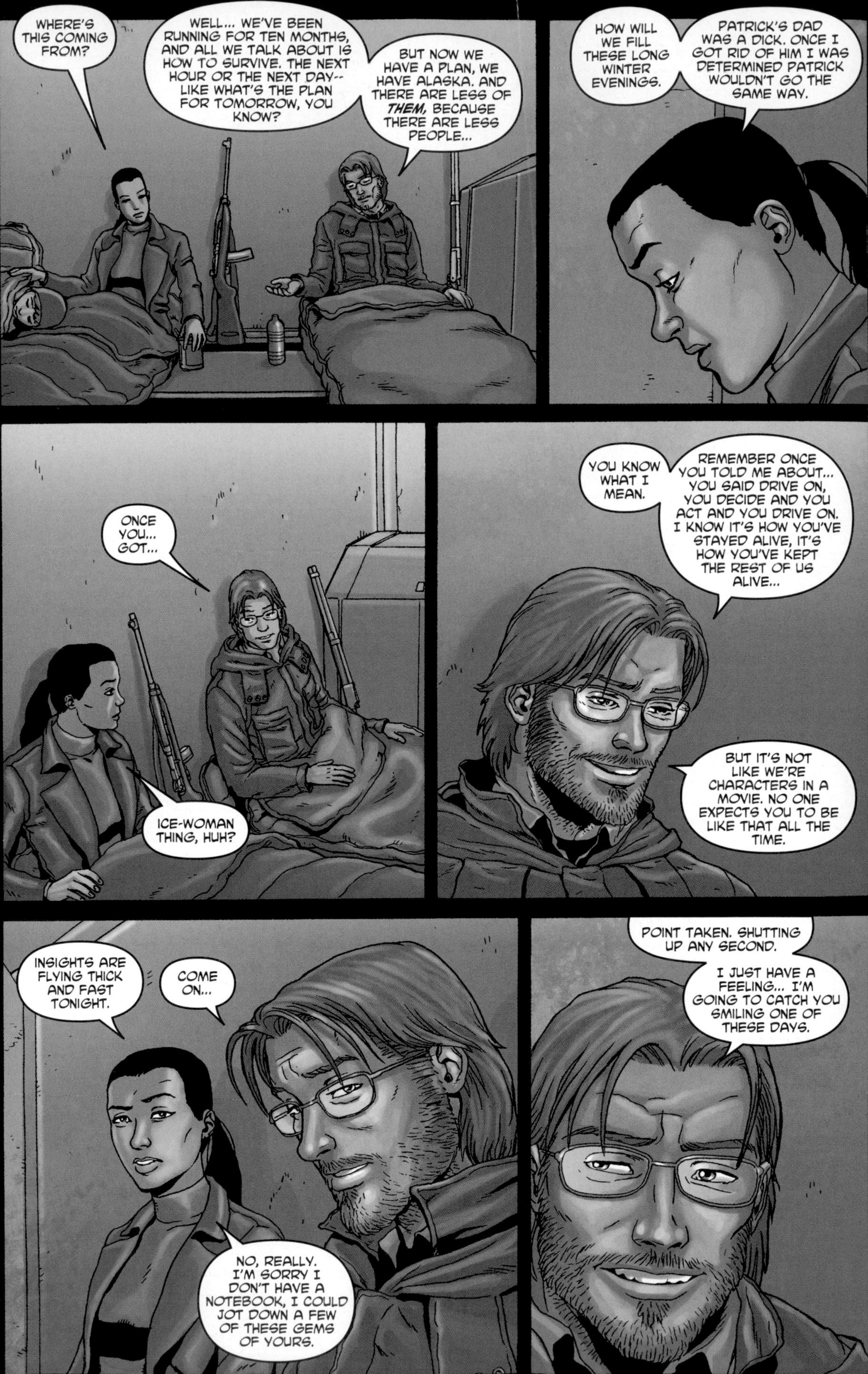
WHERE'S THIS COMING FROM?
WELL... WE'VE BEEN RUNNING FOR TEN MONTHS, AND ALL WE TALK ABOUT IS HOW TO SURVIVE. THE NEXT HOUR OR THE NEXT DAY-- LIKE WHAT'S THE PLAN FOR TOMORROW, YOU KNOW?
BUT NOW WE HAVE A PLAN, WE HAVE ALASKA. AND THERE ARE LESS OF *THEM,* BECAUSE THERE ARE LESS PEOPLE...
HOW WILL WE FILL THESE LONG WINTER EVENINGS.
PATRICK'S DAD WAS A DICK. ONCE I GOT RID OF HIM I WAS DETERMINED PATRICK WOULDN'T GO THE SAME WAY.
ONCE YOU... GOT...
ICE-WOMAN THING, HUH?
YOU KNOW WHAT I MEAN.
REMEMBER ONCE YOU TOLD ME ABOUT... YOU SAID DRIVE ON, YOU DECIDE AND YOU ACT AND YOU DRIVE ON. I KNOW IT'S HOW YOU'VE STAYED ALIVE, IT'S HOW YOU'VE KEPT THE REST OF US ALIVE...
BUT IT'S NOT LIKE WE'RE CHARACTERS IN A MOVIE. NO ONE EXPECTS YOU TO BE LIKE THAT ALL THE TIME.
INSIGHTS ARE FLYING THICK AND FAST TONIGHT.
COME ON...
NO, REALLY. I'M SORRY I DON'T HAVE A NOTEBOOK, I COULD JOT DOWN A FEW OF THESE GEMS OF YOURS.
POINT TAKEN. SHUTTING UP ANY SECOND.
I JUST HAVE A FEELING... I'M GOING TO CATCH YOU SMILING ONE OF THESE DAYS.

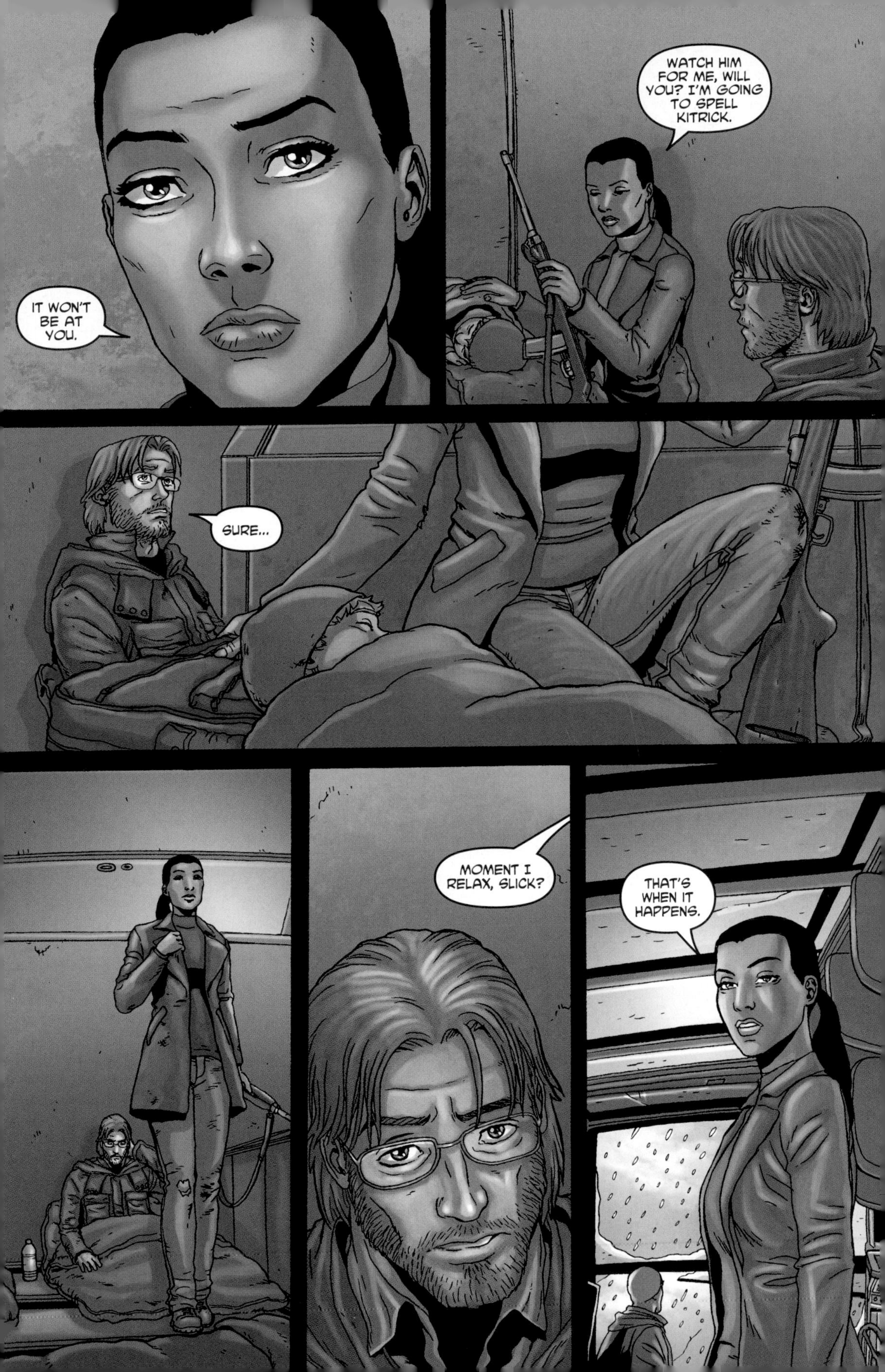
IT WON'T BE AT YOU.
WATCH HIM FOR ME, WILL YOU? I'M GOING TO SPELL KITRICK.
SURE...
MOMENT I RELAX, SLICK?
THAT'S WHEN IT HAPPENS.

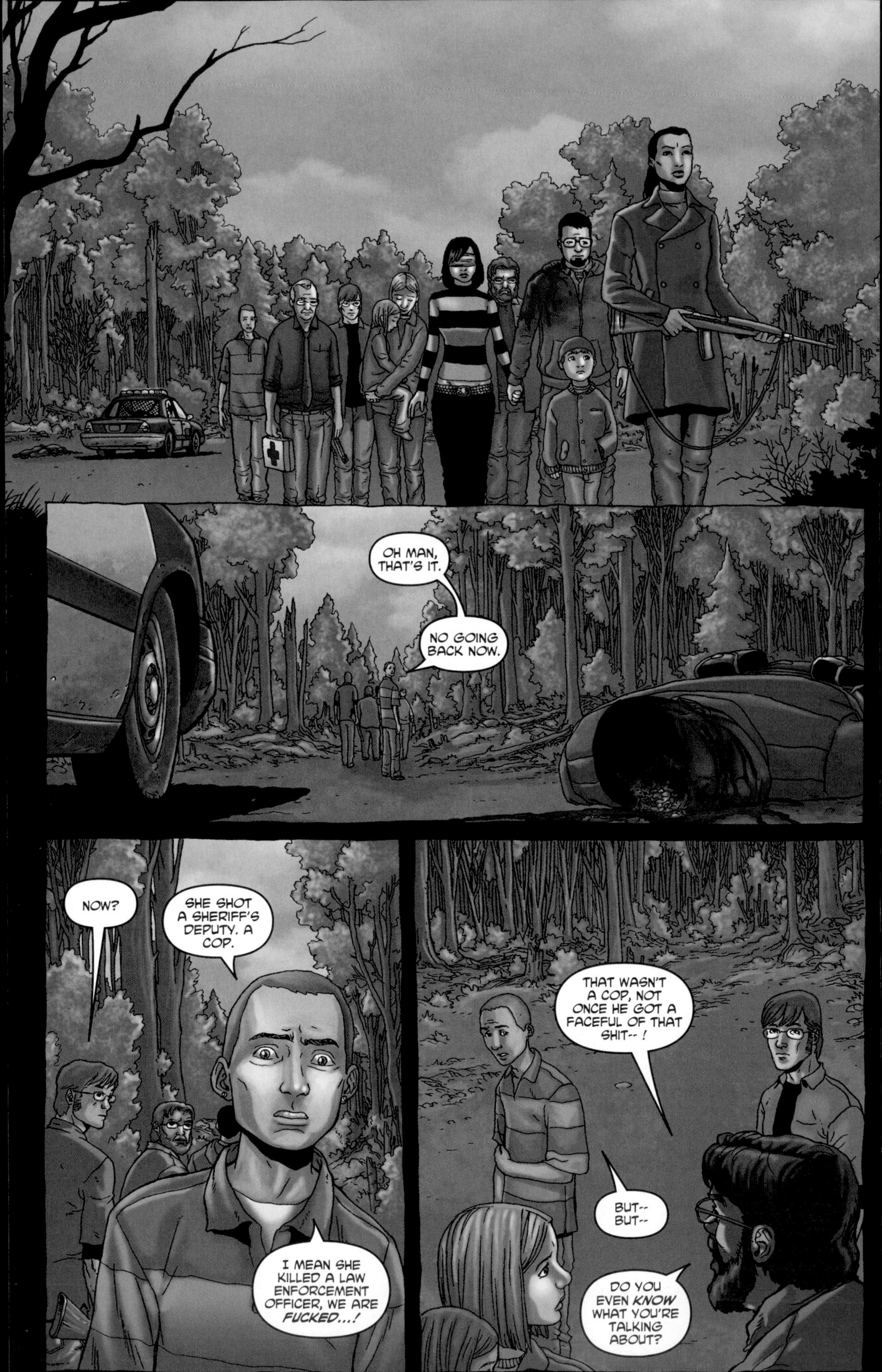
OH MAN, THAT'S IT.
NO GOING BACK NOW.
NOW?
SHE SHOT A SHERIFF'S DEPUTY. A COP.
I MEAN SHE KILLED A LAW ENFORCEMENT OFFICER, WE ARE *FUCKED...!*
THAT WASN'T A COP, NOT ONCE HE GOT A FACEFUL OF THAT SHIT-- !
BUT-- BUT--
DO YOU EVEN *KNOW* WHAT YOU'RE TALKING ABOUT?

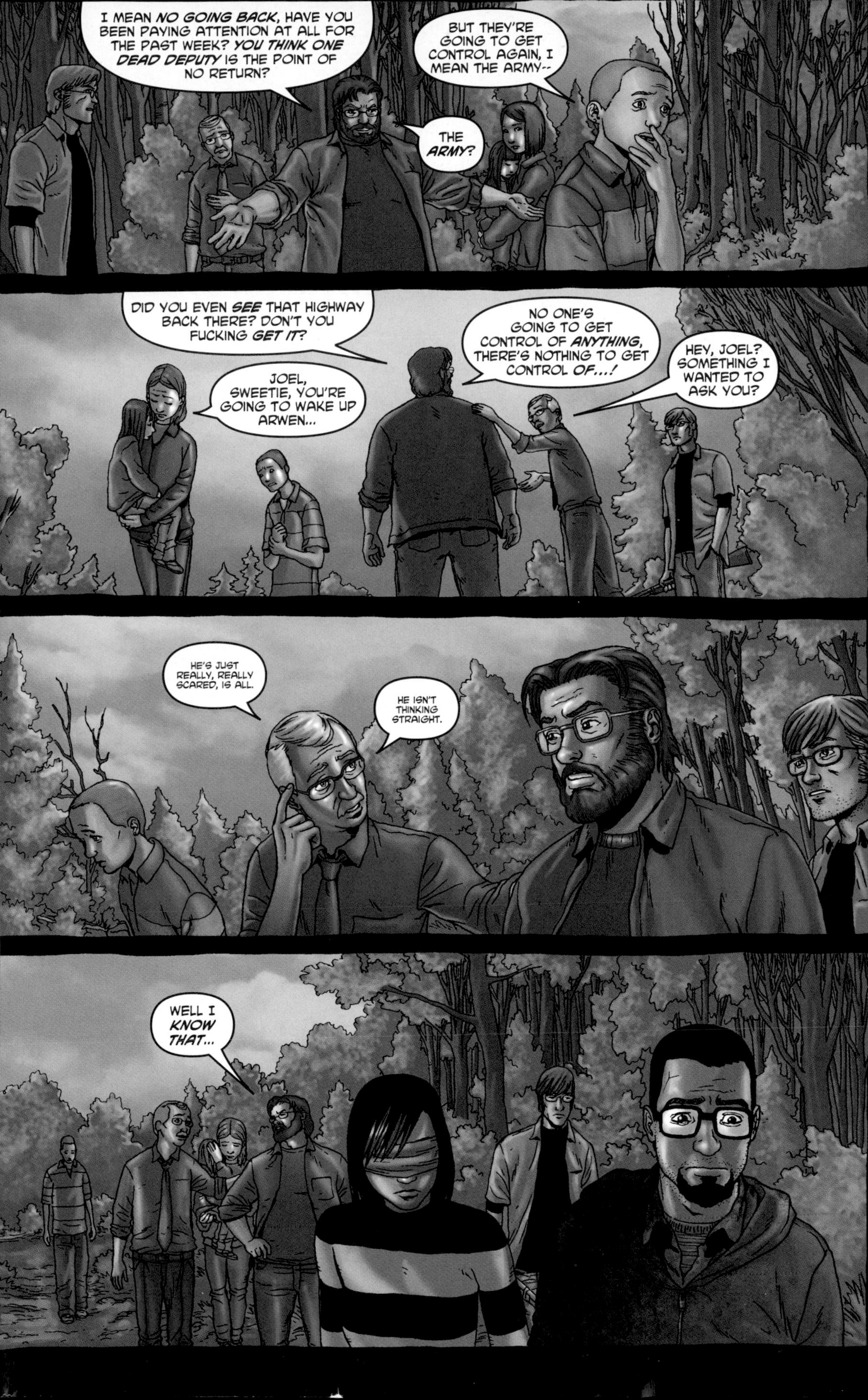
I MEAN NO GOING BACK, HAVE YOU BEEN PAYING ATTENTION AT ALL FOR THE PAST WEEK? YOU THINK ONE DEAD DEPUTY IS THE POINT OF NO RETURN?
BUT THEY'RE GOING TO GET CONTROL AGAIN, I MEAN THE ARMY--
THE ARMY?
DID YOU EVEN SEE THAT HIGHWAY BACK THERE? DON'T YOU FUCKING GET IT?
NO ONE'S GOING TO GET CONTROL OF ANYTHING, THERE'S NOTHING TO GET CONTROL OF...!
JOEL, SWEETIE, YOU'RE GOING TO WAKE UP ARWEN...
HEY, JOEL? SOMETHING I WANTED TO ASK YOU?
HE'S JUST REALLY, REALLY SCARED, IS ALL.
HE ISN'T THINKING STRAIGHT.
WELL I KNOW THAT...

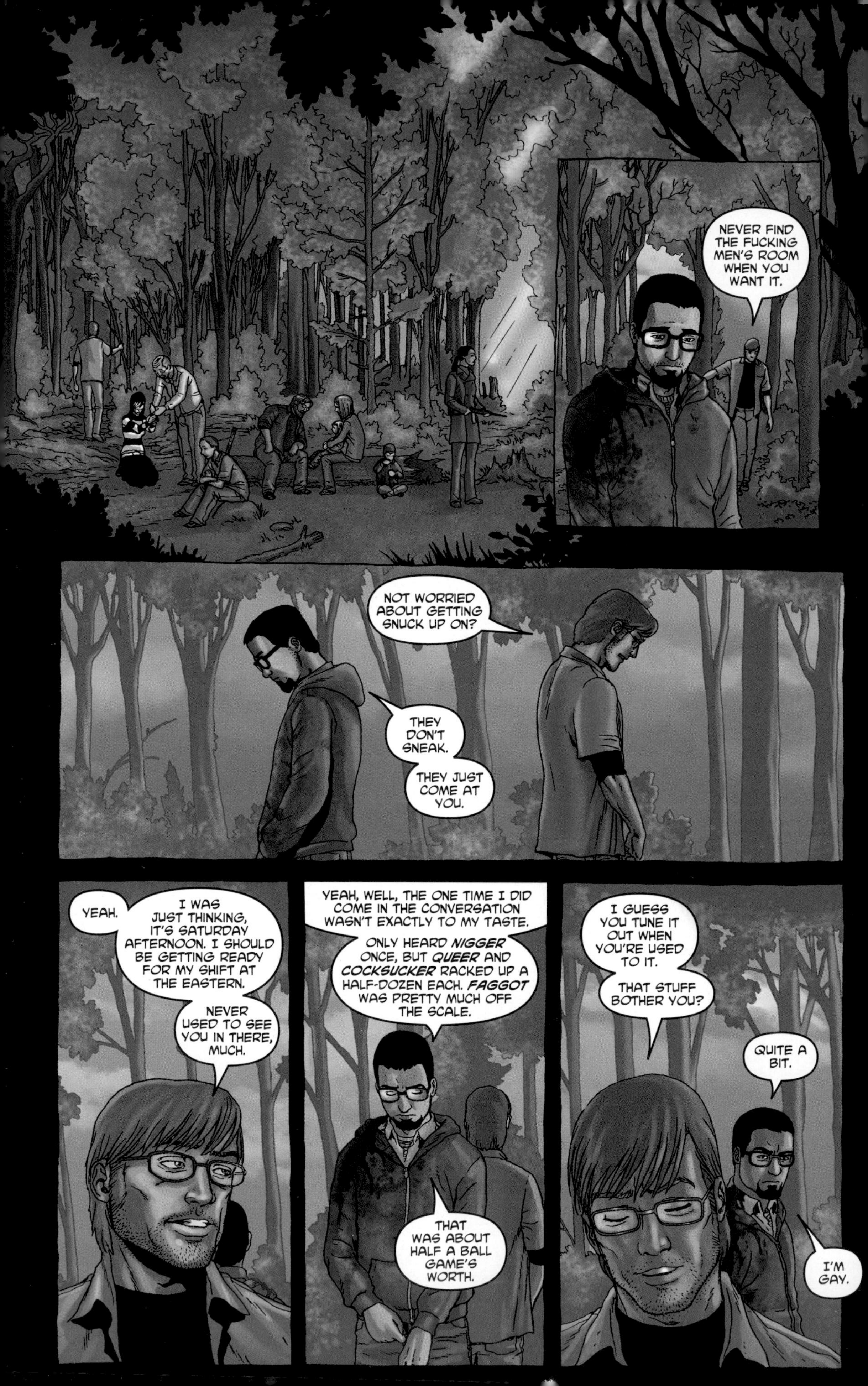
NEVER FIND THE FUCKING MEN'S ROOM WHEN YOU WANT IT.
NOT WORRIED ABOUT GETTING SNUCK UP ON?
THEY DON'T SNEAK.
THEY JUST COME AT YOU.
YEAH.
I WAS JUST THINKING, IT'S SATURDAY AFTERNOON. I SHOULD BE GETTING READY FOR MY SHIFT AT THE EASTERN.
NEVER USED TO SEE YOU IN THERE, MUCH.
YEAH, WELL, THE ONE TIME I DID COME IN THE CONVERSATION WASN'T EXACTLY TO MY TASTE.
ONLY HEARD NIGGER ONCE, BUT QUEER AND COCKSUCKER RACKED UP A HALF-DOZEN EACH. FAGGOT WAS PRETTY MUCH OFF THE SCALE.
THAT WAS ABOUT HALF A BALL GAME'S WORTH.
I GUESS YOU TUNE IT OUT WHEN YOU'RE USED TO IT.
THAT STUFF BOTHER YOU?
QUITE A BIT.
I'M GAY.

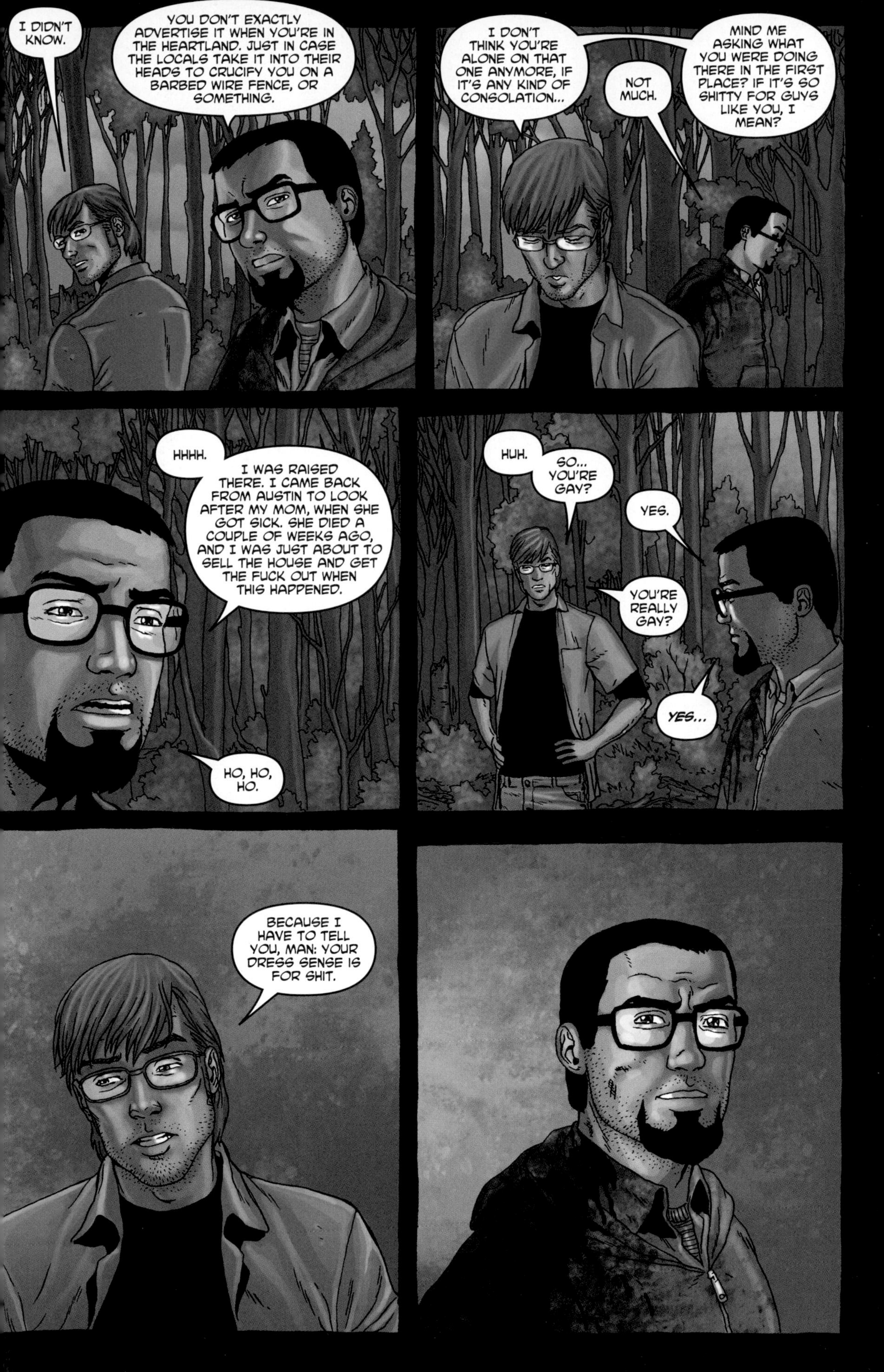
I DIDN'T KNOW.
YOU DON'T EXACTLY ADVERTISE IT WHEN YOU'RE IN THE HEARTLAND. JUST IN CASE THE LOCALS TAKE IT INTO THEIR HEADS TO CRUCIFY YOU ON A BARBED WIRE FENCE, OR SOMETHING.
I DON'T THINK YOU'RE ALONE ON THAT ONE ANYMORE, IF IT'S ANY KIND OF CONSOLATION...
NOT MUCH.
MIND ME ASKING WHAT YOU WERE DOING THERE IN THE FIRST PLACE? IF IT'S SO SHITTY FOR GUYS LIKE YOU, I MEAN?
HHHH.
I WAS RAISED THERE. I CAME BACK FROM AUSTIN TO LOOK AFTER MY MOM, WHEN SHE GOT SICK. SHE DIED A COUPLE OF WEEKS AGO, AND I WAS JUST ABOUT TO SELL THE HOUSE AND GET THE FUCK OUT WHEN THIS HAPPENED.
HO, HO, HO.
HUH.
SO... YOU'RE GAY?
YES.
YOU'RE REALLY GAY?
YES...
BECAUSE I HAVE TO TELL YOU, MAN: YOUR DRESS SENSE IS FOR SHIT.

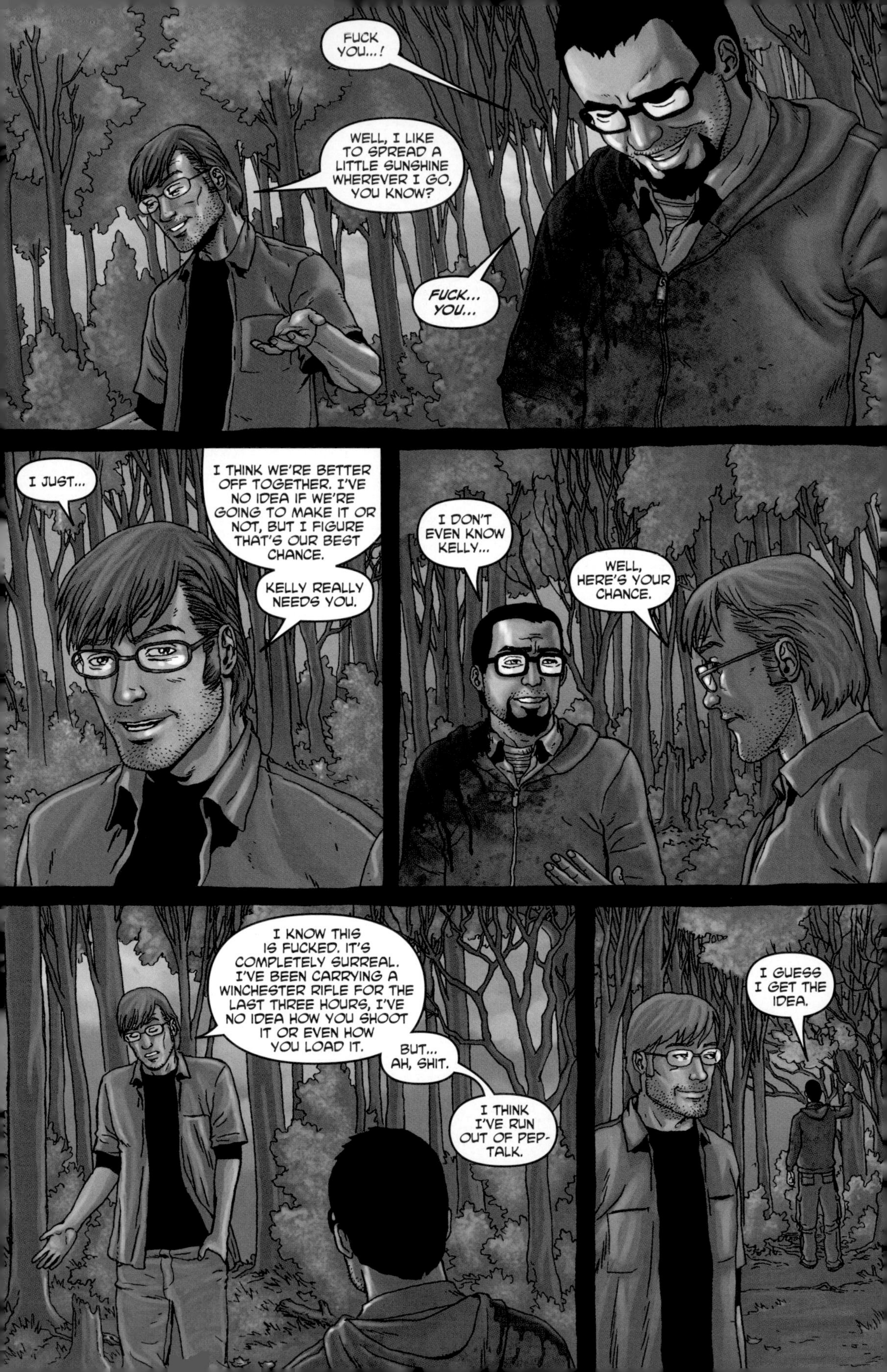
FUCK YOU...!
WELL, I LIKE TO SPREAD A LITTLE SUNSHINE WHEREVER I GO, YOU KNOW?
FUCK... YOU...
I JUST...
I THINK WE'RE BETTER OFF TOGETHER. I'VE NO IDEA IF WE'RE GOING TO MAKE IT OR NOT, BUT I FIGURE THAT'S OUR BEST CHANCE.
KELLY REALLY NEEDS YOU.
I DON'T EVEN KNOW KELLY...
WELL, HERE'S YOUR CHANCE.
I KNOW THIS IS FUCKED. IT'S COMPLETELY SURREAL. I'VE BEEN CARRYING A WINCHESTER RIFLE FOR THE LAST THREE HOURS, I'VE NO IDEA HOW YOU SHOOT IT OR EVEN HOW YOU LOAD IT.
BUT... AH, SHIT.
I THINK I'VE RUN OUT OF PEP-TALK.
I GUESS I GET THE IDEA.

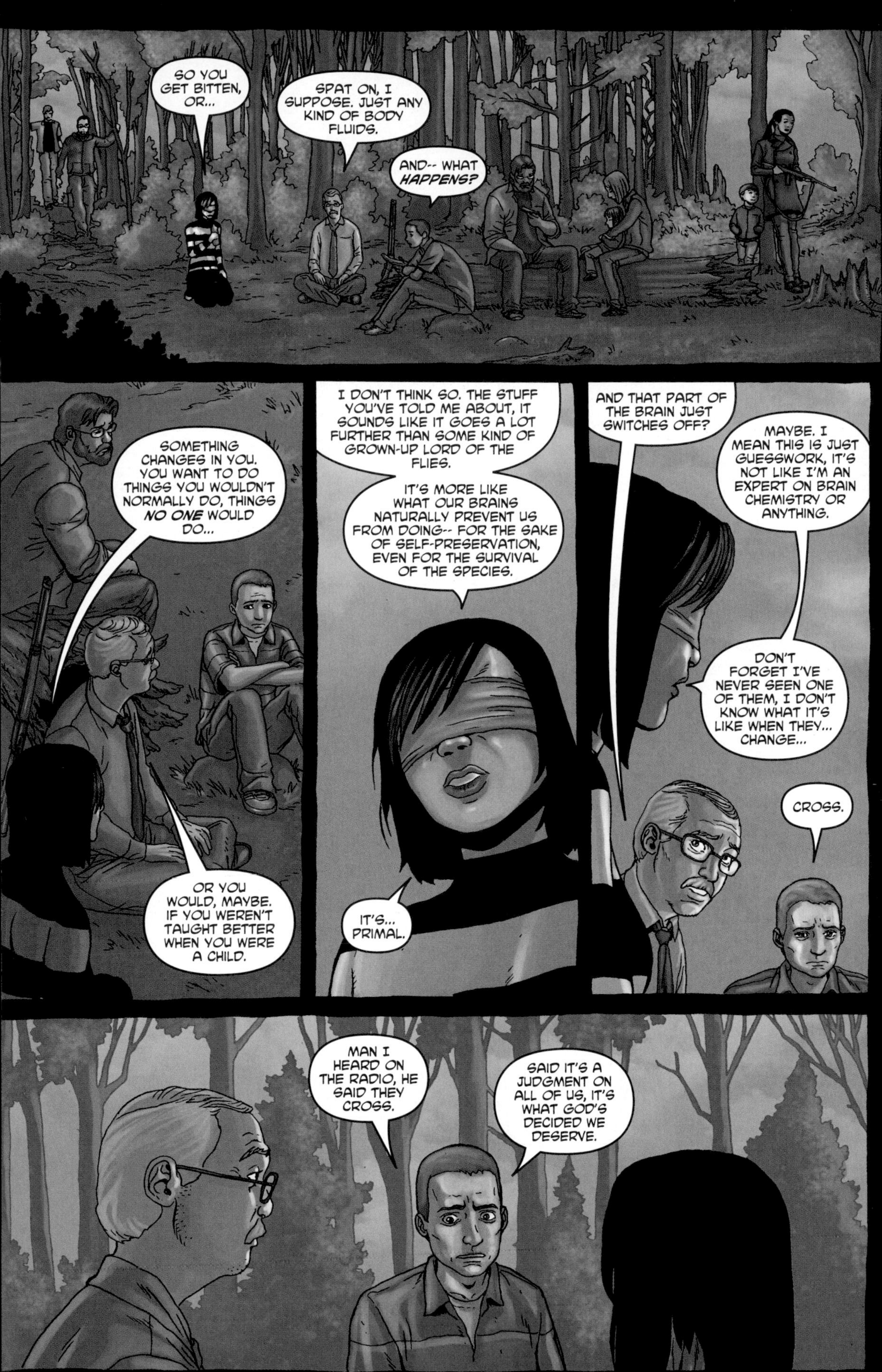
SO YOU GET BITTEN, OR...
SPAT ON, I SUPPOSE. JUST ANY KIND OF BODY FLUIDS.
AND-- WHAT HAPPENS?
SOMETHING CHANGES IN YOU. YOU WANT TO DO THINGS YOU WOULDN'T NORMALLY DO, THINGS NO ONE WOULD DO...
OR YOU WOULD, MAYBE. IF YOU WEREN'T TAUGHT BETTER WHEN YOU WERE A CHILD.
I DON'T THINK SO. THE STUFF YOU'VE TOLD ME ABOUT, IT SOUNDS LIKE IT GOES A LOT FURTHER THAN SOME KIND OF GROWN-UP LORD OF THE FLIES.
IT'S MORE LIKE WHAT OUR BRAINS NATURALLY PREVENT US FROM DOING-- FOR THE SAKE OF SELF-PRESERVATION, EVEN FOR THE SURVIVAL OF THE SPECIES.
IT'S... PRIMAL.
AND THAT PART OF THE BRAIN JUST SWITCHES OFF?
MAYBE. I MEAN THIS IS JUST GUESSWORK, IT'S NOT LIKE I'M AN EXPERT ON BRAIN CHEMISTRY OR ANYTHING.
DON'T FORGET I'VE NEVER SEEN ONE OF THEM, I DON'T KNOW WHAT IT'S LIKE WHEN THEY... CHANGE...
CROSS.
MAN I HEARD ON THE RADIO, HE SAID THEY CROSS.
SAID IT'S A JUDGMENT ON ALL OF US, IT'S WHAT GOD'S DECIDED WE DESERVE.

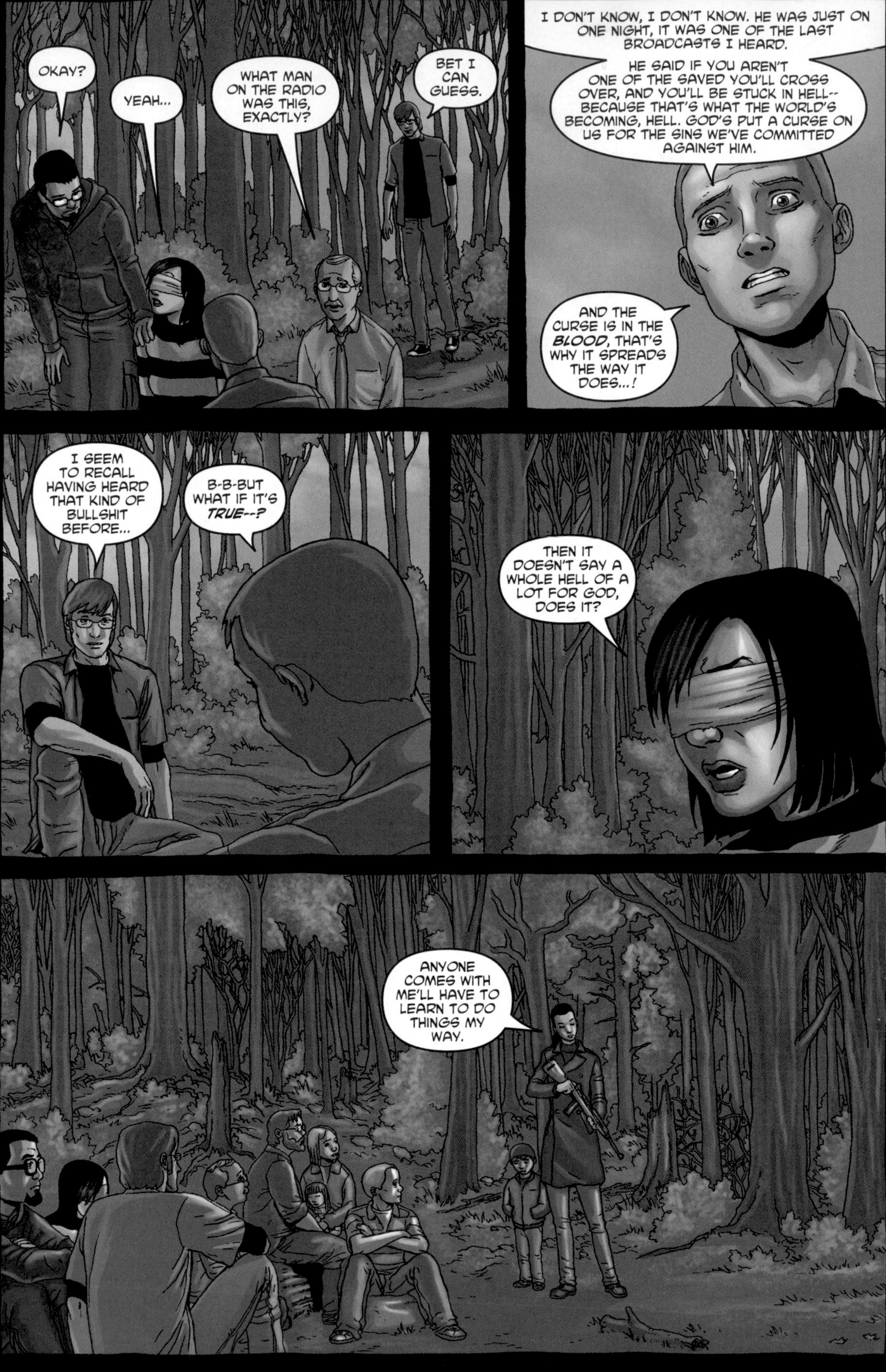
OKAY?
YEAH...
WHAT MAN ON THE RADIO WAS THIS, EXACTLY?
BET I CAN GUESS.
I DON'T KNOW, I DON'T KNOW. HE WAS JUST ON ONE NIGHT, IT WAS ONE OF THE LAST BROADCASTS I HEARD.
HE SAID IF YOU AREN'T ONE OF THE SAVED YOU'LL CROSS OVER, AND YOU'LL BE STUCK IN HELL-- BECAUSE THAT'S WHAT THE WORLD'S BECOMING, HELL. GOD'S PUT A CURSE ON US FOR THE SINS WE'VE COMMITTED AGAINST HIM.
AND THE CURSE IS IN THE *BLOOD*, THAT'S WHY IT SPREADS THE WAY IT DOES...!
I SEEM TO RECALL HAVING HEARD THAT KIND OF BULLSHIT BEFORE...
B-B-BUT WHAT IF IT'S *TRUE--?*
THEN IT DOESN'T SAY A WHOLE HELL OF A LOT FOR GOD, DOES IT?
ANYONE COMES WITH ME'LL HAVE TO LEARN TO DO THINGS MY WAY.

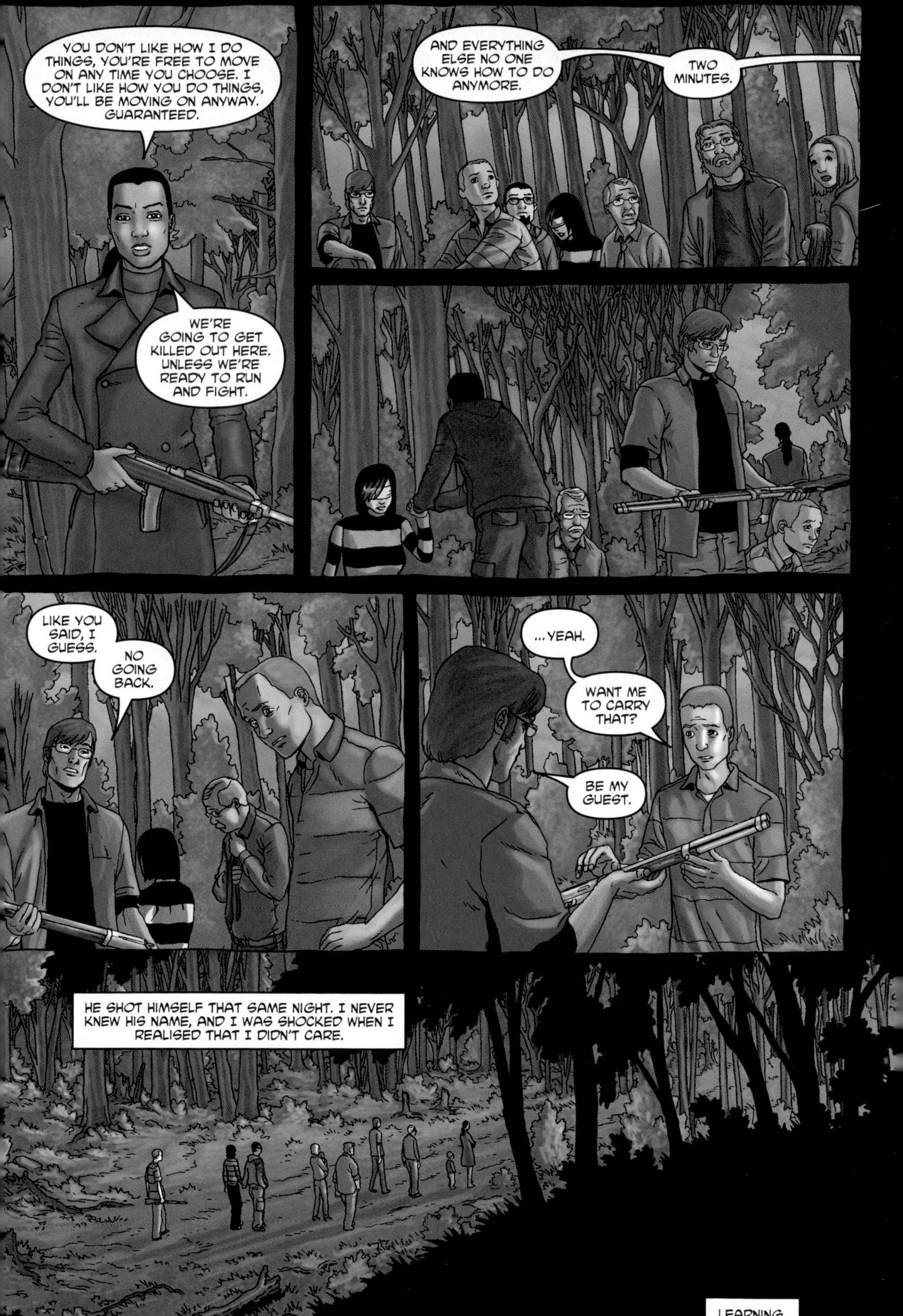

YOU DON'T LIKE HOW I DO THINGS, YOU'RE FREE TO MOVE ON ANY TIME YOU CHOOSE. I DON'T LIKE HOW YOU DO THINGS, YOU'LL BE MOVING ON ANYWAY. GUARANTEED.
WE'RE GOING TO GET KILLED OUT HERE. UNLESS WE'RE READY TO RUN AND FIGHT.
AND EVERYTHING ELSE NO ONE KNOWS HOW TO DO ANYMORE.
TWO MINUTES.
LIKE YOU SAID, I GUESS.
NO GOING BACK.
...YEAH.
WANT ME TO CARRY THAT?
BE MY GUEST.
HE SHOT HIMSELF THAT SAME NIGHT. I NEVER KNEW HIS NAME, AND I WAS SHOCKED WHEN I REALISED THAT I DIDN'T CARE.
LEARNING.

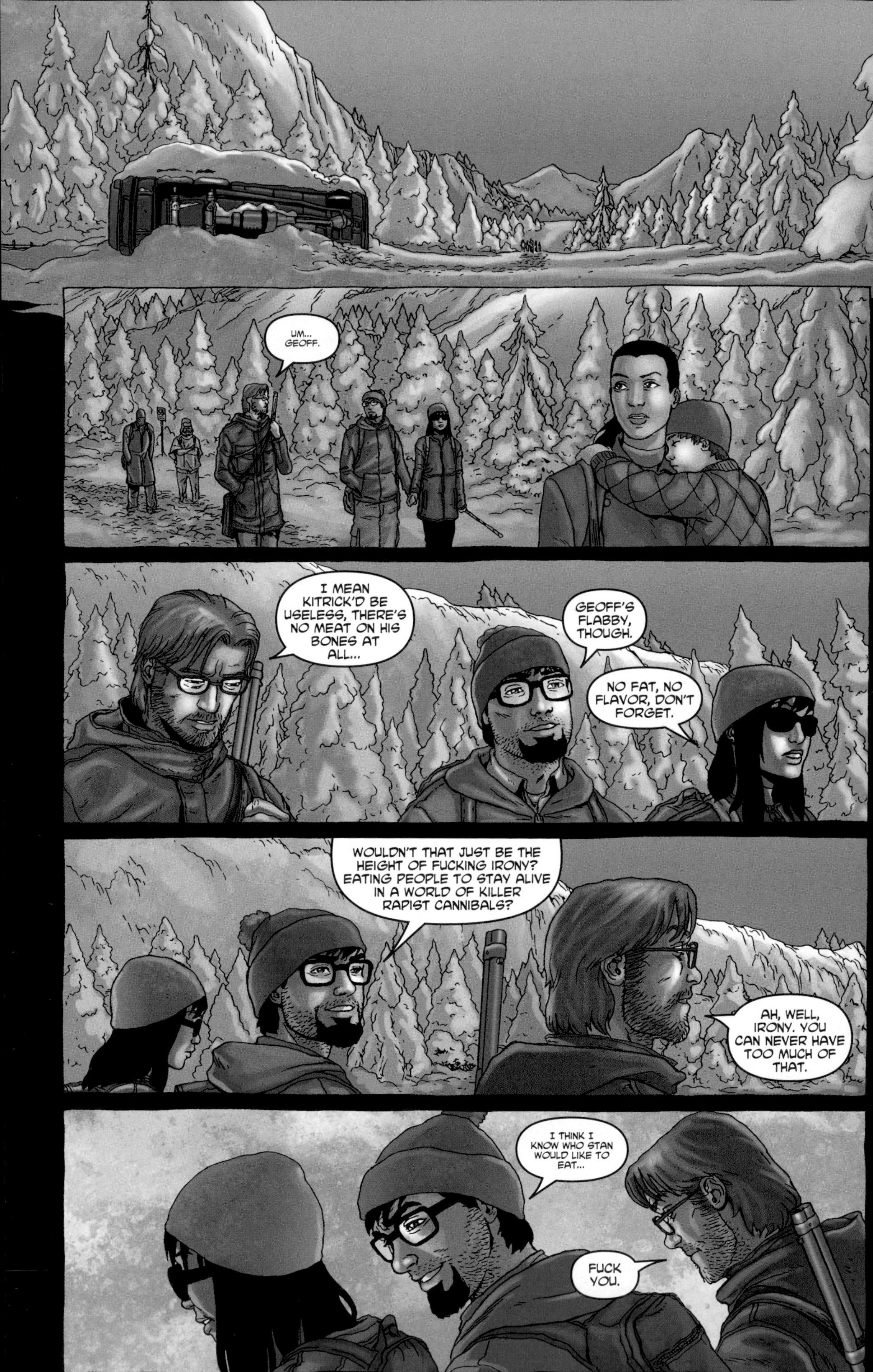
UM... GEOFF.
I MEAN KITRICK'D BE USELESS, THERE'S NO MEAT ON HIS BONES AT ALL...
GEOFF'S FLABBY, THOUGH.
NO FAT, NO FLAVOR, DON'T FORGET.
WOULDN'T THAT JUST BE THE HEIGHT OF FUCKING IRONY? EATING PEOPLE TO STAY ALIVE IN A WORLD OF KILLER RAPIST CANNIBALS?
AH, WELL, IRONY. YOU CAN NEVER HAVE TOO MUCH OF THAT.
I THINK I KNOW WHO STAN WOULD LIKE TO EAT...
FUCK YOU.

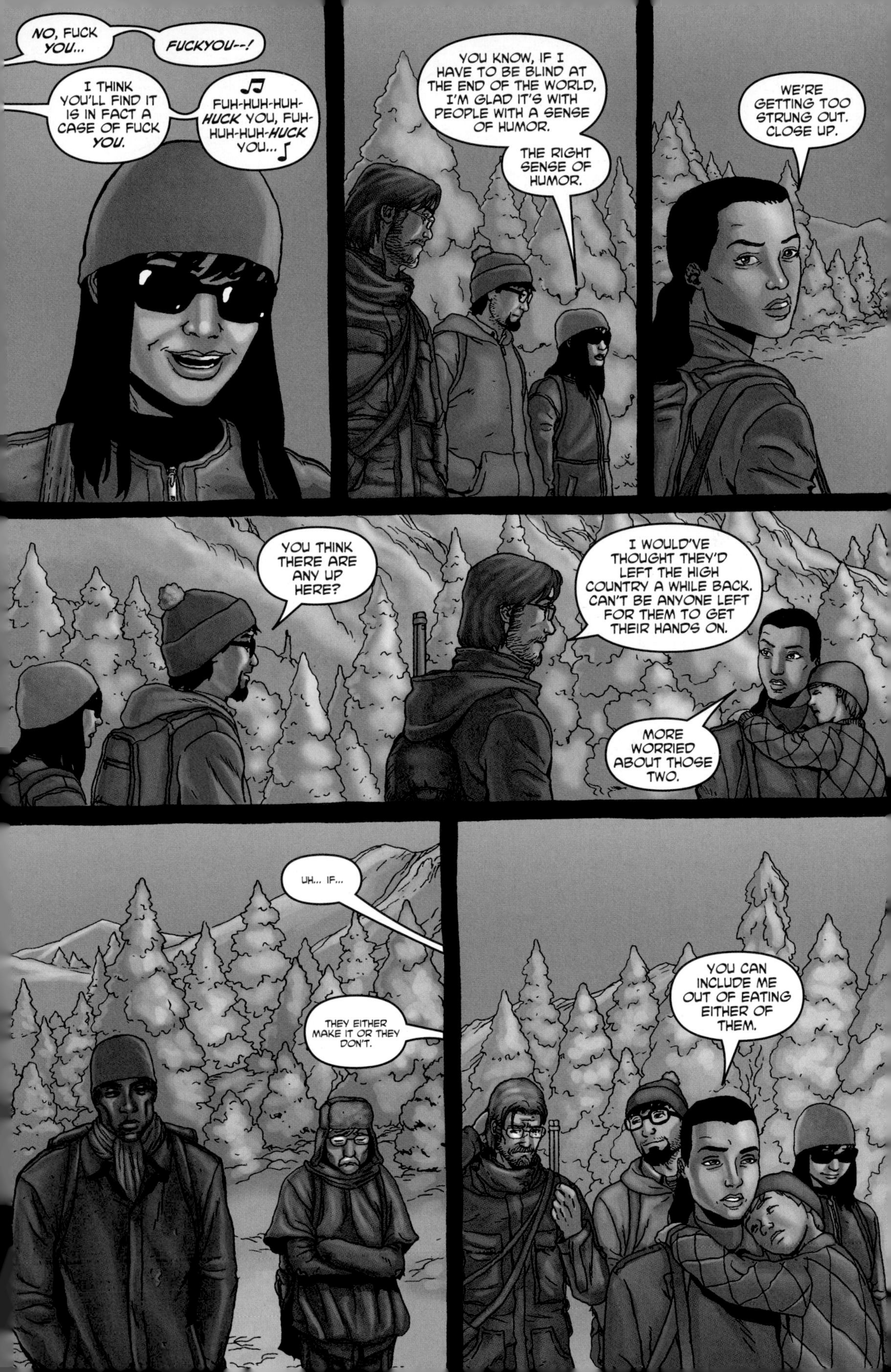
NO, FUCK YOU...
FUCKYOU--!
I THINK YOU'LL FIND IT IS IN FACT A CASE OF FUCK YOU.
FUH-HUH-HUH-HUCK YOU, FUH-HUH-HUH-HUCK YOU...
YOU KNOW, IF I HAVE TO BE BLIND AT THE END OF THE WORLD, I'M GLAD IT'S WITH PEOPLE WITH A SENSE OF HUMOR.
THE RIGHT SENSE OF HUMOR.
WE'RE GETTING TOO STRUNG OUT. CLOSE UP.
YOU THINK THERE ARE ANY UP HERE?
I WOULD'VE THOUGHT THEY'D LEFT THE HIGH COUNTRY A WHILE BACK. CAN'T BE ANYONE LEFT FOR THEM TO GET THEIR HANDS ON.
MORE WORRIED ABOUT THOSE TWO.
UH... IF...
THEY EITHER MAKE IT OR THEY DON'T.
YOU CAN INCLUDE ME OUT OF EATING EITHER OF THEM.

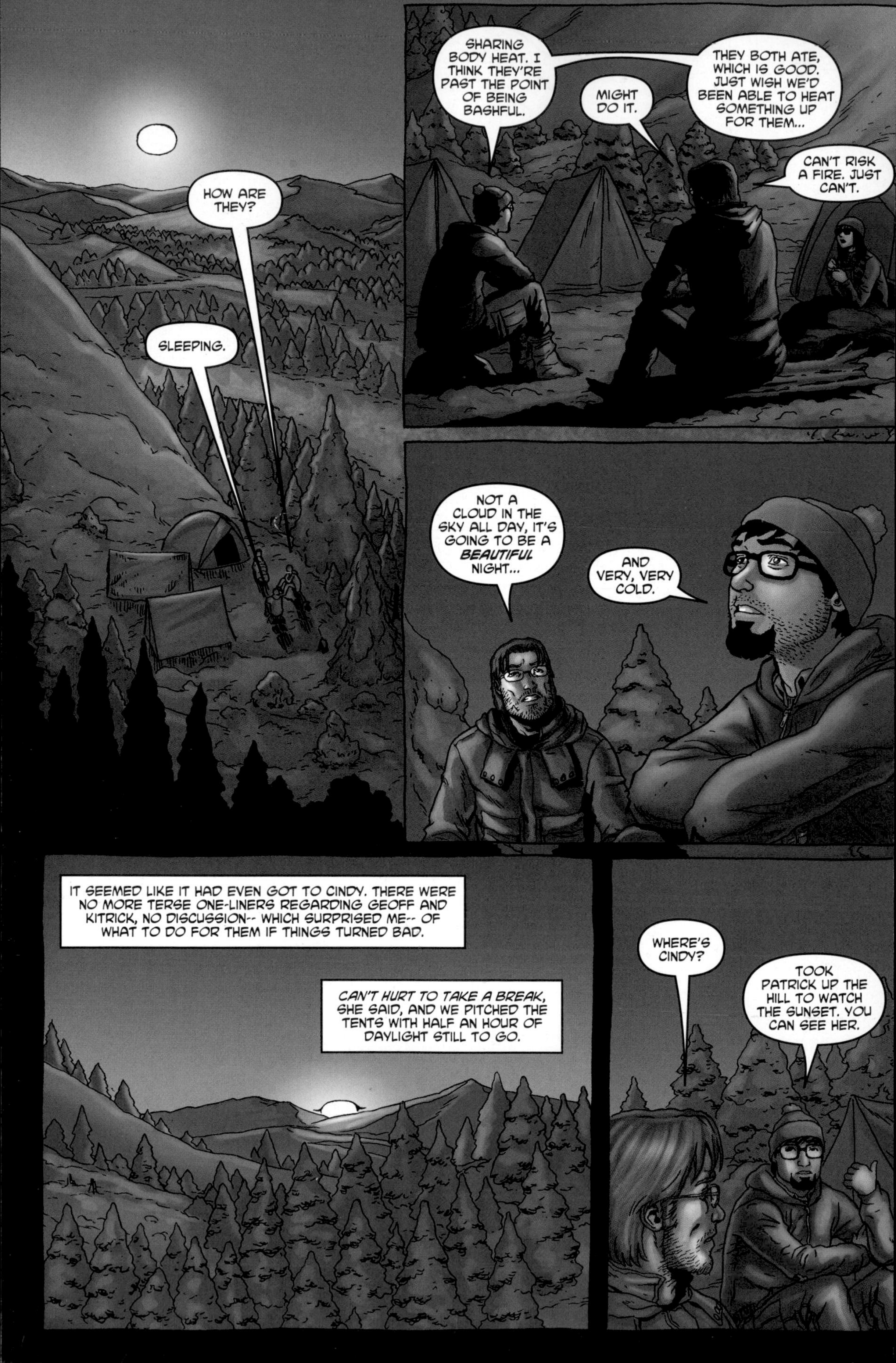

HOW ARE THEY?
SLEEPING.
SHARING BODY HEAT. I THINK THEY'RE PAST THE POINT OF BEING BASHFUL.
MIGHT DO IT.
THEY BOTH ATE, WHICH IS GOOD. JUST WISH WE'D BEEN ABLE TO HEAT SOMETHING UP FOR THEM...
CAN'T RISK A FIRE. JUST CAN'T.
NOT A CLOUD IN THE SKY ALL DAY, IT'S GOING TO BE A *BEAUTIFUL* NIGHT...
AND VERY, VERY COLD.
IT SEEMED LIKE IT HAD EVEN GOT TO CINDY. THERE WERE NO MORE TERSE ONE-LINERS REGARDING GEOFF AND KITRICK, NO DISCUSSION-- WHICH SURPRISED ME-- OF WHAT TO DO FOR THEM IF THINGS TURNED BAD.
CAN'T HURT TO TAKE A BREAK, SHE SAID, AND WE PITCHED THE TENTS WITH HALF AN HOUR OF DAYLIGHT STILL TO GO.
WHERE'S CINDY?
TOOK PATRICK UP THE HILL TO WATCH THE SUNSET. YOU CAN SEE HER.

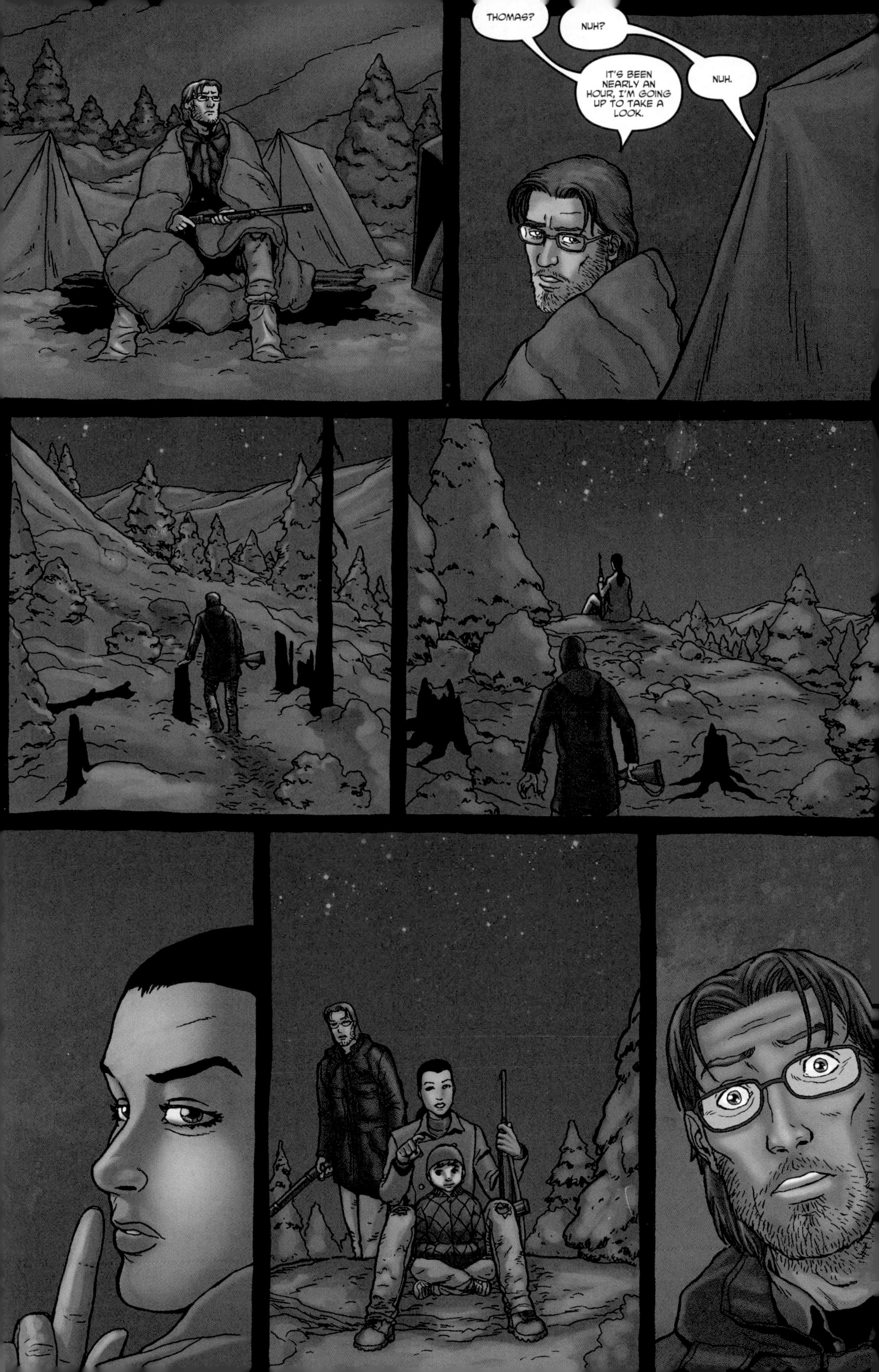
THOMAS?
NUH?
IT'S BEEN NEARLY AN HOUR, I'M GOING UP TO TAKE A LOOK.
NUH.

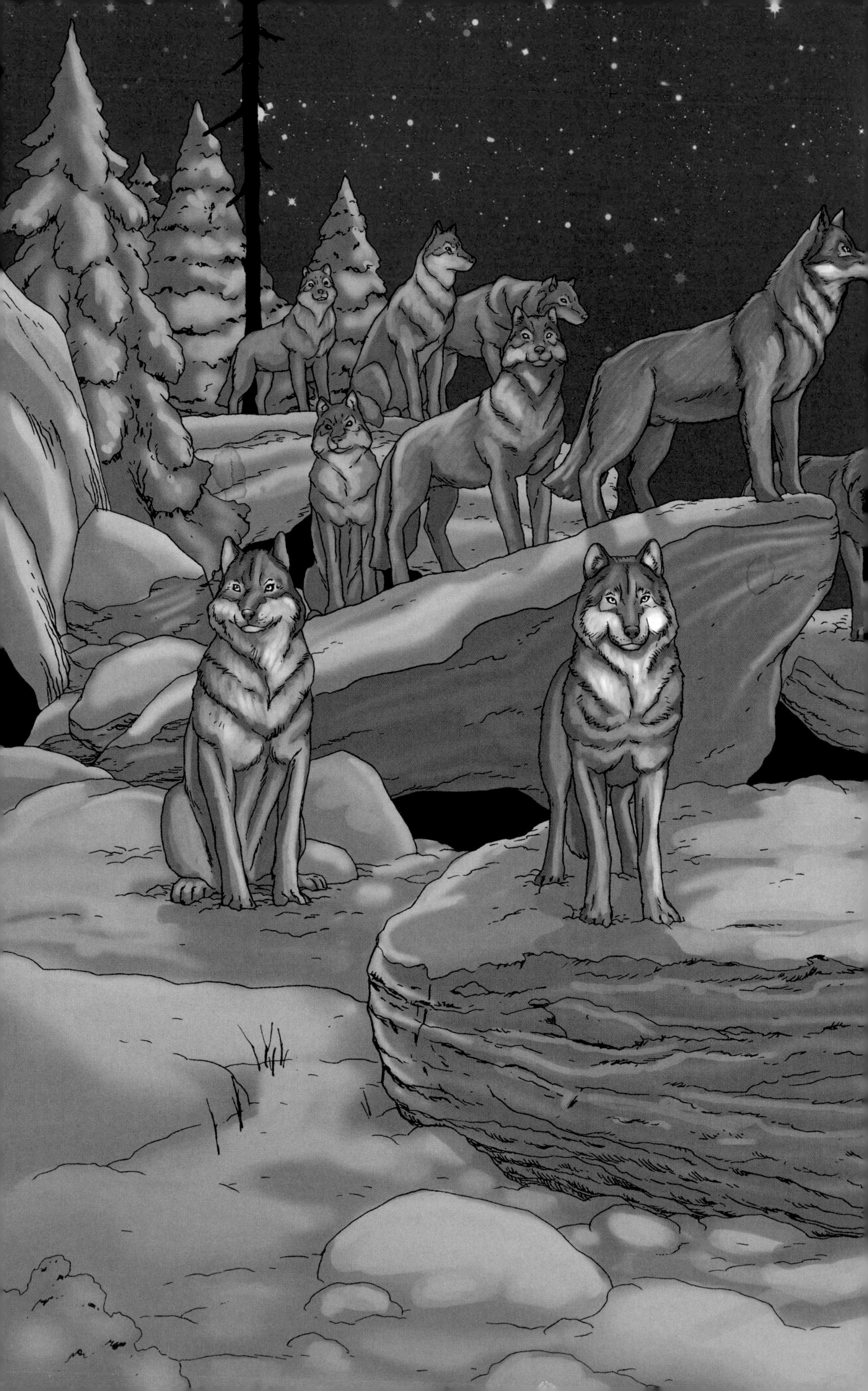

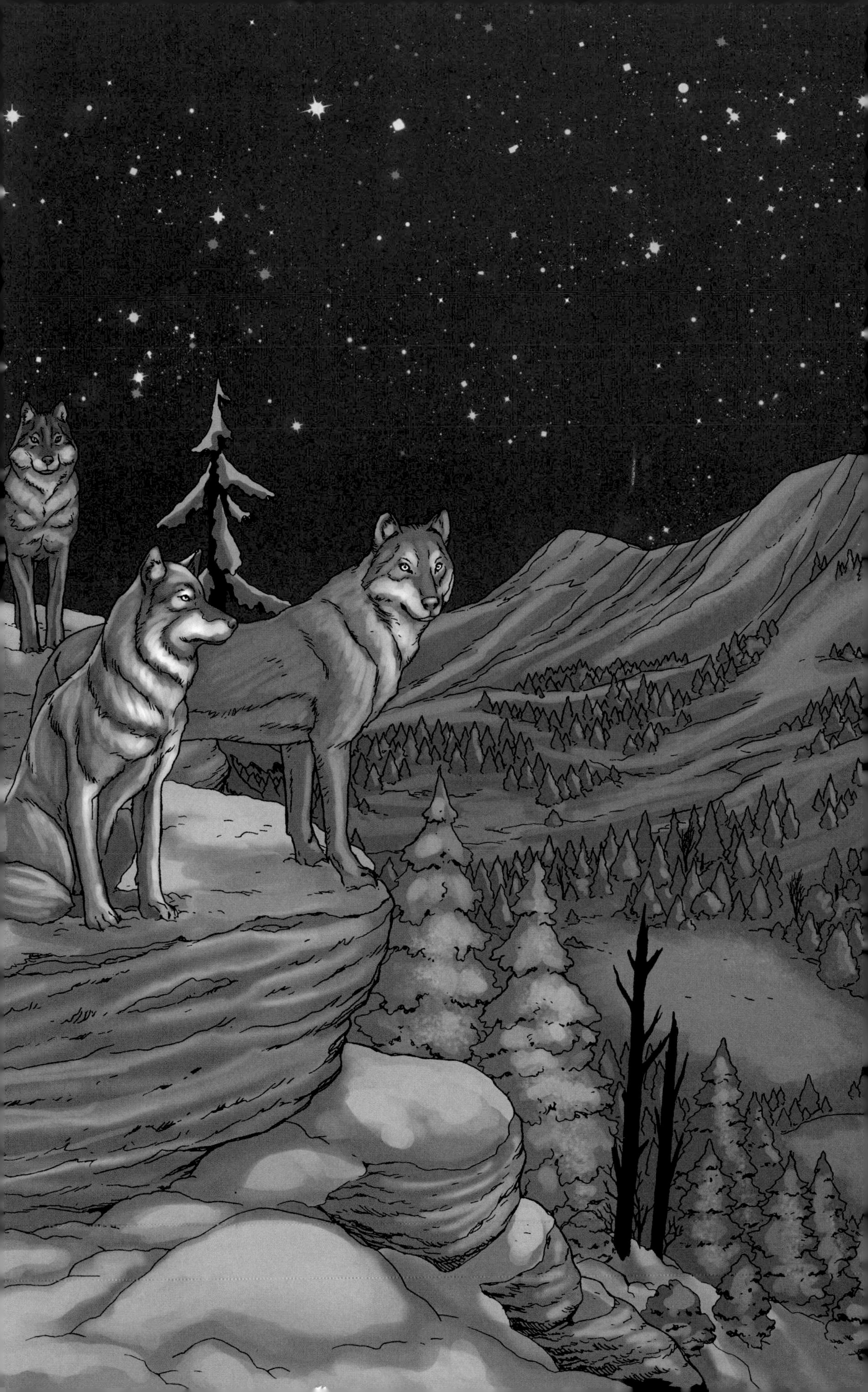

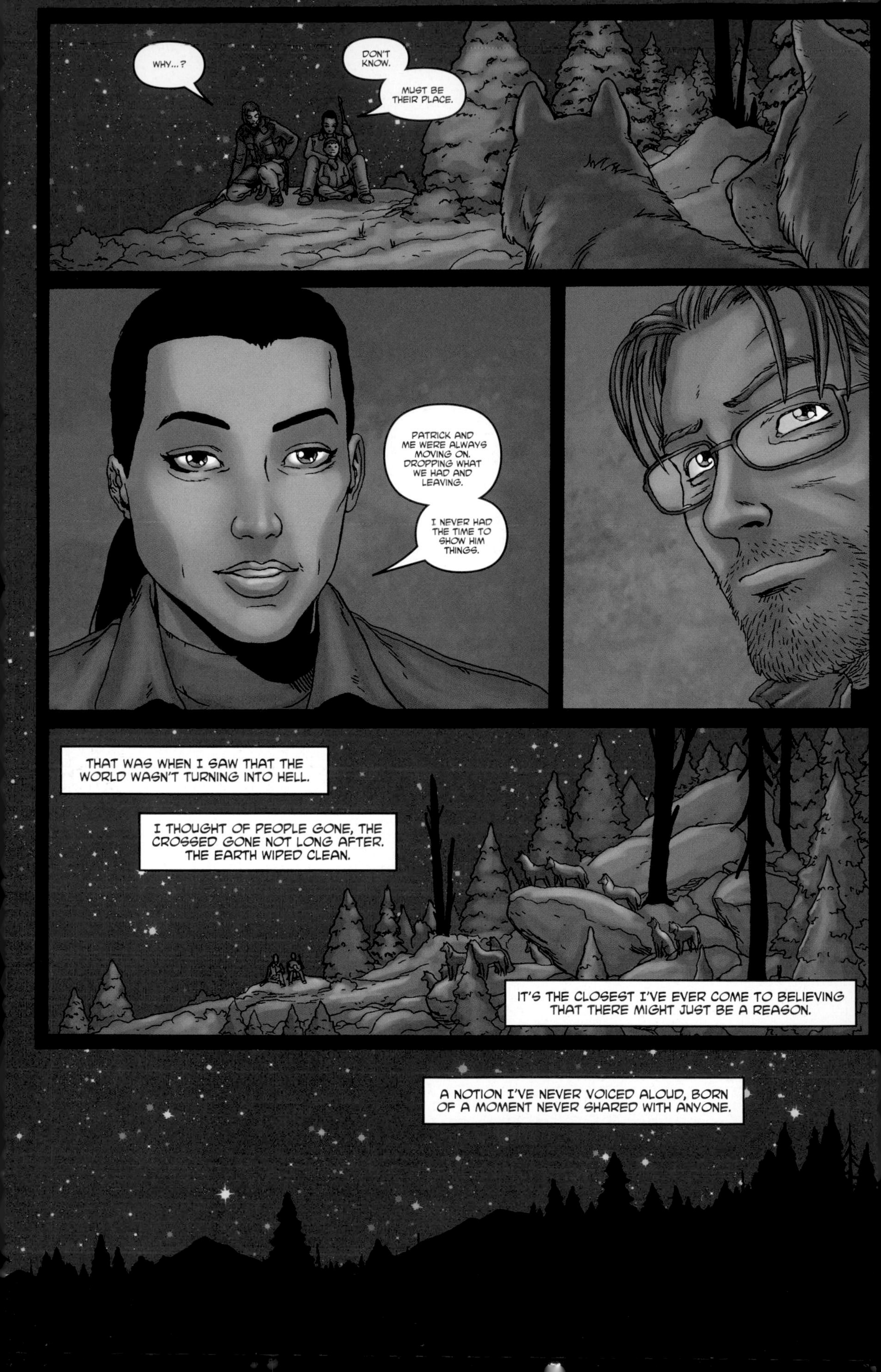
WHY...?
DON'T KNOW.
MUST BE THEIR PLACE.
PATRICK AND ME WERE ALWAYS MOVING ON. DROPPING WHAT WE HAD AND LEAVING.
I NEVER HAD THE TIME TO SHOW HIM THINGS.
THAT WAS WHEN I SAW THAT THE WORLD WASN'T TURNING INTO HELL.
I THOUGHT OF PEOPLE GONE, THE CROSSED GONE NOT LONG AFTER. THE EARTH WIPED CLEAN.
IT'S THE CLOSEST I'VE EVER COME TO BELIEVING THAT THERE MIGHT JUST BE A REASON.
A NOTION I'VE NEVER VOICED ALOUD, BORN OF A MOMENT NEVER SHARED WITH ANYONE.

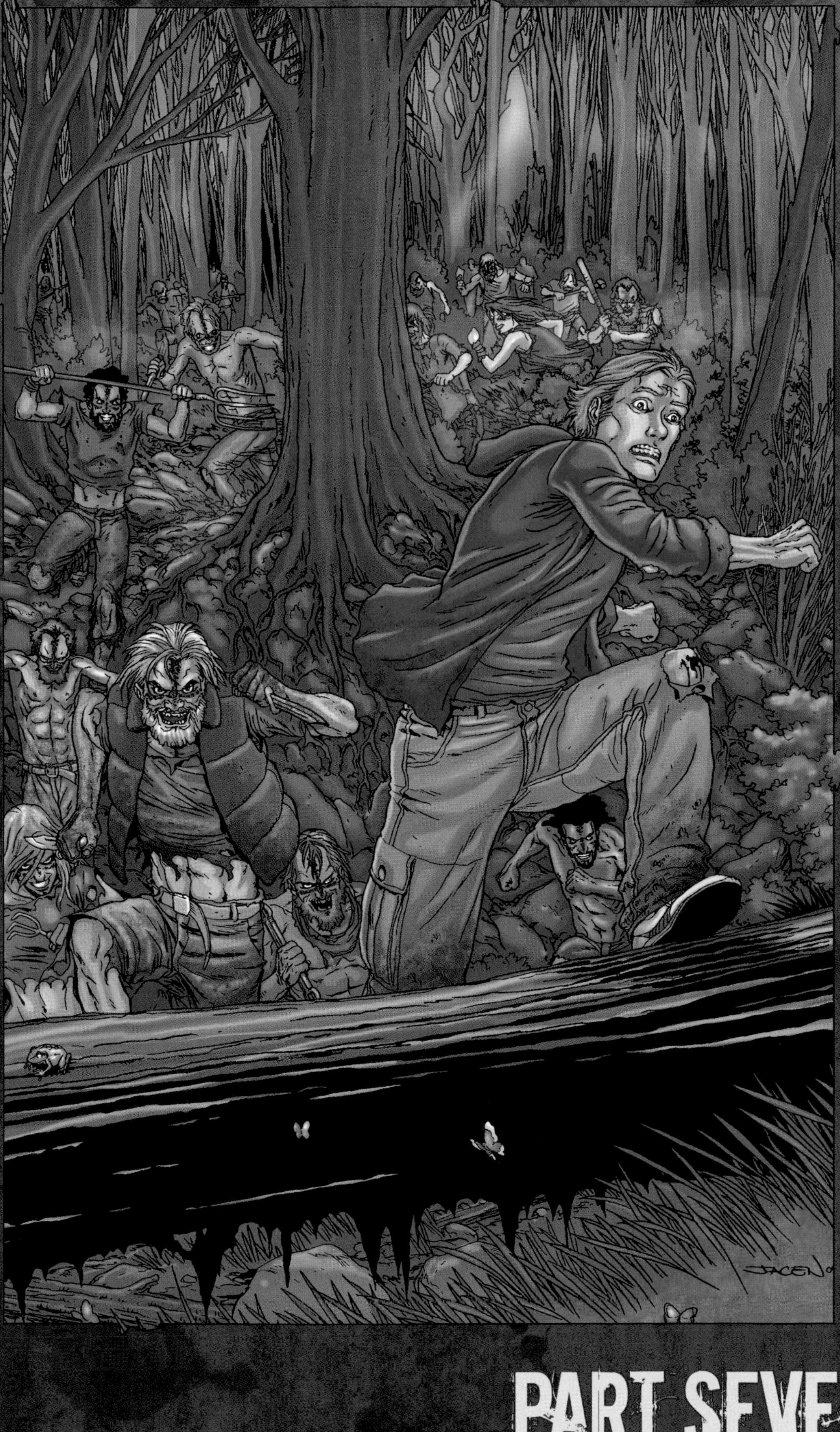

PART SEVEN

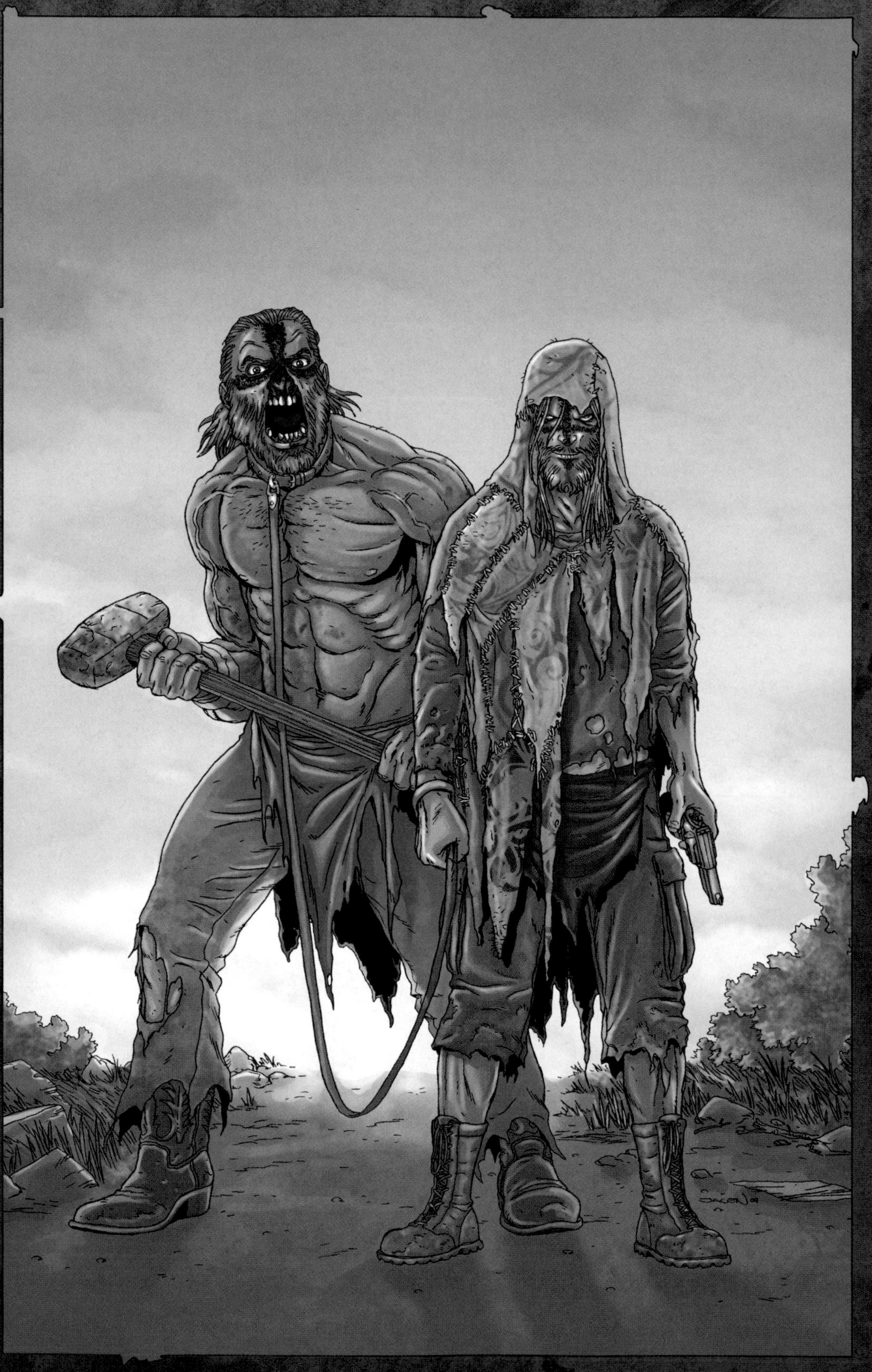

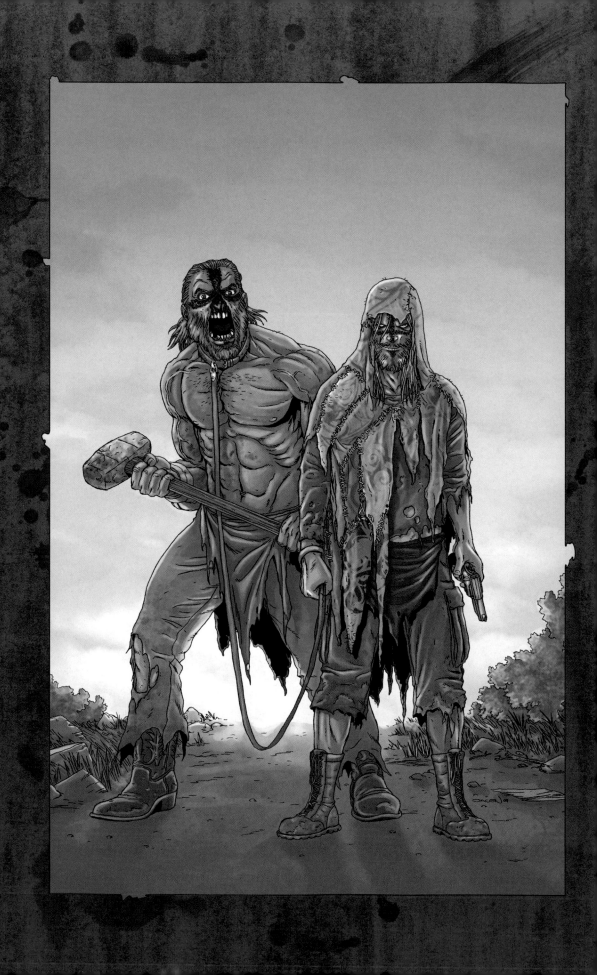

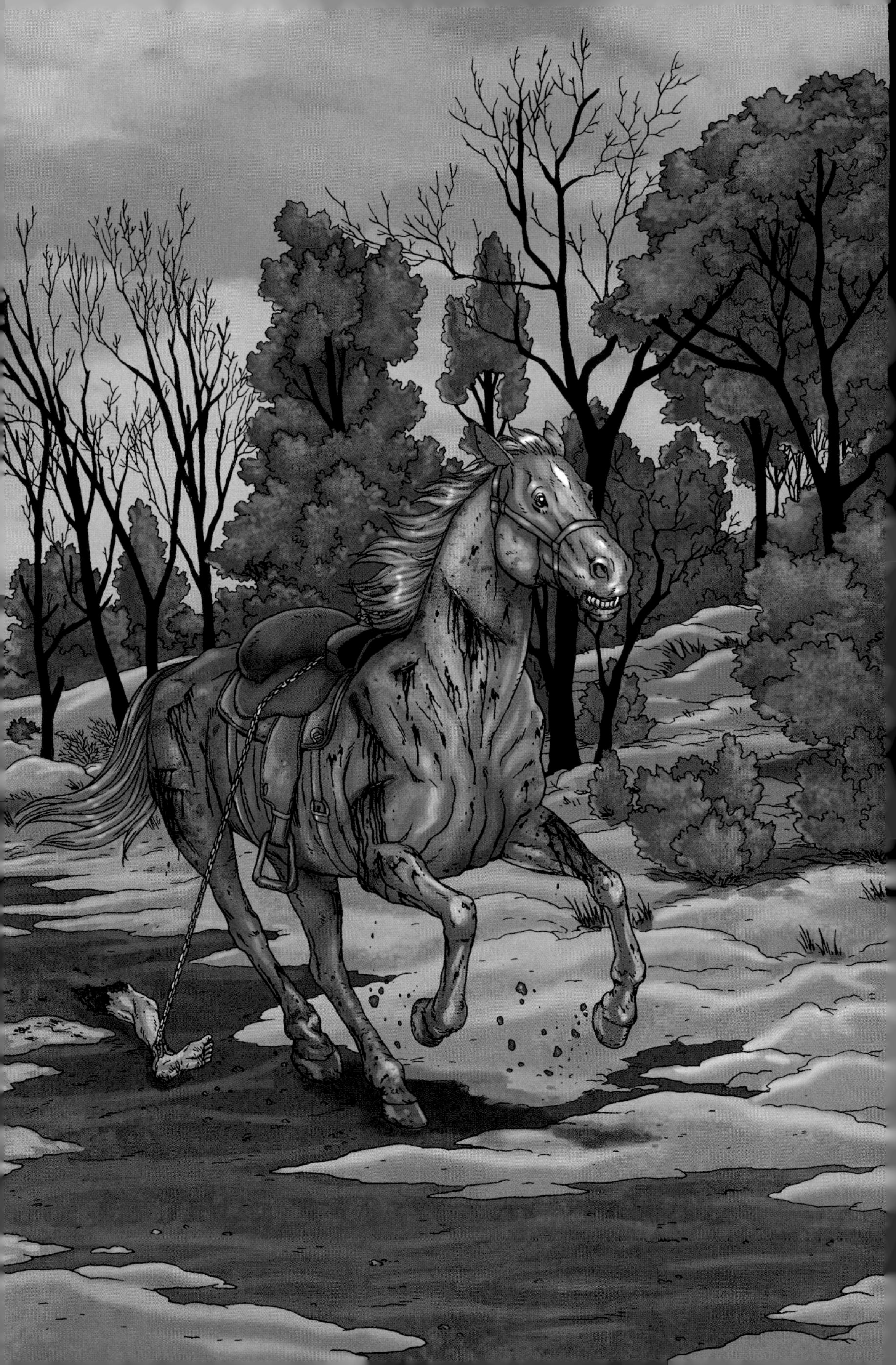

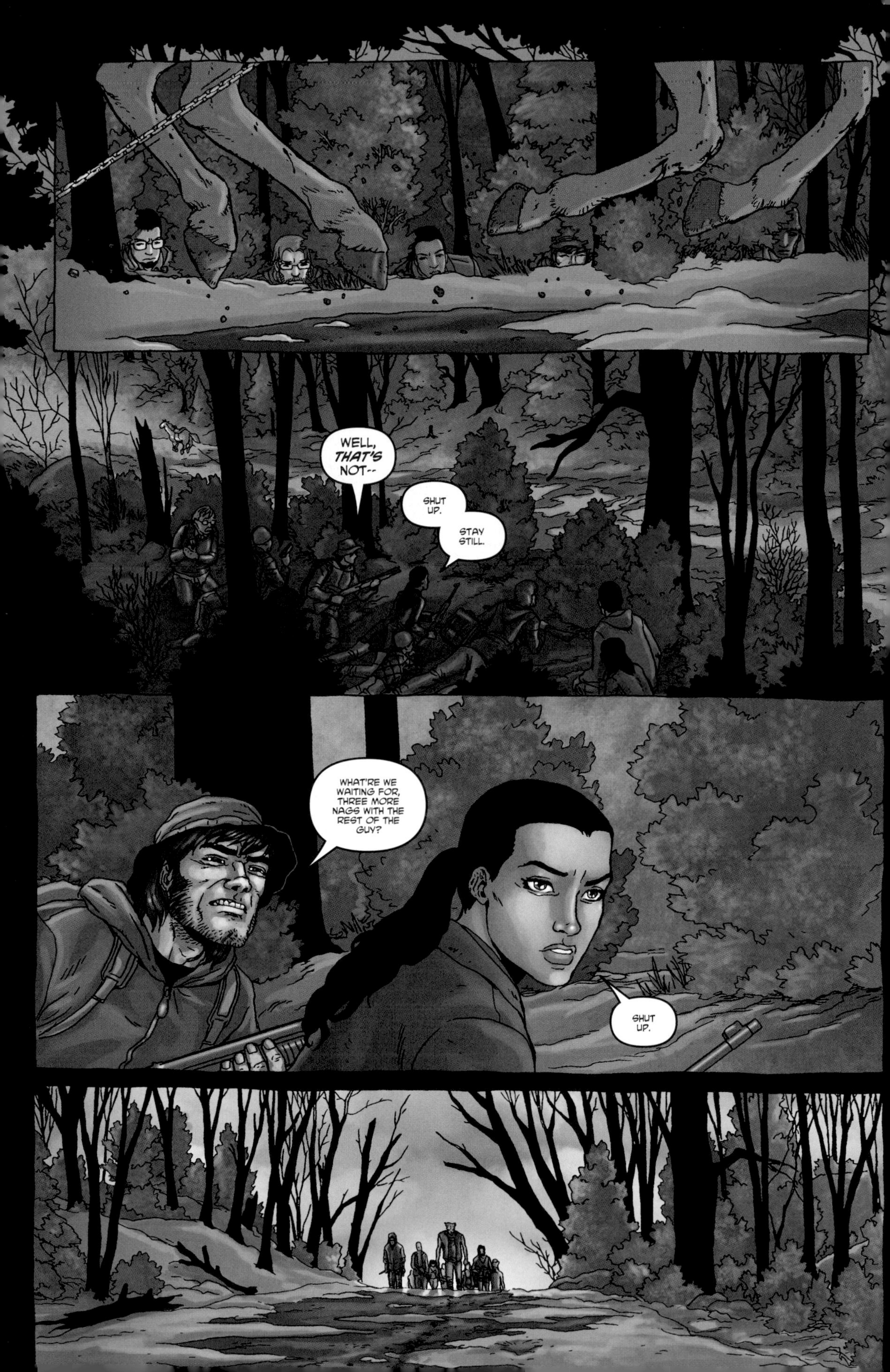

WELL, THAT'S NOT--
SHUT UP.
STAY STILL.
WHAT'RE WE WAITING FOR, THREE MORE NAGS WITH THE REST OF THE GUY?
SHUT UP.

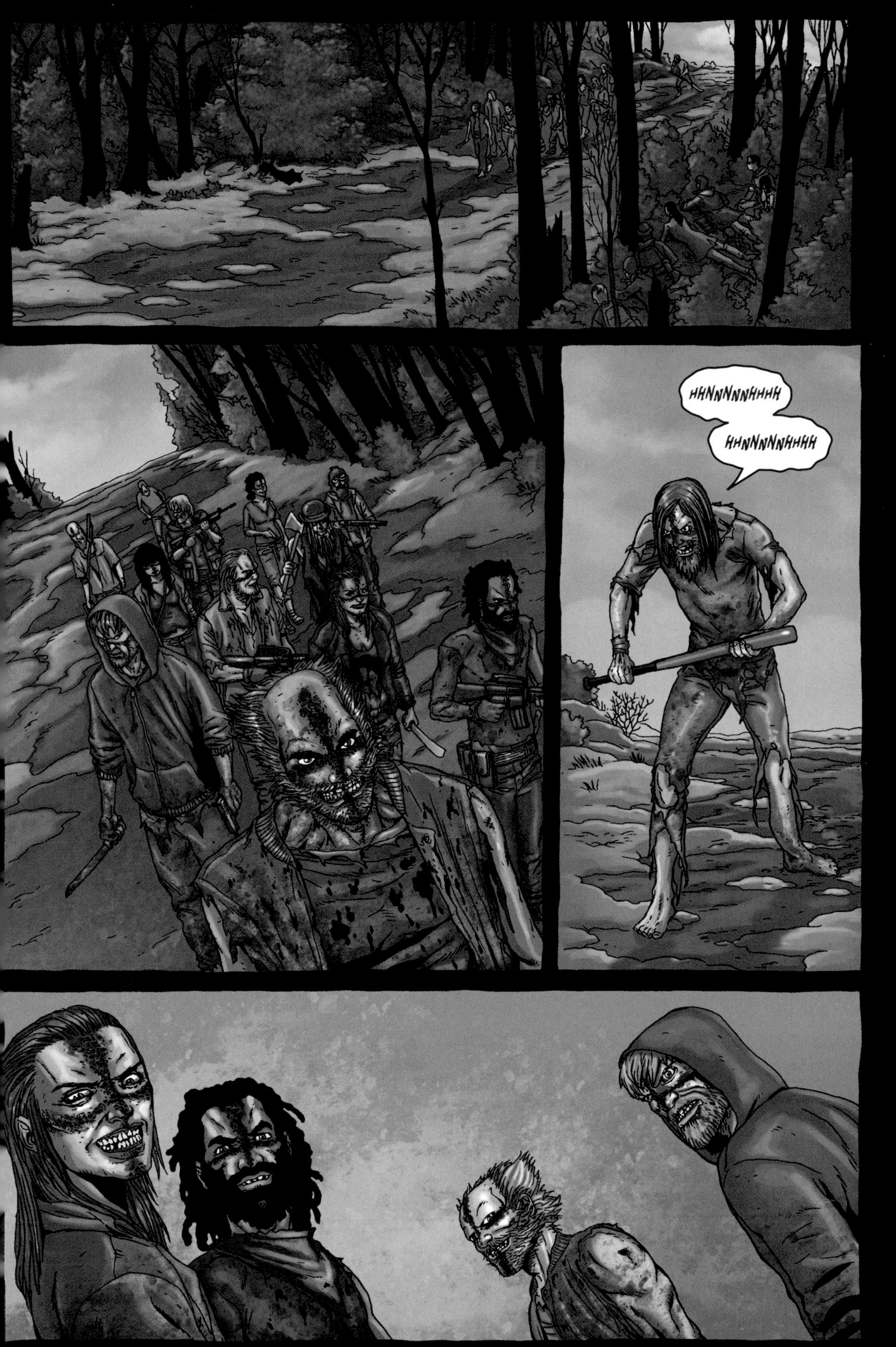
HHNNNNNHHHH
HHNNNNNHHHH

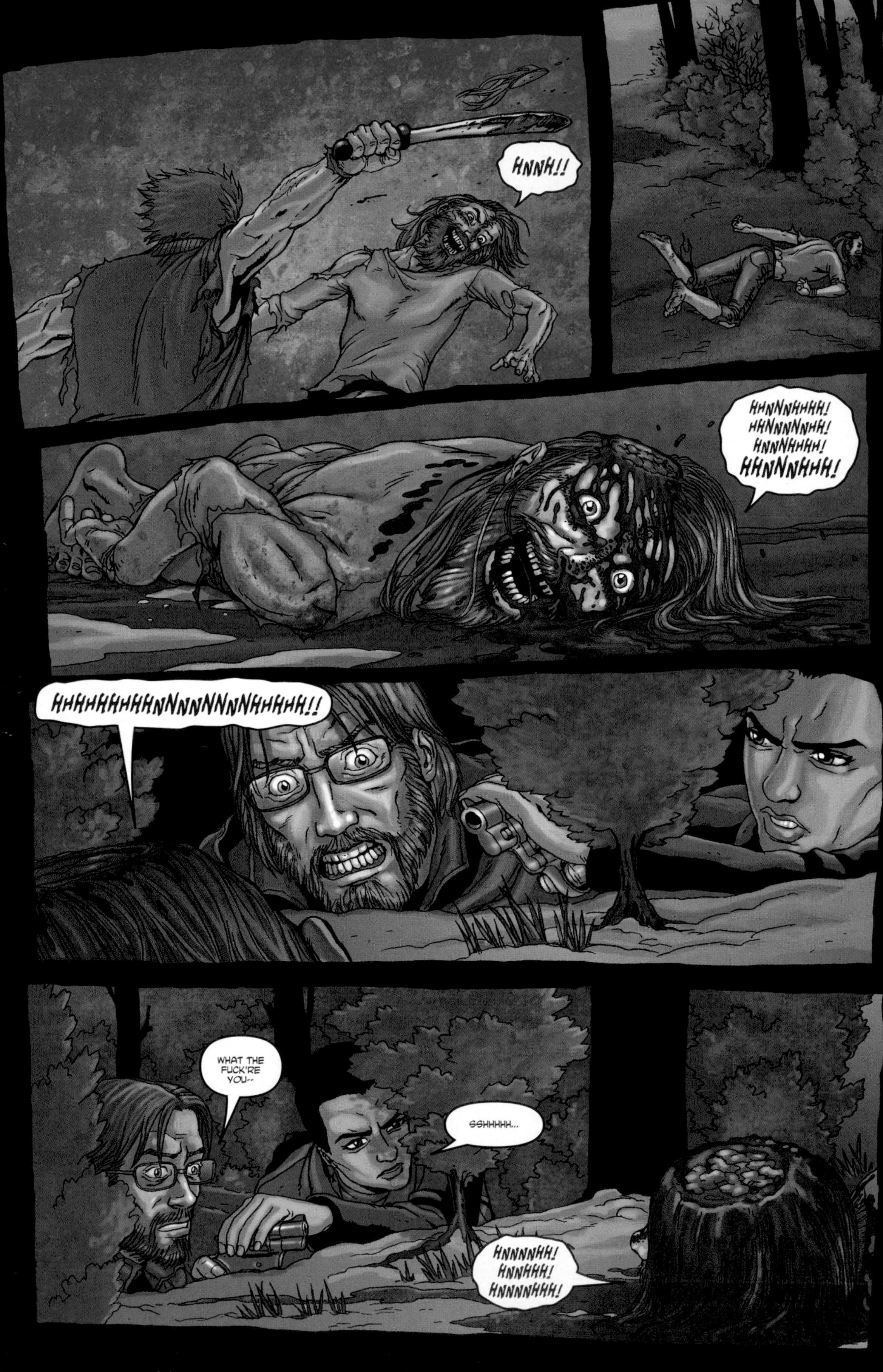
HNNH!!
HHNNNHHHH!
HHNNNNNHH!
HNNNHHHH!
HHNNHHH!
HHHHHHHHNNNNNNNHHHHH!!
WHAT THE FUCK'RE YOU--
SSHHHHH...
HNNNNHH!
HNNHHH!
HNNNNHH!

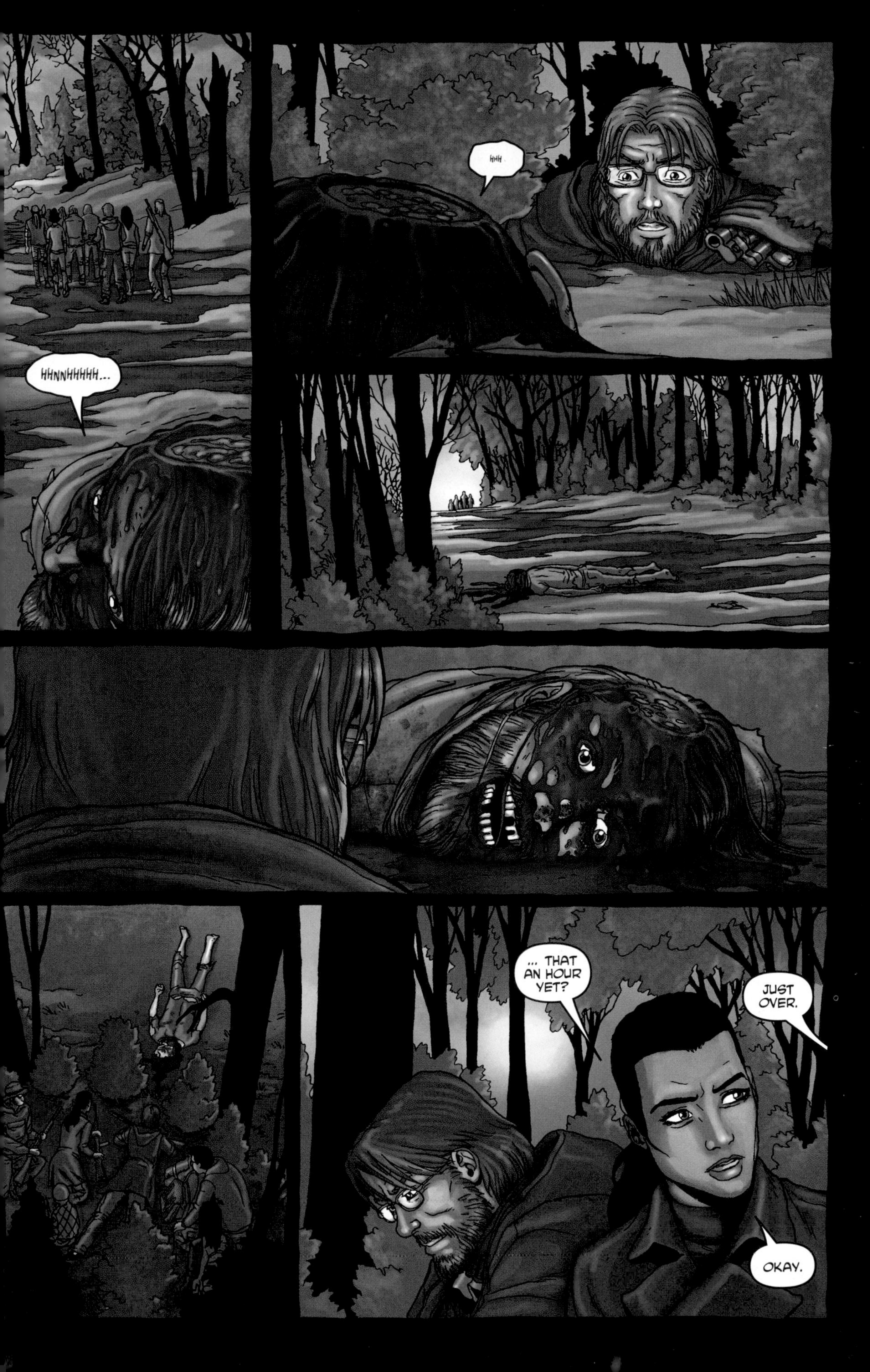
HHH.
HHNNHHHHH...
... THAT AN HOUR YET?
JUST OVER.
OKAY.

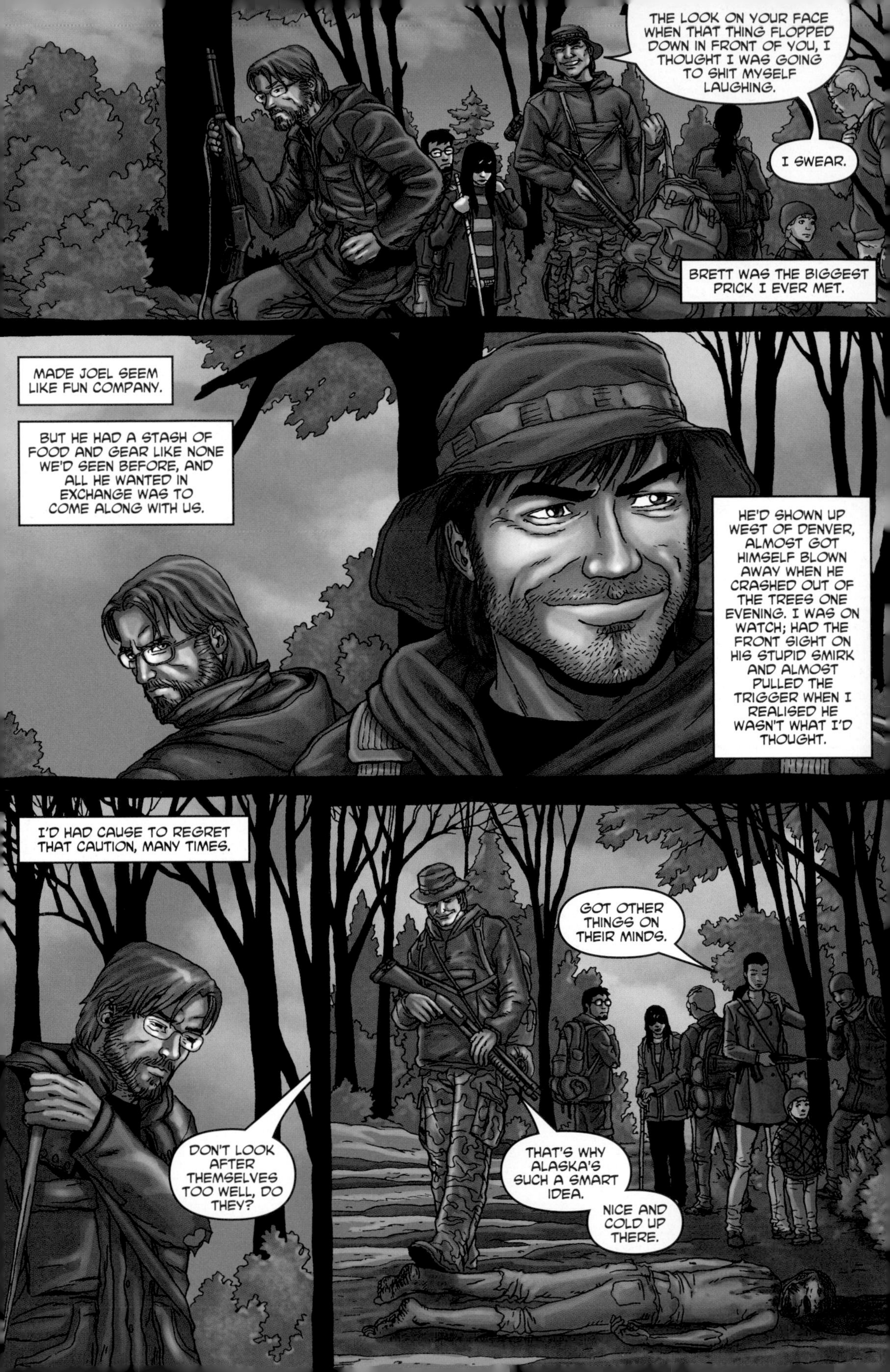
THE LOOK ON YOUR FACE WHEN THAT THING FLOPPED DOWN IN FRONT OF YOU, I THOUGHT I WAS GOING TO SHIT MYSELF LAUGHING.
I SWEAR.
BRETT WAS THE BIGGEST PRICK I EVER MET.
MADE JOEL SEEM LIKE FUN COMPANY.
BUT HE HAD A STASH OF FOOD AND GEAR LIKE NONE WE'D SEEN BEFORE, AND ALL HE WANTED IN EXCHANGE WAS TO COME ALONG WITH US.
HE'D SHOWN UP WEST OF DENVER, ALMOST GOT HIMSELF BLOWN AWAY WHEN HE CRASHED OUT OF THE TREES ONE EVENING. I WAS ON WATCH; HAD THE FRONT SIGHT ON HIS STUPID SMIRK AND ALMOST PULLED THE TRIGGER WHEN I REALISED HE WASN'T WHAT I'D THOUGHT.
I'D HAD CAUSE TO REGRET THAT CAUTION, MANY TIMES.
DON'T LOOK AFTER THEMSELVES TOO WELL, DO THEY?
GOT OTHER THINGS ON THEIR MINDS.
THAT'S WHY ALASKA'S SUCH A SMART IDEA.
NICE AND COLD UP THERE.

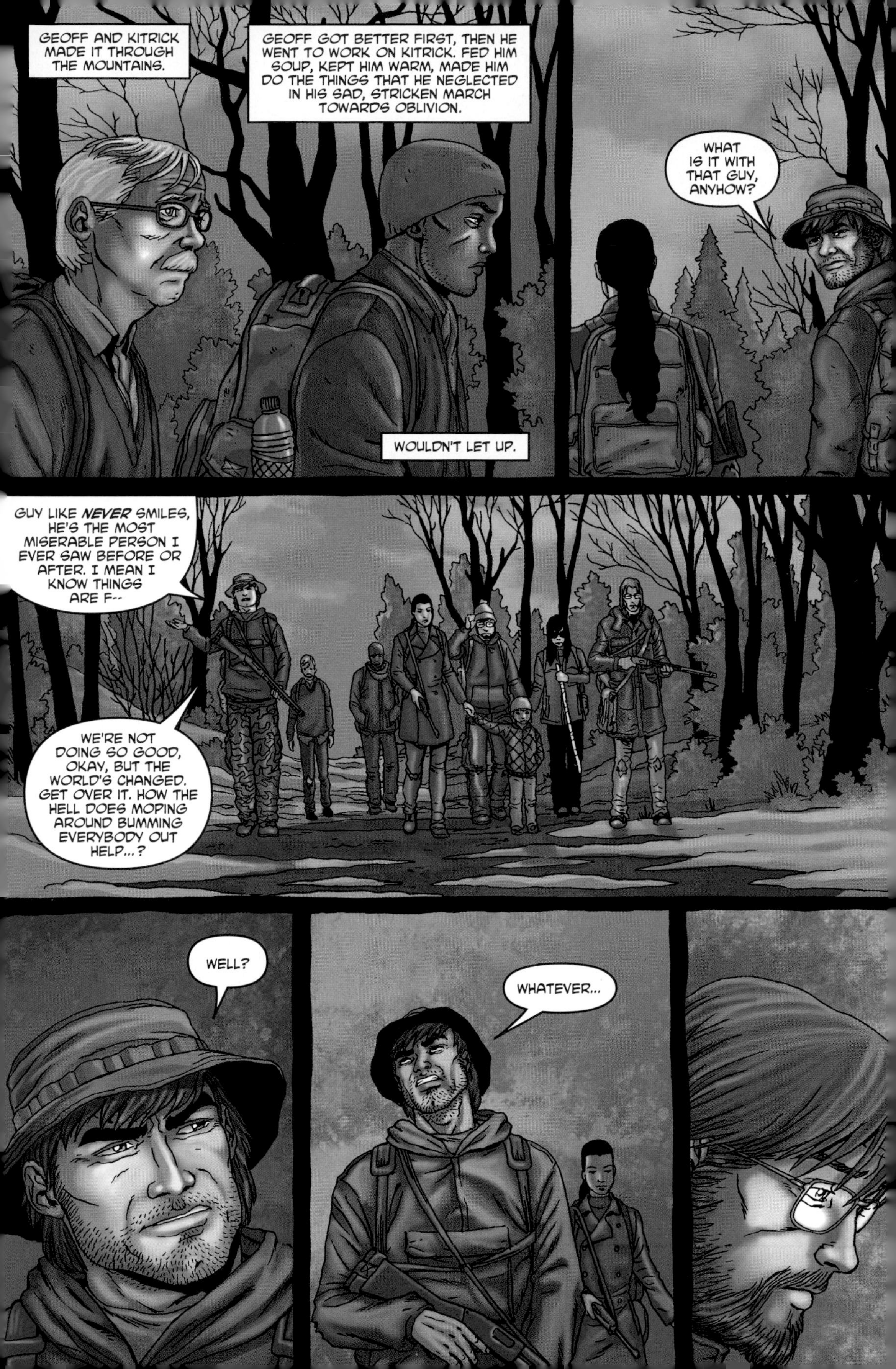
GEOFF AND KITRICK MADE IT THROUGH THE MOUNTAINS.
GEOFF GOT BETTER FIRST, THEN HE WENT TO WORK ON KITRICK. FED HIM SOUP, KEPT HIM WARM, MADE HIM DO THE THINGS THAT HE NEGLECTED IN HIS SAD, STRICKEN MARCH TOWARDS OBLIVION.
WOULDN'T LET UP.
WHAT IS IT WITH THAT GUY, ANYHOW?
GUY LIKE *NEVER* SMILES, HE'S THE MOST MISERABLE PERSON I EVER SAW BEFORE OR AFTER. I MEAN I KNOW THINGS ARE F--
WE'RE NOT DOING SO GOOD, OKAY, BUT THE WORLD'S CHANGED. GET OVER IT. HOW THE HELL DOES MOPING AROUND BUMMING EVERYBODY OUT HELP...?
WELL?
WHATEVER...

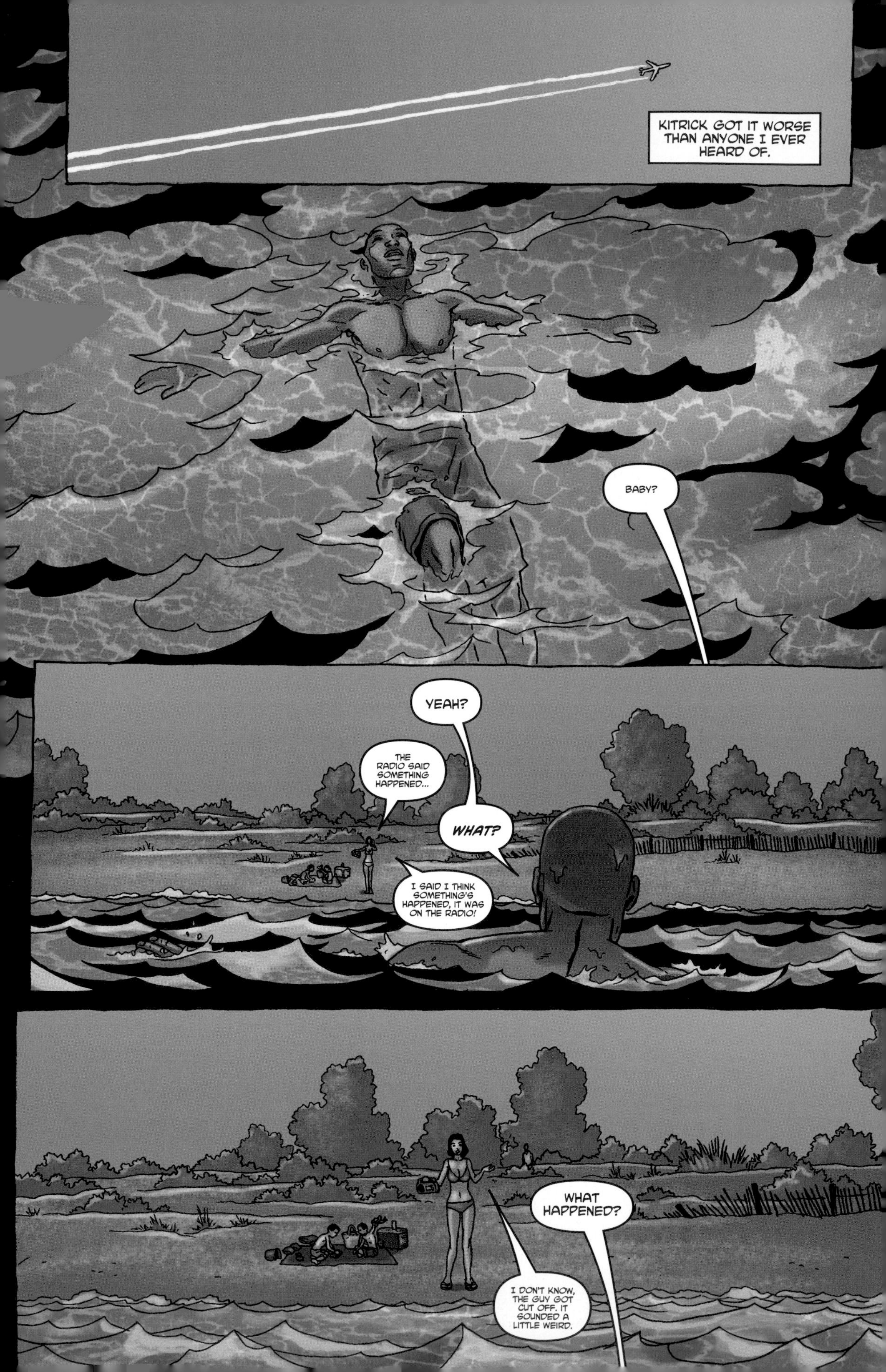
KITRICK GOT IT WORSE THAN ANYONE I EVER HEARD OF.
BABY?
YEAH?
THE RADIO SAID SOMETHING HAPPENED...
WHAT?
I SAID I THINK SOMETHING'S HAPPENED, IT WAS ON THE RADIO!
WHAT HAPPENED?
I DON'T KNOW, THE GUY GOT CUT OFF. IT SOUNDED A LITTLE WEIRD.

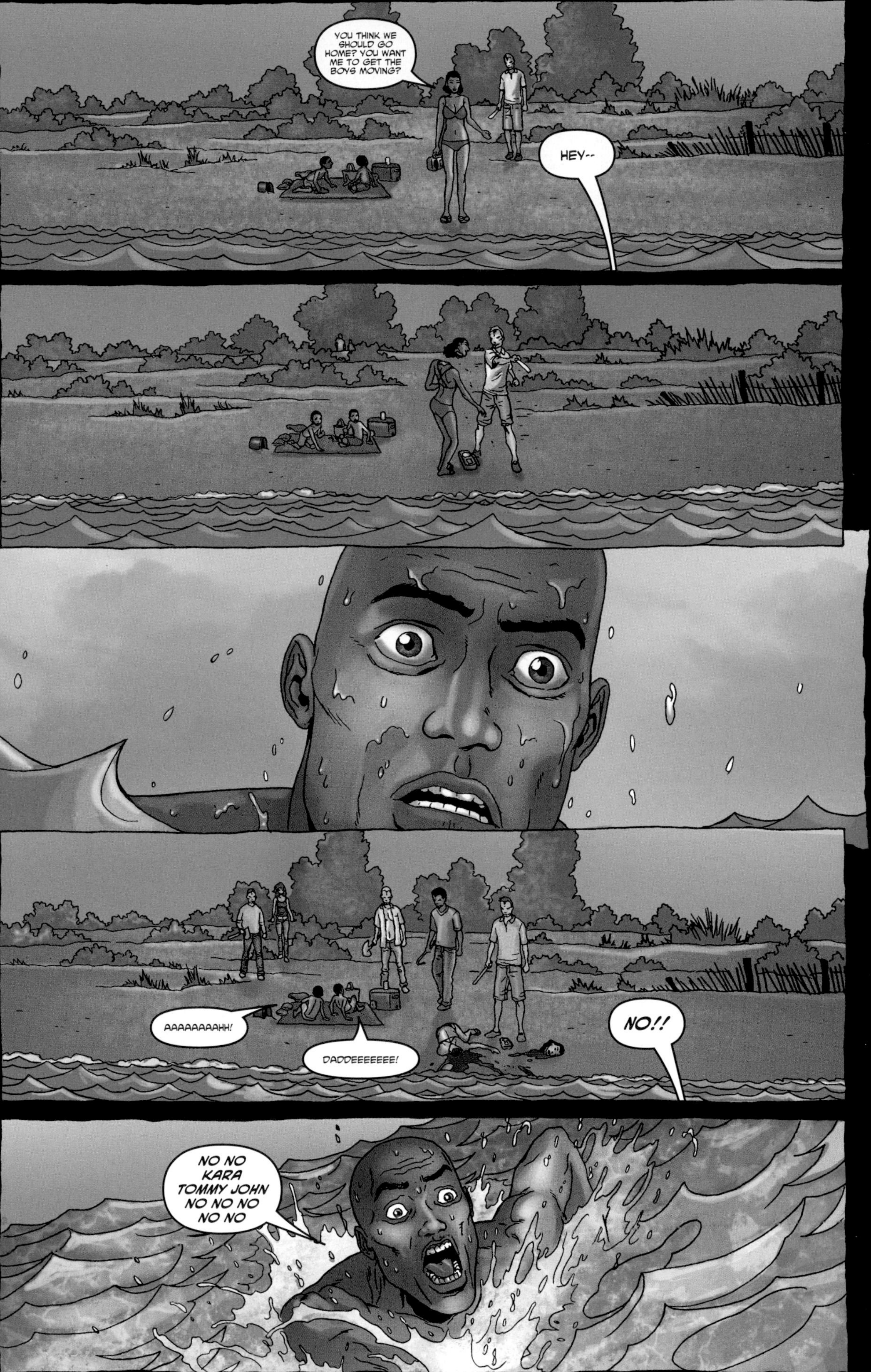
YOU THINK WE SHOULD GO HOME? YOU WANT ME TO GET THE BOYS MOVING?
HEY--
AAAAAAAAAH!
DADDEEEEEEE!
NO!!
NO NO KARA TOMMY JOHN NO NO NO NO NO

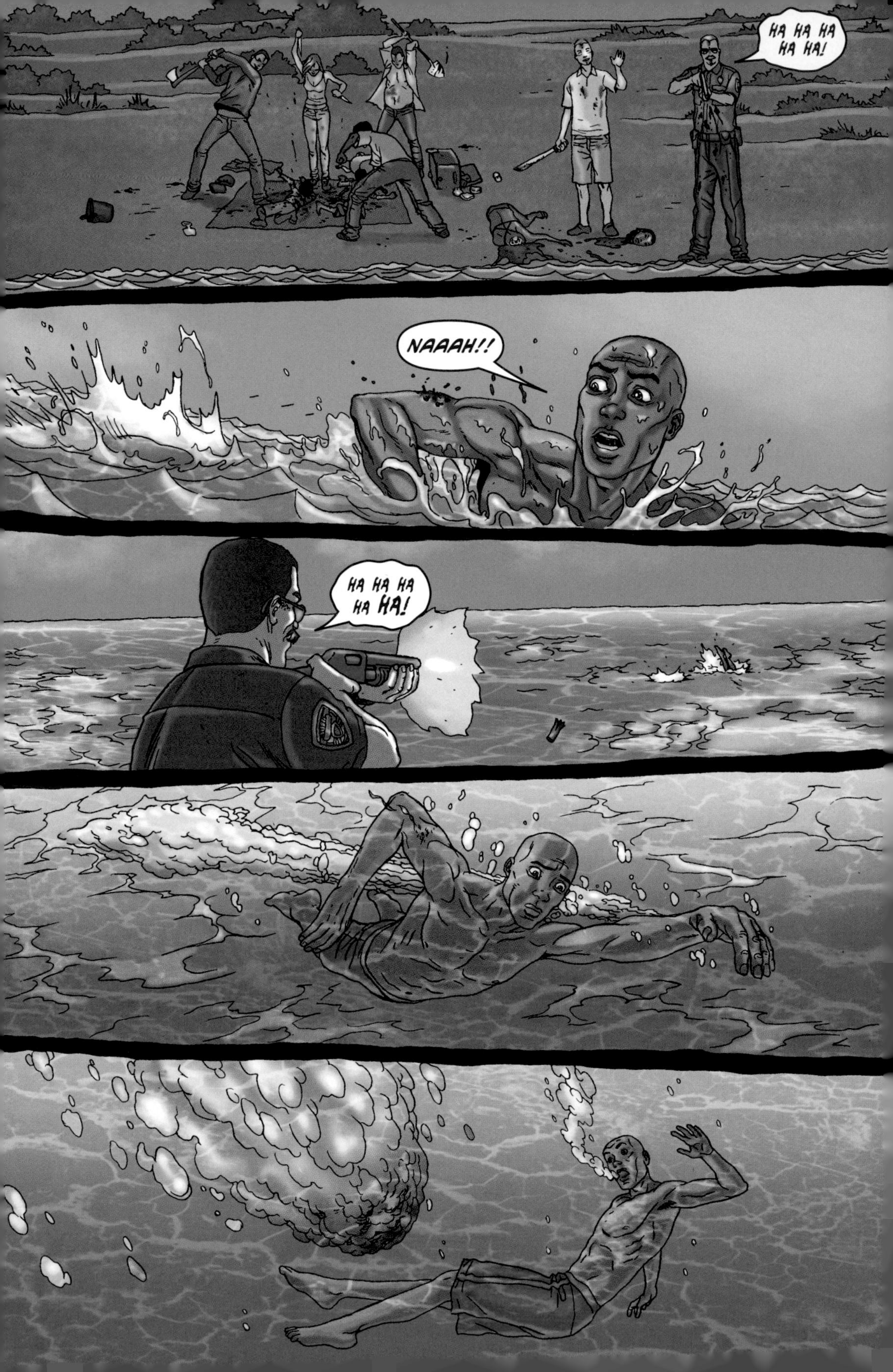
HA HA HA
HA HA!
NAAAH!!
HA HA HA
HA HA!

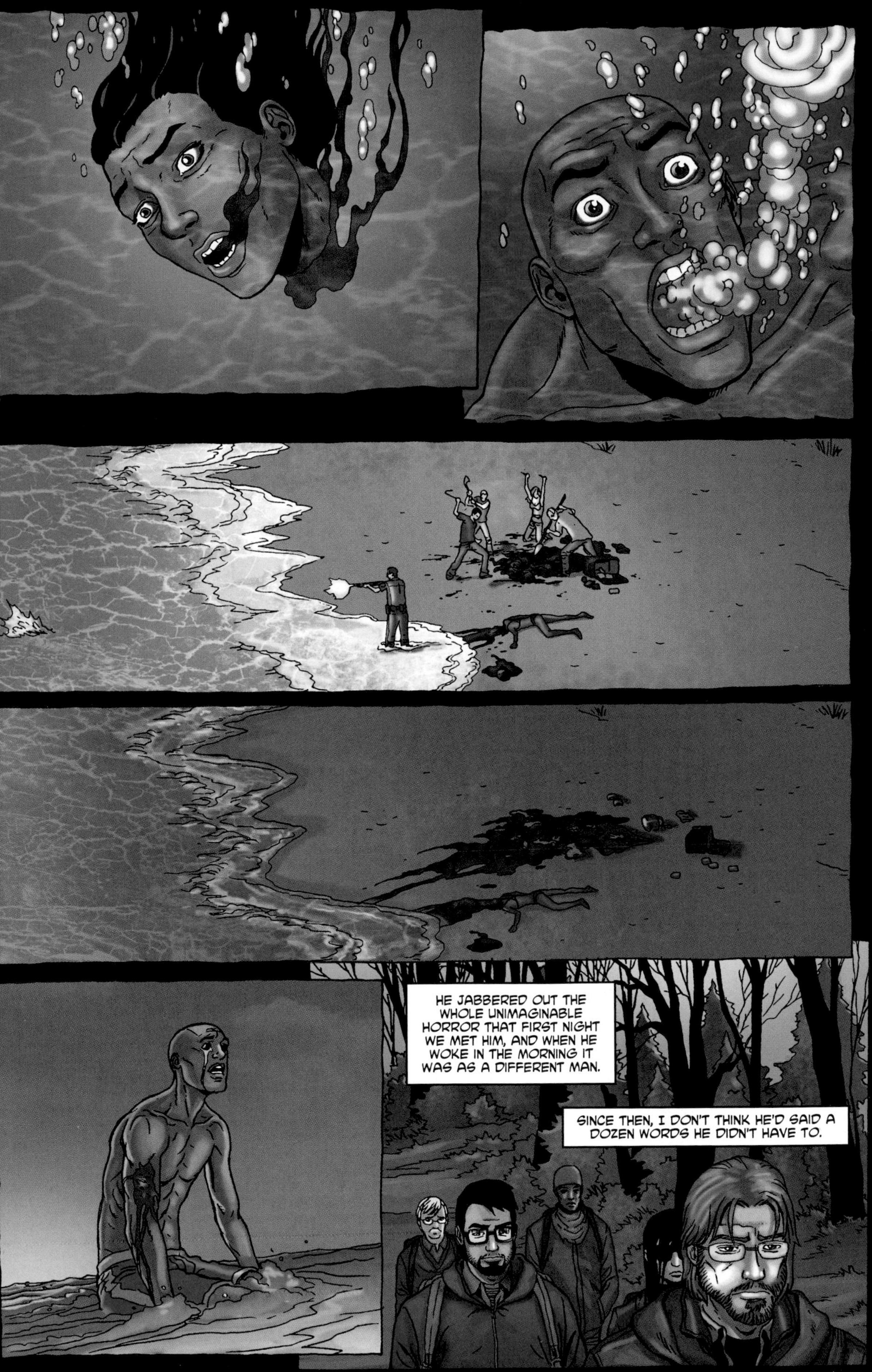
HE JABBERED OUT THE WHOLE UNIMAGINABLE HORROR THAT FIRST NIGHT WE MET HIM, AND WHEN HE WOKE IN THE MORNING IT WAS AS A DIFFERENT MAN.
SINCE THEN, I DON'T THINK HE'D SAID A DOZEN WORDS HE DIDN'T HAVE TO.

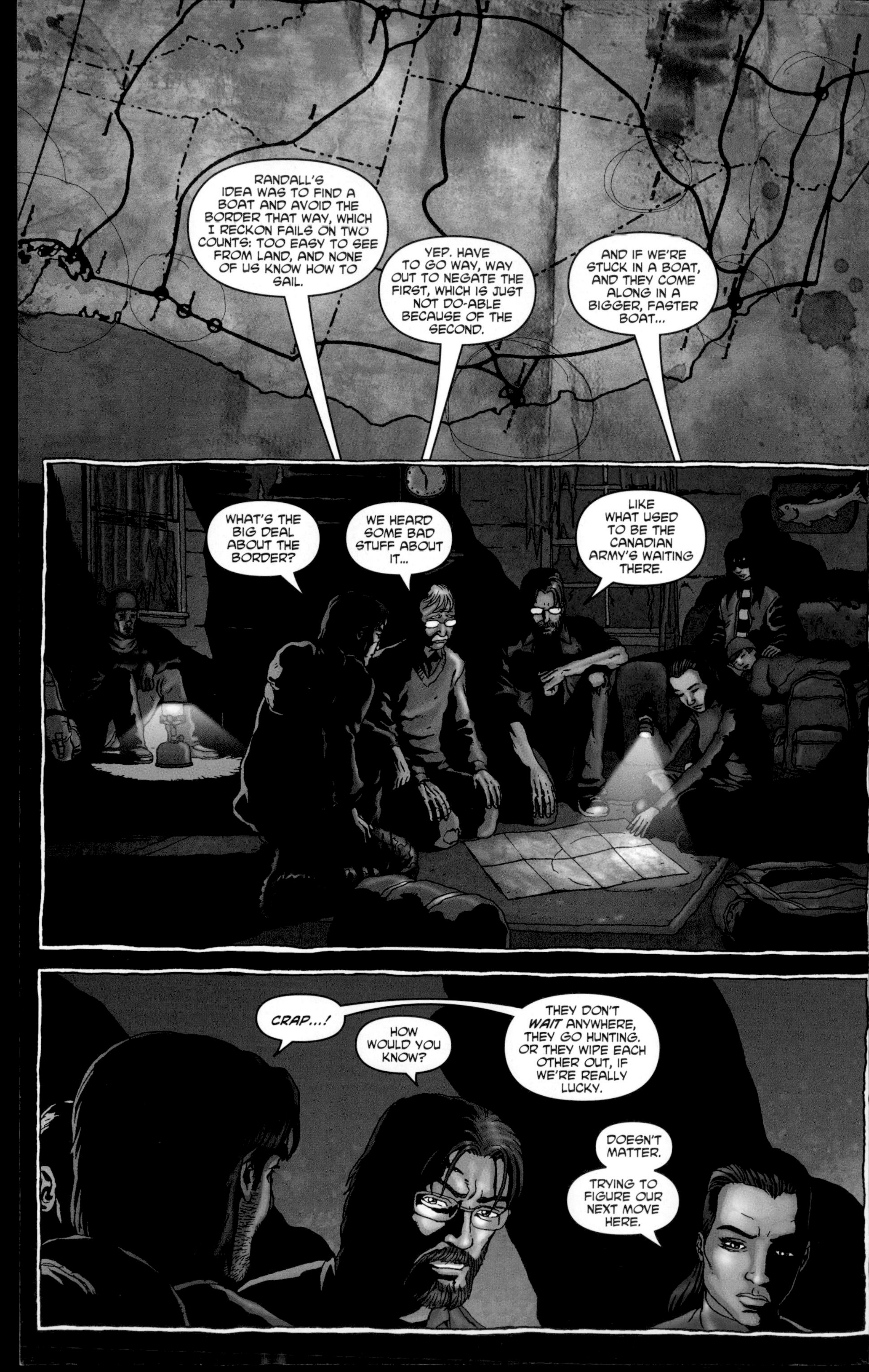
RANDALL'S IDEA WAS TO FIND A BOAT AND AVOID THE BORDER THAT WAY, WHICH I RECKON FAILS ON TWO COUNTS: TOO EASY TO SEE FROM LAND, AND NONE OF US KNOW HOW TO SAIL.
YEP. HAVE TO GO WAY, WAY OUT TO NEGATE THE FIRST, WHICH IS JUST NOT DO-ABLE BECAUSE OF THE SECOND.
AND IF WE'RE STUCK IN A BOAT, AND THEY COME ALONG IN A BIGGER, FASTER BOAT...
WHAT'S THE BIG DEAL ABOUT THE BORDER?
WE HEARD SOME BAD STUFF ABOUT IT...
LIKE WHAT USED TO BE THE CANADIAN ARMY'S WAITING THERE.
CRAP...!
HOW WOULD YOU KNOW?
THEY DON'T *WAIT* ANYWHERE, THEY GO HUNTING. OR THEY WIPE EACH OTHER OUT, IF WE'RE REALLY LUCKY.
DOESN'T MATTER.
TRYING TO FIGURE OUR NEXT MOVE HERE.

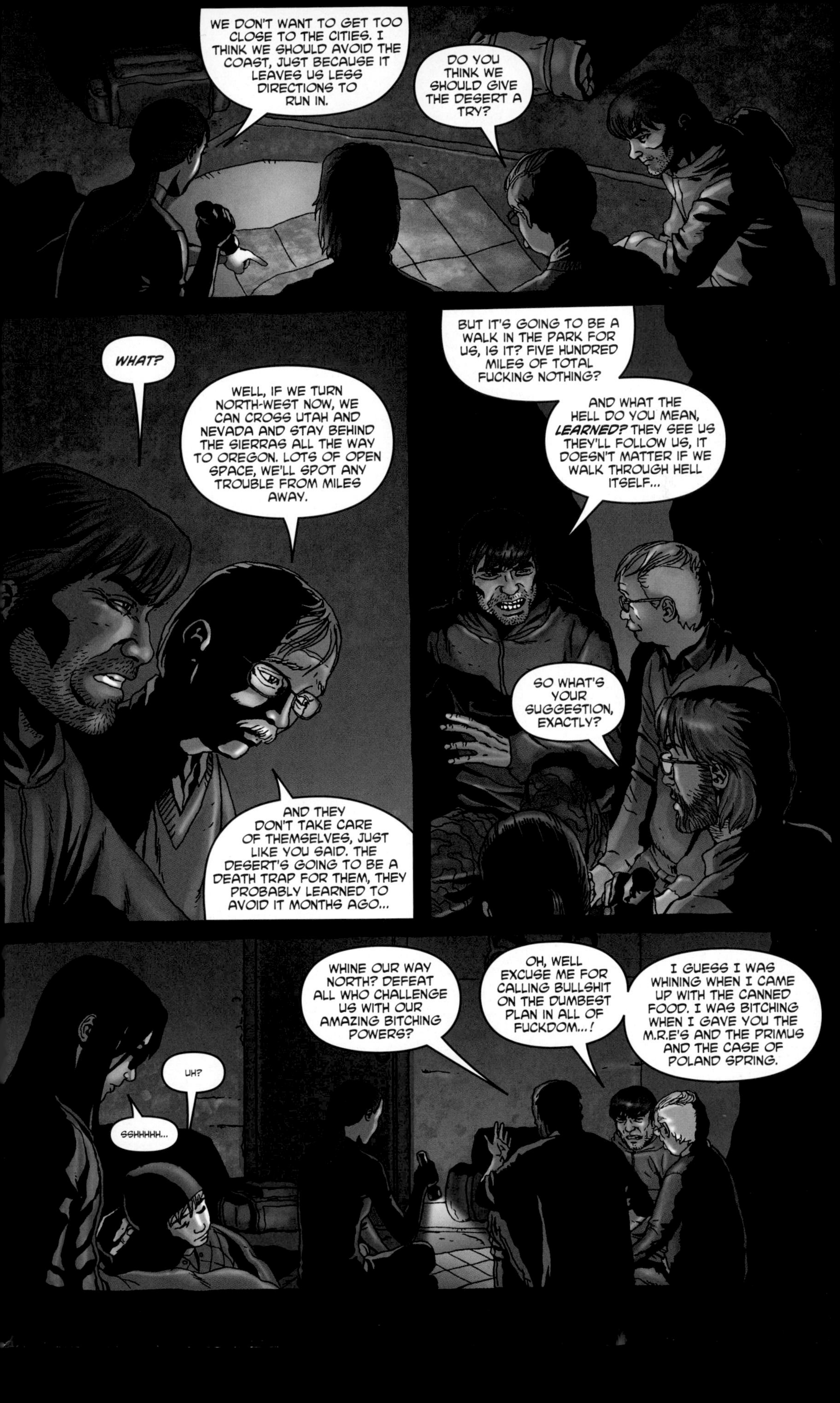

WE DON'T WANT TO GET TOO CLOSE TO THE CITIES. I THINK WE SHOULD AVOID THE COAST, JUST BECAUSE IT LEAVES US LESS DIRECTIONS TO RUN IN.
DO YOU THINK WE SHOULD GIVE THE DESERT A TRY?
WHAT?
WELL, IF WE TURN NORTH-WEST NOW, WE CAN CROSS UTAH AND NEVADA AND STAY BEHIND THE SIERRAS ALL THE WAY TO OREGON. LOTS OF OPEN SPACE, WE'LL SPOT ANY TROUBLE FROM MILES AWAY.
AND THEY DON'T TAKE CARE OF THEMSELVES, JUST LIKE YOU SAID. THE DESERT'S GOING TO BE A DEATH TRAP FOR THEM, THEY PROBABLY LEARNED TO AVOID IT MONTHS AGO...
BUT IT'S GOING TO BE A WALK IN THE PARK FOR US, IS IT? FIVE HUNDRED MILES OF TOTAL FUCKING NOTHING?
AND WHAT THE HELL DO YOU MEAN, *LEARNED?* THEY SEE US THEY'LL FOLLOW US, IT DOESN'T MATTER IF WE WALK THROUGH HELL ITSELF...
SO WHAT'S YOUR SUGGESTION, EXACTLY?
UH?
SSHHHHH...
WHINE OUR WAY NORTH? DEFEAT ALL WHO CHALLENGE US WITH OUR AMAZING BITCHING POWERS?
OH, WELL EXCUSE ME FOR CALLING BULLSHIT ON THE DUMBEST PLAN IN ALL OF FUCKDOM...!
I GUESS I WAS WHINING WHEN I CAME UP WITH THE CANNED FOOD. I WAS BITCHING WHEN I GAVE YOU THE M.R.E'S AND THE PRIMUS AND THE CASE OF POLAND SPRING.

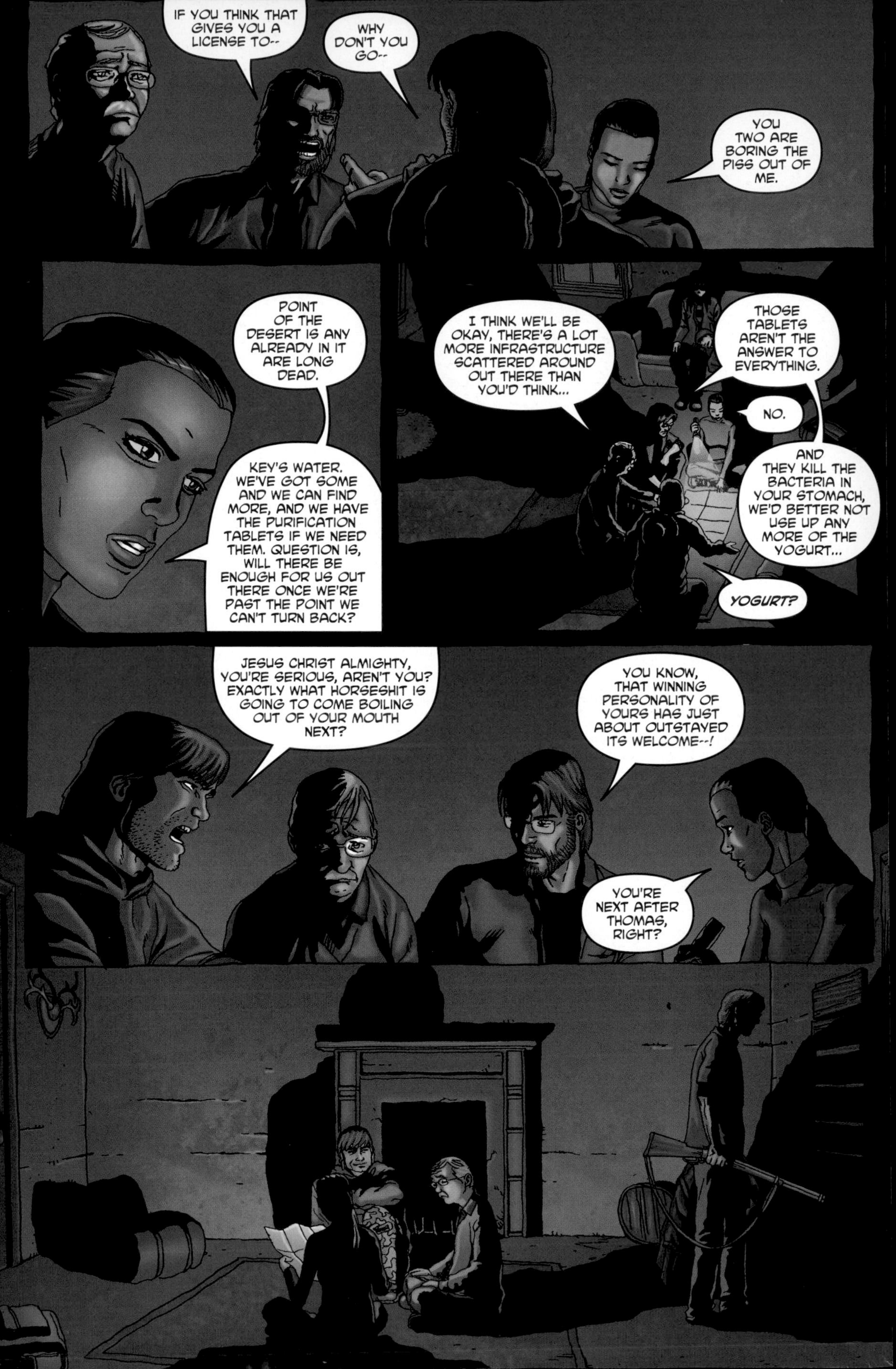

IF YOU THINK THAT GIVES YOU A LICENSE TO--
WHY DON'T YOU GO--
YOU TWO ARE BORING THE PISS OUT OF ME.
POINT OF THE DESERT IS ANY ALREADY IN IT ARE LONG DEAD.
KEY'S WATER. WE'VE GOT SOME AND WE CAN FIND MORE, AND WE HAVE THE PURIFICATION TABLETS IF WE NEED THEM. QUESTION IS, WILL THERE BE ENOUGH FOR US OUT THERE ONCE WE'RE PAST THE POINT WE CAN'T TURN BACK?
I THINK WE'LL BE OKAY, THERE'S A LOT MORE INFRASTRUCTURE SCATTERED AROUND OUT THERE THAN YOU'D THINK...
THOSE TABLETS AREN'T THE ANSWER TO EVERYTHING.
NO.
AND THEY KILL THE BACTERIA IN YOUR STOMACH, WE'D BETTER NOT USE UP ANY MORE OF THE YOGURT...
YOGURT?
JESUS CHRIST ALMIGHTY, YOU'RE SERIOUS, AREN'T YOU? EXACTLY WHAT HORSESHIT IS GOING TO COME BOILING OUT OF YOUR MOUTH NEXT?
YOU KNOW, THAT WINNING PERSONALITY OF YOURS HAS JUST ABOUT OUTSTAYED ITS WELCOME--!
YOU'RE NEXT AFTER THOMAS, RIGHT?

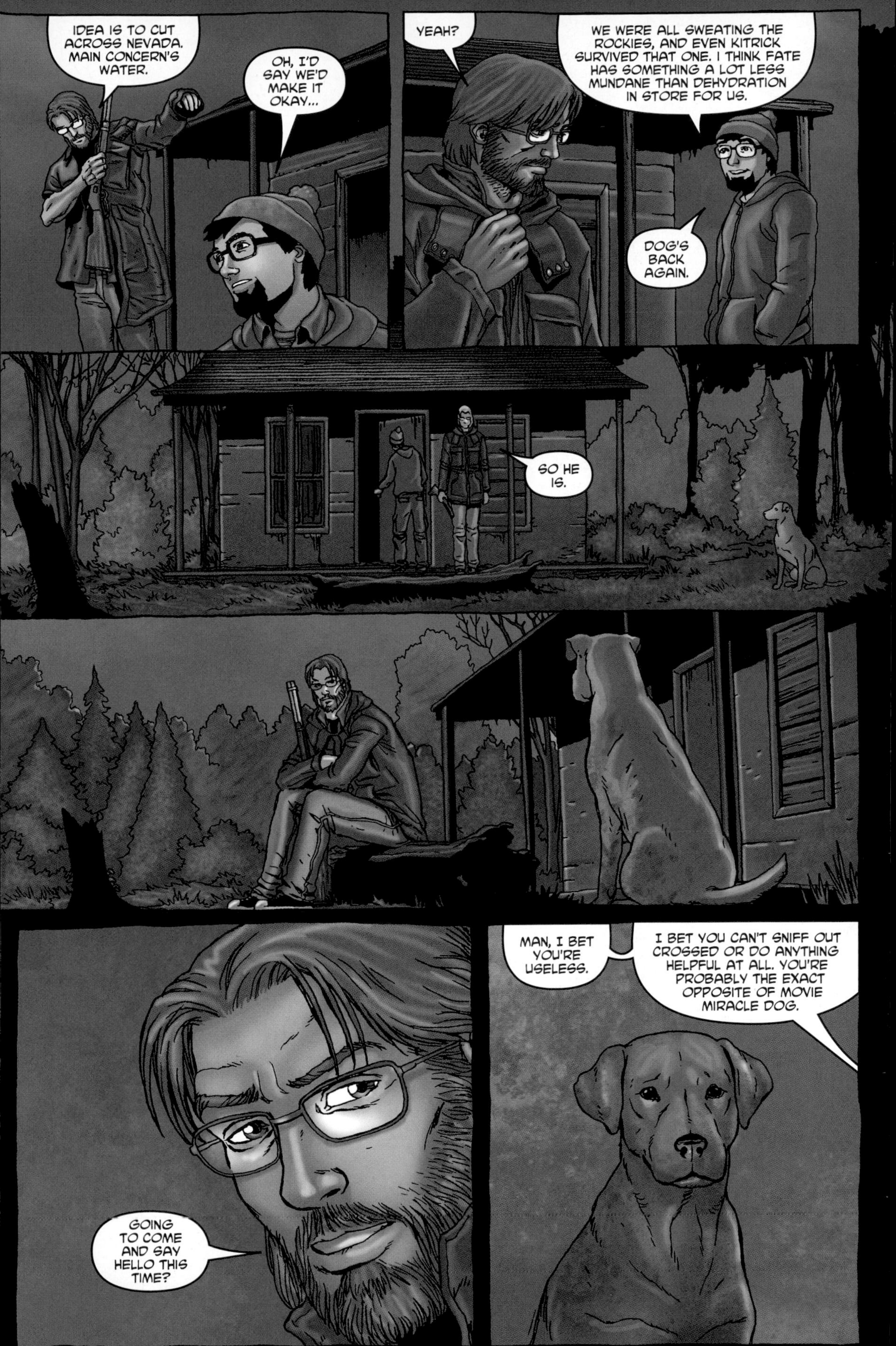
IDEA IS TO CUT ACROSS NEVADA. MAIN CONCERN'S WATER.
OH, I'D SAY WE'D MAKE IT OKAY...
YEAH?
WE WERE ALL SWEATING THE ROCKIES, AND EVEN KITRICK SURVIVED THAT ONE. I THINK FATE HAS SOMETHING A LOT LESS MUNDANE THAN DEHYDRATION IN STORE FOR US.
DOG'S BACK AGAIN.
SO HE IS.
GOING TO COME AND SAY HELLO THIS TIME?
MAN, I BET YOU'RE USELESS.
I BET YOU CAN'T SNIFF OUT CROSSED OR DO ANYTHING HELPFUL AT ALL. YOU'RE PROBABLY THE EXACT OPPOSITE OF MOVIE MIRACLE DOG.

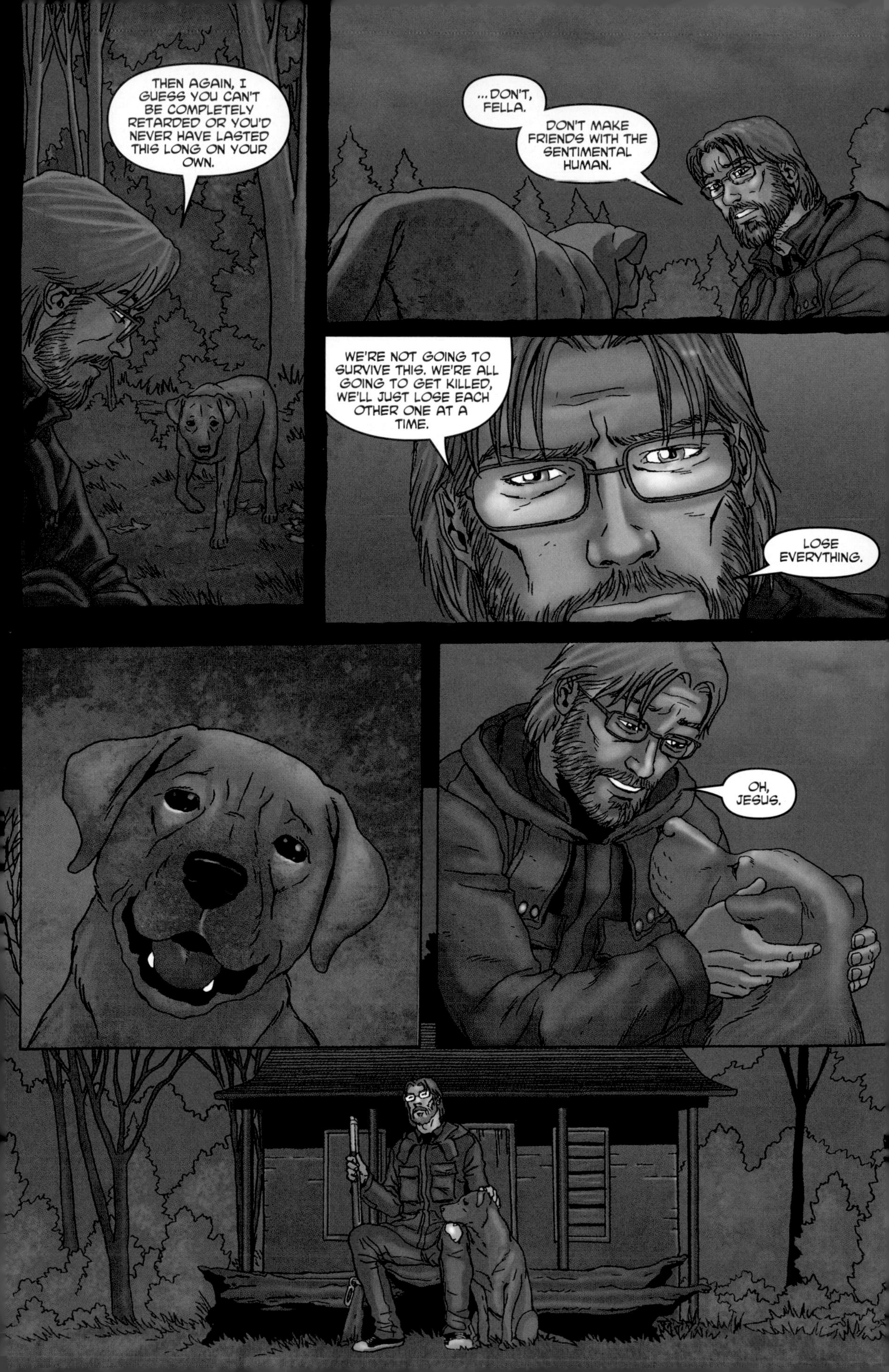
THEN AGAIN, I GUESS YOU CAN'T BE COMPLETELY RETARDED OR YOU'D NEVER HAVE LASTED THIS LONG ON YOUR OWN.
...DON'T, FELLA.
DON'T MAKE FRIENDS WITH THE SENTIMENTAL HUMAN.
WE'RE NOT GOING TO SURVIVE THIS. WE'RE ALL GOING TO GET KILLED, WE'LL JUST LOSE EACH OTHER ONE AT A TIME.
LOSE EVERYTHING.
OH, JESUS.

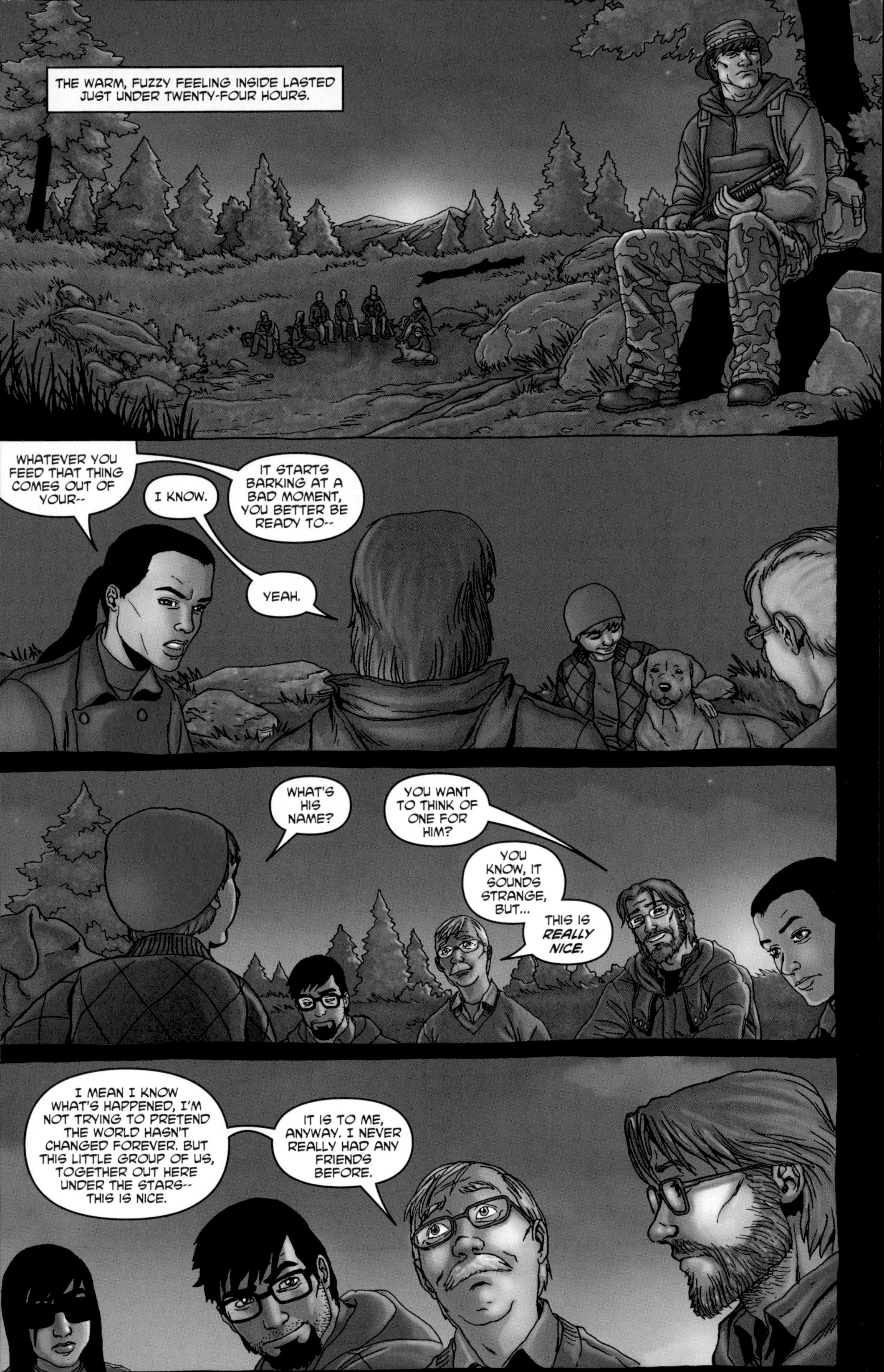
THE WARM, FUZZY FEELING INSIDE LASTED JUST UNDER TWENTY-FOUR HOURS.
WHATEVER YOU FEED THAT THING COMES OUT OF YOUR--
I KNOW.
IT STARTS BARKING AT A BAD MOMENT, YOU BETTER BE READY TO--
YEAH.
WHAT'S HIS NAME?
YOU WANT TO THINK OF ONE FOR HIM?
YOU KNOW, IT SOUNDS STRANGE, BUT...
THIS IS REALLY NICE.
I MEAN I KNOW WHAT'S HAPPENED, I'M NOT TRYING TO PRETEND THE WORLD HASN'T CHANGED FOREVER. BUT THIS LITTLE GROUP OF US, TOGETHER OUT HERE UNDER THE STARS-- THIS IS NICE.
IT IS TO ME, ANYWAY. I NEVER REALLY HAD ANY FRIENDS BEFORE.

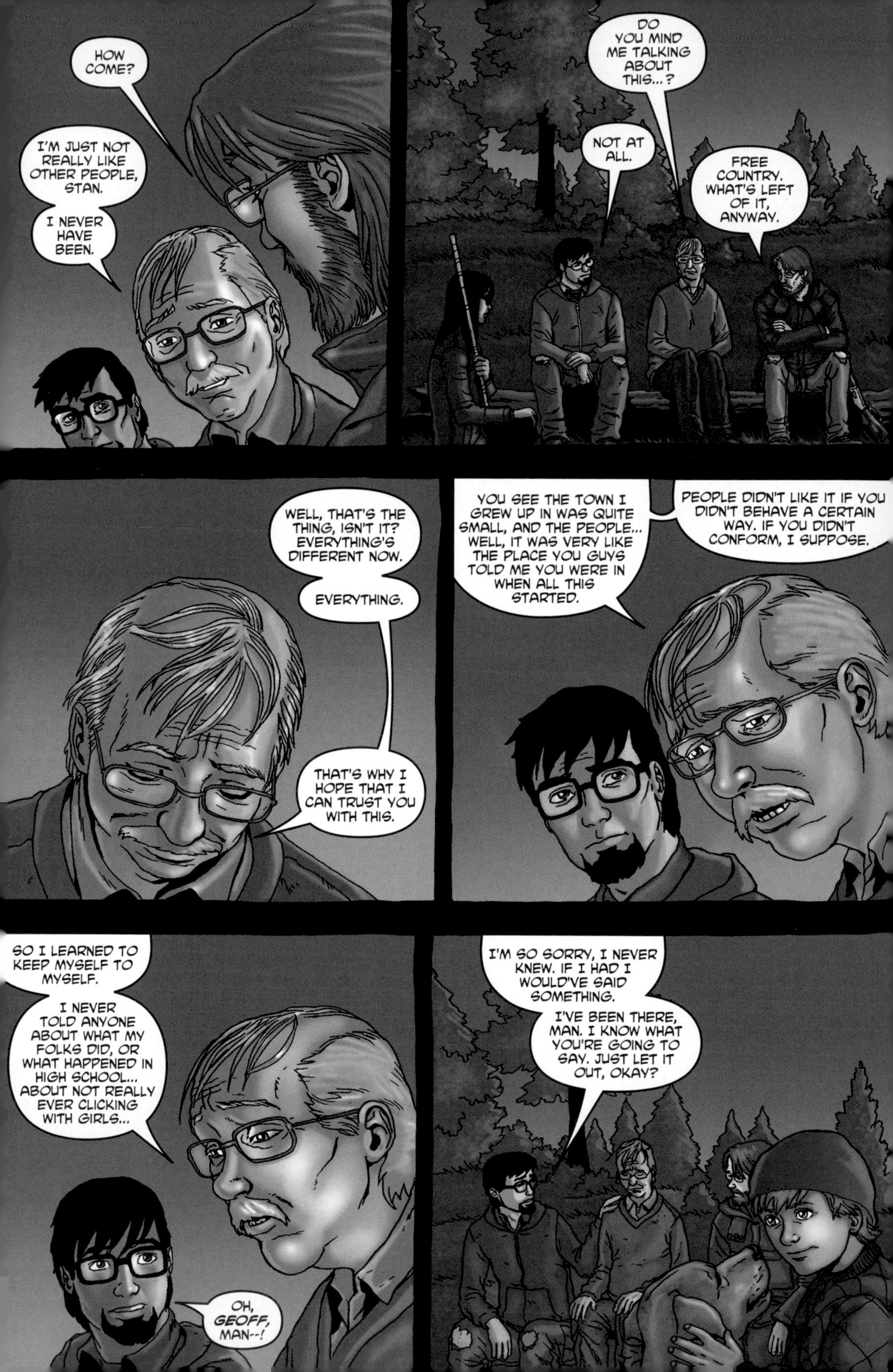
HOW COME?
I'M JUST NOT REALLY LIKE OTHER PEOPLE, STAN.
I NEVER HAVE BEEN.
DO YOU MIND ME TALKING ABOUT THIS...?
NOT AT ALL.
FREE COUNTRY. WHAT'S LEFT OF IT, ANYWAY.
WELL, THAT'S THE THING, ISN'T IT? EVERYTHING'S DIFFERENT NOW.
EVERYTHING.
THAT'S WHY I HOPE THAT I CAN TRUST YOU WITH THIS.
YOU SEE THE TOWN I GREW UP IN WAS QUITE SMALL, AND THE PEOPLE... WELL, IT WAS VERY LIKE THE PLACE YOU GUYS TOLD ME YOU WERE IN WHEN ALL THIS STARTED.
PEOPLE DIDN'T LIKE IT IF YOU DIDN'T BEHAVE A CERTAIN WAY. IF YOU DIDN'T CONFORM, I SUPPOSE.
SO I LEARNED TO KEEP MYSELF TO MYSELF.
I NEVER TOLD ANYONE ABOUT WHAT MY FOLKS DID, OR WHAT HAPPENED IN HIGH SCHOOL... ABOUT NOT REALLY EVER CLICKING WITH GIRLS...
OH, GEOFF, MAN--!
I'M SO SORRY, I NEVER KNEW. IF I HAD I WOULD'VE SAID SOMETHING.
I'VE BEEN THERE, MAN. I KNOW WHAT YOU'RE GOING TO SAY. JUST LET IT OUT, OKAY?

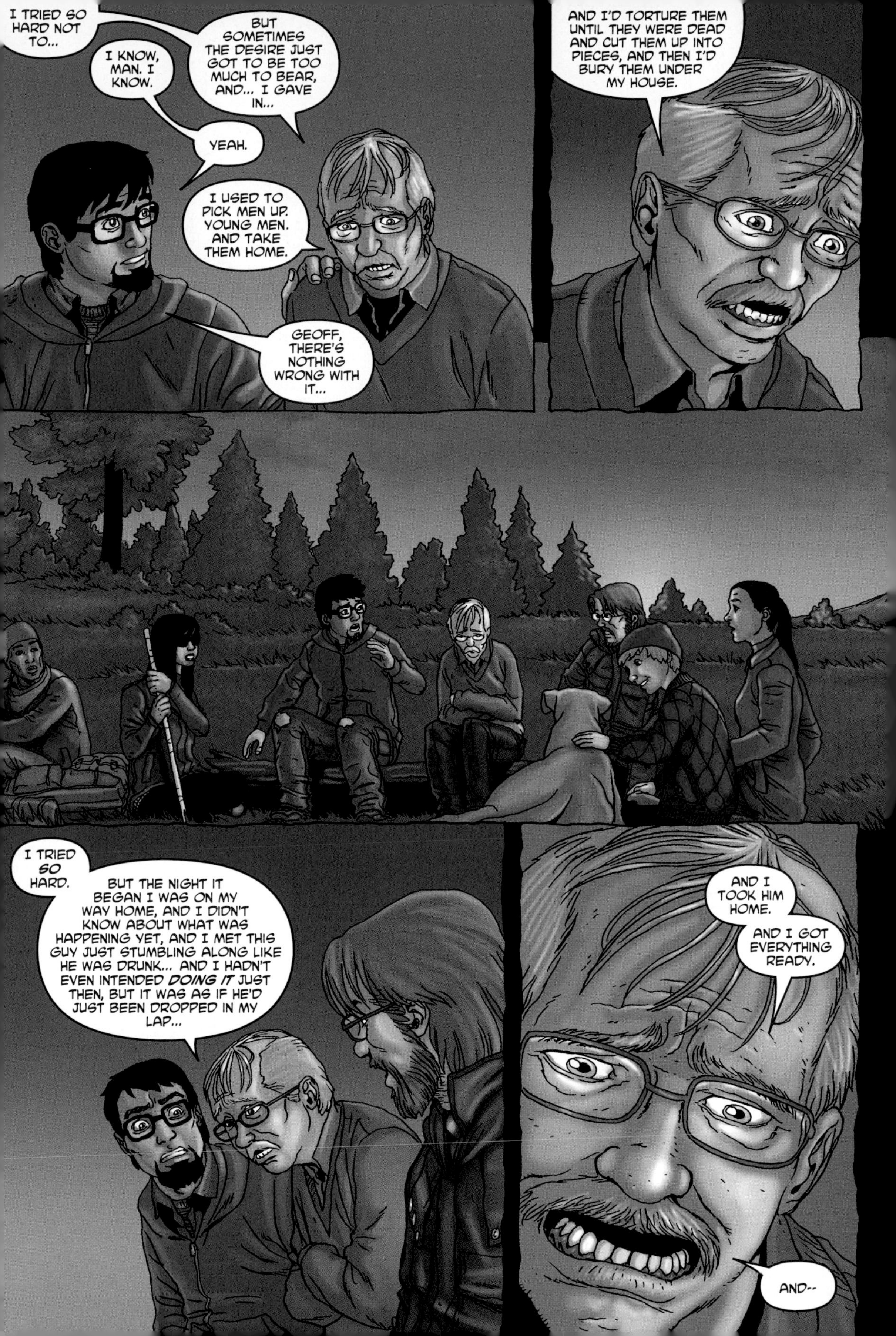
I TRIED SO HARD NOT TO...
BUT SOMETIMES THE DESIRE JUST GOT TO BE TOO MUCH TO BEAR, AND... I GAVE IN...
I KNOW, MAN. I KNOW.
YEAH.
I USED TO PICK MEN UP. YOUNG MEN. AND TAKE THEM HOME.
GEOFF, THERE'S NOTHING WRONG WITH IT...
AND I'D TORTURE THEM UNTIL THEY WERE DEAD AND CUT THEM UP INTO PIECES, AND THEN I'D BURY THEM UNDER MY HOUSE.
I TRIED *SO* HARD.
BUT THE NIGHT IT BEGAN I WAS ON MY WAY HOME, AND I DIDN'T KNOW ABOUT WHAT WAS HAPPENING YET, AND I MET THIS GUY JUST STUMBLING ALONG LIKE HE WAS DRUNK... AND I HADN'T EVEN INTENDED ***DOING IT*** JUST THEN, BUT IT WAS AS IF HE'D JUST BEEN DROPPED IN MY LAP...
AND I TOOK HIM HOME.
AND I GOT EVERYTHING READY.
AND--

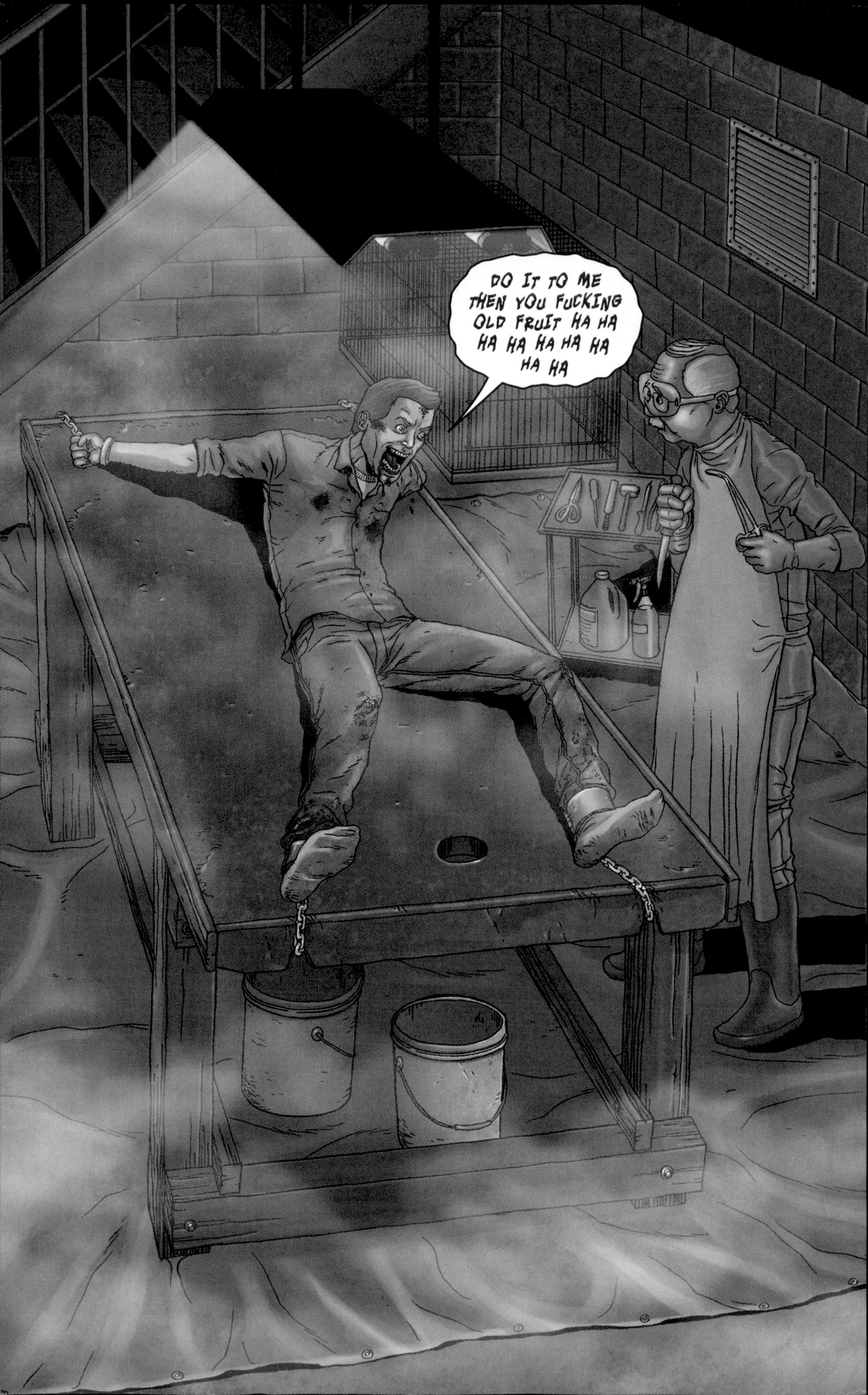
DO IT TO ME THEN YOU FUCKING OLD FRUIT HA HA HA HA HA HA HA HA HA

I LEFT HIM THERE.

I COULDN'T GET OUT FAST ENOUGH.

THIS... *CAN'T* BE...

YOU'D KNOW IF YOU COULD SEE HIM.

PATRICK, COME GET BEHIND MOMMY.

CINDY, I WOULD NEVER DO ANYTHING TO *PATRICK--!*

COME ON.

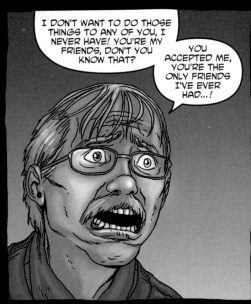

I DON'T WANT TO DO THOSE THINGS TO ANY OF YOU, I NEVER HAVE! YOU'RE MY FRIENDS, DON'T YOU KNOW THAT?

YOU ACCEPTED ME, YOU'RE THE ONLY FRIENDS I'VE EVER HAD...!

WE DIDN'T KNOW WHO YOU--

BUT--

OH, JESUS.

JESUS CHRIST ALMIGHTY.

GEOFF?

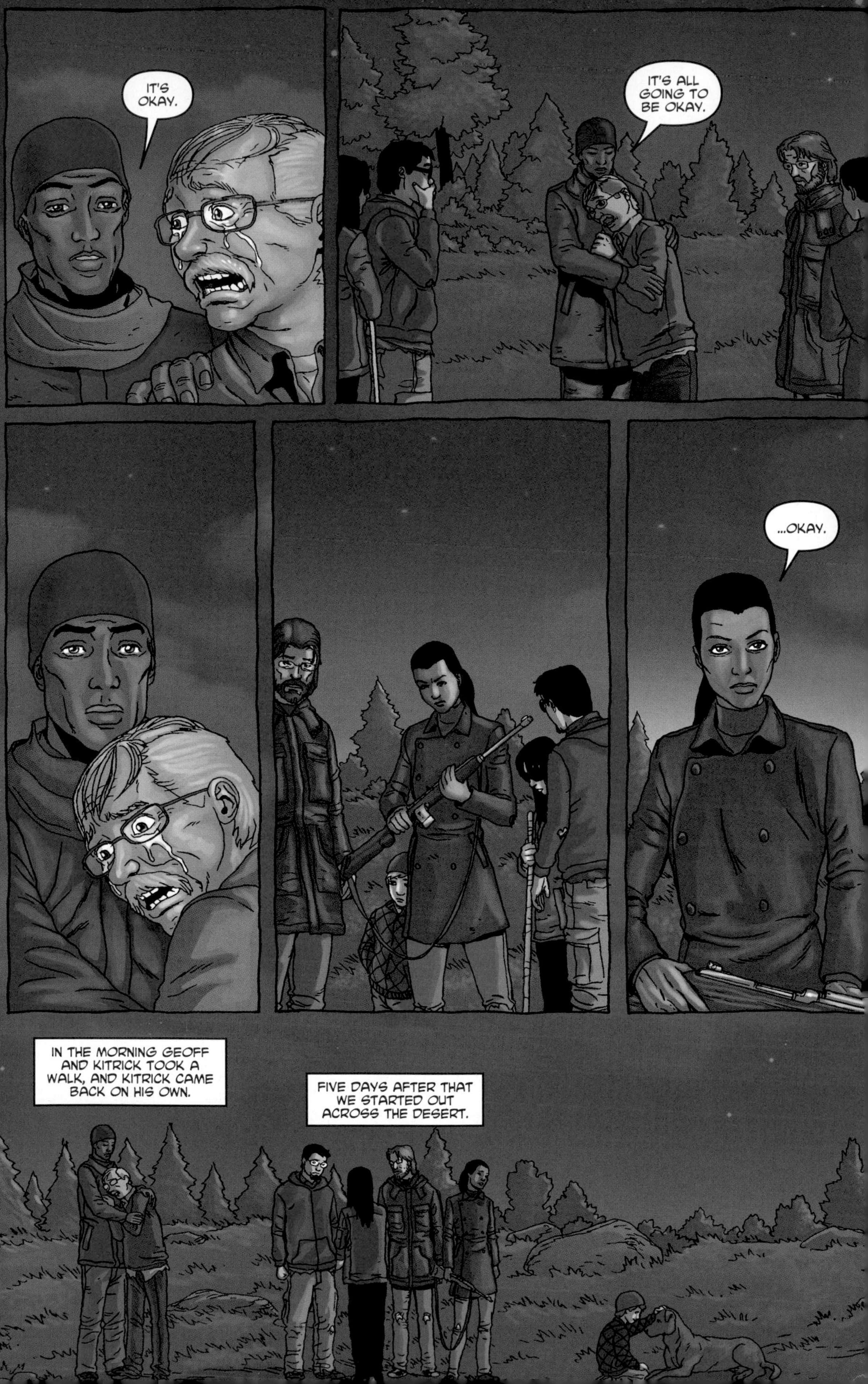
IT'S OKAY.
IT'S ALL GOING TO BE OKAY.
...OKAY.
IN THE MORNING GEOFF AND KITRICK TOOK A WALK, AND KITRICK CAME BACK ON HIS OWN.
FIVE DAYS AFTER THAT WE STARTED OUT ACROSS THE DESERT.

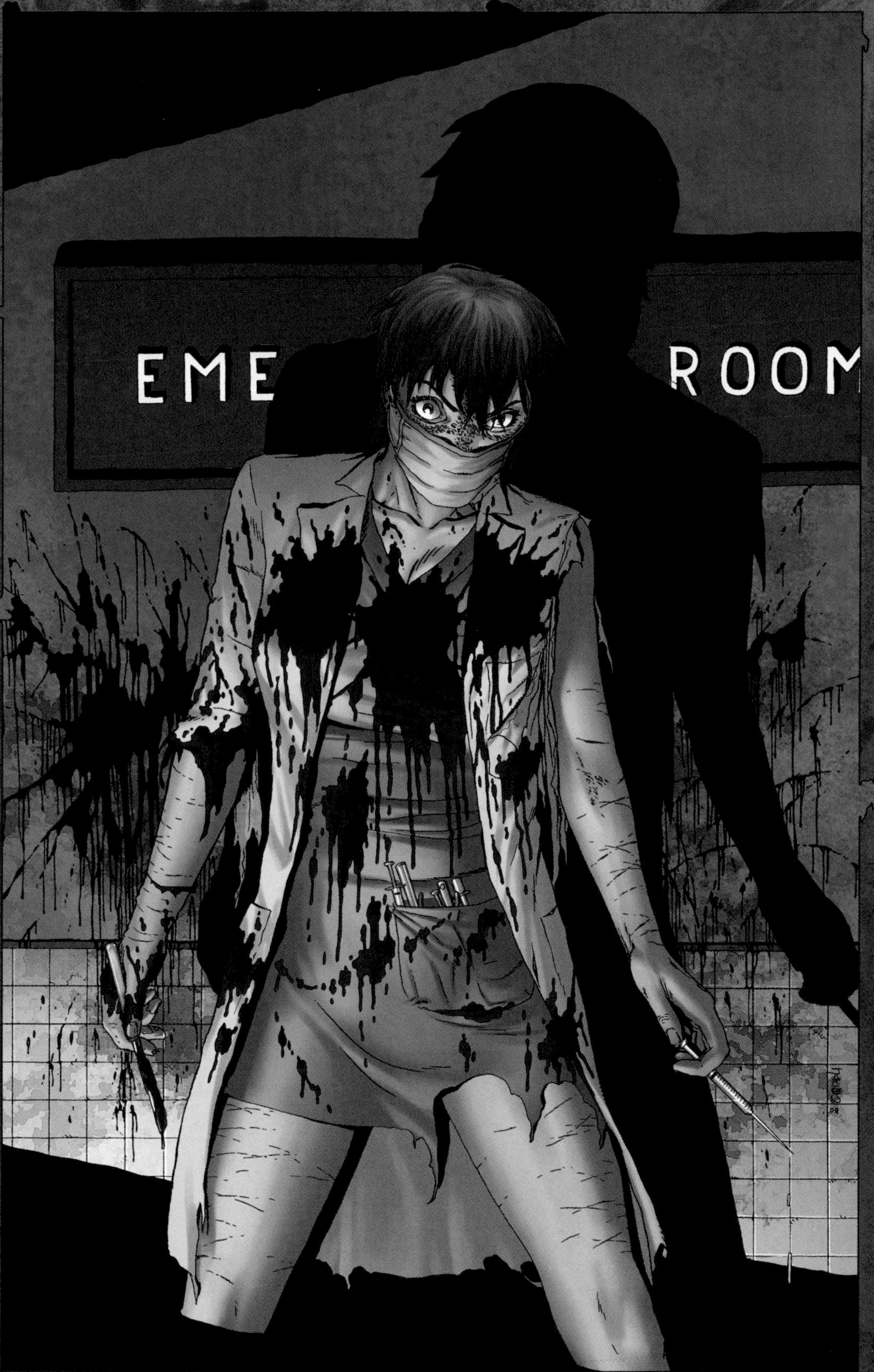
EME
ROOM

PART EIGHT

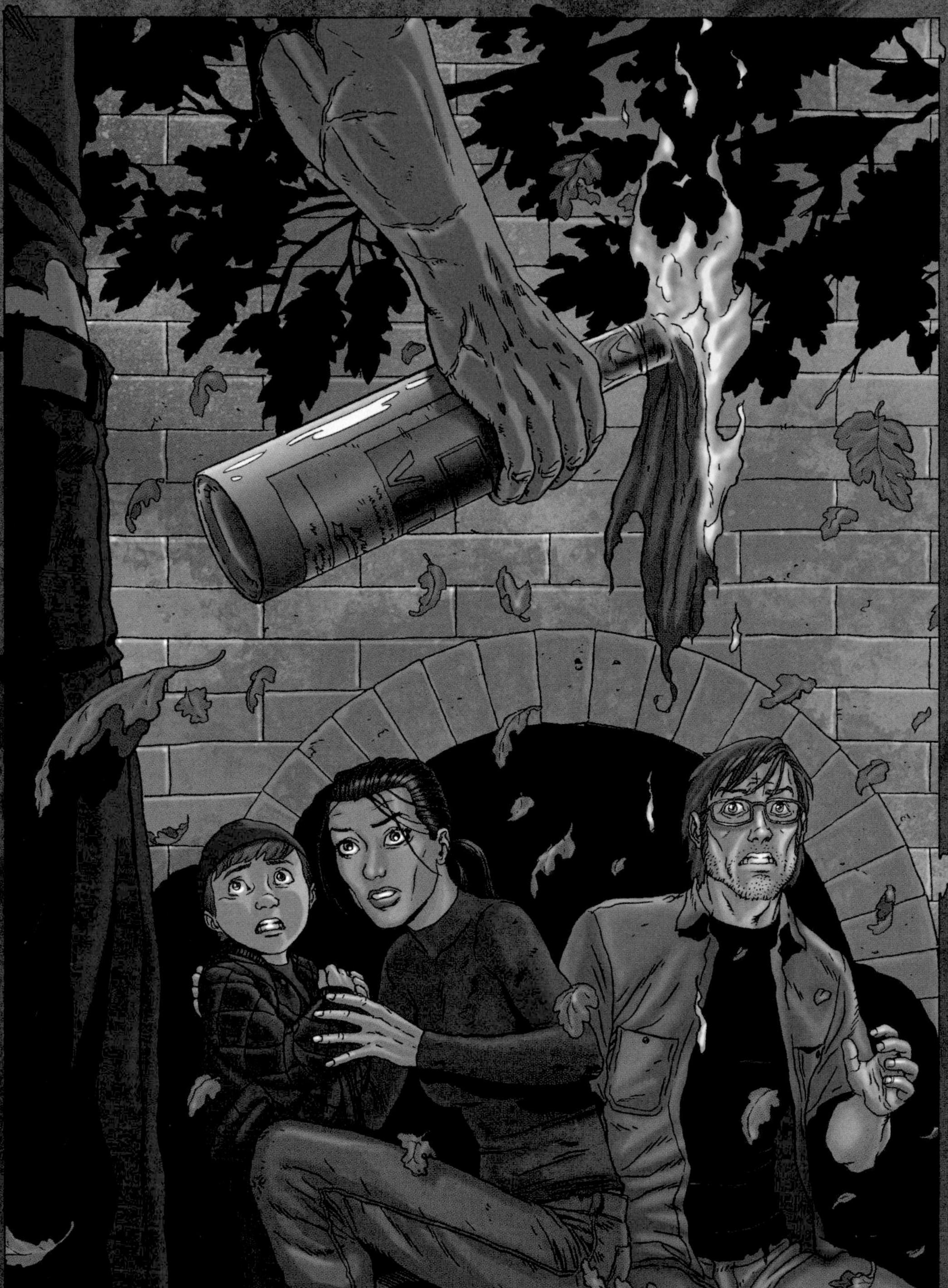

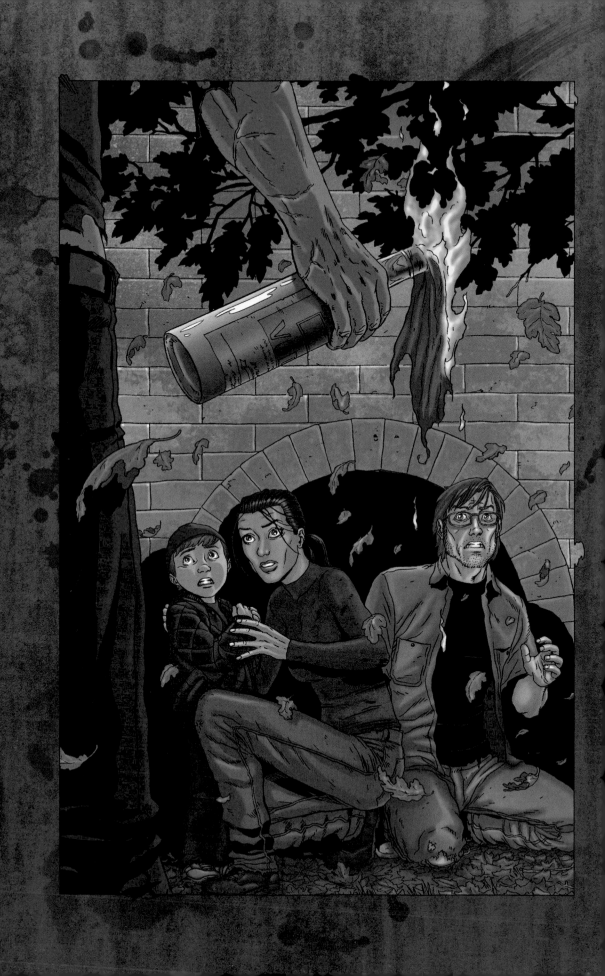

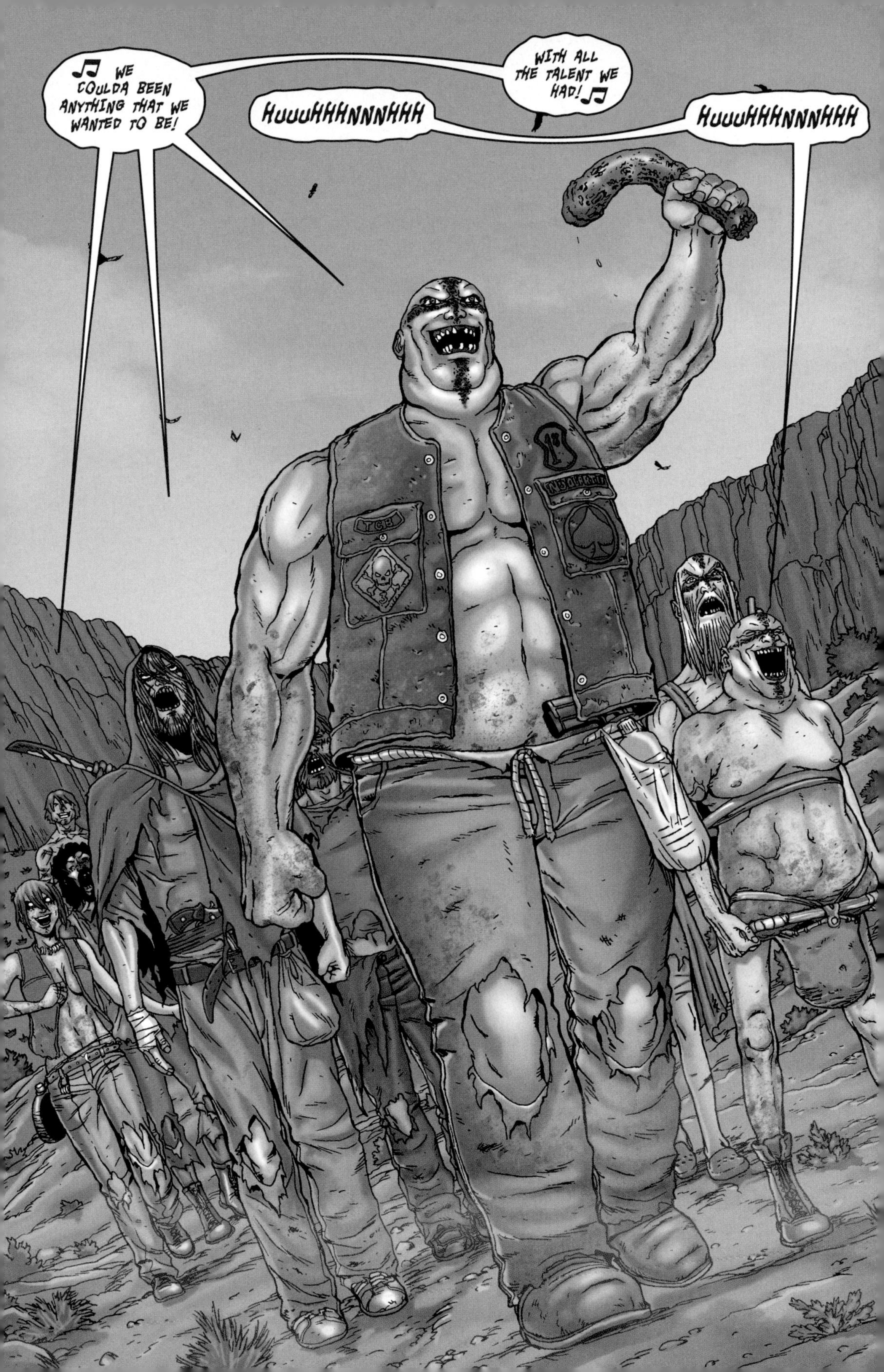
♫ WE COULDA BEEN ANYTHING THAT WE WANTED TO BE!
HUUUHHHNNNHHH
WITH ALL THE TALENT WE HAD! ♫
HUUUHHHNNNHHH

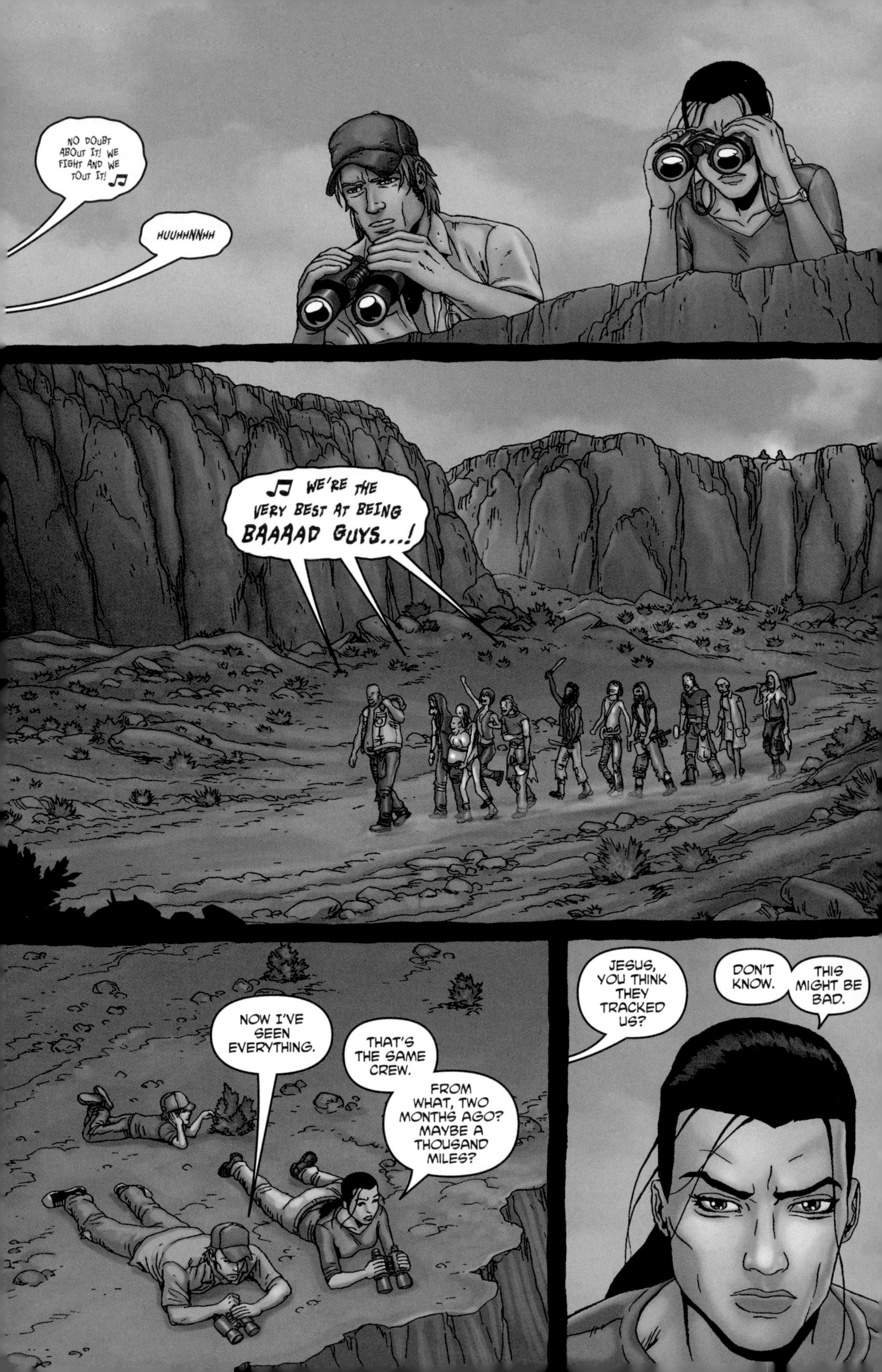

NO DOUBT ABOUT IT! WE FIGHT AND WE TOUT IT! ♫
HUUHHNNHH
♫ WE'RE THE VERY BEST AT BEING BAAAAD GUYS...!
NOW I'VE SEEN EVERYTHING.
THAT'S THE SAME CREW.
FROM WHAT, TWO MONTHS AGO? MAYBE A THOUSAND MILES?
JESUS, YOU THINK THEY TRACKED US?
DON'T KNOW.
THIS MIGHT BE BAD.

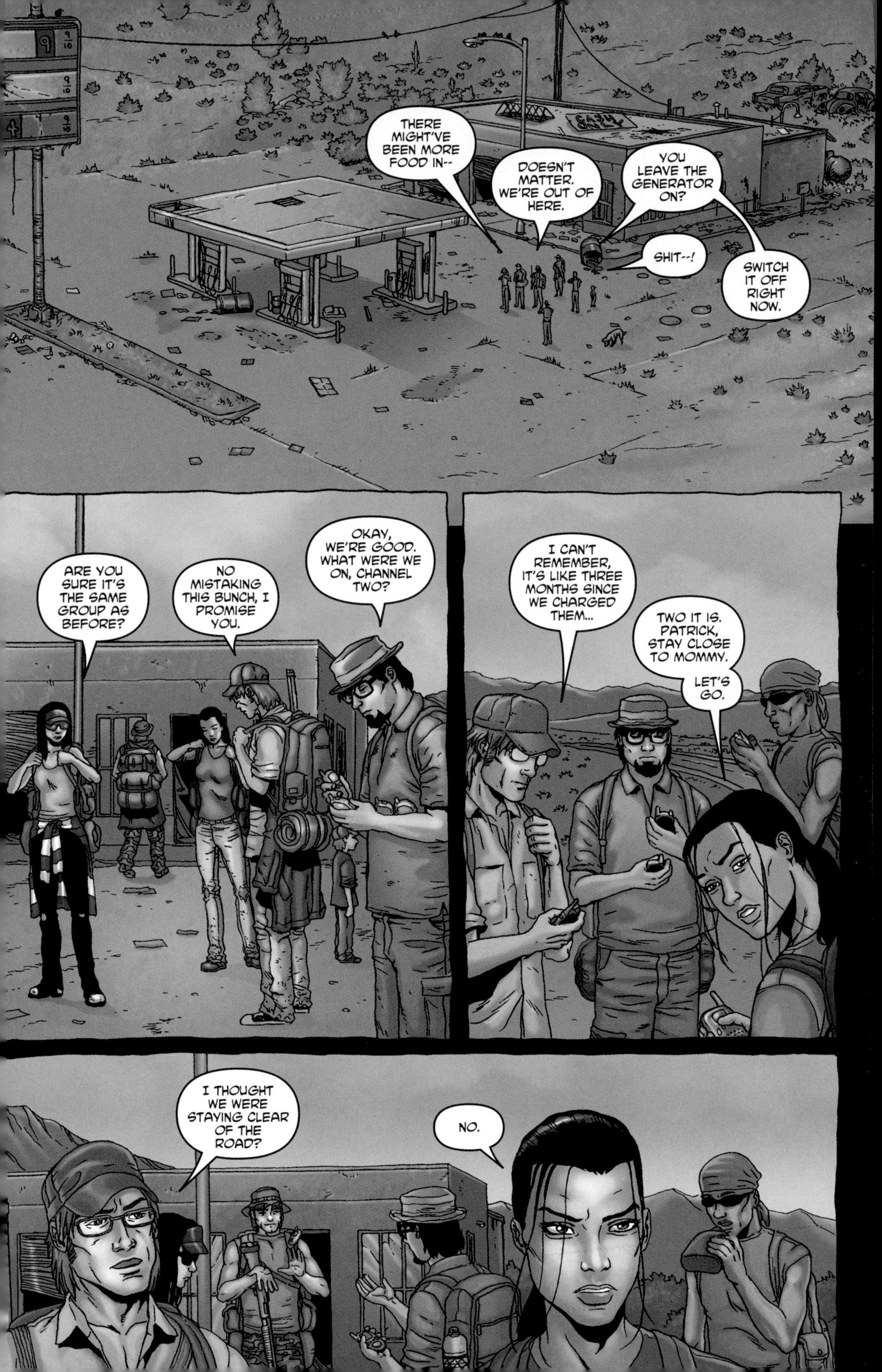

THERE MIGHT'VE BEEN MORE FOOD IN--
DOESN'T MATTER. WE'RE OUT OF HERE.
YOU LEAVE THE GENERATOR ON?
SHIT--!
SWITCH IT OFF RIGHT NOW.
ARE YOU SURE IT'S THE SAME GROUP AS BEFORE?
NO MISTAKING THIS BUNCH, I PROMISE YOU.
OKAY, WE'RE GOOD. WHAT WERE WE ON, CHANNEL TWO?
I CAN'T REMEMBER, IT'S LIKE THREE MONTHS SINCE WE CHARGED THEM...
TWO IT IS. PATRICK, STAY CLOSE TO MOMMY.
LET'S GO.
I THOUGHT WE WERE STAYING CLEAR OF THE ROAD?
NO.

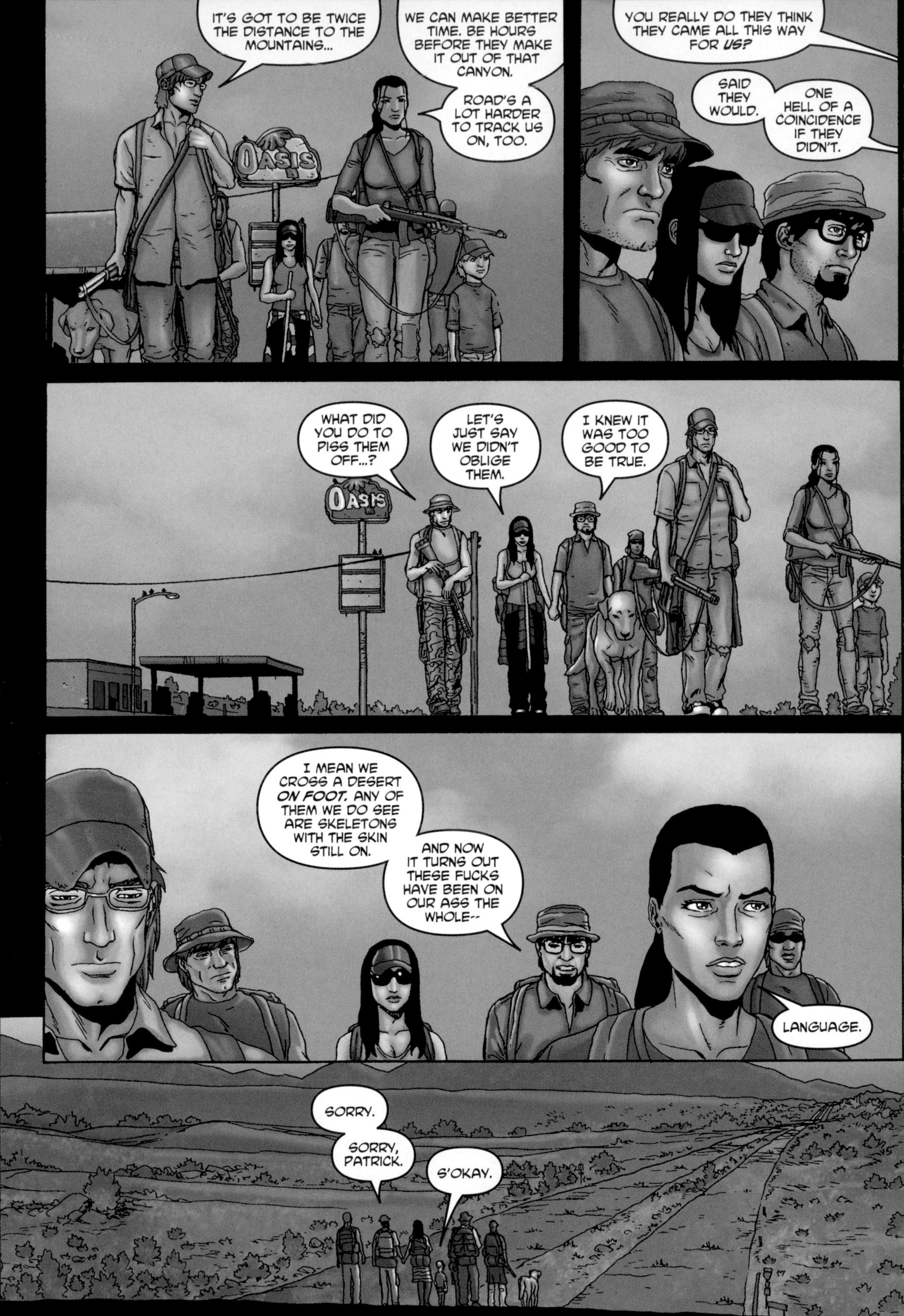

IT'S GOT TO BE TWICE THE DISTANCE TO THE MOUNTAINS...
WE CAN MAKE BETTER TIME. BE HOURS BEFORE THEY MAKE IT OUT OF THAT CANYON.
ROAD'S A LOT HARDER TO TRACK US ON, TOO.
OASIS
YOU REALLY DO THEY THINK THEY CAME ALL THIS WAY FOR *US?*
SAID THEY WOULD.
ONE HELL OF A COINCIDENCE IF THEY DIDN'T.
WHAT DID YOU DO TO PISS THEM OFF...?
LET'S JUST SAY WE DIDN'T OBLIGE THEM.
I KNEW IT WAS TOO GOOD TO BE TRUE.
OASIS
I MEAN WE CROSS A DESERT *ON FOOT.* ANY OF THEM WE DO SEE ARE SKELETONS WITH THE SKIN STILL ON.
AND NOW IT TURNS OUT THESE FUCKS HAVE BEEN ON OUR ASS THE WHOLE--
LANGUAGE.
SORRY.
SORRY, PATRICK.
S'OKAY.

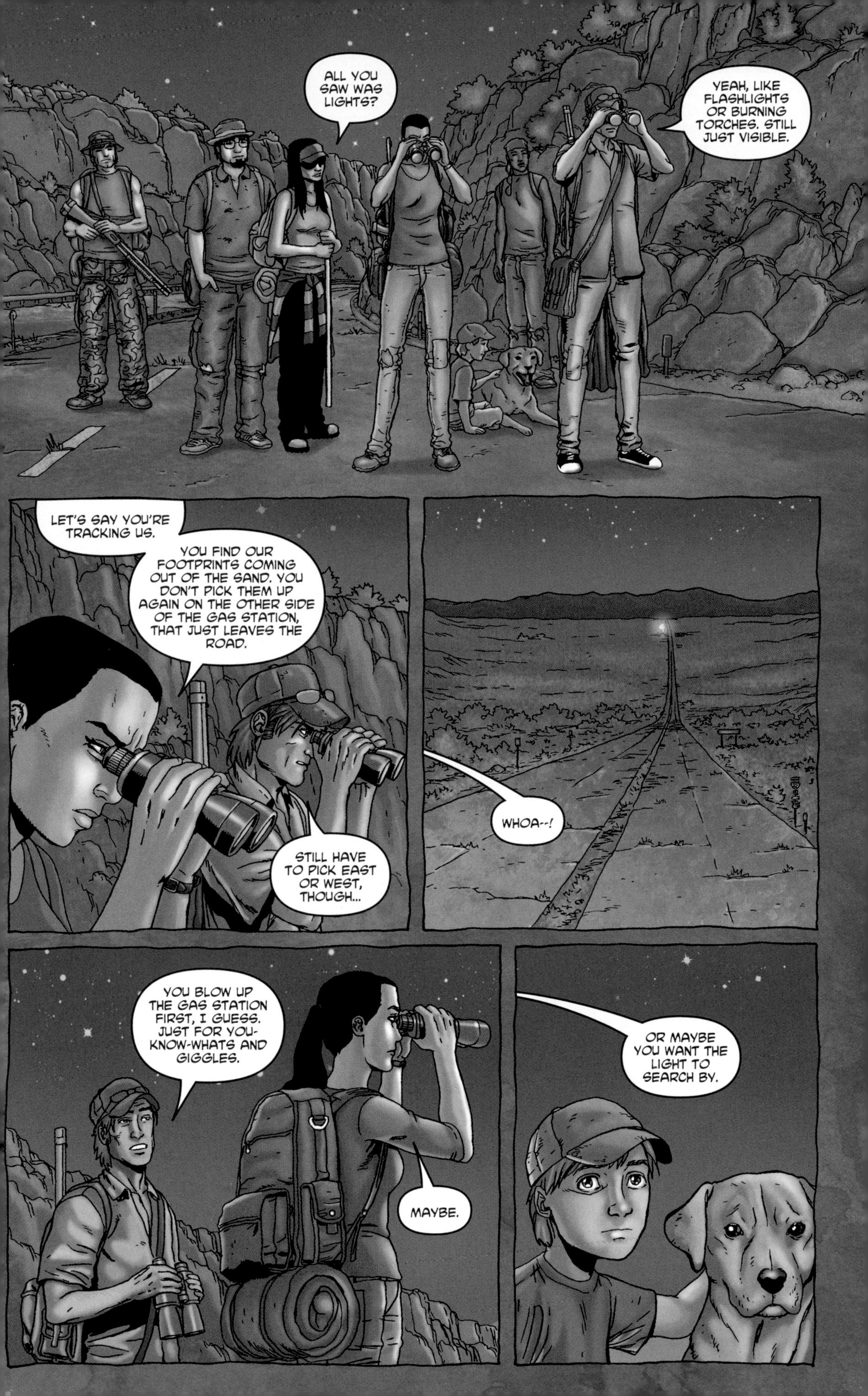
ALL YOU SAW WAS LIGHTS?
YEAH, LIKE FLASHLIGHTS OR BURNING TORCHES. STILL JUST VISIBLE.
LET'S SAY YOU'RE TRACKING US.
YOU FIND OUR FOOTPRINTS COMING OUT OF THE SAND. YOU DON'T PICK THEM UP AGAIN ON THE OTHER SIDE OF THE GAS STATION, THAT JUST LEAVES THE ROAD.
STILL HAVE TO PICK EAST OR WEST, THOUGH...
WHOA--!
YOU BLOW UP THE GAS STATION FIRST, I GUESS. JUST FOR YOU-KNOW-WHATS AND GIGGLES.
MAYBE.
OR MAYBE YOU WANT THE LIGHT TO SEARCH BY.

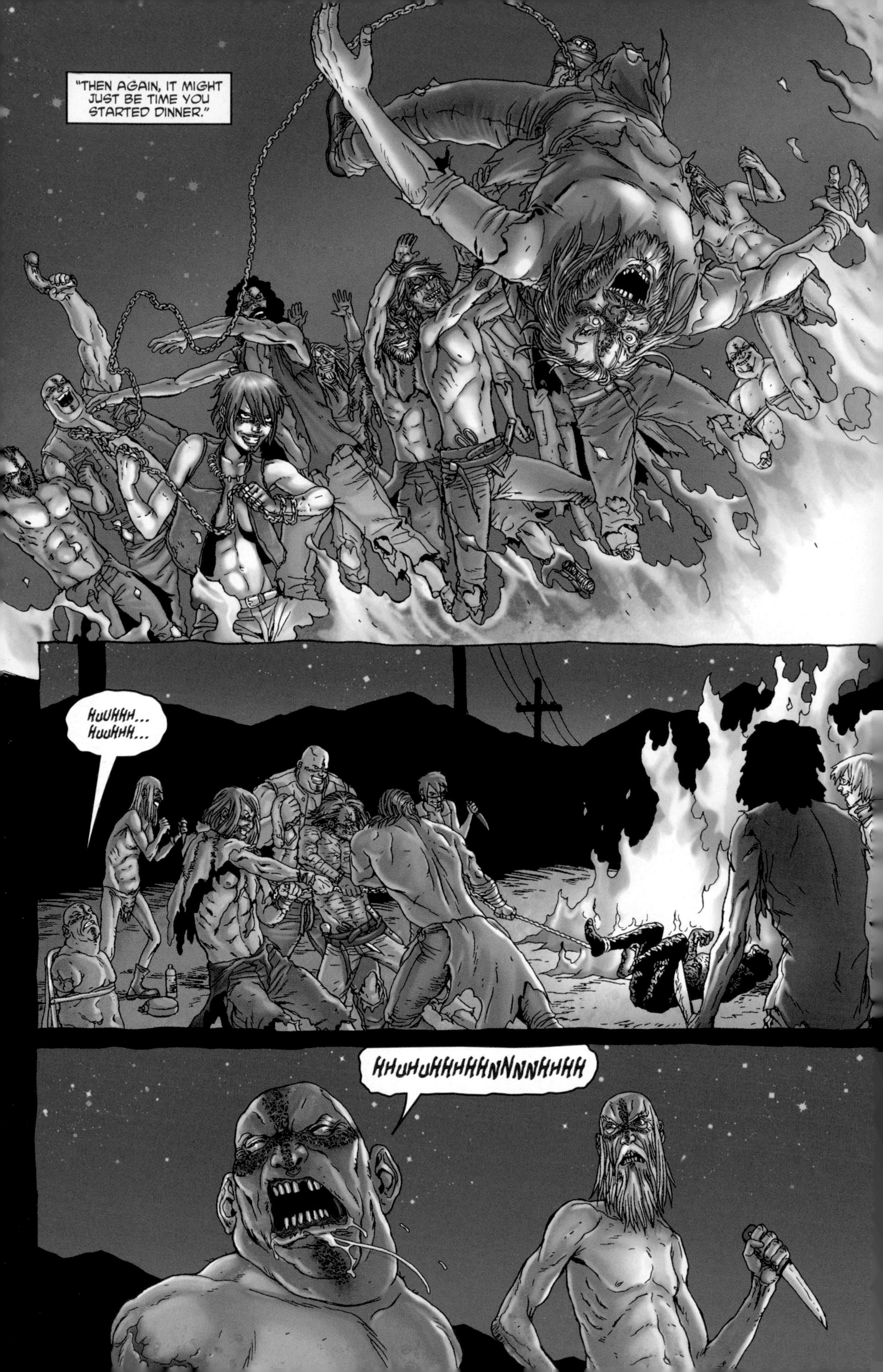
"THEN AGAIN, IT MIGHT JUST BE TIME YOU STARTED DINNER."
HUUHHH... HUUHHH...
HHUHUHHHHHNNNHHHH

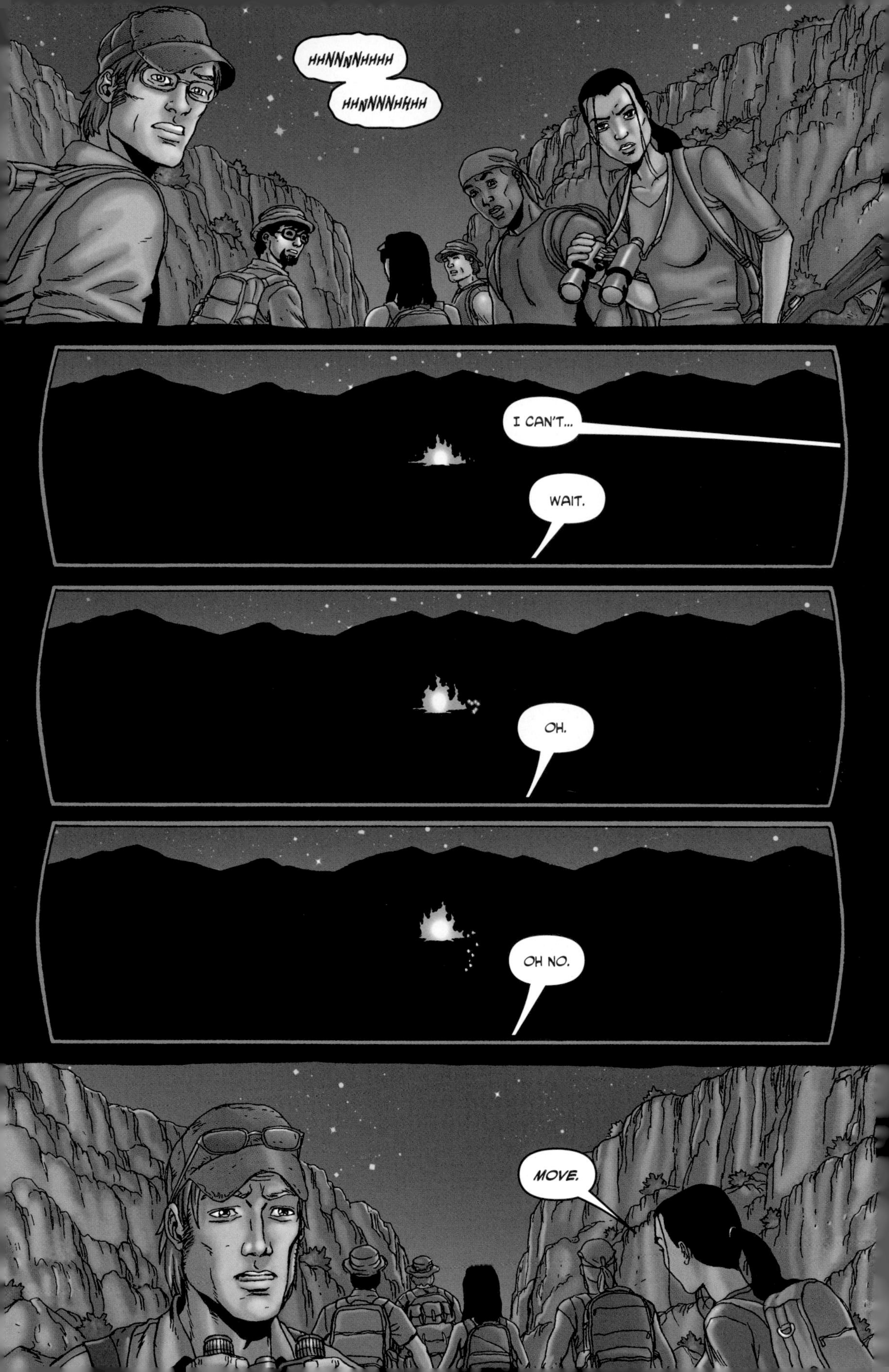
HHNNNNHHHH
HHNNNNHHHH
I CAN'T...
WAIT.
OH.
OH NO.
MOVE.

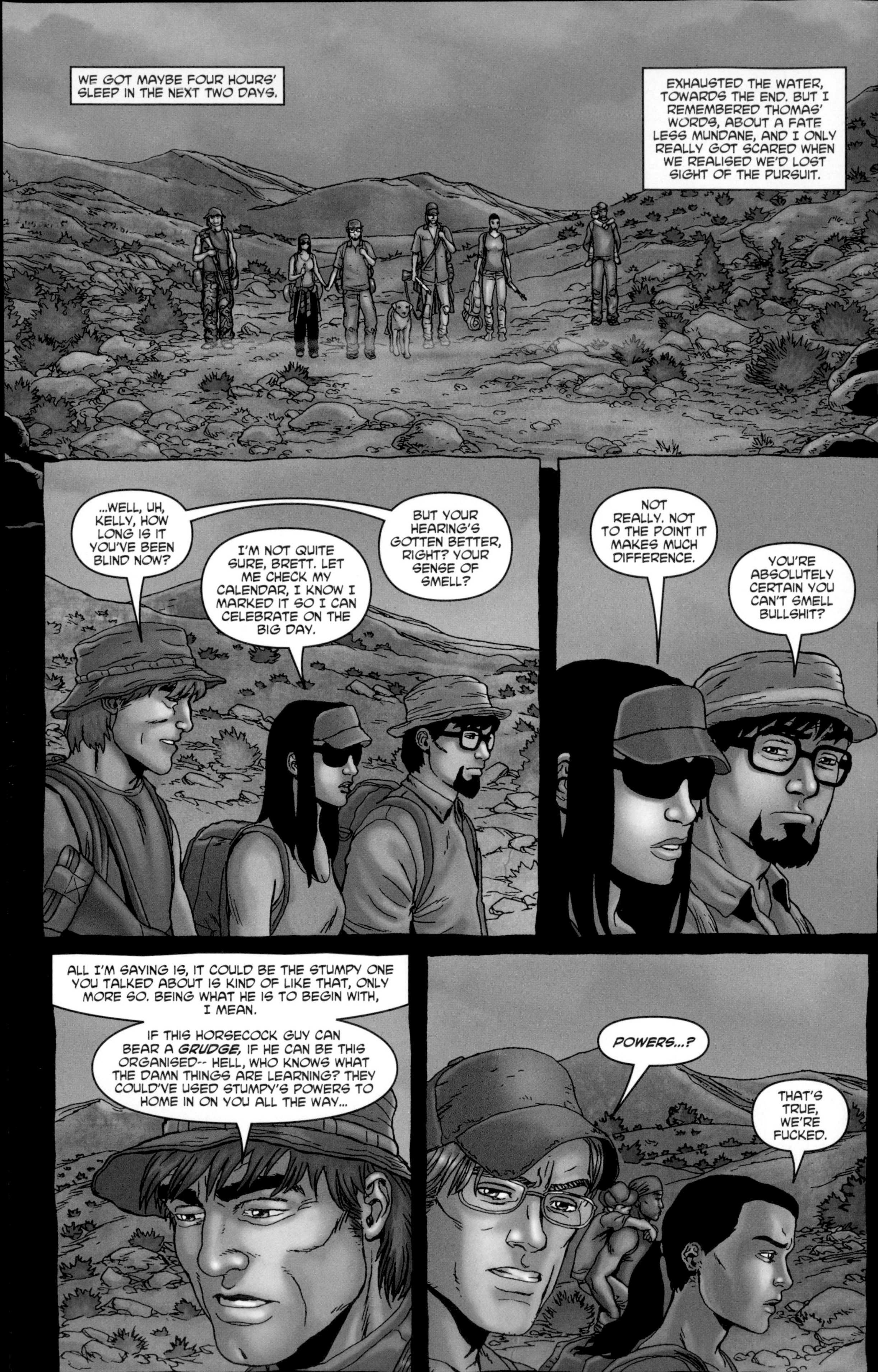
WE GOT MAYBE FOUR HOURS' SLEEP IN THE NEXT TWO DAYS.
EXHAUSTED THE WATER, TOWARDS THE END. BUT I REMEMBERED THOMAS' WORDS, ABOUT A FATE LESS MUNDANE, AND I ONLY REALLY GOT SCARED WHEN WE REALISED WE'D LOST SIGHT OF THE PURSUIT.
...WELL, UH, KELLY, HOW LONG IS IT YOU'VE BEEN BLIND NOW?
I'M NOT QUITE SURE, BRETT. LET ME CHECK MY CALENDAR, I KNOW I MARKED IT SO I CAN CELEBRATE ON THE BIG DAY.
BUT YOUR HEARING'S GOTTEN BETTER, RIGHT? YOUR SENSE OF SMELL?
NOT REALLY. NOT TO THE POINT IT MAKES MUCH DIFFERENCE.
YOU'RE ABSOLUTELY CERTAIN YOU CAN'T SMELL BULLSHIT?
ALL I'M SAYING IS, IT COULD BE THE STUMPY ONE YOU TALKED ABOUT IS KIND OF LIKE THAT, ONLY MORE SO. BEING WHAT HE IS TO BEGIN WITH, I MEAN.
IF THIS HORSECOCK GUY CAN BEAR A *GRUDGE*, IF HE CAN BE THIS ORGANISED-- HELL, WHO KNOWS WHAT THE DAMN THINGS ARE LEARNING? THEY COULD'VE USED STUMPY'S POWERS TO HOME IN ON YOU ALL THE WAY...
POWERS...?
THAT'S TRUE, WE'RE FUCKED.

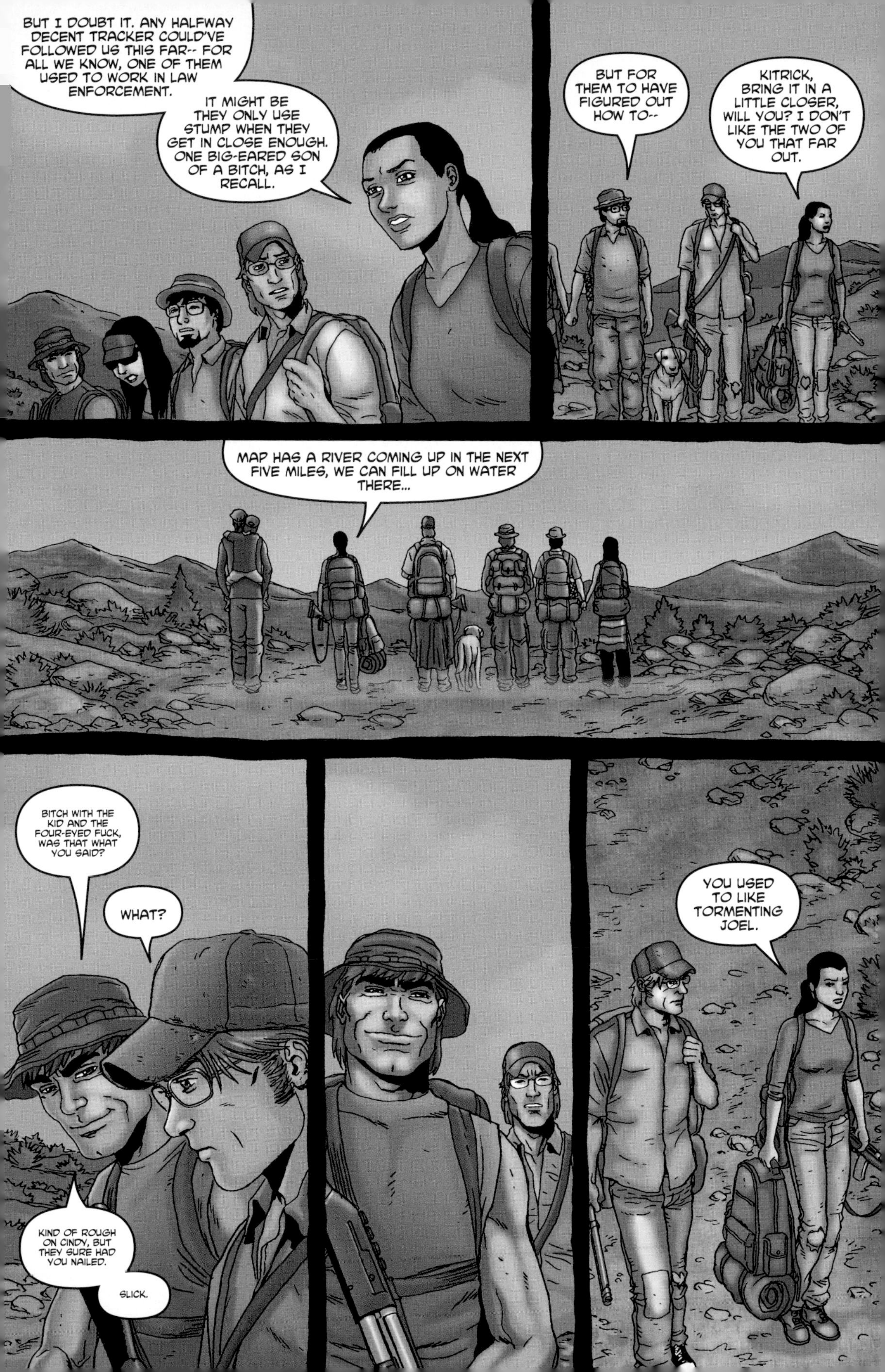

BUT I DOUBT IT. ANY HALFWAY DECENT TRACKER COULD'VE FOLLOWED US THIS FAR-- FOR ALL WE KNOW, ONE OF THEM USED TO WORK IN LAW ENFORCEMENT.
IT MIGHT BE THEY ONLY USE STUMP WHEN THEY GET IN CLOSE ENOUGH. ONE BIG-EARED SON OF A BITCH, AS I RECALL.
BUT FOR THEM TO HAVE FIGURED OUT HOW TO--
KITRICK, BRING IT IN A LITTLE CLOSER, WILL YOU? I DON'T LIKE THE TWO OF YOU THAT FAR OUT.
MAP HAS A RIVER COMING UP IN THE NEXT FIVE MILES, WE CAN FILL UP ON WATER THERE...
BITCH WITH THE KID AND THE FOUR-EYED FUCK, WAS THAT WHAT YOU SAID?
WHAT?
KIND OF ROUGH ON CINDY, BUT THEY SURE HAD YOU NAILED.
SLICK.
YOU USED TO LIKE TORMENTING JOEL.

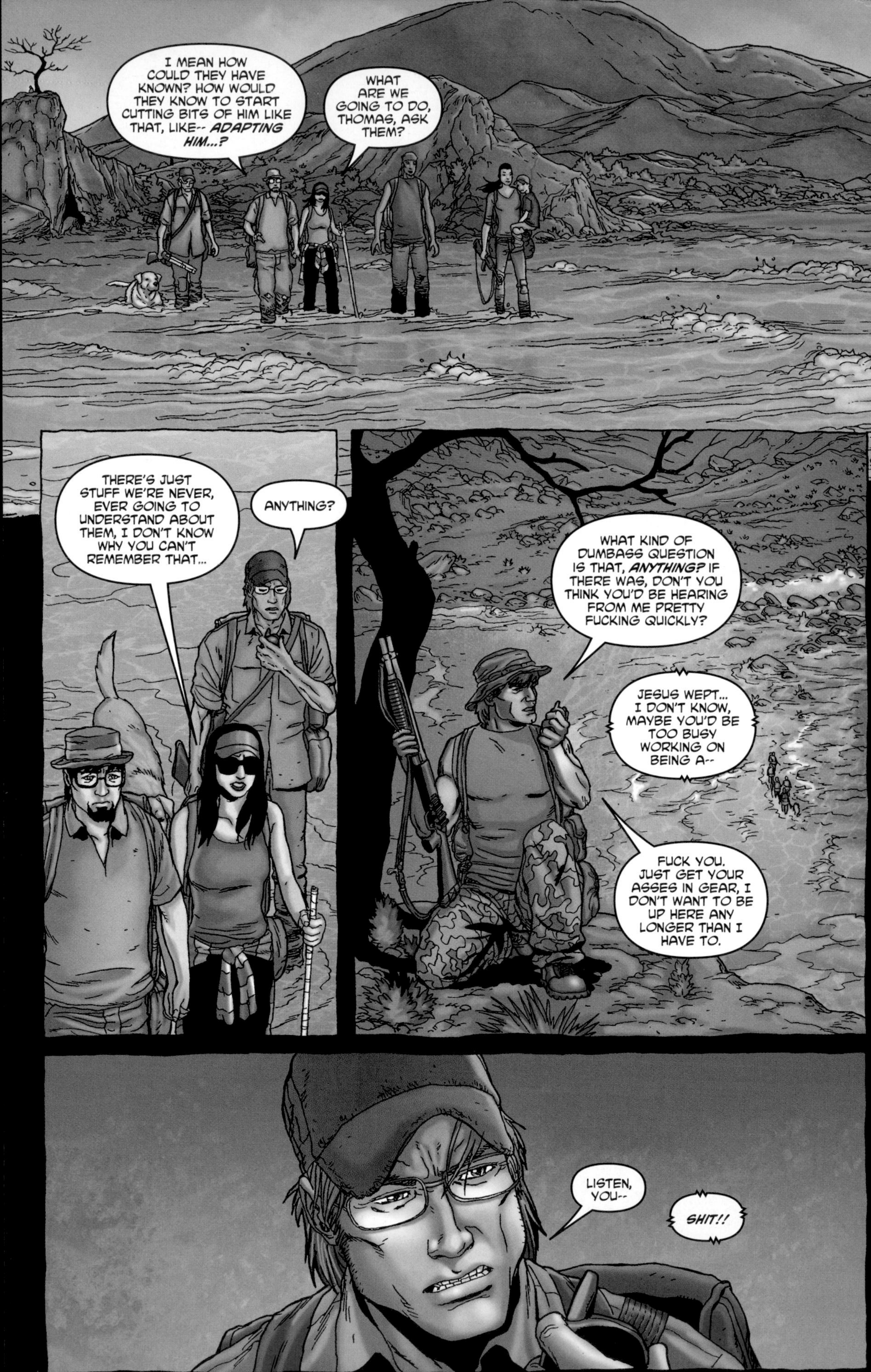
I MEAN HOW COULD THEY HAVE KNOWN? HOW WOULD THEY KNOW TO START CUTTING BITS OF HIM LIKE THAT, LIKE-- *ADAPTING HIM...?*
WHAT ARE WE GOING TO DO, THOMAS, ASK THEM?
THERE'S JUST STUFF WE'RE NEVER, EVER GOING TO UNDERSTAND ABOUT THEM, I DON'T KNOW WHY YOU CAN'T REMEMBER THAT...
ANYTHING?
WHAT KIND OF DUMBASS QUESTION IS THAT, *ANYTHING?* IF THERE WAS, DON'T YOU THINK YOU'D BE HEARING FROM ME PRETTY FUCKING QUICKLY?
JESUS WEPT... I DON'T KNOW, MAYBE YOU'D BE TOO BUSY WORKING ON BEING A--
FUCK YOU. JUST GET YOUR ASSES IN GEAR, I DON'T WANT TO BE UP HERE ANY LONGER THAN I HAVE TO.
LISTEN, YOU--
SHIT!!

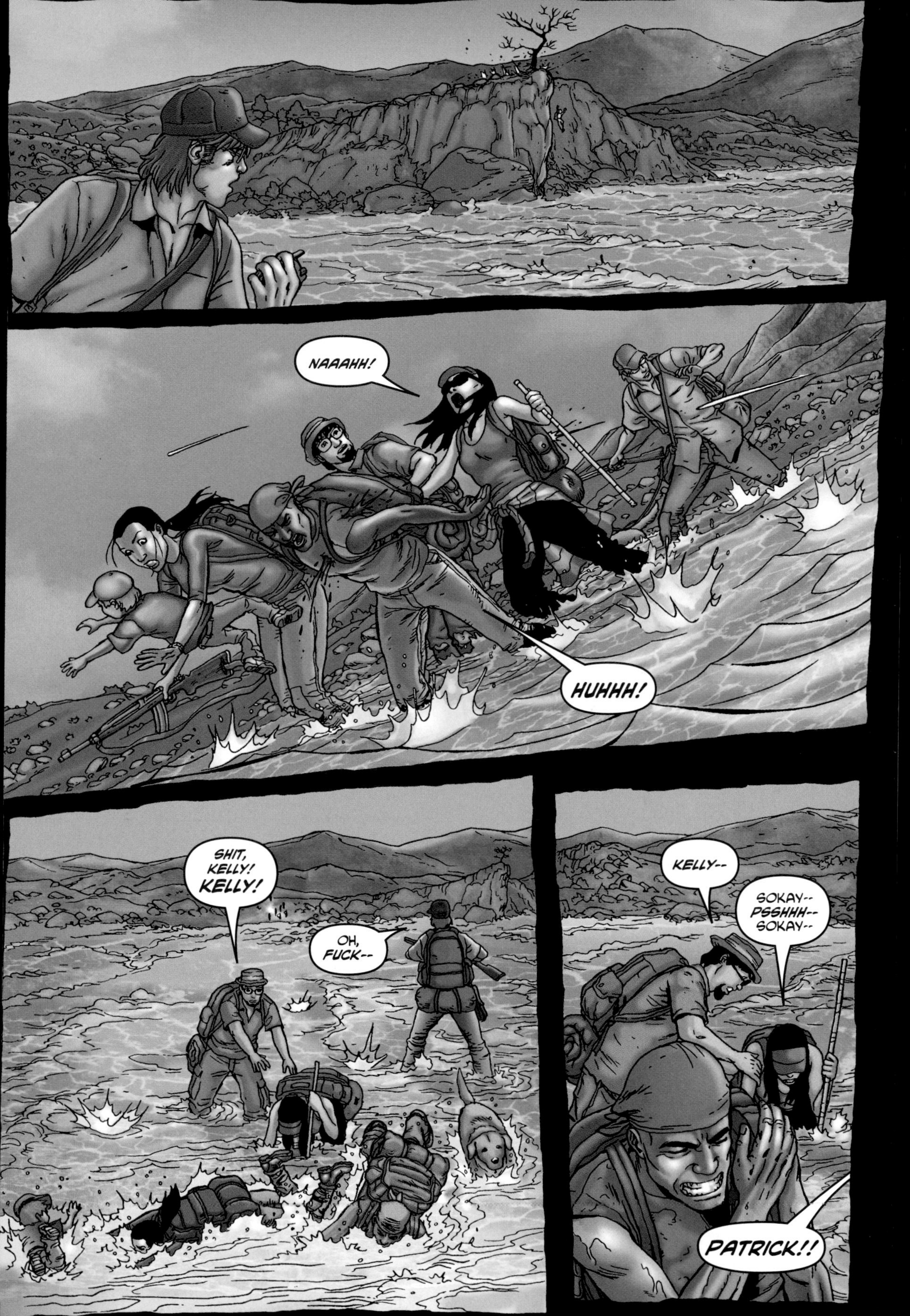
NAAAHH!
HUHHH!
SHIT, KELLY! KELLY!
OH, FUCK--
KELLY--
SOKAY-- PSSHHH-- SOKAY--
PATRICK!!

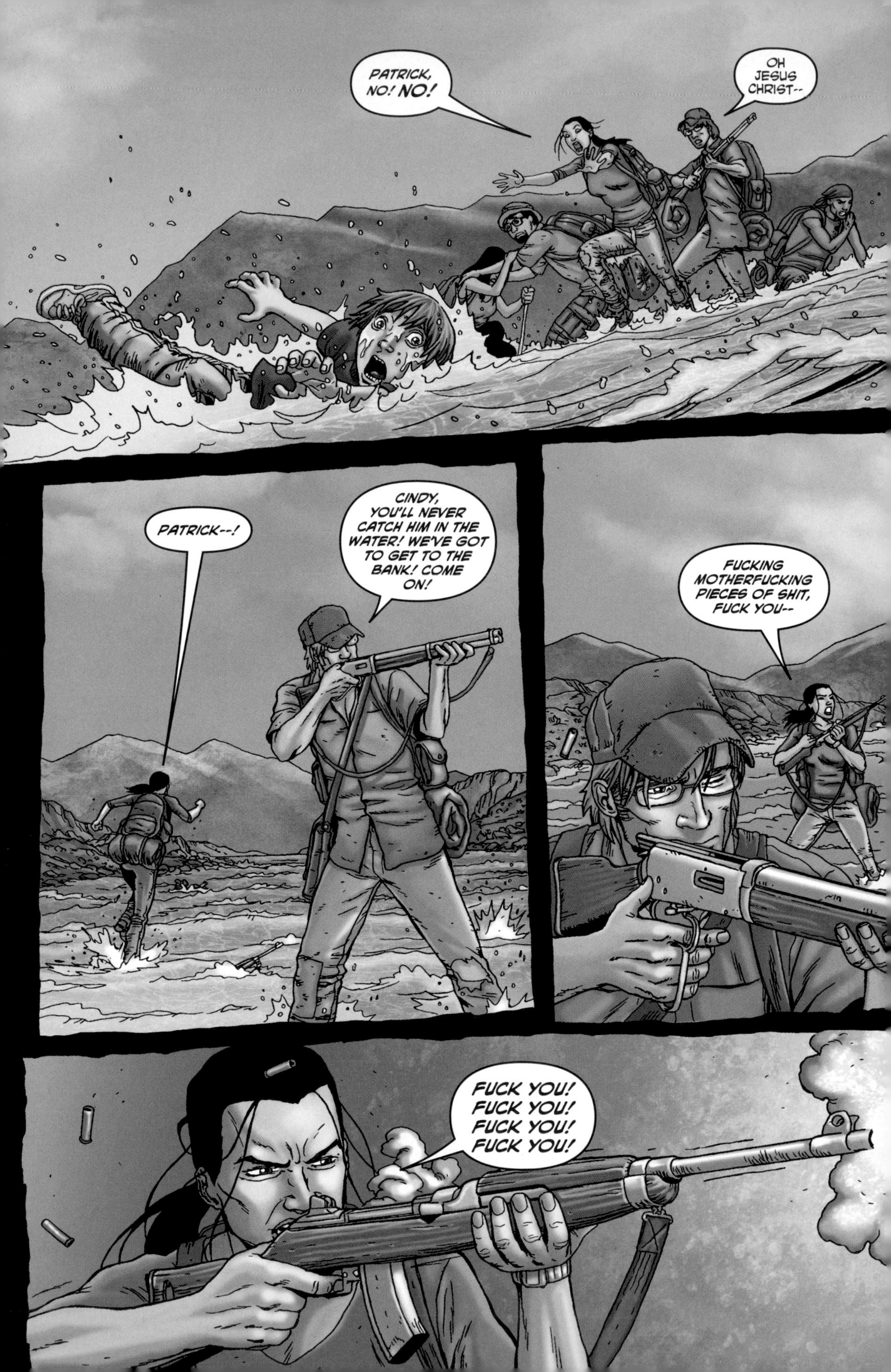
PATRICK, NO! NO!
OH JESUS CHRIST--
PATRICK--!
CINDY, YOU'LL NEVER CATCH HIM IN THE WATER! WE'VE GOT TO GET TO THE BANK! COME ON!
FUCKING MOTHERFUCKING PIECES OF SHIT, FUCK YOU--
FUCK YOU! FUCK YOU! FUCK YOU! FUCK YOU!

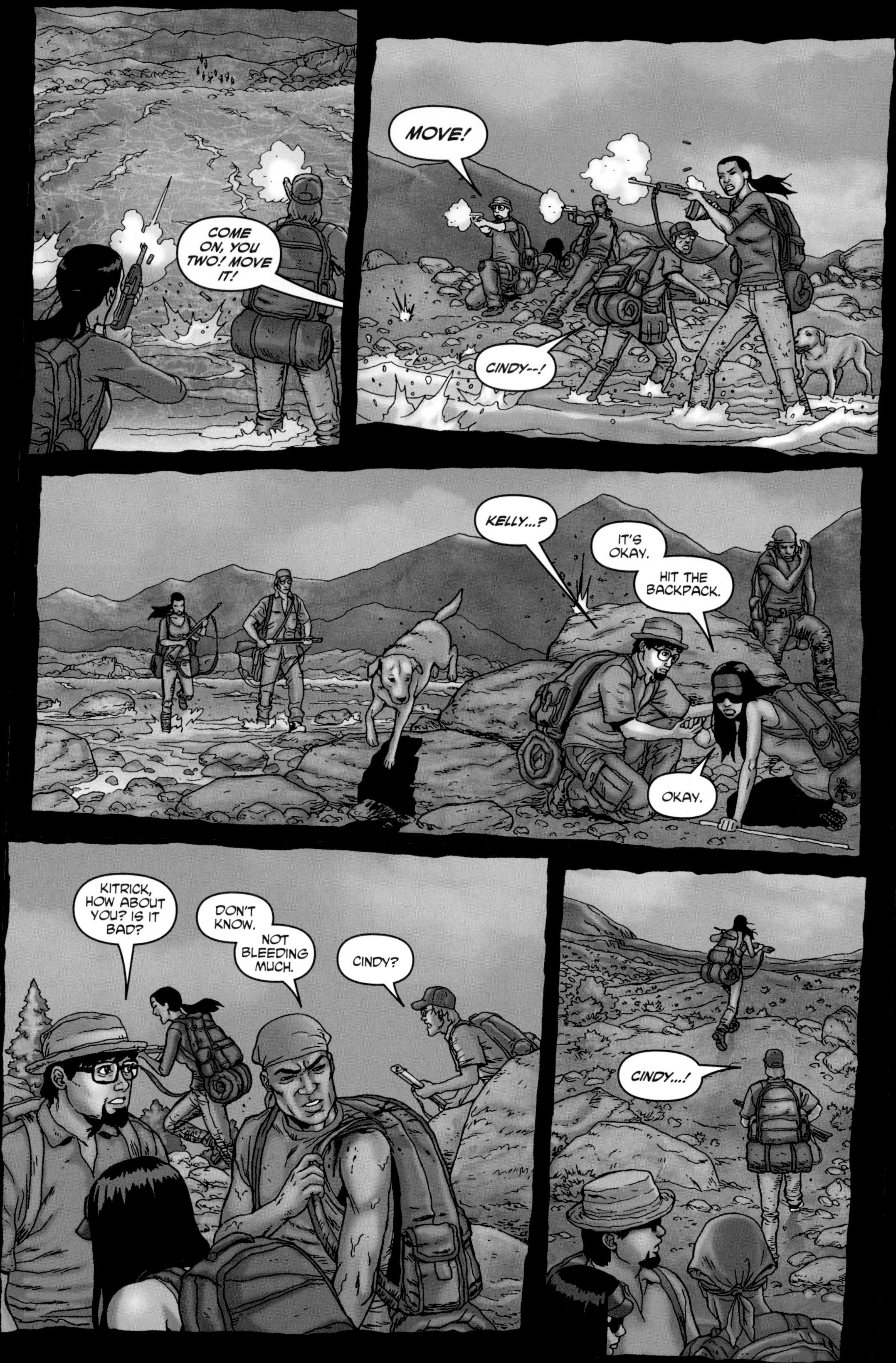
COME ON, YOU TWO! MOVE IT!
MOVE!
CINDY--!
KELLY...?
IT'S OKAY.
HIT THE BACKPACK.
OKAY.
KITRICK, HOW ABOUT YOU? IS IT BAD?
DON'T KNOW.
NOT BLEEDING MUCH.
CINDY?
CINDY...!

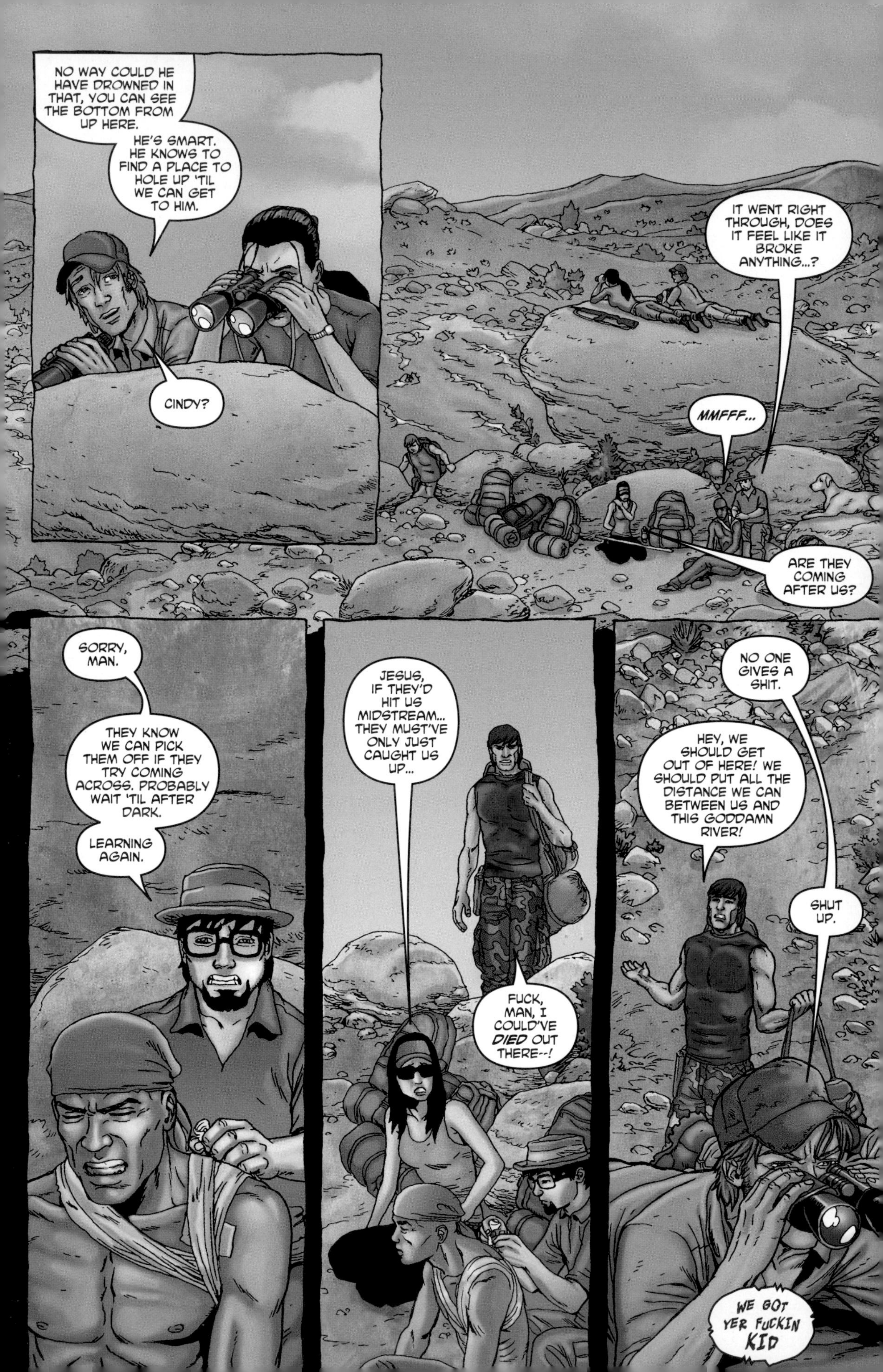
NO WAY COULD HE HAVE DROWNED IN THAT, YOU CAN SEE THE BOTTOM FROM UP HERE.
HE'S SMART. HE KNOWS TO FIND A PLACE TO HOLE UP 'TIL WE CAN GET TO HIM.
CINDY?
IT WENT RIGHT THROUGH, DOES IT FEEL LIKE IT BROKE ANYTHING...?
MMFFF...
ARE THEY COMING AFTER US?
SORRY, MAN.
THEY KNOW WE CAN PICK THEM OFF IF THEY TRY COMING ACROSS. PROBABLY WAIT 'TIL AFTER DARK.
LEARNING AGAIN.
JESUS, IF THEY'D HIT US MIDSTREAM... THEY MUST'VE ONLY JUST CAUGHT US UP...
FUCK, MAN, I COULD'VE DIED OUT THERE--!
NO ONE GIVES A SHIT.
HEY, WE SHOULD GET OUT OF HERE! WE SHOULD PUT ALL THE DISTANCE WE CAN BETWEEN US AND THIS GODDAMN RIVER!
SHUT UP.
WE GOT YER FUCKIN KID

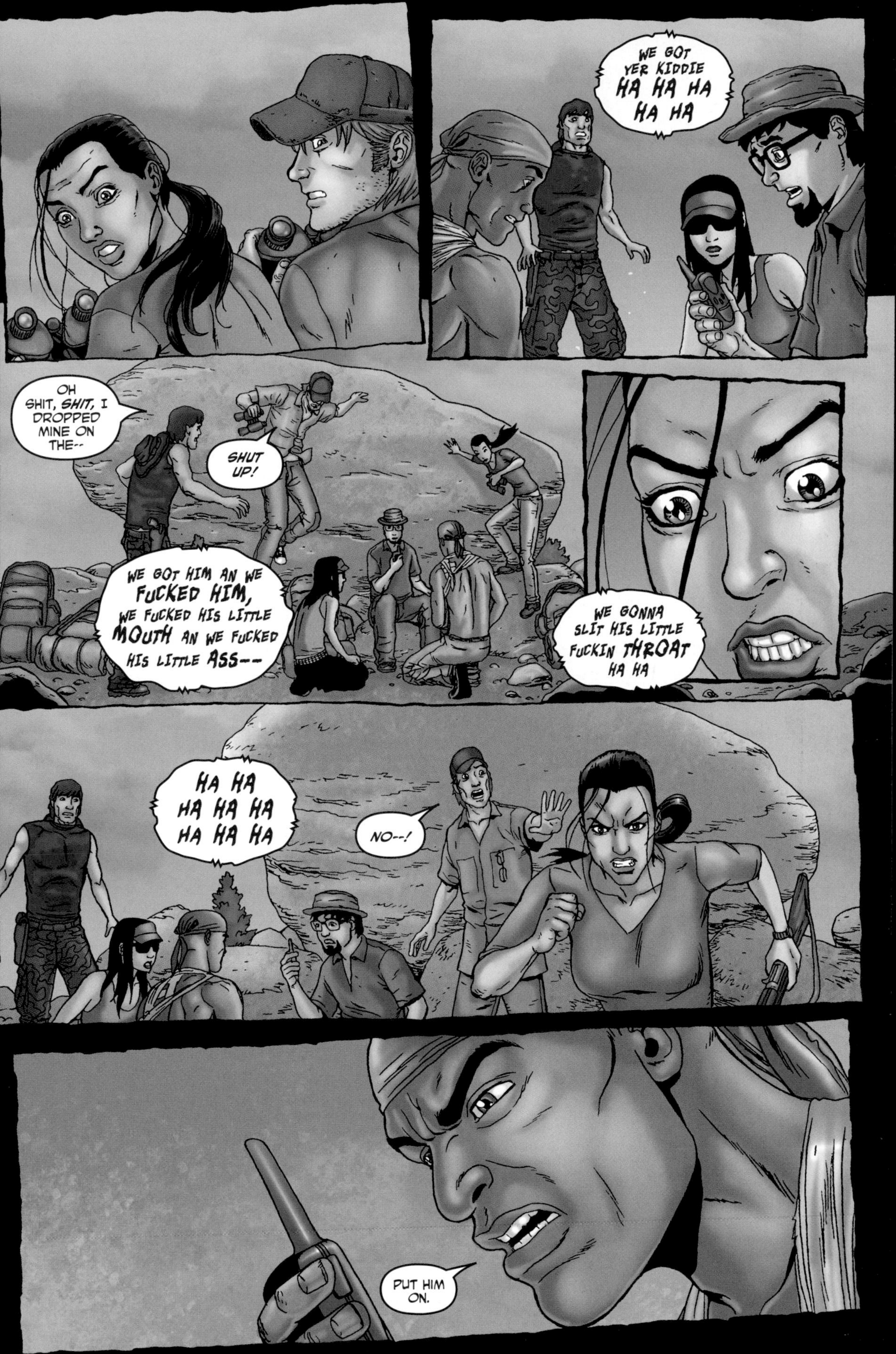
WE GOT YER KIDDIE HA HA HA HA HA
OH SHIT, *SHIT*, I DROPPED MINE ON THE--
SHUT UP!
WE GOT HIM AN WE FUCKED HIM, WE FUCKED HIS LITTLE MOUTH AN WE FUCKED HIS LITTLE ASS--
WE GONNA SLIT HIS LITTLE FUCKIN THROAT HA HA
HA HA HA HA HA HA HA HA
NO--!
PUT HIM ON.

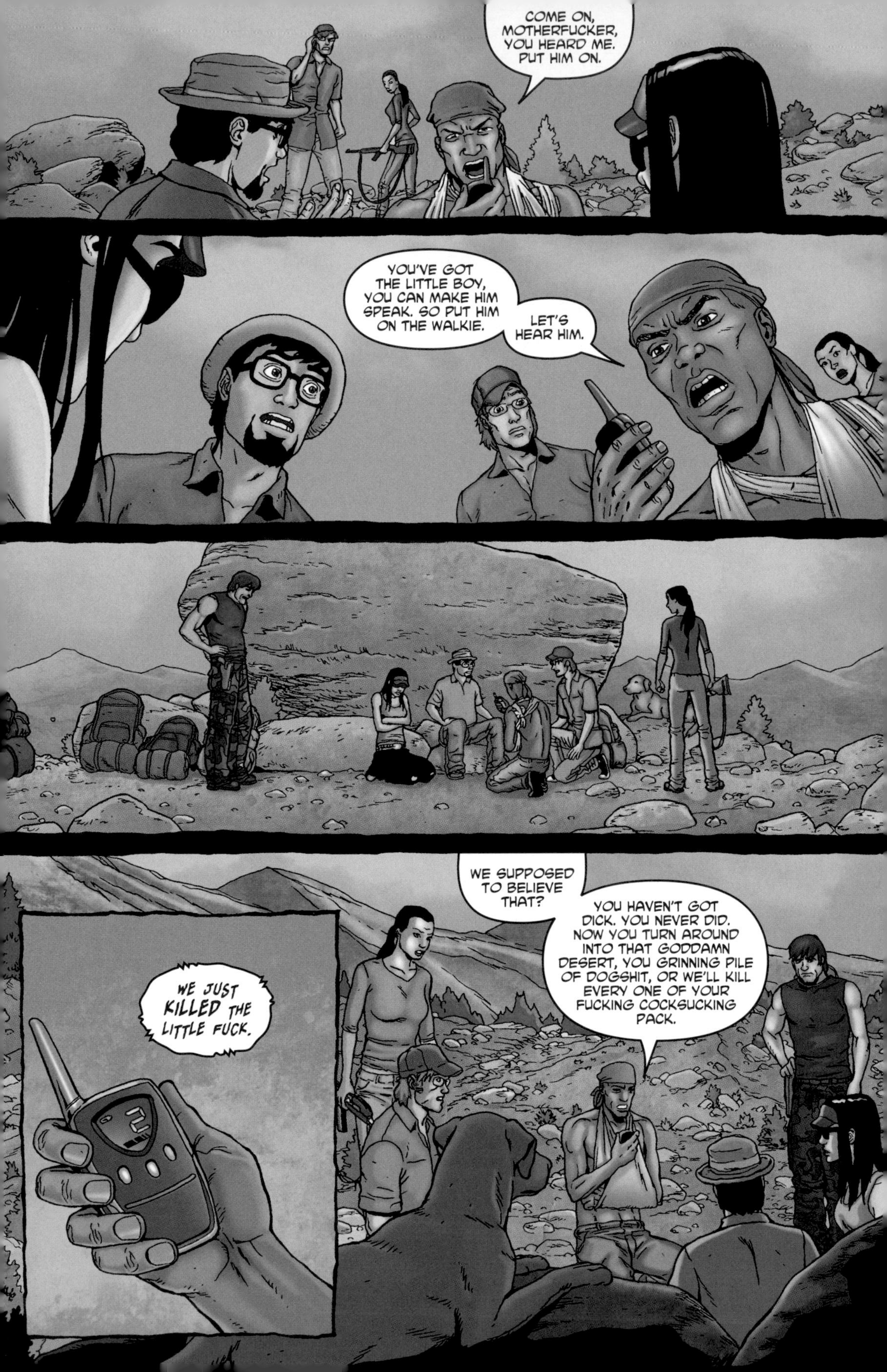
COME ON, MOTHERFUCKER, YOU HEARD ME. PUT HIM ON.
YOU'VE GOT THE LITTLE BOY, YOU CAN MAKE HIM SPEAK. SO PUT HIM ON THE WALKIE.
LET'S HEAR HIM.
WE JUST KILLED THE LITTLE FUCK.
WE SUPPOSED TO BELIEVE THAT?
YOU HAVEN'T GOT DICK. YOU NEVER DID. NOW YOU TURN AROUND INTO THAT GODDAMN DESERT, YOU GRINNING PILE OF DOGSHIT, OR WE'LL KILL EVERY ONE OF YOUR FUCKING COCKSUCKING PACK.

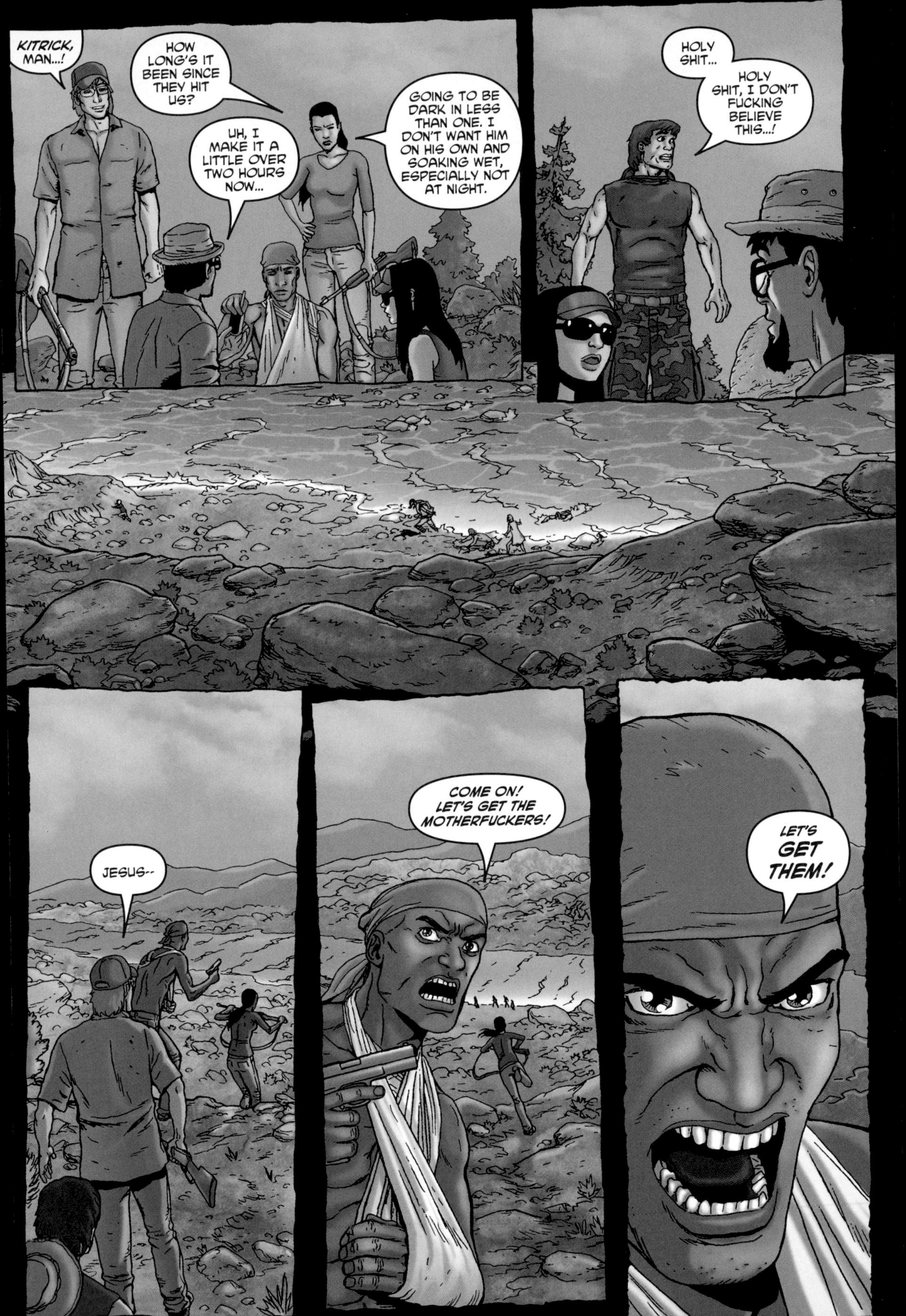
KITRICK, MAN...!
HOW LONG'S IT BEEN SINCE THEY HIT US?
UH, I MAKE IT A LITTLE OVER TWO HOURS NOW...
GOING TO BE DARK IN LESS THAN ONE. I DON'T WANT HIM ON HIS OWN AND SOAKING WET, ESPECIALLY NOT AT NIGHT.
HOLY SHIT...
HOLY SHIT, I DON'T FUCKING BELIEVE THIS...!
JESUS--
COME ON! LET'S GET THE MOTHERFUCKERS!
LET'S GET THEM!

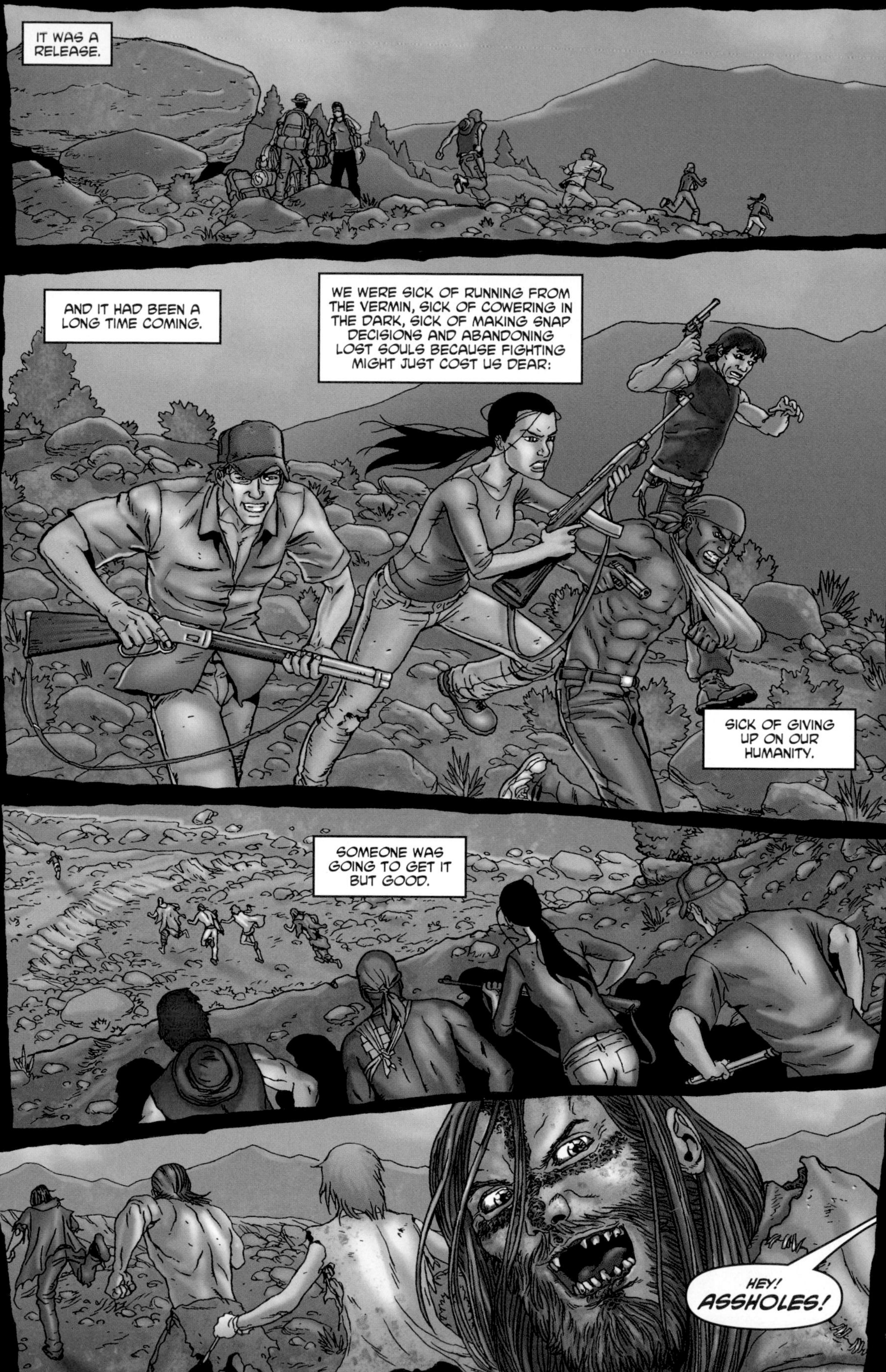
IT WAS A RELEASE.
AND IT HAD BEEN A LONG TIME COMING.
WE WERE SICK OF RUNNING FROM THE VERMIN, SICK OF COWERING IN THE DARK, SICK OF MAKING SNAP DECISIONS AND ABANDONING LOST SOULS BECAUSE FIGHTING MIGHT JUST COST US DEAR:
SICK OF GIVING UP ON OUR HUMANITY.
SOMEONE WAS GOING TO GET IT BUT GOOD.
HEY! ASSHOLES!

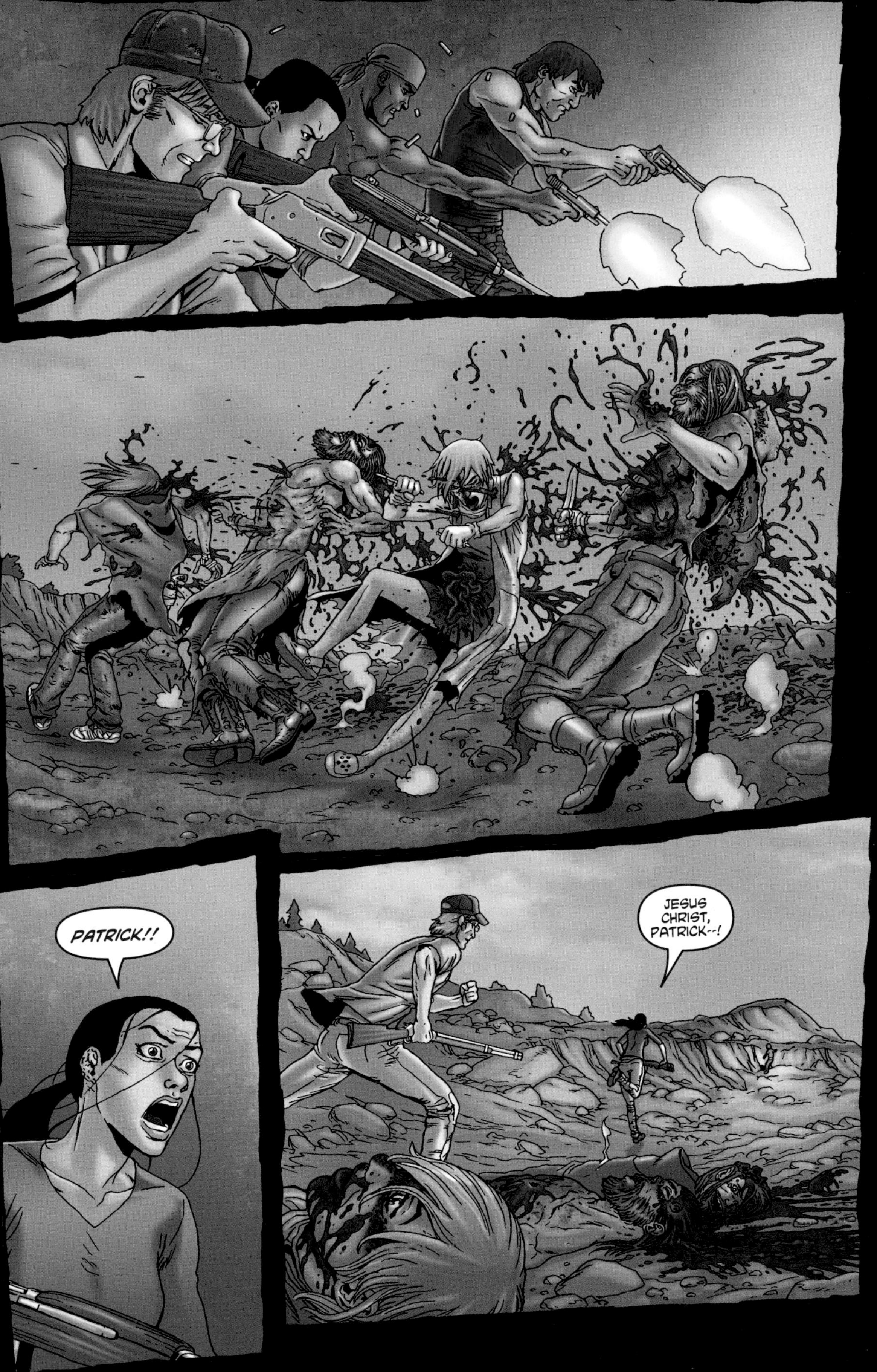
PATRICK!!
JESUS CHRIST, PATRICK--!

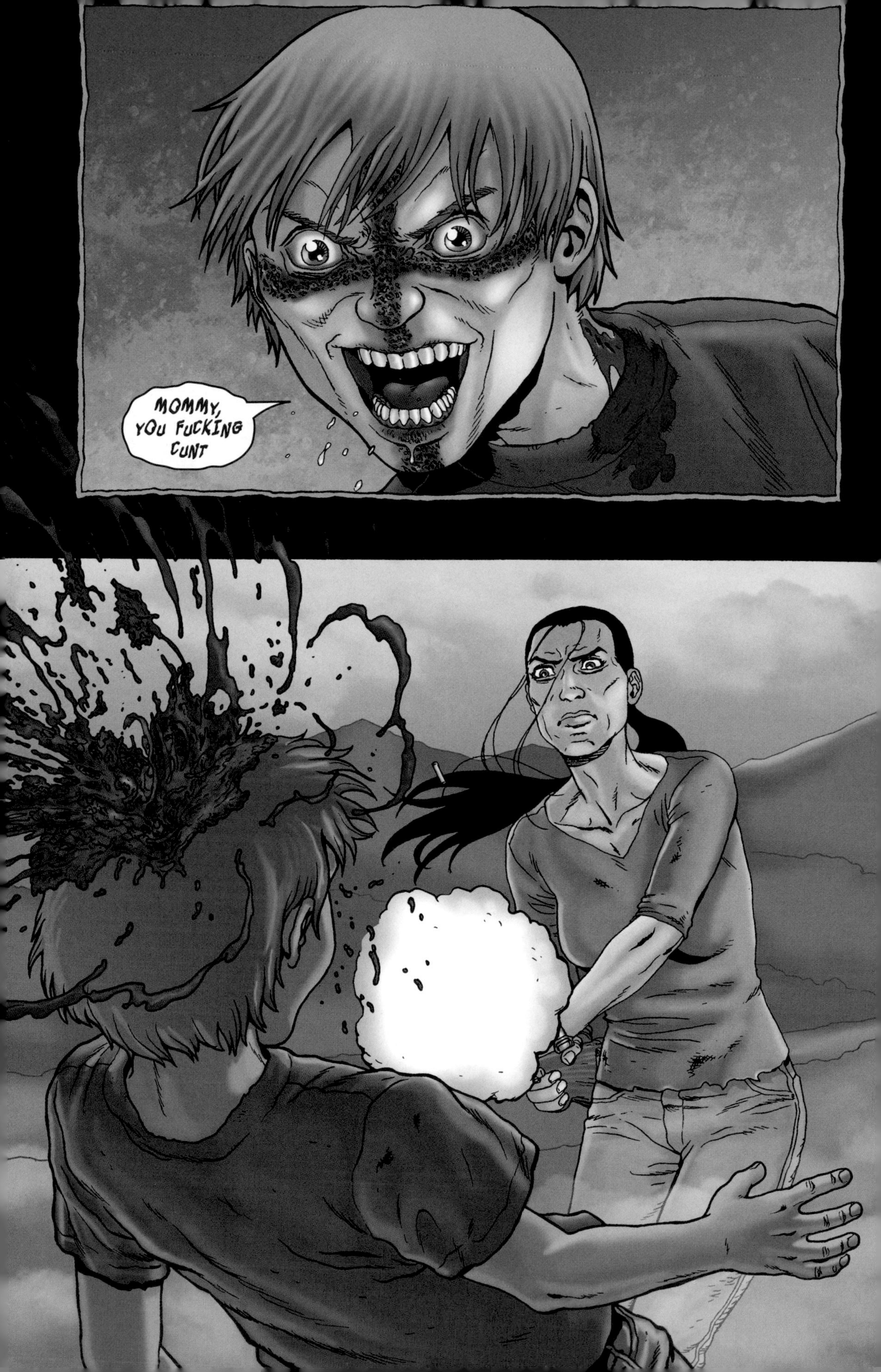
MOMMY, YOU FUCKING CUNT

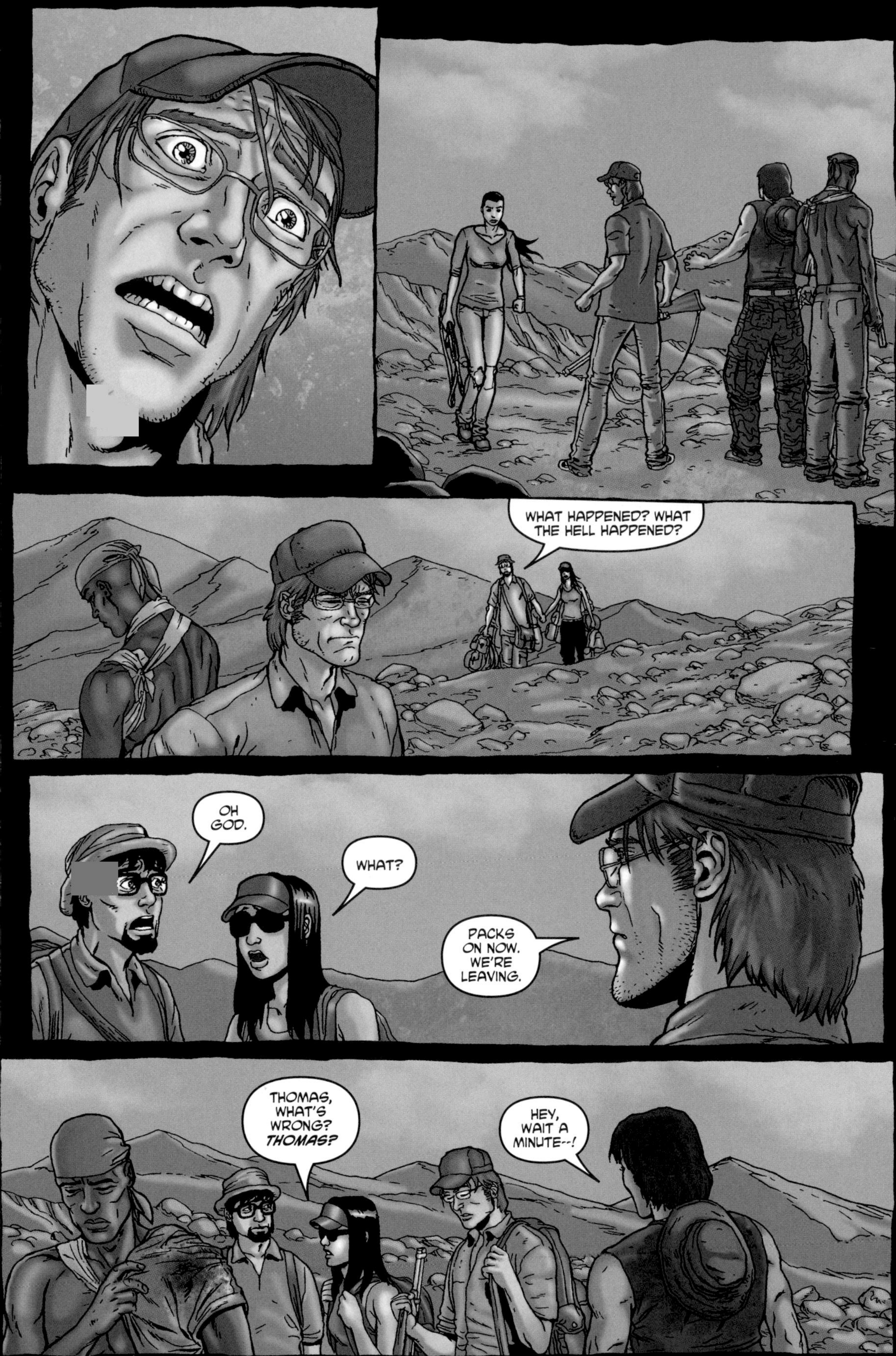
WHAT HAPPENED? WHAT THE HELL HAPPENED?
OH GOD.
WHAT?
PACKS ON NOW. WE'RE LEAVING.
THOMAS, WHAT'S WRONG? *THOMAS?*
HEY, WAIT A MINUTE--!

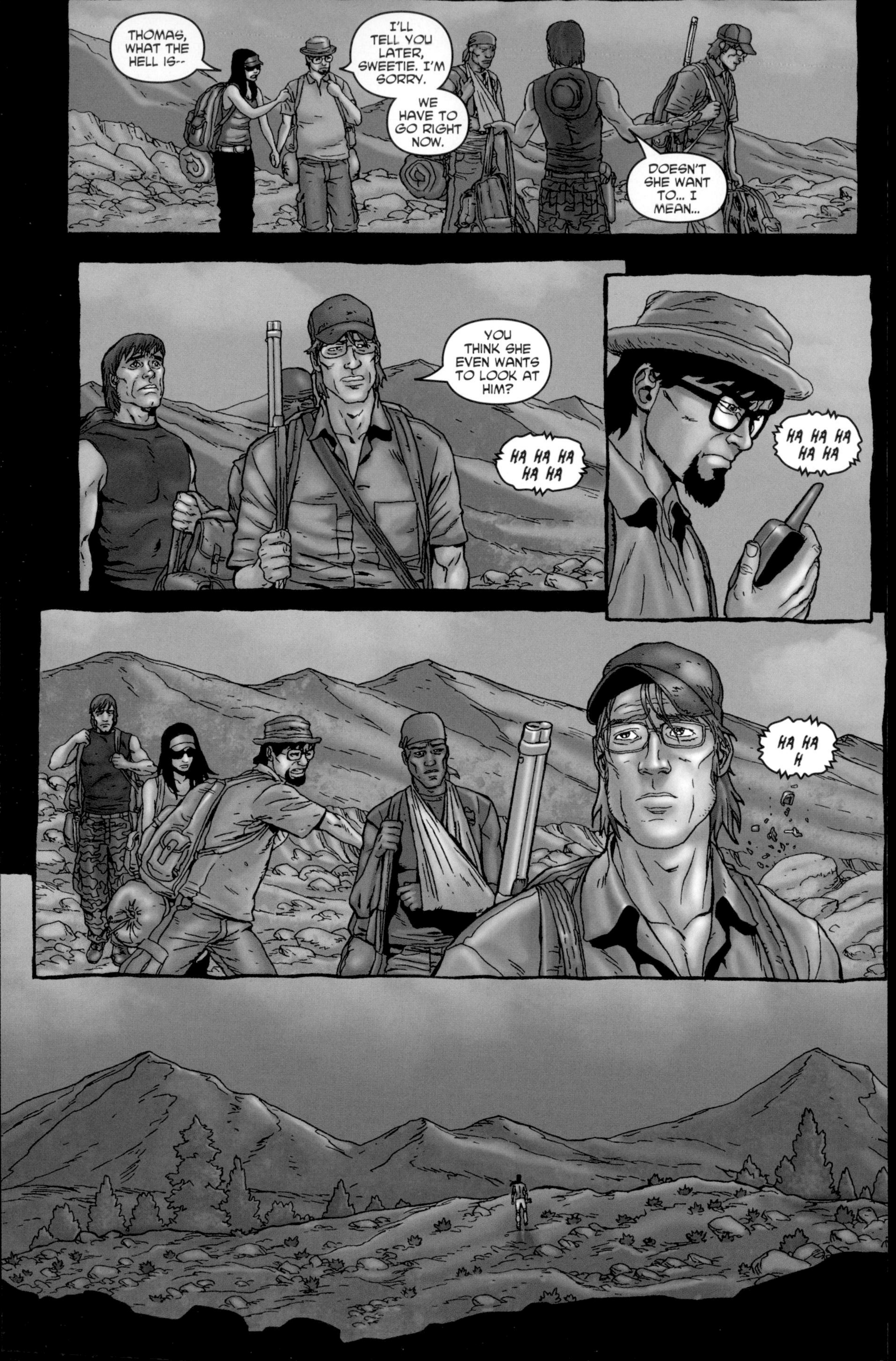
THOMAS, WHAT THE HELL IS--
I'LL TELL YOU LATER, SWEETIE. I'M SORRY.
WE HAVE TO GO RIGHT NOW.
DOESN'T SHE WANT TO... I MEAN...
YOU THINK SHE EVEN WANTS TO LOOK AT HIM?
HA HA HA HA HA
HA HA HA HA HA
HA HA H

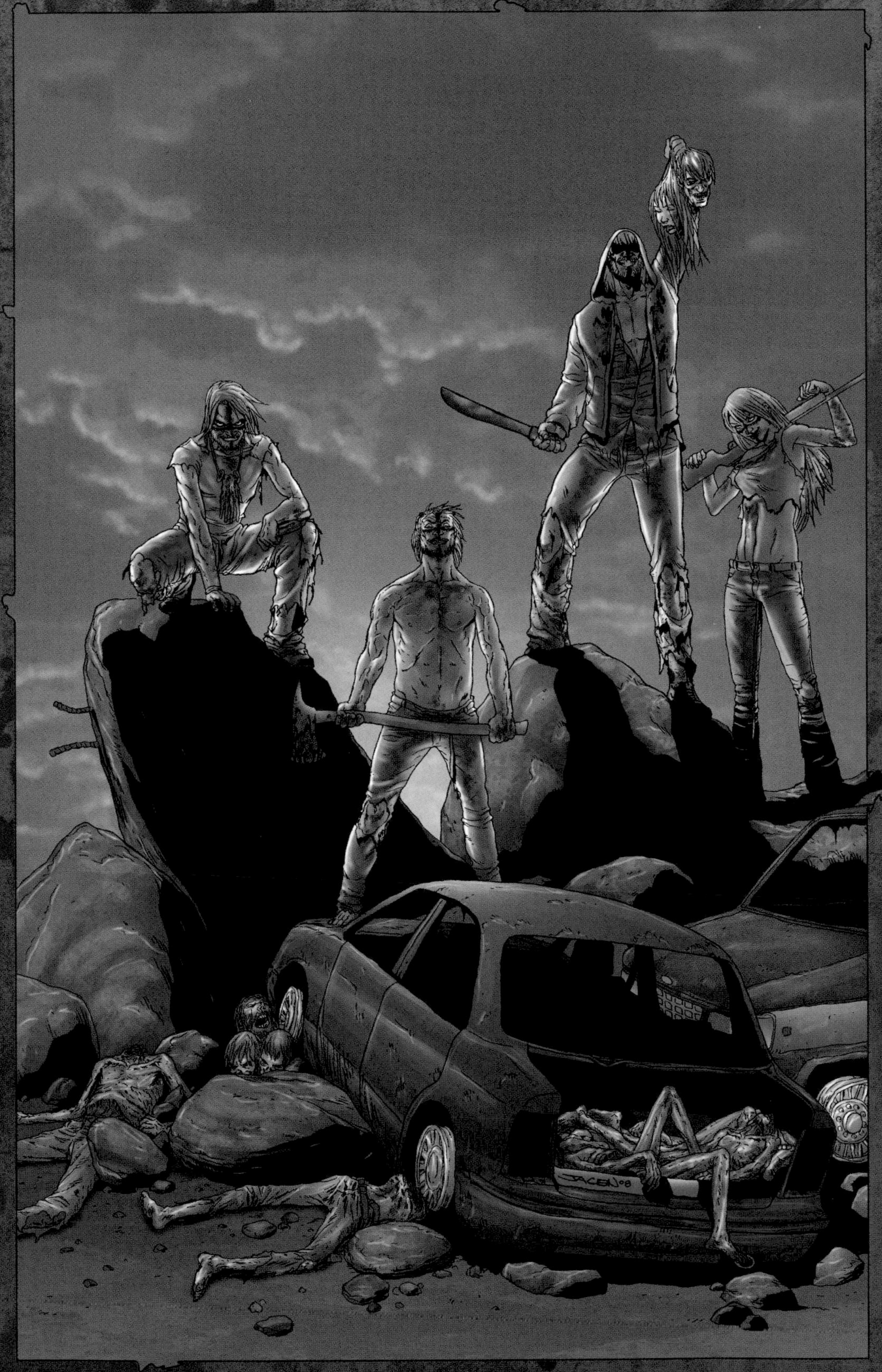
JACEN '08

PART NINE

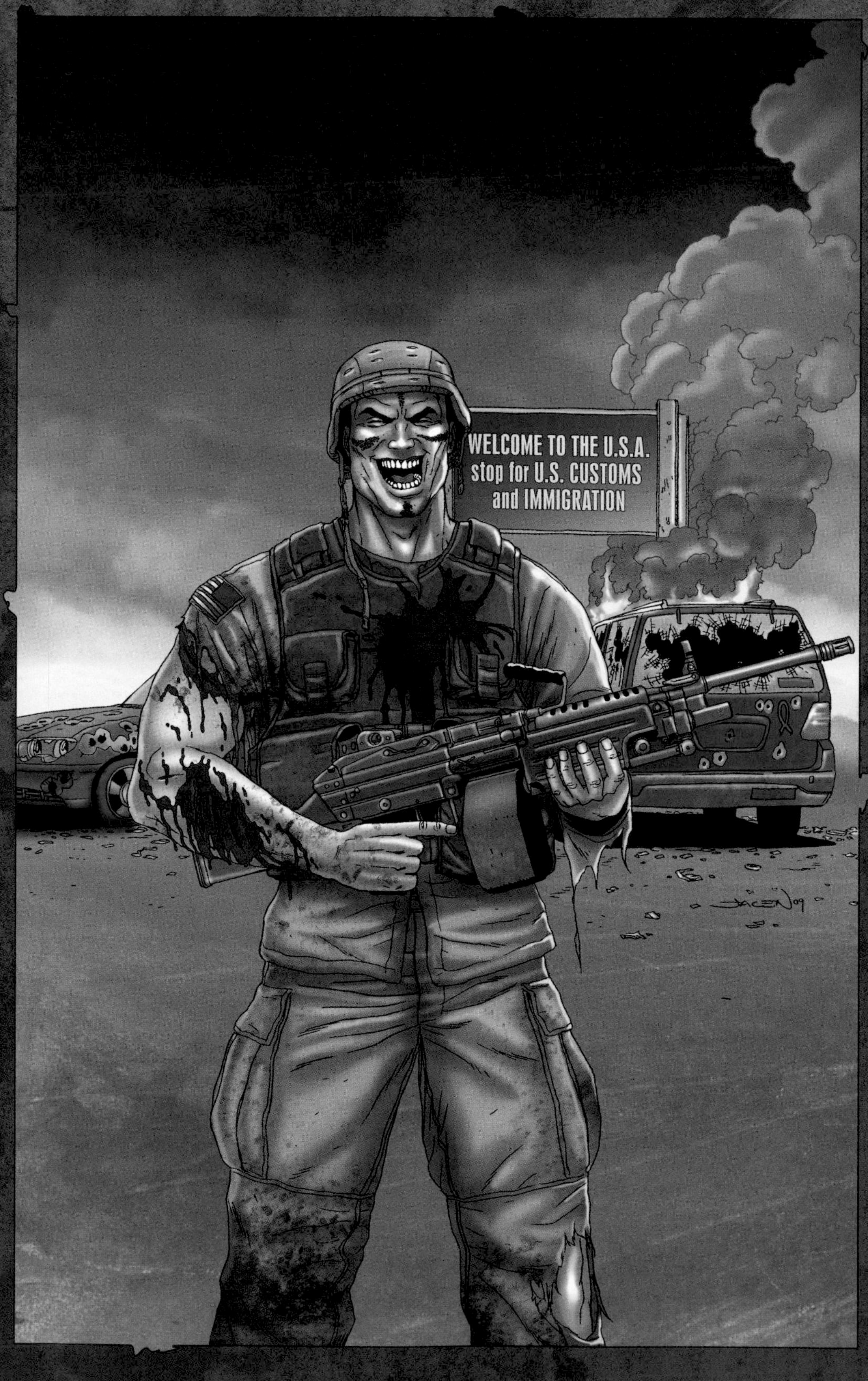
WELCOME TO THE U.S.A.
stop for U.S. CUSTOMS
and IMMIGRATION

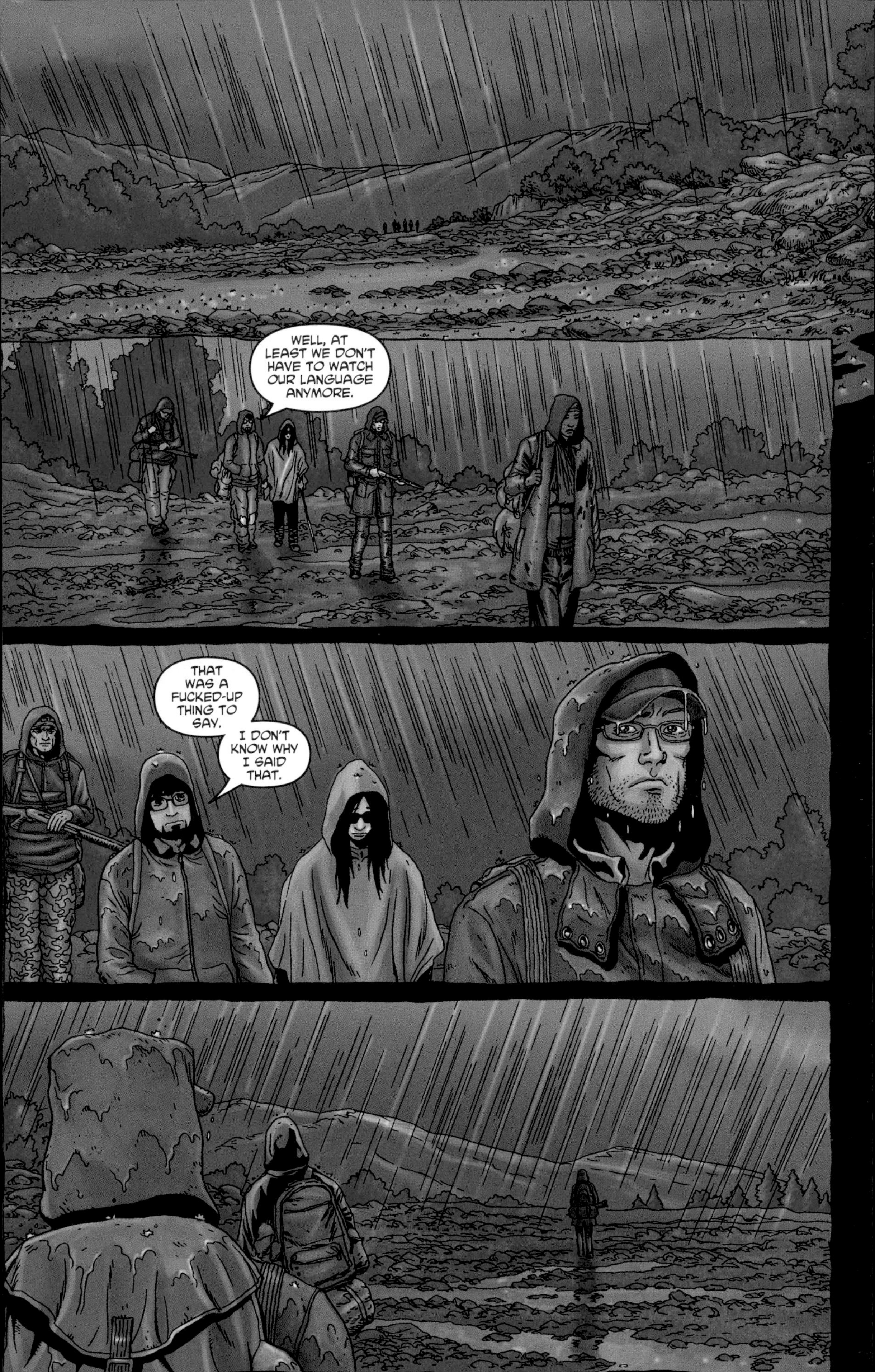
WELL, AT LEAST WE DON'T HAVE TO WATCH OUR LANGUAGE ANYMORE.
THAT WAS A FUCKED-UP THING TO SAY.
I DON'T KNOW WHY I SAID THAT.

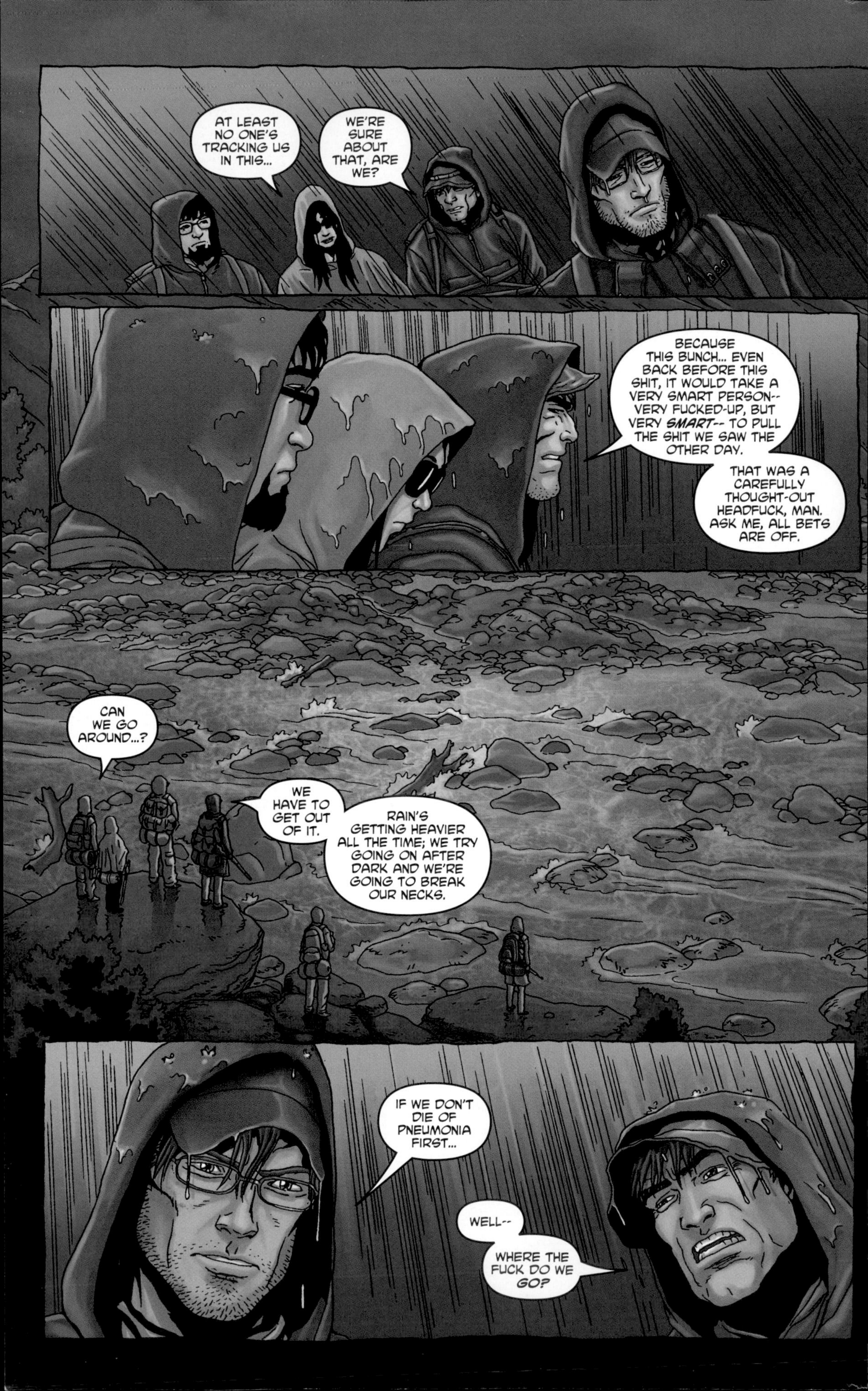
AT LEAST NO ONE'S TRACKING US IN THIS...
WE'RE SURE ABOUT THAT, ARE WE?
BECAUSE THIS BUNCH... EVEN BACK BEFORE THIS SHIT, IT WOULD TAKE A VERY SMART PERSON-- VERY FUCKED-UP, BUT VERY *SMART*-- TO PULL THE SHIT WE SAW THE OTHER DAY.
THAT WAS A CAREFULLY THOUGHT-OUT HEADFUCK, MAN. ASK ME, ALL BETS ARE OFF.
CAN WE GO AROUND...?
WE HAVE TO GET OUT OF IT.
RAIN'S GETTING HEAVIER ALL THE TIME; WE TRY GOING ON AFTER DARK AND WE'RE GOING TO BREAK OUR NECKS.
IF WE DON'T DIE OF PNEUMONIA FIRST...
WELL--
WHERE THE FUCK DO WE *GO?*

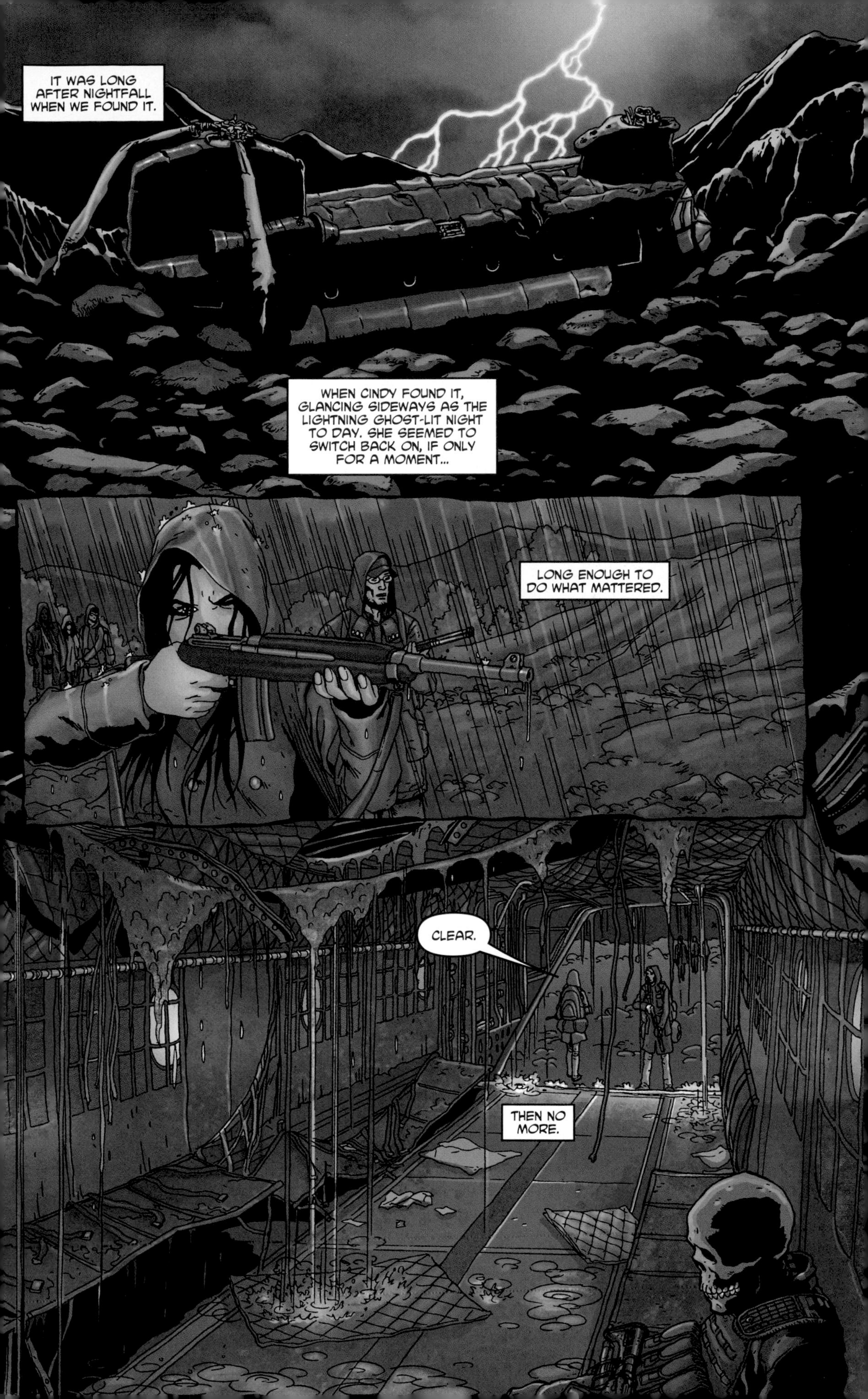
IT WAS LONG AFTER NIGHTFALL WHEN WE FOUND IT.
WHEN CINDY FOUND IT, GLANCING SIDEWAYS AS THE LIGHTNING GHOST-LIT NIGHT TO DAY. SHE SEEMED TO SWITCH BACK ON, IF ONLY FOR A MOMENT...
LONG ENOUGH TO DO WHAT MATTERED.
CLEAR.
THEN NO MORE.

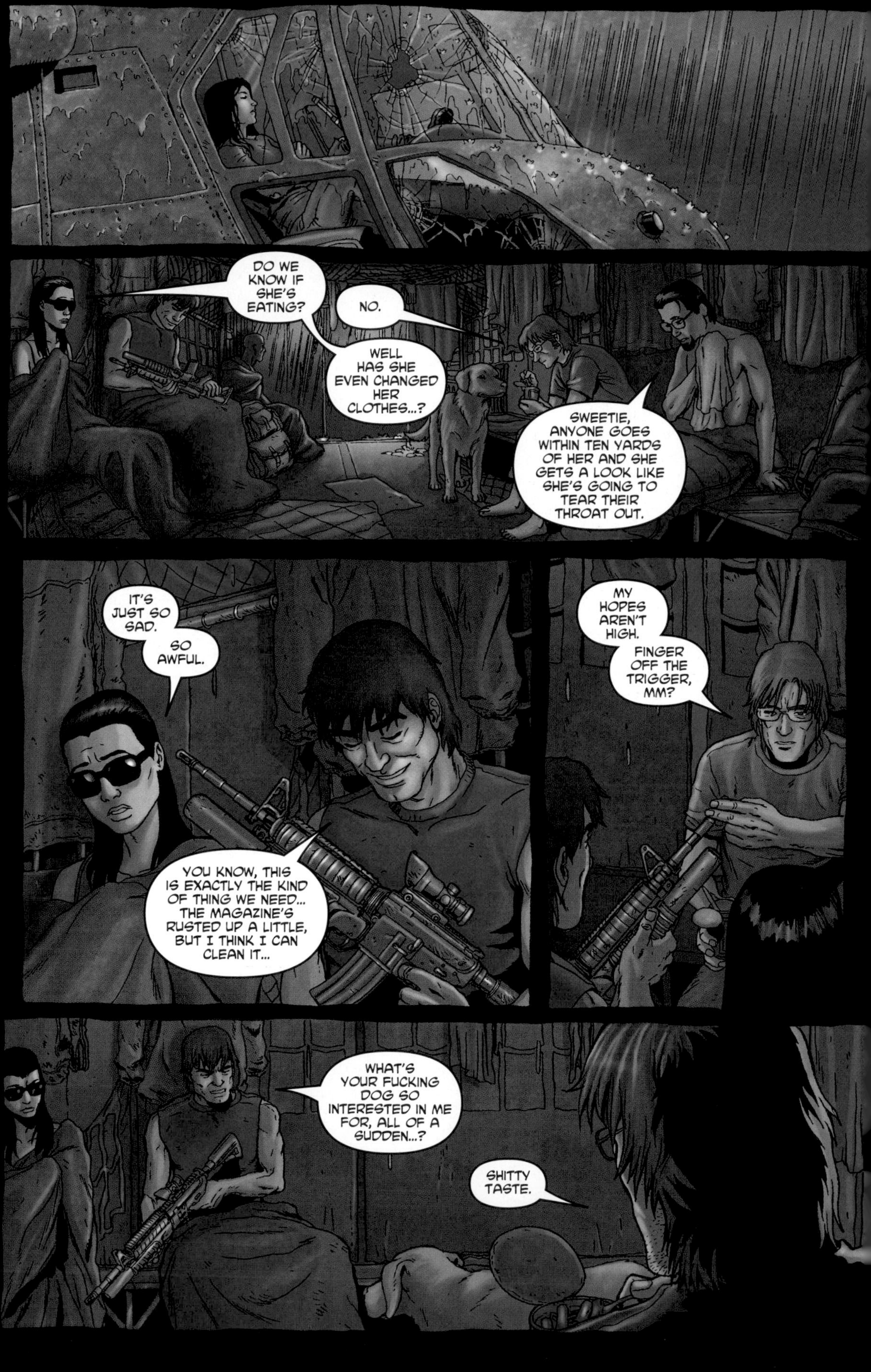
DO WE KNOW IF SHE'S EATING?
NO.
WELL HAS SHE EVEN CHANGED HER CLOTHES...?
SWEETIE, ANYONE GOES WITHIN TEN YARDS OF HER AND SHE GETS A LOOK LIKE SHE'S GOING TO TEAR THEIR THROAT OUT.
IT'S JUST SO SAD.
SO AWFUL.
YOU KNOW, THIS IS EXACTLY THE KIND OF THING WE NEED... THE MAGAZINE'S RUSTED UP A LITTLE, BUT I THINK I CAN CLEAN IT...
MY HOPES AREN'T HIGH.
FINGER OFF THE TRIGGER, MM?
WHAT'S YOUR FUCKING DOG SO INTERESTED IN ME FOR, ALL OF A SUDDEN...?
SHITTY TASTE.

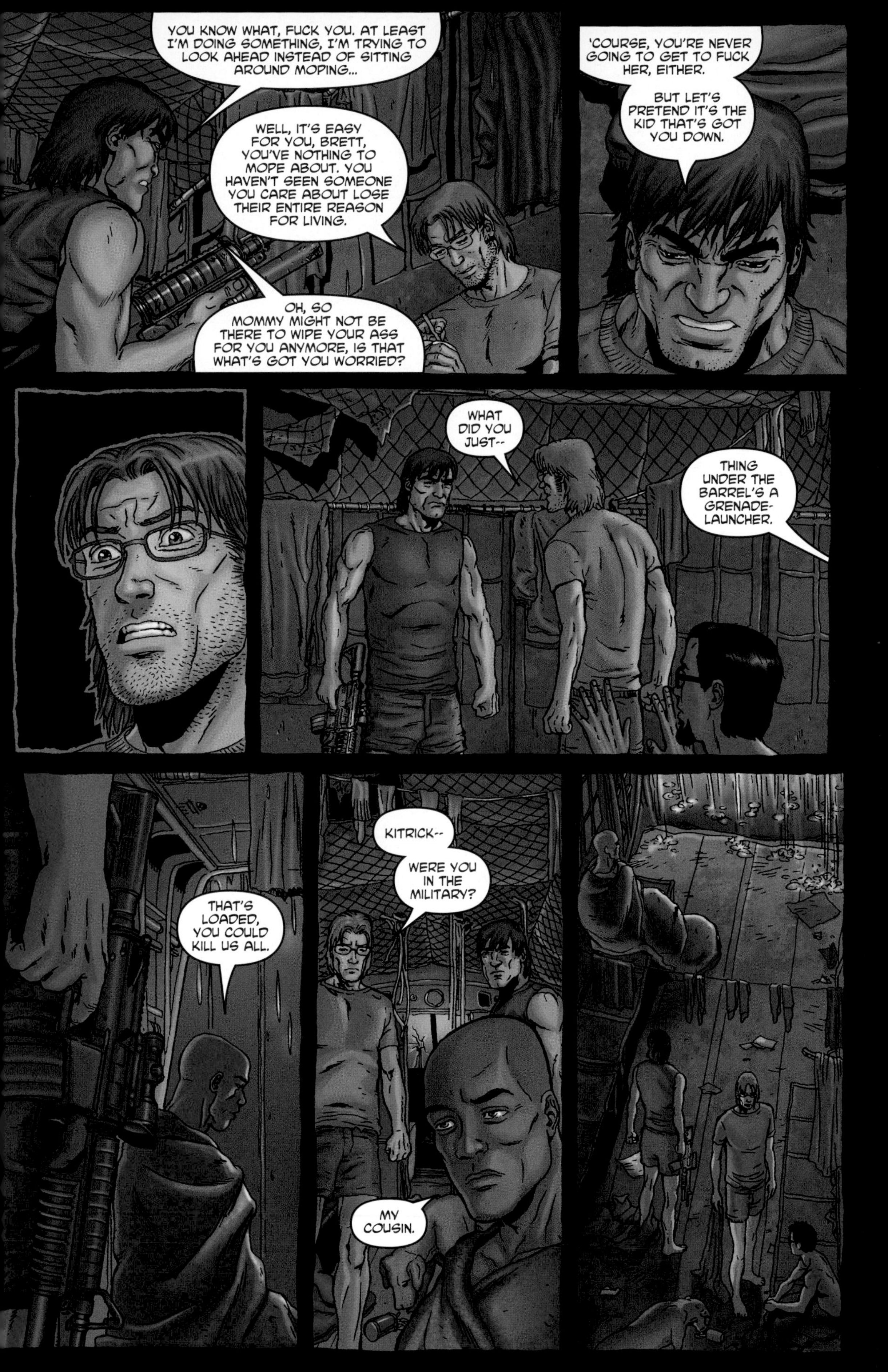
YOU KNOW WHAT, FUCK YOU. AT LEAST I'M DOING SOMETHING, I'M TRYING TO LOOK AHEAD INSTEAD OF SITTING AROUND MOPING...
WELL, IT'S EASY FOR YOU, BRETT, YOU'VE NOTHING TO MOPE ABOUT. YOU HAVEN'T SEEN SOMEONE YOU CARE ABOUT LOSE THEIR ENTIRE REASON FOR LIVING.
OH, SO MOMMY MIGHT NOT BE THERE TO WIPE YOUR ASS FOR YOU ANYMORE, IS THAT WHAT'S GOT YOU WORRIED?
'COURSE, YOU'RE NEVER GOING TO GET TO FUCK HER, EITHER.
BUT LET'S PRETEND IT'S THE KID THAT'S GOT YOU DOWN.
WHAT DID YOU JUST--
THING UNDER THE BARREL'S A GRENADE-LAUNCHER.
THAT'S LOADED, YOU COULD KILL US ALL.
KITRICK--
WERE YOU IN THE MILITARY?
MY COUSIN.

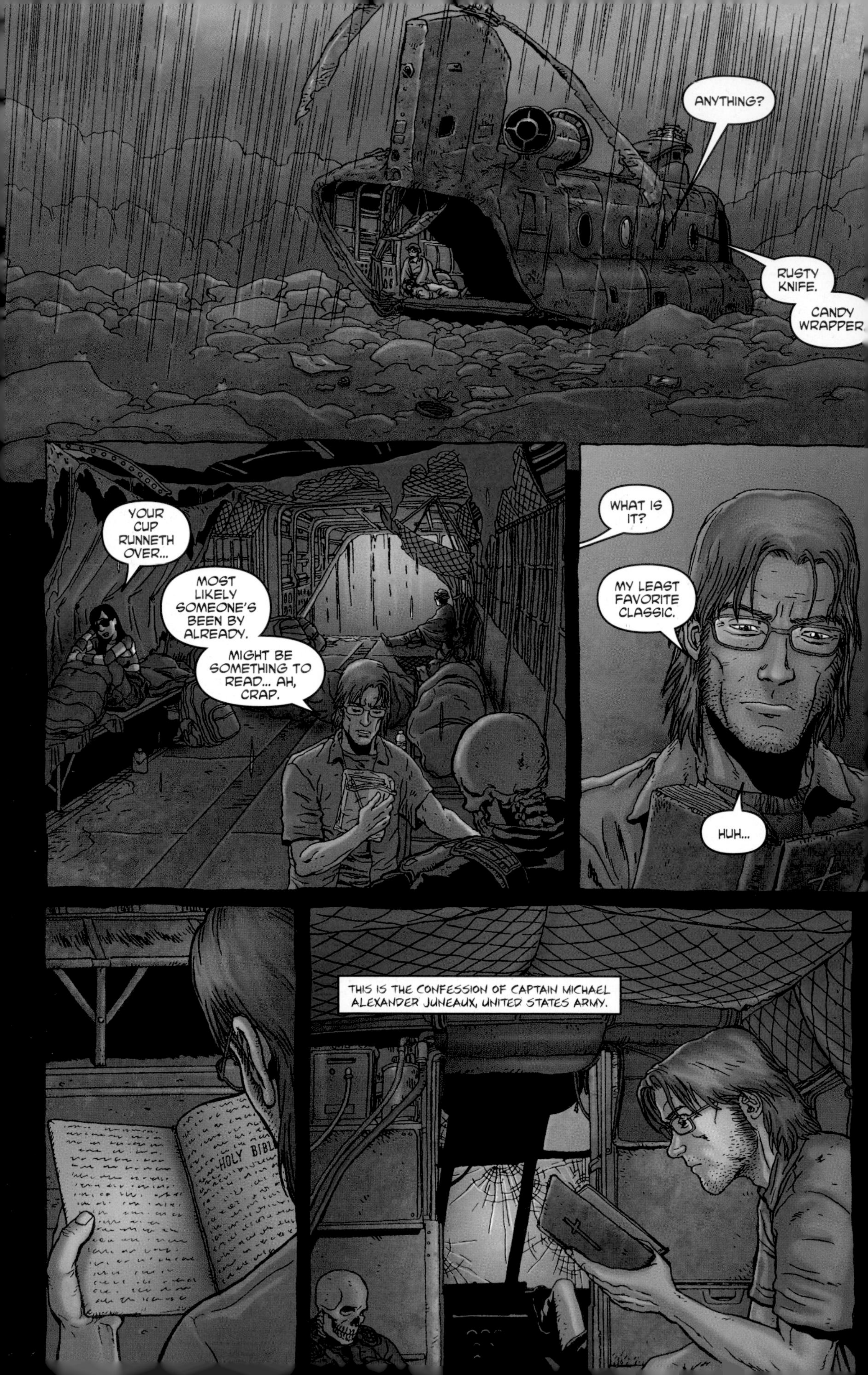
ANYTHING?
RUSTY KNIFE.
CANDY WRAPPER.
YOUR CUP RUNNETH OVER...
MOST LIKELY SOMEONE'S BEEN BY ALREADY.
MIGHT BE SOMETHING TO READ... AH, CRAP.
WHAT IS IT?
MY LEAST FAVORITE CLASSIC.
HUH...
HOLY BIBLE
THIS IS THE CONFESSION OF CAPTAIN MICHAEL ALEXANDER JUNEAUX, UNITED STATES ARMY.

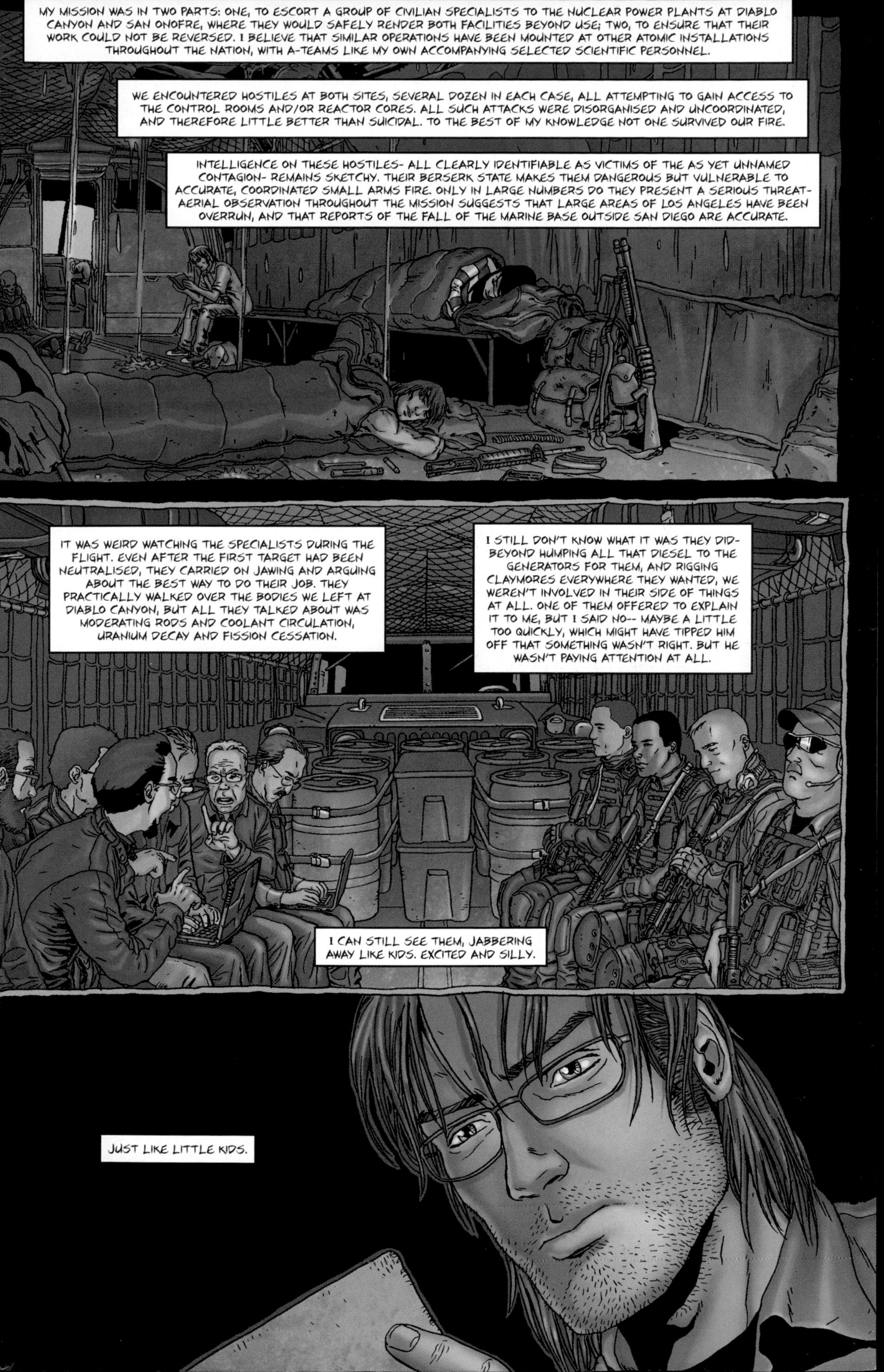
MY MISSION WAS IN TWO PARTS: ONE, TO ESCORT A GROUP OF CIVILIAN SPECIALISTS TO THE NUCLEAR POWER PLANTS AT DIABLO CANYON AND SAN ONOFRE, WHERE THEY WOULD SAFELY RENDER BOTH FACILITIES BEYOND USE; TWO, TO ENSURE THAT THEIR WORK COULD NOT BE REVERSED. I BELIEVE THAT SIMILAR OPERATIONS HAVE BEEN MOUNTED AT OTHER ATOMIC INSTALLATIONS THROUGHOUT THE NATION, WITH A-TEAMS LIKE MY OWN ACCOMPANYING SELECTED SCIENTIFIC PERSONNEL.
WE ENCOUNTERED HOSTILES AT BOTH SITES, SEVERAL DOZEN IN EACH CASE, ALL ATTEMPTING TO GAIN ACCESS TO THE CONTROL ROOMS AND/OR REACTOR CORES. ALL SUCH ATTACKS WERE DISORGANISED AND UNCOORDINATED, AND THEREFORE LITTLE BETTER THAN SUICIDAL. TO THE BEST OF MY KNOWLEDGE NOT ONE SURVIVED OUR FIRE.
INTELLIGENCE ON THESE HOSTILES- ALL CLEARLY IDENTIFIABLE AS VICTIMS OF THE AS YET UNNAMED CONTAGION- REMAINS SKETCHY. THEIR BERSERK STATE MAKES THEM DANGEROUS BUT VULNERABLE TO ACCURATE, COORDINATED SMALL ARMS FIRE. ONLY IN LARGE NUMBERS DO THEY PRESENT A SERIOUS THREAT- AERIAL OBSERVATION THROUGHOUT THE MISSION SUGGESTS THAT LARGE AREAS OF LOS ANGELES HAVE BEEN OVERRUN, AND THAT REPORTS OF THE FALL OF THE MARINE BASE OUTSIDE SAN DIEGO ARE ACCURATE.
IT WAS WEIRD WATCHING THE SPECIALISTS DURING THE FLIGHT. EVEN AFTER THE FIRST TARGET HAD BEEN NEUTRALISED, THEY CARRIED ON JAWING AND ARGUING ABOUT THE BEST WAY TO DO THEIR JOB. THEY PRACTICALLY WALKED OVER THE BODIES WE LEFT AT DIABLO CANYON, BUT ALL THEY TALKED ABOUT WAS MODERATING RODS AND COOLANT CIRCULATION, URANIUM DECAY AND FISSION CESSATION.
I STILL DON'T KNOW WHAT IT WAS THEY DID- BEYOND HUMPING ALL THAT DIESEL TO THE GENERATORS FOR THEM, AND RIGGING CLAYMORES EVERYWHERE THEY WANTED, WE WEREN'T INVOLVED IN THEIR SIDE OF THINGS AT ALL. ONE OF THEM OFFERED TO EXPLAIN IT TO ME, BUT I SAID NO-- MAYBE A LITTLE TOO QUICKLY, WHICH MIGHT HAVE TIPPED HIM OFF THAT SOMETHING WASN'T RIGHT. BUT HE WASN'T PAYING ATTENTION AT ALL.
I CAN STILL SEE THEM, JABBERING AWAY LIKE KIDS. EXCITED AND SILLY.
JUST LIKE LITTLE KIDS.

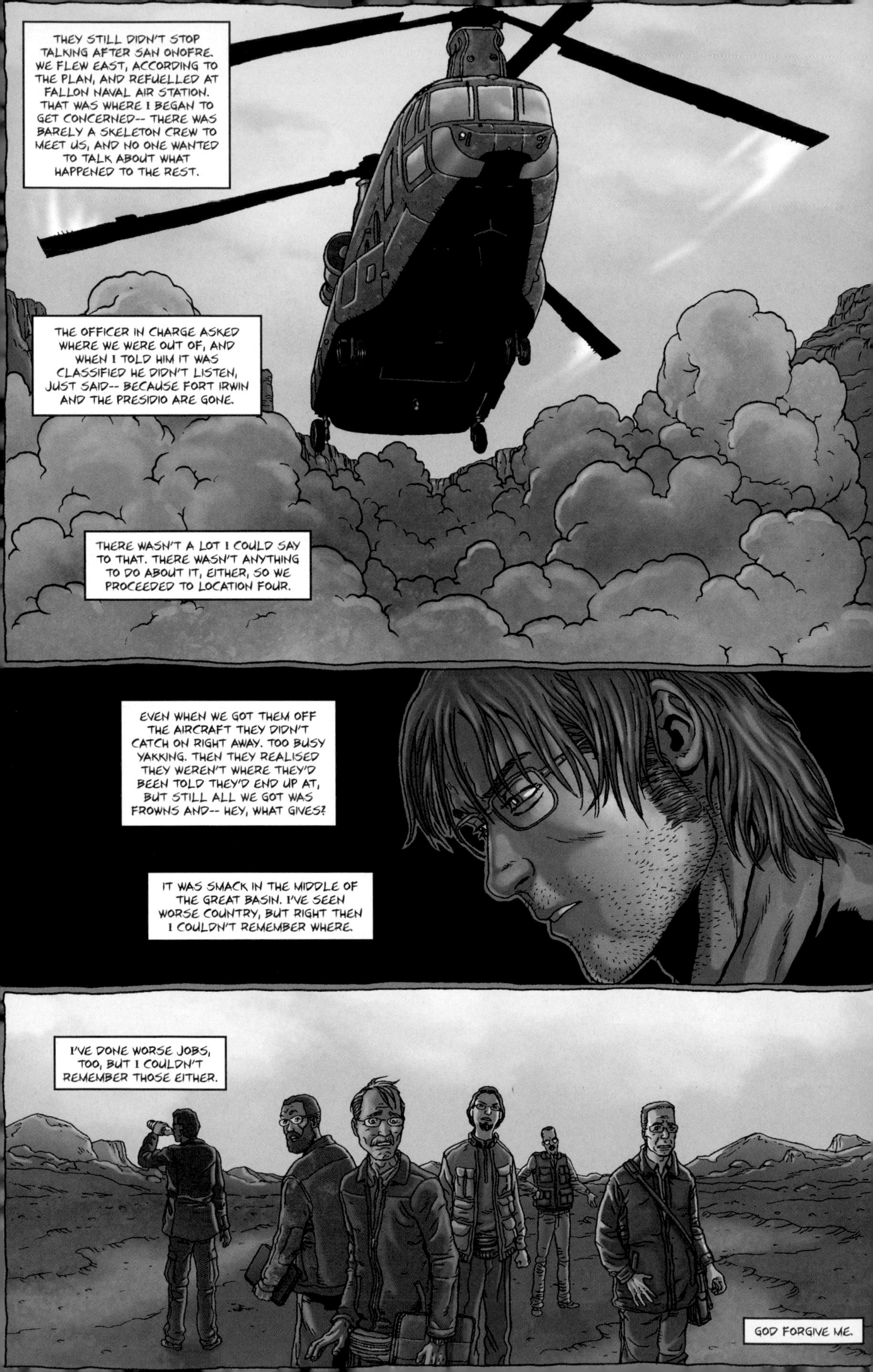
THEY STILL DIDN'T STOP TALKING AFTER SAN ONOFRE. WE FLEW EAST, ACCORDING TO THE PLAN, AND REFUELLED AT FALLON NAVAL AIR STATION. THAT WAS WHERE I BEGAN TO GET CONCERNED-- THERE WAS BARELY A SKELETON CREW TO MEET US, AND NO ONE WANTED TO TALK ABOUT WHAT HAPPENED TO THE REST.
THE OFFICER IN CHARGE ASKED WHERE WE WERE OUT OF, AND WHEN I TOLD HIM IT WAS CLASSIFIED HE DIDN'T LISTEN, JUST SAID-- BECAUSE FORT IRWIN AND THE PRESIDIO ARE GONE.
THERE WASN'T A LOT I COULD SAY TO THAT. THERE WASN'T ANYTHING TO DO ABOUT IT, EITHER, SO WE PROCEEDED TO LOCATION FOUR.
EVEN WHEN WE GOT THEM OFF THE AIRCRAFT THEY DIDN'T CATCH ON RIGHT AWAY. TOO BUSY YAKKING. THEN THEY REALISED THEY WEREN'T WHERE THEY'D BEEN TOLD THEY'D END UP AT, BUT STILL ALL WE GOT WAS FROWNS AND-- HEY, WHAT GIVES?
IT WAS SMACK IN THE MIDDLE OF THE GREAT BASIN. I'VE SEEN WORSE COUNTRY, BUT RIGHT THEN I COULDN'T REMEMBER WHERE.
I'VE DONE WORSE JOBS, TOO, BUT I COULDN'T REMEMBER THOSE EITHER.
GOD FORGIVE ME.

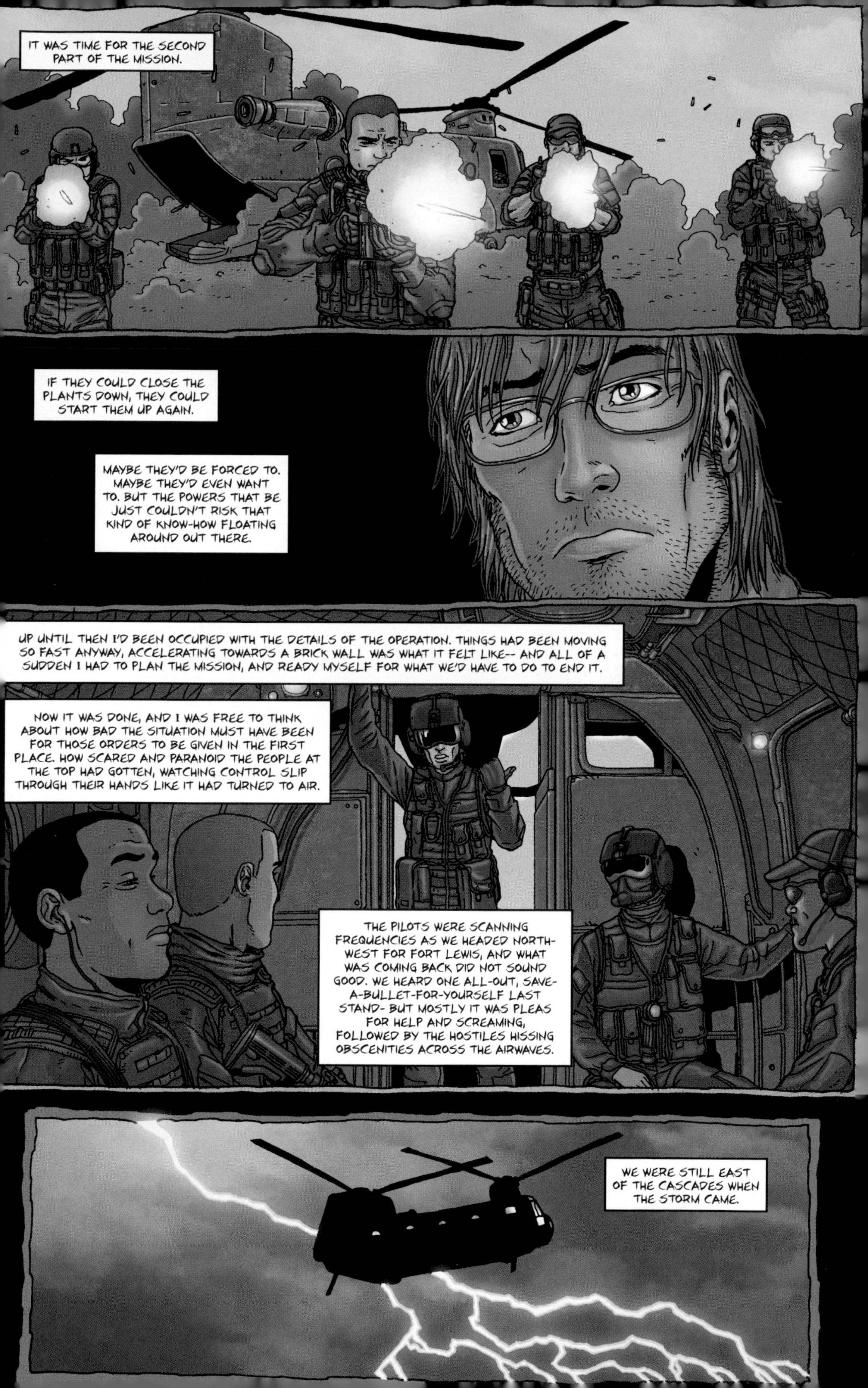
IT WAS TIME FOR THE SECOND PART OF THE MISSION.
IF THEY COULD CLOSE THE PLANTS DOWN, THEY COULD START THEM UP AGAIN.
MAYBE THEY'D BE FORCED TO. MAYBE THEY'D EVEN WANT TO. BUT THE POWERS THAT BE JUST COULDN'T RISK THAT KIND OF KNOW-HOW FLOATING AROUND OUT THERE.
UP UNTIL THEN I'D BEEN OCCUPIED WITH THE DETAILS OF THE OPERATION. THINGS HAD BEEN MOVING SO FAST ANYWAY, ACCELERATING TOWARDS A BRICK WALL WAS WHAT IT FELT LIKE-- AND ALL OF A SUDDEN I HAD TO PLAN THE MISSION, AND READY MYSELF FOR WHAT WE'D HAVE TO DO TO END IT.
NOW IT WAS DONE, AND I WAS FREE TO THINK ABOUT HOW BAD THE SITUATION MUST HAVE BEEN FOR THOSE ORDERS TO BE GIVEN IN THE FIRST PLACE. HOW SCARED AND PARANOID THE PEOPLE AT THE TOP HAD GOTTEN, WATCHING CONTROL SLIP THROUGH THEIR HANDS LIKE IT HAD TURNED TO AIR.
THE PILOTS WERE SCANNING FREQUENCIES AS WE HEADED NORTH-WEST FOR FORT LEWIS, AND WHAT WAS COMING BACK DID NOT SOUND GOOD. WE HEARD ONE ALL-OUT, SAVE-A-BULLET-FOR-YOURSELF LAST STAND- BUT MOSTLY IT WAS PLEAS FOR HELP AND SCREAMING, FOLLOWED BY THE HOSTILES HISSING OBSCENITIES ACROSS THE AIRWAVES.
WE WERE STILL EAST OF THE CASCADES WHEN THE STORM CAME.

WE JETTISONED THE HUMVEE AND ANYTHING THAT WASN'T NAILED DOWN, BUT I'VE GONE IN ENOUGH TIMES IN BLACKHAWKS THAT I KNEW THE SIGNS. ONE ENGINE WENT, AND THAT WAS ALL SHE WROTE.

STILL, THEY DID A CREDITABLE JOB OF LANDING IT. THE CREW CHIEF DIED AND I BROKE BOTH MY LEGS, BUT EVERYONE ELSE GOT OFF WITH CUTS AND BRUISES.

RECON AT FIRST LIGHT REVEALED THAT WE WERE NOWHERE IN THE WORST TERRAIN IMAGINABLE. THE PLAN WAS TO WALK OUT, CARRYING ME.

I SAID YES TO THE FIRST AND NO TO THE SECOND.

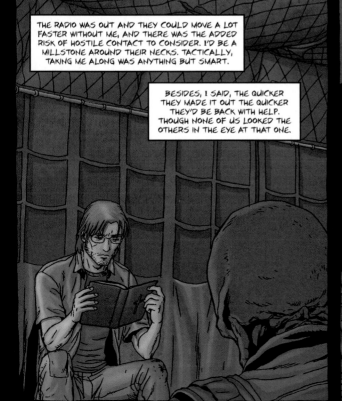

THE RADIO WAS OUT AND THEY COULD MOVE A LOT FASTER WITHOUT ME, AND THERE WAS THE ADDED RISK OF HOSTILE CONTACT TO CONSIDER. I'D BE A MILLSTONE AROUND THEIR NECKS. TACTICALLY, TAKING ME ALONG WAS ANYTHING BUT SMART.

BESIDES, I SAID, THE QUICKER THEY MADE IT OUT THE QUICKER THEY'D BE BACK WITH HELP. THOUGH NONE OF US LOOKED THE OTHERS IN THE EYE AT THAT ONE.

IN THE END I CHAMBERED A ROUND AND THEY COULD SEE I MEANT BUSINESS. FATS OFFERED ME A SECOND SHOT OF MORPHINE, BUT I WASN'T ABOUT TO FALL FOR THAT.

HE AND COTTON SAID SO LONG. BIG JOHN CURSED AT ME, THEN WALKED AWAY IN TEARS.

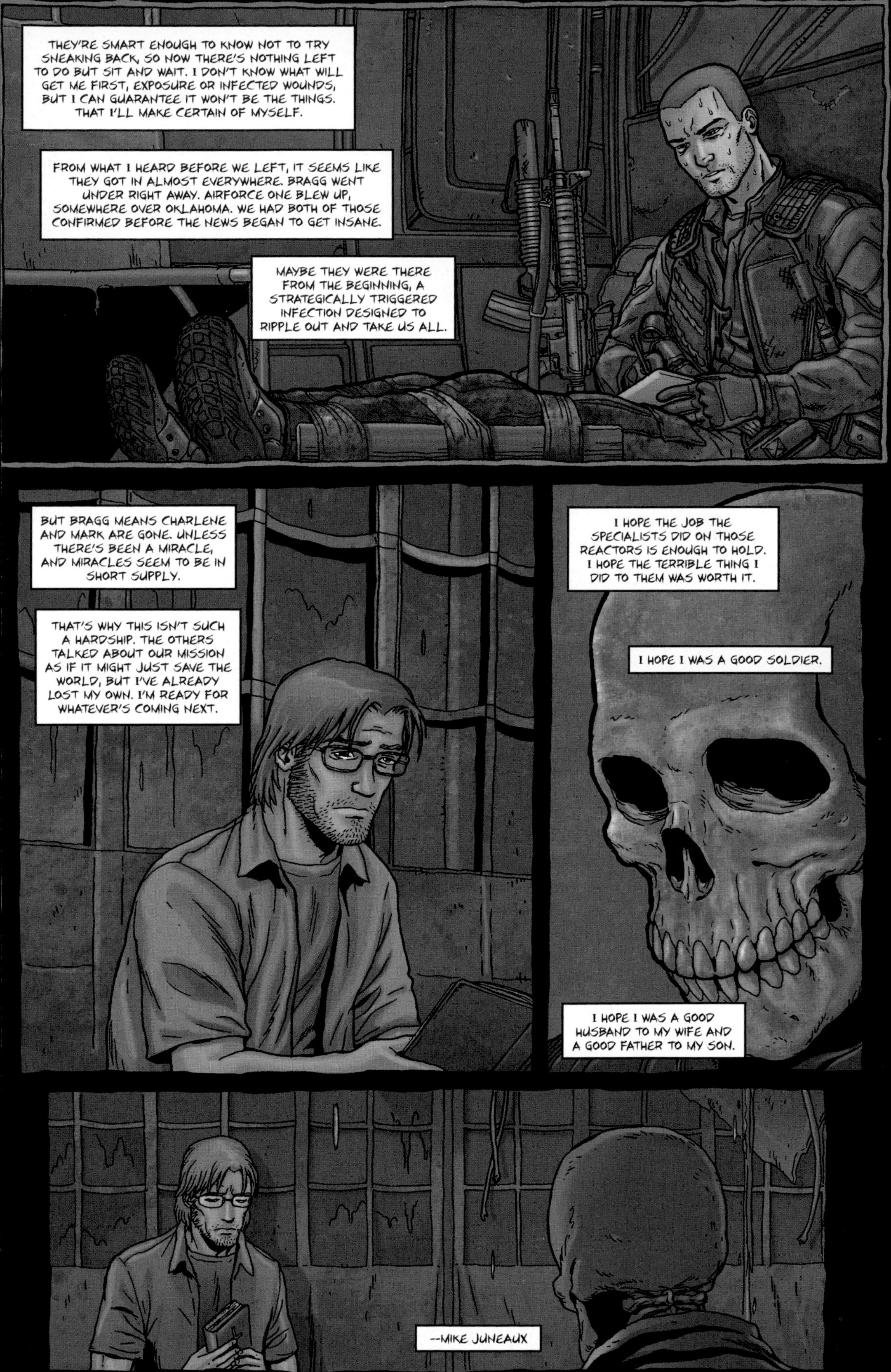
THEY'RE SMART ENOUGH TO KNOW NOT TO TRY SNEAKING BACK, SO NOW THERE'S NOTHING LEFT TO DO BUT SIT AND WAIT. I DON'T KNOW WHAT WILL GET ME FIRST, EXPOSURE OR INFECTED WOUNDS, BUT I CAN GUARANTEE IT WON'T BE THE THINGS. THAT I'LL MAKE CERTAIN OF MYSELF.
FROM WHAT I HEARD BEFORE WE LEFT, IT SEEMS LIKE THEY GOT IN ALMOST EVERYWHERE. BRAGG WENT UNDER RIGHT AWAY. AIRFORCE ONE BLEW UP, SOMEWHERE OVER OKLAHOMA. WE HAD BOTH OF THOSE CONFIRMED BEFORE THE NEWS BEGAN TO GET INSANE.
MAYBE THEY WERE THERE FROM THE BEGINNING, A STRATEGICALLY TRIGGERED INFECTION DESIGNED TO RIPPLE OUT AND TAKE US ALL.
BUT BRAGG MEANS CHARLENE AND MARK ARE GONE. UNLESS THERE'S BEEN A MIRACLE, AND MIRACLES SEEM TO BE IN SHORT SUPPLY.
THAT'S WHY THIS ISN'T SUCH A HARDSHIP. THE OTHERS TALKED ABOUT OUR MISSION AS IF IT MIGHT JUST SAVE THE WORLD, BUT I'VE ALREADY LOST MY OWN. I'M READY FOR WHATEVER'S COMING NEXT.
I HOPE THE JOB THE SPECIALISTS DID ON THOSE REACTORS IS ENOUGH TO HOLD. I HOPE THE TERRIBLE THING I DID TO THEM WAS WORTH IT.
I HOPE I WAS A GOOD SOLDIER.
I HOPE I WAS A GOOD HUSBAND TO MY WIFE AND A GOOD FATHER TO MY SON.
--MIKE JUNEAUX

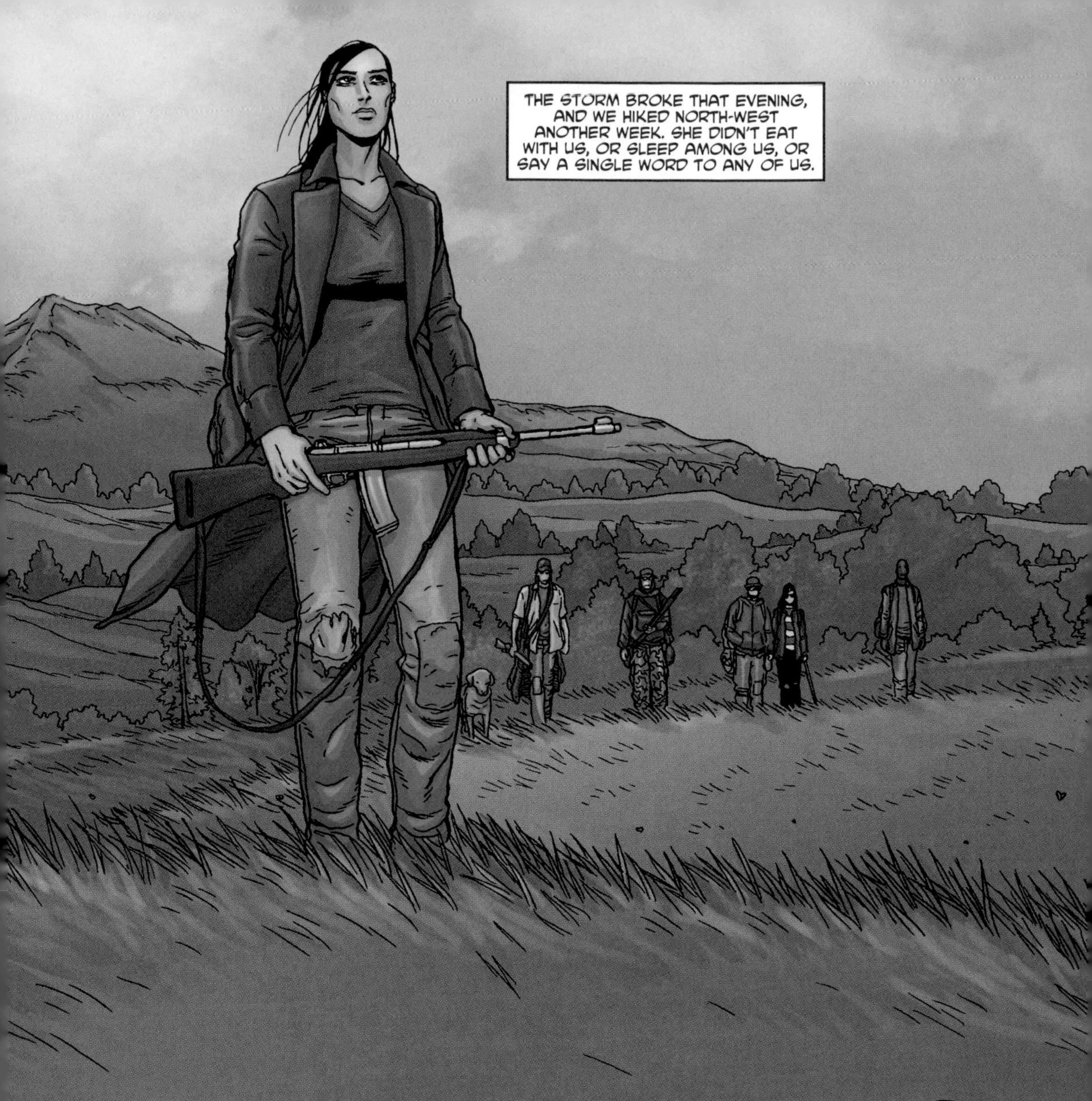
THE STORM BROKE THAT EVENING, AND WE HIKED NORTH-WEST ANOTHER WEEK. SHE DIDN'T EAT WITH US, OR SLEEP AMONG US, OR SAY A SINGLE WORD TO ANY OF US.

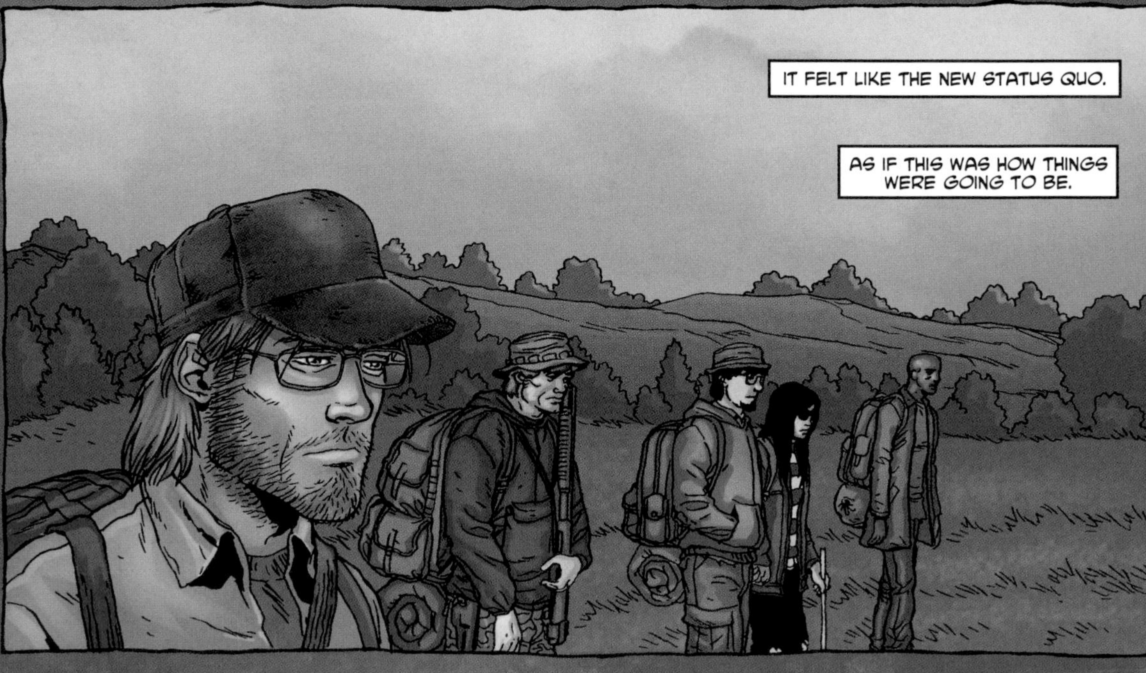
IT FELT LIKE THE NEW STATUS QUO.
AS IF THIS WAS HOW THINGS WERE GOING TO BE.

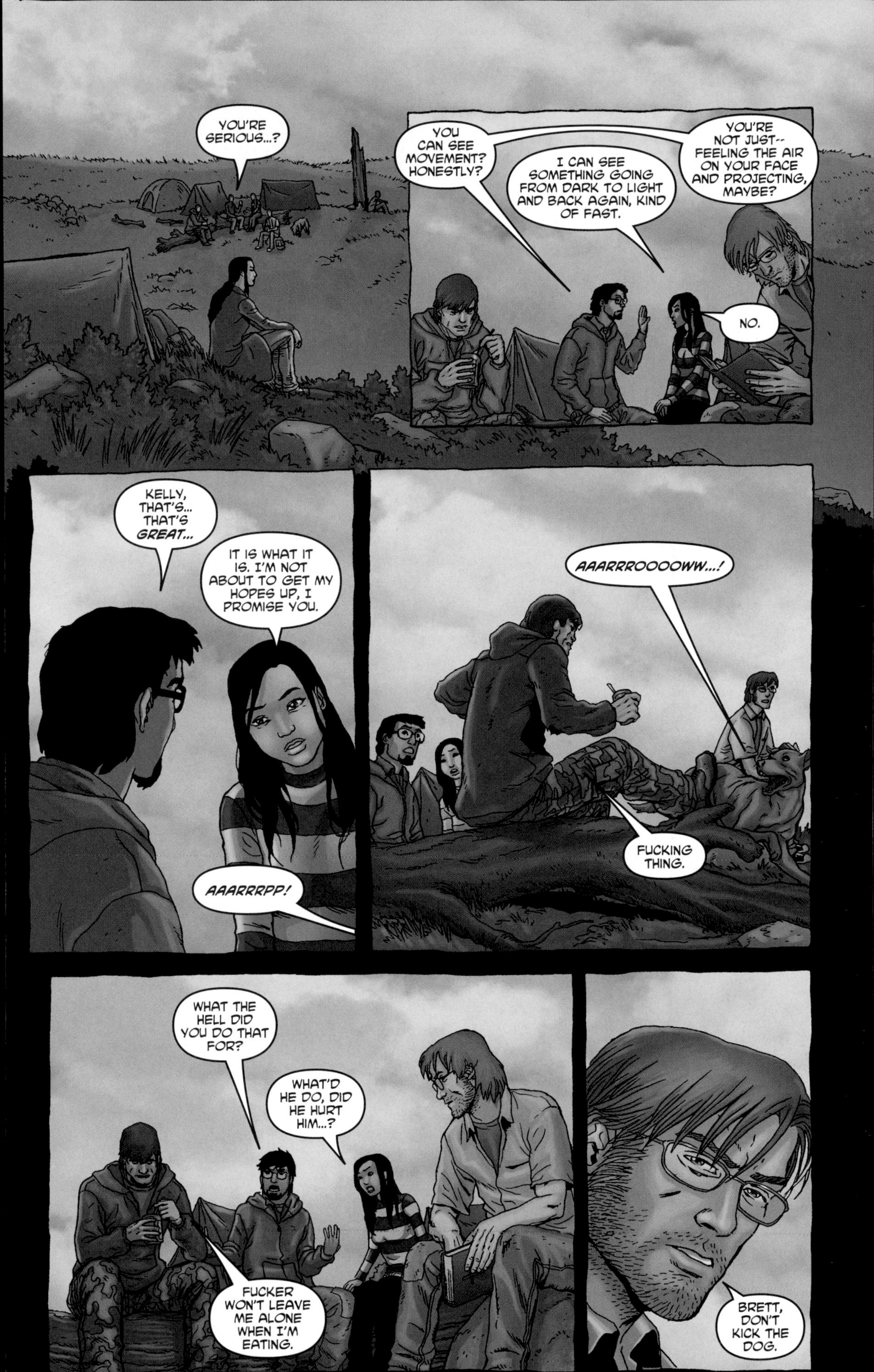
YOU'RE SERIOUS...?
YOU CAN SEE MOVEMENT? HONESTLY?
I CAN SEE SOMETHING GOING FROM DARK TO LIGHT AND BACK AGAIN, KIND OF FAST.
YOU'RE NOT JUST-- FEELING THE AIR ON YOUR FACE AND PROJECTING, MAYBE?
NO.
KELLY, THAT'S... THAT'S *GREAT*...
IT IS WHAT IT IS. I'M NOT ABOUT TO GET MY HOPES UP, I PROMISE YOU.
AAARRRPP!
AAARRROOOOWW...!
FUCKING THING.
WHAT THE HELL DID YOU DO THAT FOR?
WHAT'D HE DO, DID HE HURT HIM...?
FUCKER WON'T LEAVE ME ALONE WHEN I'M EATING.
BRETT, DON'T KICK THE DOG.

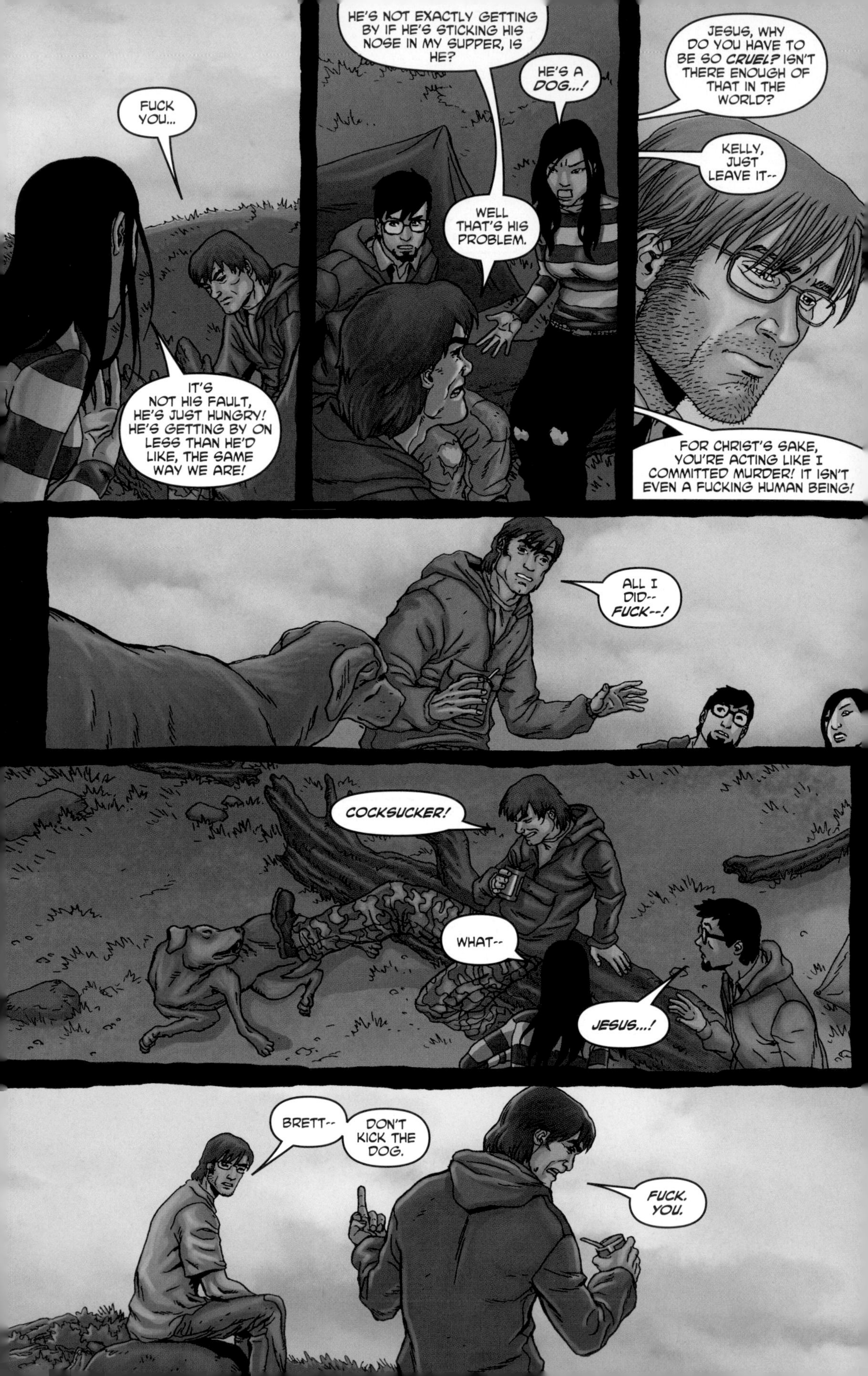
FUCK YOU...
IT'S NOT HIS FAULT, HE'S JUST HUNGRY! HE'S GETTING BY ON LESS THAN HE'D LIKE, THE SAME WAY WE ARE!
HE'S NOT EXACTLY GETTING BY IF HE'S STICKING HIS NOSE IN MY SUPPER, IS HE?
HE'S A DOG...!
WELL THAT'S HIS PROBLEM.
JESUS, WHY DO YOU HAVE TO BE SO CRUEL? ISN'T THERE ENOUGH OF THAT IN THE WORLD?
KELLY, JUST LEAVE IT--
FOR CHRIST'S SAKE, YOU'RE ACTING LIKE I COMMITTED MURDER! IT ISN'T EVEN A FUCKING HUMAN BEING!
ALL I DID-- FUCK--!
COCKSUCKER!
WHAT--
JESUS...!
BRETT--
DON'T KICK THE DOG.
FUCK. YOU.

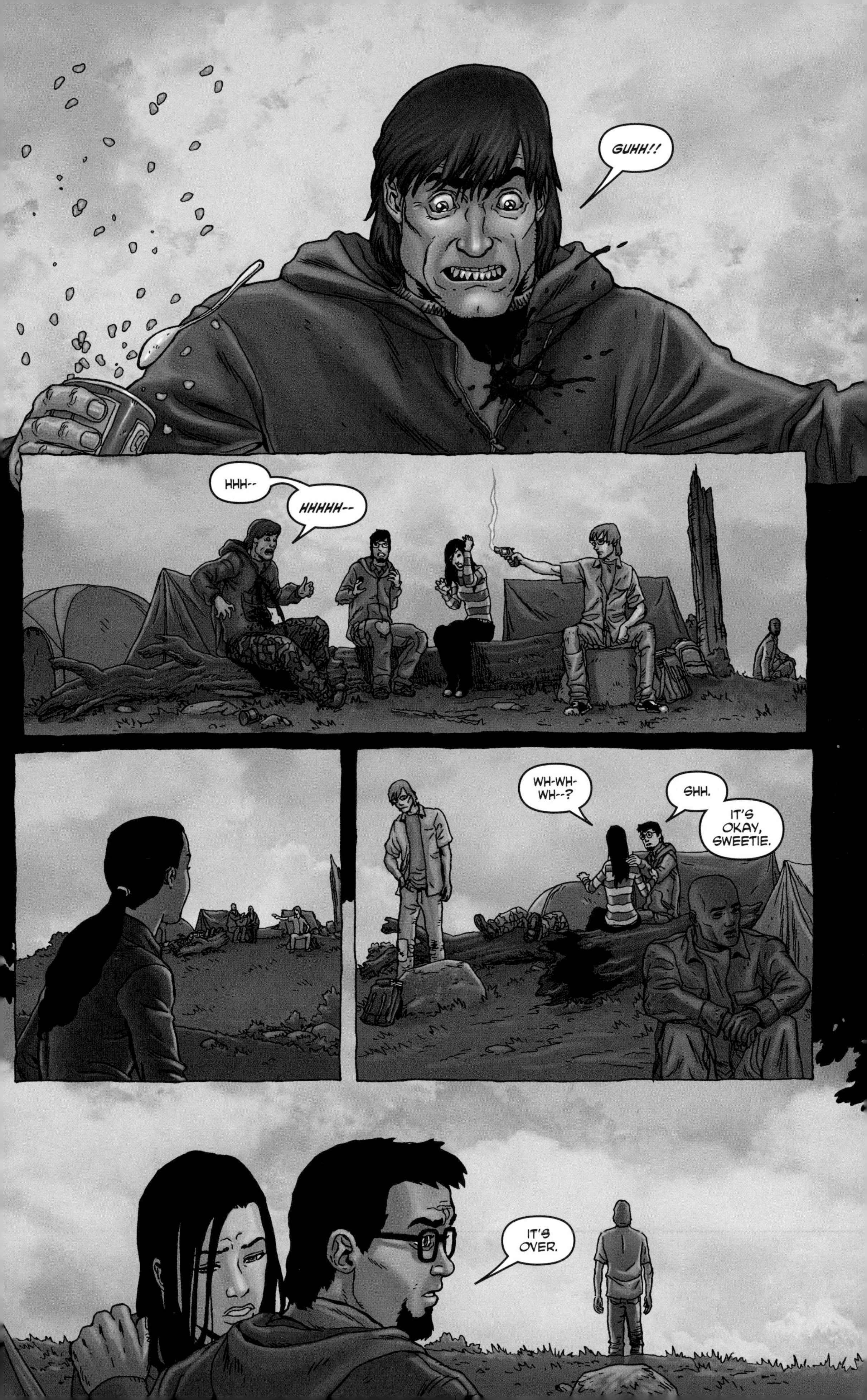
GUHH!!
HHH--
HHHHH--
WH-WH-WH--?
SHH.
IT'S OKAY, SWEETIE.
IT'S OVER.

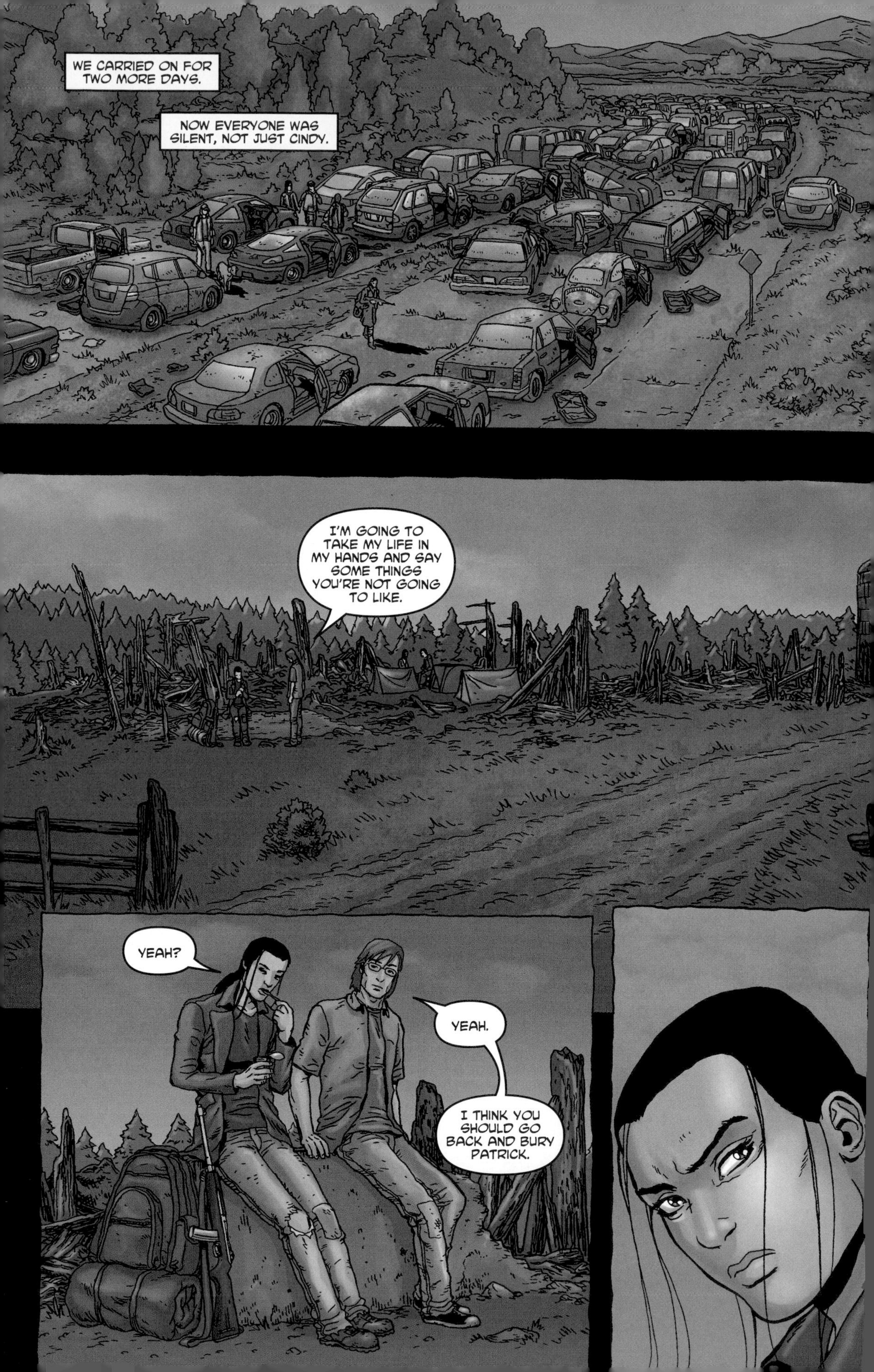
WE CARRIED ON FOR TWO MORE DAYS.
NOW EVERYONE WAS SILENT, NOT JUST CINDY.
I'M GOING TO TAKE MY LIFE IN MY HANDS AND SAY SOME THINGS YOU'RE NOT GOING TO LIKE.
YEAH?
YEAH.
I THINK YOU SHOULD GO BACK AND BURY PATRICK.

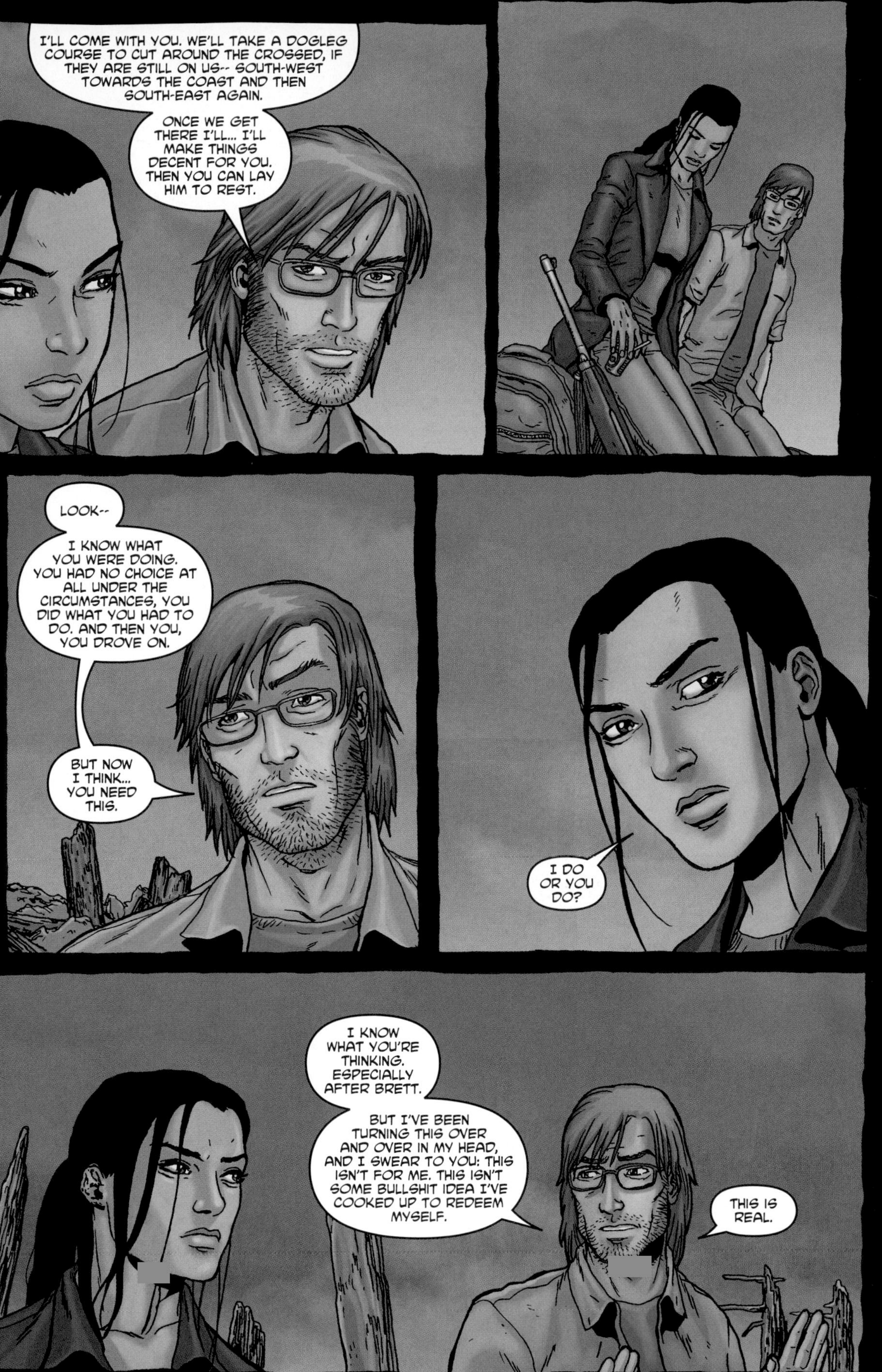
I'LL COME WITH YOU. WE'LL TAKE A DOGLEG COURSE TO CUT AROUND THE CROSSED, IF THEY ARE STILL ON US-- SOUTH-WEST TOWARDS THE COAST AND THEN SOUTH-EAST AGAIN.
ONCE WE GET THERE I'LL... I'LL MAKE THINGS DECENT FOR YOU. THEN YOU CAN LAY HIM TO REST.
LOOK--
I KNOW WHAT YOU WERE DOING. YOU HAD NO CHOICE AT ALL UNDER THE CIRCUMSTANCES, YOU DID WHAT YOU HAD TO DO. AND THEN YOU, YOU DROVE ON.
BUT NOW I THINK... YOU NEED THIS.
I DO OR YOU DO?
I KNOW WHAT YOU'RE THINKING. ESPECIALLY AFTER BRETT.
BUT I'VE BEEN TURNING THIS OVER AND OVER IN MY HEAD, AND I SWEAR TO YOU: THIS ISN'T FOR ME. THIS ISN'T SOME BULLSHIT IDEA I'VE COOKED UP TO REDEEM MYSELF.
THIS IS REAL.

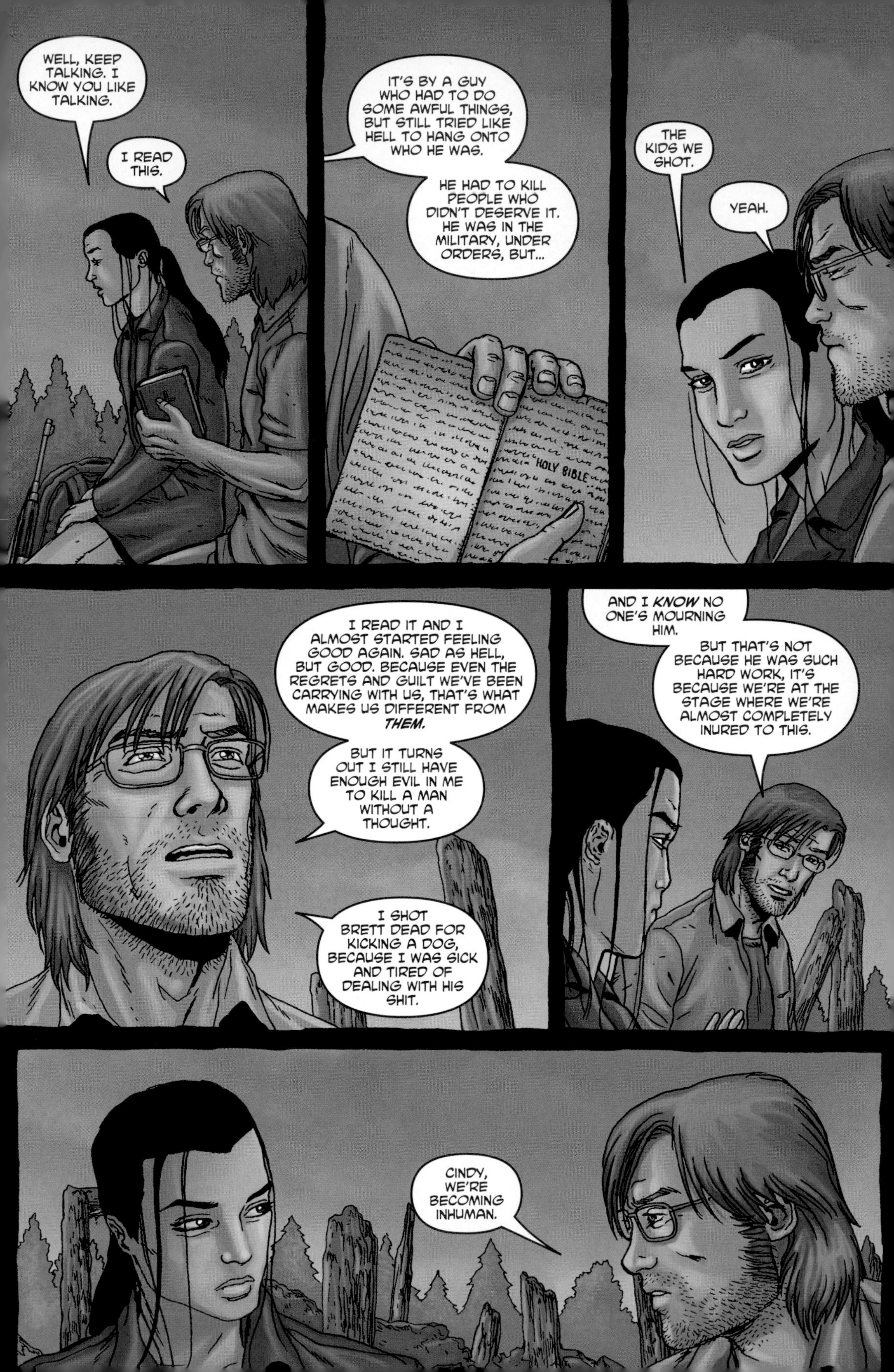
WELL, KEEP TALKING. I KNOW YOU LIKE TALKING.
I READ THIS.
IT'S BY A GUY WHO HAD TO DO SOME AWFUL THINGS, BUT STILL TRIED LIKE HELL TO HANG ONTO WHO HE WAS.
HE HAD TO KILL PEOPLE WHO DIDN'T DESERVE IT. HE WAS IN THE MILITARY, UNDER ORDERS, BUT...
HOLY BIBLE
THE KIDS WE SHOT.
YEAH.
I READ IT AND I ALMOST STARTED FEELING GOOD AGAIN. SAD AS HELL, BUT GOOD. BECAUSE EVEN THE REGRETS AND GUILT WE'VE BEEN CARRYING WITH US, THAT'S WHAT MAKES US DIFFERENT FROM *THEM.*
BUT IT TURNS OUT I STILL HAVE ENOUGH EVIL IN ME TO KILL A MAN WITHOUT A THOUGHT.
I SHOT BRETT DEAD FOR KICKING A DOG, BECAUSE I WAS SICK AND TIRED OF DEALING WITH HIS SHIT.
AND I *KNOW* NO ONE'S MOURNING HIM.
BUT THAT'S NOT BECAUSE HE WAS SUCH HARD WORK, IT'S BECAUSE WE'RE AT THE STAGE WHERE WE'RE ALMOST COMPLETELY INURED TO THIS.
CINDY, WE'RE BECOMING INHUMAN.

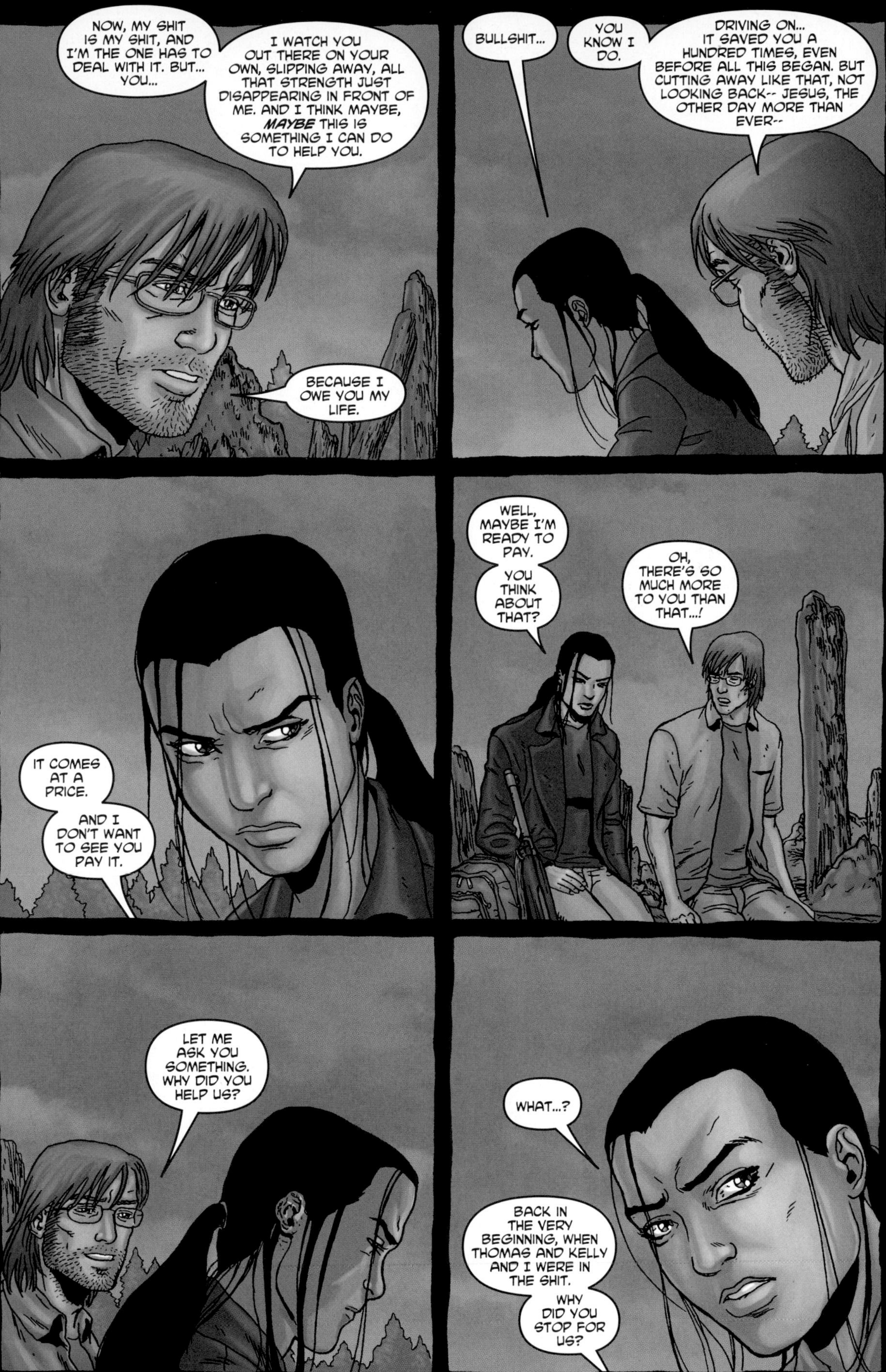
NOW, MY SHIT IS MY SHIT, AND I'M THE ONE HAS TO DEAL WITH IT. BUT... YOU...
I WATCH YOU OUT THERE ON YOUR OWN, SLIPPING AWAY, ALL THAT STRENGTH JUST DISAPPEARING IN FRONT OF ME. AND I THINK MAYBE, *MAYBE* THIS IS SOMETHING I CAN DO TO HELP YOU.
BECAUSE I OWE YOU MY LIFE.
BULLSHIT...
YOU KNOW I DO.
DRIVING ON... IT SAVED YOU A HUNDRED TIMES, EVEN BEFORE ALL THIS BEGAN. BUT CUTTING AWAY LIKE THAT, NOT LOOKING BACK-- JESUS, THE OTHER DAY MORE THAN EVER--
IT COMES AT A PRICE.
AND I DON'T WANT TO SEE YOU PAY IT.
WELL, MAYBE I'M READY TO PAY.
YOU THINK ABOUT THAT?
OH, THERE'S SO MUCH MORE TO YOU THAN THAT...!
LET ME ASK YOU SOMETHING. WHY DID YOU HELP US?
WHAT...?
BACK IN THE VERY BEGINNING, WHEN THOMAS AND KELLY AND I WERE IN THE SHIT.
WHY DID YOU STOP FOR US?

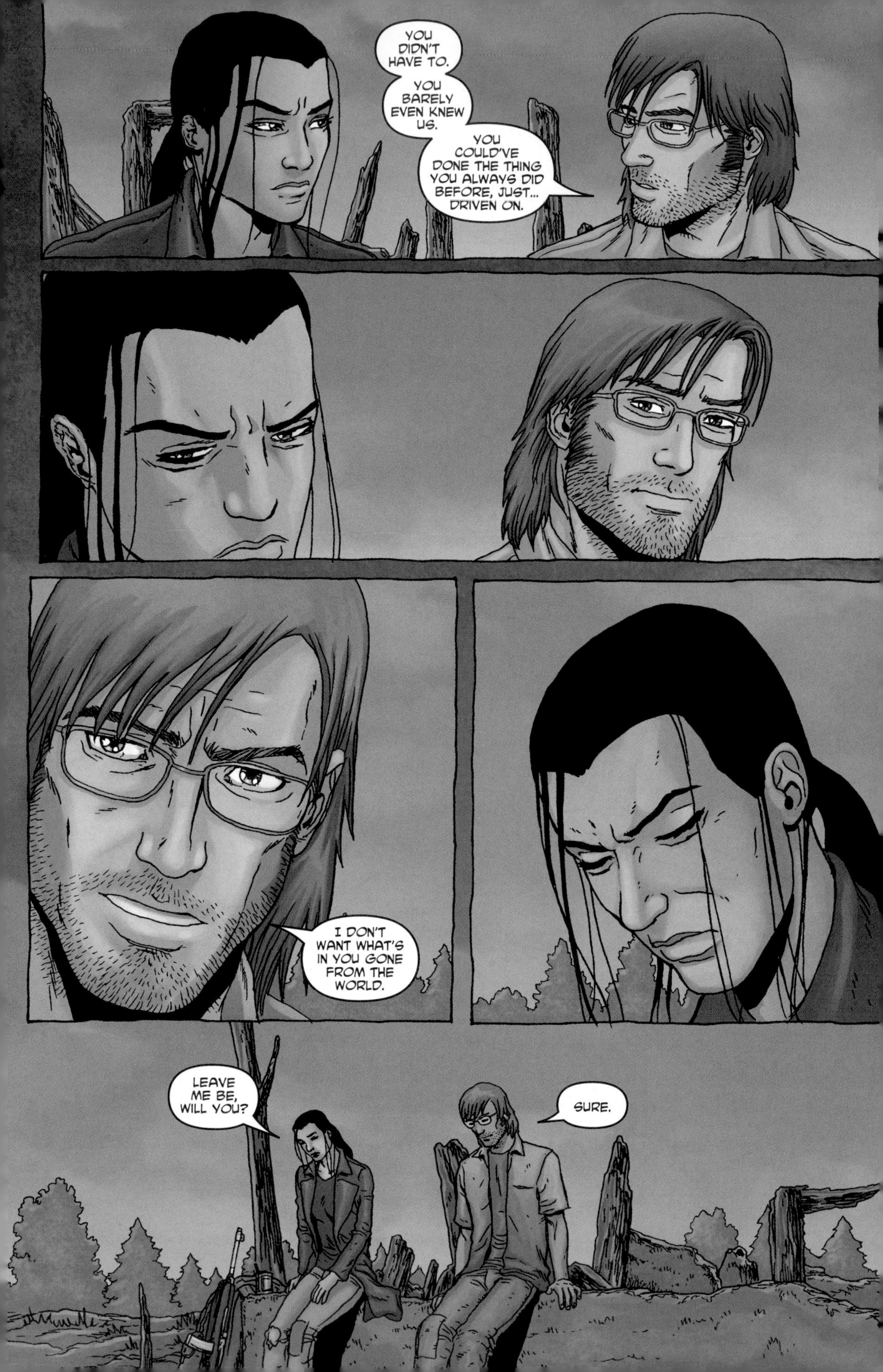
YOU DIDN'T HAVE TO.
YOU BARELY EVEN KNEW US.
YOU COULD'VE DONE THE THING YOU ALWAYS DID BEFORE, JUST... DRIVEN ON.
I DON'T WANT WHAT'S IN YOU GONE FROM THE WORLD.
LEAVE ME BE, WILL YOU?
SURE.

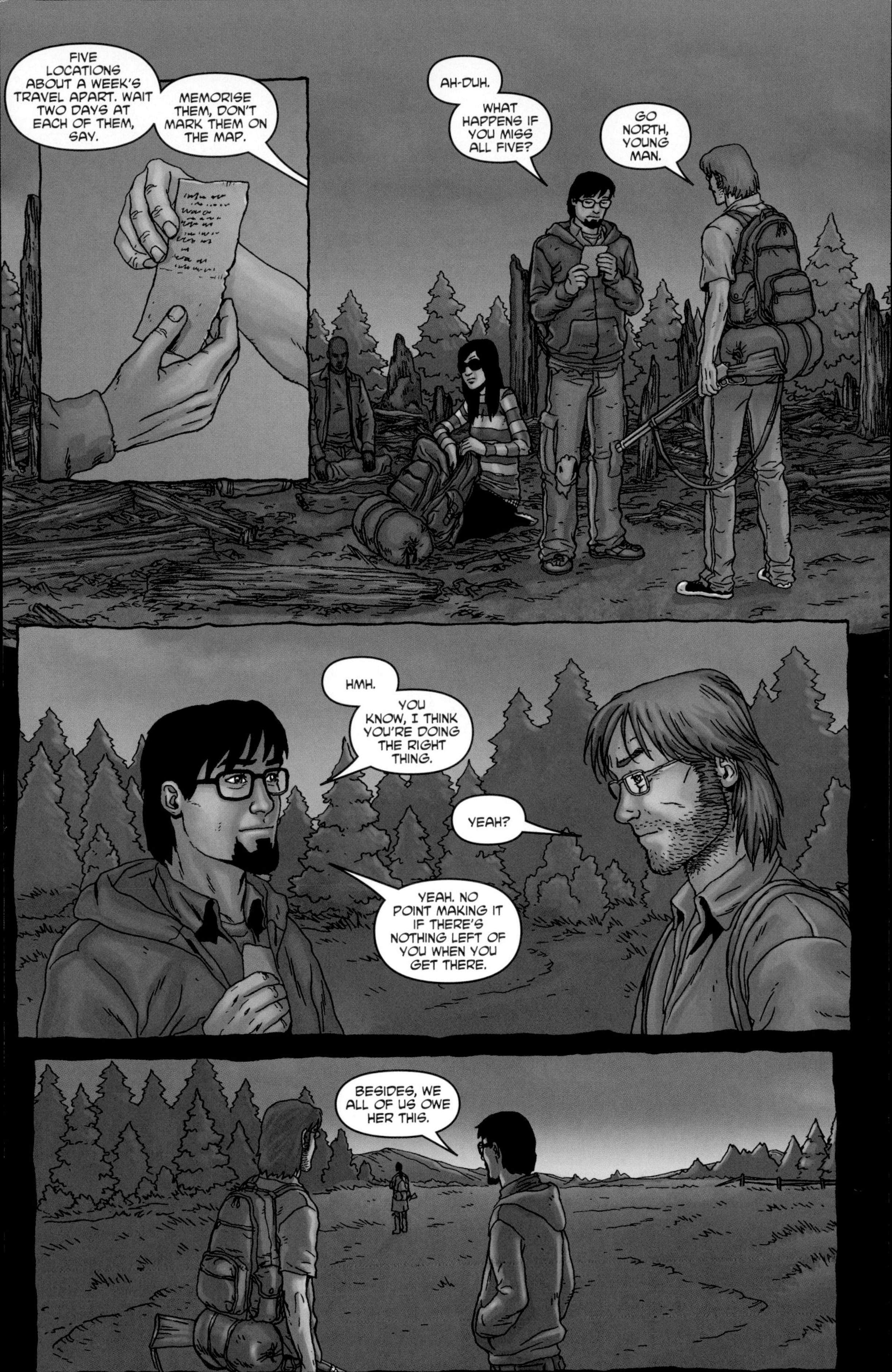
FIVE LOCATIONS ABOUT A WEEK'S TRAVEL APART. WAIT TWO DAYS AT EACH OF THEM, SAY.
MEMORISE THEM, DON'T MARK THEM ON THE MAP.
AH-DUH.
WHAT HAPPENS IF YOU MISS ALL FIVE?
GO NORTH, YOUNG MAN.
HMH.
YOU KNOW, I THINK YOU'RE DOING THE RIGHT THING.
YEAH?
YEAH. NO POINT MAKING IT IF THERE'S NOTHING LEFT OF YOU WHEN YOU GET THERE.
BESIDES, WE ALL OF US OWE HER THIS.

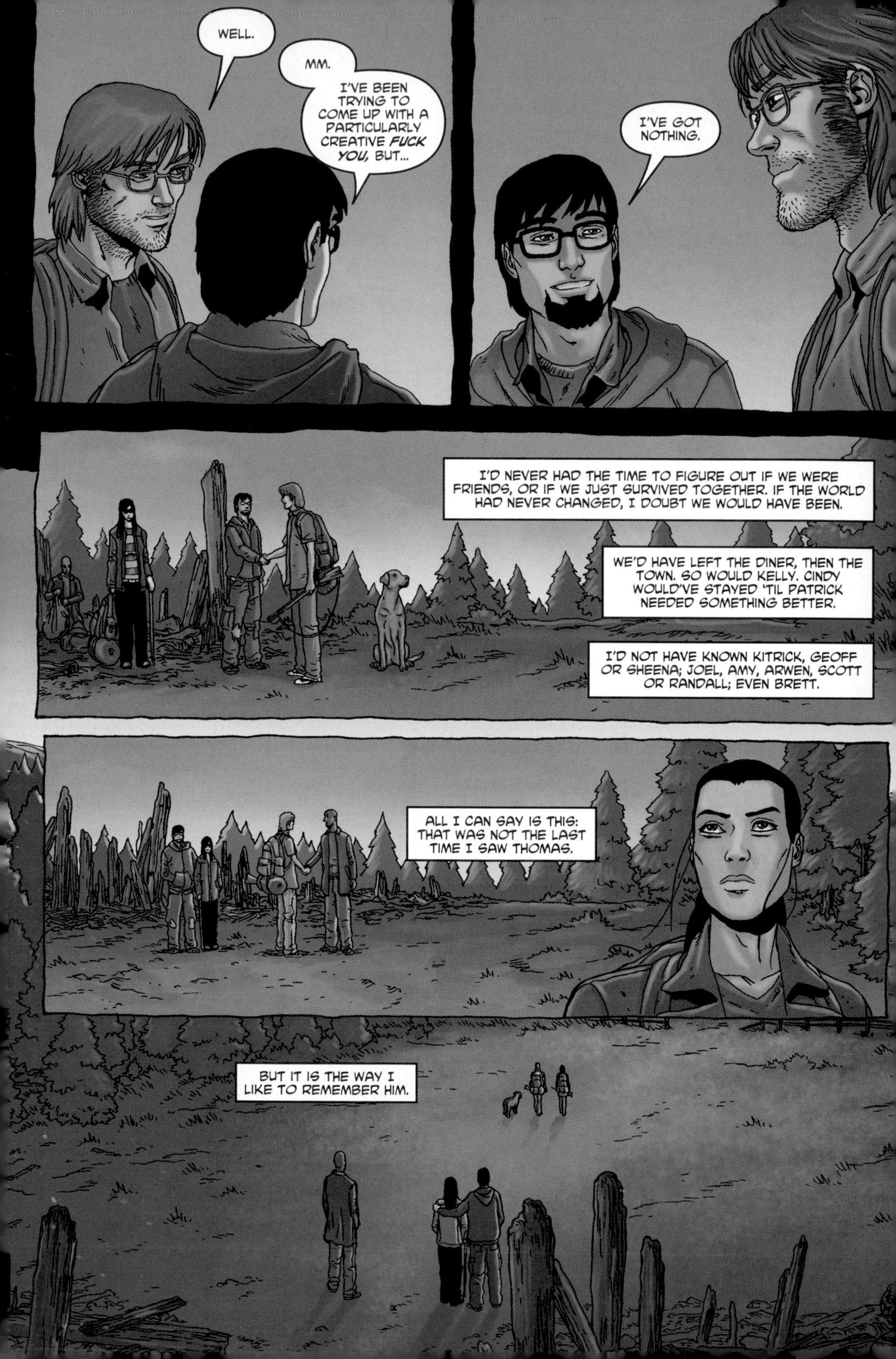
WELL.
MM.
I'VE BEEN TRYING TO COME UP WITH A PARTICULARLY CREATIVE FUCK YOU, BUT...
I'VE GOT NOTHING.
I'D NEVER HAD THE TIME TO FIGURE OUT IF WE WERE FRIENDS, OR IF WE JUST SURVIVED TOGETHER. IF THE WORLD HAD NEVER CHANGED, I DOUBT WE WOULD HAVE BEEN.
WE'D HAVE LEFT THE DINER, THEN THE TOWN. SO WOULD KELLY. CINDY WOULD'VE STAYED 'TIL PATRICK NEEDED SOMETHING BETTER.
I'D NOT HAVE KNOWN KITRICK, GEOFF OR SHEENA; JOEL, AMY, ARWEN, SCOTT OR RANDALL; EVEN BRETT.
ALL I CAN SAY IS THIS: THAT WAS NOT THE LAST TIME I SAW THOMAS.
BUT IT IS THE WAY I LIKE TO REMEMBER HIM.

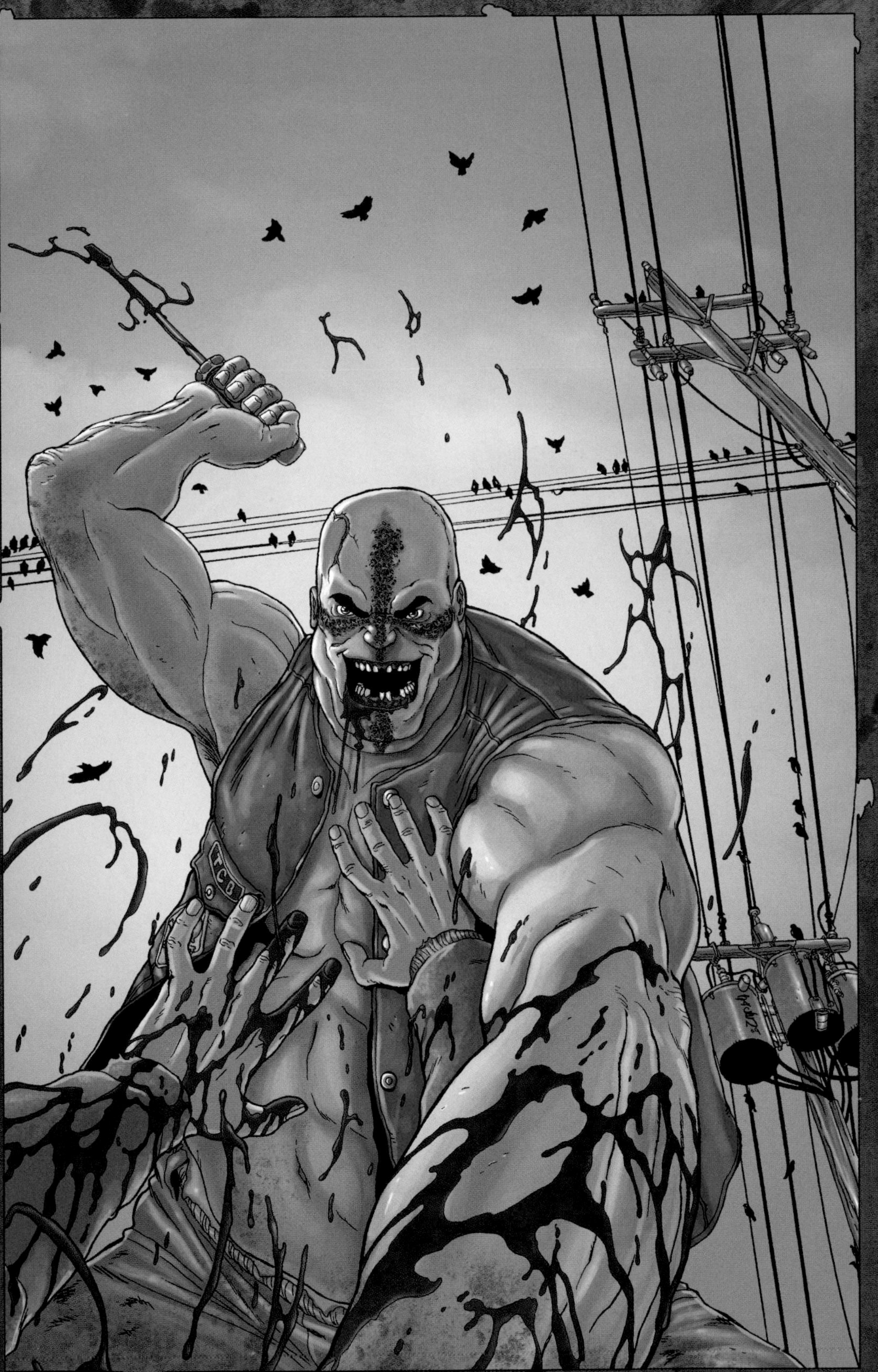

PART TEN

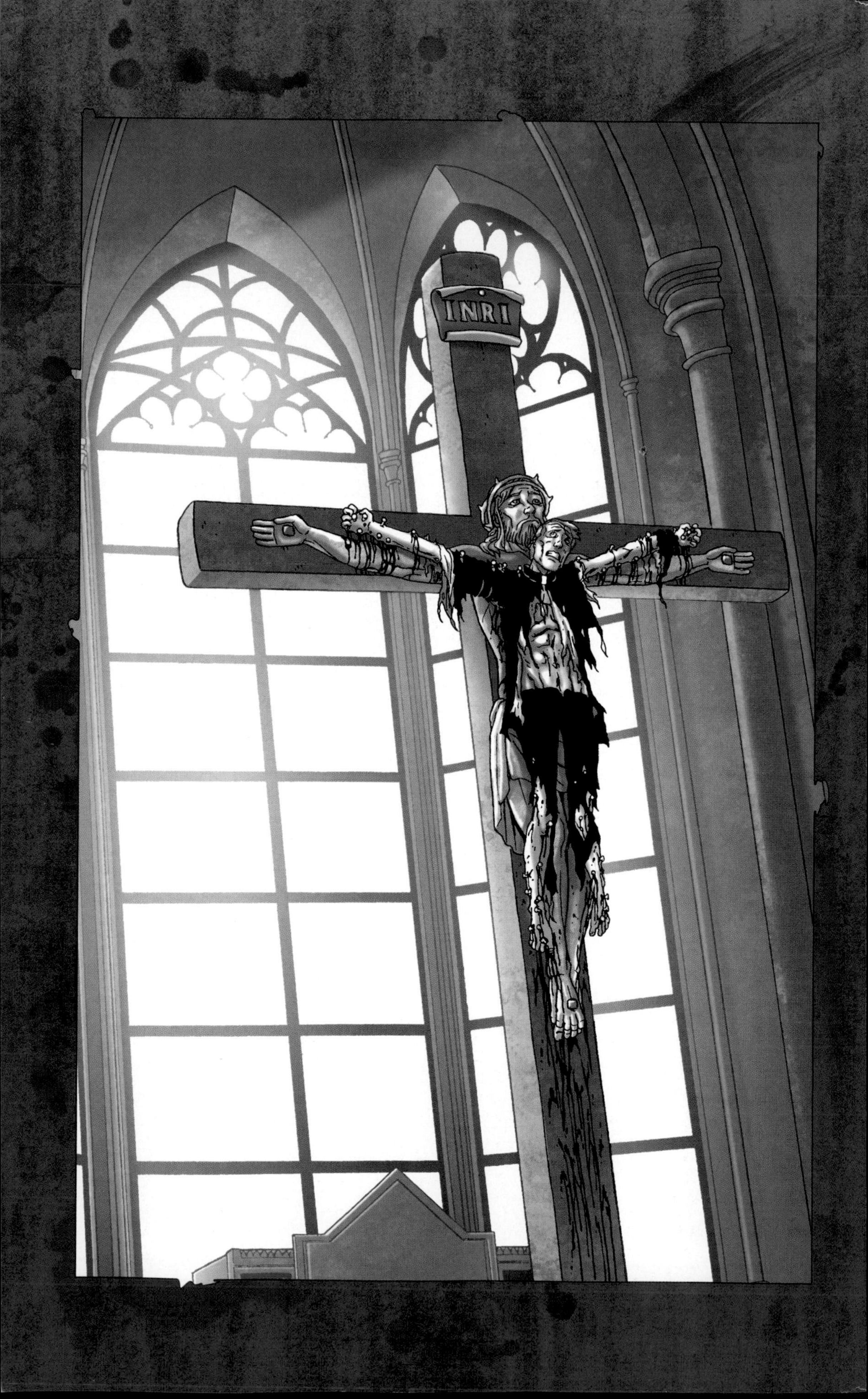
INRI

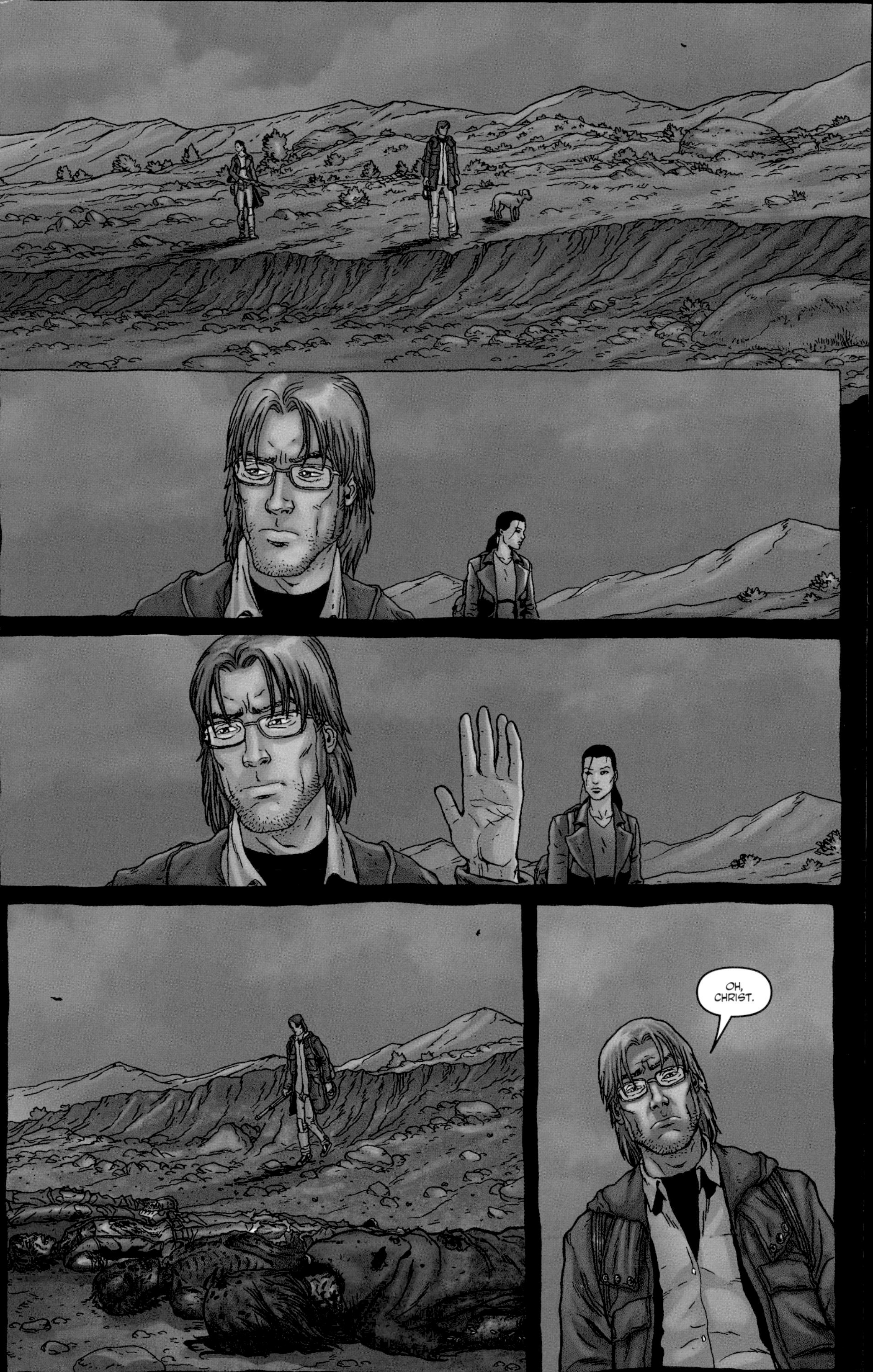
OH, CHRIST.

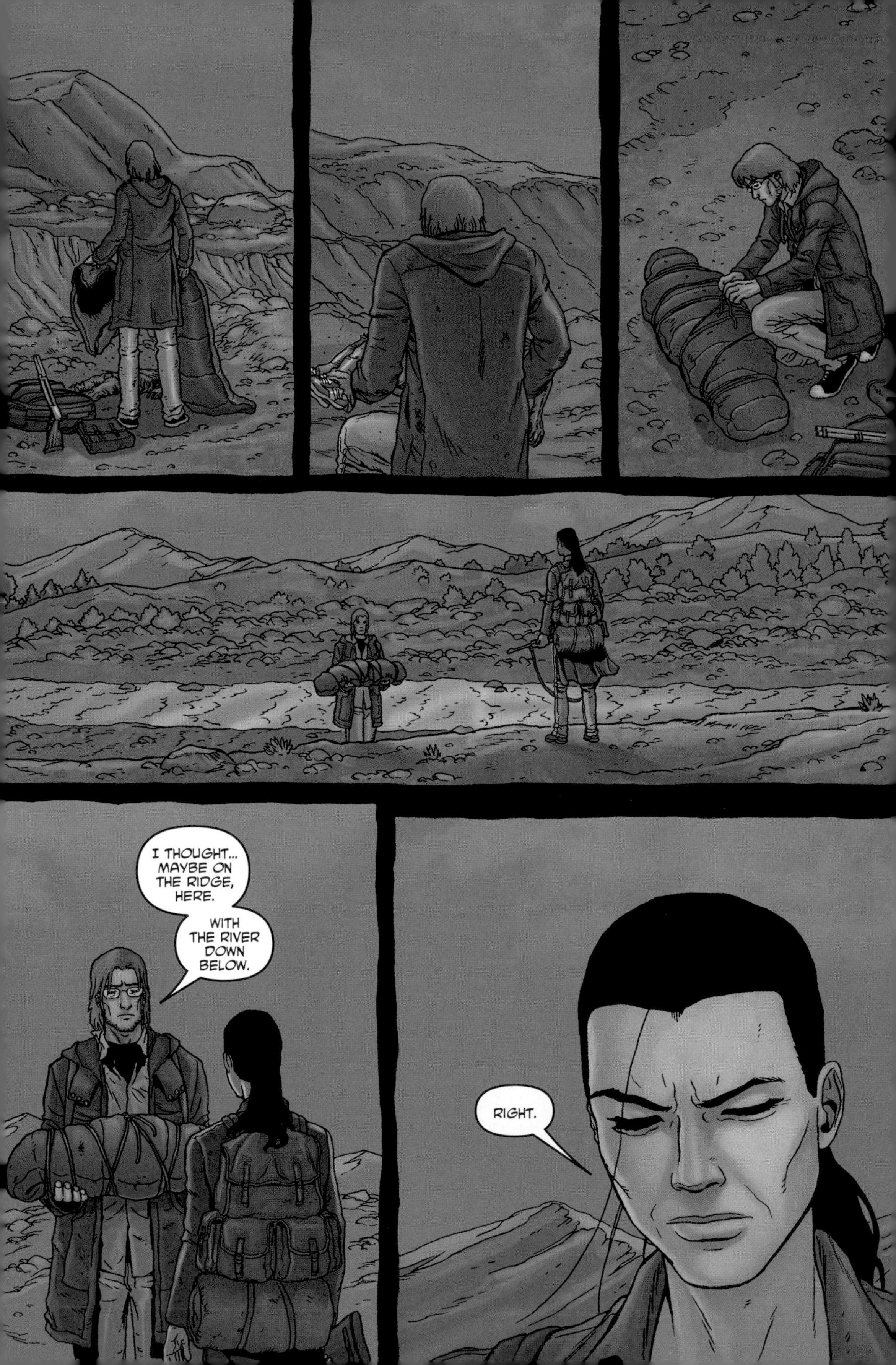
I THOUGHT... MAYBE ON THE RIDGE, HERE.
WITH THE RIVER DOWN BELOW.
RIGHT.

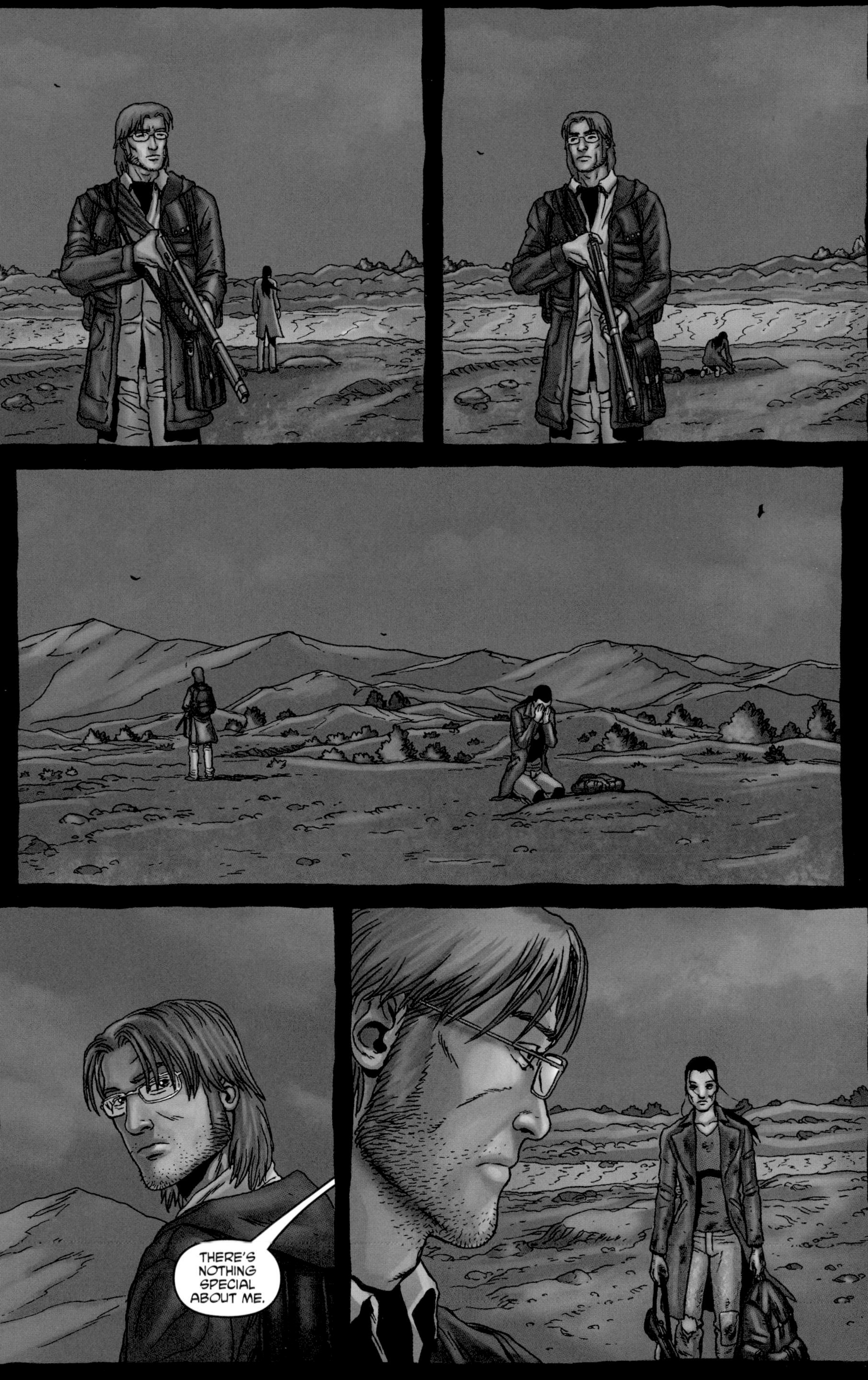
THERE'S NOTHING SPECIAL ABOUT ME.

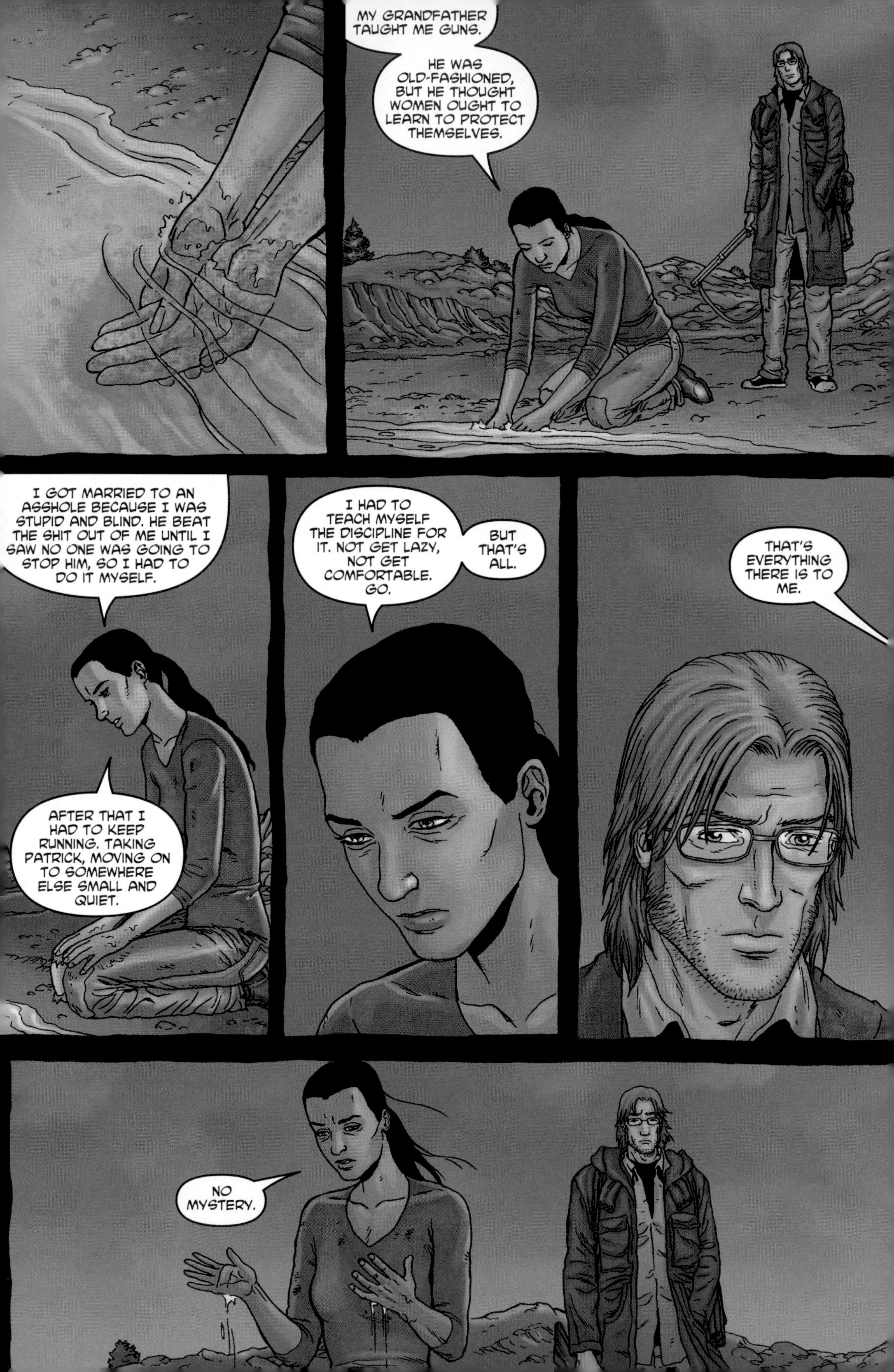

MY GRANDFATHER TAUGHT ME GUNS.
HE WAS OLD-FASHIONED, BUT HE THOUGHT WOMEN OUGHT TO LEARN TO PROTECT THEMSELVES.
I GOT MARRIED TO AN ASSHOLE BECAUSE I WAS STUPID AND BLIND. HE BEAT THE SHIT OUT OF ME UNTIL I SAW NO ONE WAS GOING TO STOP HIM, SO I HAD TO DO IT MYSELF.
AFTER THAT I HAD TO KEEP RUNNING. TAKING PATRICK, MOVING ON TO SOMEWHERE ELSE SMALL AND QUIET.
I HAD TO TEACH MYSELF THE DISCIPLINE FOR IT. NOT GET LAZY, NOT GET COMFORTABLE. GO.
BUT THAT'S ALL.
THAT'S EVERYTHING THERE IS TO ME.
NO MYSTERY.

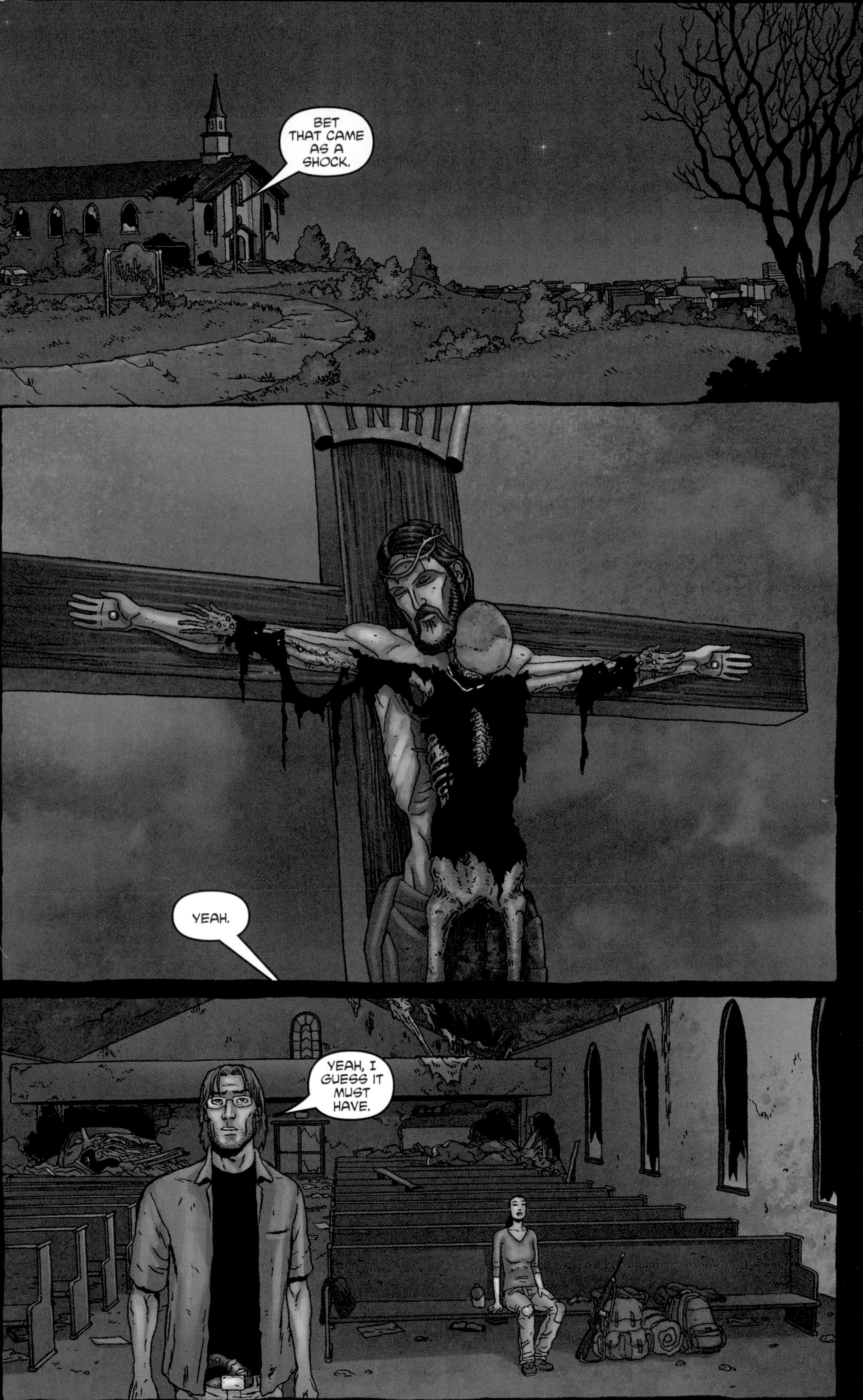

BET THAT CAME AS A SHOCK.
YEAH.
YEAH, I GUESS IT MUST HAVE.

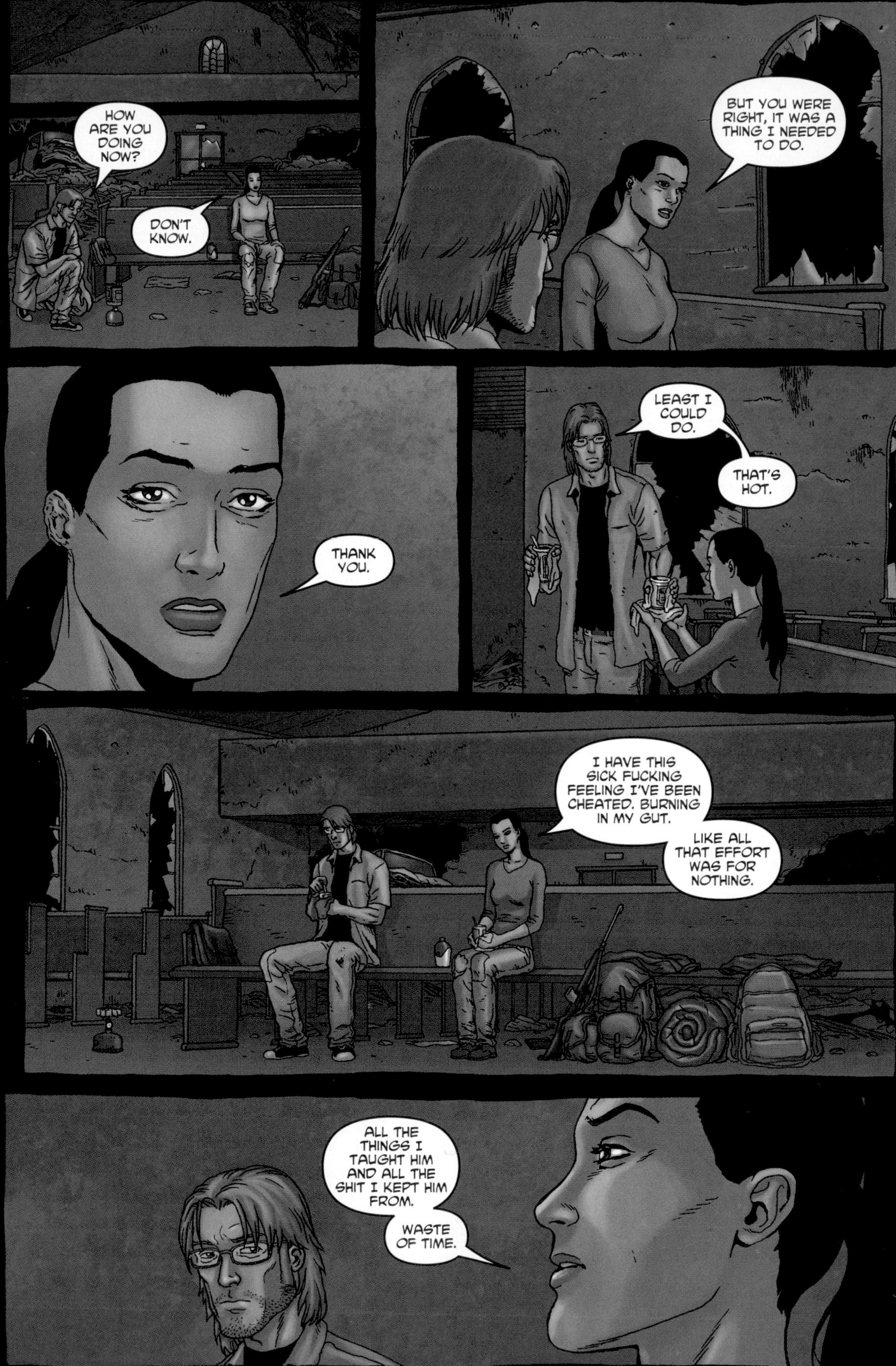
HOW ARE YOU DOING NOW?
DON'T KNOW.
BUT YOU WERE RIGHT, IT WAS A THING I NEEDED TO DO.
THANK YOU.
LEAST I COULD DO.
THAT'S HOT.
I HAVE THIS SICK FUCKING FEELING I'VE BEEN CHEATED. BURNING IN MY GUT.
LIKE ALL THAT EFFORT WAS FOR NOTHING.
ALL THE THINGS I TAUGHT HIM AND ALL THE SHIT I KEPT HIM FROM.
WASTE OF TIME.

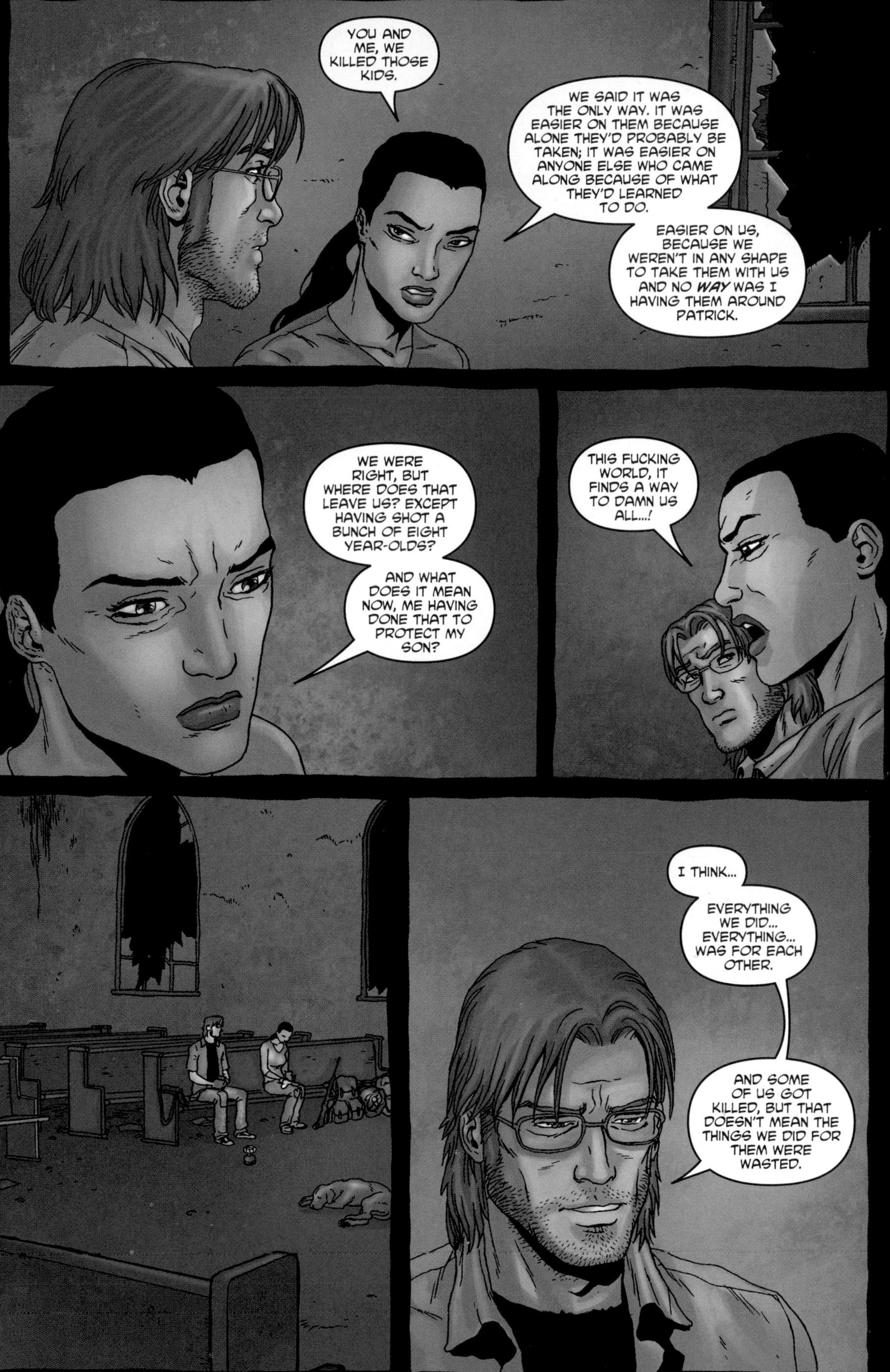

YOU AND ME, WE KILLED THOSE KIDS.
WE SAID IT WAS THE ONLY WAY. IT WAS EASIER ON THEM BECAUSE ALONE THEY'D PROBABLY BE TAKEN; IT WAS EASIER ON ANYONE ELSE WHO CAME ALONG BECAUSE OF WHAT THEY'D LEARNED TO DO.
EASIER ON US, BECAUSE WE WEREN'T IN ANY SHAPE TO TAKE THEM WITH US AND NO *WAY* WAS I HAVING THEM AROUND PATRICK.
WE WERE RIGHT, BUT WHERE DOES THAT LEAVE US? EXCEPT HAVING SHOT A BUNCH OF EIGHT YEAR-OLDS?
AND WHAT DOES IT MEAN NOW, ME HAVING DONE THAT TO PROTECT MY SON?
THIS FUCKING WORLD, IT FINDS A WAY TO DAMN US ALL...!
I THINK...
EVERYTHING WE DID... EVERYTHING... WAS FOR EACH OTHER.
AND SOME OF US GOT KILLED, BUT THAT DOESN'T MEAN THE THINGS WE DID FOR THEM WERE WASTED.

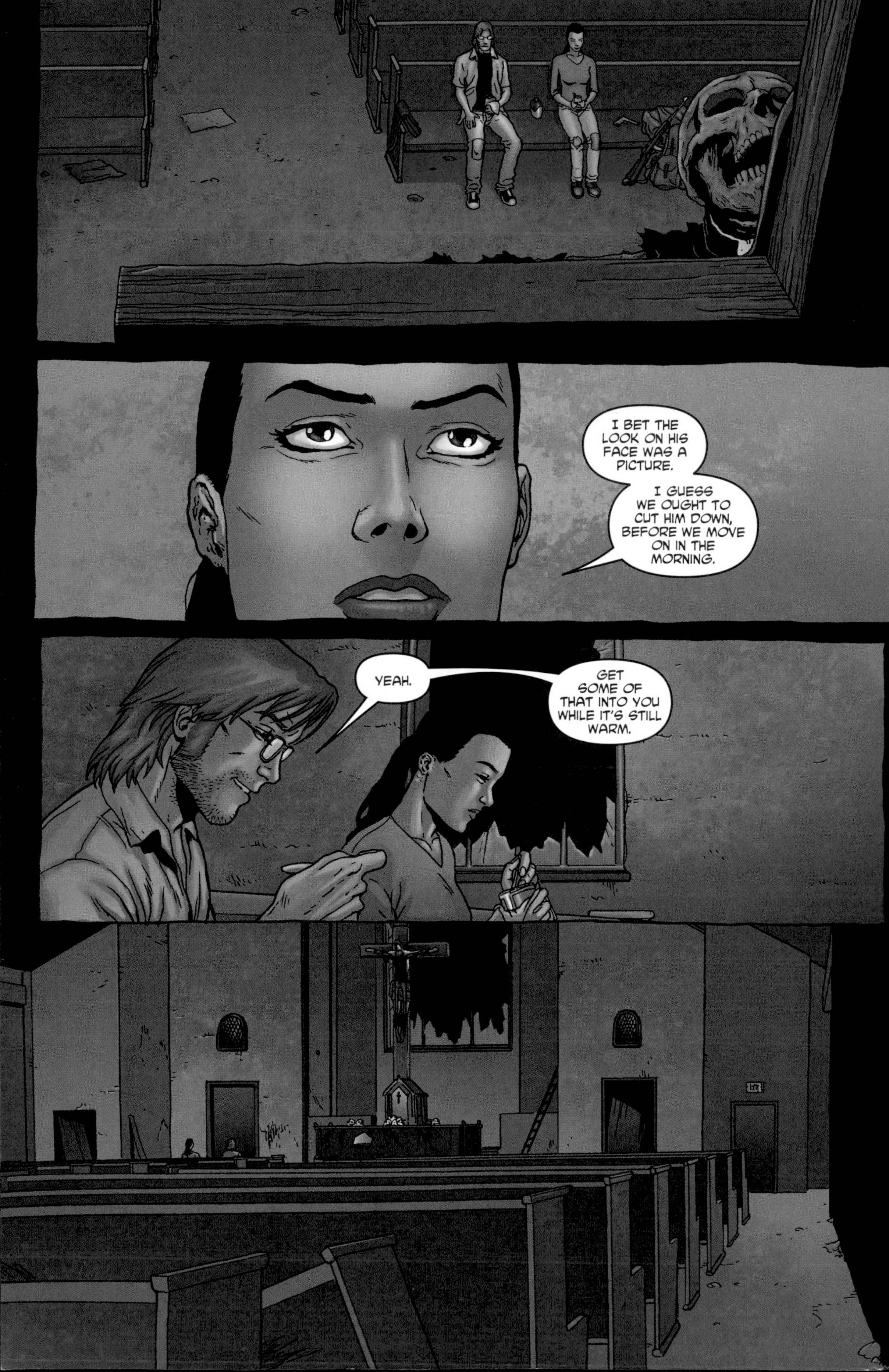
I BET THE LOOK ON HIS FACE WAS A PICTURE.
I GUESS WE OUGHT TO CUT HIM DOWN, BEFORE WE MOVE ON IN THE MORNING.
YEAH.
GET SOME OF THAT INTO YOU WHILE IT'S STILL WARM.

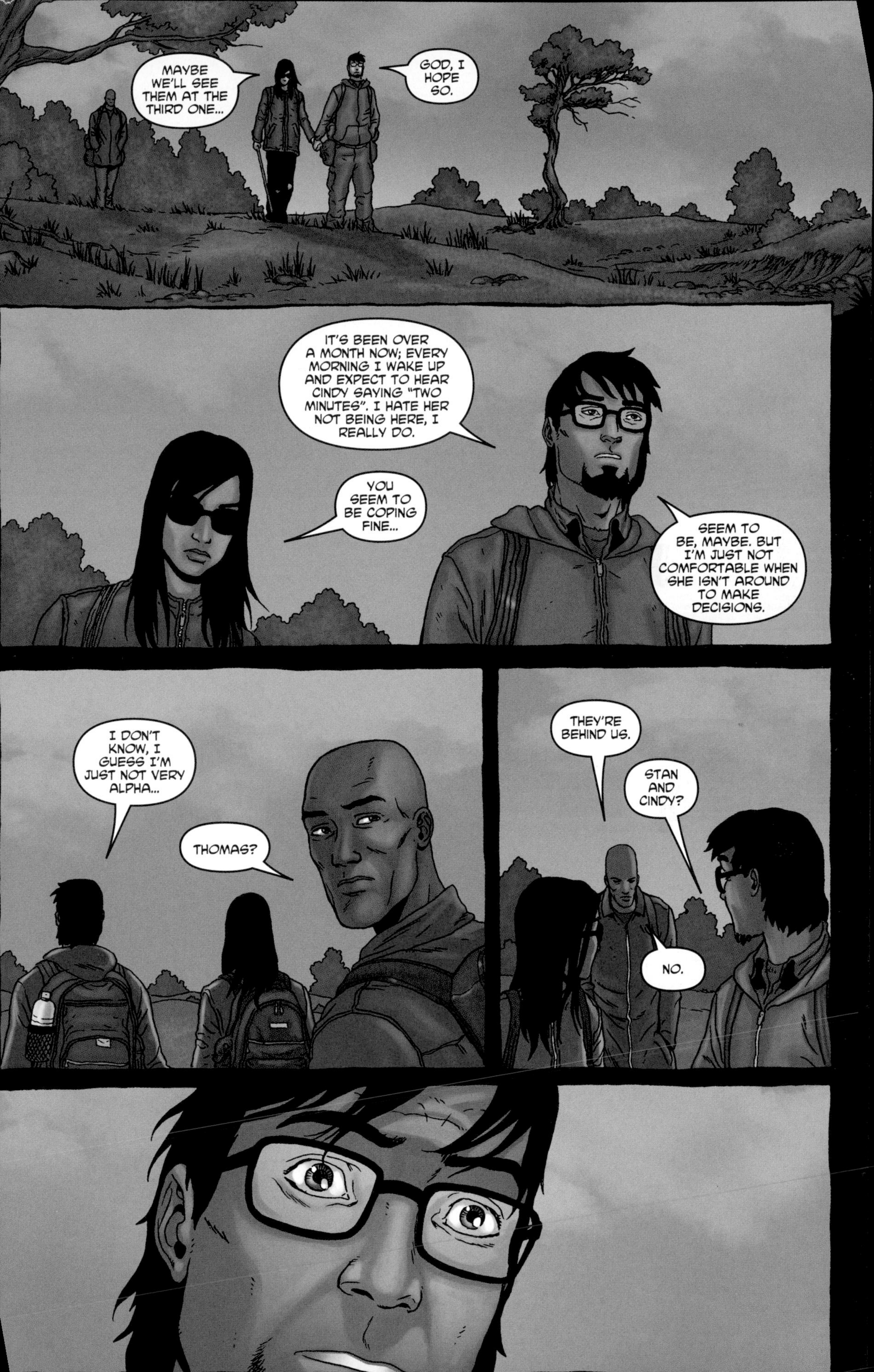
MAYBE WE'LL SEE THEM AT THE THIRD ONE...
GOD, I HOPE SO.
IT'S BEEN OVER A MONTH NOW; EVERY MORNING I WAKE UP AND EXPECT TO HEAR CINDY SAYING "TWO MINUTES". I HATE HER NOT BEING HERE, I REALLY DO.
YOU SEEM TO BE COPING FINE...
SEEM TO BE, MAYBE. BUT I'M JUST NOT COMFORTABLE WHEN SHE ISN'T AROUND TO MAKE DECISIONS.
I DON'T KNOW, I GUESS I'M JUST NOT VERY ALPHA...
THOMAS?
THEY'RE BEHIND US.
STAN AND CINDY?
NO.

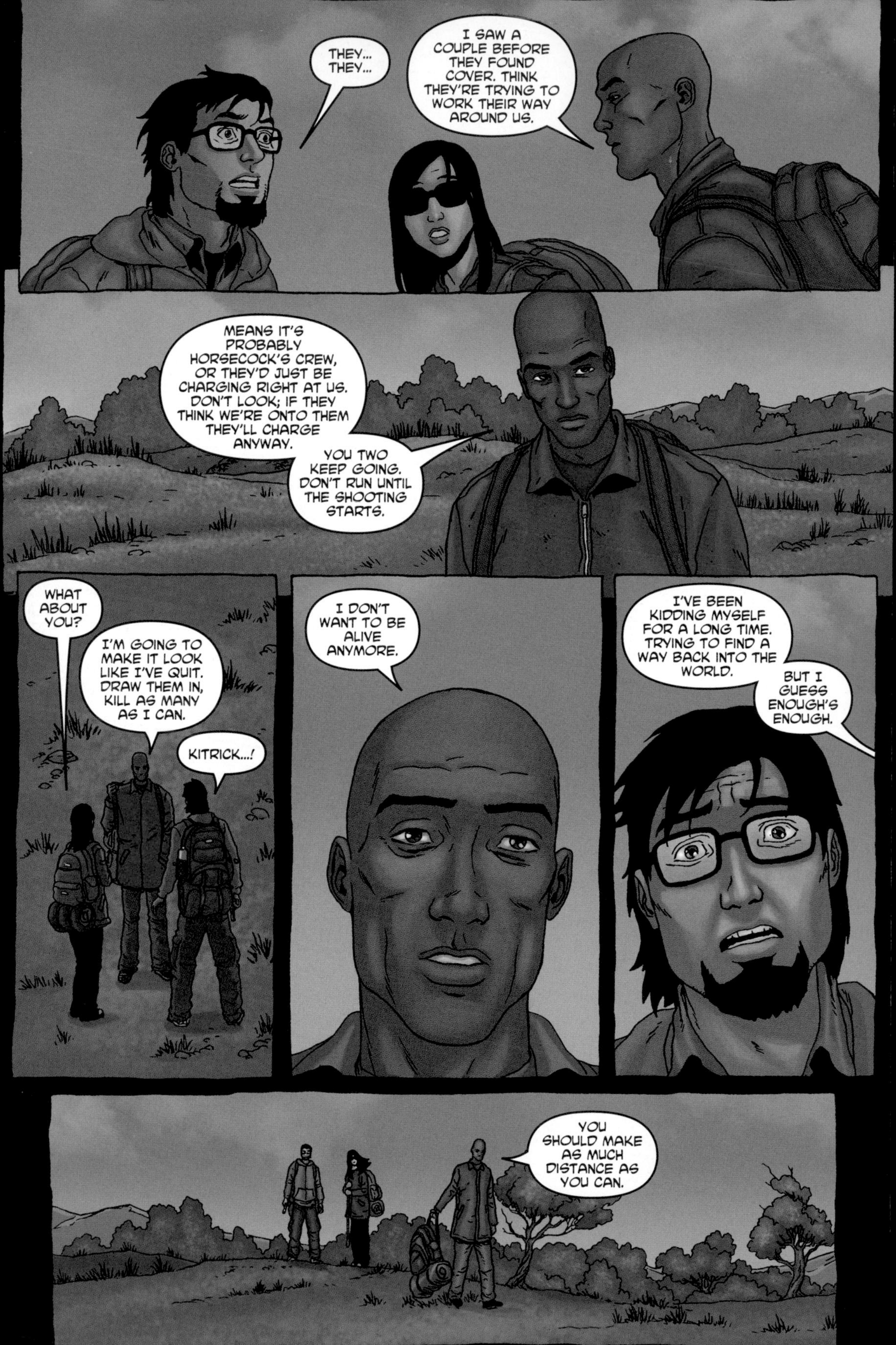

THEY... THEY...
I SAW A COUPLE BEFORE THEY FOUND COVER. THINK THEY'RE TRYING TO WORK THEIR WAY AROUND US.
MEANS IT'S PROBABLY HORSECOCK'S CREW, OR THEY'D JUST BE CHARGING RIGHT AT US. DON'T LOOK; IF THEY THINK WE'RE ONTO THEM THEY'LL CHARGE ANYWAY.
YOU TWO KEEP GOING. DON'T RUN UNTIL THE SHOOTING STARTS.
WHAT ABOUT YOU?
I'M GOING TO MAKE IT LOOK LIKE I'VE QUIT. DRAW THEM IN, KILL AS MANY AS I CAN.
KITRICK...!
I DON'T WANT TO BE ALIVE ANYMORE.
I'VE BEEN KIDDING MYSELF FOR A LONG TIME. TRYING TO FIND A WAY BACK INTO THE WORLD.
BUT I GUESS ENOUGH'S ENOUGH.
YOU SHOULD MAKE AS MUCH DISTANCE AS YOU CAN.

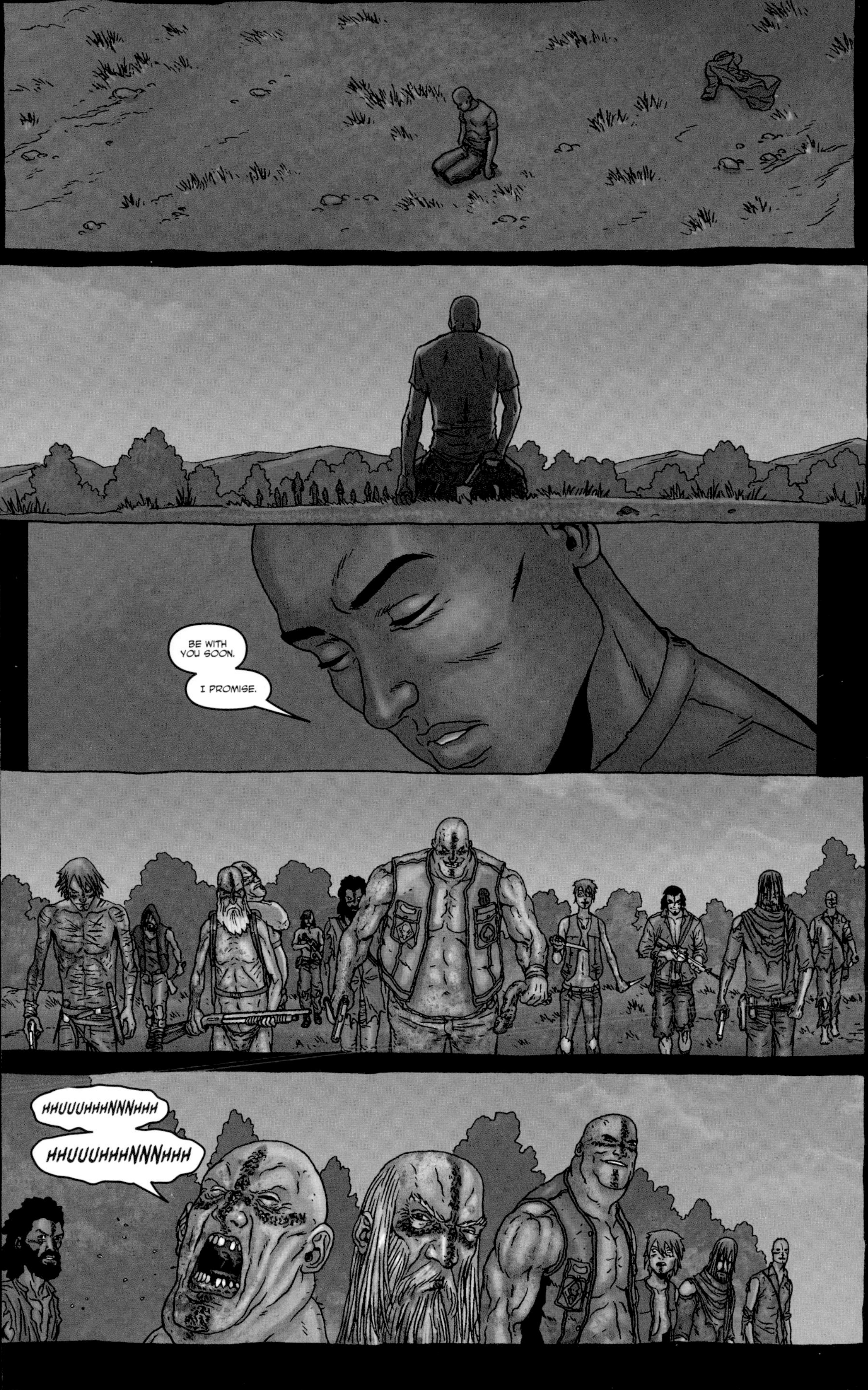
BE WITH YOU SOON.
I PROMISE.
HHUUUHHHNNNHHH
HHUUUHHHNNNHHH

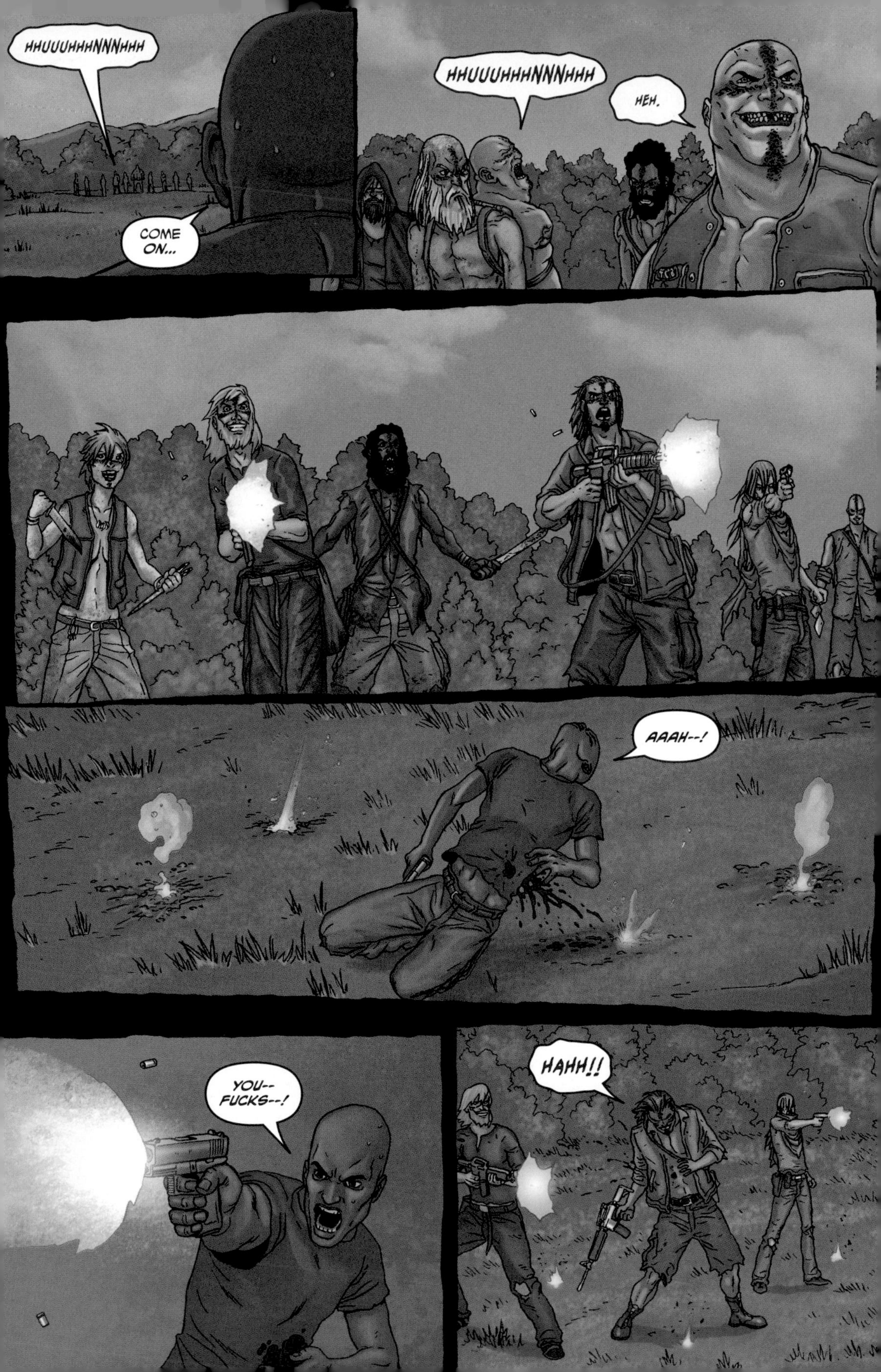
HHUUUHHHNNNHHH
COME ON...
HHUUUHHHNNNHHH
HEH.
AAAH--!
YOU-- FUCKS--!
HAHH!!

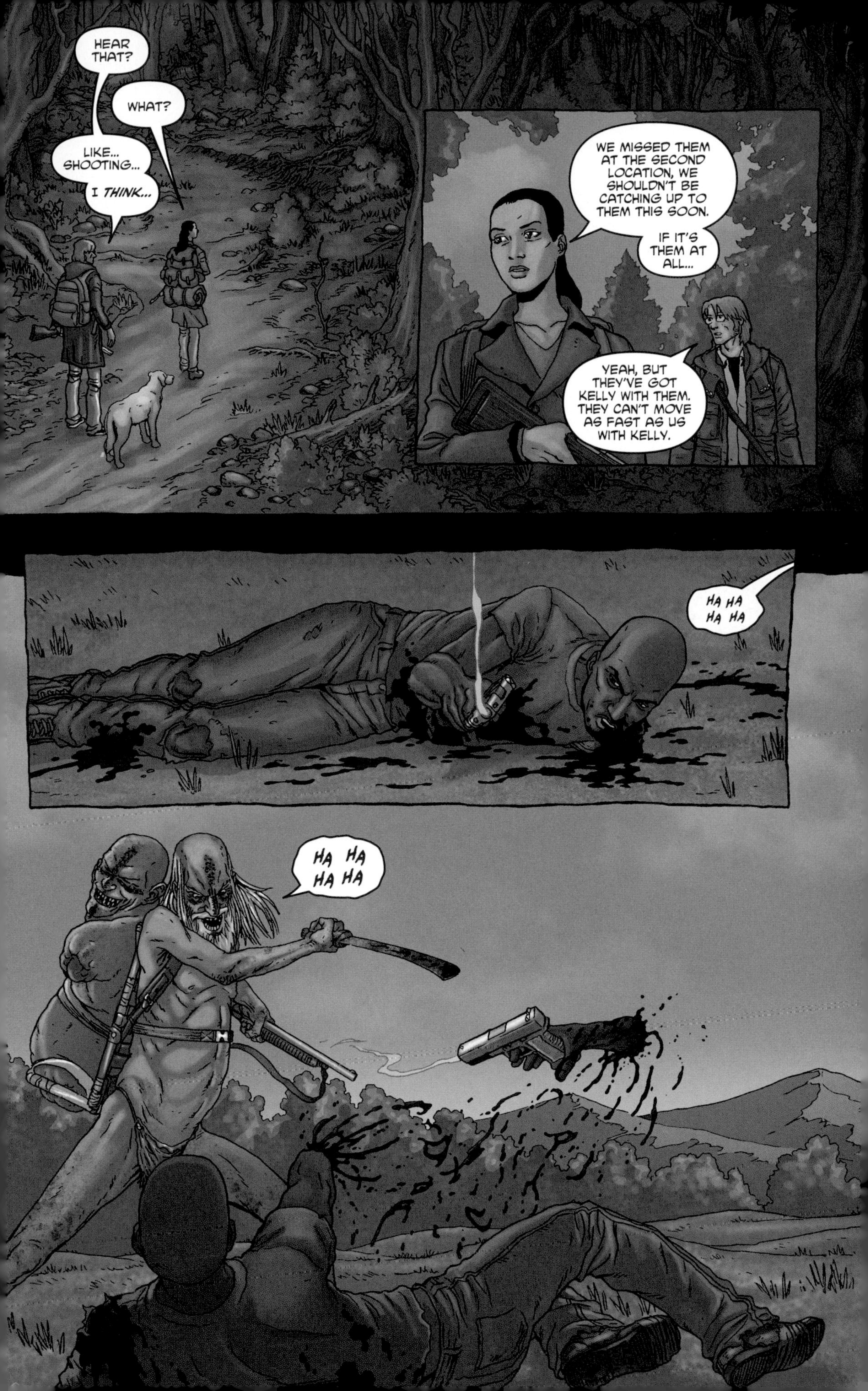
HEAR THAT?
WHAT?
LIKE... SHOOTING...
I THINK...
WE MISSED THEM AT THE SECOND LOCATION, WE SHOULDN'T BE CATCHING UP TO THEM THIS SOON.
IF IT'S THEM AT ALL...
YEAH, BUT THEY'VE GOT KELLY WITH THEM. THEY CAN'T MOVE AS FAST AS US WITH KELLY.
HA HA HA HA
HA HA HA HA

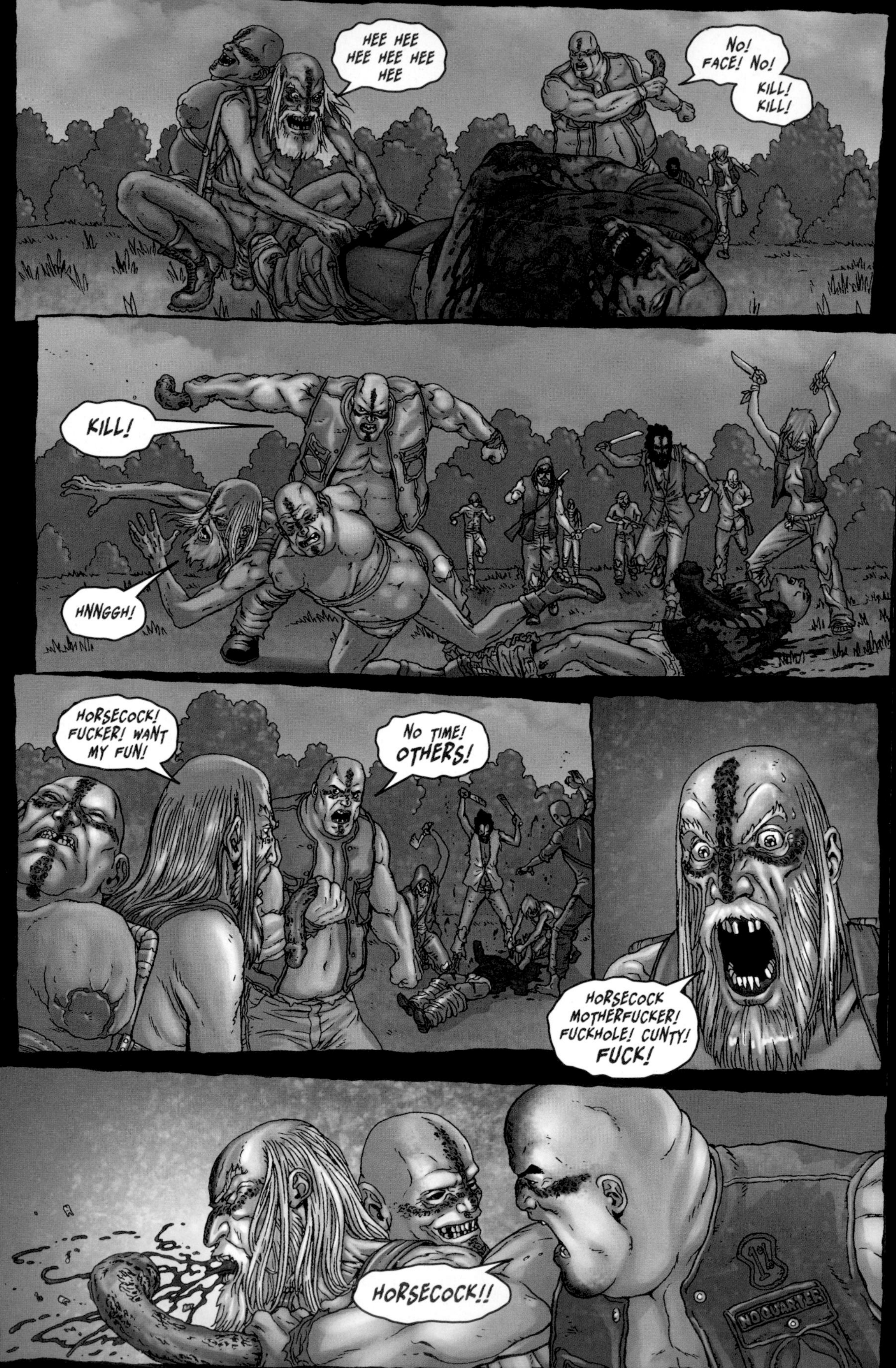
HEE HEE HEE HEE HEE HEE
NO! FACE! NO!
KILL! KILL!
KILL!
HNNGGH!
HORSECOCK! FUCKER! WANT MY FUN!
NO TIME! OTHERS!
HORSECOCK MOTHERFUCKER! FUCKHOLE! CUNTY! FUCK!
HORSECOCK!!
NO QUARTER

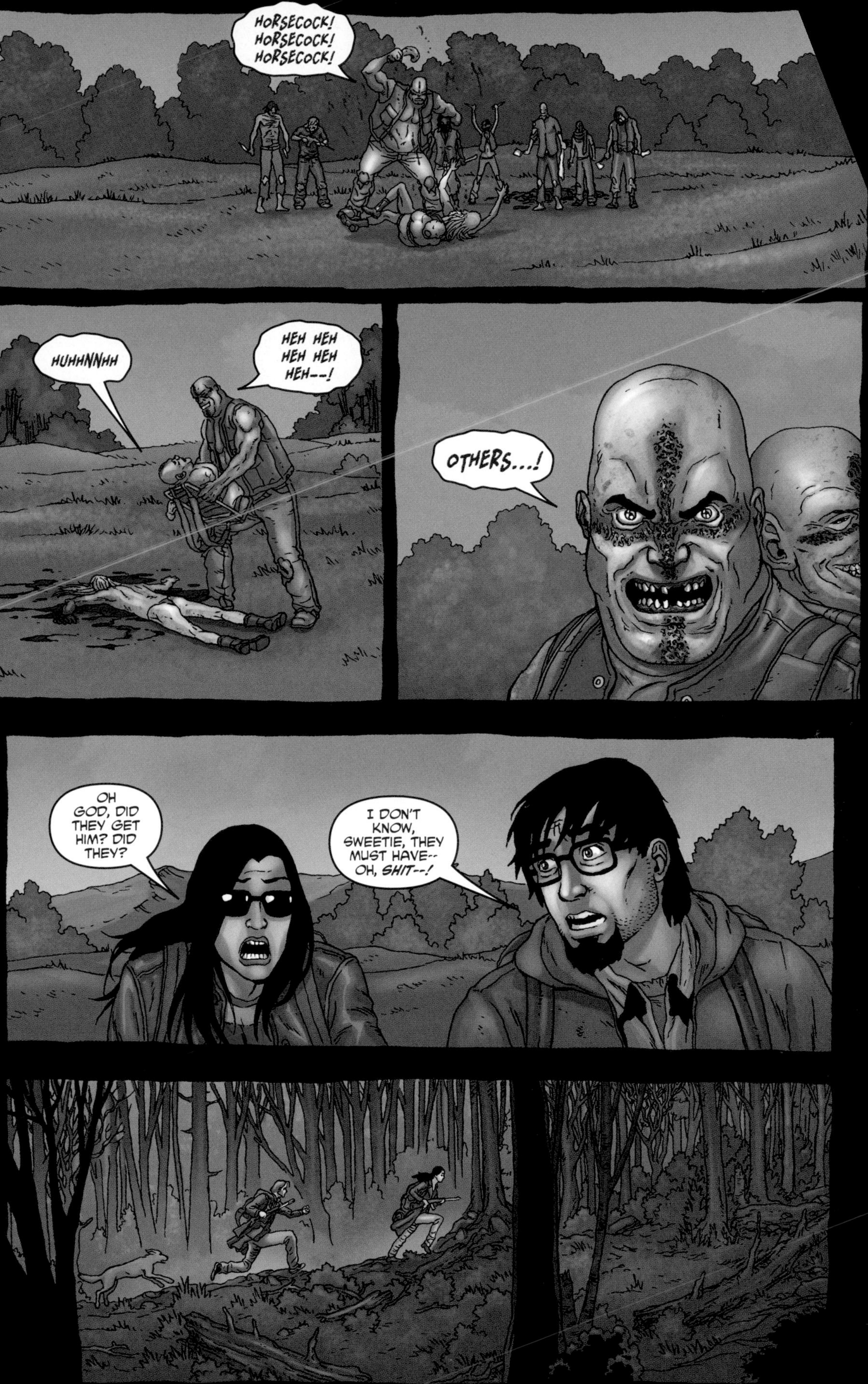
HORSECOCK!
HORSECOCK!
HORSECOCK!
HUHHNNHH
HEH HEH
HEH HEH
HEH--!
OTHERS...!
OH GOD, DID THEY GET HIM? DID THEY?
I DON'T KNOW, SWEETIE, THEY MUST HAVE-- OH, *SHIT*--!

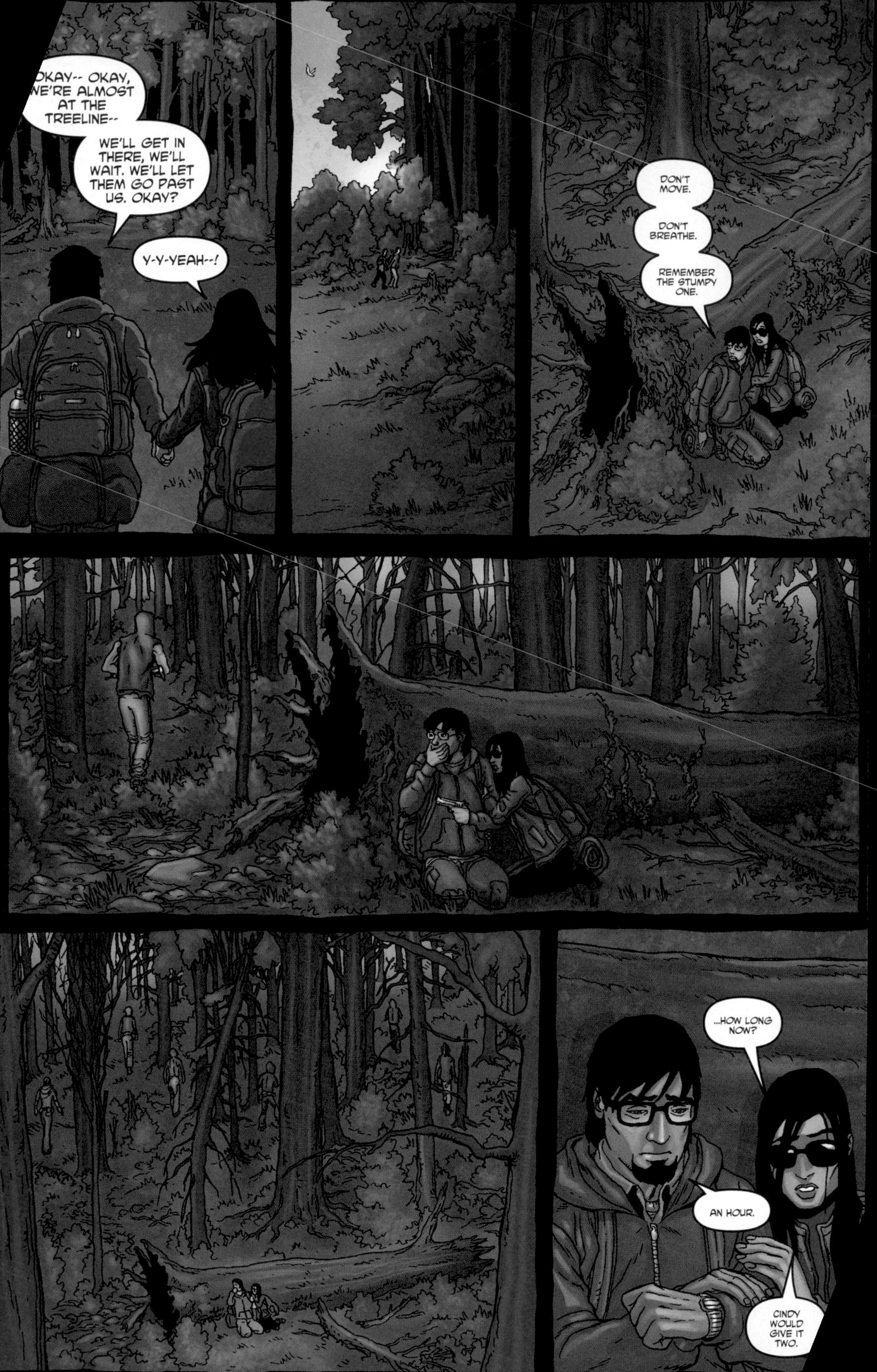
OKAY-- OKAY, WE'RE ALMOST AT THE TREELINE--
WE'LL GET IN THERE, WE'LL WAIT. WE'LL LET THEM GO PAST US. OKAY?
Y-Y-YEAH--!
DON'T MOVE.
DON'T BREATHE.
REMEMBER THE STUMPY ONE.
...HOW LONG NOW?
AN HOUR.
CINDY WOULD GIVE IT TWO.

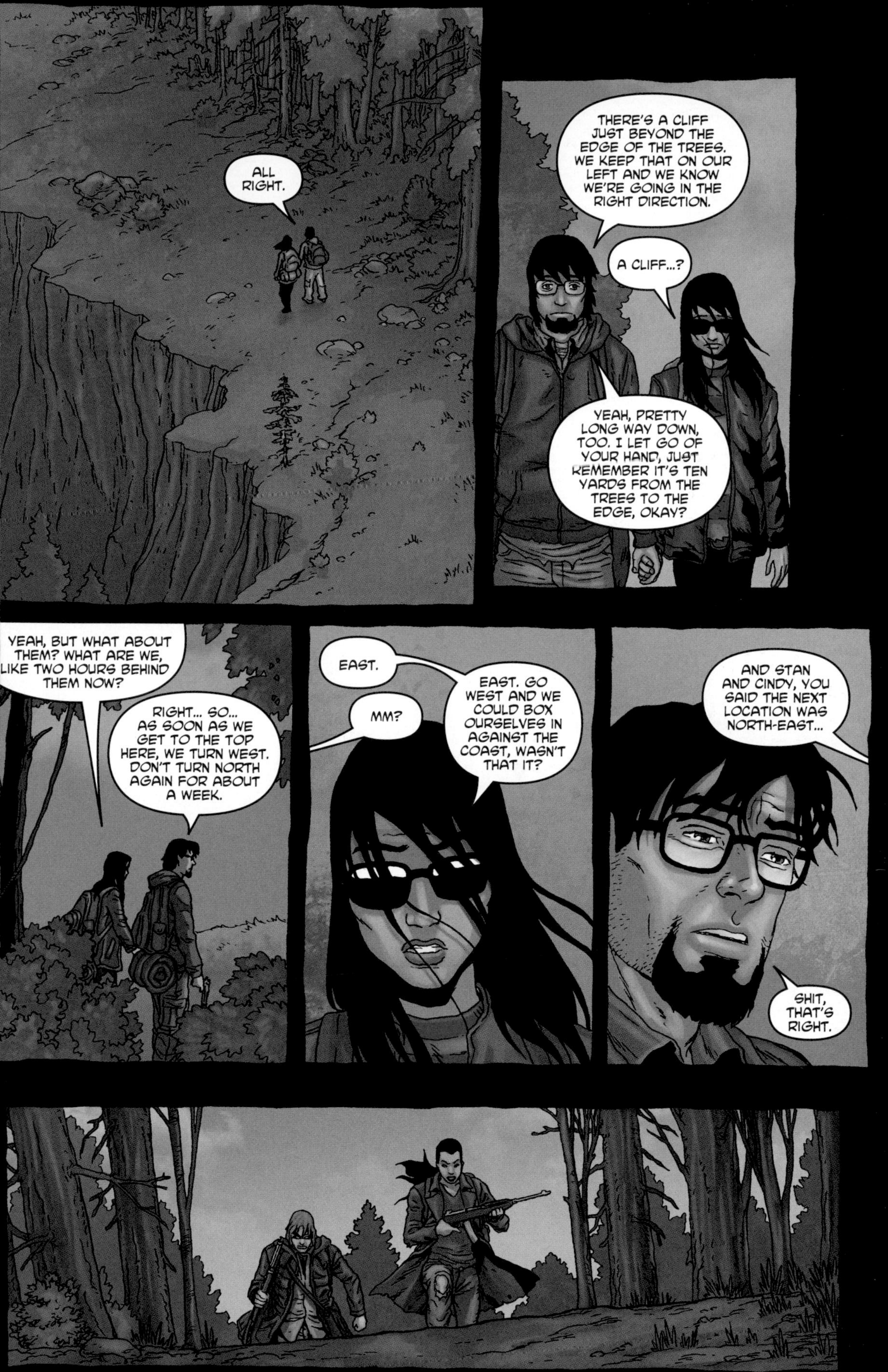
ALL RIGHT.
THERE'S A CLIFF JUST BEYOND THE EDGE OF THE TREES. WE KEEP THAT ON OUR LEFT AND WE KNOW WE'RE GOING IN THE RIGHT DIRECTION.
A CLIFF...?
YEAH, PRETTY LONG WAY DOWN, TOO. I LET GO OF YOUR HAND, JUST REMEMBER IT'S TEN YARDS FROM THE TREES TO THE EDGE, OKAY?
YEAH, BUT WHAT ABOUT THEM? WHAT ARE WE, LIKE TWO HOURS BEHIND THEM NOW?
RIGHT... SO... AS SOON AS WE GET TO THE TOP HERE, WE TURN WEST. DON'T TURN NORTH AGAIN FOR ABOUT A WEEK.
EAST.
MM?
EAST. GO WEST AND WE COULD BOX OURSELVES IN AGAINST THE COAST, WASN'T THAT IT?
AND STAN AND CINDY, YOU SAID THE NEXT LOCATION WAS NORTH-EAST...
SHIT, THAT'S RIGHT.

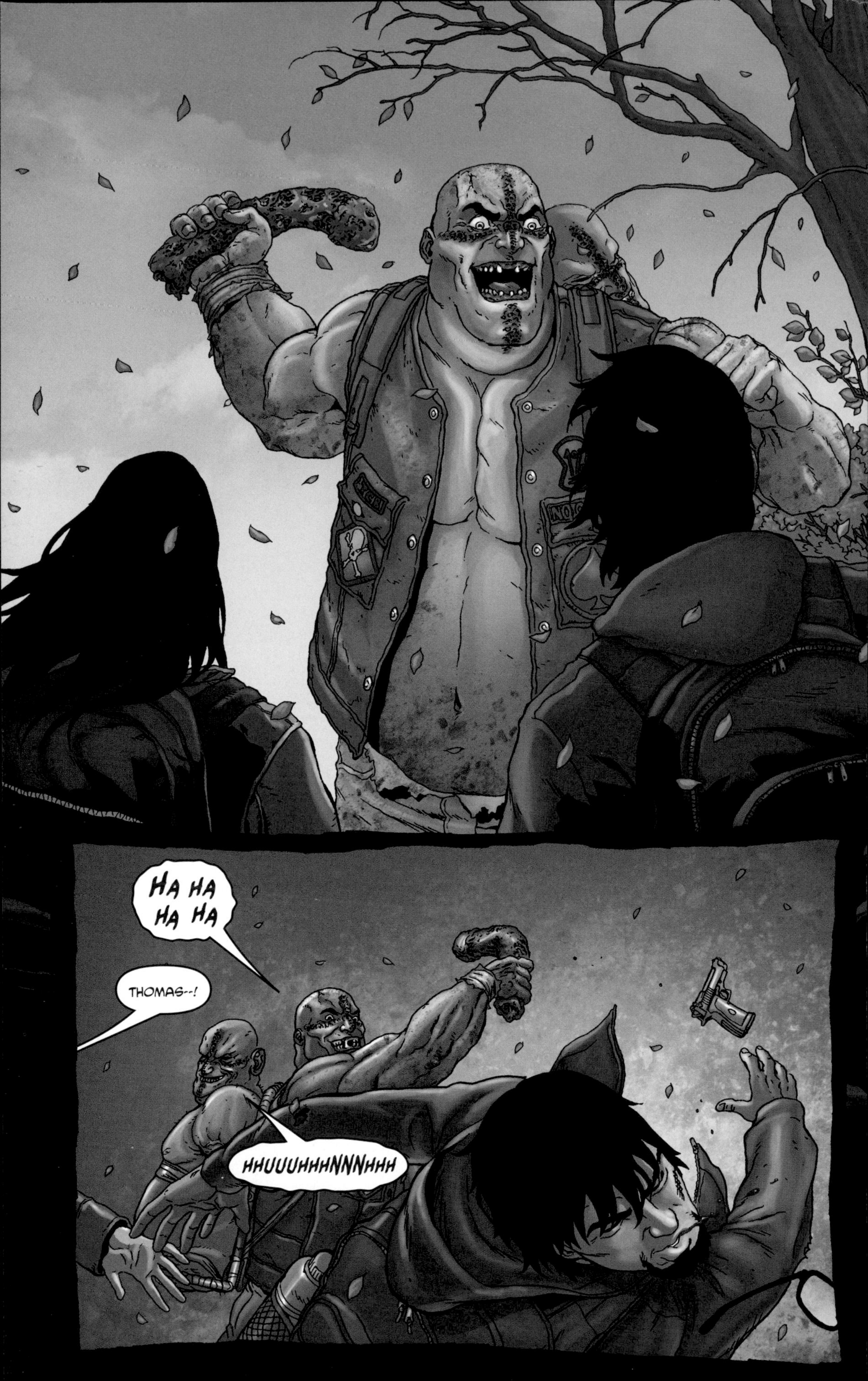
HA HA HA HA
THOMAS--!
HHUUUHHHNNNHHH

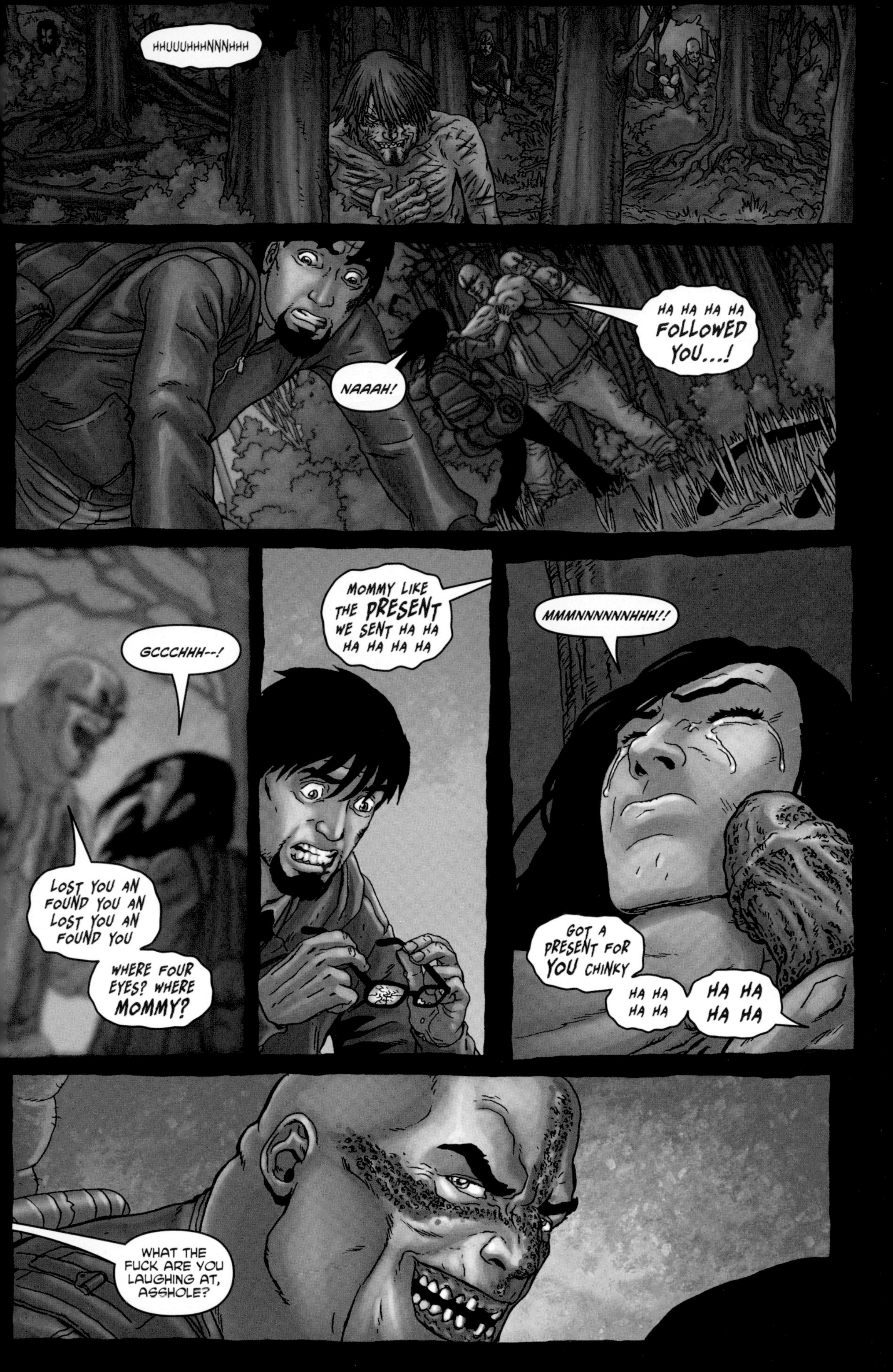
HHUUUHHHNNNHHH
HA HA HA HA FOLLOWED YOU...!
NAAAH!
GCCCHHH--!
LOST YOU AN FOUND YOU AN LOST YOU AN FOUND YOU
WHERE FOUR EYES? WHERE MOMMY?
MOMMY LIKE THE PRESENT WE SENT HA HA HA HA HA HA
MMMNNNNNNHHH!!
GOT A PRESENT FOR YOU CHINKY
HA HA HA HA
HA HA HA HA
WHAT THE FUCK ARE YOU LAUGHING AT, ASSHOLE?

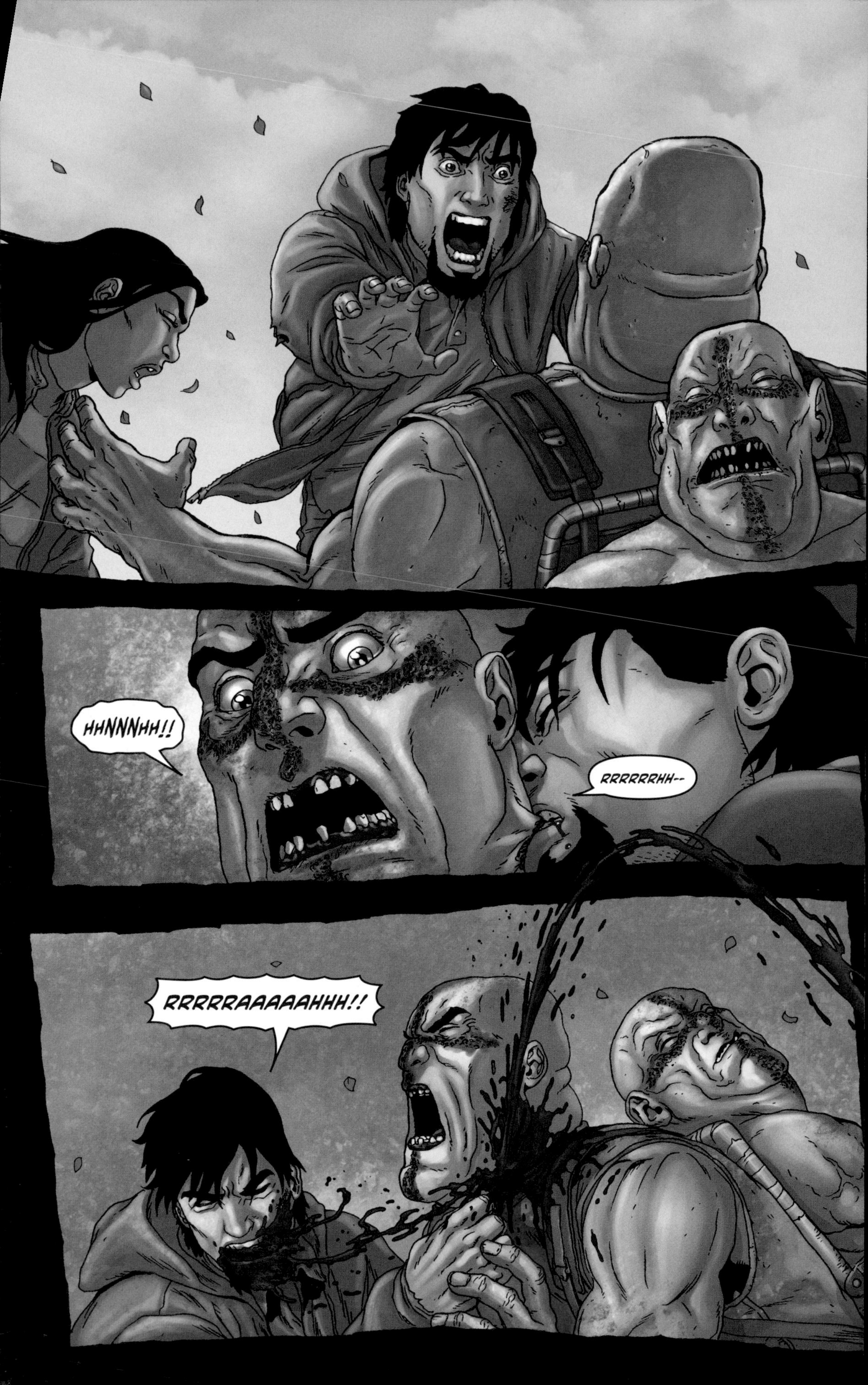
HHNNNHH!!
RRRRRRHH--
RRRRRAAAAAAHHH!!

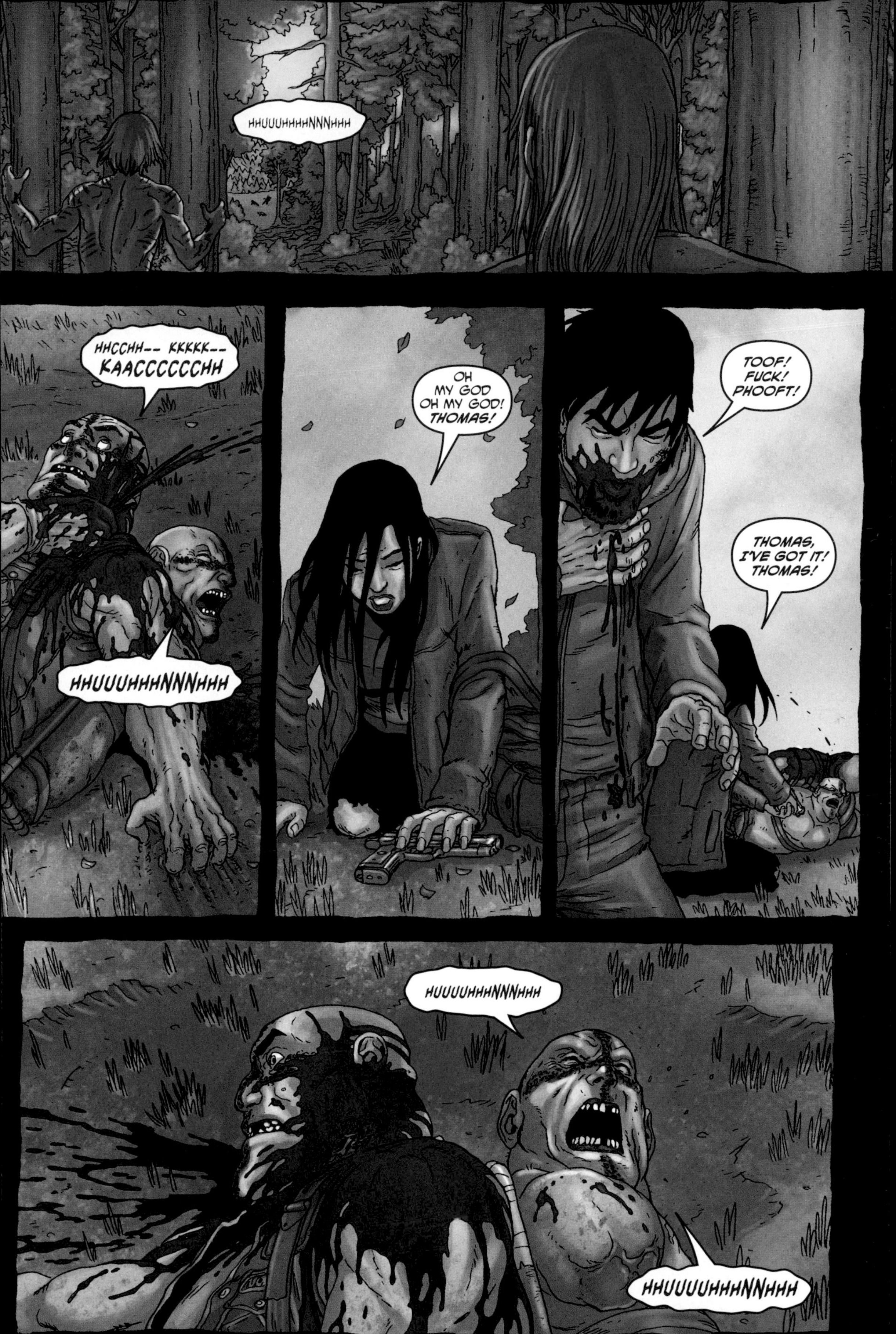
HHUUUHHHHNNHHH
HHCCHH-- KKKKK--
KAACCCCCCHH
HHUUUHHHNNHHH
OH MY GOD OH MY GOD! THOMAS!
TOOF! FUCK! PHOOFT!
THOMAS, I'VE GOT IT! THOMAS!
HHUUUHHHNNHHH
HHUUUUHHHNNHHH

SWEETIE--

AAAAAAH!

FIRE.

OH, GOD--!

SWEETIE, YOU'VE GOT TO RUN, YOU'VE GOT TO--

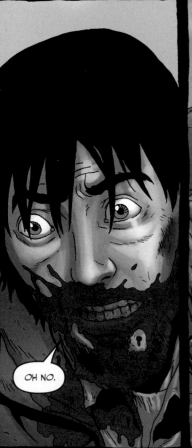

OH NO.

NO NO NNNNOOOO--!

WAAAH!

THOMAS, YOU CAN MAKE IT! SHOOT ME! JUST SHOOT ME, YOU CAN GET AWAY WITHOUT ME!

I LOVE YOU, YOU'VE BEEN SO GOOD, SO KIND! BUT YOU'VE DONE ENOUGH, YOU'VE DONE ENOUGH!

GO!!

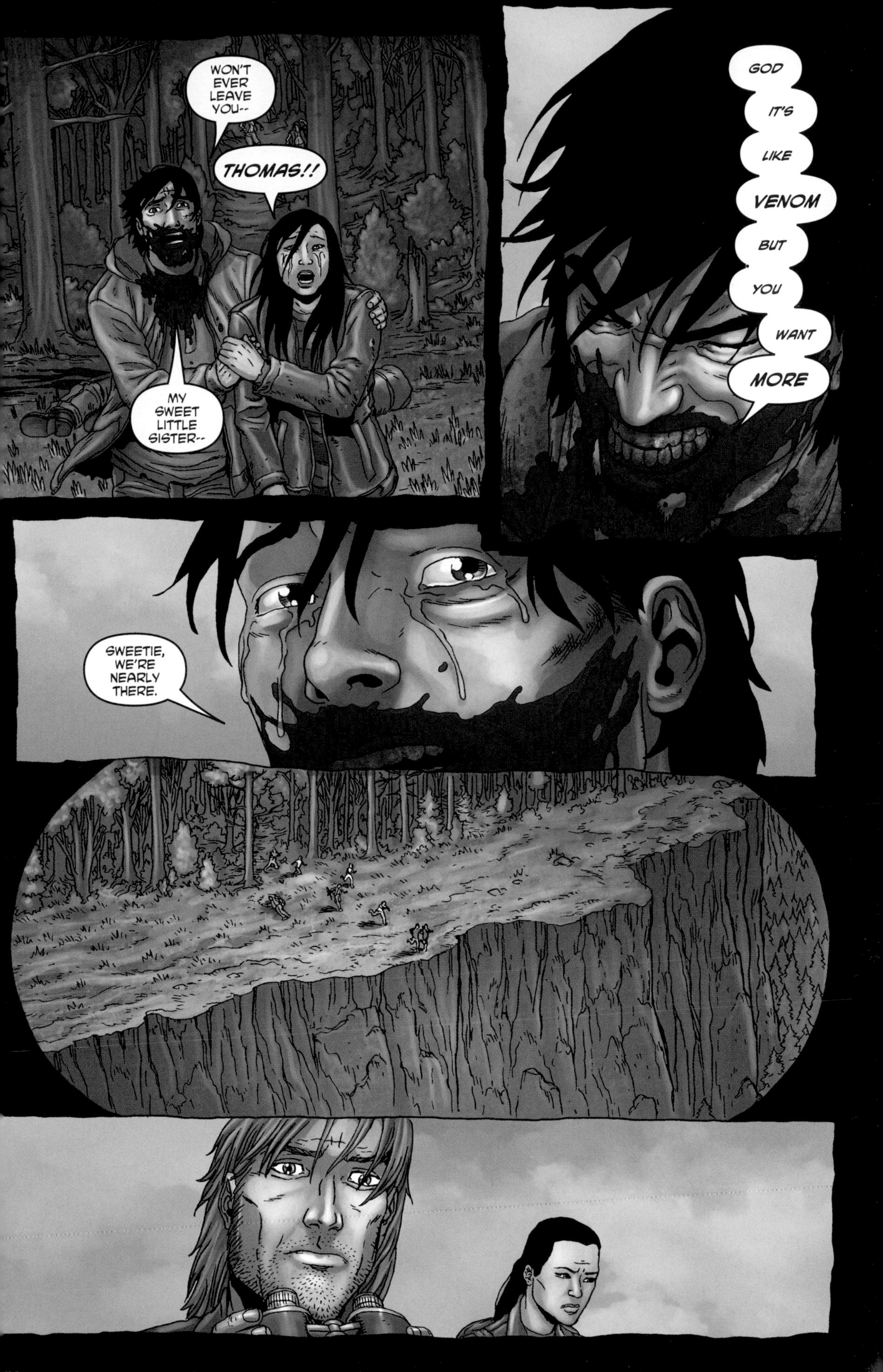
WON'T EVER LEAVE YOU--
THOMAS!!
MY SWEET LITTLE SISTER--
GOD
IT'S
LIKE
VENOM
BUT
YOU
WANT
MORE
SWEETIE, WE'RE NEARLY THERE.

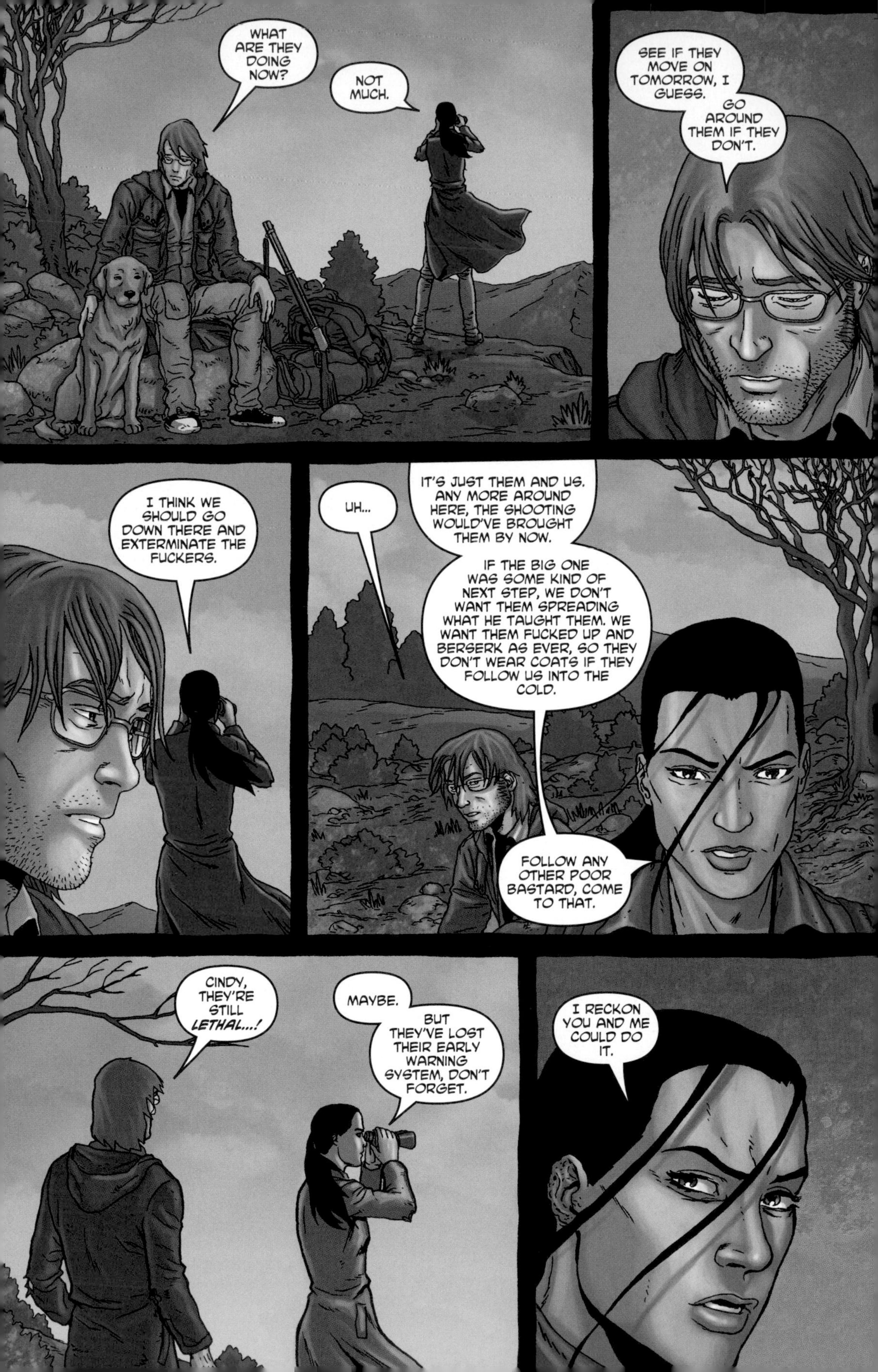
WHAT ARE THEY DOING NOW?
NOT MUCH.
SEE IF THEY MOVE ON TOMORROW, I GUESS.
GO AROUND THEM IF THEY DON'T.
I THINK WE SHOULD GO DOWN THERE AND EXTERMINATE THE FUCKERS.
UH...
IT'S JUST THEM AND US. ANY MORE AROUND HERE, THE SHOOTING WOULD'VE BROUGHT THEM BY NOW.
IF THE BIG ONE WAS SOME KIND OF NEXT STEP, WE DON'T WANT THEM SPREADING WHAT HE TAUGHT THEM. WE WANT THEM FUCKED UP AND BERSERK AS EVER, SO THEY DON'T WEAR COATS IF THEY FOLLOW US INTO THE COLD.
FOLLOW ANY OTHER POOR BASTARD, COME TO THAT.
CINDY, THEY'RE STILL *LETHAL...!*
MAYBE.
BUT THEY'VE LOST THEIR EARLY WARNING SYSTEM, DON'T FORGET.
I RECKON YOU AND ME COULD DO IT.

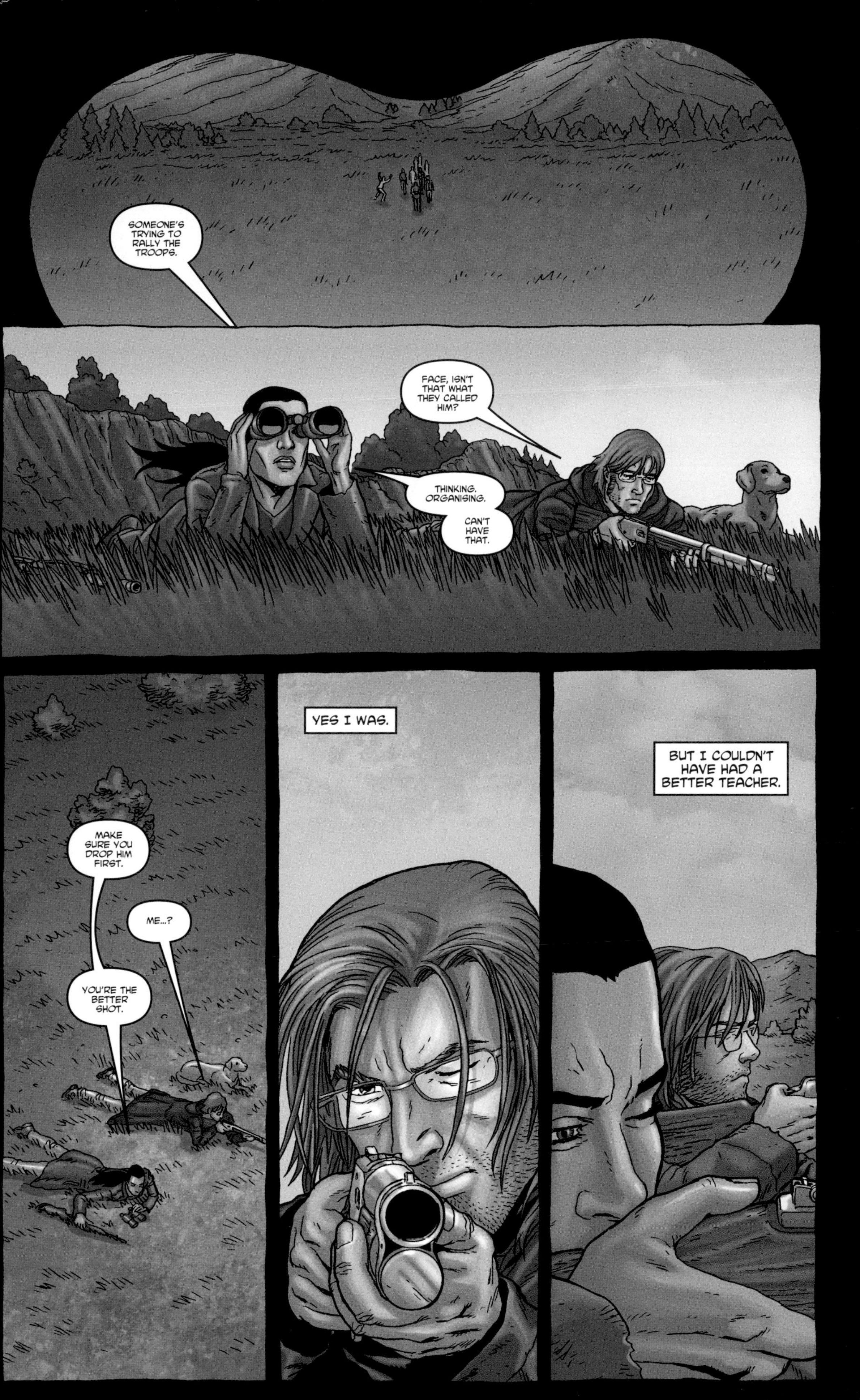
SOMEONE'S TRYING TO RALLY THE TROOPS.
FACE, ISN'T THAT WHAT THEY CALLED HIM?
THINKING. ORGANISING.
CAN'T HAVE THAT.
MAKE SURE YOU DROP HIM FIRST.
ME...?
YOU'RE THE BETTER SHOT.
YES I WAS.
BUT I COULDN'T HAVE HAD A BETTER TEACHER.

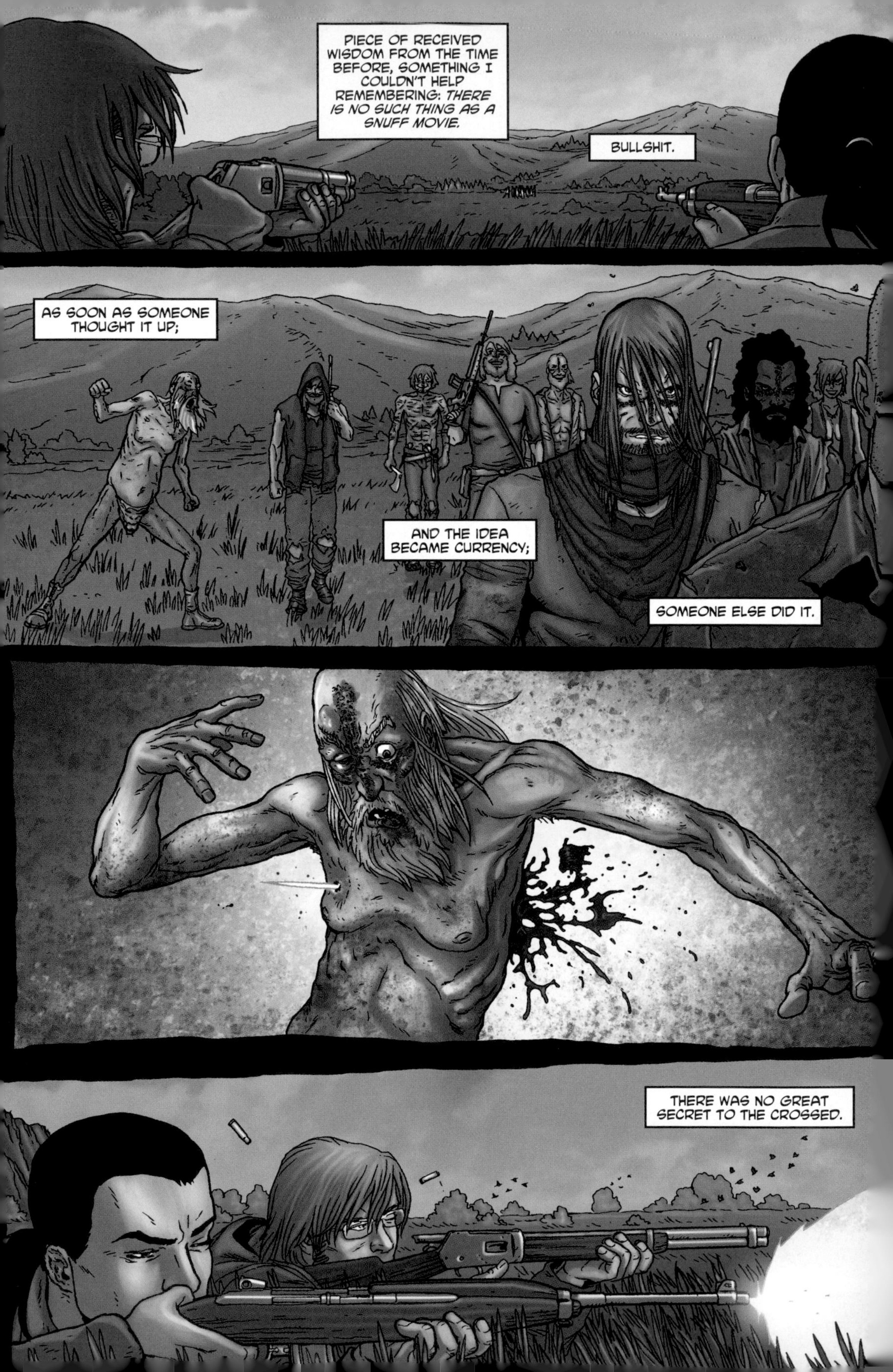
PIECE OF RECEIVED WISDOM FROM THE TIME BEFORE, SOMETHING I COULDN'T HELP REMEMBERING: *THERE IS NO SUCH THING AS A SNUFF MOVIE.*
BULLSHIT.
AS SOON AS SOMEONE THOUGHT IT UP;
AND THE IDEA BECAME CURRENCY;
SOMEONE ELSE DID IT.
THERE WAS NO GREAT SECRET TO THE CROSSED.

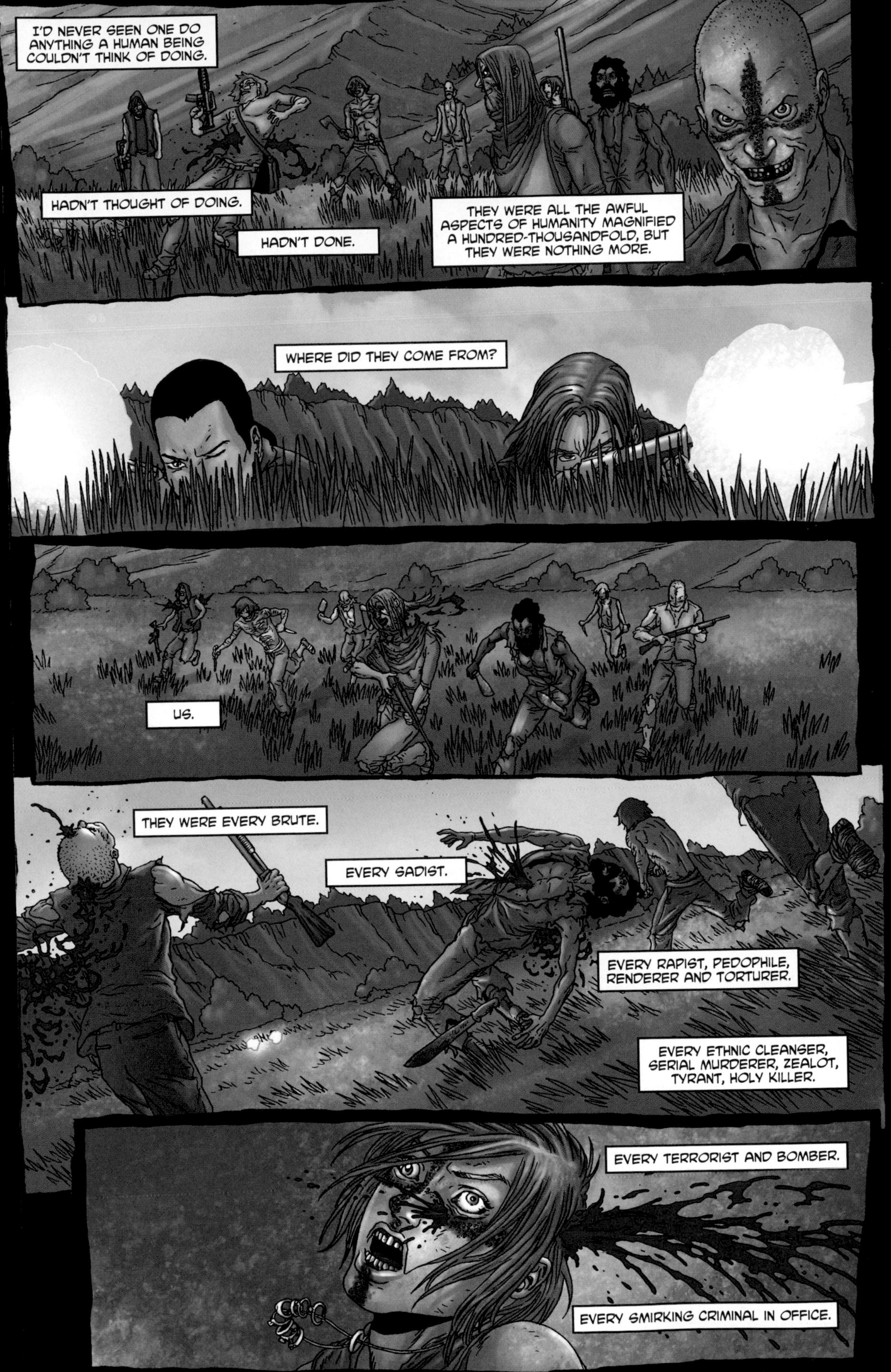
I'D NEVER SEEN ONE DO ANYTHING A HUMAN BEING COULDN'T THINK OF DOING.
HADN'T THOUGHT OF DOING.
HADN'T DONE.
THEY WERE ALL THE AWFUL ASPECTS OF HUMANITY MAGNIFIED A HUNDRED-THOUSANDFOLD, BUT THEY WERE NOTHING MORE.
WHERE DID THEY COME FROM?
US.
THEY WERE EVERY BRUTE.
EVERY SADIST.
EVERY RAPIST, PEDOPHILE, RENDERER AND TORTURER.
EVERY ETHNIC CLEANSER, SERIAL MURDERER, ZEALOT, TYRANT, HOLY KILLER.
EVERY TERRORIST AND BOMBER.
EVERY SMIRKING CRIMINAL IN OFFICE.

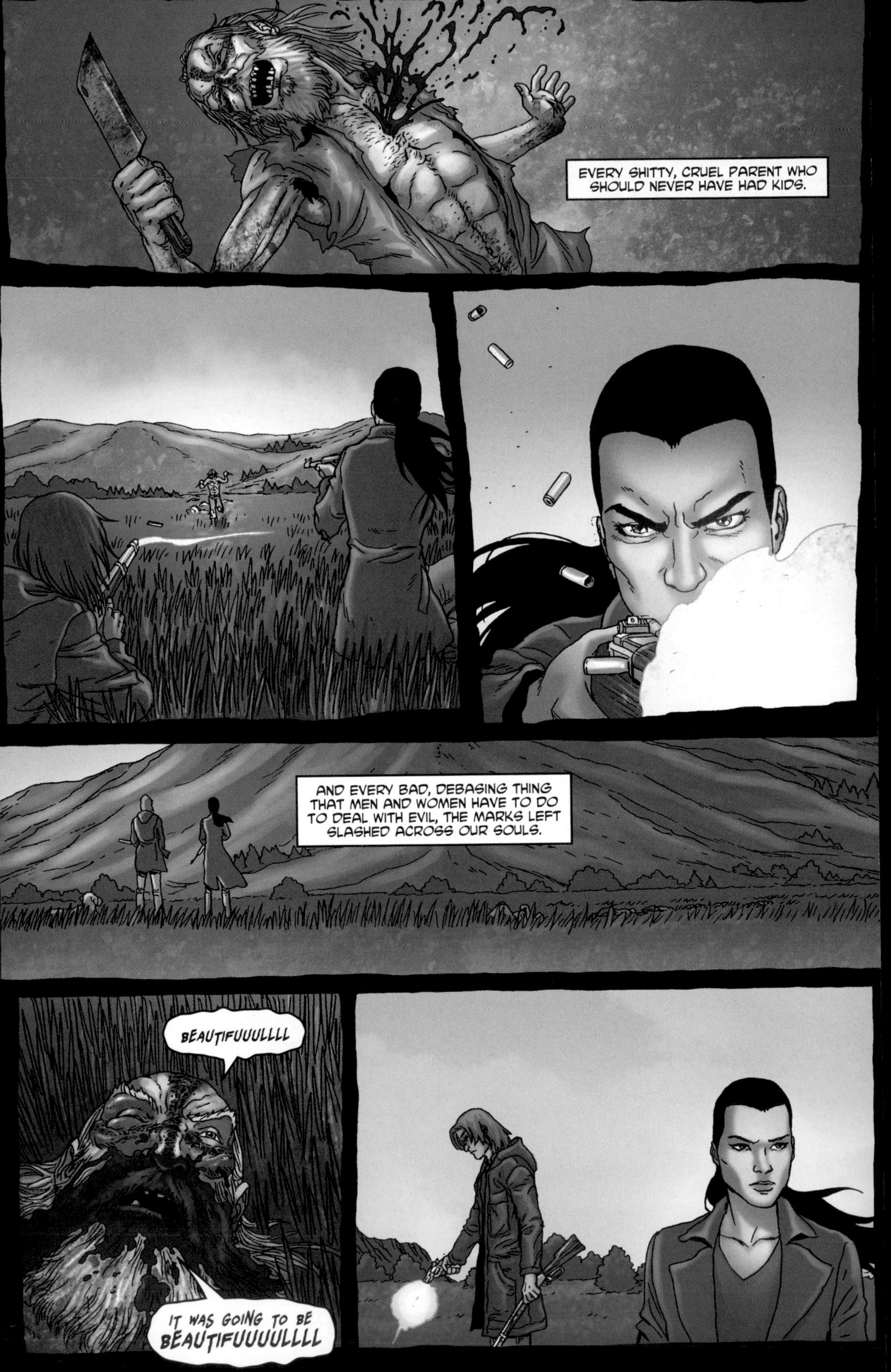
EVERY SHITTY, CRUEL PARENT WHO SHOULD NEVER HAVE HAD KIDS.
AND EVERY BAD, DEBASING THING THAT MEN AND WOMEN HAVE TO DO TO DEAL WITH EVIL, THE MARKS LEFT SLASHED ACROSS OUR SOULS.
BEAUTIFUUULLLL
IT WAS GOING TO BE BEAUTIFUUUULLLL

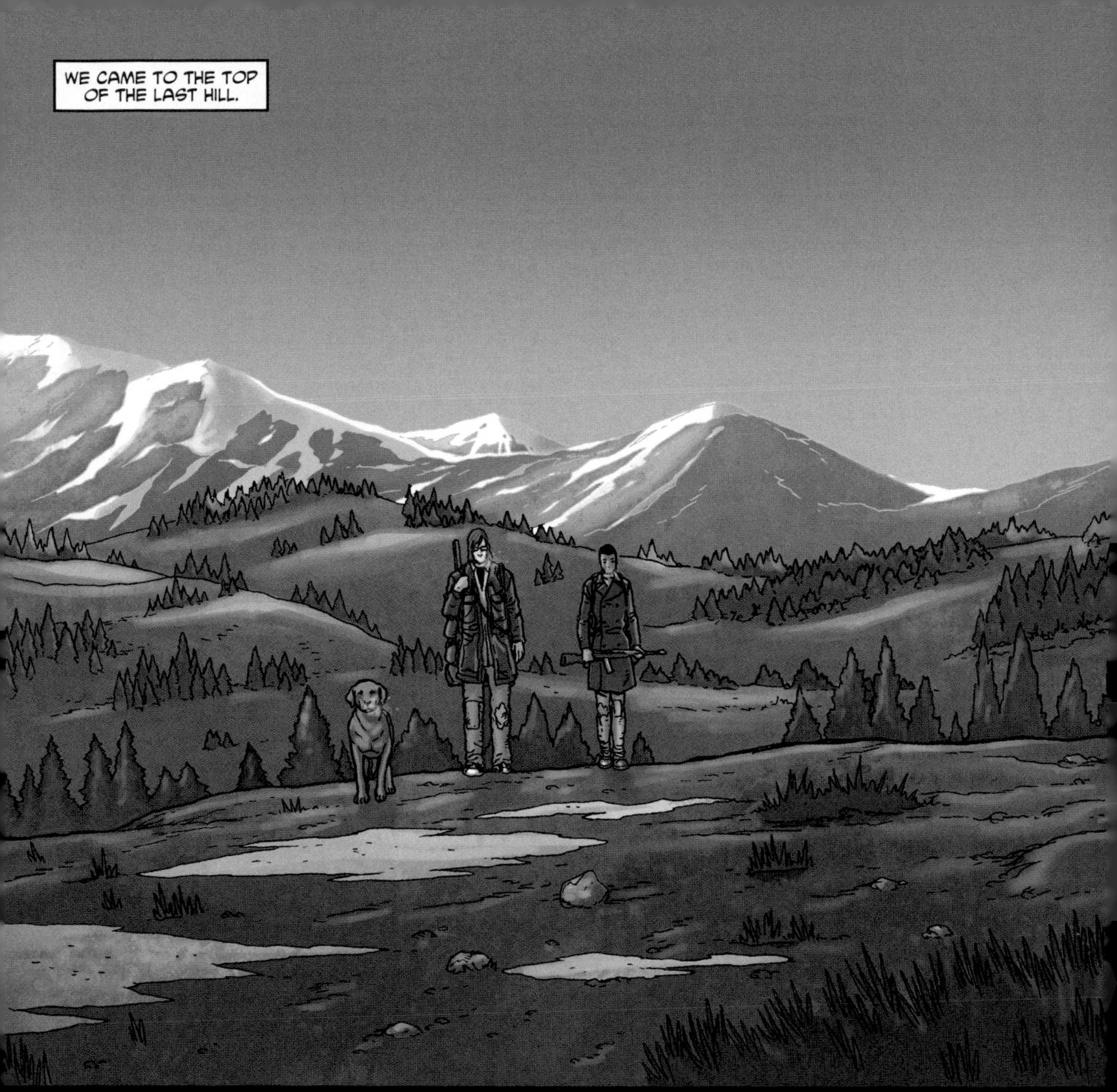
WE CAME TO THE TOP OF THE LAST HILL.

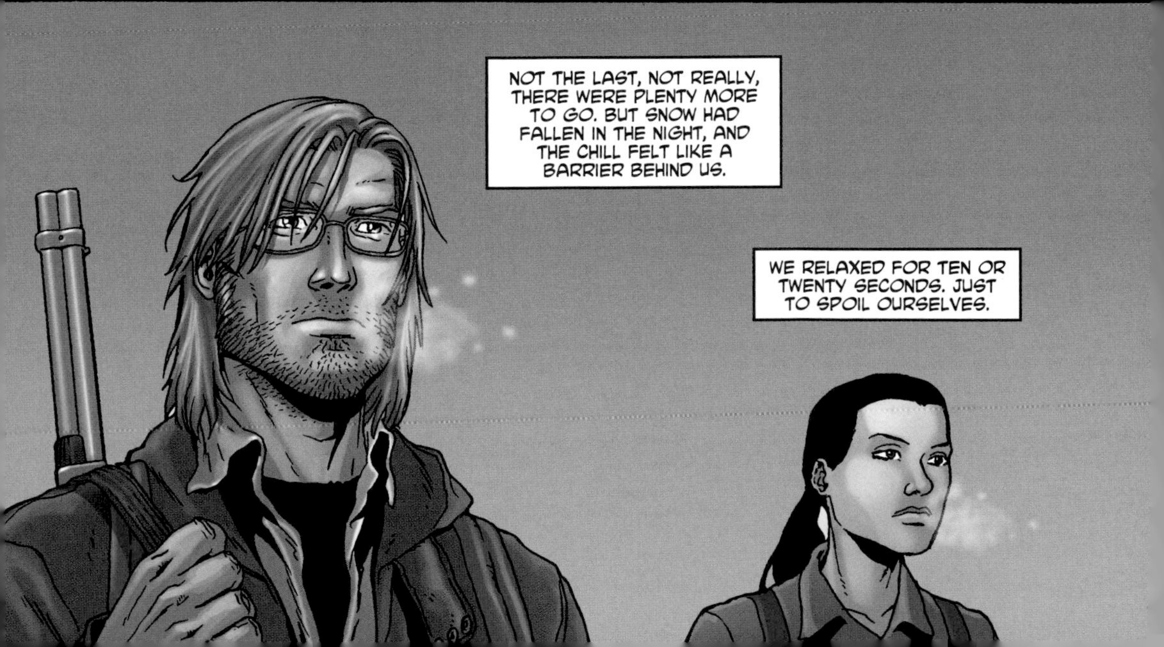
NOT THE LAST, NOT REALLY, THERE WERE PLENTY MORE TO GO. BUT SNOW HAD FALLEN IN THE NIGHT, AND THE CHILL FELT LIKE A BARRIER BEHIND US.
WE RELAXED FOR TEN OR TWENTY SECONDS. JUST TO SPOIL OURSELVES.

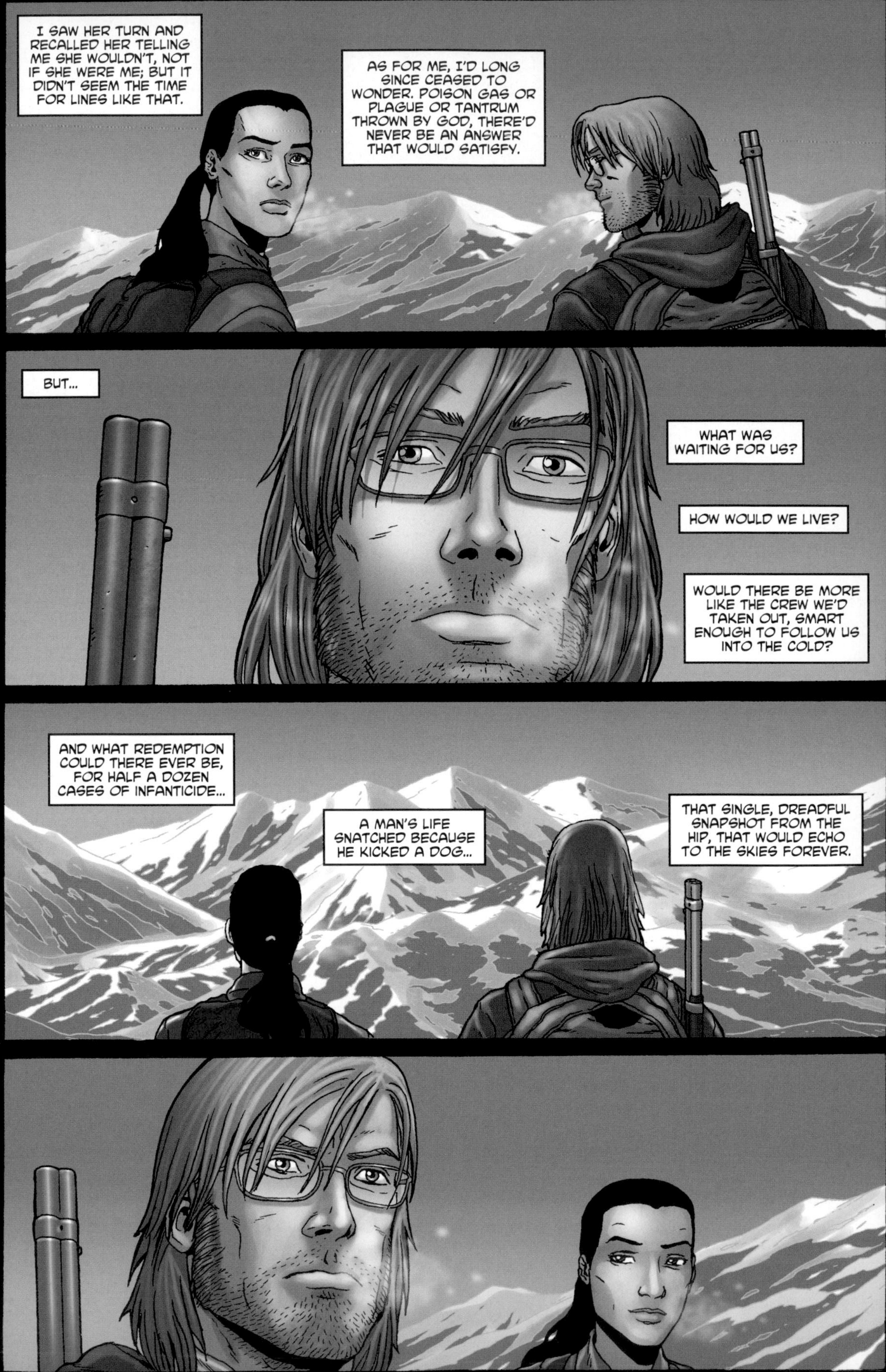

I SAW HER TURN AND RECALLED HER TELLING ME SHE WOULDN'T, NOT IF SHE WERE ME; BUT IT DIDN'T SEEM THE TIME FOR LINES LIKE THAT.
AS FOR ME, I'D LONG SINCE CEASED TO WONDER. POISON GAS OR PLAGUE OR TANTRUM THROWN BY GOD, THERE'D NEVER BE AN ANSWER THAT WOULD SATISFY.
BUT...
WHAT WAS WAITING FOR US?
HOW WOULD WE LIVE?
WOULD THERE BE MORE LIKE THE CREW WE'D TAKEN OUT, SMART ENOUGH TO FOLLOW US INTO THE COLD?
AND WHAT REDEMPTION COULD THERE EVER BE, FOR HALF A DOZEN CASES OF INFANTICIDE...
A MAN'S LIFE SNATCHED BECAUSE HE KICKED A DOG...
THAT SINGLE, DREADFUL SNAPSHOT FROM THE HIP, THAT WOULD ECHO TO THE SKIES FOREVER.

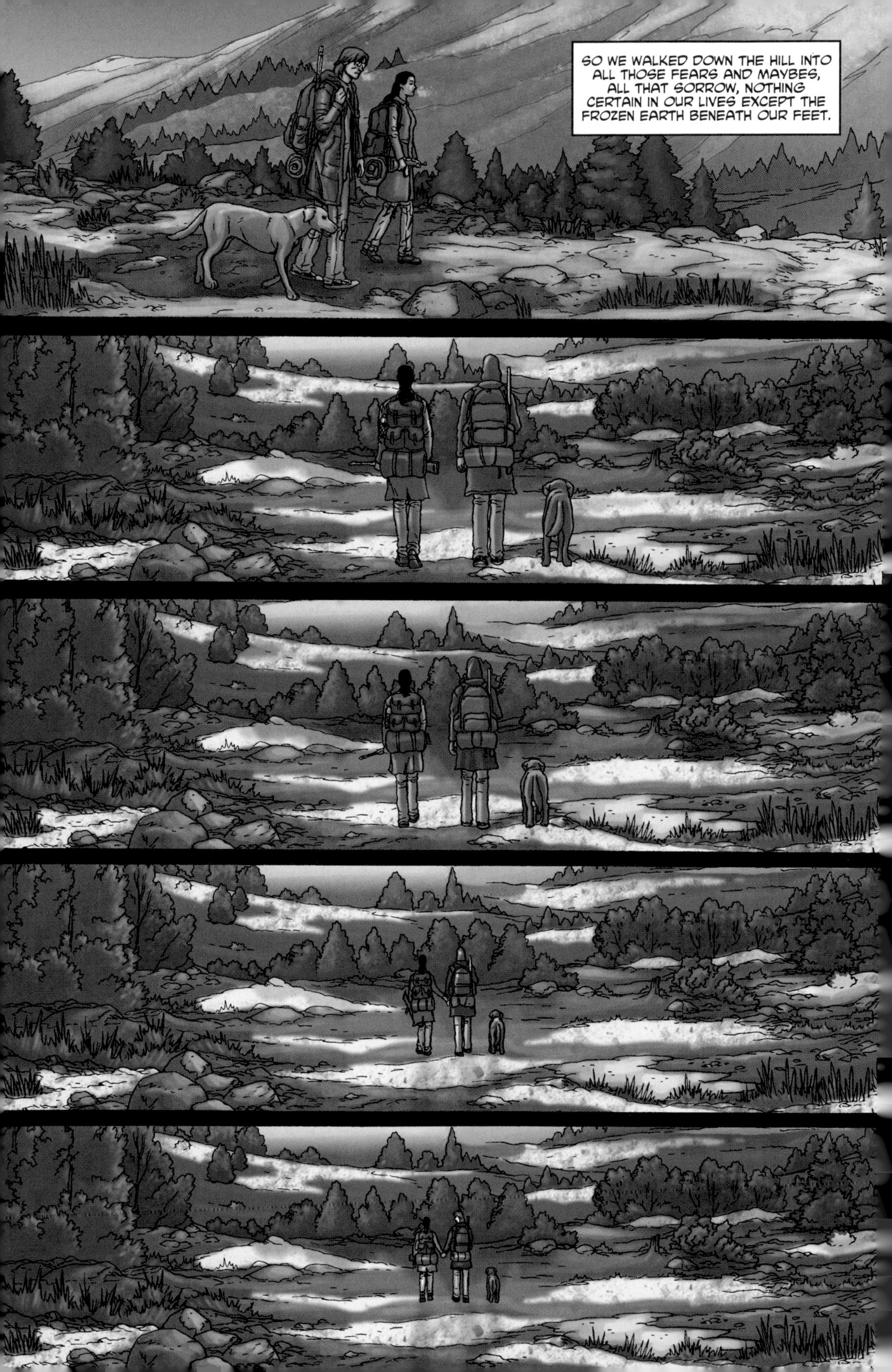
SO WE WALKED DOWN THE HILL INTO ALL THOSE FEARS AND MAYBES, ALL THAT SORROW, NOTHING CERTAIN IN OUR LIVES EXCEPT THE FROZEN EARTH BENEATH OUR FEET.

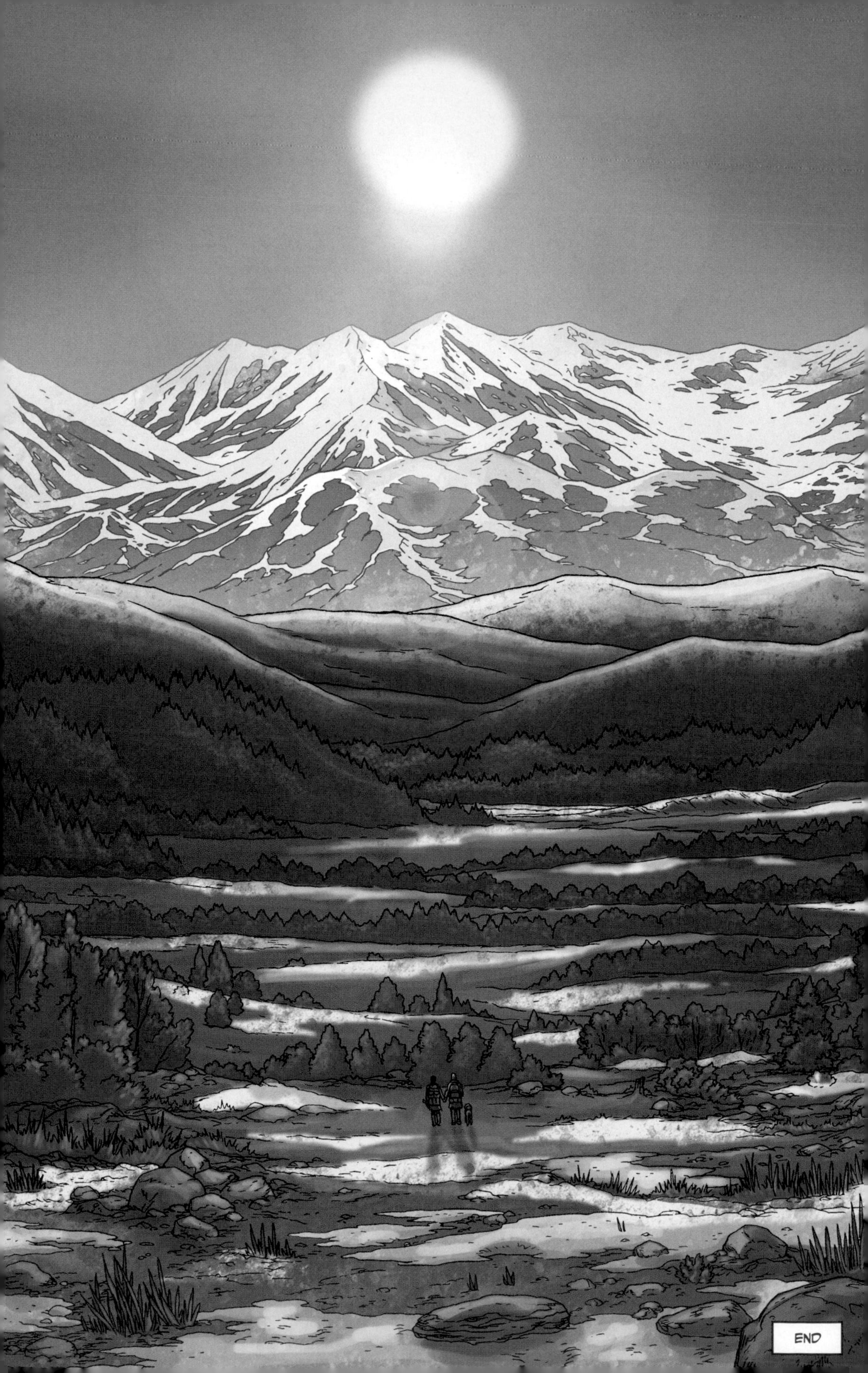
END

COVER GALLERY

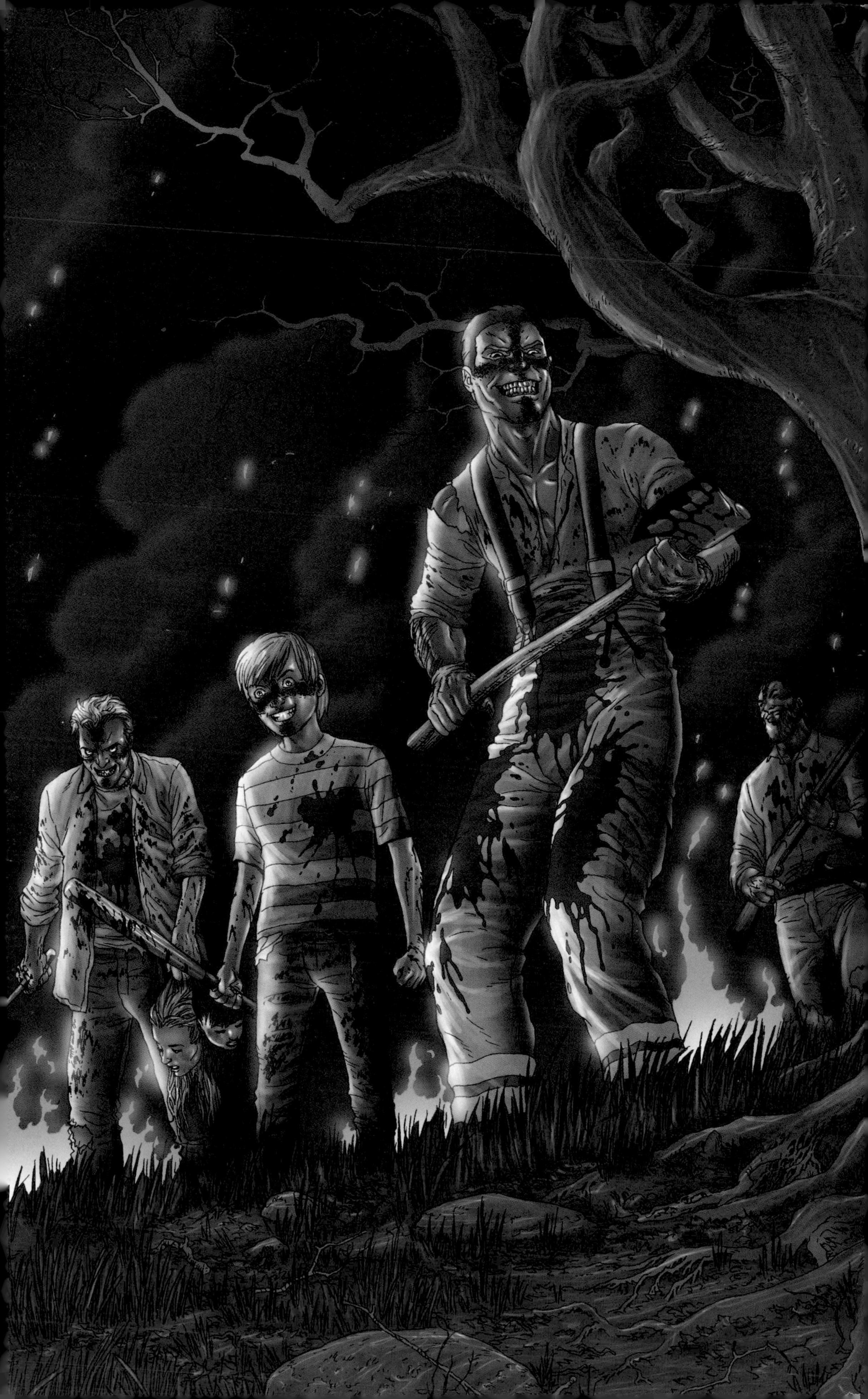

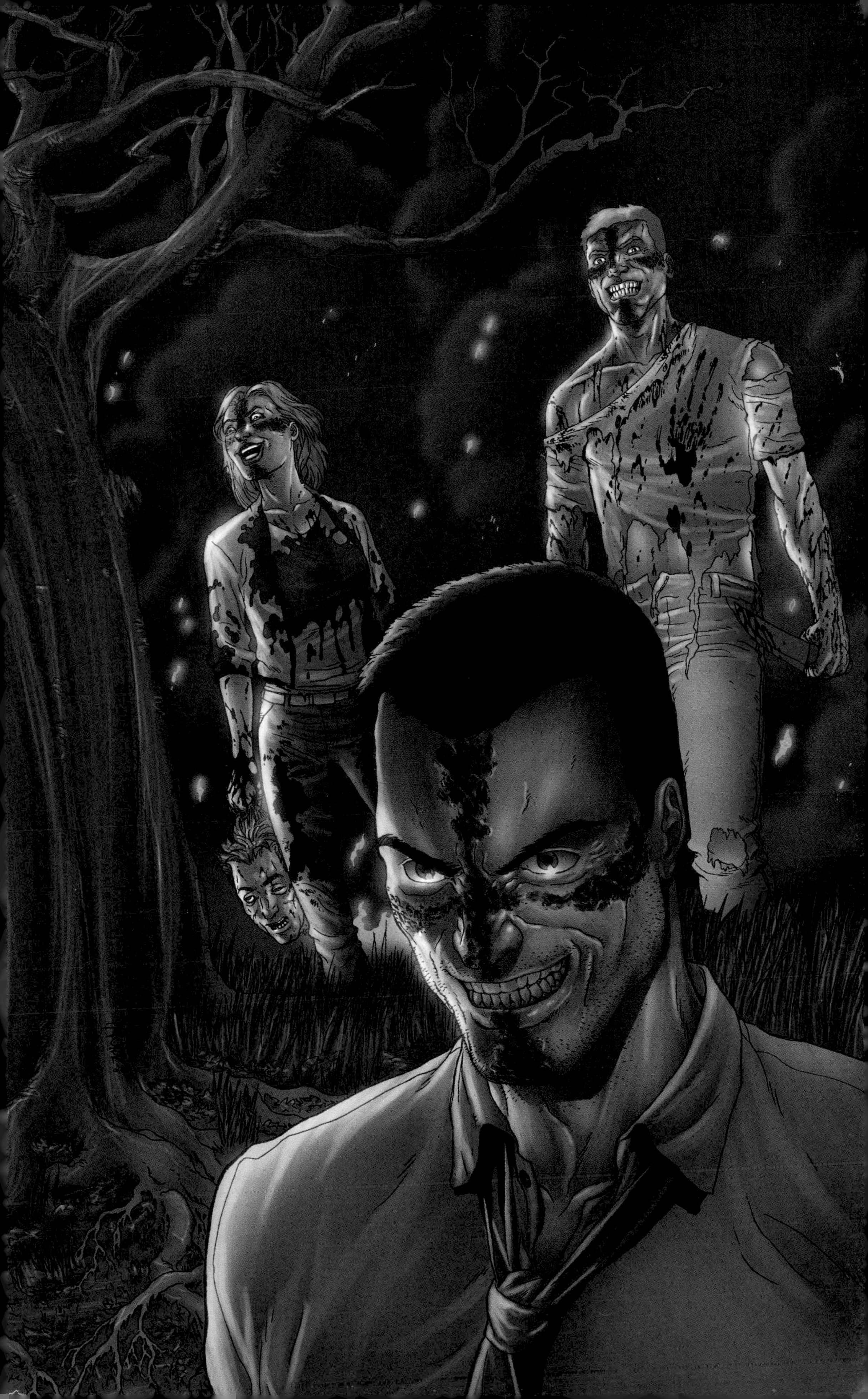

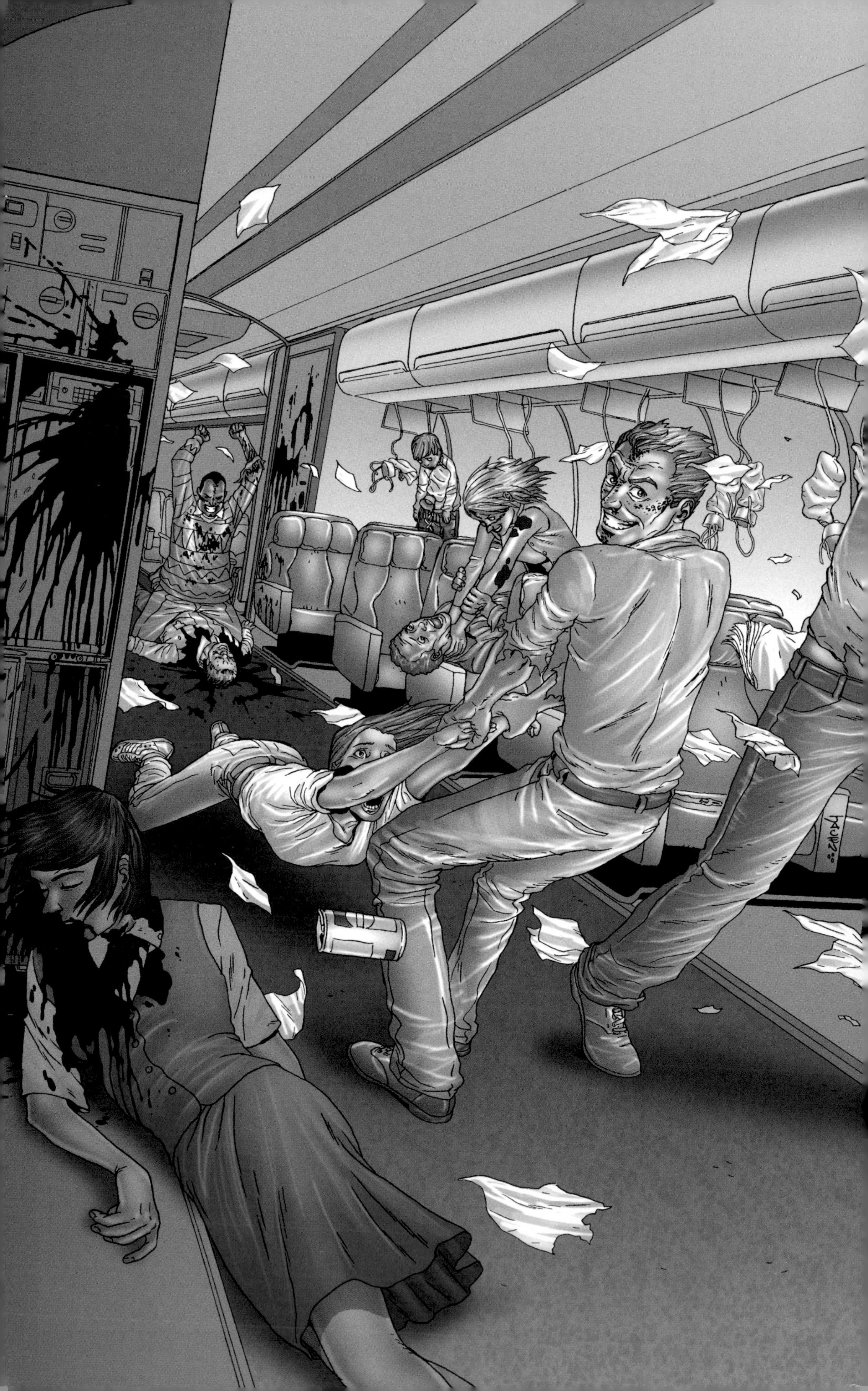

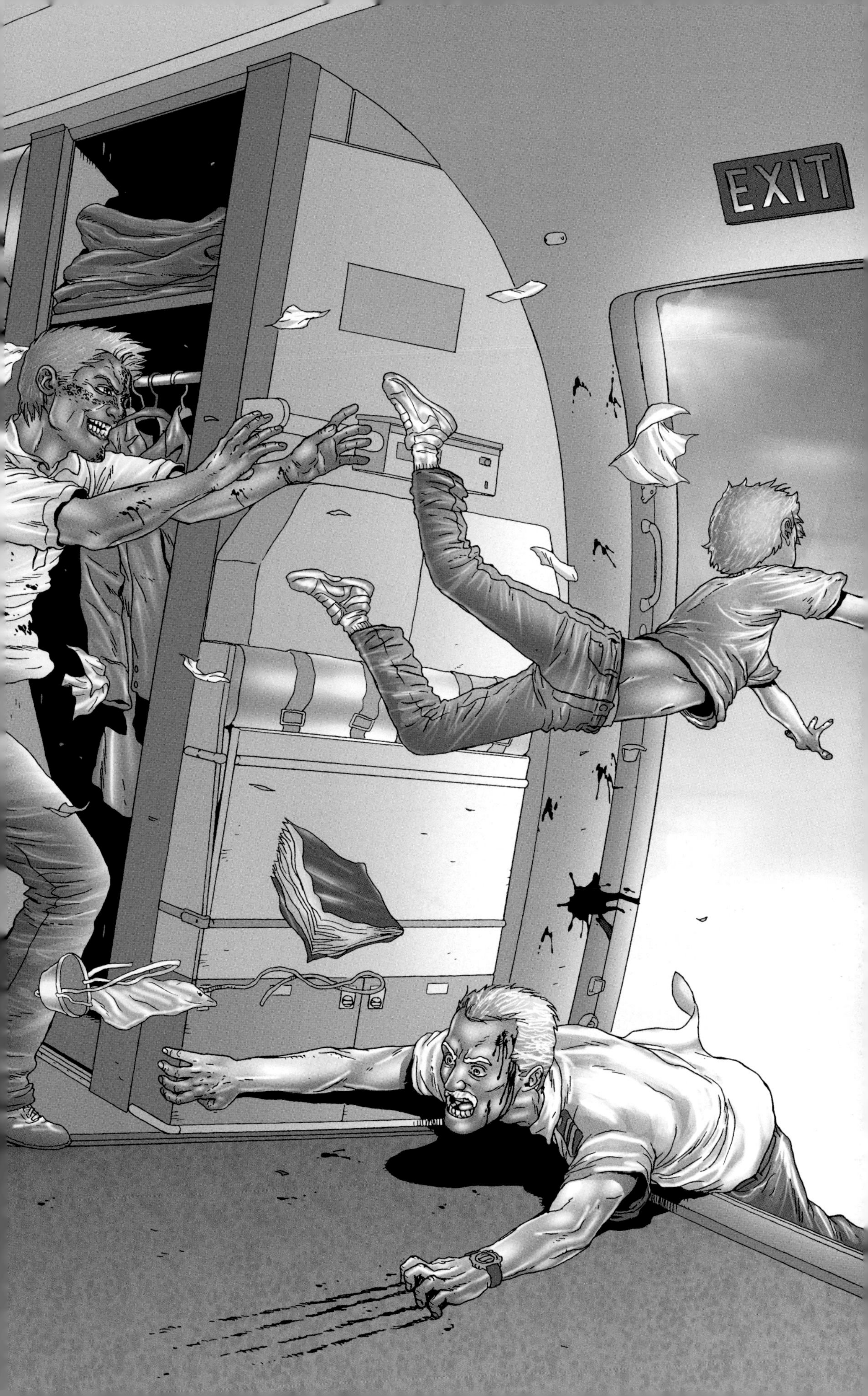
EXIT

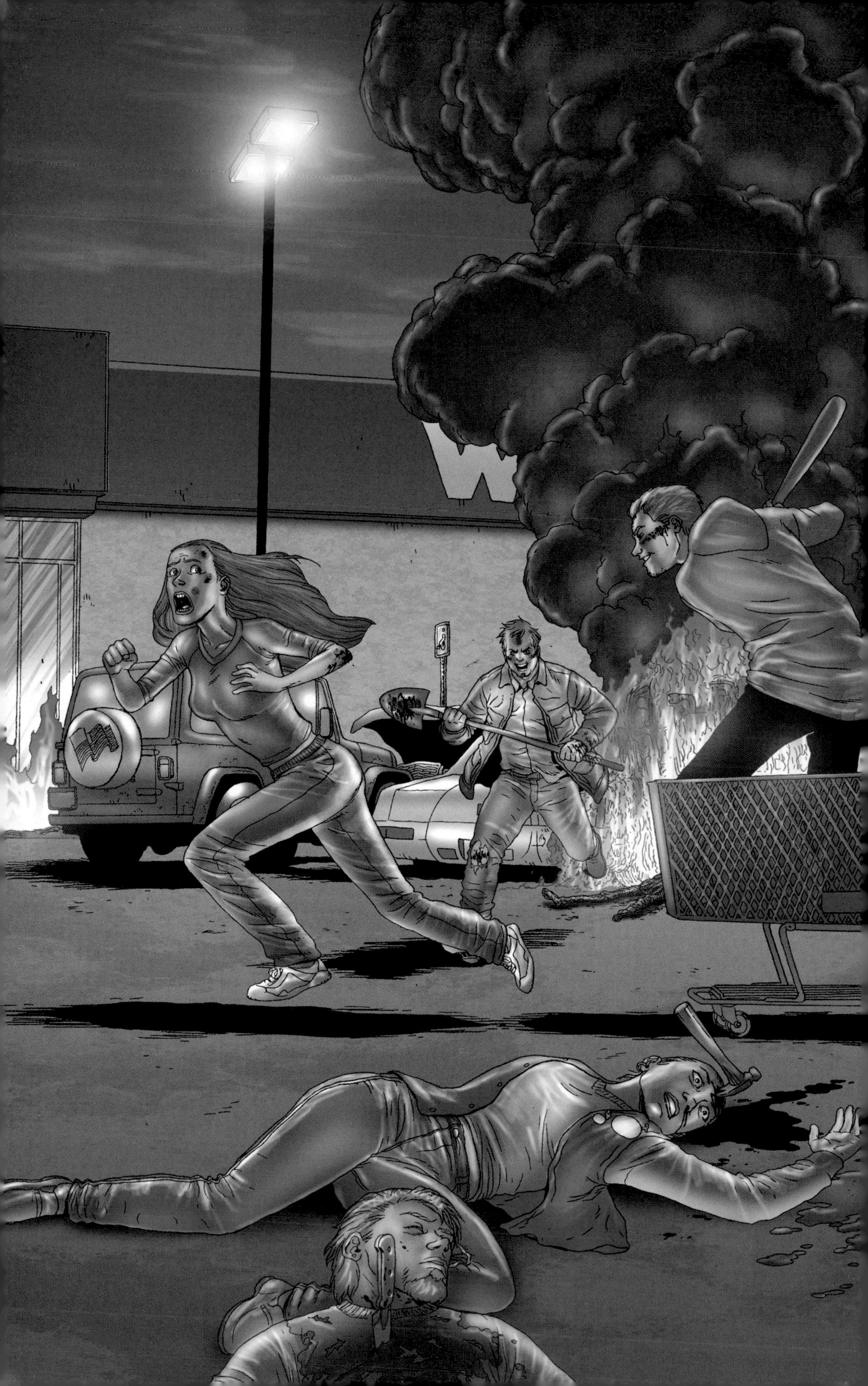

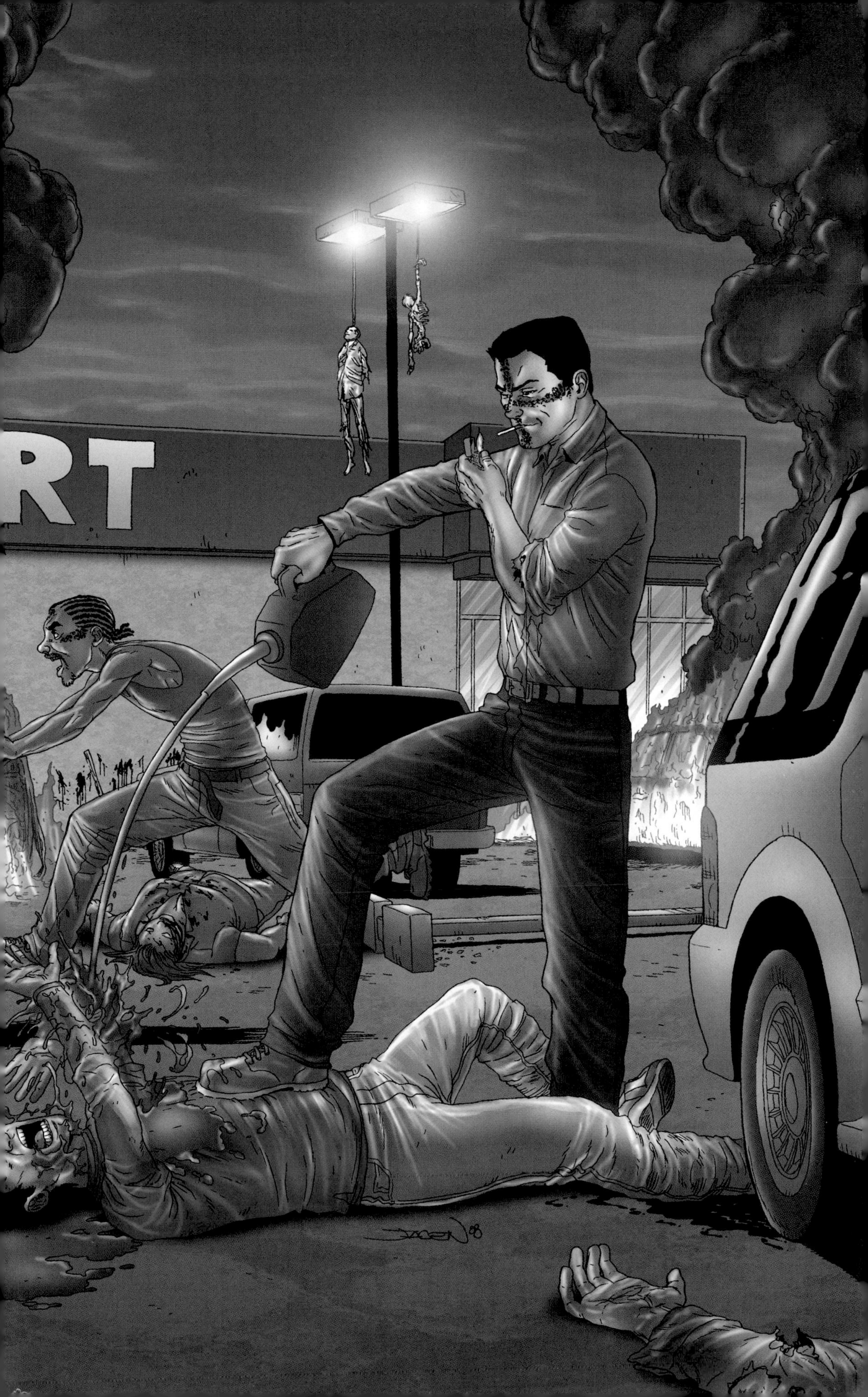
RT

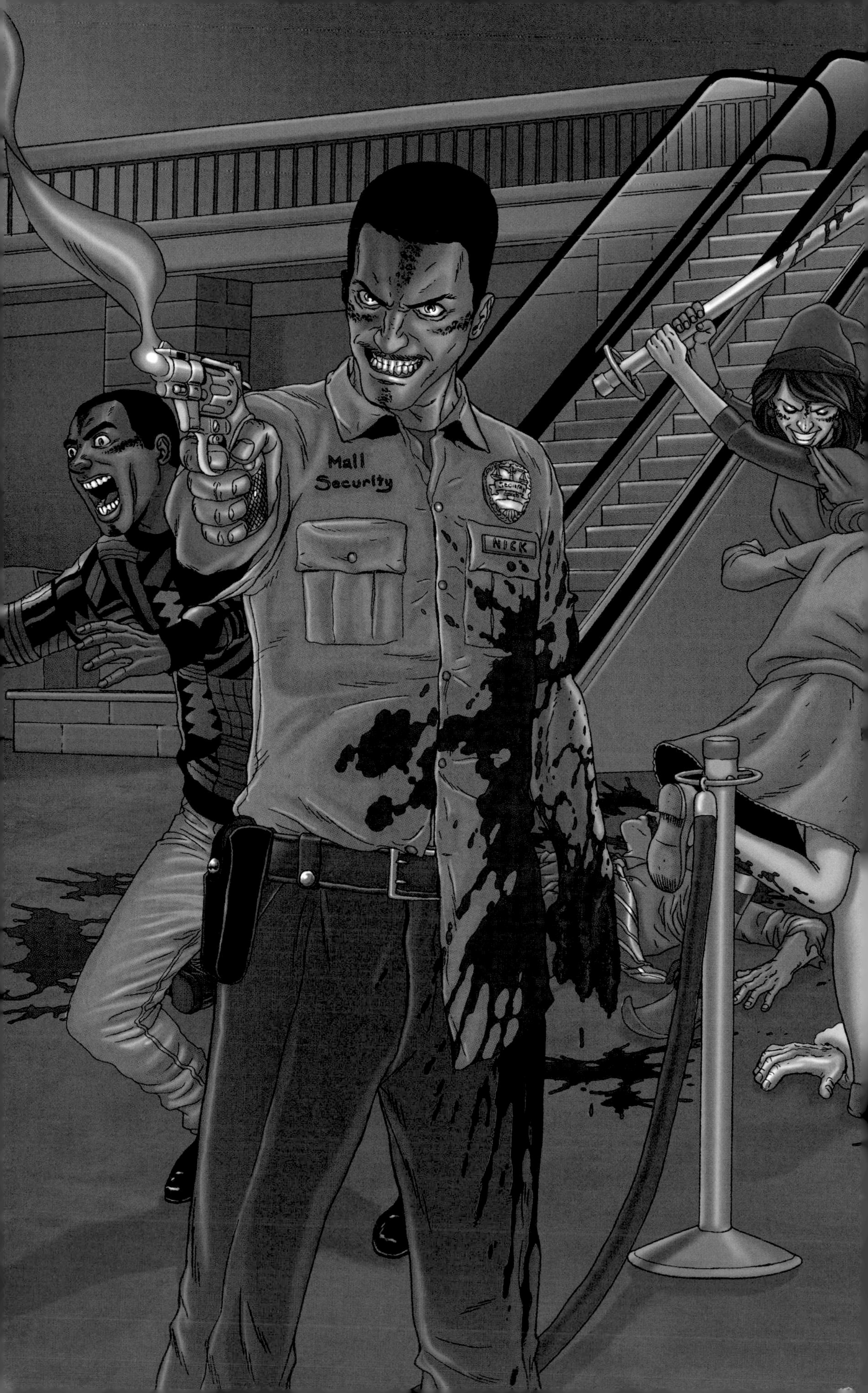
Mall
Security
NICK

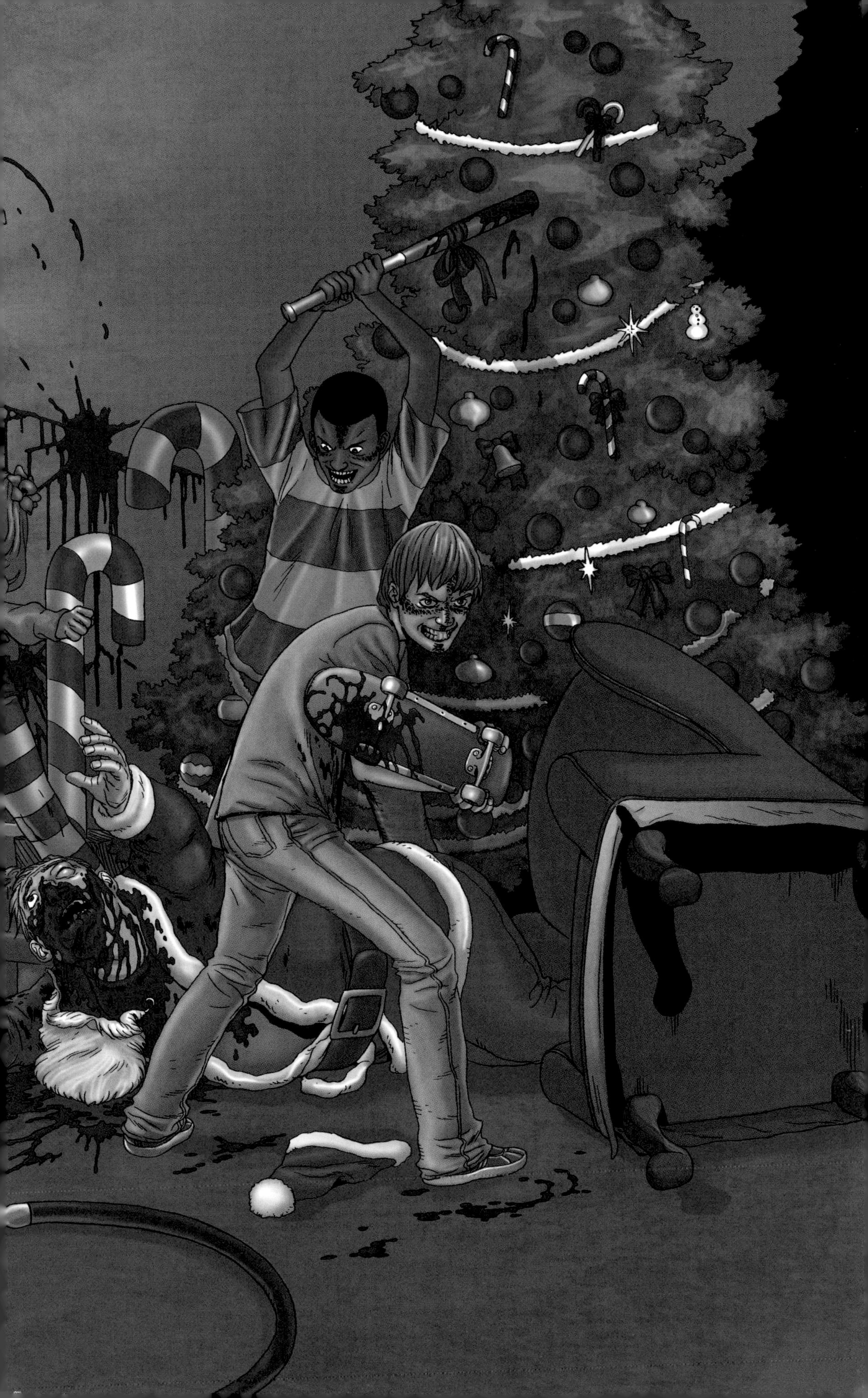

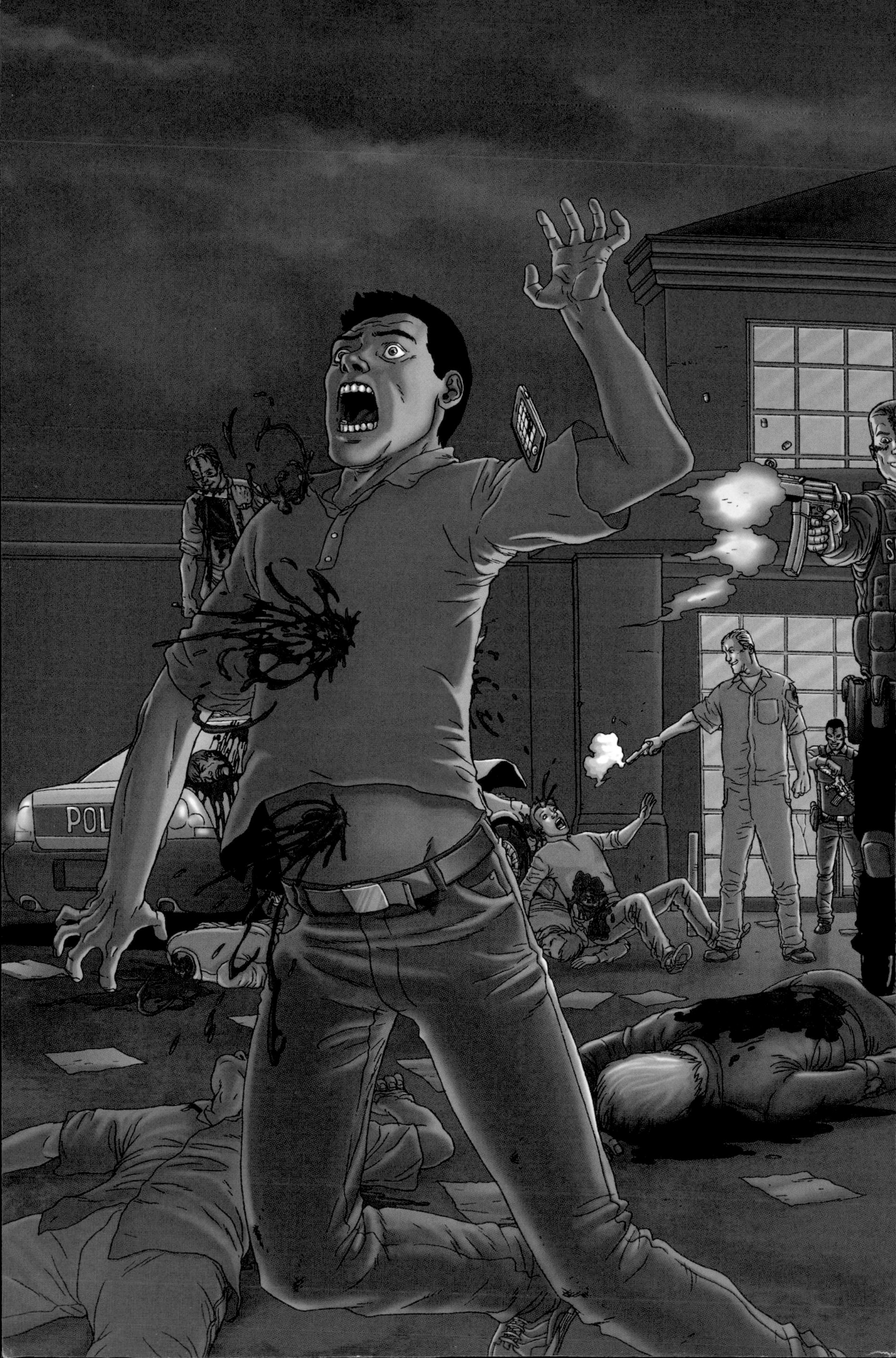
POL

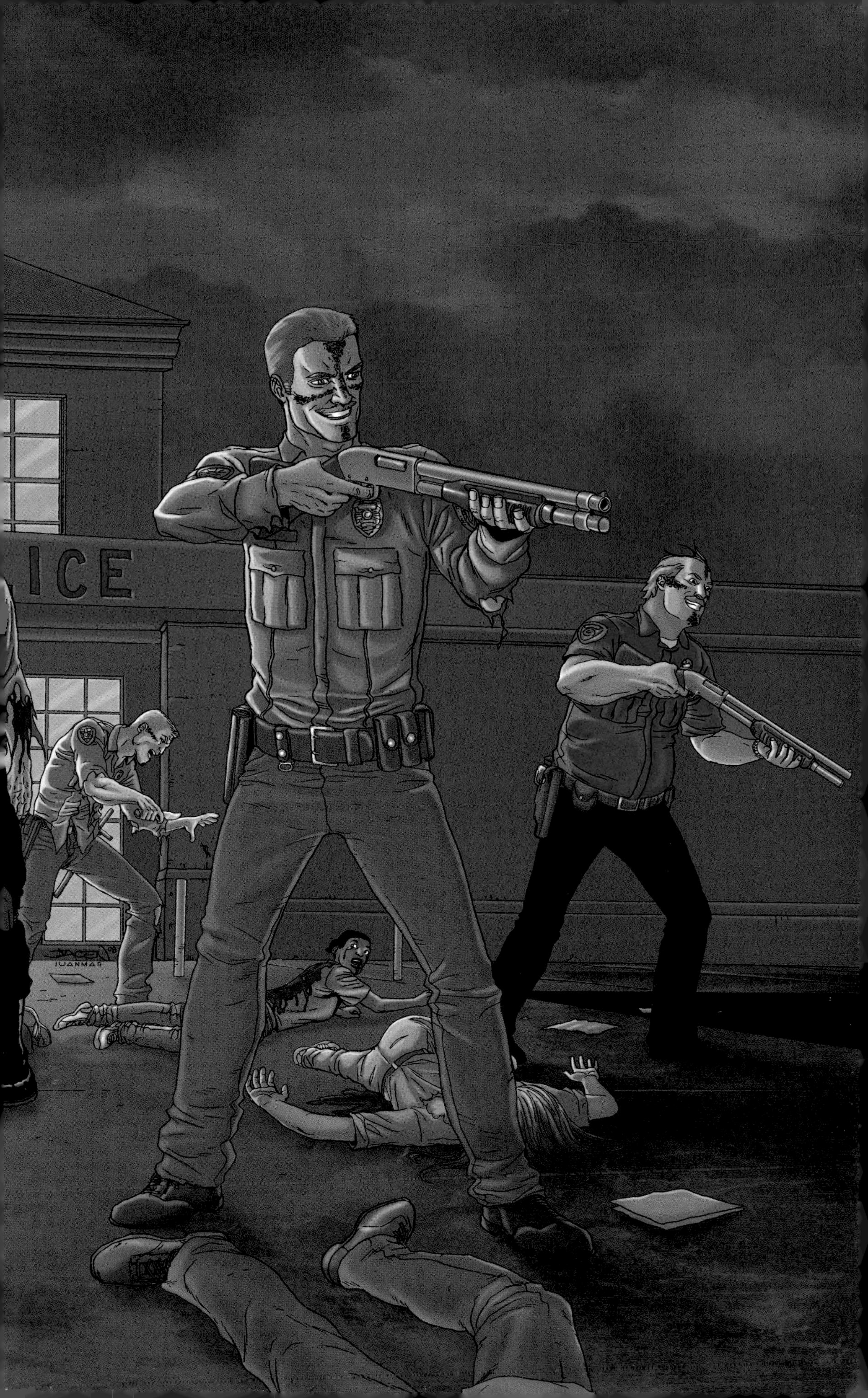
ICE
JUANMAR

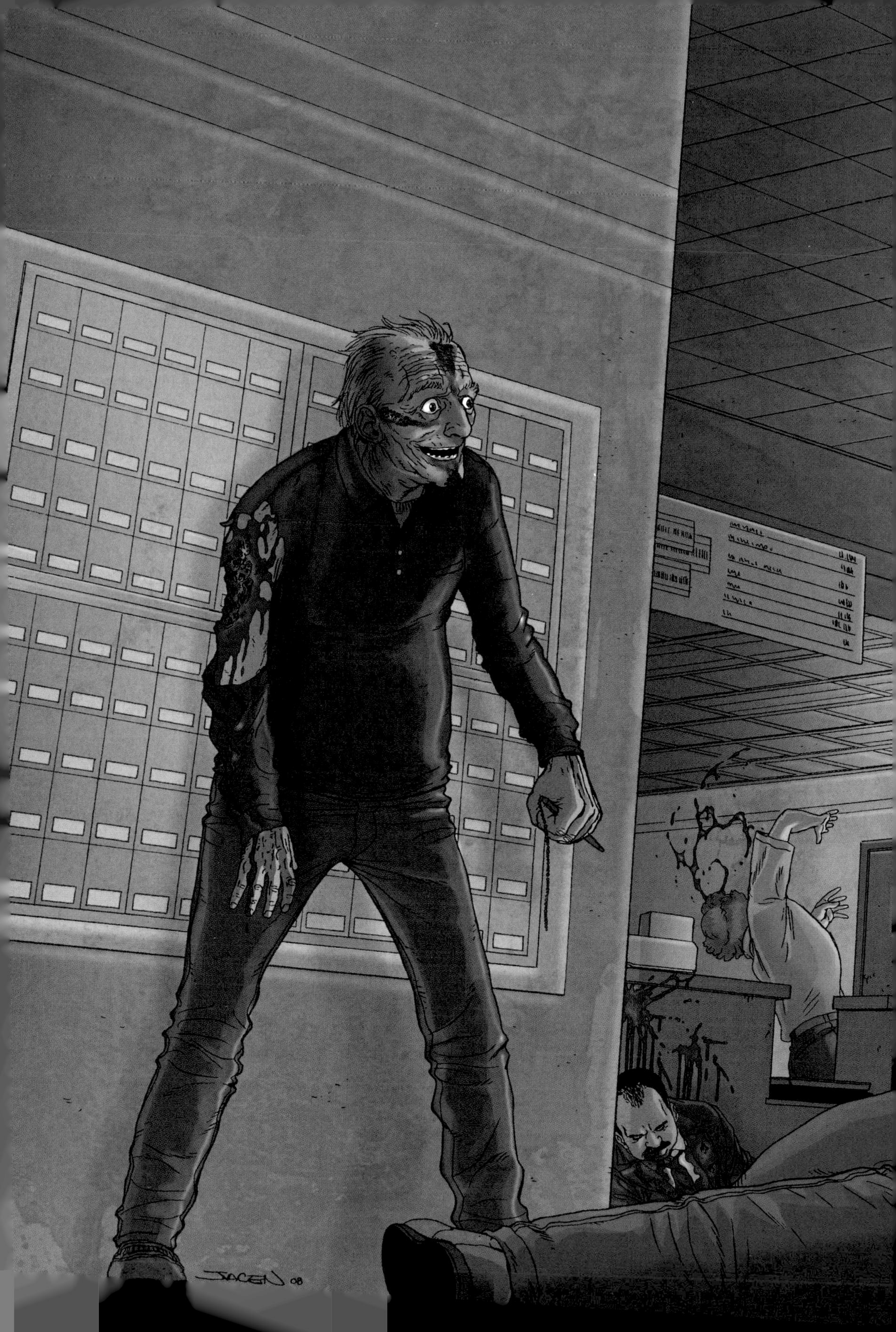
JACEN 08

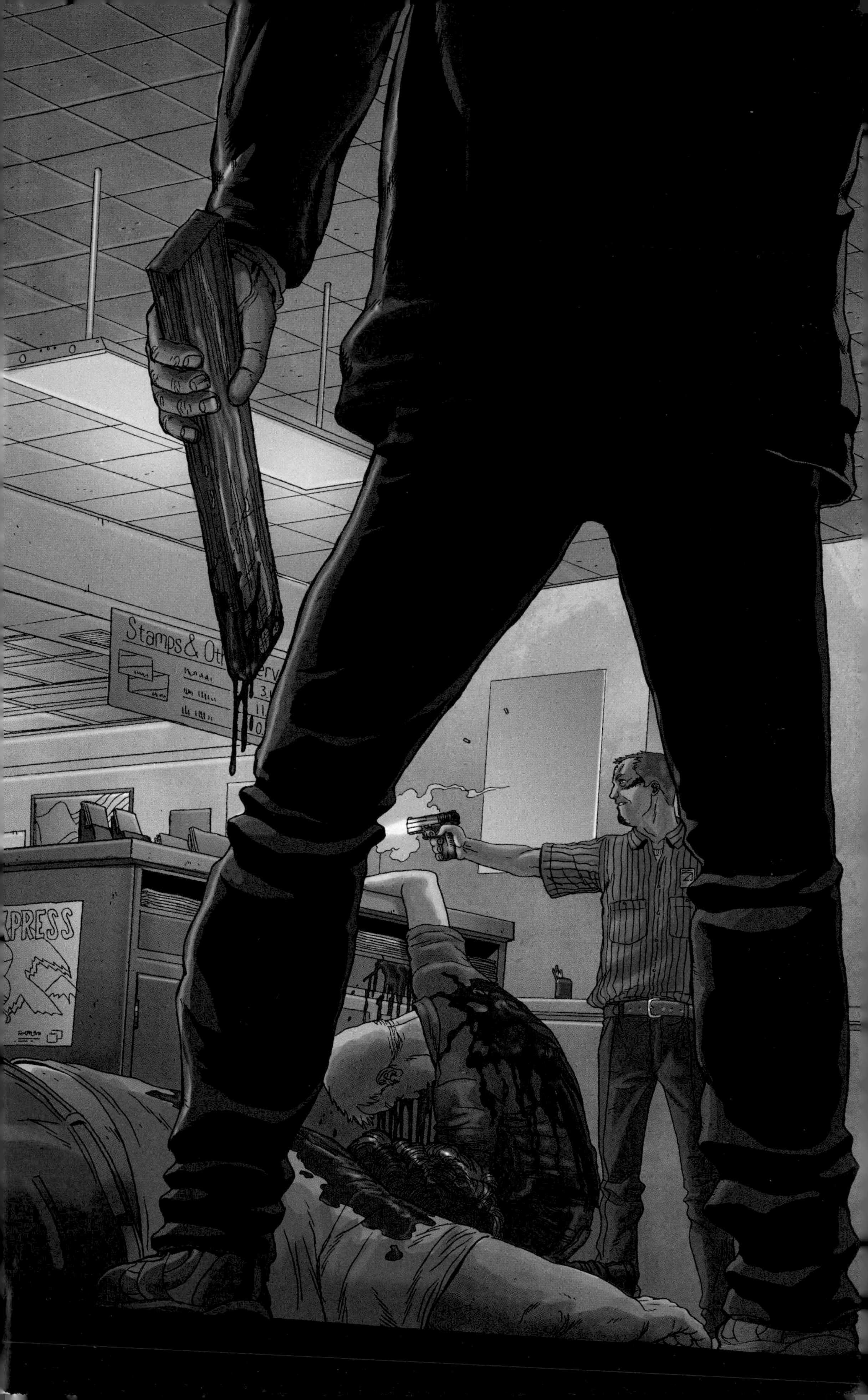
Stamps &
PRESS

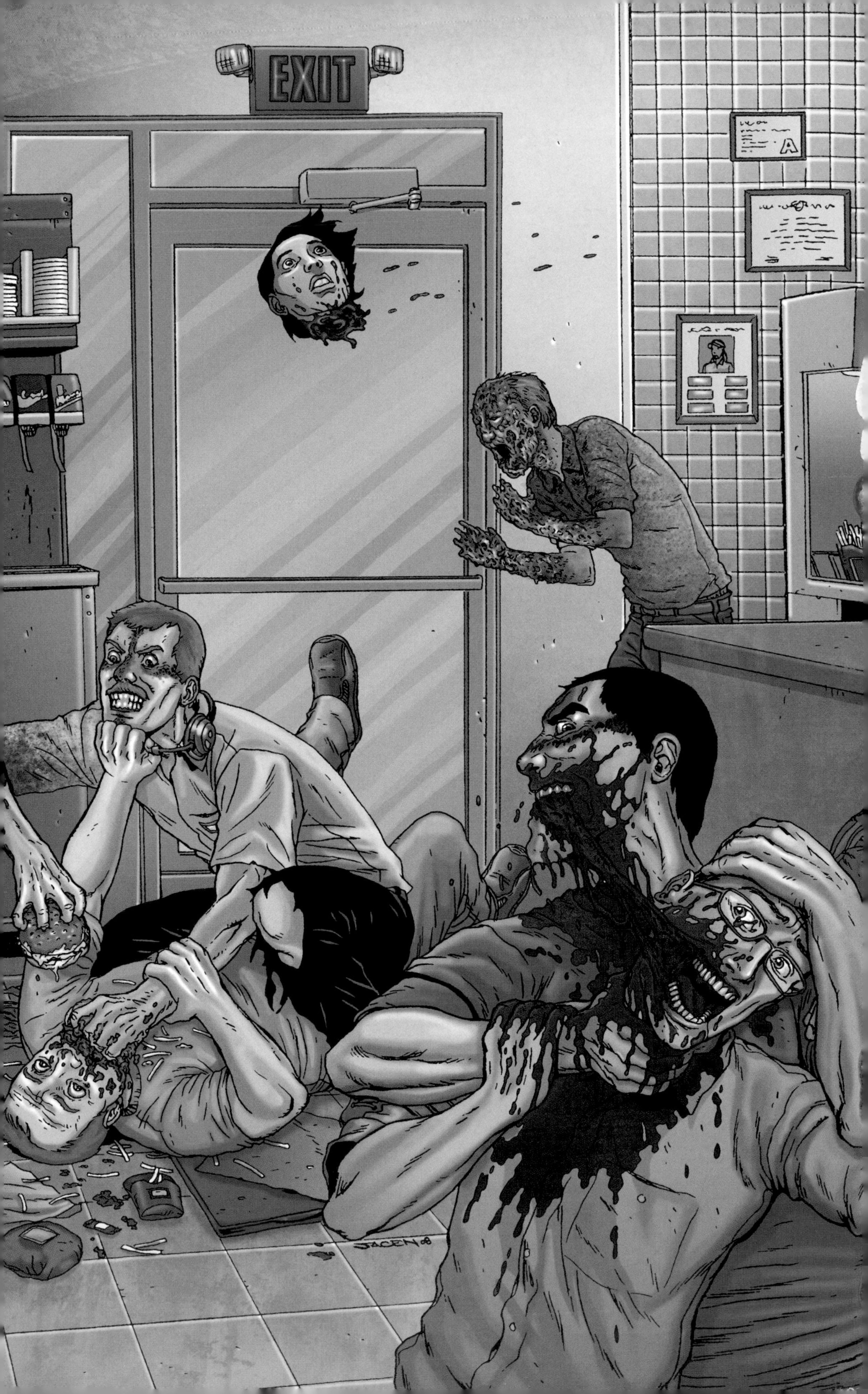
EXIT
JACEN 08

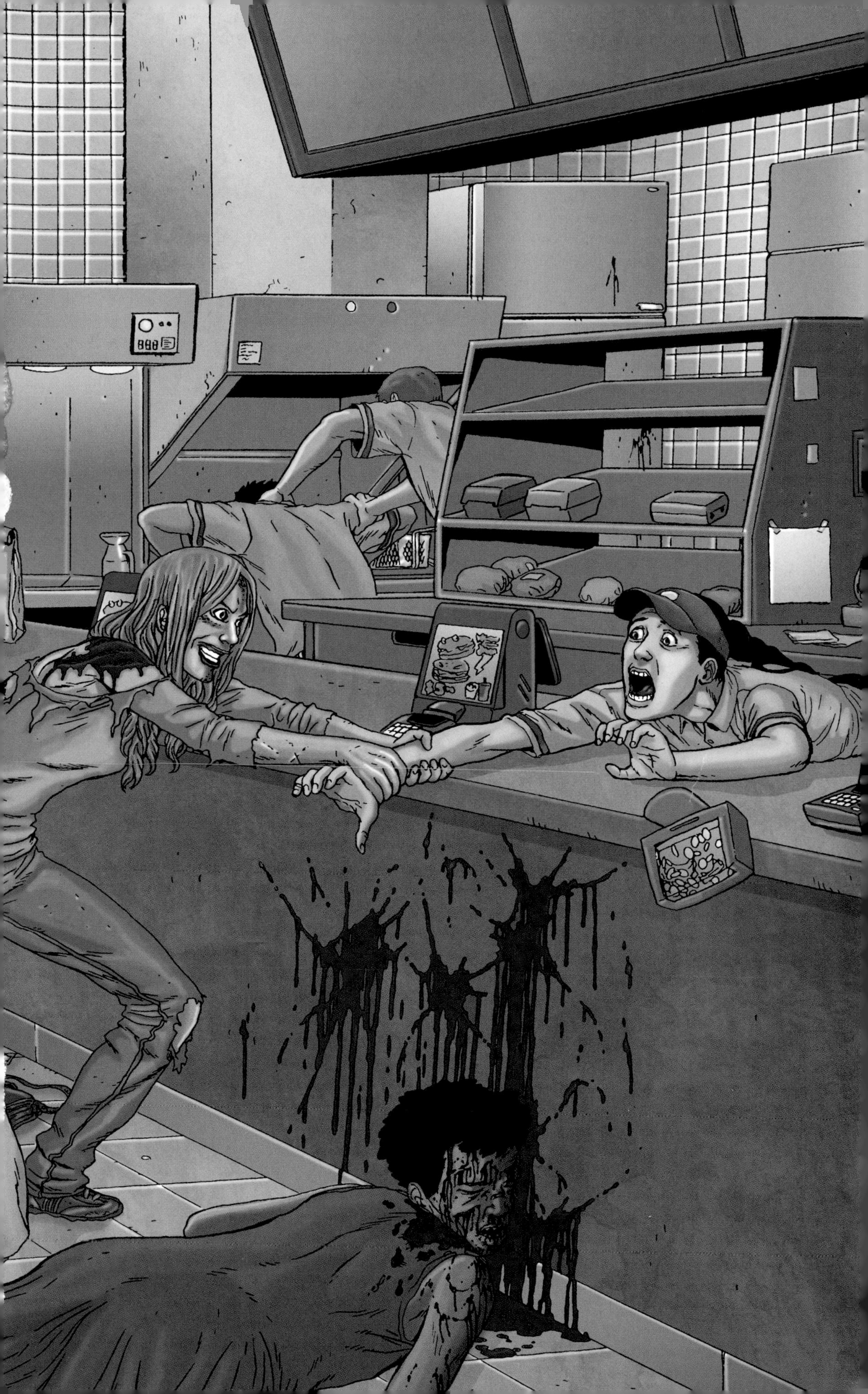

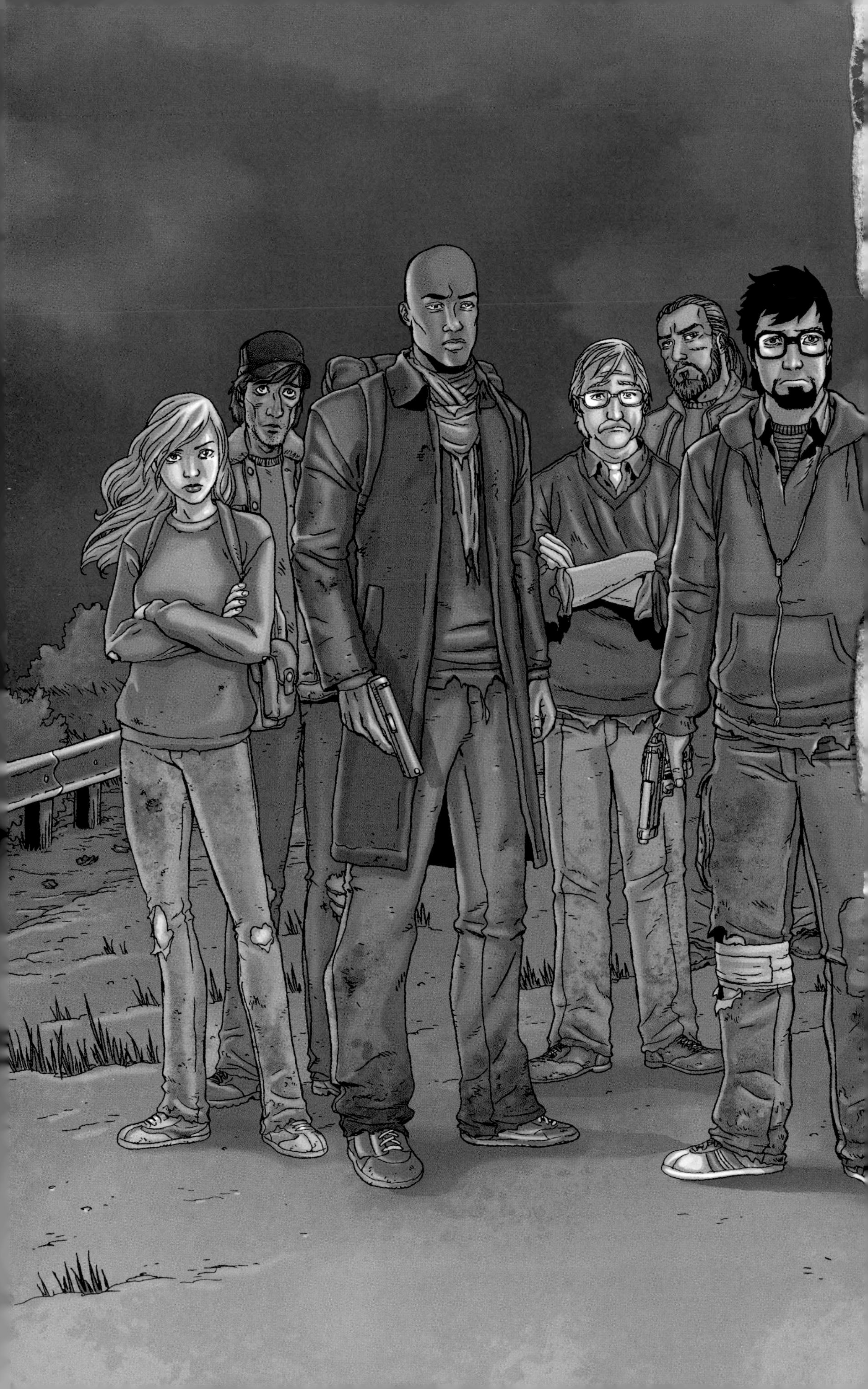

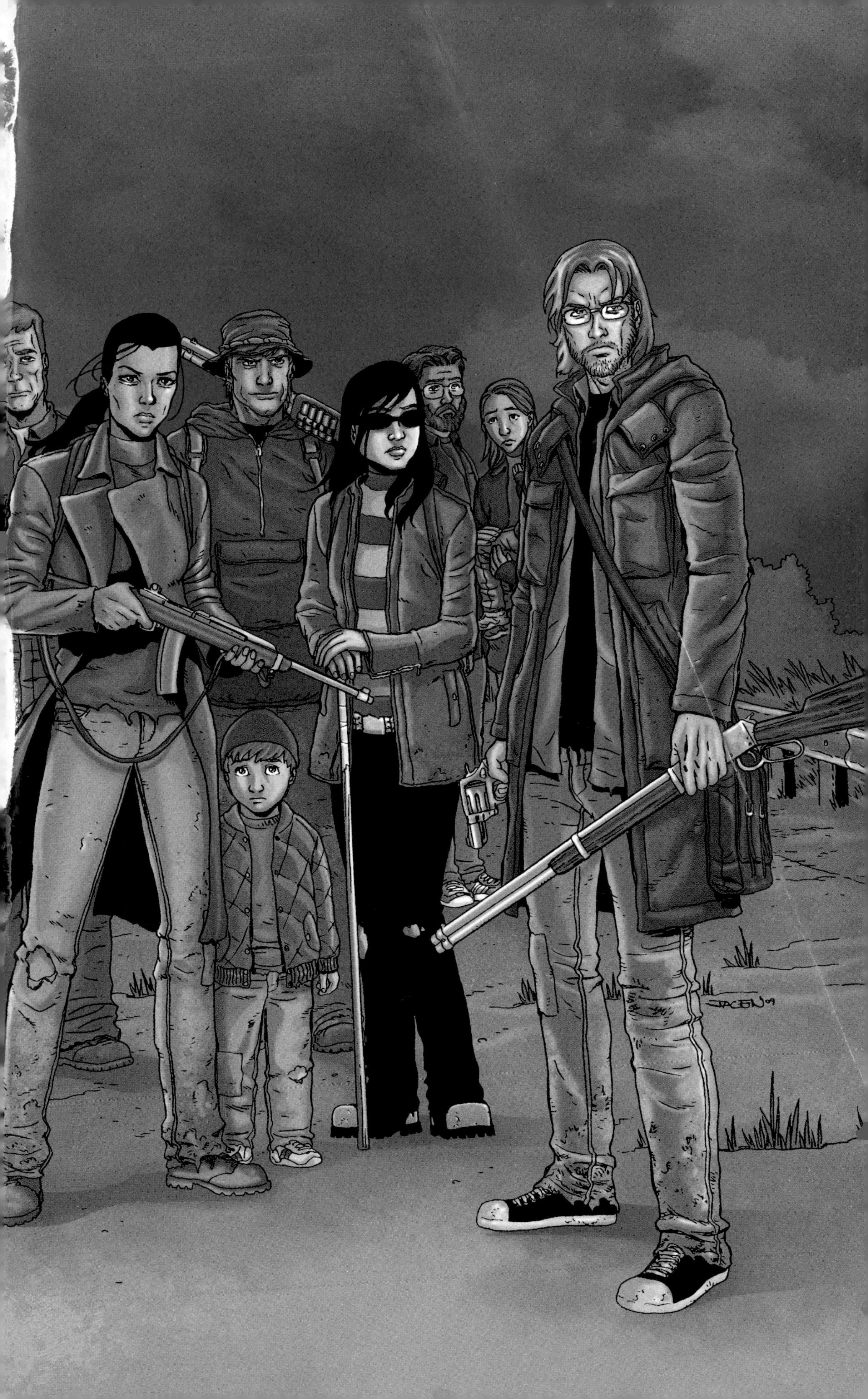

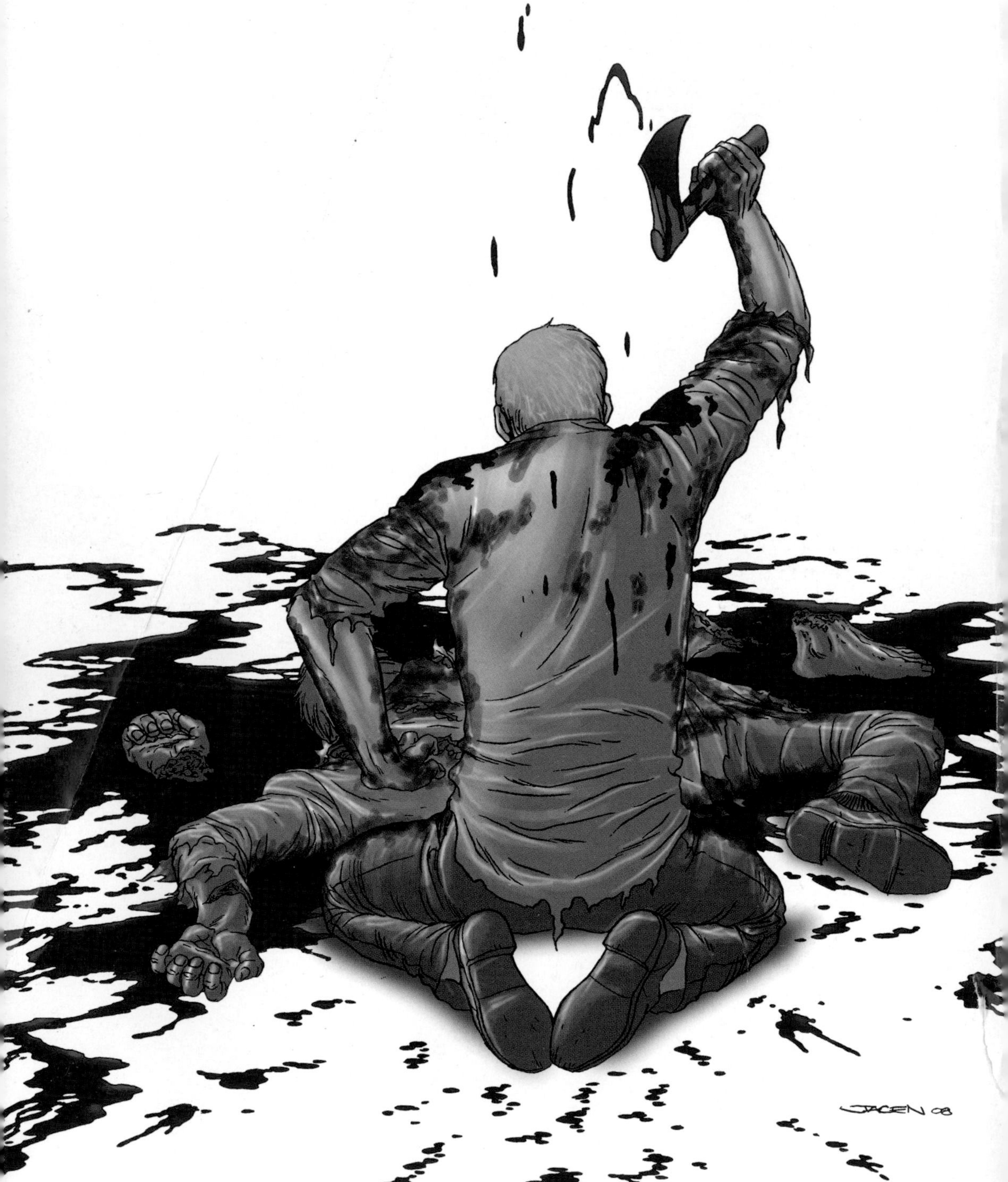